D1557785

THE DETROIT TIGERS ENCYCLOPEDIA

Jim Hawkins
Dan Ewald
With Photo & Statistical Contributions
from George Van Dusen

SPORTS PUBLISHING L.L.C.
sportspublishingllc.com

ISBN: 1-58261-222-6

Developmental editor: Erin Linden-Levy
Senior project manager and book design: Jennifer L. Polson
Statistical section designed by Greg Hickman
Dust jacket design: Kerri Baker
Insert design: Kerri Baker and Kenneth J. O'Brien
Copy editor: Cynthia L. McNew

Printed in the United States.

SPORTS PUBLISHING L.L.C.
www.sportspublishingllc.com

To Joyce,
a fellow Tigers fan,
Best wishes
Jy Van Dusen

ACKNOWLEDGMENTS

The authors are indebted to Mike Pearson, whose patience and support kept us going, and former and current members of the Detroit Tigers public relations staff who have spent endless hours over the years compiling more than a century of facts and figures so vital to this story.

CONTENTS

FOREWORD

Nothing in sports is more fun than an old baseball story. I should know. I've told a million of them. It doesn't matter if the story happened a year, 10 years or 100 years ago. All those old stories keep baseball fresh. The older the story, the better it gets. That's the beauty of baseball. It goes back more than 100 years and we still talk about all of the games and all of the characters as if they were our closest friends.

The Tigers have a tradition that goes back to the days when fans rode to the games in horse-drawn buggies. Only a handful of teams have that kind of history. Just think about some of the names. Ty Cobb. Harry Heilmann. Charlie Gehringer. Hank Greenberg. Mickey Cochrane. George Kell. Al Kaline. Hughie Jennings. Frank Navin. Walter Briggs.

I am so lucky to be a little part of it.

Dan Ewald and Jim Hawkins share a little part of that history in a different way. They've been around the Tigers writing stories and studying Tiger tradition long before I ever got to Detroit. They were around to write some of the classic stories right when they were being made.

That's what makes this Tiger encyclopedia special. It's got all the numbers that any good baseball book has to have. But the stories about the owners and players and managers are what bring the whole thing to life.

It doesn't matter when it happened. A good baseball story gives us a little picture of America and helps us to remember certain parts of our lives.

Tiger tradition makes the team so special to the city, to baseball and the whole country. Every person who ever had the privilege of putting on that uniform with the Olde English "D" should be proud. And every one of them has at least one story.

This book tells a lot of them. It's a must for every true Tiger fan.

Sparky Anderson
Tigers Manager, 1979-95

1

A BASEBALL TOWN

Detroit is a tough town. Tougher than most cities of similar size—or so say some media and political pundits who dabble from a distance in matters of social significance.

There's crime. There's drugs. There's unemployment. There are the homeless. An array of prickly social issues never seem to get resolved. Is there a metropolitan area the size of Detroit anywhere in the country that is immune to such problems, which have festered for longer than anyone cares to remember?

Nevertheless, Detroit continues to take its verbal hits. "A bar on every corner" and "a factory for every neighborhood" are two of the more caustic quips. No trip to Detroit is complete without witnessing a mugging, touring the smokestacks, watching a car roll off the assembly line or a combination of all three. The jokes come easy for those who wouldn't recognize Detroit if they were dropped on top of the Ambassador Bridge.

To know the city, one must look past the smokestacks. To feel its spirit, one must appreciate the ethics of the ordinary working man. And before trying to understand the essence of the city, one must accept the complexity of its geography. Jagged borders, like the irregular pieces of a complex jigsaw puzzle, separate the actual city from a maze of smaller towns and villages, which collectively form what is commonly known as metropolitan Detroit.

Boundaries blur when driving from one city to the next—which is the only way to get around Detroit. Connected by an intricate system of freeways—both challenging and efficient—the surrounding communities combine to form one of this nation's largest metropolitan areas.

Detroit is Los Angeles without the ocean—Chicago without the lake. It's a melting pot of nearly five million people as different from one another as the ever-changing temperatures of the Midwest climate. Yet for all of their differences, they share a tireless work ethic that has endured for more than three centuries.

Certain suburbs in the constantly expanding metropolis enjoy a significantly more affluent status than neighboring towns with a bleaker financial base. Grosse Pointe and Bloomfield Hills, for example, have become yardsticks for measuring personal affluence all across the country.

Basically, though, Detroit remains a blue-collar city. It measures time by the numbers on a punch clock. More lunches are carried to work in metal buckets than are purchased at four and five-star restaurants. Men in coats and neckties and women dressed in smart business suits and fashionable heels share the same work ethic as their lunch-bucket counterparts.

There is no question that the evolution of the auto industry at the dawn of the 20th century helped to mold the blue-collar work ethic of the city. And there's also no doubt that the evolving success of the Detroit Tigers was a direct consequence of the average working man being able to afford to share in the fortunes of his hometown team.

"That's what impresses me more than anything else about the city," remarked Sparky Anderson whose 17-year career as the Detroit Tigers' manager was the longest in team history.

An aerial view of Detroit's Tiger Stadium in 1972 reveals that the stadium and the team are truly the heart of the city. AP/Wide World Photos

"It doesn't matter if they live in Detroit or Grosse Pointe or any of the other suburbs that make up the town. These are all hard-working people. They work hard. They raise their families well. And they are some of the most generous people that I have ever seen in my whole life. Nobody does more for charity than the people of Detroit."

Besides a work ethic that seems inherent in any youngster born in the metropolitan area, Detroiters share another treasure—their Tigers.

A big-league franchise for more than a century, the Tigers cement the entire state together as no auto plant or even the surrounding Great Lakes can. Only a handful of other professional sports franchises can claim such an impact.

"I learned at least one thing during my stay in Detroit," Anderson said. "All Detroiters aren't sports fans. But all Detroiters love the Tigers."

Detroiters are living proof of what local and national sports writers have claimed for more than a century—Detroit is a "baseball town." And the Tigers were an integral part of the Detroit fabric even before automotive pioneer Henry Ford revolutionized the industrial world with the creation of the assembly line.

Throughout their history, the Tigers have been challenged for the city's attention and affection, by the Lions in football, the Pistons in basketball, the Red Wings in hockey, and at times, by the University of Michigan and Michigan State.

In the end, though, it is the Tigers—always the Tigers—who have maintained a stranglehold on the hearts of Detroit's sports-loving fans.

Perhaps the three most compelling pieces of evidence that underscore Detroit's uncompromising love affair with the Tigers occurred during the seasons of 1934, 1935 and 1968. All three were difficult, disheartening years for Detroit and for the rest of the nation. In 1934 and 1935, the nation was squeezed in the relentless vice of the Great Depression. Soup lines replaced job lines in the city. Apples and pears and precious personal items were sold to any willing buyer in desperate attempts to put food on the family table. Jobs were slashed. Families struggled for survival. With its panoply of auto plants and other factories, Detroit bled more than any other industrial city in America.

In the middle of that backbreaking social and economic misery, the Tigers—in 1934 and '35—almost miraculously lifted the spirit of a broken city by capturing consecutive American League pennants.

Managed by the colorfully pugnacious Mickey Cochrane, the Tigers won 101 games in 1934 before losing the World Series in seven games to the St. Louis Cardinals. The following year the Tigers refused to break. They needed just six games to defeat the Chicago Cubs to claim the city's first world championship. The victory celebration was long and raucous. Dealing with the misery of the Great Depression would have to wait.

Goose Goslin was a grizzled veteran outfielder by the time he was brought to Detroit in 1934 to help put the Tigers over the top. He did just that in the sixth and final game of the 1935 World Series when his ninth-inning single scored Cochrane from second base to snap a 3-3 tie.

"Oh, did those Tiger fans ever go wild," Goslin recalled later. "I'll never forget it."

While the pride of winning a world title was something new to Detroit, another phenomenon that occurred during those two pivotal years was even more enlightening.

In 1934 when the Tigers won their first pennant since the Ty Cobb days of 1909, they drew 919,161 fans to Navin Field, which eventually evolved into Tiger Stadium.

The following year was even more stunning, as the Tigers set an attendance record of 1,034,929, even before the World Series began. In the middle of America's bleakest economic quagmire, the Tigers somehow managed to provide the people of Detroit with a sense of pride and promise for tomorrow.

In 1968 when the Tigers captured their first world championship in 23 years, it was not the economy that was battered. It was, rather, the social spirit of the nation, particularly in the city of Detroit. The war in Vietnam was racing toward its deadly conclusion. Domestically, race relations plunged to their lowest, most sickening level since the Civil War. On television and in newspaper accounts throughout the mid-60s, Detroit had witnessed the rioting, looting, burning and killing that had devastated other major cities. Local politicians, police and the public quietly wondered if such insanity would strike them, too.

In 1967, the unthinkable finally happened. And the civil unrest that erupted in Detroit in midsummer

The 1934 World Series was the final World Series in which both managers were also players. Second baseman/manager Frankie Frisch's St. Louis Cardinals defeated catcher/manager Mickey Cochrane's Tigers four games to three. Burton Historical Society

exceeded all the ugly death and destruction that had broken the spirit of far too many other American cities. In Detroit, there were 43 known deaths and countless millions of dollars in destruction—some of which still lingers today.

The Tigers remained very much in the thick of the 1967 American League pennant race to the last day of the season before bowing to the Boston Red Sox. Then, reminiscent of Mickey Cochrane's Tigers 33 years earlier, the 1968 Tigers danced all the way to the pennant, and rallied for victory in the last three games of the World Series against the St. Louis Cardinals to once again launch the city of Detroit into a celebration heard round the world.

On the streets of downtown Detroit and in neighborhoods throughout the area, blacks and whites united. They danced. They hugged. They shared swigs of beer and other celebratory beverages. At least for the moment, everybody was one.

Detroit is a tough town. And it's certainly not naive. Detroiters rightfully scoff at any suggestion that a ball club can heal the wounds of a century-old social malady as serious as racism. Nevertheless, at least for that one glorious moment, the bleeding had stopped. It was a beautiful moment. One filled with pride and promise.

In that magical season of redemption, the Tigers set another attendance record of 2,031,847 as people of all colors and all walks of life took time to find some semblance of sanity in a night out at the ballpark.

Back in 1945, after the Tigers defeated the Chicago Cubs in the World Series, the *Detroit News* opined about "a strange, almost mystical connection between Detroit's fortunes in the world of sport and the state of the local mind and morale."

How can a baseball team produce such an emotional impact on the city? How can such a simple game reach out to so many who seem to be so divided in so many other measurable ways?

Maybe the answer is found in a simple conclusion that sounds as trite as the seventh-inning stretch.

Detroit is a baseball town.

What makes Detroit any more a baseball town than Chicago or Cleveland or Boston or any other city? Sociologists may suggest a theory as complex as a Latin version of the infield fly rule. The explanation may be as simple as the fact that baseball is a game that tugs at the heart of a working-class town. While other sports teams have had their moments in Detroit, none but

the Tigers have sustained it, now for more than a century.

Baseball's unique appeal is equally compelling to people of all social and economic classes. Although the price for today's game may limit the frequency of attendance for many working-class families, the game was founded upon its availability to fans from all economic strata.

From the captains of the automotive industry to the hourly workers who make the cars and trucks that roll off the line, baseball has enjoyed a unique universal appeal in Detroit. From the flannel shirts to the white collars and neckties and from the stations on the assembly line to the offices atop imposing skyscrapers, the Tigers belong to the city.

In Detroit, where generation after generation has chosen to make its home, the Tiger tradition has passed from father to son and mother to daughter year after year after year.

John E. Fetzer, the former Tiger owner who became a baseball legend through his visionary genius for televising games, succinctly captured the spirit of baseball in Detroit.

"I have never considered myself the owner of the Tigers," Fetzer observed. "I serve merely as the club's guardian. The Tigers belong to the fans. They are the true owners of this great franchise."

That sentiment is shared by all true Tiger fans. It's the underlying reason why Detroit is a baseball town.

Tiger fans can be brutally honest with the team they call their own. Promotions and gimmicks may sell tickets in some cities. In Detroit, it's wins and losses that count the most. Loyal Tiger fans also are unconditionally forgiving. Their only demand is the same honest effort from their team that is expected of them in their workplace.

Tradition is a term that is overused more than a last-place team's weary bullpen. Many teams talk about tradition. Few, however, are living examples of it.

Tradition is as tough to define as a sudden unexpected ninth-inning breeze that carries a routine fly ball barely over the fence. You can't see tradition. Certainly no one can touch it. In some inexplicable manner, however, tradition is real. And when a ball club is filled with tradition, you can feel it from the box seats behind home plate all the way to the farthest reaches of the bleachers.

Tradition is a living tribute to bygone generations of ballplayers, managers, owners and fans. Tradition is a commitment to the present and a promise for the future.

Tradition is not measured merely by games and championships won. It is, rather, a collection of characters and events that, over an extended period of time, create a living legacy.

Tradition has a beginning. But it has no real end.

Baseball is believed to have been played first in Detroit in the early 1850s. The first recorded game to appear in the *Detroit Free Press* occurred on August 15, 1857 and was played at the corner of Adams and Beaubien, just a pop fly from where the Tigers' new home, Comerica Park, stands today. That first game was more of an intramural contest played by a potpourri of citizens gathered for a fun day in the sun.

Detroit's first professional team played its first game on May 12, 1879 against Troy, New York, in the National Association of Professional Baseball Players league. The game was played at Recreation Park where the Detroit Medical Center stands today.

From 1881 through 1888, the Detroit Wolverines were part of baseball's National League. The franchise was sold after the 1888 season and later was revived as part of the minor-league Western League under the ownership of Californian George Arthur Vanderbeck.

Under Vanderbeck, Detroit played two years at League Park, which was located just outside what was then the city's eastern limit near Belle Isle. After he stated that Detroit would be "the cream of the league," Vanderbeck's ball club was quickly dubbed the "Creams."

It was Vanderbeck who first built a baseball park on property located at the corner of Michigan and Trumbull, which would become one of the most celebrated intersections in sports.

On April 13, 1896 in a spring training exhibition, the first competitive game was played at the famous "Corner." On April 28, the first official Western League game was played there and Detroit walloped Columbus, 17-2.

The park was known as Bennett Park in honor of Charlie Bennett, who had been a popular catcher for the Detroit Wolverines before losing his left foot and right leg in a freak off-season train accident.

By the time the team moved into its new home, it was already commonly known as the "Tigers." Historians differ on the origin of the name, although a

headline in the April 16, 1895 edition of the *Detroit Free Press* referred to the team as "Tigers."

With a new home and a new name, Detroit was ready to return to baseball's major leagues. On October 14, 1900, the Western League dropped smaller franchises in Buffalo, Indianapolis, Kansas City and Minneapolis in order to add the larger markets of Baltimore, Boston, Philadelphia and Washington and form the American League.

On April 25, 1901, an overflow crowd of 10,023 at cozy Bennett Park witnessed the Detroit Tigers erupt for 10 runs in the bottom of the ninth inning to nip Milwaukee, 14-13, in their first American League game.

Thus began a tradition that still lives today.

Tradition, however, is no more than a word without the characters that shape its essence. Throughout their history—which has spanned the evolution of the automobile and airline industries, two world wars and countless lesser ones, the Great Depression, Prohibition, recessions, over-the-air and cable TV, the computer explosion and the hula hoop—the Tigers have featured enough characters to fill several Damon Runyan novels.

In Frank Navin, Walter O. Briggs and John E. Fetzer, the Tigers boast three of the most influential owners the game has ever known.

Navin was the bald, bespectacled man who established the franchise at the beginning of the 20th century. Navin laid the foundation for the stadium that Detroiters would call home until the dawn of the next century. It was under Frank Navin that the Tigers won their first three pennants in 1907-08-09. They also won pennants in 1934-35, shortly before Navin's death.

Navin was a bookkeeper by trade, but a gambler at heart. Before his Tiger career, he spent time working as a croupier in one of Detroit's gambling houses. He was a regular at the racetrack and reportedly often made wagers that exceeded the yearly salaries of some of his players.

Among the many stars who played under Navin were the incomparable Ty Cobb and fellow Hall of Famers Harry Heilmann, Charlie Gehringer, Hank Greenberg and Sam Crawford.

It was under Navin, in 1924, that an upper deck down the right field line was added to the ballpark that bore his name, giving shape to the stadium that served as the Tigers' home for the rest of the century.

Walter O. Briggs was a diehard baseball fan who initially bought into the club so that he would always be guaranteed a good seat. Briggs and Navin first met in 1907 when Briggs had trouble purchasing tickets for the first game of the World Series.

During the early years of the emerging auto industry, Briggs became a multimillionaire. He founded the Briggs Manufacturing Company, which became the nation's largest independent builder of automobile bodies. The company consisted of 16 plants, including nine in Detroit and one in England.

In 1920, Briggs paid Bill Yawkey's estate $250,000 for a quarter-share of the Tigers. When Navin died in 1935, Briggs bought the rest of the team from the Navin family.

Walter O. Briggs was an enigma. He was often accused of being heartless in his dealings with his industrial laborers. The shadow of racism followed him

Tigers' owner and industrialist Walter O. Briggs, confined to a wheelchair by polio, watches a game in the rain. Collection of Jim Hawkins Productions Inc.

throughout his life. But he also was a philanthropist and reportedly had a soft spot in his heart for children.

Regardless of his personal strengths and shortcomings, Briggs was the ultimate baseball fan. After taking over the club in 1936, Briggs stated publicly that his desire was "to give Detroit the best team in the finest park in the country."

He never wavered from that commitment. He turned Navin Field, which he renamed Briggs Stadium, into the showcase of the major leagues. After the 1937 season, Briggs invested one million dollars to raze the third base pavilion and build a two-deck grandstand that wrapped all the way around to the center field upper deck, giving Detroit baseball's first full two-deck stadium. The infield and outfield grass was manicured like a putting green. The green seats and walls that Briggs had installed turned the park into a hitter's paradise. He spent lavishly on players, but remained committed to keeping ticket prices affordable for the average working man.

By design, Fetzer maintained public anonymity. He, too, was a self-made man who earned his fortune by founding and purchasing radio and television stations across the country. He was known as "Gray John" for his outwardly conservative demeanor. Over the years, he was rarely seen around the park.

But with Jim Campbell, his handpicked choice to oversee the operation of his boyhood favorite team, Fetzer carefully guided the franchise for nearly three decades through some of baseball's most turbulent economic and labor-troubled years.

It was Fetzer's vision, almost a halfcentury ago, that led major-league baseball into national television contracts that set the stage for today's abundance of televised games.

Like his predecessor, Fetzer insisted that the Tigers must remain affordable for families of every economic level. It was under his stewardship that the Tigers developed one of the most productive minorleague systems in the game.

Fetzer's dedication to the overall good health of baseball was relentless. He was considered by his fellow owners to be the "power behind the throne" and often influenced the direction of the American League president and the commissioner himself.

From Hughie Jennings to the indomitable Sparky Anderson, the Tigers have been blessed with some of the most colorful managers the game has ever known.

Jennings won pennants in each of his first three seasons (1907-08-09) and stayed at the helm through 1920. No one thought his club records for longevity and success would ever be challenged until a bubbly white-haired magician called Sparky came along in 1979 to set new club standards that will probably never be approached.

In between those two came a parade of colorful characters such as Ty Cobb, Bucky Harris, Mickey Cochrane, Steve O'Neill, Charlie Dressen, and Billy Martin, who belong as much to the history of the game as they do to the Tigers.

To paraphrase Ralph Waldo Emerson, not everyone can be a hero. There have to be some who sit at the curb and applaud. Throughout each decade of their existence, the Tigers have featured a number of heroes and a colorful cast of supporting players who captured the imaginations of fans across the country.

To this day, Tyrus Raymond Cobb remains the yardstick by which all superstar players are measured. Cobb was the fiery, enigmatic batting wizard who defined the Tigers' spirited tradition at the same time Henry Ford made Detroit the auto capital of the world by creating the assembly line.

The coupling of those two unbridled forces transcended mere coincidence. With the city's population growing exponentially from the abundance of jobs in the burgeoning auto industry, and with Cobb serving as the showcase of America's national game, Detroit was suddenly transformed into one of the most dynamic cities in the country.

It was the combination of such dynamic forces that prompted Navin, in 1912, to build Navin Field, which was initially a jewel among professional parks.

The legacy of Cobb still lives to this day. Beginning in 1907, he won nine straight batting championships. In 1916 he "slipped" to second with a .371 mark before adding three more straight titles starting in 1917.

Cobb finished his 24-year major-league career with a lifetime .367 average, by far the highest in baseball history. He had 4,191 hits, a mark that stood until Pete Rose surpassed him in 1985. At one time, Cobb owned nearly 100 major-league records.

Cobb's numbers, records and awards are staggering. But they paint only a partial portrait of perhaps the most celebrated love/hate figure ever to wear a big-league uniform.

American humorist Will Rogers once stated he never met a man he didn't like. Those who played with or against Cobb would certainly argue that Rogers never had the opportunity—or misfortune—to encounter the baseball legend from Georgia. As brilliant as he was on a diamond, Cobb was reviled by opponents and teammates alike. He played each game, each inning, each time at bat as if it were his last. And he did so with a fury that resembled a man possessed. He had a passion for excellence and total disregard for how he was perceived.

"Cobb was a very complex person," observed Davy Jones, who played with the so-called "Genius in Spikes" for six seasons. "Never did have many friends. Trouble was he had such a rotten disposition that it was damn hard to be his friend. He antagonized so many people that hardly anyone would speak to him, even among his own teammates.

"I was probably the best friend he had on the club. I used to stick up for him, sit and talk with him on the long train trips, try to understand the man.

"Ty didn't have a sense of humor, see. Especially, he could never laugh at himself. Consequently, he took a lot of things the wrong way. What would usually be an innocent enough wisecrack would become cause for a fist fight if Ty was involved."

That's because Cobb took everything seriously. Especially when it came to baseball.

While Cobb denied accusations of sharpening his spikes to terrorize infielders whenever he slid hard into a base, he certainly turned the reputation into his advantage. After sliding demonically into third baseman Frank "Home Run" Baker in Philadelphia, Cobb needed a police escort to leave the stadium.

That didn't bother Cobb. Except for a loss, nothing ever did.

He was gifted, tireless, daring, fearless, rude, vile, respected and detested. Some suspected he was possessed by the devil himself. Cobb also was one of the best players ever to set foot on a diamond. He gave shape to the Detroit franchise right from the start.

With Cobb leading the charge, the Tigers captured three straight pennants in 1907-08-09. Although they didn't win a World Series and wouldn't appear in another until 1934, it was during Cobb's years as player/manager (1921-26) that the Tigers became one of baseball's most powerful forces.

With an outfield of Cobb, future Hall of Famer Harry Heilmann, and Bobby Veach, Detroit featured a lethal offense that sent enemy pitchers scurrying for cover. In 1921, the trio combined for a .374 average and knocked in 368 runs. The team set an American League record with a .316 batting average that year. In four of Cobb's six seasons as manager, the team averaged better than a .300 batting average.

Heilmann, a husky right-handed hitter from San Francisco, was one of the few players who got along with Cobb. The master took Heilmann under his wing and adjusted his batting stroke to make more use of the entire field. The tutelage obviously worked, as Heilmann won four batting titles and finished with a .342 lifetime average.

The explosive Tiger lineup came at a magical time for the city. Thanks to the auto industry and the city's prosperous bootlegging activities during Prohibition,

In his 15 years with the Tigers, Harry Heilmann won four batting titles—1921, 1923, 1925 and 1927. Brace Photo

Detroit's economy was booming. Except for the Yankees, the Tigers drew more fans than any other team in 1922-23-24. That bonanza prompted Navin to add an upper deck to his right field grandstand, boosting seating capacity to 29,000.

"Detroit is simply baseball crazy," said a story in *The Sporting News* in 1924.

Despite the hype and hysteria, the Tigers didn't return to the winner's circle until 10 years later in 1934. By that time, the nation was being choked by the Great Depression. The economy was battered. The good times of the previous decade had been replaced with desperation and despair. Although the entire nation suffered, Detroit was leveled as if it had been punched below the belt. The most industrialized city in America suddenly found no buyers for its mechanical wonders.

Nevertheless, at least the Tigers offered the city a respite from the gloom. In 1934, the Tigers attracted 919,161 to the ballpark. The following year they set a club record by drawing 1,034,929.

Navin had assembled a talented and colorful crew led by the incomparable "G-Men" of Charlie Gehringer and Hank Greenberg. While each was bountifully gifted in his own particular way, they were bipolar in personality and in the backgrounds from which they came.

Gehringer was a quiet introspective man from the farmlands of Fowlerville, Michigan, located between Detroit and Lansing. Anything more than a soft smile and "good morning" from Gehringer was considered to be a major speech. He was signed by Frank Navin after Ty Cobb watched him play second base. At that position, some historians maintain that there has never been anyone better.

Gehringer was nicknamed the "Mechanical Man" by pitcher Lefty Gomez.

"You wind him up in the spring and he goes all summer, hits .330 or .340 or whatever, and then you shut him off in the fall," Gomez observed in his admiration of Gehringer.

Greenberg shared in the admiration of his teammate.

"I used to marvel at how smooth Charlie was with his feet from anywhere on the field," Greenberg observed. "He could move in, out and to either side so quickly and without any effort. It looked like he was playing on skates. I used to idolize him. He made everything look so easy."

From left to right, Manager Mickey Cochrane, Hank Greenberg and Charlie Gehringer share a laugh at a game with the White Sox in Chicago on April 20, 1938. AP/Wide World Photos

As brilliant as Gehringer was in the field, he was equally devastating at the plate. He drove pitchers crazy with his ability to rip line drives at will to any part of the park. He finished with a .320 average and 1,427 RBIs for his 19-year career, all with the Tigers.

For Greenberg, the game was often as difficult as it was easy for Gehringer. And it was more than just the pitchers with whom the strapping, handsome first baseman from New York had to battle.

Greenberg was one of the few Jewish players—and by far the best—in the major leagues. While he was embraced by Detroit's growing Jewish community, he was an easy target for on-field insults and racial slurs, which were far more prevalent in those days.

"I thought I handled it pretty well," Greenberg reminisced. "I never let them know they were getting to me. That way, they would have won. But it wasn't easy. I could take it because I saw others getting it, too. Italians were 'wops,' Germans were 'krauts,' and Polish players were 'dumb Polacks.' Me, I was a 'kike,' a 'sheenie,' or a 'mockie.' I was a good target. What made it tough is that there were a lot of Italians, Germans and Poles around, but I was the only Jew. They seemed to reserve a little extra for me."

While the personal attacks on Greenberg were relentless, so was his attack on American League pitchers. He led the league in home runs and RBIs four times. In 1938, he belted 58 HRs.

With Greenberg at first, Gehringer at second, Billy Rogell at shortstop and Marv Owen at third, the Tiger infield set a record with 462 RBIs in 1934.

Before that season began, Navin was concerned about how the Depression was crippling almost every business. Looking for a way to spike attendance, he tried to lure Babe Ruth into taking over as manager. When The Babe put him off, Navin, at the urging and with the financial support of his silent partner, Walter O. Briggs, turned elsewhere.

The combination of shortstop Billy Rogell and second baseman Charlie Gehringer was a key to the 1934 and 1935 pennants. Rogell played with the Tigers from 1930-39. Burton Historical Society

It may have been the most fortunate turn of events in Detroit franchise history.

Looking to unload some of his high-priced talent to pay off a bank loan, Philadelphia Athletics owner Connie Mack offered the Tigers catcher Mickey Cochrane for $100,000. Briggs loaned the ball club the money from his personal funds. The pugnacious Irishman from Massachusetts was the perfect fit for a tough town during tough times.

Cochrane, who brought his charisma, fire, inspiration, temper, leadership, stubbornness and a knack for being ornery at all the right times, led the Tigers to the pennant in his first season as player/manager.

"Cochrane was a good hitter," Charlie Gehringer recalled. "As a manager he was very good, very good. He was a tough loser and he made you fight even though you were behind 10-1. And boy, if he lost on an error and maybe the guy played it carelessly, he would stare at you and you'd know that he wouldn't have to say anything."

Shortly after purchasing Cochrane, Navin traded little-known John Stone to Washington for outfielder Goose Goslin. Goslin was nearing the end of his career, but had enough left to deliver the World Series' deciding hit in 1935 before retiring and waiting for his call into the Hall of Fame, along with Gehringer, Greenberg and Cochrane.

The Tigers lost the 1934 Series in seven games to the St. Louis Cardinals. In the celebrated finale, commissioner Kenesaw Mountain Landis removed Ducky Medwick from the game after the Cardinal left fielder was deluged with a barrage of garbage by disappointed Tiger fans. The incident occurred following an altercation between Medwick and Tiger third baseman Marv Owen the previous inning.

In 1935, however, no one could stop the Tigers. Sparked by Greenberg's league-leading 36 homers and 170 RBIs, the Tigers rambled to the pennant witnessed by a club record of 1,034,929 fans. The Tigers needed just six games to defeat the Chicago Cubs for the first world championship in Detroit baseball history.

Fearful, after four earlier setbacks, that he would never realize the joy of a world championship, Navin watched his city celebrate deliriously.

Five weeks later, on November 13, the 64-year-old suffered a heart attack while riding a horse at the Detroit Riding and Hunt Club on Belle Isle. He died a short while later at Detroit Osteopathic Hospital.

Navin's untimely death ended one of the Tigers' most colorful eras. In spite of subsequent world championships in 1945, 1968 and 1984, many historians contend that the Tigers of the 1930s were the most significant in franchise history.

Navin's passing brought an end to an era in which the Tigers had firmly established themselves as one of the most solid franchises in the major leagues. From Cobb and Heilmann to Gehringer and Greenberg, Navin's teams all shared a toughness that reflected the city they represented.

Walter O. Briggs had been Navin's silent limited partner for several years. He wasted no time purchasing total control. Immediately upon hearing of Navin's

Hank Greenberg, right, and Rudy York were a hitting force for the Tigers in the late 1930s and early '40s.
Burton Historical Society

death, Briggs sent an emissary bearing a check equal to the book value of the ball club to Navin's heirs.

"Maybe Mr. Briggs wanted to help them with the funeral expenses," cracked Harry Sisson, who served as club secretary at the time and was the alleged courier of the check.

Briggs carried on the tradition of keeping baseball a sport for the hard-working city's working men. He was lavish in his spending on players and stadium expansion and maintenance. Through Briggs's 17 years of sole ownership, however, the Tigers could manage just two pennants and one world championship.

Nevertheless, the colorful Briggs era witnessed America fight its way out of depression, return home victoriously from World War II and embark upon the "happy days" of the 1950s with prosperity, Elvis and rock 'n' roll.

In 1940, the Tigers unexpectedly nipped the Cleveland Indians by one game and the four-time defending champion New York Yankees by two for the pennant. The previous season the Tigers had finished a distant fifth, 26 games out of first.

The pitching staff was solid with Tommy Bridges, Bobo Newsom and Schoolboy Rowe. But again, it was Detroit's bruising offense that did the damage. The Tigers led the league with a .286 team average and 888 runs scored.

As usual, Hank Greenberg was the hammer. He batted .340 and led the league with 41 homers and 150 RBIs. Two years away from retirement, Charlie Gehringer was slowing slightly, but still managed a .313 mark with 108 runs and 81 RBIs.

A $10,000 investment by Briggs proved to be the best bargain of the season. That was how much the Tigers gave Greenberg to move to left field to make room for Rudy York at first base. Though he had hands of stone in the field, York was a certified executioner at the plate. Batting fifth behind Greenberg, he hit .316 with 33 homers and 134 RBIs.

Legendary sports writer Red Smith best described York:

"Rudolph Preston York, the muscular house painter of Cartersville, Georgia, was a large copper-colored man with about three fingers of Cherokee blood in his veins.

"Rudy was an outfielder, a third baseman, and a catcher as well as a first baseman. No matter where he was stationed in the field, Rudy York always played the same position.

"He played bat.

"He was slow, unskilled, awkward, sincere, tireless, and stronger than dirt. There were many things he couldn't do well on a playground and some he couldn't do at all, but when he swung a bolt of mountain ash, the baseball left the neighborhood."

Greenberg and York were a one-two combo that gave pitchers ulcers every time they faced Detroit. Nevertheless, in the 1940 World Series, the Reds rallied to win the last two games at Cincinnati to stifle Detroit's dream of a Cinderella season.

Then, suddenly, things changed. Not just for the Tigers, but for the whole world.

The nation was on the brink of war when the Tigers received their first direct hit. Greenberg was the first significant major leaguer to be drafted. He entered the army on May 17, 1941 for a six-month tour of duty. Released on December 5, Greenberg immediately reenlisted after learning of Japan's attack on Pearl Harbor.

"I wanted to get back," Greenberg recalled later. "Every day I was gone I thought about playing at Briggs Stadium in front of all of those great fans. But baseball had to take a back seat to serving the country."

For Greenberg, that back seat turned into the loss of four prime baseball years.

Greenberg, of course, had plenty of company in military service. It is estimated that by 1945, about 5,400 of 5,800 major- and minor-league players were involved with some sort of military duty.

The City of Detroit turned its attention to the war. That's what tough towns do during tough times. Proudly, the city became known as the "arsenal of democracy." After the bombing of Pearl Harbor on December 7, 1941, President Franklin D. Roosevelt ordered all production of civilian automobiles to cease on February 1, 1942. It was time for the labor force to roll up its sleeves and show America's enemies, firsthand, just what the Motor City was made of.

United Auto Workers union pioneer Walter Reuther threw down the gauntlet when he said that while England's battles were won "on the playing fields of Eton, America's can be won on the assembly lines of Detroit."

And Reuther was right.

With Detroit putting the full weight of its awesome industrial power into the war effort, the output of weapons and equipment was breathtaking. Out of the city's factories and foundries rolled jeeps, trucks, tanks, engines, airplanes, artillery, rifles and ammunition.

Detroit's Chrysler Jefferson Avenue plant produced 450-horsepower engines by the thousands. They were installed in Sherman tanks at a plant in nearby Warren. At Willow Run, west of Detroit, thousands of Ford workers produced B-24 bombers at the mind-boggling rate of one every hour.

Along with loaning the country some of their finest young men, the Tigers did their part by paying fans twenty-five cents in war stamps for every foul ball that was returned to the field from the stands. Not only were Briggs's factories producing war materials, but the steel he had purchased for the construction of stadium light towers was donated to the war effort.

The quality of baseball suffered immeasurably during the war. Nevertheless, President Roosevelt insisted that the games be played to lift the morale of the nation. Ballgames, especially in a city as committed as Detroit, were a welcome respite.

Traces of normalcy began to trickle back in 1945 as the war neared its end. In Detroit, times were anything but normal.

Greenberg returned to the lineup at Briggs Stadium on July 1, 1945 for a doubleheader against Philadelphia. Before a frenzied packed house, he belted a home run in the eighth inning of the opener. The highlight of his return, however, came on the final day of the season against the Browns at St. Louis when Greenberg belted a grand slam in the ninth inning to clinch the pennant.

It wasn't pretty, but the Tigers nipped Washington by one game with a .575 winning percentage, the lowest of any pennant winner.

Hal Newhouser led the league with 25 victories, a 1.81 ERA and 29 complete games. He thus became the only pitcher ever to win the Most Valuable Player Award two seasons in a row.

The World Series was anything but a classic. Some writers quipped that the team that made the fewest blunders would have to be considered the champion.

It took seven games, but the Tigers outlasted the Chicago Cubs. Although the victory celebration meant significantly less than the one that heralded the end of the war, it was a fitting reward for a city that, arguably, had contributed more than any other in the service of its country.

The first postwar championship would also be the last for Briggs. The Briggs era ended when he died on January 17, 1952.

Tiger manager Red Rolfe perhaps summarized Briggs's legacy best: "He was the last major-league owner with the viewpoint of the fans."

In 1952, the Tigers finished dead last. In the following four years, while the team was held in trust, the Tigers could rise no higher than fifth. The front office fell into disarray. Finally, lawyers representing the Briggs family trust deemed the team to be an unsuitable asset. The franchise was put up for auction. Spike Briggs, who had grown up with his father's team, failed in his attempts to assemble a group of investors, which would have guaranteed him control of the ball club.

Maverick owner Bill Veeck put together his own group and desperately tried to purchase the franchise. An 11-man syndicate that included John Fetzer outmaneuvered Veeck with a last-minute bid of $5.5 million. On October 1, 1956, the sale of the Tigers became official.

With its purchase of one of sports' most storied franchises, the syndicate did inherit a few valuable assets. There was Harvey Kuenn, who went on to win a batting title in 1959 and then was traded for home run champion Rocky Colavito just prior to the start of the 1960 season. There was Jim Bunning, who spent half of his career with Detroit and the other half with the Philadelphia Phillies and was elected to the U.S. House of Representatives from Kentucky, and then the U.S. Senate, before being inducted into baseball's Hall of Fame.

Most importantly, there was Al Kaline. The splendid right fielder spent his entire 22-year career with the Tigers en route to the Hall of Fame. He was the foundation upon which the championship team of 1968 was built.

The new owners of the Tigers quickly discovered—the hard way—a basic unwritten rule of baseball: an 11-partner ownership simply doesn't work.

Fetzer understood the situation better than anyone in the group and methodically went about buying up the shares of his partners. Shortly after Fred Knorr was tragically scalded to death, Fetzer negotiated a deal with the Knorr family for the remaining shares of the club. On November 14, 1961, Fetzer became sole owner of the team that he had followed since he was a young boy.

It marked the dawn of a new era in Tiger history. In many respects that era was just as significant as those that were overseen by Navin and Briggs. In some ways it was far more significant to the tradition of the Tigers and the game itself.

Fetzer was an enlightened businessman who realized that ownership of the Tigers would protect the game's broadcast rights for the radio and TV stations that he owned across the state. He also harbored a deep-rooted conviction that the game belonged to people of all economic levels throughout the state of Michigan.

He demonstrated that conviction by urging members of the dwindling syndicate to drop the name of Briggs from the ballpark. On January 1, 1961, while Fetzer was busy completing the buyouts of his remaining partners, the stadium that had carried the names of Frank Navin and Walter O. Briggs officially became Tiger Stadium.

Fetzer was a traditionalist who believed a club's most valuable asset was a productive farm system. He immediately restructured the organization to enhance its developmental capabilities.

Perhaps the most significant decision Fetzer made throughout his career was the appointment of Jim Campbell to the position of general manager at the end of the 1962 season.

Campbell was only 38 years old but had worked in the Tiger organization since 1949. Campbell served as general manager, president and chairman of the board until being fired on August 3, 1992 as part of the club's sale from Tom Monaghan to Mike and Marian Ilitch.

Throughout his entire professional career, Campbell worked for no other organization. His employment with the Tigers covered 44 years—almost 50 percent of the franchise history at that time.

A portly, bald, cigar-smoking workaholic, Campbell was a throwback to the baseball leaders of yesteryear. Although he consulted daily with Fetzer, who approved all major decisions, Campbell ran the club as if it were his own.

"That's the way all successful ball clubs were run," observed Sparky Anderson. "Jim was all baseball. None of the other stuff meant a lot to him."

Often accused of being tight with Fetzer's money, Campbell quietly withstood the barbs of media and fans. Fetzer and Campbell shared a strong conviction that only a profitable club—regardless how small the yearly profit may be—had a chance to succeed on the field. Campbell's lone concern was fielding a representative team year after year. In the mold of his boss,

Campbell appointed qualified specialists for each department of the rapidly changing industry. Then he got out of the way and let them do their jobs.

"The most important thing about Jim was his honesty," Sparky said. "His word was his bond. If he told you something, you could go to the bank with it."

The Tigers made an unexpected pennant run at the New York Yankees in 1961. Although they finished eight games back, they won 101 games on the strength of a lethal offense led by Norm Cash, Rocky Colavito and Al Kaline.

While Roger Maris drew most of baseball's attention by breaking Babe Ruth's home run record with 61, Cash was busy racing to the batting title with a .361 mark. Kaline finished second at .324. Cash belted 41 homers and knocked in 132 runs. Both marks fell slightly short of Colavito's 45 HRs and 140 RBIs.

But the good times were fleeting. That's when Fetzer and Campbell dedicated themselves to a farm system that soon produced Mickey Lolich, Bill Freehan, Willie Horton, Mickey Stanley, Jim Northrup, Dick McAuliffe and Gates Brown, among others. The process may have taken a few years longer than Tiger fans had hoped, but the commitment led to the unforgettable pennant race of 1967 and the world championship of 1968.

For once, the overworked term "classic" could legitimately be applied to the 1968 World Series. Consider the following:

- Before the Series began, Mickey Stanley was switched from center field to shortstop.
- The turning point in the Series occurred when fleet-footed Lou Brock decided not to slide into home plate and was cut down by a strong throw from Willie Horton to Bill Freehan.
- Jim Northrup's game-winning triple in the seventh game was the result of a misjudged line drive by slick-fielding St. Louis center fielder Curt Flood.
- The celebrated pitching duel between eventual Hall of Famer Bob Gibson and 31-game winner Denny McLain was overshadowed by three complete-game victories by the unheralded Mickey Lolich.
- And the Tigers' miraculous comeback occurred after they had been left for dead facing a three-games-to-one deficit.

"The Year of the Tiger," as it was dubbed by media around the state, was the result of a total organizational effort.

Despite a plethora of talent, the Tigers couldn't repeat their magic. In 1970, the club and the whole community were rocked by three suspensions of their talented but miscreant pitcher, Denny McLain.

One was the result of associating with alleged underworld figures. Following the third suspension, Campbell had his fill. He shocked the baseball world by trading McLain and a few lesser names to the Washington Senators in a deal that brought Joe Coleman, Eddie Brinkman and Aurelio Rodriguez to Detroit.

The deal turned out to be a heist for Campbell. The Tigers acquired a pitcher who would win 23 games in a season and an entirely new left side of the infield.

The fiery Billy Martin was brought in to spark one last gasp of life into the aging Tigers. And they responded with an East Division title in 1972 before losing to the Oakland A's in five games in the playoffs.

Soon the aging team would be dismantled and the Tigers again would have to rely on their farm system. It would be 14 years before the Tigers were able to make another postseason appearance.

Ralph Houk was lured from New York to manage a team in transition. The former New York Yankee boss knew it was going to be tough. Few, however, realized just how tough it would be. For the first time in history, the Tigers posted back-to-back last-place finishes in 1974 and 1975.

In 1974, Kaline reached the celebrated 3,000-hit plateau. He ended his brilliant career with 3,007 hits and a ticket to the Hall of Fame on his first ballot in 1980.

Ron LeFlore, one of the most colorful characters to play in Detroit, made his debut in 1974. He had been signed out of Jackson State Prison and soon dazzled fans with his speed and athleticism.

The 1976 season belonged to one man. Only 21 years old and not even on the roster when the season began, Mark "The Bird" Fidrych captured the imagination of the whole country with his frenetic energy, his habit of talking to the baseball and his ability to fire a baseball within a millimeter of where he was aiming.

"The Bird" became a national phenomenon that transcended baseball. His electrifying personality packed parks wherever he pitched.

"In all my years in the game, I never saw one player generate more excitement than Mark did," Campbell commented. "And the best part about it was that he really was a great kid."

After breaking into the starting rotation in May, Fidrych finished with 19 wins and a league-leading 2.34 ERA to easily capture the Rookie of the Year award.

Fidrych's flame fizzled quickly, however. Injuries struck the next spring training and he never was able to fulfill the promise he had shown.

The Tiger farm system also produced a couple of young sluggers in Steve Kemp and Jason Thompson. But the premier batch that would lead to the next world championship was still in the making.

Alan Trammell, Lou Whitaker, Jack Morris, Dan Petry, Lance Parrish, Kirk Gibson, and Tom Brookens formed the nucleus of the team that from 1980 through

Ace pitcher Mickey Lolich delivers a pitch against the Yankees in 1968.
AP/Wide World Photos

1988 won more games than anyone else in the American League.

As fresh talent began to trickle onto the scene, Jim Campbell was determined to find the leader who could best nurture all of the young prospects to their full potential. He did that in June, 1979, when he hired Sparky Anderson as manager.

Never at a loss for a few hundred well-chosen words, Sparky quickly promised that his young Tigers would be in a World Series within five years. In 1984 the Tigers made their white-haired skipper look like a genius.

They set a major-league record by jumping to a 35-5 start, won a club-record 104 games and led their division from wire to wire.

In the playoffs, the Tigers swept the Kansas City Royals in three games and then needed just five to dispose of the San Diego Padres in the World Series. Alan Trammell belted a pair of homers in Game 4 and won the Series MVP. In the Series clincher, Kirk Gibson poked two HRs, including a monstrous three-run blast with runners on second and third when Padres relief ace Goose Gossage declined to walk him intentionally.

Shortly before the season began, the Tigers picked up Dave Bergman and Willie Hernandez in a deal with Philadelphia. Bergman developed into a valuable role player and Hernandez merely turned into the best reliever since Rolaids. The lefty saved 32 games in 33 opportunities and waltzed to the Cy Young and MVP Awards.

There were a few other major changes before the season began. Veteran National League slugging first baseman Darrell Evans became Detroit's first major free agent signing with an $800,000 contract.

But the biggest change had occurred two months earlier in October 1983, when Fetzer shocked baseball by selling the ball club to his hand-picked successor, Tom Monaghan, who turned his single-shop pizzeria in Ypsilanti, Michigan, into a $1.4 billion chain known as Domino's.

As a boy, Monaghan had dreamed about playing shortstop for the Tigers. He settled for the position of owner, forking over $53 million to Fetzer, who remained as chairman of the board.

Fetzer had simply tired of the direction baseball was headed. He was convinced that out-of-control spending and too many frivolous marketing gimmicks were diluting the purity of the sport he so loved.

What looked like a dynasty in 1984, however, had trouble returning to postseason play. The Tigers finally made it back to the playoffs in 1987 with a miraculous uphill struggle after starting the season with an 11-19 record.

"I promise you that before this thing is over, we'll be in the race," Sparky proclaimed at that low point, making many people wonder what was wrong with the manager.

When it was over, Sparky was right. The Tigers swept a three-game series from the Toronto Blue Jays to clinch the division title on the season's final day. The prior weekend in Toronto, the Tigers had dropped three straight games before Kirk Gibson homered in the 13th inning of the fourth game to keep Detroit two games back of the Blue Jays with seven to play. All seven games of the home-and-home weekend series were decided by one run.

"Those were the best seven games anyone's ever seen," Sparky bubbled. "I'll always be grateful for that 1984 team. But the one in my whole career I'm proudest of is the 1987 team. We had no business winning the division, but that team refused to quit."

The Tigers were knocked out of the playoffs in five games by an upstart Minnesota team, and Detroit has not returned to the postseason since.

Players lost to free agency soon began to take a toll on the Tigers. Lance Parrish left after the 1986 season. Kirk Gibson left after 1987 and Jack Morris departed after 1990.

The biggest wave to rock the Tigers, though, occurred away from the field. Monaghan's personal finances were reeling. He was in danger of losing both the ball club and the pizza chain that he had founded.

When Jim Campbell stepped down as president to become chairman of the board and chief executive officer in 1990, legendary University of Michigan football coach Bo Schembechler was hired as president. Although his tenure was short, Schembechler proved to be adept at running a professional franchise. He immediately upgraded the scouting system, added minor-league coaches for each affiliate, and built an elaborate training facility for better conditioning.

Nothing, however, could salvage the downward financial spiral of Monaghan, the owner. On August 26, 1992, the announcement was made that Monaghan had sold the club to Mike and Marian Ilitch for $85 million.

Fans welcome the Tigers to their new home, Comerica Park. Mike Litaker

Ironically, along with the Detroit Red Wings, the Ilitches are also owners of Little Caesars, one of Domino's chief pizza competitors. On August 3, while details of the sale were being negotiated, Campbell and Schembechler were unceremoniously fired.

Thus began Detroit's first dip into what is now referred to as "corporate baseball," where success is measured by crafty marketing and promotional schemes as much as by runs, hits and errors.

Lou Whitaker retired after the 1995 season to snap the longest-running keystone combination in the game's history. Alan Trammell, his partner of 19 seasons, retired one year later.

Perhaps the most significant loss was Sparky Anderson, who stepped down after the 1995 campaign after 17 seasons at the Tiger helm. Prior to the start of the 1995 season, Sparky had refused to manage the replacement players ordered by baseball to take the places of the striking major leaguers. For months before the '95 season ended, it was widely speculated in the media that if Sparky had not stepped down, his contract would not have been renewed.

Prior to the 1995 season, John McHale Jr. was hired as Tiger president. And in 1996, former All-Star third baseman Buddy Bell was given his first managerial opportunity.

McHale, son of the former Tiger reserve first baseman and general manager, was brought to Detroit from Colorado with one principal goal: To get a new stadium built.

The struggle was painstaking and laborious, but on October 29, 1997, ground was broken for the construction of Comerica Park. On April 12, 2000, the Tigers played their first home game away from the celebrated corner of Michigan and Trumbull and came up with a 5-2 victory over the Seattle Mariners.

The new park reflects the altered face of the century-old game. Along with an array of luxury suites designed to lure corporate customers, the park features a merry-go-round and Ferris wheel, along with numerous other diversions.

McHale left the Tigers during the 2001 season and was eventually replaced at the end of that year by Dave Dombrowski, who now serves as both president and general manager.

With the hiring of Alan Trammell as manager, and the return of fellow 1984 heroes Kirk Gibson and Lance Parrish as coaches, the Tigers sought to launch a new ear in 2003.

As the cost of operating a franchise continues to rise, the Tigers apparently have moved back toward the old-fashioned method of stocking much of the major-league roster with players developed within their own organization.

Certainly Tiger owners from eras gone by would have had to stretch their imaginations to the limit to predict the astronomical amount of money necessary to operate a major-league franchise in the 21st century. Similarly, many fans today are overwhelmed by the proportionally inflated cost of spending a day at the park with the family.

But regardless of the endless labor squabbles and despite the inflated price tag on tickets, the underlying essence of the game remains the same today as when Ty Cobb was flying around the bases looking to score another run.

Throughout all the changes one thing remains the same.

Detroit is a "baseball town."

2

GREATEST TIGER OF 'EM ALL

The Ty Cobb Era, 1901-1930

As this slow-paced, horse-drawn nation slowly trotted into the 20th century, the sleepy little city of Detroit, perhaps best known up until that point for producing stoves, paint and pharmaceuticals, suddenly became fascinated with speed.

In the winter of 1904, daring, cigar-chomping Barney Oldfield, driving struggling Detroit inventor Henry Ford's newfangled motorized contraption known as the "999," set a world's record by traveling nearly 92 miles an hour over the ice of frozen Lake St. Clair, a few miles north of town.

At the University of Michigan in nearby Ann Arbor, coach Fielding "Hurry-Up" Yost's Wolverine football team was overwhelming opponents at the previously unprecedented rate of a point a minute.

And, in 1905, hell-bent, temperamental Tyrus Raymond Cobb, who would quickly become one of the most successful, and certainly the most feared, base stealer in baseball history, began his incredible, record-setting 22-year career with the Detroit Tigers.

Thanks to the advent of the automobile industry and the arrival of Cobb, the city of Detroit would never be the same again.

Baseball had never seen anyone quite like Cobb when, in August of 1905, at the urging of manager Bill Armour, the Tigers purchased the skinny 18-year-old outfielder from Augusta, Georgia, of the South Atlantic League for $750. An intense competitor, the fiery,

foul-tempered Cobb was an instant crowd pleaser. His style of play was perfectly suited to the brand of baseball played in the first quarter of the 20th century, when the emphasis was still on speed and cunning rather than on raw power.

Armour and the Tigers first spotted Cobb during spring training camp in 1905.

"Wait'll you see him," wacky infielder Germany Schaefer advised Tiger co-owner Frank Navin. "He'll give you enough laughs for a whole season. He tries to stretch every single into a double, and every double into a triple. I guess he doesn't even know there's a third base, 'cuz if he's on second when the batter hits a grounder to the infield, he keeps right on running to the plate. He's crazy as a bedbug."

Rather than pay the Augusta ball club the rent that the Tigers owed for using its minor-league facilities during spring training that year, the tight-fisted Navin offered to loan pitcher Eddie Cicotte, later of Chicago Black Sox infamy, to the Augusta team for the 1905 campaign.

In return, Augusta agreed to sell the Tigers their pick of its Class C roster for $500 at the end of the season. By late August the Tigers, ravaged by injuries, found themselves desperately short of outfielders. So Navin wired Augusta. He wanted to buy Cobb, who had batted .326 and stolen 40 bases in the low minors. The normally frugal Navin agreed to pay an extra $250

OPPOSITE: *Eighteen-year-old Ty Cobb waits on a pitch in one of his first at-bats with the Tigers in a game in Chicago against the White Sox in August 1905. AP/Wide World Photos*

if Augusta would send young Cobb north immediately, before the conclusion of the Sally League season.

Young Ty's name was not even printed on the official scorecards when he made his major-league debut at Detroit's rickety, wooden Bennett Park on August 30, 1905. A newspaper article that day referred to him, in passing, as "Cyrus Cobb."

Welcome to Detroit, kid.

On the mound for New York that historic afternoon was the Highlanders' seasoned spitball specialist Jack Chesbro, who had won 41 games the year before. Unimpressed, the brash 18-year-old Cobb stepped up to the plate in the first inning and promptly lashed a double, driving in two runs. It was but the first of Cobb's 4,191 hits. By the time he put his bat down 23 years later, he had played in more games, scored more runs, set more records and made more enemies than any man who had ever played the game.

After batting an innocuous .240 with just one stolen base in 40 games during his partial first year in the American League, Cobb quickly established himself as one of the best players in the game, and, eventually, one of the greatest of all time.

With the arrival of Cobb, the Tigers soon became a formidable force in the fledgling American League. Often, Ty won games all by himself, bunting or singling his way aboard, then stealing his way around the diamond. Thirty-five times in his illustrious career, he successfully stole home.

But Cobb was also mean, selfish, arrogant and bigoted. He didn't have a kind or compassionate bone in his body. Because of his Southern, Protestant upbringing, Cobb detested most Northerners, Catholics and African Americans. Cobb arrived in Detroit with a chip on his shoulder because he personally had not received any money from the sale of his contract and because he expected trouble from his mostly northern, Irish Catholic teammates

He quickly became one of most hated heroes in baseball history. But above all, he was obsessed with winning.

"Sure, I fought," Cobb admitted. "I had to fight all my life to survive. They were all against me. But I beat the bastards and left them in the ditch."

A bully with a demonic look in his eyes, Cobb constantly fought with opponents, teammates, fans and himself. Full of rage, some of it certainly fueled by the recent death of his beloved father who had been shot and killed by Ty's mother, Cobb was constantly at war

with the world. He was a walking powder keg with an impossibly short fuse. Some observers went so far as to suggest he may have been slightly crazy.

Cobb quickly became convinced everyone was against him. And his angry reaction to that belief soon became a self-fulfilling prophecy.

In an effort to make Cobb look bad in the field, Marty McIntyre, the Tigers' left fielder, would often give Ty the impression that he was going after fly balls and then let them drop in for base hits. After one such hit, angry pitcher Ed Siever confronted Cobb in the lobby of the Tigers' hotel, claiming the unpopular young outfielder had cost him the victory.

Cobb knocked Siever to the floor and was kicking the pitcher in the head when his teammates pulled him away. That incident was enough to convince Cobb to begin carrying a gun.

Long-ball hitting Sam Crawford was the Tigers' biggest and best-paid star until Cobb arrived. Wahoo Sam, the American League's most accomplished center fielder at the time, never really adjusted to the idea of sharing center stage. Like Joe Tinker and Johnny Evers of the Chicago Cubs' storied infield of that same era, Cobb and Crawford harbored little love for one another and rarely spoke.

"Playing by the side of two fellows like that was a good deal like being a member of the chorus in a grand opera where there are two prima donnas," observed outfielder Davy Jones, who came to the Tigers from the Chicago Cubs midway through the 1906 season and eventually became one of Cobb's few friends on the team.

"Cobb was a great ballplayer, no doubt about that," said Crawford. "But he sure wasn't easy to get along with. He wasn't a friendly, good-natured guy, like Honus Wagner or Walter Johnson or Babe Ruth."

Rival players feared Cobb. When pitcher Hub Leonard dared throw at his head, knocking Cobb to the ground, Ty purposely bunted the next pitch down the first base line so that Leonard would have to leave the mound to cover first. Leonard knew what was coming. The pitcher took the toss from his first baseman, quickly stepped on the bag, then ran full speed down the right field line, away from the hard-charging Cobb. But Ty ran after him and viciously slid into Leonard from behind, his spikes high.

Cobb's Tiger teammates regularly taunted him. They sawed his bats in half, shoved him out of the batting cage when it was his turn to hit, cut holes in the soles of his shoes, locked him out of his hotel room, refused to eat with him on the road, and mocked his Southern accent.

"We weren't cannibals or heathens," Crawford insisted. "We were all ballplayers together, trying to get along. Every rookie gets a little hazing, but most of them just take it and laugh. Cobb took it the wrong way. He came up with an antagonistic attitude, which in his mind turned any little razzing into a life-or-death struggle. He always figured everybody was ganging up on him."

In spite of all that abuse, in 1906, Cobb's first full season in the majors, he batted .320—his first of 23 consecutive seasons over .300. Nevertheless, at the conclusion of the 1906 season, the Tigers nearly gave up on Cobb, almost before his Hall of Fame career began.

Young Ty, who frequently hid in a caretaker's shed at Detroit's Bennett Park to escape the torment of his teammates, suffered a nervous breakdown during the 1906 season and spent a month in a suburban Pontiac, Michigan, sanitarium. The Tigers' top brass were convinced he would never be a long-term big-league success. Cobb, they reasoned, was too unpredictable, too irresponsible and too wild. This crazy kid, who often acted as if he was still fighting the Civil War, was more trouble than he was worth.

That winter, at the urging of manager Hughie Jennings, Tiger owner Frank Navin contacted the Cleveland Indians and offered to swap young Cobb even-up for left-handed-hitting 31-year-old outfielder Elmer Flick, who was a former batting champion and an outstanding base stealer, as well as a popular, personable player.

"It seems hard to think that such a mere boy as Cobb can make so much disturbance," Navin observed.

However, Cobb's reputation was already so rotten after only one year that Indians owner Charlie Somers rejected the proposed deal and instead offered the Tigers outfielder Bunk Congalton, who had batted .320 the previous season.

Fortunately for the Tigers, Navin nixed the counter offer. Flick developed ulcers and was out of the league by 1910. Congalton turned out to be a one-year wonder. It was quite possibly the best trade the Detroit Tigers never made.

During the 1913 season, Washington Senators owner Clark Griffith handed Navin a personal check for $100,000 in exchange for Cobb. When Navin demanded to know whether Griffith actually had the cash to back up the check, the Senators owner assured Navin the check would be good—in two weeks. Griffith then put 100,000 tickets on sale at $1 apiece to raise the cash.

Before the two weeks were up, Navin got cold feet and returned Griffith's check.

❧

One of the most popular Tiger players shortly after the turn of the century was infielder Germany Schaefer. Schaefer was not particularly talented, but he certainly was funny. As a result, Schaefer was second only to Ty Cobb as an early Tiger drawing card.

In 1906, with the Tigers trailing the White Stockings, 2-1, in the ninth inning of a game in Chicago, Tiger manager Bill Armour sent Schaefer up to the plate to pinch hit. When Schaefer reached the batter's box, he turned to face the grandstand, filled with hostile White Sox fans.

"Ladies and gentlemen," he announced, "you are now looking at Herman Schaefer, better known as Herman the Great, acknowledged by one and all to be the greatest hitter in the world. I am now going to hit the ball into the left field bleachers. Thank you."

While the partisan Chicago crowd hooted and booed, Schaefer hit the second pitch into the left field bleachers for a home run.

He stood at the plate watching the ball clear the fence, then sprinted to first base, where he slid head first into the bag. "Schaefer leading at the quarter!" he shouted to the crowd as he jumped to his feet.

He repeated that performance at second base. "Schaefer leads at the half!" he bellowed above the growing chorus of catcalls.

After sliding into home plate, he stood up and announced: "Schaefer wins by a nose!"

As he walked back to the Tigers' dugout, Schaefer doffed his cap and declared, "Ladies and gentleman, I thank you for your kind attention."

In the dugout, the Tigers were laughing hysterically. However, one player was not even smiling. Ty Cobb simply had no sense of humor.

Conversely, Davy Jones, who commented on Cobb's humorless demeanor, was himself an easy guy to get along with. Asked for the secret to his success,

Jones explained, "I have myself a Limburger sandwich and two bottles of beer before I go to bed."

Much of the credit for Cobb's early success belonged to Hughie Jennings, a former player and learned man with a law degree from Cornell University, who took over as the Tigers' manager in 1907.

Jennings, who had once worked in the Pennsylvania coal mines for 90 cents a day, knew enough to leave the high-strung Cobb alone. In the 14 years that Cobb played under Jennings, the good-humored, freckle-faced Hall of Fame Tiger manager never once told Ty what to do—either on the field, or off it.

"There isn't anything I can teach you about baseball," Jennings told his budding young superstar in 1907. "Do as you please."

Which was, of course, precisely what Cobb was going to do anyway.

Together, the fiery Cobb and the easy-going Jennings led the previously listless, lifeless Tigers to an unprecedented three consecutive American League pennants in 1907, '08 and '09.

"Cobb is the greatest ballplayer, potentially, ever to walk on a ball field," Jennings explained during his first training camp in 1907. "Everything he does is so naturally and instinctively right, that if I try to teach him anything I may spoil the genius he was born with.

"Inherently, he knows more baseball than anybody can ever teach him. That was why Bill Armour failed with him. Bill insisted on Cobb's doing things the way others did them, the old army game.

"But Cobb is a free, wild spirit. He believes the world is against him, that there is a conspiracy to prevent him from making good. This apparent arrogance is a defense mechanism by which he bolsters up his confidence."

Although he was from baseball's "old school," having played shortstop on the famed rowdy Baltimore Orioles teams of the 1890s, Jennings was a beacon of morality amidst the crude and brawling ballplayers of the day. And he had his hands full mediating the never-ending disputes between Cobb and his Tiger teammates, Cobb and the umpires, and, occasionally, between Cobb and the fans.

During spring training in Augusta, Georgia, in 1907, Jennings's first year on the job, Cobb attacked an African-American groundskeeper who made the mistake of addressing him as "you Georgia Peach" when Cobb complained about the condition of the field.

Cobb chased the man into his nearby cabin and choked the man's wife when she tried to intervene. When burly Tiger catcher Charlie "Boss" Schmidt ordered Cobb to knock if off, Ty turned on his teammate. Cobb charged Schmidt, but the 5-foot-8 Jennings broke up the fight almost before it could begin.

Not surprisingly, considering the attitude that prevailed in the South shortly after the turn of the century, the white baseball fans in town sided with Cobb and criticized Schmidt for defending a black man.

When the Tigers broke training camp and headed north to begin the regular season, Cobb was given a farewell ovation by the cheering fans. Schmidt, who had been forced to remain out of sight in his hotel room for three days after the incident, had to sneak out of town.

When the Tigers' train stopped for an exhibition game on their way north, Cobb and Schmidt went at it again. This time Jennings was not around to intercede. While the other Tiger players cheered, Schmidt, who weighed 200 pounds and had boxed professionally, beat Cobb to a pulp, breaking his nose and pounding both of his eyes shut.

He might have killed Cobb if Tiger pitcher "Wild Bill" Donovan, who had also been a prizefighter, had not grabbed Schmidt by the hair and pulled him off the beaten Ty. Years later, as a coach with the Brooklyn Dodgers, Boss Schmidt would amuse onlookers by driving nails into the floor of the clubhouse—with his fist.

The battered Cobb was taken back to the team's hotel, where Jennings summoned a doctor. The physician found no life-threatening injuries, but that was not the diagnosis Jennings delivered to his team.

"You may have killed, or probably ruined forever, the greatest ballplayer in the world," Jennings informed the Tigers when he gathered the players together. "You have badgered and abused this kid from the start of his playing with this team. You have made him the rebel that he is. Without him, we have no chance to be anywhere in this pennant race.

"Now listen, all of you," Jennings continued angrily. "This does not mean anything to me. The record books will show you where I have been. My name is safe in baseball. I have established my reputation. You have yours to make.

"Now I want all of you—every one of you—to go into Cobb's room, one by one, shake his hand, and tell him that you are sorry for what has happened this year and last, and that you are for him and want him on the team."

By the time the Tigers' train reached Detroit, Cobb's wounds had healed. On the first open date on the schedule, he and Schmidt went fishing together on nearby Lake St. Clair. Cobb then proceeded to win his first of nine consecutive batting titles. In September, the Tigers won 14 of their final 16 games, all on the road, to clinch the first pennant in franchise history.

⮾

From the beginning, Ty Cobb was a student of the game. For all of his personal flaws, he understood how baseball should be played.

During one key game late in the 1907 pennant chase, Cobb raced all the way to third on slugger Claude Rossman's sacrifice bunt. When a stunned Frank Chase, the New York Highlanders' fine-fielding first baseman, threw the ball across the diamond to third baseman George Moriarty in disgust, Cobb sprinted home.

After the game, Cobb was passing the Highlanders' locker room when he heard New York manager Clark Griffith shouting at Chase and Moriarty.

"He won't do it again," Chase promised his manager. "We'll be watching for that son of a bitch."

That evening, Cobb sought out Rossman back at the Tigers' hotel.

"Every time I get on first base tomorrow, you bunt," Cobb demanded.

"You got it," Rossman replied,

In the seventh inning, on a perfect bunt by Rossman, Cobb again scampered all the way around to third. Moriarty was so mad, he caught the belated throw and hurled the ball to the ground. By the time he retrieved it, on the first bounce, Cobb had galloped across home plate again.

The previously lackluster Tigers clinched their first pennant on the final weekend of the 1907 season, earning the right to meet the Chicago Cubs, who had been able to coast through the final month of the campaign, in the World Series.

The Tigers boasted three 20-game winners: Wild Bill Donovan (25-4), Ed Killian (25-13) and George Mullin (20-20), as well as Ed Siever (19-10). Together, long before the age of relief pitchers, that quartet accounted for all but three of the Tigers' 92 wins.

However, in spite of the offensive punch provided by the combination of Cobb and Crawford, the defensively suspect Tigers were no match for the superior pitching of the Cubs, who featured the colorfully monikered Mordacai "Three-Finger" Brown and Orval Overall, as well as the poetic infield trio of Tinker to Evers to Chance.

Before the World Series began, the always-unpredictable Germany Schaefer prophetically inquired as to what would happen to the proceeds of a Series game that ended in a tie. The players only profited from the first four games of the Series, with the rest of the money benefiting the leagues and club management. No Series game had ever ended in a draw, so there was no contingency plan in place. After considerable haggling, it was agreed that the players would share in the proceeds of the first five games, provided one of them happened to end in a draw.

Incredibly, Game 1 was called a 3-3 tie after 12 innings because of darkness. The irrepressible Schaefer later claimed the idea had come to him in a dream.

But that was as close as the Tigers would come to a victory in the 1907 World Series, as they were outscored, 16-3, in the next four games. Many observed that the Tigers looked dispirited and defeated. "We were outplayed all the time," Donovan, the Tigers' ace hurler, admitted.

The Cubs were convinced that the key to beating the Tigers was stopping Cobb. "All that talk of what Cobb was going to do to us made us sick," said Chicago's Jimmy Slagle, who swiped six bases in the Series to Cobb's none. To add insult to injury, Cubs pitcher Orvie Overall knocked in more runs with his two-run, fourth-game single than Cobb did in the entire Series. Cobb batted a mere .200 in the Fall Classic, causing many observers to credit the allegedly inferior pitching in the American League for the resounding success Ty had enjoyed during the regular season.

Tigers owner Bill Yawkey, who purchased the team at Frank Navin's urging three years earlier in hopes of winning a championship, had acquired extra bleachers to accommodate the huge crowds that were anticipated for Detroit's first World Series. However, the extra seats went unused.

There was so little interest in Detroit that when the Tigers returned home October 11, 1907, for the first World Series game ever played in the city, only 11,306 showed up on a rainy Friday afternoon. The

During the five years that they played together, Ty Cobb (left), Bobby Veach (middle) and Sam Crawford (right) were the Tigers' most dominant hitters. **Burton Historical Society**

following day a mere 7,370 turned out for the fifth and final game. In contrast, 59,392 had witnessed the first three games in Chicago.

It was embarrassing, to say the least. There were many who suggested once again that big-league baseball would never survive in Detroit.

The disappointing attendance at Bennett Park was blamed on poor weather and the Cubs' dominance during the first three games in Chicago. Certainly, the fact that there were snow flurries in the air during the final two games in Detroit didn't help.

Nevertheless, the millionaire Yawkey chipped in $15,000 out of his own pocket to sweeten the Tiger players' share of the gate receipts. As a result, the vanquished Tigers each earned $1,850, just $400 less than each player for the victorious Cubs.

In 1908, Cobb and Crawford again finished one-two in the American League batting race as the Tigers battled St. Louis, Chicago and Cleveland down the stretch in one of the closest pennant races in baseball history, defeating the White Stockings in the final game

of the season behind locked gates in Chicago to claim their second title.

The first two games of their crucial three-game season-ending series had attracted a total of 65,000 fans, and Chicago owner Charles Comiskey was afraid the emotional, capacity crowd for the finale would get out of hand and perhaps hinder the home team's chances.

Comiskey need not have worried. The visiting Tigers prevailed 7-0 behind the two-hit pitching of Wild Bill Donovan to clinch their second flag by a scant half-game.

Unfortunately, young shortstop Donie Bush, a key cog in the Tigers' pennant drive who had been acquired from Indianapolis late in the season, had arrived too late to be eligible for the 1908 World Series. As a result, the Tigers were forced to rely on Charlie O'Leary, who had injured his throwing hand during the regular season.

When second baseman Red Downs had difficulty applying the tags to the elusive Cubs runners, who again ran wild in the Series, Hughie Jennings moved Germany Schaefer from third base to second and inserted Bill Coughlin into the lineup at third. That weakened the Tigers at two more infield positions and probably sealed their fate.

The Cubs out-hit the Tigers by almost 100 points, stole nearly three times as many bases, and made only half as many errors. Thanks to Orvie Overall and Three-Finger Brown, the Cubs outpitched the Tigers as well.

Only Cobb excelled, batting .368 including four hits in Detroit's lone Series win, in Game 3. Cobb had four RBIs, stole a couple of bases, and dazzled the Cubs with his daring on the base paths—even though Ty insisted he wasn't able to get enough sleep at night.

Fans outside the Tigers' Chicago hotel made so much noise on the street that Ty couldn't sleep. He summoned Jennings to his room and demanded that the manager do something.

"What can I do?" Jennings protested.

"You're the manager, think of something," Cobb replied angrily.

The next morning, Cobb, still furious, confronted Jennings and informed him he had not been able to fall asleep until 4 a.m.

"I didn't sleep at all either," the irritated Jennings responded.

"But you're not playing," argued Cobb.

The Cubs had another advantage: An African-American teenaged mascot known as Rastus.

Cobb initially adopted the youngster as the Tigers' good-luck charm after he found him sleeping in Bennett Park that summer. The superstitious players delighted in rubbing the young man's head before every at-bat and even took him on road trips. They smuggled him aboard trains and allowed him to sleep under their hotel beds.

However, in September Rastus was accused of stealing equipment from the Tigers' clubhouse and ordered to stay away from the ballpark. He immediately offered his services as a mascot to the Cubs and sat on Chicago's bench during the 1908 World Series.

Even though the Tigers lost the Series, National League president Harry Pulliam went out of his way to praise Cobb. "That young man isn't reckless, as we were told," Pulliam said. "He's one of the wonders of baseball."

Cobb certainly thought so. He annually fought Tiger management for more money. "It isn't a question of principle with me," Ty explained. "I want the money."

Later, when Navin balked at Cobb's demands for a $2,000 raise in 1913, Hoke Smith, a U.S. Senator from Ty's native Georgia, threatened to commence a congressional investigation into baseball's violation of antitrust regulations.

Like his partner Bill Yawkey the year before, Tiger co-owner Frank Navin had erected temporary bleachers for the 1908 Series in hopeful anticipation of turnaway crowds. However, attendance in Detroit was even worse for the 1908 World Series than it had been in 1907, falling to 6,210 for the final game at Bennett Park as the Tigers again fell to the Cubs, four games to one.

Mercifully Game 5, which attracted the smallest crowd in World Series history, was also the quickest. It took just one hour and 25 minutes for the Tigers to succumb, 2-0, to the Cubs. Each Tiger's losing share of the World Series receipts amounted to a mere $870.

Sportswriters, sent to Detroit from around the country to chronicle the 1908 Series, were also displeased and disappointed. On October 14, prior to the fifth and final game, they gathered at the Pontchartrain Hotel in downtown Detroit and formed the Baseball Writers Association of America, in part to protest the woefully inadequate open-air rooftop press box facilities at Bennett Park.

As Cobb slashed his way to his third batting title in a succession, the 1909 Tigers dominated the AL from the outset, briefly relinquishing the lead just three times during the season en route to their third consecutive pennant.

George Mullin won a league-leading 29 games, heading a pitching staff that included Wild Bill Donovan, who had earned his nickname on the base paths as well as on the mound, Ed Willett, and knuckleballer Ed "Kickapoo" Summers, the first pitcher in the 20th century to homer twice in a game.

Mullin won 20 or more games five times and threw the first no-hitter at the corner of Michigan and Trumbull. Donovan, who was Frank Navin's favorite player in those early years, had been awarded to the Tigers as part of the 1903 peace treaty between the rival National and American Leagues.

In years past, the conventional wisdom in baseball had been to keep a winning team intact for as long as possible. But Hughie Jennings, frustrated by the Tigers' abject failure in their first two World Series, abandoned that theory and revamped his infield in 1909.

TY COBB

Center Field
Bats: Left ◆ Throws: Right
6'1" ◆ 175 lbs.
Played with Tigers: 1905-1926
Born: 12/18/86 ◆ Died: 7/17/61

Ty Cobb simply refused to lose.
When little Ty was in the fifth grade, he beat up a classmate whose innocent mistake had allowed the girls' team to beat the boys in a school spelling bee. Later, when he thought a butcher had insulted his wife, Cobb attacked the man with the butt of his handgun. When one of his Tiger teammates beat him in a playful outfield broad-jumping contest, Cobb practiced the feat for days, then publicly challenged the man to a rematch. Of course, Cobb won.

As a youngster, Ty Cobb played baseball with the red-suited Royston (Georgia) Rompers in his hometown. He also regularly attended Sunday school. He had no choice. The coach of the Rompers was also the assistant pastor of the Methodist Church to which the Cobb family belonged. Any player who skipped Sunday school also had to sit out the next baseball game. And young Ty loved to play ball.

His father, Herschel Cobb, was a former state senator and superintendent of schools who had been mentioned as a possible candidate for governor of Georgia. Ty idolized his father and always sought his approval. Herschel Cobb wanted Ty to go to college and become a doctor. But his stubborn son had other ideas. Young Ty wrote letters to every team in the Sally League, bragging about his ability and requesting a tryout. Not one team replied.

With the help of Rev. John Yarborough, Cobb eventually signed with the Augusta, Georgia, club. But after two games, the manager, Con Strouthers, kicked him off the team. "I only want players who follow orders," Strouthers explained. Even then, Cobb could be obstinate.

Cobb quickly caught on with another team, based in Anniston, Alabama. When he wrote his father to tell him of his change of teams, the elder Cobb wired back: "Noted new address. Do not come home a failure."

"That wire," Cobb admitted years later, "spurred me on. I carried it with me for years. I never did go back to Royston a failure."

Cobb played well enough to earn himself another chance with the Augusta club, which by then had changed managers. And news of young Cobb's exploits began to appear in Southern newspapers under the byline of influential sportswriter Grantland Rice, who, surprisingly, had heard about Ty from several of his readers. Rice did not discover until years later that Cobb himself had sent the famed scribe all of those glowing reports, signing the names of fictitious Augusta and Anniston fans.

While he was still an 18-year-old minor leaguer, Cobb's mother shot and killed Ty's father, the man he idolized.

In August, 1905—shortly before Cobb's contract was purchased by the Tigers—Herschel Cobb, who suspected that his wife, Amanda, was being unfaithful, "unexpectedly" returned home late one evening after informing his wife that he would be out of town overnight. The elder Cobb was sneaking into the house through his wife's bedroom window shortly after midnight, hoping to catch her in an indiscreet act, when Ty's mother, fearing that a burglar was breaking into her darkened room, fired the double-barreled shotgun that she kept beside her bed. The intruder, her husband, was killed instantly.

Ty's mother was charged with manslaughter, but was later acquitted. However, the tragic experience tormented Cobb for the rest of his life. "I didn't get over that," Cobb admitted much later. "I've never gotten over it. My father was the greatest man I ever knew."

Many amateur analysts later blamed that incident for Cobb's bitter personality and the fire that constantly blazed inside him. However, Cobb himself blamed his attitude on the horrible hazing he received from his Tiger teammates as a rookie. Nearly all agree he was paranoid, sometimes almost psychotic, and suffered from a persecution complex.

He also was the greatest player ever to wear a Tiger uniform.

During Cobb's final game in Augusta, after his contract had been purchased by the Tigers for $750, the appreciative fans, led by the town's mayor, marched out on the field and gave him a gold watch for good luck. The excitable young Cobb was so moved he struck out in his next at-bat. It was one of the few times in his career that the Georgia Peach failed to produce.

But Cobb didn't receive nearly such a warm reception when he reached Detroit. His new Tiger teammates picked on him unmercifully, frequently locking him out of the hotel bathroom that the players shared, shoving him out of the way during batting practice, cutting up his clothes, and hurling soggy wads of wet newspaper at him while he tried to sleep during the long, overnight train rides.

"He always figured everybody was ganging up against him," teammate Wahoo Sam Crawford observed.

"My idea was to go on the attack and never relax it," Cobb admitted.

It was not clear whether Cobb was talking about his style of play on a baseball field—or his lifestyle off it.

During the 1908 season, Cobb got into a nasty, name-calling argument with a black laborer who was working on a downtown Detroit sidewalk. Their heated conversation concluded when Cobb beat the worker up. Ty subsequently paid $75 "to be rid of the nuisance," and stay out of court.

On the road with the Tigers, Cobb once knocked a black hotel chambermaid down a flight of stairs. The maid sued for $10,000, but the case was settled out of court. Cobb also had to stay out of the state of Ohio for a year and a half to avoid arrest after he slapped a black elevator operator for being "insolent" and allegedly stabbed a hotel security guard. The Tigers paid the hotel to drop a civil suit, but the Cleveland prosecutor insisted upon pursuing assault charges. As a result, during the 1909 World Series, Cobb had to travel between Detroit and Pittsburgh by way of Canada to avoid passing through Ohio. Later, Cobb pistol-whipped a man who tried to rob him and left his assailant for dead in a Detroit alley.

The 1900 Royston baseball team sits for a team photo. Their most famous player, Ty Cobb, is in the front row on the far left. AP/Wide World Photos

Nevertheless Cobb remained with the Tigers for 22 years, then concluded his Hall of Fame career with two seasons with the Philadelphia Athletics, and established more records than any player in major-league history. More than 95 years after an inauspicious debut, players were still trying to match or surpass many of his phenomenal batting feats.

Three times, in 1911, 1912, and 1922, Cobb batted over .400. He hit above .300 for 23 consecutive years. Twelve times within a span of 13 years at the height of his career, he led the American League in hitting, amassing an amazing 4,191 hits—a record that stood until Pete Rose, another ballplayer who was driven, came along. Cobb's lifetime batting average was .367, a figure unsurpassed in baseball history. Cobb also stole 892 bases, including 96 in one season—records that stood until Lou Brock and Maury Wills surpassed them.

In the annals of baseball, only Babe Ruth and Honus Wagner begin to compare. When baseball opened its Hall of Fame in 1936, Ty Cobb was the first of five players initially ushered in.

Cobb also had a long-running feud with American League founder and president Ban Johnson.

In 1926, while baseball was still recovering from the infamous Chicago Black Sox 1919 World Series fix, another potential scandal erupted. Retired Tiger pitcher Dutch Leonard claimed Cobb and future Hall of Famer Tris Speaker, along with Cleveland outfielder Joe Wood, had been involved in a fixed game between the Tigers and Indians late in the 1919 season and produced letters from Cobb and Wood to prove it.

According to Leonard, he and Cobb met with Speaker and Wood under the stands at Navin Field on September 24, 1919, the afternoon before the final game of the season.

Since the Indians had already clinched second place behind Chicago in the American League, and the Tigers needed one more win to clinch third, the four men agreed that Detroit would be allowed to win the season finale. Third place would be worth an additional $500 to each of the Tigers as their share of the World Series proceeds.

Realizing they could also personally profit from their scheme, the four men decided to pool their money and place some wagers on the game. It was agreed that Cobb would put up $2,000, Speaker and Wood would each chip in $1,000, and Leonard would contribute $1,500. Accomplices would then wager that $5,500 with several different bookies to avoid raising suspicion. But the players' henchmen had problems getting all their bets down and the quartet won only a few hundred dollars.

Seven years later, Ban Johnson—who was no fan of either Cobb or Speaker—and Tiger owner Frank Navin paid Leonard $20,000 for the two incriminating letters that had been sent to the pitcher by Cobb and Wood after the 1919 season.

Convinced of the guilt of the two superstars, Johnson decided to allow both Cobb and Speaker to quietly "retire" after the 1926 season. However, Johnson was ordered to turn the letters over to his archrival, Kenesaw Mountain Landis, the powerful commissioner who had been hired to clean up baseball's image.

Years earlier, Navin had aligned himself with Johnson in opposing the selection of Judge Landis as commissioner. But when the pro-Landis faction threatened to retaliate by putting a new National League franchise in Detroit, Navin had quickly switched sides to make certain that didn't happen.

In 1926 Landis, aware of the devastating impact another scandal would have on the national pastime, traveled to California to personally interview Dutch Leonard. Following that meeting, Landis dismissed the letters as inconclusive and ordered both Cobb and Speaker reinstated. Landis ruled that although Cobb and Speaker may have been guilty of betting on ballgames—an indiscretion that was commonplace prior to 1920—neither was guilty of fixing games.

In addition, Landis believed that Leonard may have implicated Cobb and Speaker because he harbored grudges against both men—Cobb for releasing Leonard from the Tigers following the 1925 season and Speaker for refusing to give the pitcher a tryout with the Cleveland Indians.

Cobb had threatened to "tear Leonard apart physically," and file slander charges against Leonard and Johnson and anyone else who sided with the pitcher. Cobb also hinted that he believed Navin had embraced the charges in order to create an excuse for voiding Cobb's multiyear contract.

Since the two "retired" future Hall of Famers could hardly return to their original teams, Speaker was allowed to sign with the Washington Senators, and Cobb with Philadelphia Athletics, where they concluded their brilliant careers in something less than disgrace.

On November 3, 1926, Tiger fans were stunned by the news that Cobb was retiring as the team's manager and would not be returning to Detroit as a player either. Publicly, the 39-year-old Cobb blamed Navin's refusal to field a formidable team as his reason for leaving. Navin claimed Cobb had been let go because his abrasive personality had undermined the morale of the ball club.

Landis, who was locked in a power struggle with Johnson, accused the American League president and Navin of concocting the whole story of a "fix" to give the Tigers an excuse to void the aging Cobb's multiyear contract.

Stripped of much of his power, Johnson, who had decreed that "neither [Cobb nor Speaker] would ever play in the American League again," resigned a short while later. The other AL owners temporarily placed Navin in charge of the day-to-day operations of the league. Neither Speaker nor Cobb ever managed again.

But there was no denying Cobb's greatness or his place in baseball history.

Cobb served in the U.S. Army during World War I. He was involved in the same poison gas accident at a military testing laboratory in France that damaged Hall of Fame pitcher Christy Mathewson's lungs and significantly shortened the famed hurler's life.

In the fall of 1941, Cobb returned to Detroit to play a golf match on Grosse Isle against his old rival, Babe Ruth. The 55-year-old Cobb approached the exhibition as he did everything else in his life. He went on a diet and practiced for weeks. When the match with the fun-loving Ruth began, Cobb conceded nothing. He fought for every hole and put maximum effort into every shot. Inevitably, perhaps, he won the match.

That evening, a small group of Cobb's old acquaintances gathered for a quiet dinner at the Statler Hilton Hotel in downtown Detroit. Among those present was a major in the Air Reserve Corps named Jimmy Doolittle.

Babe Ruth, left, and Ty Cobb choose up to tee off at an exhibition charity golf match at Fresh Meadow Country Club in New York on June 27, 1941. The two baseball legends played in a charity grudge tournament with proceeds going to the United Service Organizations. Ruth won the match in New York and Cobb won the first match held in Boston on July 26, 1940. AP/Wide World Photos

"As a kid in St. Louis I never missed a game in which Cobb played," Doolittle explained to those assembled. "I wanted to see him go around the bases. I have never known any other man who had such complete coordination of mind and body."

Later the whole country would be moved by the headline: "Doolittle Bombs Tokyo!"

Cobb remained crotchety, even in retirement. The year before he died in 1961, Cobb and Hall of Fame slugger Ted Williams, who over the years had grown quite close, were debating the greatest players of all time. Williams argued that Rogers Hornsby was the best second baseman ever. Cobb disagreed. When Williams pointed out that Hornsby once batted .424, a figure even the great Cobb never reached, Ty ended the conversation and never spoke to Williams again.

Even before he retired from baseball, Cobb had become a very rich man, a millionaire many times over. But early in his career, he would collect the straw hats that Tiger fans flung out on the field and take them home to Georgia for the mules on his farm to wear. He also gathered up the scraps of soap left behind in the showers of the Tigers' locker room, and took them home for his field hands.

However, Cobb also had the foresight to invest heavily in Coca-Cola and General Motors stock. As the Tigers manager, Cobb repeatedly urged his players to "Buy a few shares of Coca-Cola." Stock in the new soft drink company was selling for $1.18 a share at the time. Less than 10 years later it was at $181. At the time of Cobb's death, estimates placed his worth at more than $12 million.

But money couldn't buy Cobb happiness or friends. He was twice divorced and eventually became estranged from his children. Family life, Ty explained, was almost impossible for a ballplayer.

In his final years, in considerable pain and aware that the end was near, Cobb consumed a quart of Jack Daniels mixed with a quart of milk each day to numb his pain.

Tragically, after Cobb died of cancer on July 17, 1961, embittered and alone, only three men from the baseball world—Mickey Cochrane, Ray Schalk and Hall of Fame director Sid Keener—cared enough to attend the funeral of the greatest Tiger of them all.

Versatile fielder George Moriarty played with the Tigers from 1909 to 1915. His specialty was baserunning and he stole 34 bases during the 1909 AL championship season. Burton Historical Society

In an effort to find somebody who could catch ground balls, Jennings replaced Coughlin at third base with George Moriarty, who had been purchased from New York for $5,000. He installed Jim Delahanty at second in place of the departed Schaefer, and put Tom Jones on first instead of Claude Rossman. Only Bush, the sure-handed shortstop who had been summoned late in the 1908 season, was retained. The radical changes soon paid big dividends.

The 1909 World Series featured the first and only head-to-head confrontation between baseball's two premier players of the day: Ty Cobb, the Tigers' much-despised Triple Crown winner, and Honus Wagner, the Pittsburgh Pirates' lovable, bowlegged shortstop who was, arguably, at least Cobb's equal.

In many ways Wagner, the 35-year-old "Flying Dutchman," was the exact opposite of the 22-year-old

Cobb. He was quiet, even-tempered, sociable, and popular with teammates, opponents, and fans alike, not only in Pittsburgh, but all around the National League.

Wagner had just won his seventh of eight batting titles and was generally regarded as the best shortstop in the game. Moreover, at six feet and 200 pounds, the barrel-chested Wagner was not intimidated by anyone, including Cobb, even though he was 12 years older than Ty.

Popular legend has it that when Cobb reached first base for the first time in the 1909 Series, he shouted at Wagner, "Watch out, Krauthead, I'm coming down on the next pitch. I'll cut you to pieces."

"I'll be ready for you, Rebel," Wagner replied.

True to his word, Cobb slid hard into second base, his sharpened spikes high in the air. But Wagner, moving with his awkward grace, held his ground, applying the tag so vigorously to Cobb's face that several of Ty's teeth were reportedly jarred loose.

"He split my lip for me," Cobb admitted afterwards, flashing a grin of admiration.

The confrontation attracted a new invention called "a moving picture camera," and the two baseball heroes made a short, silent film together. The Series results, however, were the same for the Tigers as they had been the two previous years as Pittsburgh prevailed thanks to three wins by unheralded 27-year-old rookie pitcher Babe Adams. Wagner upstaged Cobb, batting .333 to Cobb's .231, and stole six bases—a record that stood until 1967—to Ty's two.

Thanks to the opening of Pittsburgh's new, state-of-the-art Forbes Field, with its elevators, grandstand lighting and upper deck ramps, it was the richest, best-attended World Series in the brief six-year history of the event. Those record gate receipts would have been even greater had Bennett Park, which was sold out for a change for three of the four games played in Detroit, offered more seating. Instead, fans who had been unable to buy tickets ringed the outfield, sat atop the fence, and climbed up on utility poles and roofs near the corner of Michigan and Trumbull.

It marked the first time the World Series had gone the full seven games. Since the situation had never arisen before, the two teams flipped a coin to see who would host the seventh and deciding game. The Tigers won the coin flip, but lost the contest, and the Series.

Despite winning three pennants in a row, the Tigers were still winless in the World Series. To his friends,

Frank Navin muttered, "I'd like to win one World Series before I die." But it would be a full quarter-century before the Tigers would get another opportunity to redeem themselves.

≫

The owner of the Tigers at the time of Ty Cobb's arrival and the emergence of baseball as a major player on the Detroit sports scene was millionaire playboy Bill Yawkey, whose adopted nephew Tom would later own the Boston Red Sox.

But the real brains behind the Tigers' ball club, from shortly after the turn of the century until his death in 1935, was a bespectacled, owlish-looking bookkeeper named Frank Navin.

Navin, who had graduated from law school and once unsuccessfully ran for the office of justice of the peace, had previously worked as a clerk for Samuel F. Angus, the insurance man who briefly owned the Tigers in 1902-03

The 32-year-old Navin kept Angus's books. He knew in 1903 that his boss, woefully under-financed from the outset, was nearly out of money. And Navin also knew that the 28-year-old Yawkey, who fancied himself as a sportsman, had recently inherited $10 million from his deceased lumber baron father, the richest man in Michigan at the time.

Navin knew Yawkey was a vain man who had no real desire to own a professional baseball team. He also knew young Bill loved to frolic in the company of sports heroes. Yawkey had once hired Tommy Ryan, the light heavyweight champion of the world, to teach him how to box.

So through mutual acquaintances Navin cleverly planted the idea in Yawkey's head that Detroit, which had won the National League pennant in 1887, deserved another title. Wouldn't it be wonderful, Navin suggested, if Yawkey owned a world championship baseball team? And, of course, Navin would be only too happy to run that ball club for him. Navin appealed to Yawkey's vanity and his sense of civic responsibility. It worked.

In 1904, Yawkey purchased the team for $50,000 and immediately named Navin president and chief executive officer. Yawkey insisted upon remaining in the background as a "silent partner." As guardian of the family fortune, he didn't want his name associated too closely with a sports venture that he still feared

might fail. For bringing Angus and Yawkey together and brokering the deal, Yawkey gave his bookkeeper 10 percent ownership—or $5,000 worth of stock—and total control of the team.

Money didn't matter much to Yawkey. He had plenty. The Tigers were just another toy. Occasionally, he would slip hundred dollar bills into the pockets of players or take them out for a night on the town to celebrate a big win or a good play. But money meant everything to Navin, an avid gambler and former bookie. Before teaming up with Yawkey, Navin had worked in a popular downtown Detroit gambling establishment.

For years, Navin was a well-known regular at the horse races across the Detroit River in Windsor, Canada. Horse racing, at that time, was illegal in Detroit. Navin would board the ferry, not far from the ballpark that would eventually bear his name, and venture across the border where, observers said, somehow he always seemed to know when a particular race was "fixed."

According to legend, shortly after Yawkey purchased the Tigers, Navin won $5,000 in an all-night poker game. The next day he gave that five grand to Yawkey as a downpayment on his eventual half-ownership of the team.

Navin also won a two-year power struggle with bushy-browed Tigers manager Ed Barrow, who had been given $2,500 worth of stock when Yawkey purchased the team. Ousted by Navin in Detroit, Barrow later became famous as the manager of the Boston Red Sox and then GM of the New York Yankees.

When the Tigers, led by the fiery young Ty Cobb, won the pennant and set a team record for attendance in 1907, Navin used his share of the profits to pay the $40,000 balance due on his half-interest in the ball club. Finally, there was some semblance of stability in the Tigers' front office, which had previously been a self-serving, muddled mess.

The Tigers' first owner was Jimmy Burns, a quick-tempered 34-year-old wrestler, prizefighter and saloon-keeper, who later became sheriff of Wayne County, Michigan. Burns's father was a brick manufacturer, who had provided the material that built many of early Detroit's downtown buildings.

On March 6, 1900, Burns purchased the Tigers from former West Coast real estate magnate George Vanderbeck for $12,000 when Vanderbeck was forced to sell because of a messy divorce. Vanderbeck's wife was suing him for $8,500 in overdue alimony and Vanderbeck saw selling the ball club as a way out of his financial woes.

The turn-of-the-century Tigers played in Bennett Park, a wobbly, rapidly rotting wooden structure that had been erected by Vanderbeck at the intersection of Michigan and Trumbull in 1896, just seven weeks after the first horseless carriage had rumbled through the streets of Detroit.

The Tigers played their inaugural American League game on April 25, 1901. Players on both teams, accompanied by the mayor, other city officials, and thousands of fans marched in a parade from City Hall to the ballpark. Although it had recently been expanded to seat 8,500, Bennett Park was still the smallest facility in the major leagues.

But 10,023 fans came from as far away as Mt. Clemens, Michigan, for that first AL game. Thousands of patrons overflowed the still unfinished stands onto the wet, muddy field, and the game was halted several times because fans, restrained by ropes, kept crowding the outfielders.

By the time the Tigers came to bat in the bottom of the ninth, trailing Milwaukee, 13-4, many in the throng, disgusted by the Tigers' poor play, were already heading home in their buggies and on bicycles. Suddenly the Tigers erupted for 10 runs in the bottom of the ninth, to grab a 14-13 victory.

The fans who remained threw their hats in the air and ran out on the field, where they mobbed the players and carried first baseman Frank "Pop" Dillon, who had doubled home the winning run, away on their shoulders. Sportswriters of that day called it "the grandest and greatest finish ever seen at Bennett Park."

Burns's partner in that early venture was Tiger manager George "Tweedy" Stallings, who had once studied medicine at the College of Physicians and Surgeons in Baltimore. Stallings had played for the Tigers prior to the turn of the century before leaving to manage the Philadelphia entry in the National League, where he had been accused of stealing signs by using a telescope and moving the letters in the scoreboard to relay signals to the hitters. Years later, after leaving the Tigers again, Stallings would gain fame as manager of the 1914 "Miracle Braves."

A complex personality, Stallings could be personable and charming away from the ballpark. But he was a cutthroat competitor in uniform.

Although the issue remains in dispute to this day, Stallings always maintained that he was responsible for the nickname "Tigers" when he had his players don orange and black stockings similar to those worn by Princeton University. A Detroit newspaper also claimed credit for the name.

Burns and Stallings were hardly the models of upstanding citizenship that Ban Johnson had in mind when he founded the American League in 1901 as a more "genteel" alternative to the often rowdy rival National League. Among other things, Johnson insisted the players and managers in his new league refrain from abusing the umpires and take pains not to offend any women who might be attending the game.

But Stallings had surrounded himself with ballplayers who enjoyed the rough-and-tumble style of play almost as much as he did, and the American League president found himself repeatedly reprimanding and disciplining the Tiger manager. During one weekend series, a different Tiger player was ejected from the game each day.

To circumvent the prevailing ban on Sunday baseball, which was strictly enforced within the city limits of Detroit, the Tigers played their Sunday home games at Burns Park. The primitive field next door to a stockyard was located on land that belonged to the Burns family just beyond Detroit's western border. Burns Park's other neighbor was a tavern where fans and gamblers—and ballplayers—often gathered and did business before and after games.

"You used to see more fights there on a Sunday afternoon than you see now in the big leagues in five years," recalled one of the patrons, turn-of-the-century industrialist Walter O. Briggs, who would later own the Tigers. "The players fought each other and the fans. The fans fought the gate tenders. And the tenders fought the ground keeper."

Meanwhile, Burns and Stallings frequently feuded over the Tigers' finances and stole from one another at every opportunity. They "had a simple system of bookkeeping," wrote Detroit newspaperman Malcolm Bingay, who would later become famous as the popular Tiger critic Iffy the Dopester. "Whichever one got to the cash box first, got the money."

Salaries, taxes and stadium upkeep took second place behind their personal profits. It was not a savory situation. Disturbed by the drunken rowdiness at Tiger games and the shabby condition of Bennett Park,

Johnson made no secret of the fact that he wanted Burns out of his league. On November 14, 1901, the powerful Johnson traveled to Detroit to personally find a new owner for the team.

Privately, Johnson already planned to move the Detroit franchise to Pittsburgh as soon as possible. Like many in the early 1900s, Johnson did not believe that the city of Detroit, which had failed to rally behind earlier teams in the National and International Leagues, would ever adequately support major-league baseball.

Johnson quickly convinced Michigander Ed Doyle, who had earned a small fortune in the lumber industry, that it was his civic duty to seize control of the team and save major-league baseball in the city of Detroit. Johnson neglected to inform Doyle of his plans to relocate the Detroit franchise at the first opportunity.

Doyle reluctantly agreed to the purchase—Johnson could be very persuasive—but Doyle had second thoughts and backed out before the sale could be consummated.

Next, Johnson turned to Sam Angus, a Detroit insurance man. Johnson talked Angus into buying the team with the promise the franchise would soon be moved to presumably more profitable Pittsburgh.

However, when Johnson's American League made peace with the National League in 1903, one of the key provisions of that truce was an agreement that the AL would stay out of Pittsburgh, which was NL territory. Sam Angus was "stuck" in Detroit.

Despite the change in ownership, the decorum in Detroit did not noticeably improve. Provoked by a jeering fan one afternoon in 1903, Tiger manager Ed Barrow dumped a bucket of water on the patron's head and ended up in jail.

On January 22, 1904, with Frank Navin lurking in the wings, the financially strapped Angus sold the Tigers to Bill Yawkey for $50,000. For the next 32 years, Navin ruled the Tigers with an iron fist, especially when it came to the club's finances.

Typical was the letter Navin sent to future Hall of Famer Sam Crawford in February, 1904. At the conclusion of the 1903 season, Crawford's first as a Tiger, in which he batted a hearty .335 and led the American League with 25 triples, Wahoo Sam stuffed his soiled, well-worn wool uniform into his suitcase and went home to Nebraska. That winter, Navin sent his star outfielder the following letter:

"Kindly forward last season's uniform and coat to the Detroit Baseball Club at once, so it can be put in shape for spring practice. As those uniforms are paid for by the Detroit club, they are, of course, the property of the Detroit club, and should have been returned at the close of last season."

Donie Bush, who later managed in both the American and National Leagues, played shortstop well enough on the Tigers' pennant-winning teams of 1907-09 to rank among the Tigers' all-time best at that pivotal position. Although he lacked power, Bush was an excellent leadoff batter and stole 403 bases in his career.

However, that didn't stop Navin from grousing in a March 16, 1911 letter to manager Hughie Jennings:

"[Bush] received $4,200 [in 1910], which was way too much money, considering the class of ball he played. He was of absolutely no use to us from an offensive standpoint. Besides, he did not take as good care of himself as he should have."

Even Cobb was not immune to Navin's devious, penurious ways. When Navin learned that his superstar was being wooed by the upstart Federal League, the Tiger owner ordered all of Cobb's incoming telegrams intercepted and forwarded to Navin's home so that Frank could stay one step ahead of the competition.

Navin concurred completely with Ban Johnson's drive to make baseball an acceptable, attractive form of entertainment for the average American family. He detested rowdy behavior in his ballpark. In 1907, when patrons seated in the right field pavilion at Bennett Park began hurling bottles out onto the field, Navin stationed three security guards there. Periodically, on orders from Navin, a popcorn vendor would pick up a megaphone and inform the crowd that bottle throwing would not be tolerated.

"No game is cleaner, healthier or more scientific [than baseball]," Frank Navin wrote. Baseball, according to Navin, attracted "thousands of devotees out into the open air and the sunshine and distracts them from every contaminating influence."

Detroit's fabled corner of Michigan and Trumbull, the site of Bennett Park, and later Navin Field, Briggs Stadium and Tiger Stadium, had once belonged to

William Woodbridge, the son of a Revolutionary War hero, who would later serve as one of Michigan's first governors and a United States Senator. In 1819, Woodbridge purchased the large plot of land that bordered Michigan Grand Avenue, then the main artery connecting Detroit with Chicago.

Once an Indian footpath known as the Sauk Trail, the log and dirt road stretched for 300 miles to the west, through the heavily wooded wilderness and was regularly traversed by traders, trappers and travelers.

In 1837, the name of the historic road was shortened to Michigan Avenue. In 1858, Woodbridge named the dirt road that formed the eastern boundary of his farm Trumbull Avenue, in honor of his father-in-law, Revolutionary War poet John Trumbull. Following Woodbridge's death in 1860, the site at the intersection of Michigan and Trumbull became a public picnic grounds called Woodbridge Grove.

There on the outskirts of the city, where according to legend the Ottawa Indian chief Pontiac had convened his war councils 100 years earlier, the citizens of Detroit ate and drank and frolicked under the towering oak and elm trees.

Woodbridge Grove eventually became Western Market, site of the city's thriving haymarket, a lumber planing mill and a dog pound. By 1895, the cobblestone-covered haymarket had been abandoned.

Long before it became synonymous with baseball, the neighborhood bordering the corner of Michigan and Trumbull was the land of the Irish. Hundreds of families, fleeing Ireland's infamous potato famine, found refuge in the small wooden cottages that sprang up along what was then the western city limit of Detroit. They called the area Cork Town in memory of County Cork back home in their beloved Ireland.

The residents were poor, but fiercely proud. When the horse-drawn cars that served as public transportation in that section of the city were mistakenly painted yellow one year, the citizens tipped the cars over and chased the drivers away. Eventually the company saw the error of its ways and repainted all of the cars that ran through Cork Town green, like the seats in the ballpark that would serve Tiger fans and the neighborhood for much of the next century.

Hastily constructed Bennett Park, built in 1896 by George Vanderbeck partially out of lumber from trees that grew near the corner of Michigan and Trumbull, was never meant to be a permanent structure. From the day it opened it was a rickety edifice. It soon became a dangerously outdated fire hazard.

A few trees were even left standing in the outfield until 1900, making it look more like a cow pasture than a big-league ballpark. The field, atop the old cobblestones of the haymarket, offered an uneven surface at best. Bad bounces and bruised shins soon became a way of life at Bennett Park.

Whenever it rained, the sponge-like mixture of clay and silt and sand that covered the cobblestones turned the outfield into a swamp. In the winter months, Bennett Park was flooded and used as a skating rink.

When Bennett Park opened in 1896, amidst much hoopla and ceremony, the seating capacity was 5,000. By 1908, after the Tigers won their first pennant, that was doubled to 10,000. Prior to the opening of the 1910 season, following the Tigers' third American League championship in a row, it was increased to 13,000. Still, as much as many fans loved the quaint little ballpark, where the operator of the primitive scoreboard had to climb up and down a ladder to post the hand-painted numbers, nearly everyone readily agreed it had to be replaced.

The Tigers' locker room, located in distant center field some 490 feet from home plate, was woefully inadequate. There was only one showerhead to accommodate the entire team. After peeling off their sweaty, scratchy, heavy wool uniforms, the Tiger players had to stand in line, waiting to bathe. Visiting teams dressed at the downtown Cadillac Hotel where they all stayed, then rode along Michigan Avenue to the ballpark in horse-drawn trolleys. Worst of all, from Tiger owner Frank Navin's point of view, the cramped facility was costing him money.

Attendance was always a problem at rickety Bennett Park, where the best seats sold for 75 cents and the cheapest cost a quarter. On those days when the Tigers did attract good crowds, fans unable to find seats in the L-shaped grandstand or first base bleachers were often forced to stand behind ropes in the outfield, alongside the parked horses and carriages. There they frequently interfered with fielders trying to track down fly balls.

To make matters worse, a half-dozen towering, teetering "wildcat stands" had been erected in the backyards of residents living along National Avenue beyond Bennett Park's billboard-covered, 12-foot-high left field fence. There fans could watch the Tiger games at a cost of five or ten cents without paying the ball club a penny.

A chagrined Navin went to court in an effort to get those bandit bleachers torn down. When that legal challenge failed, Navin sought to thwart the freeloading wildcatters by hanging huge strips of canvas above the outfield fence to block their view. Angry fans, many of whom were young and undisciplined, retaliated by throwing bottles and rotten vegetables onto the field. When the police were called, spectators seated in the wildcat stands would spit tobacco juice down upon them.

Navin calculated that the wildcat bleachers were costing him 400 admissions per game. Because of their three pennants in a row, the Tigers had become a hot commodity.

Thanks in no small part to the presence of Ty Cobb, nearly 485,000 paying customers passed through the Bennett Park turnstiles in 1911. But Navin was dazzled by the huge crowds of 30,000 and more that were flocking game after game to the comfortable new state-of-the-art steel and concrete sports palaces in Pittsburgh, St. Louis, and Philadelphia. Navin looked at those new ballparks and saw dollar signs.

By now the Motor City was booming. No longer merely a quiet, Midwestern outpost, Detroit had become the noisy, congested automotive capital of the world. Two streetcar lines served Bennett Park.

The city was on the cutting edge. The country's first stop signs and the first traffic lights were developed in Detroit to control the growing deluge of motorized vehicles. Snowplows and concrete roads debuted in Detroit, too. By 1910, there were 23 different companies in the city of Detroit manufacturing automobiles. That surge in employment opportunities had sent the population soaring, from 286,000 in 1900 to 466,000 by 1910. To accommodate the flood of immigrants, work signs in the plants had to be posted in several languages.

Ty Cobb always drew a crowd, thanks to his incredible skills and his unpredictable attitude. Brace Photo

In 1911, weary of battling the wildcatters, Navin bought out the property owners beyond the left and right field fences and tore down the houses, barns and towers that bordered the ballpark. Bennett Park was razed as soon as the 1911 season ended and work began immediately on a modern new ballpark on the same site.

Construction was completed in one winter, at a cost of $300,000, as men worked around the clock to get the new ballpark finished in time. Home plate was moved from what would later become right field at Tiger Stadium so that batters would no longer have to stare into the late afternoon sun. A giant scoreboard, which could display the scores of all of the out-of-town games, was erected in left field and a 125-foot flagpole, the tallest object ever placed in fair territory inside a major-league ballpark, was situated in center.

Navin even installed enough showers in the new clubhouses to accommodate both teams. Never again would visiting ballplayers have to dress at their hotel or return to their rooms to bathe after the games.

However, co-owner Bill Yawkey still feared that the fledgling franchise might fail. He insisted the new ballpark not bear his family name. "That would not be in keeping with the dignity of the Yawkey name," he explained. Yawkey preferred that Navin, his powerful partner, put his name and reputation on the line.

Privately, Navin loved the idea. But he feared the public repercussions. Bennett Park had been named in honor of Charlie Bennett, the beloved catcher from Detroit's 1887 National League championship team who had lost parts of both legs in an 1894 train accident. Bennett remained a popular figure around town, both with the public and the press, and Navin worried that there would be an angry backlash.

Bennett had slipped while boarding a train in Kansas and fallen beneath the heavy metal wheels of the moving train. The train cut off his left foot and crushed his right leg, which later had to be amputated below the knee. The former ballplayer was forced to sell cigars and painted china dishes from a downtown Detroit shop to support himself. Each spring, with the aid of a cane, Bennett would hobble up to home plate on his two artificial limbs to catch the ceremonial first pitch on Opening Day in the ballpark that bore his name.

In addition, Navin realized that he had earlier made many enemies among Detroit's most powerful political figures. Navin's well-known penchant for gambling, both on horses and on cards, had tarnished his reputation in the eyes of many of the city's influential, upstanding citizens. Frank Croul, Detroit's new police commissioner, claimed Navin had cheated him out of his rightful winnings years earlier when Navin worked at Alvord's, a local gambling parlor. Croul, one of the city's leading aristocrats and quite a gambler himself, had placed a $500 bet on a horse, at odds of three to one. The horse won, but Navin claimed that Croul had been late in placing his wager and merely returned his $500 bet.

Croul publicly called Navin a crook and later made a point of refusing to frequent his ballpark. Even-

tually, in 1907, Navin agreed to donate the disputed $1,500, with compound interest, to charity. In exchange, Croul withdrew his objection to the Tigers playing games at Bennett Park on Sunday.

Sunday was traditionally a day of rest, and cities throughout the East and Midwest had laws prohibiting the playing of baseball on Sunday. Ministers usually led the crusade. They wanted people to spend the day in church and in spiritual reflection. Baseball was still viewed in many quarters as a crude, raucous, unsavory form of amusement, barely one step above burlesque or vaudeville. Ballplayers who dared break that law ran the risk of being hauled off to jail.

In Detroit, St. Peter's Episcopal Church, the red brick house of worship that still stands on the southeast corner of Michigan and Trumbull across the street from abandoned Tiger Stadium, led the civic fight against Sunday baseball. When the "blue laws" banning Sunday baseball were relaxed, St. Peter's profited for nearly a century by charging ballpark patrons to park their cars on church property.

On August 18, 1907, the first Sunday game of baseball was played at the corner of Michigan and Trumbull with police commissioner Croul in attendance.

Rather than simply name Detroit's new baseball stadium after himself, Navin secretly sought the assistance of a sympathetic friend who wrote for one of Detroit's daily newspapers. The reporter in turn suggested to an acquaintance on the Detroit City Council that a resolution should be introduced, proclaiming that the new ballpark ought to be named Navin Field.

The Council, many of whose members had climbed on the Tigers' bandwagon along with most of the rest of the city during the team's 1907-08-09 pennants, did not want to appear disloyal. It passed the resolution unanimously.

The next day, Navin modestly accepted congratulations on the great honor and "reluctantly" agreed to allow the eagerly awaited new structure to bear his name.

Navin Field, nearly five times the size of the original Bennett Park, was scheduled to open on April 18, 1912, Frank Navin's 41st birthday. However, rain washed out the inaugural game, and Navin, ever the superstitious gambler, refused to open the season the following day because that was a Friday. In Navin's mind, Fridays were synonymous with bad luck. Navin also avoided cross-eyed people and always put his left shoe on first.

"Those men, who were sports people, were quite superstitious," explained Joanna Navin-Monaghan, granddaughter of Navin's older brother, Thomas, the former mayor of Adrian, Michigan, who served six years in prison for embezzlement and who was briefly involved with George Vanderbeck in an effort to save professional baseball in Detroit at the turn of the century. "When the Tigers were winning, Frank Navin wouldn't change his hat.

"He had great humor. He didn't look it. He certainly looked like a stiff guy. He was very fastidious. He liked to gamble. He loved horses. He and Al Jolson were great friends. He dressed for ballgames and all that. And he built that team. He was a true sports person. He loved the game and he loved owning the team. And he acted like an owner. He did not miss ballgames. It was his life.

"I think those men were visionaries, if you will, in another time," continued Navin-Monaghan, whose father, also named Thomas, was Frank Navin's godson and "kind of the darling of the team." Years later, Joanna's dad would sit in Navin's stadium office and read the newspaper to the Tiger owner and help him conduct business meetings.

"They were kind of adventurous. They wanted to build something and be a part of something. They did vest their time and their life and their money in baseball. They took care of players and made a lot of people happy. They were great builders of community. They'd didn't just say, 'Gee, we own a baseball team.' Sure, they wanted to win the World Series. And they did. But they also were very active in the community. They shared their time and wealth."

Rather than debut his new namesake ballpark on Friday, the superstitious Navin claimed that the new field was still too wet from the rain to permit play and postponed the opening of Navin Field until Saturday, April 20. Then the Tigers marked the occasion with a 6-5, 11-inning triumph over the Cleveland Indians. The next morning, however, that historic victory was overshadowed by the news that the Titanic had sunk.

Officially, a sellout crowd of 24,384, many of whom marched down Michigan Avenue to the new ballpark along with the players and assorted dignitaries, saw Cleveland's "Shoeless Joe" Jackson score the first run in the new ballpark and Ty Cobb steal home with one of his signature hook slides. Cobb also was thrown out at the plate trying to score from second on an infield out. Estimates placed the actual size of the day's crowd at more than 26,000.

The seats in new Navin Field, by the way, were painted yellow, not the traditional green for which Briggs Stadium and Tiger Stadium would later become known.

The starting time for games at Bennett Park had been 3:30 p.m. But, with the opening of Navin Field, that was switched to three o'clock. According to published reports, the change was made "to allow fans to reach home before supper gets cold, thus avoiding much domestic commotion and lightening the work load of divorce courts."

One of the customers in the overflow crowd in the new park on that momentous afternoon was Walter O. Briggs, a well-to-do former switchman on the Central Michigan Railroad, who had been a Bennett Park regular from its earliest days.

Briggs once became so vociferous that umpire Tom Connolly interrupted a game and walked over to the grandstand to warn Briggs that he would be ejected if he didn't quiet down. Briggs, who got his big break in the business world when he took over a small buggy and wagon shop and began making bodies for automobiles, was undeniably an ardent baseball fan.

Like the rest of Detroit, Briggs had been overjoyed when the Tigers won their first American League pennant in 1907. But that happiness turned to anger when young Briggs, who had grown accustomed to getting his way because of his new wealth, discovered he wouldn't be able to occupy his regular box seats at the World Series. The best seats in tiny Bennett Park were already sold out.

With the aid of a mutual acquaintance, Briggs wrangled a meeting with Navin. Navin was immediately impressed with Briggs's love of baseball—and with his money. While Navin was a notorious tightwad, Briggs was a hopeless spendthrift. For some reason, the two men hit it off. Briggs got his box seat at the World Series.

Friends later said that from that day forward, Briggs vowed he would someday own the Detroit Tigers. And when he did, there would be room in his ballpark for everyone who wanted to come.

❦

Ty Cobb continued to be the Tigers' principal draw—and baseball's biggest problem child.

In 1909, after Cobb slid particularly high into popular Philadelphia third baseman Frank "Home Run" Baker, spiking Baker's arm, he received several

SAM CRAWFORD

Right Field
Bats: Left ♦ Throws: Left
6'0" ♦ 190 lbs.
Played with Tigers: 1903-17
Born: 4/18/80 ♦ Died: 6/15/68

Sam Crawford was awarded to the Tigers as part of the 1903 peace agreement between the National and American Leagues—the same agreement that derailed AL president Ban Johnson's grand scheme to relocate the struggling Detroit baseball franchise in Pittsburgh.

In 1903, Crawford, who had earned a mere $150 a month while batting .333 at Cincinnati the summer before, signed contracts with both the Tigers and the Reds. When the AL and NL reluctantly agreed to peacefully coexist, Crawford and pitcher "Wild Bill" Donovan were awarded to the Tigers as part of that settlement.

Although he was uncomfortably relegated to the shadow of Ty Cobb throughout most of his career, "Wahoo Sam" nevertheless compiled a .309 lifetime average and a reputation as one of the hardest hitters in the dead-ball era. He batted over .300 eleven times, including a resounding .378 average in 1911.

Once an aspiring apprentice barber in Wahoo, Neb., (hence his nickname), where he cut the hair of wandering hobos for practice, Crawford is best remembered as the most prolific triples hitter of all time.

Crawford was so fond of his nickname that throughout his later life he continued to sign all correspondence and autographs as "Wahoo Sam Crawford." When he was elected to the Hall of Fame in 1957, he asked that he be inducted as "Wahoo Sam."

Five times with the Tigers, and once with Cincinnati, the slope-shouldered slugger with unusually large hands and feet led the league in three-baggers. Crawford smacked 312 triples in his career, a major-league record that still stands and a most remarkable feat considering that Crawford played in the era of the dead ball. He is the only player ever to lead both leagues in home runs and triples during the course of his career.

A favorite among Bennett Park fans, the surprisingly fast Crawford also delivered a record 51 inside-the-park home runs and swiped 366 bases during his 19-year career.

Crawford collected 2,964 hits. But some statisticians have argued he actually should have received credit for the 87 hits he delivered at Grand Rapids in the Western League, forerunner of the AL, in 1899. In 1901, the National Commission, the three-man body that ruled baseball in those days, ordered that any Western League performers who moved on to the American or National Leagues, were entitled to have their Western League statistics counted as major-league totals. However, for some reason league officials ignored that ruling in Crawford's case. Otherwise, Wahoo Sam's hit total would be 3,051.

Although he and Cobb rarely mingled socially and seldom spoke, they frequently teamed up to befuddle the opposition. If Crawford drew a walk when Cobb was perched on third base, the two men had a secret signal. As soon as Crawford reached first base he would take off for second. If a fielder threw the ball to second to try to catch Crawford, Cobb would take off for the plate.

"They didn't know what the devil to do," Crawford recalled. "Sometimes they'd catch him, and sometimes they'd catch me, and sometimes they wouldn't get either of us. Most of the time they were too paralyzed to do anything and I'd wind up on second on a base on balls."

In 1957, after he had been elected to baseball's Hall of Fame, Crawford was invited back to Detroit for a 50th reunion of the 1907 pennant winners. However, Wahoo Sam vainly refused to put on a uniform.

"I want to be remembered the way I used to be," he said. "When they think of Sam Crawford in a Detroit uniform, I want them to think of me the way I was back then."

"Wahoo Sam" Crawford became famous mostly for hitting triples. He is first on the all-time list with 312 triples over a 19-year career. Fourteen of those years were spent with the Tigers. Burton Historical Society

death threats, and the Athletics clamored that Cobb should be suspended from baseball for life. However, a photograph of that play clearly showed that Cobb's slide had been his famed "fade-away," and that Baker was actually out of the base path. Nevertheless, for the rest of that series, Cobb needed a police escort to take him to and from Shibe Park, and several officers stood behind him in the outfield to protect Ty from the enraged Philadelphia fans.

"They always talked about Cobb playing dirty, trying to spike guys and all that," said Sam Crawford. "Cobb never tried to spike anybody. The base line belongs to the runner. If the infielders get in the way, that's their lookout.

"But Ty was dynamite on the base paths," continued Crawford. "Talk about strategy and playing with your head, that was Cobb all the way. It wasn't that he was so fast on his feet. He was fast on his thinking. He didn't out-hit the opposition and he didn't out-run them. He out-thought them."

Cobb didn't worry about making friends. During a doubleheader on the final day of the 1910 season, in an effort to prevent Cobb from winning his fourth batting crown in a row, St. Louis Browns manager Jack O'Connor ordered third baseman Red Corriden to play so deep that Cleveland's Nap Lajoie would be able to bunt for a base hit on every at-bat and thus finish the season with a higher average than Ty.

Lajoie collected eight hits that day—six of them were bunts. But Cobb won the title anyway, by less than one point. O'Connor wasn't so lucky. American League president Ban Johnson banned the manager from the game and kicked out Browns' pitching coach Harry Howell, too, for offering the official scorer a new suit of clothes if he would change an obvious error to a hit for Lajoie.

Seventy years later, a researcher discovered that Cobb had been inadvertently awarded two extra hits, which meant that Lajoie actually had won the batting crown. But baseball commissioner Bowie Kuhn ruled that Cobb could keep the tainted title.

Never a natural athlete, Cobb worked tirelessly to hone his skills. When he discovered that he had trouble hitting low pitches and spitballs, he practiced for hours until he learned to handle those pitches. He kept his hands well apart on his bat, shortening or lengthening his grip depending upon the pitch and the situation.

Although he was far from the fastest man in the majors, Cobb made a science of stealing bases. He studied the pitchers in order to get a better jump and slid into the bases with reckless abandon, daring the opposing fielders to stand their ground.

To assist Cobb, not that he needed a whole lot of help, the Tigers' groundskeepers regularly soaked the ground in front of home plate with so much water that it became known as "Cobb's Lake." The strategy worked. It slowed down Cobb's bunts and frequently caused rival fielders to slip and fall.

Cobb was often thrown out trying to steal. It was all part of his strategy. He would take off and run even when the Tigers were way ahead. He didn't want the opposing pitcher and catcher to get a moment's rest. He wanted them to be constantly worrying about him. And Ty's teammates frequently fared better at bat because the pitcher was concentrating on Cobb on base.

Often he scored from second on a sacrifice fly. Several times he started out on first base and then swiped second, third and home,

"Tighten your belts, boys," teammate Germany Schaefer would holler, "or he'll steal your pants."

Cobb didn't miss a trick. He would often limp out on the field at the start of a game. He would keep limping and complaining to the opposing players about how much his legs hurt until the right situation arose. Then Ty would take off, running as fast as ever.

Often criticized for sliding with his feet turned up and his spikes high, Cobb later insisted that he was not trying to injure anyone, but rather trying to keep his spikes from getting caught in the dirt, possibly fracturing his ankle.

"Baseball is a red-blooded game for red-blooded men," Cobb declared. "Baseball is like war. It's no pink tea. Mollycoddlers had better stay out. It's a struggle for supremacy. A survival of the fittest."

In May of 1912, while the Tigers were in New York to play the Highlanders, Cobb climbed into the stands to attack a fan who had been taunting him. The victim, a minor New York politician named Claude Luecker who had lost his left hand and three fingers off his right hand in a printing press accident a year earlier, began berating Cobb as soon as the Tigers stepped on the field. "He had been picking on me every trip," Cobb explained later.

At first Cobb tried to ignore him. But the verbal barrage, which according to Cobb included racial insults, continued throughout the first seven innings.

Tiger shortstop Donie Bush urged Luecker to be quiet, but to no avail. Finally Cobb walked to the edge of the grandstand and retaliated with some profanity of his own. When Luecker responded in kind, Cobb climbed into the stands and began punching and kicking his antagonist. Luecker later insisted Cobb had spiked him after knocking him to the ground.

According to Luecker, when someone in the crowd yelled, "Don't kick him! He has no hands!" Cobb supposedly replied, "I don't care if he has no feet!"

Umpire Silk O'Loughlin immediately ejected Cobb from the game. American League president Ban Johnson, who was sitting in the stands, suspended Cobb—although Johnson privately remarked that he "did not blame him a bit."

In a rare display of support for Cobb, Ty's Tiger teammates—led by Sam Crawford, one of the leaders of the anti-Cobb faction on the team—refused to take the field for the next game, which was against the Philadelphia Athletics. To avoid a $5,000 fine from the league for forfeiting the game, the Tigers assembled an impromptu team that included 50-year-old Tiger coach Deacon McGuire, plus collegians and semipro players. That odd, inept assortment of alleged athletes, most of whom were paid $10 each to replace the striking Tigers, lost to the Athletics, 24-2. The pitcher, a Jesuit seminarian named Albert Travers, received $50 for tossing a complete game. His penance completed, Travers resumed his preparations for the priesthood.

Another of the players was a teenager using the pseudonym of Billy Maharg, an anagram for his real name, which was Graham. Maharg later became the only one of the pickup Tigers ever to appear again in a major-league lineup when he played one game with the Philadelphia Phillies in 1916.

Maharg was also a part-time prizefighter and small-time gambler who later acted as a go-between and whistle blower in the Chicago Black Sox fix of the 1919 World Series.

Many of the fans who had purchased tickets to the boycotted Tigers/Athletics game demanded refunds, believing they had been gypped. American League president Ban Johnson rushed to Philadelphia and warned the striking Tigers that they would be banned for life if they sat out another game. Cobb himself appealed to his teammates to return to the field.

As a result of his unexpected efforts as a mediator, Cobb was fined only $50 for the attack. His 10-day suspension was made retroactive so that he didn't miss another game. Meanwhile, Cobb's striking teammates, who had sent an angry telegram to Johnson demanding that the suspension be lifted, were fined $100 apiece.

The brief strike led to the formation of the Baseball Players Fraternity, forerunner of today's powerful Major League Baseball Players Association. It also prompted major-league teams to hire ushers to oversee the crowds.

But it did nothing to repair Cobb's relationship with his Tiger teammates.

Prior to the 1917 season, the Tigers met the New York Giants in a series of exhibition games. Led by Buck Herzog, the Giants rode Cobb relentlessly from the bench until Cobb exploded, attacking Herzog at second base. That evening, at the teams' hotel, Herzog approached Cobb's table and informed him that he would meet him in Ty's room. Cobb rushed through the rest of his meal, then raced back to his room. He moved the furniture to one side and rolled up the rug.

Peering through his keyhole, Cobb spied Herzog coming down the hall. Cobb noticed his would-be opponent was wearing rubber-soled shoes. Ty quickly emptied a pitcher of water on the floor, knowing his own leather-soled shoes would grip the wet floor better than Herzog's rubber soles. According to eyewitness reports, Cobb savagely beat his smaller opponent, nearly breaking his back. The next day, Cobb refused to take the field against the Giants, citing their "roughhouse stuff."

In 1920, after Bill Yawkey had passed away, baseball-minded Walter O. Briggs and millionaire industrialist John Kelsey each bought quarter-shares of the Detroit Tiger franchise from the Yawkey estate for $250,000 apiece. Frank Navin, who owned the other 50 percent, continued to run the team. In fact, Kelsey, who had pitched and played third base on the Detroit Athletic Club team that won the national amateur championship in 1892, carried business cards that read: "Ask Navin, he's the owner."

Detroit's population now topped one million. In 1919 the Tigers led the American League in attendance, attracting 643,805 fans. Before the 1923 season began an upper deck was added to the grandstand, increasing Navin Field's capacity to 29,000. In 1924 Detroit was the nation's fourth-largest city thanks to a large influx of European immigrants and Southern blacks seeking work. That influx helped the Tigers become just the second big-league team to top the one million mark in attendance. "Detroit," observed baseball's self-appointed bible, *The Sporting News,* "is simply baseball crazy."

The No. 1 team in attendance, of course, was the New York Yankees, who by then featured baseball's two most popular stars, Babe Ruth and Lou Gehrig.

Cobb bitterly resented all of the attention Ruth received. As the Tigers' player-manager, Ty once sent an obvious signal from his position in the outfield, ordering the Detroit pitcher to intentionally walk The Babe. At the plate, Ruth relaxed. The Babe was stunned when the Tiger hurler unexpectedly fired the first pitch past him for a called strike.

Pretending to be incensed at his pitcher's insubordination, Cobb called time out and ran in from the outfield to castigate his hurler on the mound, right in front of Ruth. As soon as Cobb returned to his position, the pitcher proceeded to throw another perfect strike past the unsuspecting Babe.

Acting thoroughly outraged, Cobb again raced to the mound where he screamed at the Tigers' battery and replaced them both, bringing a new pitcher and catcher into the game.

When play resumed, the new Tiger hurler threw strike three past the unsuspecting Ruth.

The Babe walked slowly back to the Yankee dugout, knowing he had been had.

For some reason, Cobb seemed to harbor a special hatred for Lou Gehrig. He probably was the only player who ever made the mild-mannered Gehrig really mad.

"You're a bum!" Cobb would shout, whenever the Tigers and Yankees clashed. "You're a thick-headed, no-good Dutchman! Get out of here, you lousy Kraut!"

One day Gehrig decided he had heard enough. Passing the Tiger dugout while Cobb spewed out his epithets, Gehrig suddenly lowered his head, clenched his fists, and charged Cobb.

Ty stepped out of the way, causing Gehrig to smack his head against an iron stanchion in the dugout. Stunned, the Yankee first baseman fell to the ground. Gehrig staggered to his feet and, like a punch-drunk boxer, went after Cobb again. Finally the Tiger players pulled the two men apart.

In spite of the presence of Cobb, until 1934-35 the Tigers never again achieved the level of success that they had reached in 1907-08-09. But the Tigers continued to pound the baseball. Between 1910 and 1919, they finished either first or second in the league in hit-

ting seven times. But as Hughie Jennings discovered, when the pitching soured, powerful hitting was not enough.

The Detroit press blamed Jennings, who continued to practice law during the off season. Jennings grew increasingly sarcastic and began to drink heavily. The media claimed he couldn't handle the Tigers' pitching staff. The problem was, the Tigers didn't have much pitching to handle. And the Tigers' defense was often suspect, at best.

Against that backdrop, at the urging of both Briggs and Kelsey, Navin dismissed Jennings, who had been known as a defensive specialist since his playing days with the Baltimore Orioles in the 1890s, and hired Cobb, who had always been obsessed with hitting.

Years later, Cobb, who was initially reluctant to accept the job, would call his decision to manage the Tigers while continuing to play the field "the biggest mistake of my life."

His decision was influenced by the fact that Tris Speaker, one of Cobb's principal batting rivals, had managed the Cleveland Indians to the world championship the previous year while hitting .388. Never one to let another player outdo him, Cobb was determined to prove he could do the same thing. Besides, Cobb yearned to finally win the one prize that had eluded him throughout his career: A World Series championship.

When Cobb learned that the Tigers were thinking of hiring Chicago White Sox manager Pants Rowland in the event he turned them down, Ty realized he had no choice. Cobb hated Rowland. He felt he was a fraud. And he had vowed he would never play for Rowland. Fearing Rowland might accept Navin's offer, Cobb had no choice but to take the job himself.

Tigers fans and the city of Detroit agreed with Briggs and Kelsey. Ty Cobb was just the man to bring home the title that the team and the town coveted. Bands, speeches, a banquet and a parade surrounded Cobb's return to Detroit during the off season to sign his contract to manage the team. Sportswriters traveled from the East Coast to cover the signing. Cobb himself vowed he would quit if the Tigers did not immediately improve upon their wretched seventh-place finish under Jennings in 1920.

Under Cobb, the 1921 Tigers batted .316, a franchise record that still stands. They hammered out 1,724 hits and scored 883 runs, but still finished no better than sixth, 27 games behind the New York Yankees.

Future Hall of Famer Harry Heilmann profited most from Cobb's managerial advice, but rookie first baseman Lu Blue (.308), rookie catcher Johnny Bassler (.307), third baseman Bobby Jones (.303) and outfielder Ira Flagstead (.305) all benefited. Meanwhile, the outfield of Cobb, Heilmann, and Bobby Veach batted a hearty .374 collectively. Cobb himself enjoyed a banner year, hitting .389 with 101 RBIs and 12 homers despite the added pressures of managing.

In fact, in six seasons under manager Cobb, the Tigers, as a team, batted an amazing .302, exciting fans and making Detroit the second most profitable franchise in the American League during the 1920s.

Under Cobb's watchful, demanding eye, the Tigers led the league in hitting and in scoring twice and boasted four individual batting champions in those six seasons—not one of them named Ty Cobb.

Whenever a hard-hitting team came to town to play the Tigers, Cobb would instruct the groundskeepers to erect temporary bleachers in the outfield to turn long drives into ground-rule doubles instead of triples and home runs. When crowds were small, Cobb would order the groundskeepers to sit in the temporary stands themselves so that the umpires would not be tempted to order them removed.

However, Cobb's disposition didn't improve as the Tigers' manager. "He was the same off the field as he was on," said Hall of Famer second baseman Charlie Gehringer, who played for Cobb. "He was always fighting with somebody."

Hall of Famer Billy Evans was one of the best liked, most respected umpires in the American League. In 1909, Evans brought about the introduction of four-man umpiring crews. Working the World Series between the Tigers and Pirates with the famed Bill Klem, Evans lost sight of a line drive by Pittsburgh's Dot Miller down the right field line and polled fans in the grandstand as to whether the ball had been foul or fair. American League president Ban Johnson was so enraged that he assigned four umpires to the next game.

None of that mattered in 1921, however, when after a hotly contested game in Cleveland Cobb challenged Evans to "meet me under the grandstand."

The two men stripped to the waist and went at it while a group of Tigers and Indians watched. Cobb's five-year-old son, Ty Jr., cheered his father on, shouting, "Come on, Daddy." Cobb had a firm grip on the umpire's neck and was banging Evans's head against the cinders when the Tiger players pulled the two men

apart. Neither side reported the ugly incident to the league office. Ironically, Evans—who had been suspended in 1912 following an angry confrontation with Tiger outfielder Davy Jones—later served as the Tigers' general manager from 1946 to 1951.

The 1923 season was Cobb's most successful as a manager, as he guided the Tigers to a second-place finish. But in spite of the presence of Heilmann, Heinie Manush, Veach and Bob Fothergill, not to mention the still formidable Cobb himself, the Tigers wound up 16 games behind the New York Yankees.

Fothergill, who at five foot ten and 240 pounds was usually referred to as "Fats," or "Fatty," or "Rotund Robert," was one of the Tigers' greatest pinch hitters, compiling a .327 average in that role in his nine seasons with the team. During a five-year span he batted .350.

Late one season, the Tigers were playing the Yankees, who as usual were in the thick of the pennant race, when Fothergill stepped up to the plate with two out and the winning run on base in the ninth inning. Suddenly, the Yankees' future Hall of Famer Leo Durocher called time and raced toward the home plate umpire. "There's a man batting out of turn here!" Durocher bellowed.

The umpire pulled his copy of the lineup card out of his back pocket, examined it for a moment, then shook his head. "Fothergill is the right batter," he said.

"Fothergill?" Durocher exclaimed, doing his best to appear astonished. "Is that Fothergill? I'm sorry. From where I was standing it looked like there were two men standing at the plate."

Fothergill was so furious that he had to be restrained. When play resumed, Fothergill was so busy glaring at Durocher that the Yankee pitcher fired three quick strikes past him. The inning over, the rally killed, Fothergill dropped his bat and charged out on the field after Durocher, who was running as fast as he could back to the safety of the Yankee dugout.

Cobb's simmering rivalry with Babe Ruth erupted on June 13, 1924, in the ninth inning of a game at Navin Field. New York Yankee outfielder Bob Meusel was hit by a pitch, presumably on orders from Cobb, and immediately charged the mound. Both benches emptied for a typical baseball brawl. Ruth and Cobb squared off and wrestled one another to the ground while fans ripped out seats and hurled them onto the field. The police had to be summoned, and it was half an hour before peace was restored. Bruised and battered, Cobb and Ruth returned to their respective dugouts as the umpires awarded the game to the Yankees by forfeit.

"The Babe was a great ballplayer, sure," Hall of Famer Tris Speaker once observed, "but Cobb was even greater. Babe could knock your brains out, but Cobb would drive you crazy."

The Tigers' box office boom was particularly pleasing to the always-shrewd Cobb, who had a clause in his contract that gave him 10 cents for every ticket over 700,000 that the Tigers sold. Perhaps that was what prompted player/manager Cobb to bench himself in June of 1926—even though he was hitting .392 at the time—because the Tigers' three other outfielders, Harry Heilmann, Heinie Manush, and Fatty Fothergill, were all batting over .400.

However, in spite of their fan support and the cajoling of Cobb, the Tigers continued to struggle on the field.

As Tiger manager, Cobb squabbled constantly with team owner Frank Navin. Cobb later claimed the frugal Navin had cost the Tigers the chance to win several pennants by refusing to purchase future Hall of Famer Paul Waner from San Francisco of the Pacific Coast League for $45,000. Cobb also complained publicly in 1924 when Navin refused to summon promising first baseman Johnny Neun from the minor leagues to replace injured Lu Blue when the Tigers still had a chance to win the pennant. Neun did join the Tigers the following year. But without him the Tigers finished third in 1924, six games behind the Washington Senators.

On May 31, 1927, Neun validated Cobb's high opinion of him by pulling off an unassisted triple play. There were two Indians on base and nobody out in the top half of the ninth inning, with the Tigers nursing a 1-0 lead, when Cleveland's Homer Summa pulled a drive down the first base line. Neun grabbed the line drive for one out and quickly tagged Charlie Jamieson, who was caught several steps off first base for out number two.

Meanwhile, Indians catcher George Myatt, who had been on second base, representing the tying run, had raced all the way to third in an effort to score on Summa's drive.

Neun could easily have tossed the ball to Tiger shortstop Jackie Tavener, who was standing on second base shouting for the ball. However, earlier that day, Neun had read a newspaper account of an unassisted

triple play that had been pulled off the previous afternoon by Johnny Cooney of the Chicago Cubs. So the significance of such a rare feat was fresh in Neun's mind.

Shouting, "Triple play, unassisted! Triple play, unassisted!" Neun himself raced to second base, easily beating the slow-footed Myatt for the third out.

On April 20, 1927, Ty Tyson broadcast the first Tiger game on radio on station WWJ. This was the height of Prohibition and an estimated 25,000 "blind pigs" flourished throughout the city of Detroit, serving far more liquor than the 1,200 bars shut down by Prohibition ever had.

Harry Heilmann, whose fondness for the nightlife was well known, once drove his Austin roadster, which had been presented to him on "Harry Heilmann Day," down the steps of a basement speakeasy and right up to the bar, where he purchased an illegal beverage. Members of the notorious Purple Gang, an all-Jewish mob of thugs famed for their cold-blooded violence, were frequently present at Navin Field, cheering for the Tigers, and sometimes celebrating with the players in illicit saloons afterwards.

But overall, Cobb ran a tight ship. He demanded that the Tigers be all business on the field, hustling at all times. He forbade fraternization with opposing players.

Convinced that Bobby Veach was not playing up to his potential because he lacked the necessary competitive fire, Cobb ordered the good-natured Heilmann, who batted behind Veach in the Tigers' lineup, to constantly ride his teammate from the on-deck circle and accuse him, among other things, of being gutless. Cobb assured Heilmann that once the ploy worked and Veach responded, he would explain the situation to Veach and take Heilmann off the hook.

Heilmann did as he was instructed. And the strategy succeeded. Veach batted .338 in 1921 and enjoyed career highs in hits (207), home runs (16), and RBIs (128). However, Cobb failed to keep his end of the bargain. At the end of the season, he failed to tell Veach about the scheme. When Heilmann tried to explain himself, and apologize, Veach advised him not to "come sucking around me with that phony line." The two men never did make up.

Cobb frequently infuriated the Tiger pitchers, especially proven veterans like Hooks Dauss, Howard Ehmke and Dutch Leonard, who would win a total of 526 games in their combined careers. Cobb would call

Veach was the Tigers' lefthanded-hitting left fielder for more than 11 years and he batted .306 or better in eight of them. While Veach was a solid hitter, he was usually overshadowed by his more famous teammates Sam Crawford, Ty Cobb and Harry Heilmann. Burton Historical Society

pitcher who was revolutionizing the game with his booming bat. Cobb claimed he could have hit 30 to 40 home runs a year if he had tried.

"Gentlemen," the obviously envious Cobb informed the writers on the field before the day's game, "I would like you to pay particular attention today because for the first time in my career I will be deliberately going for home runs."

In the first inning against St. Louis, Cobb belted one of Joe Bush's fastballs over the fence in right field. The second time up, he hit a slow curve for another home run. In the eighth inning he connected again for his third home run of the afternoon, off three different pitchers. Sandwiched in between those three homers were a double and two singles. The following day, Cobb singled his first time up, then added two more HRs.

Five home runs in two days—Ty Cobb had proven his point. He went back to hitting singles and smacked only seven more homers the rest of the year.

At the time, Ty Cobb was 38 years old.

But Babe Ruth was not impressed. "Hell," the Babe grumbled, "I could hit .600! But I'm paid to hit homers."

Hooks Dauss was the first of Detroit's six long-term one-team-only players. Dauss played from 1912-26. His nickname was derived from his arsenal of sharp-breaking curve ball pitches. Burton Historical Society

time, jog in from the outfield, and tell the pitcher, no matter how experienced, exactly how to deal with the next batter.

Although he never played on or managed a World Series-winning team, Cobb never considered himself a failure as a manager. "I took over a seventh-place club in 1921 and, with one exception, all my clubs won more games that they lost," he insisted. "We were in the first division four times. We played interesting and exciting ball."

Never known as a home run hitter, Cobb announced in May of 1925 that he was going to start swinging for the fences. Ty was tired of hearing all of the talk about the sensational Babe Ruth, the former

HARRY HEILMANN

Right Field
Bats: Right ♦ Throws: Right
6'1" ♦ 195 lbs.
Played with Tigers: 1914-29
Born: 8/3/94 ♦ Died: 7/9/51

Harry Heilmann, Ty Cobb's prize pupil, succeeded his demanding mentor as the Tigers' leading hitting hero. But he did so without most of the character flaws and personal baggage that so tainted Cobb's image. "Slug," as Heilmann was affectionately known, may have been the only ballplayer who was a friend of both Cobb and Babe Ruth.

Heilmann, who couldn't even make his own high school team and eventually flunked out of school, was working as a bookkeeper for the Mutual Biscuit Co. in San Francisco in 1913 when he was spotted playing semipro ball and signed to his first professional contract. His bonus: A spaghetti dinner.

Heilmann was already a decent hitter when he was drafted by the Portland Tigers of the Northwestern League in 1914. However, his defense was a different matter. Slow afoot, Heilmann was quickly nicknamed "Harry the Horse" by his Tiger teammates. Nevertheless, as a rookie he was called upon to play first base, second base, and the outfield. On May 22, 1914, he committed three errors in the outfield in the first inning, setting a major-league record.

Although Cobb and Heilmann had played side by side in the Tigers' outfield since 1916, sharing the same locker rooms and the long, late-night train rides, it was not until Cobb took over as manager, replacing Hughie Jennings in 1921, that he began to counsel the raw slugger on pitch selection and stance. Cobb taught Heilmann to move his feet closer together and to put more weight on his front foot. He coached him to keep his elbows high and his arms away from his body. He also urged him to study catchers, some of whom habitually called for the same pitch in certain situations.

Heilmann was a willing, eager pupil. He even imitated Cobb's stance, sometimes crouching to reduce the strike zone and gripping the bat with his hands a few inches apart. The results were dramatic.

Heilmann, one of the few players who actually got along with the irascible Cobb, didn't bat over .300 until 1919, his fifth year in the big leagues. His best batting average, before Cobb took him under his wing, had been a respectable .320. In 1921, his first season under Ty's tutelage, Heilmann soared to .394 to lead the American League. Ironically, the player Heilmann beat to win the batting title that year was none other than his teacher, Cobb himself.

Actually, the "unofficial" batting averages, posted at the end of the 1921 season, credited Cobb with a mark of .391 and Heilmann with .390. But when the season's box scores were examined further and the official averages came out, Heilmann's average had been elevated to .394 and Cobb reduced to .389. Cobb reportedly called up the statistics bureau that serviced the American League and verbally attacked the employee who answered the phone.

In light of Heilmann's dramatic improvement, Cobb was asked why he had not come to Harry's aid earlier. Cobb explained that as a teammate and peer, it would have been presumptuous for him to offer advice. But as the Tigers' manager, that was part of his job.

By today's standards, Heilmann's batting prowess bordered on the unbelievable. A lashing, line drive hitter, Heilmann repeatedly led the AL in hitting in odd-numbered years, 1921 (.394), 1923 (.403), 1925 (.393), and 1927 (.398). With a little luck—or more specifically, nine additional hits—he could have been the only hitter to bat over .400 four times. This despite the fact that the lead-footed Heilmann rarely enjoyed the benefits of beating out an infield hit.

Some cynically suggested that Heilmann's two-year contracts, which regularly expired in odd-numbered years, accounted for that hitting oddity. Heilmann himself joked about it. However, the fact that in his "off" years, Heilmann posted averages of .356 (1922), .346 (1924), and .367 (1928) suggested otherwise. He finished with a lifetime average of .342

Heilmann fell just four hits short of the mythical .400 mark in both 1921 and 1925, despite going seven for nine in a doubleheader on the last day of the season in 1925. And in 1927, he collected six hits in eight at-bats on the final day to fall just one hit shy of .400.

In 1927, Philadelphia's Al Simmons, who would later close out his career with the Tigers, led Heilmann by .002 entering the final day of the season. In Washington, where the Athletics were playing, Simmons went two-for-five to boost his average to .392.

Word of Simmons's performance had been telegraphed to Navin Field by the time Heilmann concluded his three-for-four effort in the first game of a doubleheader against Cleveland. Heilmann knew that all he had to do to win the AL batting title was sit idle on the Tiger bench during the second game. But he insisted on playing anyway.

The Navin Field crowd, informed of what was happening in the batting race, cheered when Heilmann assumed his position in right field for the second game. And when Heilmann again went three-for-four, with a home run, a double, and a single, the batting crown was unquestionably his.

Weak in the field, although he did possess a strong throwing arm, Heilmann spent 15 seasons in the Tigers outfield. He became renowned as one of the greatest right-handed hitters in the game. He reigned as the Tigers' premier slugger until Hank Greenberg arrived on the scene. Heilmann then spent 17 years (1934-51) behind the microphone as the Tigers' most popular radio announcer until Ernie Harwell came along.

When Heilmann was dying of lung cancer in 1951, Ty Cobb visited him in the hospital. Ty leaned over and whispered in Heilmann's ear, informing Harry that he had just been elected to baseball's Hall of Fame. Heilmann died a happy man. But Cobb had lied. In fact, Heilmann was not inducted into baseball's shrine in Cooperstown until 1952, one year after his death.

Tigers' slugger Harry Heilmann kneels with the bat in 1926. AP/Wide World Photos

Briggs Stadium in July 1951 was triple-decked and had a seating capacity of 52,000. AP/Wide World Photos

3

THE GLORIOUS G-MEN

The Greenberg, Gehringer & Goslin Era, 1931-1950

It was the height of the Great Depression and the entire nation was gripped in its horrible throes. No city had been hit harder than Detroit, where automobile production, by then the city's primary industry, had dropped by more than 75 percent. Most Americans didn't have money to buy food, much less new cars.

The banks were closed. The soup kitchens were full. The factories were idle. The office buildings in downtown Detroit were deserted. Former corporate executives sold apples on the street. The city was forced to pay its employees with script. Laid-off workers huddled around fires outside the factories' front gates. When desperate unemployed workers marched on Ford's massive River Rouge plant, they were actually fired upon with live ammunition. Several workers were killed.

Needless to say, few in the Motor City could afford to go to baseball games. Like the industrial city that they represented, the Detroit Tigers were in dire straits. By 1933, attendance at Navin Field had nose-dived to one-third of its lofty 1924 level. Tight-fisted team owner Frank Navin had been forced to borrow money to send the Tigers south for spring training. Ever the penny pincher, Navin banned radio broadcasts on weekends and holidays rather than risk "giving the game away."

After languishing in the American League's second division for six consecutive seasons following the departure of Ty Cobb, never once finishing closer than 25 games behind the pennant winner from 1928 through 1933, the Tigers were desperately in need of a shake-up, a wake-up call.

The team needed a lift—and so did the city.

Navin, who had run the Tigers almost single-handedly since 1904, was desperate, too. He had lost much of his own carefully accumulated personal fortune when the country's economy turned sour.

At the conclusion of the 1933 campaign, in which the Tigers finished fifth and attracted only 320,972 fans—their poorest showing at the box office since the war-shortened 1918 season—a forlorn Navin met with his wealthy partner, Tigers co-owner Walter O. Briggs.

"Let's quit," Navin glumly suggested.

A syndicate, headed by Ty Cobb, the wealthy, although somewhat disgraced, former Tiger great, had quietly offered Navin $2 million for the Detroit franchise, and Frank figured, with that much money, he would be set for the rest of his life.

"I'm not selling," the wealthy Briggs insisted. "And you're not selling, either. What we need is a new manager."

The dollar-conscious Navin suggested the Tigers hire Babe Ruth. The larger-than-life former New York Yankee home run hero would have been a huge drawing card. He would have put people in the Navin Field seats. Furthermore, the 39-year-old Ruth desperately wanted to manage in the major leagues and Navin assumed he would be willing to work cheap. And, incredibly, Yankee management was eager to be rid of the Bambino, who had become a burden in New York.

Navin went so far as to send Ruth a telegram, inviting The Babe to travel to Detroit as soon as possible to discuss the Tiger manager's job. But the free-spirited Ruth inexplicably put the Tiger owner on hold, insisting he first had to travel to the West Coast for a series of exhibition games and then on to Hawaii for some relaxation and fun.

In a letter to Navin, Ruth—who was suddenly playing hard to get—hinted that if he did take the Detroit job, he would want a percentage of the Tigers' ticket sales in addition to his salary. Needless to say, that demand, however veiled, didn't sit well with the tight-fisted Navin. Nor did the delay that Ruth, rudely in Navin's mind, demanded.

Meanwhile, Briggs, Navin's normally silent partner, had some ideas of his own. Briggs, an ardent baseball fan as well as a highly successful businessman, believed the downtrodden Tigers needed more than a popular figurehead. Briggs felt they needed a manager who would breathe fire and life back into the listless Tigers, much as future Hall of Famer Hughie Jennings had done when he was hired in 1907.

In 1920, when Briggs first purchased 25 percent of the team, he agreed that he would not meddle in baseball affairs. When he became an equal partner seven years later, he promised he would continue to let Navin call all the shots.

But now Briggs was convinced he could no longer remain silent. Briggs urgently wanted to hire Mickey Cochrane, the scowling Irishman known as "Black Mike." Cochrane was an intense competitor and a natural leader, who had established himself as the premier catcher in the game while playing for the Philadelphia Athletics. And Cochrane was available. Athletics owner Connie Mack, in dire financial straights himself, was selling off his best ballplayers in an effort to pay off a $400,000 bank loan and keep his once highly successful franchise afloat.

The problem was Cochrane's price tag: $100,000. One hundred thousand Depression-era dollars was the equivalent of several million bucks today. The financially strapped Navin couldn't afford anything close to that. Furthermore, he wouldn't have been inclined to pay that kind of money for any manager, even if he could.

"We haven't got a hundred thousand cents," Navin protested.

"That's all right," replied Briggs, whose Commercial and Development Company and other assets had continued to prosper despite the Depression. "I'll pay for him. I want him. I'll lend the club $100,000, but I'll only do it on one condition: That you use the $100,000 to get Mickey Cochrane. You get him, and we'll win a pennant."

At the time, workers at Briggs's huge auto body plant in Highland Park, Michigan, on the edge of Detroit, were earning 25 cents an hour.

On December 12, 1933, the Tigers acquired Mickey Cochrane for $100,000, plus backup catcher Johnny Pasek. Eight days later, Navin traded unheralded outfielder John "Rocky" Stone to Washington for future Hall of Famer Leon "Goose" Goslin.

Like Cochrane, Goslin—who was affectionately known as "Goose" because of the size of his nose—had become available because Senators owner Clark Griffith ran short of money despite winning the 1933 pennant.

Both deals turned out to be steals.

Connie Mack had also wanted to sell the Tigers pitcher Lefty Grove for an additional $100,000. But Navin, who years earlier had passed on the opportunity to sign a hard-throwing young right-hander named Walter Johnson, was convinced that Grove was past his prime and rejected Mack's offer. En route to the Hall of Fame, Grove went on to win 105 more games on behalf of the Boston Red Sox.

Cochrane, with considerable help from Goslin, a fellow old pro who knew how to win, took the lethargic fifth-place Tigers and almost overnight transformed them into pennant winners and, a year later, world champs.

"He was a great leader," pitcher Elden Auker recalled. "He wanted things done his way. He told us the very first day on the job that it would be a $50 fine for anyone not wearing a shirt, tie and jacket at the ballpark, on the road, or in the hotels.

"He said, 'If you lose the games, it's your fault, not mine. So you better not lose them.'"

The addition of Cochrane improved the 1934 Tigers dramatically in several ways. First, Cochrane himself was already established as one of the finest catchers ever to play the game. His presence behind the plate and in the dugout greatly enhanced the Tigers' talented young pitching staff of Schoolboy Rowe, who won a

record 16 games in a row, curveball specialist Tommy
Bridges, and submariner Elden Auker. In addition,
Cochrane's will to win and his good judgment and
understanding of the game helped drive and guide the
Tigers forward to respectability and beyond.

The Tiger infield, in particular, benefited from
his leadership. So devastating was the infielders' hitting that they became known around the American
League as "The Battalion of Death." Hank Greenberg,
the first baseman, was a tall, powerful but awkward
slugger when Cochrane took over. Under Cochrane's
guidance, Greenberg became a dedicated, productive,
winning ballplayer. Charlie Gehringer, the steady, silent, smooth-fielding second baseman who had broken into the big leagues under Ty Cobb, was already
focused and driven to excel, but he was further spurred
on by his fiery new manager. Shortstop Billy Rogell
had never been anything more than an adequate, ordinary ballplayer until Cochrane turned him into a champion. Under Cochrane's constant glare, Marv Owen,
the previously undependable, light-hitting third
baseman, became one of the steadiest hitters on the
team.

Suddenly, Depression-weary Detroiters forgot
about their miseries at home and flocked, by car, foot,
and trolley, to the corner of Michigan and Trumbull.

It cost a buck to get into the ballpark—fifty cents
for the bleachers. That was big money in those days
when dinner at a fancy restaurant cost $1.25 and a
nickel was considered a big tip.

And the fans weren't the only ones forced to count
their pennies.

"We looked for cheap hotels to stay at," Hank
Greenberg recalled. "When I first got to Detroit, I
stayed at the Wolverine Hotel for eight bucks a week.
They gave you a room with a bed, but no closet. We
just hung our clothes on the curtain rod in our bathroom. Since we took most of our showers at the
ballpark, our bathrooms in the hotel became our clos-
ets."

As the once-timid Tigers continued to win game
after game, week after week, during the 1934 season,
their confidence began to grow.

Detroit's "G-Men," Greenberg, Gehringer and
Goslin, the future Hall of Famer who had been labeled
over the hill in Washington, each knocked in more than
100 runs. They won a club-record 101 games and
claimed the pennant with ease—perhaps too easily.

*Submarine pitcher Elden Auker played for the Tigers from 1933-
38. His pitching style developed from a shoulder injury incurred
while playing football for Kansas State University, where he
starred in basketball as well as baseball.* Burton Historical Society

The Tigers, flushed with their own stunning success, simply were not prepared to cope with the swag-
gering, rambunctious Gas House Gang from St. Louis,
who went out of their way to antagonize the Tigers
during the hard-fought, seven-game World Series.

Earlier in the season, Rowe, the Tigers' home-
spun six-foot-four hurler from Arkansas, had concluded
a network radio interview with an impromptu question for his fiancee, Edna Mae Skinner, who was listening at home: "How'm I doing, Edna?" Rowe na-
ively asked, over the national airways.

Once the World Series began, the brash, unbridled Cardinals, many of whom had heard the broadcast, refused to let Rowe forget his off-the-cuff remark.

"How'm I doing, Edna?" they bellowed from the
St. Louis dugout when Schoolboy took the mound in
Games 2, 6 and 7.

Before the Series began, Dizzy Dean, the Cardinals' swashbuckling, fun-loving 23-year-old right-

MICKEY COCHRANE

Catcher
Bats: Left ♦ Throws: Right
5'10" ♦ 180 lbs
Played with Tigers: 1934-37
Born: 4/6/03 ♦ Died: 6/28/62

Mickey Cochrane was the right man, in the right place, at the right time.

Although his best days as a ballplayer had been spent with the Philadelphia Athletics, Cochrane's fiery temper and his overwhelming will to win made him the ideal manager for the lethargic Tigers and Depression-ravaged Detroit when he was hired as player-manager in 1934.

Cochrane, an intense competitor and a natural leader, lit a fire under both the Tigers and the town. Pennant fever soon lifted the city and let fans forget their Depression-era woes.

Purchased from the Athletics for $100,000, Cochrane, who became the everyday catcher in addition to managing the team, immediately drove the Tigers, who had been picked to finish fourth or fifth, to the 1934 pennant—their first flag in 25 years.

Attendance at Navin Field nearly tripled to 919,161, and Cochrane was named the American League's Most Valuable Player, a truly amazing accomplishment in a season in which Lou Gehrig won the Triple Crown with the second-place New York Yankees.

The following season, with Cochrane at the helm, the Tigers won the World Series for the first time.

In the 1935 World Series, Cochrane scored the winning run in the bottom of the ninth inning of the sixth and deciding game. "It was my greatest day in baseball," Cochrane declared. It was also one of his last happy moments in the game.

Mickey Cochrane was one of the most popular Tigers of his day, even though he spent only four of his 13 big league seasons in a Detroit uniform. Cochrane had unusual speed for a catcher and probably could have excelled at several other positions. As a student at Boston University he participated in baseball, track, football, basketball and boxing. Cochrane worked his

way through college playing saxophone in a jazz band and washing dishes. He also secretly played semipro baseball on the side, using the name "Frank King" to protect his amateur status.

Cochrane continued to use that pseudonym when he signed his first professional contract, even though he had already received his degree and exhausted his college eligibility. Cochrane reasoned that if he failed as "Frank King" he could always try again, using his real name. Instead, he went on to become one of the best catchers in baseball history.

In 1934, Tiger co-owner Frank Navin wanted to hire Babe Ruth to manage the Tigers. But Navin's partner, Walter O. Briggs, insisted on Cochrane and loaned the team $100,000 to purchase his contract from financially strapped Philadelphia. Cochrane quickly made Tiger fans forget all about the aging Sultan of Swat. Nevertheless, when the team continued to flounder in 1938, Cochrane, who had suffered a nervous breakdown in 1936 and a near-fatal beaning in 1937, was unceremoniously fired.

Detroit fans, many of whom had turned against Cochrane during his final year at the helm, nevertheless gave "Black Mike" a rousing farewell when he left town two days later.

"He never got over being let go as manager by Mr. Briggs," Tiger Hall of Famer Hank Greenberg observed years later. "He never got over the hurt. And this wasn't getting hit on the head by Bump Hadley. Mike's hurt was in his heart, not his head."

After Cochrane was unexpectedly fired as the Tigers' manager, he volunteered for the navy in 1941, shortly after Pearl Harbor. Mickey managed the Great Lakes Naval Base baseball team to 166 wins and 26 losses during the first three seasons at that post. His 1944 Great Lakes team included Tigers Schoolboy Rowe, Virgil Trucks, Pinky Higgins, and Dick

Wakefield. Trucks later claimed that 1944 service team "could have won the American League pennant, or the National League, for that matter."

Under Cochrane's leadership, they compiled a 48-2 record. One of those losses occurred at the hands of the Brooklyn Dodgers. The other came, in Dearborn, Michigan, against a team of Ford Motor Company employees. Returning to the Detroit area, where he was still hailed as a hero, Cochrane inserted himself into the lineup as the starting catcher. In the bottom of the ninth, with the score tied at 1-1 and Schoolboy Rowe pitching, Cochrane called for a fastball. Instead, the playful Rowe threw a blooper pitch, which the Ford worker blasted for a game-winning inside-the-park home run.

"Mickey Cochrane was so mad at Schoolboy Rowe he could have killed him," Trucks recalled. "When we got back on the bus I thought Cochrane was going to give Rowe a dishonorable discharge. He said, 'If I ever catch another ballgame, and I call for a fastball, you better throw it. Or I'll have you shipped out so far you'll never get back.'"

Back when he was still a brash young catcher with the Philadelphia Athletics, Cochrane once ignored manager Connie Mack's warning not to provoke aging Tiger legend Ty Cobb. When Ty stepped up to bat against the Athletics, Cochrane, crouching behind home plate, boldly suggested aloud that Cobb was washed up. Cochrane urged him to sit down and let some younger guys play. Cochrane went so far as to declare that Cobb probably had never been a very good player anyway.

Cobb, his eyes blazing, stepped out of the batter's box and informed Cochrane that he was going to hit the next pitch and would be soon on third base, waiting to score. Cochrane, convinced he had thoroughly upset the Tiger veteran, called for a pitch-out to frustrate Ty further.

But Cobb threw his bat at the ball, knocking it over the pitcher's head, then sprinted all the way to third before the Athletics fielders could retrieve the ball. Mickey Cochrane never challenged Ty Cobb again.

Cochrane scouted for the Tigers in 1960 and served briefly as the team's vice president before his death in 1962. After Cochrane passed away, the street along the left field line at Tiger Stadium was renamed in his honor.

Although he never once led the American League in any offensive category and managed to hit as many as 20 home runs and drive in 100 runs only once in his career, Cochrane is still regarded as one of the greatest catchers of all time.

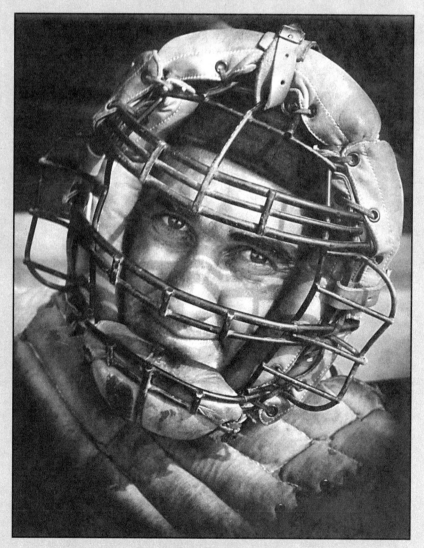

Hall of Fame catcher and manager Mickey Cochrane was with the Tigers from 1934-38. Collection of Jim Hawkins Productions Inc.

hander, predicted that he and his younger brother Paul, also known as Daffy, would defeat the Tigers all by themselves.

Dizzy, who won 30 games and lost only seven in 1934, was widely heralded as the best pitcher in the game, and one of the best of all time. However, to hear Dizzy tell it, he was "just a sem-eye pro alongside Paul."

Dean was quoted in all the newspapers prior to the start of the Series, boasting about himself and his brother. He belittled Rowe, the Tigers' ace 24-game winner, noting, "With a wind behind him, he's pretty near as fast as my brother Paul."

On the morning of the World Series opener, the Dean brothers were invited to have breakfast with Henry Ford, the world-famous Detroit carmaker whose company had paid $100,000 to sponsor the national radio broadcast of the 1934 Fall Classic.

When the two Cardinal pitchers arrived at the Ford mansion in nearby Dearborn, Michigan, their host extended his hand. "Welcome, Mr. Dean," Ford said.

Schoolboy Rowe, remembered for his powerful right arm and for his naive "How'm I doin', Edna?" shored up the pitching staff from 1933-42. Burton Historical Society

"Put 'er there," Dizzy replied, vigorously pumping the old man's hand. "I'm sure glad to be here because I heard so much about you. But I'm sorry I'm gonna have to make pussycats out of your Tigers."

Arriving at Navin Field, Dean immediately strolled through the Tigers' clubhouse, introducing himself to anyone who would shake his hand, as "the Great Dean."

Still wearing his street clothes, Dean interrupted the Tigers' batting practice by jumping into the batting cage. The Cardinal pitcher then astounded and probably intimidated the stunned Tigers by lashing out several line drives.

Dean offered advice, unsolicited of course, to several Detroit batsmen. And he playfully asked permission to hold the bat that belonged to Hank Greenberg, the Tigers' home run hitting giant.

Dizzy hefted the bat, stepped back into the batting cage, and smacked the next pitch into the left field bleachers. Then he handed the bat back to a speechless Greenberg.

"Throw it away," Dean suggested. "I'm pitchin'."

Later, Dean draped a tiger skin over his gray traveling uniform and playfully joined a band on the field. "I got me a tiger skin already," Dizzy declared. Then he proceeded to win the Series opener, 8-3.

The Tigers, who had won seven more games than the Cardinals during the regular season, appeared nervous, committing five costly errors. The Detroit fans, who had come to view their hometown team as almost invincible, seemed stunned that the hometown favorites could be routed so convincingly.

When Schoolboy Rowe won the second game of the Series, 3-2, in 12 innings, some disgruntled Tiger fans wondered aloud why Mickey Cochrane hadn't started him in the opening game. Even Cochrane began to second-guess himself, dropping Greenberg from the cleanup spot in the batting order down to sixth for Game 4.

Inserted in the fourth inning of Game 4 as a pinch runner, Dizzy Dean was knocked unconscious and carried off the field on a stretcher after he was struck on the head by a ball thrown by Tiger shortstop Billy Rogell. The Cardinals' Pepper Martin had hit a tailor-made double play grounder toward Charlie Gehringer, the Tigers' sure-handed second baseman. Gehringer routinely flipped the ball to Rogell, who stepped on the bag, forcing Dean, and fired to first. However, Dean had decided to try to break up the double play by going into second base standing up and was beaned by the throw.

After Dean was released from the hospital the next day, Rogell presented him with a World War I soldier's helmet. "They X-rayed my head," Dean proudly reported, "and they didn't find anything."

Tiger manager and catcher Mickey Cochrane himself spent each night during the World Series in the hospital. Cochrane checked himself in each evening to make certain he got enough rest, then checked himself out in the morning.

Tensions ran high. Goose Goslin engaged umpire Bill Klem in a heated argument, and called him "Catfish"—a nickname Klem detested and a sure way to provoke the famed umpire's anger. The next day, Goslin tried to apologize, but Klem called him every name in the book. Bystanders reported the incident to baseball commissioner Kenesaw Landis, who fined Klem $200.

A controversial call in Game 6 by umpire Brick Owens may have cost the Tigers the World Series when Cochrane was called out at third base even though newspaper photos later showed that he clearly was safe.

That evening former umpire and future Tiger front office executive Billy Evans sought to console Frank Navin, reminding him that the setback in the sixth game meant the Tiger owner would reap an additional $50,000 in revenue from the seventh and deciding game, which was played in Detroit.

"To hell with the $50,000," grumbled the penny-pinching Navin. "I'd give five times that much to have won today. I've been wait-ing 35 years to see Detroit win a world's championship and here we have one within our grasp and that umpire blows it for us."

In the end, the Dean brothers made good on Dizzy's promise, as they each won two games in the Series. Ol' Diz himself won the seventh game, beating Elden Auker, 11-0.

When Auker began to warm up for the final game, the irrepressible Dean hollered over at Cochrane, "He won't do, Mickey!"

And Dean started celebrating long before the rout was over, laughing and clowning on the mound, taunting the vanquished Tigers.

Game 7, however, will forever be remembered in World Series annals, not because of the shutout pitching of Dean, but rather for the near-riot that erupted at Navin Field during the seventh inning.

In the sixth inning, expecting a close play, the Cardinals' Joe "Ducky" Medwick slid hard into Marv Owen, spiking the Tigers' third baseman. Owen, who had suffered through a frustrating Series, responded with a particularly hard tag, then stepped on Medwick's

In the sixth inning of Game 7 of the 1934 World Series, Cardinal Joe Medwick tripled and slid into third, spiking third baseman Marv Owens. They began fighting and the umpire broke it up. When Medwick took his position in left field, the Tigers' fans pelted him with bottles and fruit. Commissioner Landis, sitting in the stands, ordered Medwick ejected to keep the peace.
Burton Historical Society

foot. Owen later claimed that Medwick kicked him three times while still lying on the ground. The two men traded punches, but teammates quickly pulled them apart.

However, when Medwick trotted out to his position in left field, the frustrated Tiger fans pelted him with a barrage of bananas, vegetables, fruit and half-eaten sandwiches. When they ran out of perishables, they began throwing empty boxes, milk bottles and even chairs. Like Frank Navin some 24 hours earlier, the crowd of 40,902 was understandably in a foul mood.

Medwick stood in the outfield, his hands on his hips, grinning, just out of range of the debris that was raining down on the field.

Seated in the front row of the Navin Field stands, baseball czar Judge Kenesaw Mountain Landis wasn't laughing. With the Cardinals already comfortably leading in the game, 9-0, Landis was understandably eager to avoid a forfeit. Tiger manager Mickey Cochrane even ran halfway out into left field in an effort to pacify the angry mob.

After the barrage had continued for 20 minutes, the commissioner ordered Medwick to leave the field, even though Medwick had been the Cardinals' best hitter in the Series and had done nothing more egregious than slide hard into third base.

"For your own sake, Medwick," Landis declared, "you're out of the game."

"Why should I take him out?" Cardinals manager Frankie Frisch wanted to know.

"Because I say so," the all-powerful Landis replied.

Following the game, two Detroit detectives ate dinner with Medwick and stayed by his side until the victorious Cardinals boarded their midnight train for the trip back to St. Louis.

"Are we destined never to win one of these things?" Frank Navin wondered aloud.

The World Series may not have been an artistic success from the Tigers' point of view, but it certainly was worth their while financially, topping $1 million in gate receipts.

Although they won eight fewer games, the 1935 Tigers, with a hard-hitting outfield of Goslin, Pete Fox and Gee Walker, were an even better team than their 1934 predecessors.

Early in the 1935 season, when the Tigers were buried in last place, manager Mickey Cochrane was asked if he had lost confidence in his club.

"I said at Lakeland, down in Florida, where we trained for this campaign, that I would bet my last pair of socks that we would win the pennant again," the Tiger manager declared. And Cochrane was sticking to it.

When the 1935 season concluded, Cochrane's prediction had come true. Greenberg, by now one of baseball's biggest stars, belted 36 homers and drove in 170 runs to lead the league while hitting .328. The pitching staff of Schoolboy Rowe (19-13), Tommy Bridges (21-10), Elden Auker (18-7) and General Crowder (16-10) was solid.

And this time, when the Tigers reached the World Series, they didn't have to contend with the Dean brothers. To a man, they were determined to make the most of their opportunity.

In 1935, it was the Chicago Cubs who came into the World Series brimming with confidence. Too much confidence, as it turned out. This time it was the Tigers who were the battle-hardened Series veterans.

The Cubs were convinced—and rightly so—that the Tigers were intimidated by the trash-talking Cardinals in 1934. So they began the '35 Series with a steady stream of verbal abuse. The heckling got so bad that Landis, baseball's no-nonsense commissioner, summoned both managers and umpire George Moriarty before the third game and ordered the extraneous noise stopped.

After the Tigers and Schoolboy Rowe were shut out, 3-0, by Chicago ace Lon Warneke in the Series opener, they began the second game with four first-inning runs, including a two-run HR by Hank Greenberg, before Chicago starter Charlie Root was able to get anyone out.

When Greenberg broke his wrist in a home plate collision with Cubs catcher Gabby Hartnett later in the 8-3 Tiger victory, Cochrane toyed with the idea of playing first base himself for the remainder of the Series and letting veteran Ray Hayworth catch. But Navin overruled him. Navin instructed Cochrane to move Marv Owen to first base and station light-hitting Flea Clifton at third. "If we lose the Series," the Tigers' owner boldly said, "it'll be on my head."

Clifton didn't get a hit in 16 trips to the plate and Owen went one for 20. But it didn't matter.

The Tigers took a three-games-to-one lead in Game 4 behind the five-hit pitching of General Crowder, who wore a tattoo of a naked woman on his right arm, a souvenir of his World War I Navy days, and who dedicated the victory to his seriously ill wife, who was at home listening to the Series on the radio.

In Game 6, with Hank Greenberg out of the lineup because of his broken hand and the potential winning run in the person of Mickey Cochrane waiting on second base, Goose Goslin stepped up to the plate with two out in the bottom of the ninth inning.

Moments earlier, perched on the top step of the Tigers' dugout, Goslin had turned to pitcher Elden Auker and said, "I've got a feeling we're going to win the world championship this inning and I'm going to get the winning hit."

At bat, Goslin sized up the situation, glanced back at the umpire and said, "If they pitch that ball over this plate, you can take that monkey suit off."

Chicago manager Charlie Grimm elected to pitch to Goslin rather than issue an intentional walk. And Goose smacked Larry French's first pitch over the Cubs' second baseman's head and into right center field for a game-winning single, as the determined Cochrane, not about to be denied, raced all the way home.

There, Cochrane jumped up and down several times on home plate, as if to emphasize the point. Cochrane, who had previously won a pair of world championships with Philadelphia, proclaimed the moment, "My greatest day in baseball!"

Goslin galloped off the field and leaped into Auker's arms.

"Didn't I tell you?!" he screamed. "Didn't I tell you?!"

"Lucky hit, that's all it was," Goslin modestly insisted later. "I mean, at least you're lucky to get up to bat at just the right time. I hadn't had a hit all day."

At first, the frenzied Detroit fans, who finally had their first world championship, refused to leave the ballpark. After Cochrane addressed the crowd over a loudspeaker, they spilled out into the streets. Thousands of others, who had been listening to the game at home, soon joined in the revelry, banging on dishpans and honking car horns.

That night, joyous Tiger fans paraded through the streets of downtown Detroit, which were filled with ticker tape and confetti, chanting Goslin's name. Crowds filled Cadillac Square and Grand Circus Park, guns were fired into the air, and bars stayed open all night. The city remained a madhouse until dawn.

The Tigers had delivered the perfect antidote to the woes of the Great Depression.

"I played with the Senators for 12 years, the Browns for two and the Tigers for four," declared

Goose Goslin—so named because of the size and shape of his nose—was always a huge hit with young fans. Brace Photo

Goslin, who had injured his arm seven years earlier while fooling around with a shot put in spring training. "And the best baseball town I ever played in was Detroit. The fans there were great. I always had a rooting section behind me in those left field stands in Detroit. Mostly school kids. When I came up they'd all yell, 'Yea, Goose!' I loved it."

For winning their first World Series, each Tiger collected $6,544.

"I waited 30 years for this day," a smiling Frank Navin said. "I can now die in peace."

Ironically, 37 days later, the Tiger owner was, indeed, dead.

Navin was an avid horseman, who loved to ride horses as well as wager on them. He owned six racehorses and went horseback riding nearly every day for exercise.

CHARLIE GEHRINGER

Second Base
Bats: Left ♦ Throws: Right
5'11" ♦ 180 lbs.
Played with Tigers: 1924-42
Born: 5/11/03 ♦ Died: 1/21/93

It was New York Yankees Hall of Famer Lefty Gomez who nicknamed Charlie Gehringer "The Mechanical Man."

"You wind him up in the spring," the colorful Yankees pitcher explained, "and he goes all summer. He hits .330 or .340 or whatever, and then you shut him off in the fall."

With Gehringer, baseball often appeared that simple, that automatic, that easy. In Gehringer's 16 full seasons, he hit .320, batting over .300 13 times, and played his position with elegance and grace. He was simply the best-fielding second baseman of his day. What's more, he made it look easy.

"I could never figure out when to go for ground balls and when to leave them for Charlie," Hank Greenberg, the Tigers' slugging Hall of Fame first baseman, would lament. "I would dive for one and it would bounce off my glove. Charlie would be standing there, right behind me, and he'd say, 'I could've gotten that one.' The man was amazing."

In 1937, Gehringer was named the American League Most Valuable Player after batting .371.

Cobb, who managed the Tigers during Gehringer's first three seasons, declared that, aside from turn-of-the-century Hall of Famer Eddie Collins, Charlie was "the greatest second baseman [he] ever saw."

At the urging of former Tiger outfielder Bobby Veach, Cobb had invited the quiet farm boy from Fowlerville, Michigan, who was then a third baseman, to come to Navin Field for a tryout in 1923.

"Cobb couldn't take his eyes off me," Gehringer later recalled. "It was eerie. The only sound in the big, empty ballpark, was me standing there, hitting line drives, with the whole Tigers club watching me."

Signed by the Tigers in 1924, after his freshman year at the University of Michigan, Gehringer became the Tigers' everyday second baseman in 1926 when Frank O'Rourke came down with the measles.

Gehringer, advised by Cobb to ignore those who might try to change his batting stance, quickly became one of the best two-strike hitters in the game. No batter in the AL was more reliable when there were men on base and the game was on the line. And no player was more unassuming.

When the Tigers held a day in Gehringer's honor late in his career, the left-handed-hitting second baseman was presented with a set of right-handed golf clubs. Charlie never said a word. Years later, he admitted that he had learned how to play golf right-handed rather than risk embarrassing the people who had given him the gift.

Following the 1942 season, Gehringer joined the navy. After two years' duty in California, he was transferred to the naval air station in Jacksonville, Fla. When his commanding officer announced plans to form a baseball team, Gehringer, who had spent 19 years at second base for the Tigers, said he would be happy to merely coach the team. That was hardly what the base brass had in mind.

"If you don't play," the officer in charge informed him, "I'll send you so far away they won't know where to find you."

Suffice to say Charlie played.

Gehringer later served as the Tigers' general manager from 1951 to 1953.

Soft-spoken second baseman Charlie Gehringer looks out from the Tigers' dugout on September 27, 1934. AP/Wide World Photos

On November 13, 1935, five weeks after he had celebrated the happiest moment in Tiger history, Navin suffered a heart attack while riding one of his horses at the Detroit Riding and Hunt Club on Belle Isle. The 64-year-old Tiger owner, who had controlled the team since 1904, died a short while later at Detroit Osteopathic Hospital. Navin was buried at Holy Sepulchre Cemetery with two huge stone tigers guarding his final resting place.

Immediately upon learning of Navin's death, Walter O. Briggs, Frank's silent partner and lifelong Tiger fan, ordered club secretary Harry Sisson to seek out Navin's widow and present her with a check for $1 million for Frank's half of the team.

Detroit sport fans enjoyed a great year in 1935. In addition to the Tigers, the Detroit Lions won the championship in the National Football League and the Detroit Red Wings won hockey's Stanley Cup.

Basil "Mickey" Briggs was still in his mother's womb when the Tigers won the 1935 American League pennant. It had already been decided that the Briggs family's new baby would be named after his maternal grandfather. But the unborn infant's proud father-to-be, Spike Briggs—whose own father, Walter O., owned half of the Detroit Tigers—had promised Tiger manager and catcher Mickey Cochrane that if the team also won the World Series he would nickname his new son in honor of the fiery Tiger leader.

"That," said 65-year-old Basil Briggs, now a Michigan attorney, "was how I became 'Mickey.' The Tigers winning that 1935 World Series saved me from a lot of fights while I was growing up."

Unfortunately, 12 games into the 1936 campaign, Hank Greenberg broke his hand again in a first base collision with Washington's Jake Powell, forcing the popular, powerful slugger to miss the rest of the '36 season.

Meanwhile, the pressure of playing and managing caught up with the high-strung Mickey Cochrane and, in June 1936, he suffered a nervous breakdown. Tiger coach Del Baker took over the team while Cochrane went to a friend's ranch in Wyoming to recover. For Cochrane, things were never quite the same again.

Cochrane's playing career came to an abrupt end on May 25, 1937, when he was beaned while batting against New York Yankee pitcher Bump Hadley. At the last second, Cochrane threw up his hand in front of his face, but the ball struck his temple with a sickening thud. Cochrane fell to the ground, face first.

Cochrane's skull was fractured in three places and he remained unconscious for 10 days. For four days, his life was very much in doubt. Cochrane had already been plagued by eye and stomach problems and various other injuries. His playing days were over.

Cochrane's managerial career soon ended on a sour note, too.

In four and a half seasons at the helm of the Tigers, "Black Mike" won two pennants, finished second twice and guided the Tigers to their first world championship. But in 1937, when he traded away popular players Gee Walker, Marv Owen and Mike Tresh, the fans began to openly question his judgment. In 1938, the normally benevolent Briggs, who had personally insisted upon hiring him less than five years earlier, fired Mickey Cochrane.

"According to Charlie Gehringer, when Cochrane got hit in the head he became a totally different kind of manager," Mickey Briggs, Walter Briggs's grandson, explained. "He couldn't take his anger out on the playing field any more, so he would take it out on players. Gehringer said, after the beaning, Cochrane became more like Cobb. That's the reason he was discharged as manager in 1938."

Walter Briggs, who had stubbornly stuck by his popular manager even after many of the Tiger players, the press, and the fans had turned against him, summoned Cochrane to his office on August 6, 1938.

"Well, what is the alibi for today?" the boss demanded.

"To tell you the plain truth, Mr. Briggs, you haven't got the players to win," replied Cochrane.

"That's not what you said in the spring," Briggs snapped back. "Maybe it isn't the players. Maybe you are the cause and it would help matters if you quit."

The man who four years earlier had helped lift the city out of its darkest era, was suddenly out of a job.

Many whispered it never would have happened if Frank Navin had still been alive.

❧

Walter O. Briggs was a former railroad worker who, in 1909, took control of a small buggy and wagon shop and soon struck it rich in Detroit's automotive boom.

As a youngster during Detroit's early National League days, Briggs had often peered through the knotholes in the fence that surrounded primitive Recreation Park. Though earning only $18 a week as a switchman on the Central Michigan Railroad, he was a frequent, faithful patron of the bleachers at the Tigers' rickety, wooden Bennett Park.

Briggs first met Frank Navin in 1907, when Briggs, by then an ambitious and successful young businessman, was unable to buy a ticket to sit in his usual box seat at the Tigers' first World Series.

The angry Briggs demanded a face-to-face meeting with Navin to plead his case.

"Who the hell is Walter Briggs?" Frank Navin inquired.

However, through the intercession of a mutual friend, Briggs got his meeting with Navin—and his box seat tickets. Navin was no dummy. He knew any man who loved baseball and was willing to spend money the way Briggs did was a good friend to have.

Over the years, the well-to-do Briggs bailed Navin out of numerous financial jams, but Briggs never concealed his burning desire to own the ball club someday. He assured friends that when that opportunity occurred, he would build the best team and the best ballpark in the game.

After Tigers co-owner Bill Yawkey passed away in 1919, Briggs, already a multimillionaire, and fellow automotive magnate John Kelsey each purchased 25 percent ownership of the Tigers for $250,000 apiece. The Tigers had led the American League in attendance in 1919, attracting 643,805 fans, and Navin was anxious to expand the stadium that bore his name. Briggs was only too happy to provide the capital to make that expansion possible.

Before the 1923 season began, an upper deck was added to the grandstand, increasing Navin Field's capacity to 23,000. In 1924 Detroit, by now the nation's fourth largest city, made the Tigers the second big-league team, after the New York Yankees, to top the one million mark in attendance.

When Kelsey passed away in 1927, Briggs purchased his share of the team from his estate. That gave Briggs, along with Navin, 50 percent ownership of the Tigers. However, both men agreed that Navin would remain in complete control of the ball club.

Although Briggs was supposed to be Navin's "silent partner," he frequently gave the Tiger players free suits of clothes, made by the best tailors in town, whenever they swept an important series.

However, when a $2 million fire swept through one of Briggs's Detroit factories that same year, killing 21 workers and critically burning many others, Briggs was publicly accused of ignoring unsafe working conditions in the plant. Outside the baseball world, he was not a popular boss.

Before Navin's untimely death, he and Briggs had agreed to plow the profits from the 1934 and 1935 World Series back into improving the ball club and the ballpark. After Navin's passing, Briggs proceeded to carry out those plans.

In fact, Briggs publicly vowed he would never take a penny of profit from the ball club. Instead, he spent the $150,000 in profits from the 1935 World Series to add second decks in right field and in the bleachers. Briggs also spent $40,000 building powder rooms to accommodate and cater to the growing number of women who patronized his ballpark.

After the 1937 season, Briggs spent an additional $1 million to further expand the stadium. He added upper deck stands in left field and toyed with the idea of covering the outfield walls with ivy and installing escalators. Engineers quickly talked him out of the latter idea.

On April 22, 1938, the enlarged edifice was renamed Briggs Stadium. "I want to build the finest ball club in the finest ballpark in America," Briggs declared. "And money doesn't matter."

In honor of the occasion, Briggs ordered a reenactment of the original American League Opening Day at tiny Bennett Park in 1901, complete with horse-drawn carriages. A record crowd of 54,500 showed to sit in the newly repainted green seats and watch the Tigers fall to Cleveland, 4-3.

Briggs increased the number of scouts on the Tigers' payroll to 12, three more than employed by the hated New York Yankees. And he ordered them to spare no expense in scouring the sandlots in search of young talent. Barney McCoskey, Hoot Evers, Johnny Lipon, Johnny Groth, Art Houtteman, Billy Piece and Hal Newhouser all became Tigers as a result of that effort.

Unlike the penny-pinching Navin, Briggs pampered and overpaid his players. He hurled bonuses at prospects such as Lou Kretlow and Frank House, many of whom didn't pan out. On the advice of Mickey Cochrane, Briggs paid $75,000 in 1936 for over-the-

Rocket-armed Hal Newhouser pitched for the Tigers from 1939-53 and is the only Tiger pitcher to win back-to-back MVP awards. Brace Photo

hill slugger Al Simmons, who had starred with "Black Mike" in Philadelphia. In 1939 he gave Seattle of the Pacific Coast League $55,000 plus five players for pitcher Fred Hutchinson, who at first flopped as a Tiger. In 1941, Briggs signed bonus baby Dick Wakefield off the University of Michigan campus for an unheard-of $52,000 bonus.

In 1940 Commissioner Landis, hired to clean up the sport after the 1919 Black Sox scandal, fined the free-spending Tigers $47,250 for a violation of the minor-league rules. Landis declared 91 players in the Tigers' farm system to be free agents and released them. Undaunted, Briggs continued to spend in pursuit of his lifelong dream.

By far, the Tigers' biggest star of the pre-World War II era was Hank Greenberg.

Greenberg, who worked exceedingly hard to make himself into a formidable major leaguer, would regu-larly take hours of extra batting practice whenever the Tigers were at home. Tiger employees would visit the schools and playgrounds in the historic Cork Town area, inviting young, neighborhood ballplayers to shag balls for the popular Greenberg. Greenberg would hit and hit and hit, often until his hands bled. And the young boys would chase and chase and chase his line drives and towering flies.

One of those wide-eyed shaggers was a young man named Mike Ilitch, who would grow up to play mi-nor-league baseball for the Tigers and eventually buy the team.

"I was dumbfounded," Ilitch recalled years later. "When Greenberg stepped into the batting cage, he couldn't get the ball out of the infield. I'd be waiting in the outfield but the balls would barely reach the out-field grass. Then I noticed the balls looked dark. When I picked one up, it was wet. It was heavy. It was water-logged.

"It turned out Hank used three sets of balls: The waterlogged ones, slightly older balls and some brand new ones. It was like swinging a heavier bat before step-ping in to hit. When he got to the new balls, they'd go flying into the upper deck. What a smart man."

Greenberg always considered 1937, not his MVP years of 1935 and 1940, to have been his finest season. Even more than hitting homers, Greenberg loved to drive in runs. He often told teammate Charlie Gehringer, who batted ahead of him in the Tigers' or-der, to try to move runners around to third so that Greenberg could bring them home.

In 1937, "Hankus Pankus," as he was affection-ately known, drove in 183 runs, one short of Lou Gehrig's American League record. That, not Greenberg's near-miss in 1938 when he belted 58 home runs, just two shy of Babe Ruth's record at the time, stood out in his mind as the biggest disappointment of his brilliant career.

In 1938, the first season that Briggs Stadium was completely enclosed, Greenberg smacked his 58th home run with five games to go. The whole country was watching to see if he could break Babe Ruth's monu-mental record of 60.

Greenberg went homerless in the next three games, and on October 3, 1938, the last day of the season, he still had 58 homers. But he still had a chance to break Babe's mark.

Greenberg's quest for what was then baseball's greatest record came down to a Sunday doubleheader in Cleveland's massive Municipal Stadium. Anticipating a historic moment, newsreel cameras were dispatched to the ballpark.

Greenberg failed to connect in the opener, settling for a double in four trips to the plate. But the news crews did not go home disappointed. Bob Feller, the Cleveland Indians' 19-year-old ace right-hander, struck out a record 18 Tigers. Greenberg himself fell victim to Feller twice.

In the nightcap, Greenberg doubled twice off pitcher Johnny Humphries. One of those two-baggers bounced off the outfield fence, 420 feet away, and would have been a home run in any other park in the league.

However, by the sixth inning of the nightcap, darkness was beginning to descend on Cleveland's cavernous lakefront stadium.

"I'm sorry, Hank," umpire George Moriarty, himself a former Tiger player, apologized, moments before he called off the game. "This is as far as I can go."

"That's okay," said the gracious Greenberg. "This is as far as I can go, too."

Years later, Greenberg insisted, "I always felt Walter Briggs was almost pulling for me not to break Ruth's record because that might mean $5,000 or $10,000 more in salary for me."

Strange sentiments, indeed, because Walter O. Briggs was not only the Tigers' owner until his death in 1952, he was also the team's No. 1 fan.

Shortly after noon one Sunday, when the Tigers were scheduled to host the Boston Red Sox, Briggs looked out his third floor office windows down at the corner of Michigan and Trumbull, and saw that the street outside the ballpark was filled with people.

There had been a heavy rainstorm that morning. But at the last minute the skies had cleared and a bright sun had appeared. Thousands of people who had planned to spend Sunday at home suddenly decided it was a perfect day to see a ballgame. As a result, the bulk of the day's crowd was unusually late in arriving.

Briggs picked up the phone and called the Tigers' general manager, Jack Zeller, who was in his office next door.

"There are a million people out there!" Briggs shouted into the telephone.

"The gates are all open," Zeller replied calmly. "Those people are waiting to buy tickets."

Hank Greenberg was named Most Valuable Player on July 24, 1936. He won the MVP award again in 1940. Brace Photo

"You can't keep those people waiting," Briggs responded. "They want to see a ballgame. Let 'em all in for free."

In 1939, when baseball was celebrating its 100th anniversary, Briggs spent $10,000 to print 75,000 souvenir books, chronicling the history of the sport, and gave them away to fans, compliments of the ball club, as a gesture of goodwill.

Briggs, who lived in a 40-room mansion in one of Detroit's most fashionable neighborhoods and enjoyed a 140-acre estate in one of the city's richest suburbs as well as a lavish winter residence in Florida, installed the major leagues' first underground sprinkling system. He was the first owner to hire attendants to keep the washrooms clean, and introduced the idea of

HANK GREENBERG

First Base/Outfield
Bats: Right ♦ Throws: Right
6'3" ♦ 210 lbs.
Played with Tigers: 1930-46
Born: 1/1/11 ♦ Died: 9/4/86

The 1934 Tigers, driven by their fiery new manager and catcher Mickey Cochrane, were closing in on their first American League pennant in a quarter-century when Hank Greenberg, their mild-mannered, slugging first baseman suddenly found himself in the midst of a raging controversy.

Although Greenberg's parents were Orthodox Jews, Hank himself had never been a particularly religious person. Now he suddenly found himself torn apart, pulled in opposite directions by the demands of his religion and his chosen profession.

The Tigers and their fans were understandably anxious to see the mighty Greenberg in the lineup for every game as they pursued their first pennant since 1909. But Jewish leaders were pressuring young Greenberg not to play on Rosh Hashanah, the first day of the Jewish New Year. The debate quickly became front-page news in Detroit.

In a quandary, Greenberg consulted a Detroit rabbi who discovered a precedent in the Talmud. In ancient times there were references to Jewish children playing in the streets of Jerusalem on that holy day. The rabbi gave Greenberg permission to play.

On Rosh Hashanah, September 10, 1934, "Hammerin' Hank" appeared at his usual position at first base. What's more, he smacked a couple of homers, including the game winner in the bottom of the ninth, as the Tigers beat Boston, 2-1.

However, Greenberg later declined to play on Yom Kippur, the Jewish Day of Atonement. Instead, he visited his synagogue, where the congregation gave him a rousing ovation.

Greenberg's principled stand made him a hero to millions in the Jewish community, but it also made him a target for bench jockeys around the American League.

During the 1934 World Series, Dizzy Dean, the St. Louis Cardinals' nonstop-talking 30-game winner, repeatedly referred to Greenberg as "Moe."

"The worst team was the Yankees," Greenberg recalled years later. "They brought up a guy from the minor leagues just to heckle me. But I never let it show that it bothered me. I couldn't.

"There was added pressure, being Jewish," Greenberg acknowledged. "How the hell could you get up to home [plate] every day and have some SOB call you a Jew bastard and a kike and a sheeny without feeling pressure? If the ballplayers weren't doing it, the fans were. I used to get frustrated as hell. Sometimes, I wanted to go into the stands."

Although Greenberg never wanted to be anything but a big-league baseball player, he was not blessed with an abundance of natural talent. Tall and gangly, he lacked both speed and grace. As a youngster, Hank was often teased about his awkwardness. When he began playing baseball, he was relegated to first base, where his lack of speed and his clumsiness would not be so glaring.

Greenberg was the son of Romanian immigrants. His father was very successful in the garment industry in New York. The friends and neighbors of Greenberg's family in the Bronx, New York, not far from Yankee Stadium, all wanted their sons to grow up to become doctors or lawyers. "I," Greenberg later admitted, "was a disgrace."

Greenberg's primary asset was his power. At six foot four and 210 pounds, he could belt a baseball out of sight. But when John McGraw, the legendary manager of the New York Giants, personally scouted young Greenberg, he deemed the lad too awkward to ever become a big-league ballplayer—even though the Giants desperately wanted to find a Jewish star. The New

York Yankees were very interested in Greenberg, but they already had Lou Gehrig firmly entrenched at first base and Hank didn't know if he could play anywhere else on the field.

When the Tigers offered Greenberg a contract that would allow him to complete his college education, thereby appeasing his father, Hank signed with Detroit.

Even after turning professional, Greenberg continued to work at the game. Early in his career, he often took so much batting practice that his hands bled. He spread sawdust on the lawn in front of his house to practice sliding. Quickly, he became the most feared right-handed hitter in the American League.

He muscled the Tigers to their first world championship in 1935, when he led the American League with 36 home runs and 170 RBIs and was unanimously voted the Most Valuable Player. In 1937, he knocked in 183 runs, one shy of Lou Gehrig's American League record. In 1938 he belted 58 homers, nearly breaking Babe Ruth's record.

Greenberg grabbed MVP honors again in 1940, batting a career-high .340 with 41 homers and 150 RBIs, powering the Tigers to another pennant. And in 1945, after more than four years in the army, he smacked a grand slam HR on the final day of the season to put the Tigers back into the World Series, where they succeeded for the second time.

Like most ballplayers of his era, Greenberg constantly had to fight with the front office to get a salary that he thought was fair.

When Greenberg hammered 58 home runs in 1938, normally free-spending Tiger owner Walter O. Briggs didn't offer him a raise for 1939. "He said he didn't have the money to give me a raise because he needed it to paint the stadium," Greenberg recalled. Hank eventually settled for a $5,000 raise.

When his home run production dropped to 33 the following year, Briggs sought to cut his salary by

Hank Greenberg follows through on his swing circa September 1940.
AP/Wide World Photos

$10,000. But Greenberg knew the Tigers wanted him to move to left field to make room at first base for young Rudy York. So he agreed to move to the outfield—provided the Tigers would give him a $10,000 raise. At $50,000, Greenberg became the highest-paid player in the American League.

Relocated into left field, Greenberg produced another MVP season, leading the League in home runs, RBIs, doubles and slugging average.

There simply is no telling how many home runs Greenberg would have hit, or how many runs he would have batted in, had he not missed more than four years because of military service at the height of his career and having spent another season on the sidelines with a broken wrist.

Hank Greenberg shows off his jumping ability during spring training in Lakeland, Florida on February 25, 1940. Greenberg switched from first base to outfield. AP/Wide World Photos

covering the infield with a heavy tarp during rain delays.

Long considered a ruthless, cold-hearted employer by workers at his Briggs Manufacturing Co., which at its zenith comprised 16 plants and employed 40,000 people, Briggs lavished his ballplayers with bonuses and perks and let 100,000 youngsters into his ballpark each summer for free.

"We treated our players very well," said Walter Briggs's grandson, Mickey Briggs, who as a youngster had his own little Tiger uniform and grew up hanging around the team. "We had one of the highest payrolls in the major leagues. We were usually one-two with the Yankees.

"When my grandfather would send out a contract to Charlie Gehringer he used to send it out blank and tell Charlie to fill in the amount. 'Name your price,' my grandfather would say. 'I know you'll be fair.' That used to upset Gehringer because it put the pressure on him."

However, as Detroit darlings Mickey Cochrane and Hank Greenberg discovered when they were both unceremoniously let go despite their considerable contributions, Briggs could also be a demanding, unforgiving boss.

Although the 1939 Tigers had finished a distant 26 1/2 games behind the New York Yankees, they suddenly awoke the following year. Led by home run champ Hank Greenberg and a .340-hitting young outfielder named Barney McCoskey, the Tigers grabbed the 1940 pennant, nipping the Cleveland Indians by one game.

The pennant race came down to a three-game series between the Tigers and Indians in Cleveland during the last week in September. The Tigers needed just one victory in the three games to clinch the title and earn their sixth trip to the World Series.

The Indians, with their backs to the wall, sent their ace fireballer, 27-10 Bob Feller, to the mound in the opener. Rather than waste either of his two best pitchers, Schoolboy Rowe or Bobo Newsom, Tiger manager Del Baker served up journeyman Floyd Giebell, who had been called up from the minors late in the season, as a sacrificial lamb to face Feller.

But the 31-year-old Giebell surprised everyone by shutting the Indians out on six hits. The overpowering Feller only yielded three hits to the Tigers, but one of those was a decisive two-run homer by Rudy York.

Floyd Giebell, by the way, never won another ballgame the rest of his life.

Baker, the Tigers' pennant-winning manager in 1940, was a longtime coach and a master at stealing signs. And Greenberg, for one, loved knowing in advance what a pitcher was about to throw.

Mired in a slump during the 1940 season, Greenberg complained to Baker because the Tiger manager wasn't stealing any signs.

"Come on, Del," Greenberg groaned. "What's going on here? You're not giving me any signs."

"I'll tell you the truth," Baker replied. "I'm not getting any."

"Well," pleaded Greenberg, "guess."

A giant of a man at six-foot-four and 210 pounds, Greenberg could be as gentle as he was large.

In 1940, with Washington's George Case aboard at first base and one out, the Senators' next batter lofted a long fly ball to right. Quickly realizing that Case had lost track of the number of outs, Greenberg shouted, "Two outs, get going!"

Case, foolishly believing Greenberg was doing him a favor, took off for second base.

The Tiger right fielder caught the ball and hurriedly threw to Greenberg at first base, completing the double play.

"You big son of a bitch," the embarrassed Case shouted, as Greenberg trotted off the field. "I'm going to cut your leg off the next time I come down there."

His next time up, Case slapped a little grounder between first base and the pitcher's mound. As Greenberg stretched to keep his foot on the bag while he took the throw, Case purposely stepped on his heel, tearing off Hank's shoe.

As Case walked back past Greenberg on his way to the Washington dugout, the Tigers' first baseman simply said, "Well, young fellow, I hope you're satisfied."

After Baker unexpectedly guided the Tigers to the 1940 pennant, Briggs generously rewarded him with a $40,000 contract. By comparison, Joe McCarthy, the legendary Hall of Fame manager of the perennially successful New York Yankees made only $27,500 that year.

Baker received the big bucks, but it was Briggs himself who deserved much of the credit for the 1940 pennant. Over the objection of both Baker and general manager Jack Zeller, Briggs had insisted on trading for journeyman pitcher Bobo Newsom in 1939.

The colorful, outspoken Newsom, who called himself and everyone else "Bobo" was one of the St. Louis Browns' few stars. He knew it. And, never at a loss for confidence, he often acted accordingly.

Browns owner Don Barnes had promised Newsom he would buy him a new suit if Bobo won on Opening Day. Newsom held up his end of the bargain and Barnes went down to the St. Louis clubhouse after the game to give Bobo some cash.

"Don't worry about it," Newsom shrugged.

"What do you mean, 'Don't worry about it?'" said Barnes. "I promised you a new suit if you won the game."

"I already bought it," Newsom replied. "The bill is on your desk."

Briggs knew Newsom had dug himself a deep hole in St. Louis Browns manager Fred Haney's doghouse. One afternoon, when the Brownies were being bombarded as usual by the Yankees, Newsom had taken it upon himself to walk down to the St. Louis bullpen in the middle of the game to begin warming up. In Haney's mind, Newsom was sending a message, showing him up.

"Who told you to warm up?" Haney demanded.

"I did," Bobo replied. "I was getting ready in case you needed me."

"Well, I give the orders around here," Haney barked.

On May 31, 1939, after a full day of wrangling with St. Louis GM Bill DeWitt, Zeller traded Tiger pitchers Vern Kennedy, Bob Harris, George Gill and Roxie Lawson, outfielder Chet Laabs, and infielder Mark Christman to the Browns for outfielder Beau Bell, infielder Red Kress, pitcher Jim Walkup, and Newsom. The 10-player swap was the largest in Tigers history up until that time.

Typically, the wacky Newsom ignored the fact that he would be fleeing the downtrodden St. Louis Browns and refused to report until the Tigers gave him a $3,500 bonus to compensate him for having to give up his St. Louis radio show.

At first, Zeller refused the ridiculous demand. But when Zeller reported the stalemate to Briggs, the Tiger

Rudy York played in two World Series with Detroit—1940 and 1945—before he was traded to Boston, where he played in the 1946 World Series. Brace Photo

owner declared, "We're out to win a pennant and we can't afford to have any discontented ballplayers on the club. Pay him $4,000."

When Newsom won 20 and lost 11 in '39, Briggs told the pitcher he could name his own price the following year. Surprisingly, Newsom only asked for $25,000, a mere $5,000 raise. Briggs felt so guilty he gave Newsom another $5,000 raise midway through the 1940 season, when Newsom won 21 and lost five.

That winter, Bobo, whose given name was Louis Norman Newsom, celebrated by buying a new automobile. He had it equipped with a loud, custom-made horn that played "Hold That Tiger!" whenever Bobo tooted.

First baseman Rudy York, hitting hero of that pennant-clinching game in 1940, was another intriguing character. A third-grade dropout with a distinctive scar on his face where he had been struck with an axe as a youngster, the six-foot-one, 200-pound York was a formidable figure when he stepped up to the plate. "I just shut my eyes and swing," Rudy was fond of saying.

In August of 1937, York belted 18 homers—a record that stood until 1998 when Chicago's Sammy Sosa smacked 20—and batted .363 that month, with 50 RBIs.

York was one of the Tiger players commissioner Kenesaw Landis initially emancipated in 1940 because of bookkeeping shenanigans in the Tigers' farm system. However, Landis relented in York's case because he had already reached the parent club by the time the evidence surfaced.

Although he bounced from first base to the outfield in addition to occasionally playing third base and catching as the Tigers sought a way to keep his potent bat in the lineup, York smacked 277 homers in his 13-year career.

In 1937, York replaced the injured Cochrane behind the plate, and came up with 35 homers and 103 RBIs. The 1940 season was the year of the Tigers' so-called "noble experiment," which saw Greenberg shift from first base to left field and York move from behind home plate to first base.

The daring double shift was a smashing success. Not only did Greenberg continue to pound the ball, he also turned out to be an outstanding left fielder. Meanwhile, York continued his slugging, batting .316 with 33 HRs and 134 RBIs, and played an almost flawless first base.

York, who had grown up dirt poor in rural Georgia, loved the good life as much as he enjoyed a good ballgame. Years later, he admitted he earned and spent at least $250,000 in his career on booze, women and a new automobile every year.

Liquor, in particular, probably hindered York's career and reduced his accomplishments. "If I had it to do all over again, that's one thing I'd use a lot less," York conceded later. "I'd have had a couple more years of baseball left in me if I had stayed away from it."

Charlie Gehringer was still a fixture at second base in 1940 when York, shortstop Dick Bartell and third baseman Pinky Higgins joined him in the Tiger infield.

The pitching staff, anchored by Schoolboy Rowe and Tommy Bridges, now had a new ace, the well-traveled, irrepressible Newsom, who toiled for 18 different teams, nine in the majors and nine in the minors, in his nomadic 26-year career in organized baseball.

Newsom once sought to discover Joe DiMaggio's weakness by throwing him a different pitch each time he came to bat. In four trips to the plate against Newsom that afternoon, DiMaggio delivered a home run, two triples and a single.

"I've got it," Bobo declared. "His weakness is two-base hits."

Newsom was never better than he was in 1940, when he won 21 games, losing only five, despite missing two weeks with a busted thumb. And, in spite of the sudden death of his father, Newsom almost won the 1940 World Series for the Tigers, too.

Although the Cincinnati Reds boasted only two solid hitters, Ernie Lombardi and Frank McCormick, they bested the Tigers in the seven-game Series, thanks to pitchers Paul Derringer and Bucky Walters, who was actually a converted infielder.

Before the World Series began, Newsom was asked whom he thought should start the opening game for the Tigers. "Who else but Bobo?" Bobo replied.

The Tigers got off to a fine start, winning 7-2, behind Newsom. Unfortunately, in the wee hours of the following morning, after much celebration, Newsom's father, who had traveled to Cincinnati from South Carolina along with the rest of the family to watch Bobo win the first game, died of a heart attack at the Tigers' downtown Cincinnati hotel.

After burying his father, Newsom made his second start of the Series in Game 5. And he conquered the Reds again, 8-0, before a Briggs Stadium-record

Rudy York swings for the camera on March 7, 1938 during spring training in Lakeland, Florida. AP/Wide World Photos

throng of 55,189. With tears in his eyes, Bobo tossed a three-hit shutout in which only one Cincinnati runner got as far as second base. Newsom declared, "I won one for Dad."

After Schoolboy Rowe, who had returned from a stint in the minors to post a 16-3 record, failed to finish off the Reds in the sixth game, the Tigers again turned to Newsom in Game 7, even though he had only had one day's rest.

It turned out to be too much to ask, even from Bobo.

The weary, emotionally drained Newsom held the Reds at bay until the seventh inning before succumbing 2-1. The Reds' first run came when Frank McCormick scored from second base while Tiger shortstop Dick Bartell, his back to home plate, held the ball on the relay from right field. Because of the noise of the Briggs Stadium crowd, Bartell couldn't hear

HAL NEWHOUSER

Pitcher
Bats: Left ♦ Throws: Left
6'2" ♦ 192 lbs.
Played with Tigers: 1939-53
Born: 5/20/21 ♦ Died: 11/10/98

Detroit-born Hal Newhouser was a child prodigy, arriving in the big leagues with his live fastball in 1939, at the tender age of 18.

The fact that he signed with the Tigers at all said a lot about young Newhouser's character. The Cleveland Indians had offered more money—$15,000, which was a bundle in those post-Depression days. But Newhouser felt an obligation to Detroit scout Wish Egan, who had first spotted him on the sandlots when he was only 16 and followed him throughout his high

"Prince Hal" Newhouser pitched two complete-game victories, including the seventh-game clincher in the 1945 World Series against the Cubs. Burton Historical Society

school career. Newhouser, who would become a Hall of Famer, signed with the Tigers for a mere $4,000.

Imagine what might have happened if Prince Hal had joined Indians Hall of Famer Bob Feller in Cleveland in the primes of their careers. Instead, Newhouser was frequently pitted against Feller, often on Sunday afternoons, as the two teams rearranged their pitching rotations in an effort to boost attendance in both Detroit and Cleveland. Their duels became legendary.

Rejected for military service because of a heart problem, Newhouser overcame his early wildness and in 1944 he won 29 games while losing only nine and compiling an ERA of 2.22. He also led the American League in strikeouts (187) and shutouts (6), and was voted the Most Valuable Player.

The following season Newhouser pitched the Tigers to the pennant, with a 25-9 record, 212 strikeouts, eight shutouts, 29 complete games and a 1.81 ERA.

Again Newhouser was named MVP, the AL's first back-to-back winner of that coveted award since Hall of Famer Jimmy Foxx in 1932-33.

As if to prove those two MVP seasons were not just wartime flukes, Newhouser posted a 26-9 record, with 275 strikeouts and a 1.94 ERA in 1946, after the major-league stars had returned from military service.

A shoulder injury, aggravated when Newhouser was called upon to face Feller with only two days' rest in the final game of the 1948 season, prevented Hal from ever scaling those lofty peaks again, although he did lead the league in victories for the fourth time in five years when he won 21 games in 1948.

"Some of my fondest memories were the Ladies Day games," recalled Newhouser, who often claimed his mother, Emilie, was his biggest fan. "My mother would always come with a bunch of women. They'd sit at the 325-foot mark in right field and she'd always wear the same hat. It was her lucky hat. Dad never got into it because we played all day games back then, at three o'clock, and he had to work."

Gehringer screaming at him to throw the ball home, where he could have nailed McCormick, who had momentarily stopped at third.

Afterwards, in the Tigers' locker room, Newsom was visibly distraught.

"I really wanted this one," the big right-hander said.

"For your dad?" a reporter asked.

"Naw," Newsom replied. "I wanted this one for Bobo."

When Newsom slipped to 12-20 the following year, Briggs slashed his salary from $30,000 to $12,500. Then he sold the 35-year-old pitcher to the Washington Senators for $40,000. That same season, Senators owner Clark Griffith sold the Tigers' 1940 World Series hero to the Brooklyn Dodgers for 25 grand.

But Newsom had the last laugh. He continued to pitch in the big leagues until 1953, when he was 46 years old.

Baseball commissioner Kenesaw Landis, hired to clean up the image of the national pastime in the wake of the infamous 1919 Black Sox scandal, focused his attention on the Tigers' flourishing farm system in 1940.

Declaring the Tigers guilty of manipulating the paperwork to illegally keep many promising young players captive in the minor leagues, Landis freed 91 Detroit farmhands and players. He also ordered the Tigers to compensate 15 other minor leaguers who had been treated unfairly.

General manager Jack Zeller—who had reportedly acted in cahoots with Cecil Coombs, business manager of the Tigers' farm club in Fort Worth, Texas—publicly bore the brunt of the blame.

But when Briggs declined to punish or even criticize his GM, many believed Zeller—who had been hired in 1926 to clean up another scandal in the Tigers' farm system, involving scouts who had been soliciting bribes from amateur prospects—may have been simply following Briggs's orders all along.

Only one of the Tiger farmhands who was released—outfielder Roy Cullenbine—ever enjoyed significant major-league success.

Dick Wakefield became baseball's first "bonus baby" when he signed with the Tigers for $52,000 in 1941. A left-handed slugger, who had been scouted since he was in high school, Wakefield reminded many people of Ted Williams.

Many baseball owners, fearing the unprecedented bonus would set a costly precedent, criticized Briggs for his largess.

The first thing Wakefield did after signing for that unprecedented bonus was to buy a Lincoln Zephyr for $1,400. He then asked the salesman to drive him from the dealership to the Leland Hotel in downtown Detroit, where Dick was staying. Bonus baby Dick Wakefield owned a car, but he didn't yet know how to drive.

When Wakefield proudly drove his prize vehicle to Briggs Stadium for the first time, Tiger scout Wish Egan went bonkers.

"For God's sake, what have you done, Dick?" Egan exclaimed.

"What's the matter?" Wakefield asked innocently.

"Do you know what kind of a car you've got there?" Egan asked angrily. "That's a Lincoln. Ford makes that. Don't you know that Mr. Briggs makes Chryslers and Packards? Mr. Briggs and Henry Ford are having a feud. They hate each other."

Wakefield showed signs of living up to his advance billing in 1943, when he collected 200 hits, including 38 doubles and batted .316. The following year, he was hitting .355 with 12 HRs and 53 RBIs when he was summoned for military service.

While in the service, the precocious Wakefield encountered Ted Williams in Hawaii and boldly bet the Boston superstar that he would hit more home runs, drive in more runs, and post a better batting average than Ted when both men returned to the major leagues. "We bet a thousand dollars each on RBIs, home runs and batting average," Wakefield boasted.

Baseball commissioner Happy Chandler quickly informed Wakefield he didn't consider such wagers to be in the best interest of the grand ol' game.

In any event, Wakefield lost all three bets. Although he hit well for several years, Wakefield never fulfilled his earlier promise. By 1952, at age 31, Wakefield's career was over.

Wakefield later claimed the press had placed too much pressure on him because of his bonus money. "I had a bad press in Detroit," he explained after his career had ended. "It was brutal. Some of those writers were making $8,000 a year and they resented an untried kid getting a $52,000 bonus."

He also believed that the baseball owners had blackballed him because of his efforts to establish a pension plan for players. "A lot of strife and effort went into that thing," he said. "I guess a lot of the owners didn't like what I was doing. The idea of a pension fund was an anathema to them. I suppose, in the owners' estimation, I was something of a radical."

However, Wakefield had invested his record-setting bonus money wisely.

"Before the games, the players would all be talking about last night's game, or who was pitching today," recalled Mickey Briggs.

"But not Wakefield. He would call me over and ask, 'When are you guys going to raise the dividend at Briggs Manufacturing Company?' He took the $52,000 that my grandfather gave him and bought Briggs Manufacturing Company stock. He did very well with it. He always wanted to know when they were going to declare a dividend, or when the stock was going to split.

"I would say to him, 'How the hell do I know? I'm 14 years old. I don't even know if the company has any stock.' And Wakefield would say, 'Go ask your old man.' That's where his mind was."

Hank Greenberg was the first of baseball's big-name stars to enter military service for World War II. His was the 621st number to be drawn out of a total of 9,000 in the peacetime lottery.

Greenberg was drafted on May 7, 1941 and missed all but 19 games of the 1941 season. He was discharged on December 5, 1941. But when the Japanese attacked Pearl Harbor two days later, he immediately re-enlisted and did not return to the Tigers until July, 1945.

At Greenberg's first draft physical, conducted in Lakeland, Florida, during the Tigers' 1941 spring training camp, it was discovered that Hank, the most feared slugger in the American League and the 1940 Most Valuable Player, actually had flat feet. The doctors recommended that he be limited to light duty. But a second physical, ordered by the politically motivated Michigan draft board and conducted April 18 in Detroit, declared Greenberg fit for full military service.

The Tigers' famed $55,000-a-year power hitter was about to become a $21-a-month army private.

Two days before Greenberg was due to report for duty, his Tiger teammates threw a gala party for him at the exclusive Franklin Hills Country Club in one of Detroit's most fashionable suburbs. They even invited the New York Yankee players, who were in town at the time to play the Tigers.

The next afternoon, Greenberg bid farewell to baseball in grand fashion, belting a pair of home runs in a 7-4 Tiger victory.

At the last minute, his draft board, perhaps feeling a bit guilty, offered to delay his induction for one day so that Greenberg could attend ceremonies raising the 1940 pennant at Briggs Stadium. But Greenberg declined the offer.

"I have been ordered to report May 7, and I will do so," the 30-year-old Tiger superstar said. "I want no favors."

The Detroit induction center was packed the next morning. Pvt. Henry Greenberg posed for newsreel cameras and signed more than 1,000 autographs for fellow GIs, processing sergeants, and women workers from a nearby corset factory.

When Greenberg reported to Camp Custer in Battle Creek, Michigan, a couple of hours west of Detroit, one-third of the 15,000-man Fifth Division turned out at the train station to welcome him.

By November, Greenberg, an anti-tank gunner, had risen to the rank of sergeant. Because of his age, he was discharged from active duty on December 5.

Two days later, the Japanese attacked Pearl Harbor. Without waiting for a formal summons, Greenberg reported back to the army, which soon sent him to the China-Burma-India theater in an administrative capacity.

When he was finally discharged, Greenberg, who had not swung at a major-league pitch for more than four years and was nearing his 35th birthday, took batting practice for six hours a day for a full week. When his hands blistered and bled, he wrapped them in tape and kept slugging away, struggling to regain his timing and his form.

Incredibly, on July 1, 1945, in his first game back in a baseball uniform, Greenberg hit a home run.

Although hampered by blistered hands, a sore arm, a sprained ankle and several charley horses, Greenberg finished the season with 13 home runs, 60 RBIs and a .311 average. His final blow, a bases-loaded blast against the St. Louis Browns on the final day of the season, returned the Tigers to the World Series.

Critical shortages caused by World War II had forced major-league teams to curtail their spring training trips to Florida. In 1943-45, the Tigers trained in Evansville, Indiana. However, in 1945, under the rules imposed by the Office of Defense Transportation, even the Tigers' limited schedule of exhibition games in the Midwest appeared to be in jeopardy.

But Tiger GM Jack Zeller had an idea: The Tigers could walk from Evansville to the Chicago White Sox training camp in Terre Haute, Indiana, a mere 112 miles away.

"Have them carry their uniforms, bats and toilet articles on their backs," Zeller ordered manager Steve O'Neill. "The players are supposed to be athletes in good condition. There are a few million boys who aren't athletes who are walking 10 to 20 miles a days in training camps and they're carrying something heavier than uniforms and bats. They're carrying 45- to 60-pound packs on their backs. You could take five to six days to get there, stopping along the way."

"If they walk," the 53-year-old O'Neill replied, "they have to go without a manager. I can't foot it that far."

Second baseman Eddie Mayo proposed a compromise. "Why should we do all the walking?" Mayo asked. "Why can't we meet the White Sox halfway and play them on the most convenient hayfield?"

The Tigers eventually got to Terre Haute. They took a train. They stayed for several days, playing exhibition games against the White Sox, then continued on to St. Louis for their regular season opener.

Later that summer, on an East Coast road trip in July, the Tigers asked the government for permission to make a 66-mile detour by train to play an exhibition game in Pittsburgh to benefit various servicemen's welfare agencies. Permission was denied. For a while it appeared the 1945 World Series might also have to be canceled, a casualty of the war.

Nevertheless, the Tigers were among baseball's biggest money makers during World War II. The population of the Detroit and its surrounding suburbs increased by more than 200,000 as factories worked overtime to produce much-needed war materials. Bolstered by a boomtown economy, the Tigers led the majors in attendance in both 1944 and 1945. The team reported an overall profit of $532,810 during World War II.

On the field, the 1945 Tigers, like every other team in baseball, were an odd collection of kids too young to be drafted, old timers, and players who had been rejected for military service because they were classified 4F.

The pitching staff featured temperamental lefty and future Hall of Famer Hal Newhouser and colorful

right-hander Dizzy Trout. Newhouser, who had planned to be sworn into the Army Air Corps on the Briggs Stadium pitching mound, was unexpectedly deferred because of a heart murmur. So "Prince Hal" pitched baseballs by day and worked at a defense plant at night. The bespectacled Trout, who pitched with a red handkerchief hanging out of his back pocket, was rejected because of poor eyesight. Rudy York, ineligible for military service because of an old knee injury, played first base.

The 1945 season also marked the arrival of 17-year-old Art Houtteman and 18-year-old Billy Pierce. And it featured the rebirth of Hank "Prince" Oana, who may or may not have been of royal blood.

Oana, who knocked around the minor leagues as an outfielder for 13 years, was converted into a pitcher in 1942 and toiled for the Tigers in 1943-45. Oana repeatedly denied that he was Hawaiian royalty, but the Tigers' Virgil Trucks later claimed the pitcher had confided to him that he really was a prince.

"Not like being next to a king or queen or something like that," Trucks explained. "He wasn't that kind of a prince. He was just a minor-league prince."

The Tigers' 1945 double play combination featured a pair of 35-year-olds, second baseman Eddie Mayo, who had been dismissed in Philadelphia because of poor eyesight, and shortstop Skeeter Webb, who also happened to be manager Steve O'Neill's son-in-law.

Thirty-six year-old Paul Richards, who had been out of the major leagues for eight years and a minor-league manager for five before he was lured back to active duty, did much of the catching. Forty-three-year-old Doc Cramer roamed the outfield. By the time Hank Greenberg returned from active duty in July, after more than four years had been cut from the heart of his career by military service, he was nearly 35 years old.

On July 1, 1945, on his first day back in a Tiger uniform, Greenberg delighted the war-weary Briggs Stadium crowd by belting an eighth-inning home run.

"I was just glad to be back alive," Hammerin' Hank sighed.

It wasn't so much a case of the Tigers winning the 1945 pennant. More accurately, the Washington Senators lost it.

In order to get the regular season finished early so he could lease his ballpark to the pro football Washington Redskins, Senators owner Clark Griffith scheduled a series of late-season doubleheaders.

The pace and the pressure took its toll. The Senators collapsed down the stretch and the lumbering, slumbering Tigers stumbled into the title by a game and a half.

Greenberg, who had been discharged in midsummer, belted a grand slam home run and Virgil Trucks, who had been released from the navy less than a week earlier, did the pitching as the Tigers downed the St. Louis Browns, 6-3, to win the pennant.

Back in Detroit, where thousands of fans had gathered outside the Telenews Theater on Woodward Avenue to listen to the broadcast of the game, the crowd exploded with joy.

"Quick, put on the National Anthem," the panicked theater owner shouted, "before they get out of hand."

Because of travel restrictions still in effect, the first three games of the World Series were to be played in Detroit and the remainder in Chicago.

World War II was still very much in evidence at the 1945 Series. More than 700 Tiger fans returned tickets they had purchased so that wounded servicemen could watch the games. Spectators were asked to toss foul balls back onto the field so they could be sent to soldiers still in military camps. Throughout the war, the Tigers had offered a 25-cent war bond stamp for every foul ball that was turned in.

However, not all of those balls found their way into servicemen's pick-up games. Tiger pitcher Virgil Trucks, who joined the navy after the 1943 season, revealed the baseball-playing servicemen overseas often gave bomber pilots autographed baseballs to drop on their bombing missions. According to Trucks, they often were inscribed to the Japanese prime minister, "To Tojo, With Love," and other more X-rated messages.

The 1945 World Series between the Tigers and the Chicago Cubs certainly was not marked by stellar play. Many said it may have been the worst-played World Series in baseball history. It was a comedy of errors.

In Game 5, which was won by the Tigers, 8-4, aging outfielders Doc Cramer and Roy Cullenbine allowed a routine fly ball by Chicago's Phil Caverretta to drop between them for a base hit.

"I could have caught the ball," Cramer explained, "but Cullenbine kept shouting, 'All right! All right!' When I heard this, I stopped and the ball plopped to the ground. I asked Cullenbine why he didn't make the catch and he said, 'When I called all right, I meant, all right, you catch it.'"

The Tigers lost the sixth game, 8-7, in 12 innings, but went on to win the Series in the seventh game when Hal Newhouser, working with only two days' rest, conquered the Cubs, 9-3. Greenberg, batted .304 in the Series with five key extra-base hits and a team-leading seven RBIs.

But the '45 Series is, perhaps, best remembered for the pratfall that Tigers outfielder Chuck Hostetler, representing the Series-winning run, took when he tried to stop after rounding third base in the seventh inning of Game 6. Had Hostetler scored on the play, there would have been no need for a seventh game. Hostetler, a 42-year-old retired minor-league journeyman, had been working in a Boeing plant and playing semipro ball when the Tigers called. He never played in another major-league game.

Nevertheless, tens of thousands of fans were waiting at Michigan Central Station for the triumphant Tigers when they returned by train from Chicago following the final game. Thousands of others lined Michigan Avenue, cheering as the Tigers made the short trip past the ballpark to the Book-Cadillac Hotel downtown.

The 1935 world championship had belonged to Frank Navin, even though Walter O. Briggs had been instrumental in signing Cochrane.

But the 1945 world championship belonged to Briggs.

By then Briggs, once a dashing, robust man, was confined to a wheelchair. His legs had been paralyzed by polio and he obviously was not in good health. He would sit in his wheelchair, a blanket draped across his lap, puffing on a cigar, watching his team proceed toward the pennant.

Briggs, who was further crippled by arthritis, ignored doctors' orders and attended the team's victory banquet, where 1,200 fans paid $10 apiece to celebrate with their heroes. Briggs, who had cheered for the Tigers since their fledgling Bennett Park days, finally had fulfilled his life-long dream.

But it would be 23 years before the Tigers would partake in another World Series.

Although the postwar Tigers continued to be financially successful, selling discounted standing-room-only admissions to further pack the park on special occasions, they frequently floundered on the playing field.

Following the 1946 season, Greenberg, who led the American League in home runs (44) and RBIs (127), was suddenly sold to the Pittsburgh Pirates, after the entire American League mysteriously waived him.

"I couldn't believe it," admitted Greenberg, who first heard about the sale on his car radio. "Detroit was my team. I identified 100 percent with the Tigers."

Perhaps the ailing Briggs had grown weary of his salary squabbles with his popular slugger. Or maybe he was alarmed by Greenberg's announced desire to become the Tigers' general manager. There had been growing speculation that Greenberg, backed by the financial support of his in-laws, who owned Gimbel's department store, might attempt to buy the Tigers franchise.

In any event, in Pittsburgh, Greenberg immediately became baseball's first $100,000-a-year ballplayer. In Detroit, attendance immediately dropped more than 300,000.

"My grandfather and father ran the team hands-on," recalled Mickey Briggs. "There was one of them and a general manager and a business manager—three people, period. Today, with these gigantic salaries and having to deal with agents and lawyers, I don't know if my father and grandfather would criticize what's going on now so much as they would be appalled."

In 1948, against Briggs's better judgment, Briggs Stadium became the last ballpark in the American League to install lights. Reluctantly, Briggs had been planning to install lights for the 1942 season. In fact, he had already ordered the steel for the light towers. But after the attack on Pearl Harbor he gladly donated that steel to the war effort.

"Baseball belongs to the sun," Briggs had maintained over the years, as, one by one, all of the other big-league baseball teams except the Tigers and Chicago Cubs installed lights in their stadiums and scheduled the more financially lucrative night games. "And the sun to baseball. Baseball is artificial without the sun. The people are entitled to see it played as it should be. Night baseball is the beginning of the end of baseball."

Nevertheless, in 1948, Briggs himself threw the switch, lighting the stadium that bore his name for the first time. A crowd of 54,480 showed up on the evening of June 15 to watch Hal Newhouser defeat the Philadelphia Athletics, 4-1.

New Tiger heroes emerged. Slick-fielding future Hall of Famer George Kell, acquired from Philadel-

phia for Barney McCoskey midway through the 1946 season, nipped Boston great Ted Williams to win the 1949 batting championship.

Entering the final day of the season, Kell trailed Williams by two points. "Whoever thought of beating out Williams for anything?" Kell later recounted. "I didn't give myself much of a chance."

However, as Kell was putting on his uniform for the Tigers' final game against the Cleveland Indians, teammate Hoot Evers turned to him and said, "You know something, you're going to win this thing."

The unassuming Kell looked at Evers and shook his head. "No way," he said.

After all, the Tigers would be facing Indians ace Bob Lemon, who had always given Kell trouble, while Williams and the Red Sox were playing the Yankees in New York, where the short right field fence favored Williams.

Kell singled and doubled his first two times up against Lemon, then struck out against Bob Feller, who had been summoned in relief. From New York came word that the Yankees had blanked Boston, 5-0, and Williams had gone hitless in two official trips.

Upstairs, in the Briggs Stadium press box, calculations were quickly made. If Kell didn't step up to bat again and risk making another out, he would automatically win the American League batting crown. That information was immediately relayed to the Tiger dugout.

The Tigers were trailing the Indians and Kell was scheduled to be the fourth batter up in the bottom of the ninth. After pinch hitter Dick Wakefield singled with one away, Tiger manager Red Rolfe approached Kell in the dugout. It was time to make a decision.

"What do you want to do?" Rolfe asked. "Do you want to hit, or do you want me to use somebody for you?"

"I'll hit," Kell said. He didn't want anyone to accuse him of backing into the championship.

Nevertheless, no one was happier than George Kell, who was waiting in the on-deck circle, when weak-hitting Eddie Lake grounded into a game-ending double play.

Kell yelled and hurled his bat high into the air. However unlikely, he was officially the American League batting king by .0002 percentage points: .3429 to .3427. In 522 at-bats that season, Kell had struck out a mere 13 times.

Although he only starred for the Tigers for six years, between 1946 and 1952, George Kell reigned as one of the best third basemen in the game. Five times, during those years, he was named to the American League All-Star team.

Kell was acquired from the Philadelphia Athletics for popular, hard-hitting veteran Barney McCoskey on May 18, 1946. "I couldn't understand why the Tigers would trade somebody like him for an unknown third baseman," Kell admitted in his autobiography. "That's what I felt like in the deal—the unknown third baseman."

Financially strapped Athletics owner Connie Mack told Kell he had traded him because he couldn't afford to pay young George the salary that he was worth. When Kell reported to the Tigers, Detroit GM George Trautman asked him how much money he had been making in Philadelphia.

"I told him that the first year I played in Philadelphia I made $3,000," Kell recalled. "I made $5,000 the second. The previous winter Mr. Mack had sent me a contract for $6,500. Mr. Mack told me that if I kept hustling and improving like I had, he'd give me an extra $2,000 at the end of the 1946 season."

Trautman surprised Kell by saying, "You've already hustled and improved more than you realize. If you weren't a good player already, I wouldn't have traded for you."

Trautman immediately gave Kell a contract for $8,500. At the end of the 1946 season, after Kell batted .327, Trautman rewarded him with a $2,500 bonus and an $11,500 contract for 1947.

Like Dick Wakefield before him, George Kell quickly became one of Tigers owner Walter O. Briggs's favorite ballplayers—but only from afar. The closest actual contact between the two men came between games of a particular doubleheader.

Kell, his uniform soiled as usual from diving after balls in the first game, was on the field, warming up for the second game when he heard someone calling his name.

Will Harridge, right, president of the American League, presents the silver bat to third baseman George Kell for leading the league in 1949 with a batting average of .343. The presentation was made on July 3, 1950 at Comiskey Park in Chicago before the White Sox-Tigers game. AP/Wide World Photos

Briggs had been stricken with polio and was confined to a wheelchair, but his attendant had wheeled him down next to the railing between games. "Mr. Kell," the attendant shouted, "Mr. Briggs would like to have a brief word with you."

Not knowing what to expect, Kell sprinted over to the edge of the grandstand.

"George," Briggs said quietly and politely, "don't you have a clean uniform to put on for the second game?"

After edging Boston Red Sox superstar Ted Williams to win the 1949 AL batting crown by .0002, Kell almost won the title again in 1950 when he led the league in base hits (218) and doubles (56). However, he lost the batting crown by .014 to Billy Goodman, who had 217 fewer at-bats.

Not bad for a fellow who was labeled "good field, no hit," when he broke into the big leagues with the Philadelphia Athletics in 1943.

As his hitting prowess improved, mostly through long hours of hard work, Kell remained one of the game's premier defensive third basemen. Seven times, he led all AL third basemen in fielding.

Few balls ever got by Kell. In 1948, Joe DiMaggio hit a rocket toward third. The ball took a sudden bad hop and struck Kell in the face, breaking his jaw. Undaunted, George picked the ball up and threw DiMaggio out at first base.

When the Tigers opened the 1952 season by losing 10 of their first 13 games, they shipped Kell to the Boston Red Sox as part of a nine-player swap that management hoped would turn the season around. It didn't. The Tigers finished the season 50-104, losing 100 games for the first time in history, while Kell batted .311 on behalf of the Bosox.

Soon after he retired as a player, Kell was hired as a Tigers radio announcer in 1959. Except for 1964, Kell broadcast the Tigers games, first on radio and later on TV, every season until he retired in 1996.

In addition to George Kell, the hard-hitting Hoot Evers, Vic Wertz and Johnny Groth often brought Tiger fans to their feet in the post-World War II years. Hal Newhouser, Fred Hutchinson and Virgil Trucks headed the pitching staff.

"The war was over and everyone was getting back on their feet and they were getting into recreation," Evers recalled. "There was a kind of general craziness about baseball in the city."

But the team was on a downhill slide.

In 1952, the year Walter O. Briggs died at his winter home in Miami, the Tigers lost more than 100 games for the first time in team history, despite a pair of no-hitters by hard-throwing Virgil Trucks.

Only 2,215 fans were at the ballpark to witness Trucks's first gem against the Washington Senators on May 15, 1952. But tens of thousands of people lined the streets of downtown Detroit, a few blocks away, that afternoon for a parade in honor of war hero Gen-

eral Douglas MacArthur. "We were playing so badly," Trucks later recalled, "that nobody wanted to see us play."

Trucks and Senators hurler Bob Porterfield were locked in a scoreless pitchers' duel when Vic Wertz won the game with a two-out home run in the bottom of the ninth. "I jumped up in the dugout and bumped my head on the ceiling," Trucks confessed. "I didn't draw blood but I sure saw some stars."

Prior to the game, Trucks, who had been complaining that his spikes were pinching his feet, borrowed a pair of shoes from fellow pitcher Art Houtteman. Ironically, they were the same shoes Houtteman was wearing the previous year when he lost a bid for a no-hitter with two out in the ninth.

After throwing his no-hitter, Trucks refused to give Houtteman his shoes back.

Even the New York fans were on their feet, applauding, as Trucks doffed his cap and walked off the Yankee Stadium mound on August 25, 1952 after crafting his second no-hitter of the season.

In the third inning, Yankee shortstop Phil Rizzuto was called safe on a close play at first base after Tiger shortstop Johnny Pesky was unable to get the ball out of his glove cleanly. *New York Times* sportswriter John Drebinger, who was serving as the official scorer that day, initially ruled the play an error but then changed his mind and called it a hit. At the urging of colleagues in the press box, Drebinger phoned Pesky in the Tiger dugout several innings later. Pesky admitted he had juggled the ball and should have made the play. Again, Drebinger reversed his decision, restoring the no-hitter. When word that the play had been ruled an error was relayed to the crowd, the normally partisan Yankee fans cheered.

Four months later Trucks, who won only three other games that season in addition to his two no-hitters, was banished to the St. Louis Browns.

The Detroit Tigers franchise was floundering. Thirty-three players changed teams in 1952 as a result of the Tigers' four trades with the St. Louis Browns and one with the Boston Red Sox. Even so, the Tigers finished 45 games behind the Yanks.

A country club atmosphere prevailed in the Tigers' locker room. The ownership situation became muddled. A probate court informed the Briggs family that the Tigers were not a prudent investment for Walter O. Briggs's grandchildren and ordered the team sold. A family feud erupted.

GEORGE KELL

Third Base
Bats: Right ♦ Throws: Right
5'9" ♦ 175 lbs.
Played with Tigers: 1946-52
Born: 8/23/22

After almost six decades in major-league baseball as a player and a broadcaster, George Kell retired with only one regret.

"If I have one regret from my playing career, it's the fact that I never had the opportunity to play in a World Series," he said. "Every player wants to get that chance at least once in his career. So getting into one as a broadcaster for the Tigers was very special to me."

Kell got two opportunities at baseball's biggest prize. The first came in 1968 when the Tigers miraculously rallied to win the final three games over the St. Louis Cardinals to claim the world championship. The second shot came in 1984 when the Tigers defeated the San Diego Padres in five games after waltzing their way through the season and the playoffs.

Even now, the taste of victory remains as sweet as ever.

"Those were special times for me," Kell said. "I felt just as proud of those teams as if I had been on the field."

Kell, of course, accomplished far more than most players ever did on the field. In 1949, he edged Ted Williams for the American League batting title. In 1983, he was inducted into baseball's Hall of Fame.

When his playing career was over, he spent 38 distinguished years as the revered "voice of the Tigers," creating countless cherished memories for generations of Tiger fans.

Kell was one of the best third basemen ever to play the game. He was tough and relentless in his pursuit of excellence. His uncompromising doggedness belied his laid-back, caring personality off the field.

"I always felt that if a player is getting paid to play baseball—no matter at what level—then he owes it to his owner, manager, the fans and himself to give everything he has every time he steps on to that field," Kell said.

"I know when I broke into the big leagues, I felt there were a whole lot of players who had more natural talent than I did. But I promised myself that no one was going to work harder than I did. I played like that for my entire career."

Kell got his first taste of the big leagues at the end of the 1943 season. Playing for Lancaster (Penn.), Kell led all of minor-league baseball with a .396 batting average. On the final day of the minor-league season, as Lancaster was preparing for the playoffs, Kell got a visit from the legendary Connie Mack. Mack's Philadelphia Athletics had a working agreement with Lancaster, and the owner invited Kell to play in Philadelphia once the playoffs finished.

"I can't remember if I was sitting or standing at the time," Kell recalled. "When I heard his voice and shook his hand, I actually felt like I was floating in mid-air. He was wearing a necktie and that famous straw hat. This was the great Connie Mack. There was no owner bigger than him. In fact, I can't think of anybody in the game that he didn't overshadow in his own quiet and gentle way."

On the last day of Philadelphia's season, Kell made his big-league debut at old Shibe Park. Playing against the St. Louis Browns, Kell sliced a line drive into the right field corner for a triple off Al Milner his first time up.

It was the start of a major-league career that ran for the next 15 years and eventually landed Kell in baseball's Hall of Fame.

Kell played for the Athletics until early in the 1946, season when he was traded to Detroit in a stunning deal for Barney McCosky.

"I didn't want to trade you," Connie Mack explained to Kell. "But you are going to be a very good ballplayer and you are going to make a lot of money. You will be much better off playing for Detroit. I can't afford to pay the kind of money you have a chance to make. This is a tremendous opportunity for you."

Kell made the most of that opportunity. He played a little more than six seasons for the Tigers, which were the finest of his Hall of Fame career.

"There wasn't a day I didn't enjoy playing in Detroit," Kell said. "Detroit was the perfect place for me to play. It's always been a great sports town. The fans there know their sports and appreciate players who perform like they want to be there.

"Detroit is a big city without all the hassles of New York or the frills of Chicago or some other major cities. It was easy for me to identify with all the Detroit fans. I think they appreciated my work ethic. I may have gone hitless or made an error in a game, but I never cheated them out of their money."

As much as Kell loved Detroit, that's how much the fans enjoyed watching him perform. He gave them a special treat in 1949 when he became the first third baseman to win the American League batting title. He edged Ted Williams by the slimmest margin on the last day of the season.

Williams drew two walks and went hitless in two other at-bats in New York on that day. Playing Cleveland in Detroit, Kell went two for three against 22-game winner Bob Lemon. Kell finished with a .3429 average to Williams's .3427. Kell's title also prevented Williams from winning his third Triple Crown.

"I wanted that title real bad," Kell said. "Not just for me, but also for my father. He helped me so much when I was just a kid. I do remember thinking that the title belonged as much to him as it did to me."

In six seasons for the Tigers, Kell never batted below .304. He led the league in hits and doubles in 1950 (218 and 56) and 1951 (191 and 36).

Stellar third baseman George Kell joined the Tigers in 1946 and became a Tigers' broadcaster after his playing days. **Brace Photo**

Early in the 1952 season, with the Tigers heading nowhere and eventually finishing there, Kell was part of a nine-player trade with the Boston Red Sox in an effort to shake up the team. Later he was traded to the Chicago White Sox and finished his playing career with the Baltimore Orioles in 1957.

Kell posted a career .306 batting average. He scored 881 runs and knocked in 870. In 6,702 at-bats, he struck out only 287 times. He also was an excellent third baseman.

Kell joined the Tiger broadcast team in 1959, serving as Van Patrick's partner on radio and a handful of telecasts. From 1960 through 1963, Kell worked with Ernie Harwell. Kell sat out the 1964 season, choosing to spend time with his family instead of the Tigers for the whole year. He returned as a TV commentator only in 1965 and remained in the position until retiring after the 1996 campaign.

Kell was so accomplished as a broadcaster for so long that some younger fans never realized he had starred as a player for Detroit.

"I made a speech in Lansing [Mich] once," Kell said. "There were a lot of young people in the audience. After the speech, a young lady told me that she had enjoyed listening to my broadcasts for so long. She said she didn't know I had ever actually played.

"I was not offended by her remark. In fact, I took it as a compliment. If I was that good of an announcer that she accepted me for those skills and not just the fact that I was a former player, then I had to feel good.

"I was blessed. I can't think of a better place to work in baseball than in Detroit. The fans are so good there."

George Kell was good to them, too.

Walter's son, Spike Briggs, who also pampered his favorite players and loved to socialize with them, assembled a group of interested buyers and offered the estate $3.5 million for the franchise. But Spike's four sisters, who disapproved of their brother's heavy drinking, refused to sell.

In 1956, an 11-man syndicate of radio and TV moguls, headed by John E. Fetzer, Fred Knorr and Kenyon Brown, finally purchased the Tigers and Briggs Stadium for $5.5 million, cleverly outmaneuvering baseball maverick Bill Veeck.

Actually, Fetzer and Knorr, both of whom owned radio stations that carried the Tigers' games, were more interested in acquiring control of the broadcast rights than they were in owning the ball club. They feared that if the ball club fell into the "wrong" hands, they would lose the right to broadcast the games.

"I had always liked baseball and followed the Tigers and that sort of thing," Fetzer later confessed. "But the last thing I wanted to do at this juncture in my life was to own a baseball team."

Although all bids to buy the ball club were supposed to be sealed and secret, Veeck eagerly campaigned for himself in public, through the press. He bragged about bringing clowns and fireworks and exploding scoreboards to Detroit. He talked about waking up the dormant baseball team, and the town. Veeck also boasted that he had been given a $2.5 million line of credit by the National Bank of Detroit.

"It seemed like he was holding a press conference every hour, on the hour," Fetzer remarked. "I think he held one press conference too many."

Fetzer, an astute and highly successful businessman, knew that banks normally required customers to match their credit line with an equal amount of cash. Fetzer did the math. He guessed that Veeck's bid would be about $5 million.

Fetzer's group had been planning to bid $4.8 million. Now Fetzer hastily contacted his partners and informed them they would have to up the ante. He suggested they had to bid $5.5 to have a chance. Otherwise, Fetzer argued, they should "get out of the game."

Up until that time, no team in baseball history had ever sold for such a lofty sum. The previous record was $4.5 million, set by beer baron August Busch in 1953 when he purchased the St. Louis Cardinals.

The gamble took guts. What if Fetzer's hunch was off base and Veeck's bid was actually way below theirs? Nevertheless, the group agreed with Fetzer. And they won.

Veeck, who had bid $5.2, cried foul. He verbally increased his offer to $6 million, and later to $6.75 million. But the ground rules had been set. And the future of the Detroit Tigers franchise was forever altered.

Ironically, prior to the start of the 2002 season, the Tigers—by then owned by Mike Ilitch and under the command of new team president Dave Dombrowski—hired Bill Veeck's son, Mike, to interject some "controlled craziness" into the marketing and promotion of the franchise.

Another of the unsuccessful 1956 bidders, by the way, was a Chicago insurance executive named Charles O. Finley, who later became infamous as the outrageous owner of the Kansas City and Oakland Athletics.

In 1999, as the Tigers prepared to play their final game in Tiger Stadium, the storied ballpark that once bore his influential family's name, Mickey Briggs was asked if he wished his family still owned the team.

"I sure as hell wish they had waited another 15 years to sell," Briggs replied, "so we could have gotten $50 million for the team instead of $5.5 million."

4

NUMBER 6

The Al Kaline Era, 1951 - 1975

By 1968, the city of Detroit was again a town in desperate need of a sports team to wrap its arms around—a team that would help the city heal its ugly racial wounds.

It was the era of the divisive Vietnam War. President John F. Kennedy, Martin Luther King Jr. and Bobby Kennedy had all been assassinated. There was anger and unrest everywhere, against the government and between the races—especially in Detroit.

"I don't want to use the word 'hatred,'" Gates Brown, the Tigers' popular pinch hitter deluxe, recalled. "But everywhere I went in the summer of '67, people were just against everything connected with the city—anti-black, anti-white, anti-police, anti-Tigers."

The devastating Detroit riots in the summer of 1967, ignited by a police raid on an illegal after-hours drinking and gambling establishment in a black neighborhood, had resulted in a recorded 43 deaths, 7,231 arrests, and $200 million in damage. At the time, it ranked as the bloodiest racial riot in American history. Everyone who lived or worked in the city was on edge.

Furthermore, although it paled in comparison to that catastrophe, the Tigers' heartbreaking failure to capture the 1967 American League pennant had left the members of the team personally devastated.

After battling Boston, Minnesota and Chicago down to the final day of the regular season, the Tigers were stunned when Dick McAuliffe grounded into a

season-ending double play, unexpectedly relegating them to second place. Their disappointment ran deep. The Tigers were convinced they had been the best team in baseball. And they had nothing to show for it.

In a letter to himself, penned minutes after the Tigers' season-ending loss to the California Angels, Tigers owner John Fetzer wrote: "John Fetzer has just died. This is his ghost speaking."

Downstairs at Tiger Stadium, in their small, somber locker room, the players were similarly depressed.

"I can't believe it," said Tiger catcher Bill Freehan. "There is no tomorrow."

The Tigers' 1967 final-game failure ignited its own minor riot at the ballpark as frustrated fans stormed the field, ripped up home plate and the pitcher's rubber, and battled with stadium guards, city police, and one another. It was a nasty scene and yet another black eye for the city of Detroit.

Because of the near miss in 1967, Tiger manager Mayo Smith worried about his team's state of mind for the following year. So, instead of summoning the pitchers and catchers to training camp in Lakeland, Florida, a week or so ahead of the rest of the squad, as was the usual practice, Smith ordered everybody to report a week early in February of 1968.

"I wanted to get us all started off together," he explained. "The theme was to generate that motivation just a little more, to start right off from scratch

OPPOSITE: *Star outfielder Al Kaline watches the flight of a hard-hit ball.* AP/Wide World Photos

getting each and every man to believe that all he had to do was play just a little bit harder and we'd win it."

To a man, the Tigers reported to Lakeland, the sleepy, central Florida community that has served as the team's spring home away from home since 1934, determined to make amends in 1968.

"Inwardly, we came out of spring training determined to prove that we were the best team in the American League," pitcher Mickey Lolich admitted.

"We should have won it in 1967, but we didn't," recalled outfielder Jim Northrup. "We lost on the last day of the season in '67 and in '68 we decided we were going to win it."

The deadly riots and the disappointment of the previous pennant race were still fresh in everyone's minds and hearts when 1968 Tigers, including future first-ballot Hall of Famer Al Kaline, Willie Horton, the team's first bona fide black hero, 31-game winner Denny McLain, pot-bellied Mickey Lolich, and color-

Mickey Lolich captured the hearts of Detroit fans in 1968 when his pitching helped the Tigers win the World Series. Brace Photo

ful, carefree Norm Cash, gave the citizens of Detroit good reason to forget their racial differences and focus on their common cause: Winning the World Series.

"We were able to give people a positive diversion," said Gates Brown, one of three black stars on the '68 Tigers team. "Now, when I went into the neighborhoods I heard people talking Tigers nonstop. None of that other stuff mattered, at least for the time being."

"Let's be realistic," said pitcher Earl Wilson, another of the Tigers' black stars. "A baseball team isn't going to cure the racial ills affecting a community. But we made everyone temporarily forget our differences and provided a little pride and a little hope."

"Sock it to 'em, Tigers" bumper stickers and signs were everywhere. Everyone, it seemed, wanted to get in on the act. Over and over, radio stations played the Tigers' 1968 theme song:

We're all behind our baseball team.
Go get 'em Tigers!
World Series bound and pickin' up steam.
Go get 'em Tigers!

When the riot erupted the previous summer, Willie Horton, who had grown up in one of Detroit's housing projects and still lived in the city, tried in vain to reason with some of the looters. As an impoverished, inner-city youngster, Horton once hung around Briggs Stadium until he was hired to wash the Tiger players' uniforms and shine their shoes.

"I thought the players were gods," Horton recalled. "I couldn't believe I could get that close to them.

"I'm no implanted player," Horton continued. "I grew up here. I used to slip in [Briggs Stadium] when I was 12 years old. I don't think I ever paid to get in. We slipped in all the time until John Hand gave us a job working in the clubhouse."

When Horton was 13 years old, he snuck across the Detroit River and unbeknownst to his father participated in a boxing tournament in Canada. In the finals, Horton easily pounded his burly 18-year-old opponent into submission.

When Horton was a 14-year-old freshman playing in a high school all-star game at Tiger Stadium, he blasted a home run into the right center field bleachers.

"It scared me so much the umpire had to tell me to run," Willie later recalled. "That was when everybody started talking about Willie Horton."

Now, in 1968, Horton was leading the team, batting .285 with a career-high 36 homers and reuniting his battle-scarred city.

When the Tigers, after hovering on the brink of elimination against the St. Louis Cardinals in the 1968 World Series, rallied to win three straight games behind the clutch pitching of Mickey Lolich, the hitting of Jim Northrup, and a stunning defensive play by Horton and Bill Freehan, the city of Detroit erupted again.

Only this time whites and blacks embraced one another in jubilant celebration. Fifty thousand fans flooded the runway at Metro Airport to await the team's triumphant return from St. Louis, forcing the Tigers to land, instead, at Willow Run airport near Ann Arbor. Even there they found 5,000 frenzied fans crowding the runway.

"I had a couple of police officers who worked at Tiger Stadium tell me that in 1967 there would be three or four guys standing on the street corner, looking for trouble," said Lolich, the 1968 World Series hero. "In 1968, those same guys were standing on the corner, but they had a transistor radio and were listening to the ballgame. We, as a team, embodied what this city was all about. We were a blue-collar, working-class team who loved being a part of this city."

When Bill Freehan awoke the morning following the Tigers' World Series victory and the all-night celebration that followed, he was greeted by the voices of a large group of children and nuns from a nearby Catholic school. They were all singing, "We love you, Freehan."

"I believe," Willie Horton declared, "the '68 Tigers were put here by God to heal this city."

Hometown hero Willie Horton played outfield for the Tigers from 1963-77 when he was traded to Texas. Brace Photo

❧

The 1968 World Series will long be remembered for four things: Mickey Lolich's duels with St. Louis Cardinals ace Bob Gibson; Willie Horton's throw that nailed Lou Brock at home plate; the Tigers' gallant comeback; and manager Mayo Smith's daring decision to play center fielder Mickey Stanley at shortstop.

For much of the '68 season, the Tigers' outfield had featured future Hall of Famer Al Kaline in right field and Willie Horton in left, with Stanley and Jim Northrup alternating in center. When Kaline was sidelined for five weeks with a busted hand, Northrup took over in right field and played extremely well. When Kaline returned late in the season, Smith alternated him with Norm Cash at first base.

Smith knew he had to find a way to get Kaline back into the everyday lineup. That would only be fair. Al had been the Tigers' best player since 1955 and he had waited his entire career for the chance to play in the World Series. And Mayo realized sure-handed shortstop Ray Oyler was, without a doubt, the weak link in the Tigers' potent batting order.

On the road, late in the regular season, Smith summoned Stanley, his Golden Glove center fielder who hadn't made an error all year, to his hotel room.

"You're always popping off to me about how you can play shortstop, second base and third base," Smith chided. "Well, how would you like to play shortstop in the World Series?"

Stanley was stunned. A gifted, all-around athlete, he frequently positioned himself on the infield during batting practice and scooped up ground balls. But that had never been anything more than a way to loosen up and ease the tension before games. Stanley was just having fun. He had never seriously entertained the idea of playing shortstop—especially in the World Series.

"Mayo saw me do that," said Stanley. "He wanted to get Al back into the lineup. He told me I could do the job. But I wasn't so sure. To be taken out of center field and put at shortstop was like landing in alien territory."

What's more, the whole country would be watching.

"If you can play shortstop, I can put Kaline in the outfield and I think our ball club would be better offensively than it's ever been," Smith explained.

Stanley gave Smith a sly grin. "When do I start?" he said.

Smith kept his plan secret. Stanley and second baseman Dick McAuliffe worked out alone in the infield each afternoon, long before the other players and members of the media arrived at the ballpark. After the pennant had been clinched, Smith started Stanley at shortstop in one game. Attempting to complete a first-inning double play, Stanley heaved the ball into the stands.

With time running out, Smith summoned McAuliffe to his office. "What do you think?" the Tiger manager asked. "Can he do the job?"

"Mayo," the always-intense McAuliffe replied, "you've got to be kidding."

"Well, let's keep working on it," Smith ordered.

When the Tigers' stunning starting lineup for the opening game of the World Series was announced, with Stanley at short in place of Oyler, Hall of Fame shortstop-turned-announcer Pee Wee Reese approached Smith in the Detroit dugout.

"Mayo, you're not serious, are you?" Reese asked.

"The hell I'm not!" Smith replied.

In the opening game, the first Cardinal batter, Lou Brock, bounced an easy grounder to Stanley, who proceeded to throw him out with no problem.

Mayo Smith's daring switch worked perfectly.

"I was scared stiff all the time because I didn't want to let the guys down," Stanley later confessed. "I didn't enjoy the Series at all."

Neither did Denny McLain, the Tigers' brash, outspoken 31-game winner.

"I'm sick of hearing what a great team the Cardinals are," declared McLain with typical bravado on the eve of the Series opener. "I don't want to just beat them. I want to demolish them."

But, as usual, McLain wasn't telling the whole story.

Detroit's two daily newspapers had been on strike during most of the 1968 season, which made it easier to conceal the fact that McLain was regularly receiving cortisone shots in his talented right arm as he reeled off his historic 31 victories while losing only six times. Privately, doctors warned Mayo Smith that the cortisone shots would only work their magic for so long. Sooner or later, they predicted, McLain would have to pay the price. True to that diagnosis, Denny won 24 games for the Tigers in 1969, but 1970 was a nightmare. He was suspended for the first half of the season for gambling activities and when he returned on July 1, he was far from his former self. People blamed the suspension and the long layoff, but the Tigers knew better. By then McLain's arm was dead.

However, late in the summer of 1968, Dennis Dale McLain was sitting on top of the world.

As much as Mayo Smith appreciated McLain's mastery on the mound, the unbridled Tiger right-hander and his manager were often at odds.

On a miserably hot summer afternoon in Chicago, McLain took a one-run lead into the ninth inning. With one out in the top of the ninth, it was McLain's turn to bat. This, of course, was in the days before the designated hitter.

"Go up there, take three strikes, then come sit back down," Smith ordered. In the intense heat, he wanted his star pitcher to save his strength for the bottom of the ninth.

"Everybody on the bench heard me tell him that," Smith recalled. "He walks up there, and on the second pitch, hits a ground ball to shortstop and has to run. He comes back to the bench and the sweat is pouring off him."

In the bottom of the ninth, McLain got into trouble and Smith had to summon a relief pitcher to preserve the victory. As soon as the Tigers returned to the cool of their air-conditioned clubhouse, Smith told an attendant to send McLain into his office.

"You want to see me?" McLain said, grinning when he stuck his head in the door.

"Yeah," Smith growled. "That little episode will cost you $200."

"What?" McLain shrieked in mock disbelief.

"What did I tell you about going up there and taking three strikes?" the Tiger manager snapped.

"I didn't think you were serious," McLain replied.

On September 14, 1968, the flamboyant Denny McLain became baseball's first 30-game winner since Dizzy Dean in 1934. With Dean—who had so convincingly conquered the Tigers in the 1934 World Series—looking on, the Tigers rallied for two runs in the bottom of the ninth inning against the Oakland A's, after Denny had been removed for a pinch hitter, to make McLain a winner.

A Detroit newspaper had flown the colorful Dean into town to collaborate with a ghostwriter and report on the historic event. But that newspaper's own reporter threw Dizzy out of the Tiger Stadium press box, claiming he wasn't a bona fide member of the Baseball Writers Association of America, which had been founded in Detroit 60 years earlier.

Despite the bragging of McLain, the St. Louis Cardinals built up a seemly insurmountable lead of three games to one in the '68 Series as, more often than not, the Tigers looked hopelessly overmatched.

Bob Gibson shut the helpless Tigers out in the opener, fanning a record 17, then struck out 10 more while winning Game 4 for St. Louis.

Lefty Mickey Lolich grabbed a victory for the Tigers in Game 2, even though he didn't think he would be able to answer the bell. Lolich had a boil lanced before the game, and the surgery left him woozy.

"I was groggy," Mickey admitted after the 8-1 win. "But once I began to warm up, I felt a little better."

Lolich also belted an unlikely home run, his first in 10 years of professional baseball. He became so excited watching the ball disappear into the Busch Stadium stands that he missed first base and had to retrace his steps.

"I still won't believe he hit a home run," quipped McLain, "until I see a replay."

Back in Detroit, where Washington Boulevard had temporarily been renamed Tiger Drive and the downtown business district had been decorated with bunting and banners, both Lolich and McLain, who had lost the Series opener, criticized Cardinals speedster Lou Brock for continuing to steal bases even after his team was comfortably ahead.

"It definitely was for his own self-glory," Lolich declared. "He wants to set a record for stolen bases or something."

What neither hurler knew was that, before the World Series began, Brock had made an extensive study of the Tiger pitchers' moves to first base and felt confident he could steal at will. Brock's diligence paid dividends as he stole seven bases during the Series to none for the entire Tiger team.

Ironically, the turning point in the Series came in the fifth inning of Game 5, when, with the Tigers trailing three games to one, Willie Horton gunned down Brock, trying to score, in a close play at home plate.

The Cardinals were leading in the game, 3-2, at the time, and appeared on the brink of clinching the world championship. But Bill Freehan effectively blocked the plate and Horton's throw from left field was perfect as the speedy Brock defiantly sought to score standing up.

Even as Brock had been busy studying the Tiger pitchers, the Tigers had been busy studying him.

"We studied film on Brock and we knew he always went in standing up at home, coming from second base," explained Horton. "I think he was so successful throughout his career that coaches relaxed when he would come around third base and he didn't get any help from the hitter on deck. I would say that was the play that did it for us."

"If Brock scores, we might never have gotten out of the inning," agreed Jim Northrup. "Then Al [Kaline] gets the hit to win the game."

"At the time, we had no idea it would be a turning point," Bill Freehan admitted. "In retrospect, from then on, everything went our way."

The winning pitcher in Game 5, as he had been in Game 2, was Mickey Lolich, who had played second fiddle to the far more flamboyant McLain throughout his career. It had all been up to Lolich. Win the fifth game or the Tigers would be eliminated and humiliated.

"I had a special routine for warming up," Lolich recalled. "I would go down to the bullpen 15 minutes before the game and throw a certain amount of warmup pitches that usually took 12 minutes.

"I started warming up and I got halfway through my routine, and all of a sudden they're doing the National Anthem. Jose Feliciano is singing and it lasts forever. He goes on and on. I started cooling down.

"Then the umpire comes out and says, 'Come on, Mick. We gotta get the game started.'

"So I go to the mound and all I can throw right away are fastballs. Orlando Cepeda smacked a three-

Right-handed pitcher Denny McLain throws to a batter in the first game of the World Series against the St. Louis Cardinals at Busch Stadium in St. Louis, Missouri on October 2, 1968. AP/Wide World Photos

nals, were all trying to figure out who would start for Detroit in Game 6. Everyone assumed they had seen the last of the suddenly struggling McLain in the Series.

Mayo Smith was on the field during an off day workout, talking to the press, when a reporter raised the question of the Tigers' Game 6 starter.

"I'm not sure," Smith said soberly. "Maybe Earl Wilson."

Just then McLain walked by, looked at the Tiger manager, and winked. "I didn't say anything to the reporters," Smith recalled later. "But I thought to myself, 'By God, there's my pitcher.'"

The always unpredictable McLain whipped the Cardinals with ease, 13-1, to even the Series at three wins apiece.

"I remember the Cardinals coming out and watching us taking batting practice before the sixth game," Al Kaline recalled. "They were all joking and having a lot of fun. Then all of a sudden we scored 10 runs in [the third] inning, and the next game those guys weren't joking around anymore."

"When we went out and got 10 runs in one inning and beat them 13-1 we all knew [the Cardinals] were just waiting to get beat," said Jim Northrup. "And we were going to beat 'em."

"I noticed in the fifth game, after we threw Brock out at the plate, a little bit of the aggressiveness of the St. Louis hitters changed," observed Lolich. "When we blew them away in the sixth game, and I went out to pitch in the seventh game, their hitters were totally different.

run homer into the left field seats. Luckily I was able to settle down and we won the game."

McLain had been pounded in each of his first two starts in the Series, in Games 1 and 4. His once-magic arm ached. He could barely raise it above his head. After the rain-delayed 10-1 drubbing in Game 4, McLain went to the hospital for yet another shot of cortisone.

With the Tigers trailing the Cardinals three games to two, the sportswriters and fans, as well as the Cardi-

"They had become defensive hitters. They started swinging at bad pitches. When I saw that, I started to keep the ball down and I actually started to go below the strike zone. And they were swinging at it. They were under a tremendous amount of pressure in the seventh game and I knew, by the second inning, that if we could just score, which was going to be difficult because we were up against Gibson, we had a very good chance of beating them."

In the deciding seventh game, the rubber-armed Lolich, working with only two days' rest, bested the previously untouchable Gibson, who had won seven World Series games in a row. For Lolich, it was his third victory in eight days. Jim Northrup, who had belted a grand slam in Game 6 to help even the Series, lined a clutch two-out seventh-inning triple off the normally unhittable Gibson, over the head of normally sure-fielding center fielder Curt Flood, for two runs and a 4-1 Tiger victory.

When Tim McCarver's high pop foul nestled securely in Bill Freehan's glove, the Tigers won their first world championship in 23 years and only the third in their long history. "All I could think," admitted Freehan, "was: 'Don't drop this one, dummy.'"

The ample Lolich, who liked to ride his motorcycle to the ballpark, leaped into Freehan's arms, setting off the wildest celebration Detroit had witnessed in years. It was easily one of the finest moments in Detroit baseball history.

"All my life, someone else was the big star and I was number two," observed Lolich. "There's always been somebody ahead of me. A hitter like Al Kaline. A pitcher like Denny. It was always somebody else—never Mickey Lolich. But now my day has finally come."

Before the 1968 World Series began, some people had suggested that Mayo Smith should avoid the ballyhooed confrontation between Denny McLain and Bob Gibson in the first, fourth and possibly seventh games, and use Mickey Lolich as a sacrificial lamb instead, saving mighty McLain for easier victories against the Cardinals' lesser pitchers. Instead, Lolich upstaged both Gibson and McLain, hurling three complete-game victories and posting a 1.67 ERA with 21 strikeouts.

A natural right-hander, Lolich broke his left collarbone in a bicycle accident as a child and the rehabilitation made his left arm stronger than his right. In time, with the arguable exception of Hall of Famer Hal Newhouser, he became the Tigers' best left-handed pitcher of all time.

In his 13 seasons, the portly left-hander started more games (459), struck out more enemy batters (2,679), and tossed more shut-outs (39) than any pitcher in Tiger history. "Fat guys need idols, too," Lolich explained.

John Fetzer had always been a hands-off owner, leaving general manager Jim Campbell to run the ball club. Fetzer rarely set foot in the clubhouse or mingled with the players. When the Tigers won the 1968 World Series, the jubilant players threw their soft-spoken, seldom-seen owner into the whirlpool with all of his clothes on. Fetzer loved it.

"I actually thought of the World Series as basically being anticlimactic," admitted Lolich. "When we lost [the American League pennant] on the last day of the season in '67, I think that really hurt us. When we finally won it in '68 I got the feeling we had accomplished our mission. That was what we were all geared for, after what happened in '67. After we won the 1968 pennant, then it was like, 'Oh, gee, now we've got to play in the World Series.' Personally, I hoped we could play a good Series and not embarrass ourselves.

Al Kaline was named to 18 All-Star games during his career with the Tigers. Brace Photo

"Without sounding too conceited, the '68 Series was what made me famous," Lolich continued. "I actually had a better year in 1971, but nobody remembers that. All that anybody remembers is the World Series. I sometimes kid people that that was the only week I ever pitched in baseball. It might just as well have been."

To this day, the players on the 1968 Tiger team refer to themselves as baseball's "last true champions." In 1969, because of expansion, baseball introduced its playoff system, which has since been expanded to include wild cards. No longer would the two winners of the season-long pennant races proceed directly to the ultimate showdown—the World Series.

"It was the last year that the regular season had total meaning," Bill Freehan declared.

"You had to battle all year long to get to that point," explained Al Kaline, who rose to the occasion in the first and only World Series of his brilliant career, batting .379 with two homers and eight RBIs. "Now you have to get to the playoffs and get lucky to have a chance to get to the World Series.

"But coming so close, like we did in 1967, then losing on the last day, was such a devastating thing that the guys were not going to be denied in '68. It was amazing how everybody participated and did their job. Everybody forgot about their batting averages and their win-loss records and their salaries. Everybody just gave 100 percent. Everybody did something to help us win. Every game. It was a great feeling just to be a part of that team. I had never been a part of a team like that before, where everybody had one goal, where everybody was just focused on winning. And I was never on another one after that."

❧

The long drought was over. After 23 years, the Tigers were champions again.

In spite of the largess of Walter Briggs and the business acumen of John Fetzer, the Tigers had floundered from 1946 until 1967. During those 22 seasons, they employed 13 different managers and hundreds of disappointing ballplayers. Ten times they languished in the second division. In only five seasons did they finish as high as second.

Desperate to win one more pennant before he passed away, Briggs forgot about the future and traded away dozens of key prospects and made other mistakes that would cost the Tigers dearly for years to come. Briggs also had no interest in pursuing African-American players, even though they were making a significant impact on other teams throughout the major leagues. It was hardly the Tigers' finest hour.

"When I think of Tiger Stadium," African-American Tiger pitcher Earl Wilson once remarked, "I think of Briggs saying no blacks would ever play in this stadium."

In 1952, the Tigers finished last and lost more than 100 games, 104 to be exact, for the first time in franchise history. All too often in those glum days, the situation was borderline comical.

On August 19, 1951, in an effort to stimulate attendance, St. Louis Browns owner Bill Veeck, who would fail five years later in his bid to buy the Detroit franchise, signed 26-year-old, three-foot-seven Eddie Gaedel and sent him to the plate to bat against the Tigers.

At first, Gaedel was skeptical. After all, he wasn't a baseball player. He wasn't even an athlete. When Veeck asked Eddie what he knew about baseball, Eddie replied, "I know you're supposed to hit the white ball with the bat, and then you run somewhere."

But Gaedel was an actor—an entertainer. The more Veeck talked about Gaedel's eventual place in history as the shortest person ever to step up to the plate in a major-league baseball game, the more Eddie liked the idea. "You'll be famous," Veeck assured him. "You'll be immortal."

Gaedel was sold. He was ready.

In his office, Veeck showed Gaedel how to crouch over to further reduce his already tiny strike zone. Veeck picked up a ruler off his desk and measured the distance between the bent-over Gaedel's armpits and his knees. It measured a mere 1 1/2 inches.

Veeck borrowed a uniform from Bill DeWitt Jr., the seven-year-old son of the Browns' vice president, and had the number "1/8" sewn on the back. The whole caper was kept top secret. Gaedel signed the standard major-league player's contract and Veeck agreed to pay him $100, which was the going rate at the time for one day's work.

In the bottom of the first inning against the Tigers, Browns manager Zack Taylor, who was in on the gag, sent Gaedel out to bat for center fielder Frank Saucier.

"For the Browns," the public address announcer intoned, trying hard to sound serious, "number one-eighth, Eddie Gaedel, batting for Saucier."

Home plate umpire Ed Hurley immediately objected and impatiently looked toward the Browns' dugout.

"What's going on?" bewildered Tiger catcher Bob Swift demanded to know.

But Taylor produced Gaedel's contract, and reluctantly the umpire ordered the game to continue.

Swift, who would become the Tigers' manager in 1966, walked to the mound with a grin on his face. "Pitch him low," Swift advised pitcher Bob Cain.

"I thought maybe we should hit him," Swift cracked later. "But I didn't want to face a homicide charge."

Cain, who was laughing out loud, hurled four soft pitches high over the head of the three-foot seven-inch, 65-pound batter—even though, in his excitement, Gaedel forgot to crouch as Veeck had ordered.

Little Eddie trotted down to first base, waited for pinch runner Jim Delsing to replace him, then shook hands with the Browns' first base coach and waved to the 18,000 cheering fans. Gaedel's big-league career was over.

The next day, Veeck received an angry telegram from American League president Will Harridge, condemning such "stunts." When Gaedel died in June 1961, only one baseball figure, Tiger pitcher Bob Cain, went to his funeral.

Walter O. Briggs passed away on January 17, 1952, and was succeeded at the Tigers' helm by his

Eddie Gaedel, a three-foot-seven stuntman pinch hits for the St. Louis Browns in a game against Detroit at Sportsman's Park, in St. Louis, on August 19, 1951. Gaedel walked on four pitches and was replaced by a pinch runner. AP/Wide World Photos

son, Spike. Former pitcher Fred Hutchinson took over for Red Rolfe as the Tigers' manager during the 1952, 104-loss debacle.

Spike Briggs initially offered the job to former Chicago White Sox Hall of Fame pitcher Ted Lyons, but he turned it down. Briggs then tried to contact former Tiger pitching star Schoolboy Rowe. But Schoolboy was on a fishing trip and couldn't be reached, so Spike turned to Hutchinson, his third choice.

Many felt that Hutchinson could have become one of the finest Tiger managers ever. But Briggs elected to continue his deceased father's cautious policy of never giving any manager more than a two-year contract.

When Hutchinson's contract was up at the end of the 1954 season, he asked for a new three-to-five-year agreement for security. But the Tigers refused to commit to more than two more years, and Hutchinson departed, replaced by seasoned veteran Bucky Harris, who had managed the Tigers more than two decades earlier, from 1929-33.

Walter Briggs had left the Tigers in trust to his son, Spike, and his three daughters. However, the bank, which served as executor of the estate, went to court and obtained a ruling that a baseball team was "not a prudent investment" for the elder Briggs's grandchildren.

Spike Briggs offered his sisters $2.5 million for their share of the Tigers. When they turned him down, he gathered some investors and raised his offer to $3.5 million. When his sisters, who didn't approve of Spike's heavy drinking and frequent carousing, rejected that bid, too, brother and sisters stopped speaking and the Detroit Tigers went on the auction block.

Rather than continue to try to put together the necessary financing to buy the club, Spike Briggs became convinced he would be better served to sell the club to an outsider, reap the financial rewards, and arrange things so that he would be allowed to continue to run the team. It would be the best of both worlds.

Privately, broadcaster Fred Knorr, who was part of a group of interested investors headed by Kalamazoo, Michigan, radio and TV pioneer John Fetzer, assured Briggs that if his group's bid was successful, Spike would remain in control of the team. Coincidentally, Briggs, a wealthy man in his own right, happened to own seven percent of Knorr Broadcasting Co.

Baseball maverick Bill Veeck, another eager bidder, vowed that if he won he would run the Tigers himself. "Watch out," Veeck warned Briggs. "These guys are going to get the club and then throw you out."

When the Tigers went on the auction block, eight syndicates participated in the bidding. Detroit banker Chick Fisher, who was married to one of Spike Briggs's sisters and also served as treasurer of the Tigers, authorized multimillion-dollar loans to both Veeck and the rival group that included Fetzer, Knorr, and Kenyan Brown. Veeck, citing a potential conflict of interest, later claimed he had been merely used as a shill to drive up the price for the Briggs family.

When the Fetzer/Knorr group won, they did, indeed, retain Briggs as the team's general manager and executive vice president—temporarily.

Like his father before him, Spike Briggs was a fan first and foremost. His life revolved around the Tigers. He loved the limelight and enjoyed pampering his players. The fun-loving, impulsive, and freely-imbibing Briggs and the disciplined, highly private Fetzer were exact opposites. It was inevitable that, sooner or later, they would clash.

That happened in 1957 after Briggs fired Bucky Harris, a future Hall of Famer, who managed for 29 years in the big leagues—longer than anyone except Connie Mack and John McGraw. Fetzer wanted to hire Al Lopez, who also was later elected to baseball's Hall of Fame. But Briggs insisted on promoting the Tigers' personable former minor-league manager, coach and scout Jack Tighe.

Angrily, Fetzer immediately called a meeting of the Tigers' board of directors. At Fetzer's urging, they voted to fire Briggs. Tiger president Fred Knorr, Briggs's close friend, resigned rather than personally wield the ax. On April 26, 1957, Fetzer and fellow owner Harvey Hanson met with Briggs and "invited" him to resign.

In Briggs's place, they hired former Tiger first baseman John McHale, whose son, John Jr., later served as the Tigers president and CEO under Mike Ilitch and was instrumental in making Comerica Park a reality.

Later in the summer of 1957, the Tigers made a road trip on an airplane for the first time. Times were changing.

In 1953, the Tigers signed a shy, skinny 18-year-old kid off the Baltimore sandlots for $35,000, including bonus, and brought him straight to the big leagues. Two years later, Al Kaline became the youngest American League batting champ in history, edging the immortal Ty Cobb for that distinction by a single day.

A year before Kaline arrived, the Tigers signed shortstop Harvey Kuenn off the campus of the University of Wisconsin for a fat $52,000 bonus. After just 63 games in the minors, the hard-drinking, tobacco-chewing Kuenn became the Tigers' leadoff batter and starting shortstop. In 1953, Kuenn batted .308, with a league-leading 209 hits, and was named Rookie of the Year.

The press called Kuenn and Kaline the "K-K Kids," and along with pitchers Jim Bunning and Frank Lary, they formed the nucleus as the Tigers slowly crept back to respectability. Bunning, who would later be elected to the United States Senate from Kentucky, won 118 games for the Tigers between 1955 and 1963.

"I remember when Al Kaline was brought up," Mickey Briggs, Spike's son, recalled. "He was a skinny kid out of high school. He was my age. It marveled me to see a kid who was my age play like he could. When he was 19,

Shortstop Harvey Kuenn only hit below .300 once during his seven-year career with the Tigers.
Brace Photo

you knew he was an All-Star. He is the quality, class player that epitomizes Detroit Tiger baseball at its best.

"The two greatest days of my father's reign were when he signed Harvey Kuenn and Al Kaline. I think the good Tiger teams of the '60s were the result of my father starting that program in the 1950s."

In 1955, the streetcar line that had ferried so many millions of fans to the ballpark over the years ceased operations. Like the baseball team that cavorted at the corner of Michigan and Trumbull, the city of Detroit was changing. Fans had fled to the suburbs and now traveled to the ballpark almost exclusively by automobile, along high-speed thoroughfares called freeways.

On August 27, 1953—19 months after Walter Briggs's death—the Tigers became the last major-league team to sign an African-American player when Claude Agee signed a minor-league contract and began to play in the farm system. Despite Detroit's growing African-American population, as late as 1958 there were only 19 black players in the Tigers' entire farm system.

On June 6, 1958, more than 10 years after the debut of Jackie Robinson—who by then had already retired—the Tigers finally fielded their first ballplayer of color at the major-league level.

The belated trailblazer was 25-year-old third baseman Ozzie Virgil, who was also the first player from the Dominican Republic to reach the big leagues. In all of baseball, only the Boston Red Sox waited longer than the Tigers to integrate.

In his first Briggs Stadium start, Virgil, who had been acquired in a trade with the San Francisco Giants, went five-for-five. Virgil, who had grown up in New York City, appeared in 131 games for the Tigers over three seasons, batting a meager .228. He was never embraced by Detroit's African-American community, which always suspected that the Tigers had only selected Virgil because of his relatively light skin coloring. "The only thing I didn't like," Virgil admitted years later, "was that the black people in Detroit didn't accept me."

Earlier in that 1958 season, the Tigers snubbed a young African-American speedster in their farm system named Maury Wills, preferring to play Coot Veal at shortstop. Four years later, Wills, who was lost on waivers to the Los Angeles Dodgers, shattered Ty Cobb's single-season stolen base record.

Not that the Tigers of the 1950s didn't have their moments.

Frank Lary, the "Yankee Killer," was 5-1 against the mighty Bronx Bombers in 1956 and 7-0 against them in 1958—the best effort against New York by any opposing pitcher since 1916. The slightly built right-hander, known as "Taters," or "Mule," was an unlikely workhorse, leading the AL in innings pitched and complete games three times.

Charlie Maxwell, another Tiger hero during the 1950s, famed for his "Sunday Punch," was a much better hitter than many people realized. In 1956, he batted .326 with 28 homers. But Maxwell's claim to fame was the fact that he smacked 40 of his 148 career homers on Sunday. Oddly enough, Charlie rarely went to church during the baseball season.

"I never could understand why I did it," admitted Maxwell. "But I guess I did it a lot. It started on May 3, 1959. I hit four home runs in a row in a Sunday doubleheader—my last time up in the first game and then three in a row to start the second game. Van Patrick [the Tigers' radio announcer at the time] made a big deal out of it."

In 1958, J. W. Porter, the Tigers' freckle-faced reserve catcher who frequently ate two dozen eggs for breakfast, set out to drive from his home in Oregon to spring training in Lakeland, Florida. After driving down the West Coast, Porter cut across Arizona, where he stopped in Tucson to visit friends in the Cleveland Indians' training camp. Then he resumed his long, arduous cross-country journey.

An hour outside Lakeland, a weary Porter turned on his car radio and learned that the Tigers had just

Charlie Maxwell played for the Tigers from 1955-62 and was well-known for hitting particularly well on Sundays.
Burton Historical Society

traded him and pitcher Hal Woodeshick to those same Cleveland Indians for pitcher Hank Aguirre and catcher Jim Hegan. Porter made a U-turn and headed back to Arizona.

From 1958 through 1967, Aquirre was one of the worst hitters in baseball history, going 2-for-75.

One afternoon at Yankee Stadium, Aguirre stunned the New York outfielders by driving a ball over their heads into deep right center field. While the outfielders chased down the ball, Aquirre chugged all the way around the base path to third.

After he dusted himself off, Aguirre turned to Tigers third base coach Tony Cuccinello and asked, "Hey, Tony, do you want me to steal home?"

"It took you eight years to get this far," Cuccinello replied, with a straight face. "Don't spoil it now."

Harvey Kuenn, the Tigers' line drive-hitting shortstop, led the American league in hitting with a .353 average in 1959. On Easter Sunday, the eve of the 1960 season opener, the Tigers traded Kuenn to Cleveland for popular American League home run king Rocky Colavito. In all of baseball history, there had never been a trade quite like it.

Kuenn had been a hero in Detroit. He was a ballplayer's ballplayer. But Colavito had been a god, a matinee idol, in Cleveland. He had good looks. He smacked homers. The fans loved him, especially the women and young girls. Nevertheless, Cleveland general manager Frank Lane defended the blockbuster deal, describing the trade as, "Hamburger for steak."

Colavito, "the hamburger," never did enjoy the success or the stardom in Detroit that had been his in Cleveland. He smacked 139 HRs in his four years with the Tigers, but more often than not he was treated like ground chuck.

Following the 1963 season, Colavito was traded to Kansas City in another curious deal for light-hitting second-baseman Jerry Lumpe. The Tigers even threw in $50,000 to sweeten the swap.

Also just prior to the start of the 1960 season, another bizarre series of events occurred that would significantly impact the Tigers' future.

Bill Veeck, who wound up purchasing the Chicago White Sox after being thwarted by Fetzer in his effort to buy the Tigers, was anxious to trade catcher John Romano to Cleveland for the ageless box office draw Minnie Minoso. But the Indians wanted some cash as well. Financially strapped, Veeck offered to throw in a nondescript first baseman named Norm Cash instead.

But before Cash had even had time to unpack, Cleveland GM Frank Lane swapped Cash to the Tigers for rookie infielder Steve Demeter. In 1961, Cash made both Veeck and Lane look stupid when he exceeded everyone's expectations, batting a league-leading .361 with 41 homers and 132 RBIs.

Years later, Cash confessed he had illegally hollowed out his bats to help make that sensational season happen.

Late in the 1960 season, Tiger general manager Bill DeWitt—who had traded for both Cash and Colavito—and Cleveland's Frank Lane made headlines again, swapping Detroit manager Jimmy Dykes for the Indians' skipper Joe Gordon. By the end of the year, Gordon and DeWitt were both gone. At the conclusion of the 1960 season, the thoroughly frustrated Gordon barricaded himself in his apartment and refused to speak to anyone. He quit and was replaced by Bob Scheffing.

Meanwhile, John Fetzer continued to quietly buy out his fellow owners. After Fred Knorr was tragically scalded to death late in 1960, Fetzer purchased the balance of the ball club from Knorr's estate, giving him total control of the Tigers.

Unlike Frank Navin and Walter Briggs, Fetzer had no interest in seeing his own name on the storied sporting structure at the intersection of Michigan and Trumbull. In fact, he found the very idea abhorrent. So, in 1961 when Fetzer became sole owner of the team, the 50-year-old ballpark was quickly renamed Tiger Stadium. Although no one named Briggs had been associated with the ball club for four years, many longtime Tiger fans were jolted by the change.

They were also pleasantly surprised by the performance of the Tigers' new first baseman, 26-year-old Norm Cash, who took the city and the American League by storm in 1961. "Stormin' Norman," as he was known, lived life to its fullest. On the field he played with flair, frequently doffing his cap to the crowd. In 1973, as Hall of Famer Nolan Ryan was hurling a no-hitter at the Tigers, Cash playfully stepped up to the plate carrying a table leg instead of a bat.

"I couldn't get a hit off him with a bat, so I might as well use this," Cash explained.

Nevertheless, umpire Ron Luciano, quite a showman himself, ordered Norm back to the dugout to get a real bat.

Off the field, Cash loved his liquor and was not opposed to partying all night, even when he had a game to play the next afternoon.

Shortly after daybreak one Sunday morning, Cash returned in a rather inebriated state to the Kansas City hotel room he was sharing with Tiger backup catcher Jim Price, who was still sound asleep. Minutes later, Cash's wife called to check up on her husband's whereabouts. Norm became so enraged at the intrusion that he ripped off his wristwatch and hurled it out the hotel window.

A stunned Price, who by now was wide awake, looked out the window and spotted the watch in the middle of the deserted street. While Cash crashed back onto his waiting bed and passed out, Price rushed out of the room, rode the elevator down to the lobby, and proceeded directly to the street.

Price, now a Tigers radio announcer, was retrieving Cash's watch when he felt a tap on his shoulder. "I think you had better come with me," the Kansas City cop said.

In his haste to help his roommate, Price had left the hotel wearing only his pajama bottoms. No shoes. No shirt. No identification. He was arrested for indecent exposure.

At the police station, Price somehow talked himself out of the jam, just in time to rush to the ballpark and crouch behind home plate for both halves of that afternoon's doubleheader. Price went zero-for-eight that hot, dreadful day while Cash, armed with only a few hours of sleep, somehow managed six hits.

Cash himself called his unexpected 1961 heroics "a freak."

"Everything I hit seemed to drop in," he admitted.

Unfortunately, the next season, nothing did. And Cash's batting average nose-dived 118 points to .243—the biggest drop by any batting champion in baseball history.

Whenever anyone mentions Al Kaline, they, of course, think of his 1955 batting title, when he was not yet 21 years of age, and the Tigers' triumph in the 1968 World Series, when Mickey Stanley was shifted to shortstop to make room in the outfield for the veteran Number Six. However, 1962 could have been Kaline's greatest personal season, had not injury intervened, as it so often did in his nevertheless brilliant career.

Less than two months into the 1962 campaign, with the Tigers very much in contention for the American League pennant, Kaline had already belted 13 home runs. Only Jim Gentile of the Baltimore Orioles had more. Kaline led the league in runs batted in with 38. His .345 batting average was third best in the league behind nobodies Chuck Essegian and Manny Jiminez.

Although it was only late May, all around the American League people were talking Triple Crown. The normally reserved Kaline himself was convinced that 1962 was going to be his best year yet.

Then, on May 26, diving for a sinking pop fly off the bat of the New York Yankees' Elston Howard in the ninth inning, Kaline landed on his right shoulder. He felt the ball nestle into his glove, meaning the game was over and the Tigers had won. But he also felt a burning pain in his arm. He tried to get to his feet but couldn't. The pain was so intense, Kaline was certain he was going to black out.

"Are you okay?" asked first baseman Norm Cash, the first Tiger to reach the fallen right fielder.

"I don't know," Kaline whispered in anguish. "Get [Tiger trainer] Jack Homel. I'm hurt."

By the time Homel reached Kaline's side, Tigers Billy Bruton and Jake Wood were already on the scene. Homel cautiously touched Kaline's shoulder. "I'm afraid it's broken," the trainer said as he turned to tell someone to signal for a stretcher.

"Just get me up," Kaline said, still barely speaking above a whisper. "I can walk. There's nothing the matter with my legs."

Kaline's concerned teammates helped him to his feet. As the Yankee Stadium crowd applauded in appreciation, Kaline walked slowly off the field.

When he finally reached the dugout steps, several Tigers grabbed hold of him. It was a good thing they did, because Kaline immediately collapsed. He was out cold.

Kaline regained consciousness while his teammates were carrying him through the tunnel to the clubhouse. Once in the locker room, lying on the trainer's table, he passed out from the pain again.

As the Tigers milled about the locker room knowing their high hopes for the 1962 season would be greatly diminished without their superstar, Kaline passed out for the third time. Finally, the ambulance arrived to carry Kaline to Lenox Hill Hospital. As the ambulance, its lights flashing and siren blaring, pulled away from Yankee Stadium, Tiger manager Bob Scheffing groaned, "There goes our pennant, riding off in that ambulance."

"I sat on the bench that day, hoping Al would catch that ball," future Hall of Fame Tiger pitcher Jim Bunning recalled. "And I spent the rest of the season wishing he hadn't."

The freak injury sidelined Kaline for eight weeks, causing him to miss 57 games. And when he finally did return, on July 23, he still couldn't throw and his swing was noticeably altered. The 1962 Tigers finished fourth, 10 1/2 games behind the Yankees.

In 1967, Kaline was sidelined again. After striking out against Cleveland's Sam McDowell, Al slammed his bat into the rack in the dugout so hard that he busted a bone in his hand.

Although John Fetzer preferred to remain in the background, operating behind the scenes and leaving the day-to-day management of the Tigers to his general manager, Jim Campbell, the Tigers' mild-mannered new owner soon became a major force in baseball. In 1965, armed with knowledge gained during his lifelong career in broadcasting, he negotiated baseball's first national television contract, sharing the revenue equally among all of the major-league clubs.

From that modest first agreement, which awarded each club $300,000, the pot of gold the visionary Fetzer arranged has grown to tens of millions of dollars per team, per year.

On August 9, 1964, the Tigers held the first of their many annual "Bat Day" giveaways to boost attendance and promote the game at the sandlot level. The popular practice was discontinued a decade later because management feared the fans' rhythmic pounding of bats might damage the aging structure of Tiger Stadium.

In 1965, Tiger manager Chuck Dressen suffered a heart attack in spring training. Dressen returned after three months, but on May 16, 1966, he suffered a second heart attack and died on August 10. Dressen's replacement, former coach Bob Swift, who had been the Tiger catcher the day Bill Veeck sent Eddie Gaedel up to bat, was diagnosed with lung cancer and replaced by Frank Skaff midway through the 1966 season. Swift died on October 17. Somehow, despite tragically losing two managers, the 1966 Tigers managed to finish third.

Meanwhile, Jim Campbell, the former director of the Tigers' farm system, had set about rebuilding the ball club.

One by one, Mickey Lolich, Bill Freehan, Willie Horton, Dick McAuliffe, Gates Brown, Mickey Stanley,

Jim Northrup, Pat Dobson, Ray Oyler and John Hiller—the nucleus of the 1968 world championship team—began arriving at the corner of Michigan and Trumbull.

It soon became obvious that they were a special group of guys.

"I keep looking back at all the jerks we had on that team," said Hiller. "I don't mean that meanly—I mean it affectionately. I just can't imagine another mix of personalities like we had. We had more characters on that team than has ever been assembled on any one team anywhere. You forget about the games. You forget about the bobbles and the good plays and the good hits. What you remember are the pranks and the good times."

Like the time Gates Brown suddenly heard his sizeable stomach growling in the middle of a game. No problem, said Northrup, ever the instigator. "I leaned out of the dugout and asked a fan to go buy us a hot dog," Northrup recalled. "I traded him a baseball for it. We did that all the time. Mayo [Smith] never did figure it out."

However, before Brown could take his first bite of his hot dog, the Tiger manager hollered for him to pinch hit.

"I offered to hold the hot dog for him," said Northrup, "but you know Gates. Once he's got his hands on something to eat, he's not going to let go."

Instead, Brown tucked his hot dog, mustard and all, inside his shirt, and headed for home plate. Of course, he got a hit. He was, after all, the Tigers' top pinch hitter. But Gates was forced to do a head-first slide into second base, hot dog and all.

"When Gates stood up," Northrup recalled, "he had a big splotch of mustard, about six inches across, on the front of his uniform. Mayo went ballistic."

The fun-loving 1968 Tigers were an unusually close-knit group.

"We were like family," Northrup said. "We barbecued together with our wives and kids. We partied together. When we had problems, we talked to each other.

"Hell, we even loaned each other money when things got tight—although we'd run the other way when McLain came along. He was constantly looking for a few bucks. He always said he needed the money to buy a little something for his wife. But it wasn't a loan with Denny. It was more like a gift."

The average major-league baseball player was paid $22,000 in 1968. The average Tiger earned less than

Pitcher John Hiller came back from a heart attack at age 27 to become the best relief pitcher in baseball. Brace Photo

that. The payroll of the entire 1968 world championship Tiger team was $980,000. Today, the average major-league player makes more than $2 million per year. Al Kaline, the future Hall of Famer, was the top-paid Tiger at $93,000, far less than the major-league minimum today.

"We had a lot of guys like me who were barely making the minimum," John Hiller recalled.

In 1967, Hiller made the major-league minimum salary: Six thousand dollars. That winter, the Tigers sent him a contract for $12,000. "Of course, I signed it right away," Hiller recalled. "I couldn't believe they were doubling my pay. Later that winter, I read in the paper that the major-league minimum had been raised to $10,000. So I actually only got a $2,000 raise."

"We knew the owners were making money—we just didn't know how much," said Northrup. "And we had no way of finding out. Jim Campbell would always say, 'Do you want to play baseball or not? If you don't like what I'm paying you, go out and get a job.'"

"In 1968, I was making $30,000," recalled Mickey Lolich. After the Tigers came from behind to upset Bob Gibson and the St. Louis Cardinals in the World Series, thanks in no small part to Lolich's three heroic Series victories, Mickey was offered a $10,000 raise.

"I jumped all the way up to $40,000," he said, smiling. "But I took it. It was better than digging ditches."

One member of that 1968 team later got even. In 1973, the Michigan Bureau of Workmen's Compensation ruled in favor of left-handed pitcher Les Cain's claim that Tiger manager Billy Martin had curtailed Cain's career by forcing him to pitch with a sore arm.

The Tigers were ordered to pay Cain $111 per week for the rest of his life. The two sides later agreed on a lump-sum settlement.

Earl Wilson was the first Tiger player to hire an agent, Boston-based Bob Woolf, to help him negotiate his contract. But Tigers GM Jim Campbell wouldn't allow the highly respected Woolf to set foot in his office, much less talk to him. So Wilson would negotiate with Campbell for a while, then excuse himself under the guise of visiting the restroom and dash to the nearest telephone to call Woolf back in Boston to confer. How times have changed.

The '68 Tigers thrived in an age before playoffs and interleague play, before free agency and salary arbitration, before seven-figure contracts became commonplace. Unlike today's teams, which are often products of free agency, most of the '68 Tigers were developed in the Detroit farm system. Only two front-line performers, Norm Cash and Wilson, had ever worn another uniform prior to 1968.

There were many times earlier in his career when Al Kaline secretly wished he could play with a better ball club. "In the back of my mind, I would wonder, 'Man, am I ever going to get a chance to play in the World Series?'" he admitted. "Yeah, there were second thoughts. I'd think, 'Man, if I could only play for the Yankees.'"

In fact, in the late 1950s, Mickey Mantle and Whitey Ford told Kaline the Yankees had offered the Tigers' first baseman Moose Skowron and a couple of minor leaguers in exchange for Al. And Tiger management supposedly was interested. Then Skowron broke his wrist and the trade talks stopped.

In 1968, Kaline finally reached the World Series for the first and only time in his career.

"Quite frankly it put a lot of pressure on me," Kaline admitted. "It took me so long to get to the World Series. With the big buildup the media gave it—'Kaline Finally Gets to World Series'—I kept thinking, 'Man, what if I screw up? What if I have a bad World Series?' Fortunately, it turned out the other way."

In fact, Kaline batted .379 with two homers and eight RBIs as the Tigers won their first World Series in 23 years.

"It was a joy and a delight just to play on that team," he said.

For winning the 1968 Series, the Tigers each received an extra $8,300 after taxes. "The paper boy cashed my Series check for me," joked Northrup, who made a total of $418,000 in 16 years of playing baseball. "A rookie today will make more money in two years than I made in my entire career, counting major leagues, minor leagues and bonuses."

But the 1968 Tigers didn't play solely for money.

"We all grew up together," said Lolich. "We were all friends. We knew each other's wives. We knew each other's families. It was great just to be around those guys. We always stuck together. On the road, when the games were over, we had our spots in every town. You always knew where to find us. And we always knew where to find one another. Nobody ever felt bad about a mistake they made in a game. Because we talked it out among ourselves. We were real close. Then all of a sudden we were there, in the World Series. And we won."

Mayo Smith, a career minor-league player and big-league scout, was from baseball's old school. He was a laissez faire manager who believed in leaving his players alone to do their jobs as much as possible. But the party-loving '68 Tigers, led by the likes of Denny McLain and Pat Dobson, frequently pushed the envelope and tried their manager's patience.

At the height of the torrid 1967 pennant race, which the Tigers lost on the final day of the season, McLain was suddenly sidelined with a mysterious foot injury, which was later linked to his involvement with gamblers.

One night, in the heat of the '68 pennant race, aware that many of the Tigers liked to sample life on the road in the wee hours of the morning, Smith pulled a surprise bed check to make certain his talented team was all tucked in. Somehow, Mayo, who enjoyed a nightcap or two himself, forgot to call pitcher Fred Lasher's room.

When Lasher learned he had been overlooked, he became angry and confronted the Tiger manager in the clubhouse the next day. "What about me?" the reliever demanded. "I'm a part of this team, too, you know."

Each of the '68 Tigers had a nickname—most of which were awarded by pitcher Pat Dobson, who was himself known as "Cobra."

Norm Cash was "Beagle." Dick McAuliffe was "Mad Dog." Earl Wilson was "Duke." Mickey Stanley was "Squirrely." Don Wert was "Coyote." Jim Price was "Big Guy." Joe Sparma was "Square Deal." Wayne Comer was "Bush Hog." Darryl Patterson was "Chief." Tom Matchick was "Pizza." Ray Oyler was "Oil Can." John Hiller was "Ratso." Willie Horton was "Boomer." Denny McLain was "Dolphin." Bill Freehan was "Big Ten." Jim Northrup was "Fox." Mickey Lolich was "Condor." Gates Brown was, of course, "Gator." Al Kaline was, simply, "Line."

To this day, those nicknames have stuck. The '68 Tigers were that close.

"A bunch of us were sitting around, playing poker on the bed in somebody's room one night, like we did a lot of nights, when Jim Northrup caught Denny McLain cheating," recalled Hiller, the Tiger pitcher who later shook off a heart attack to become one of the most effective relievers in club history. "Northrup jumped across the bed and grabbed Denny by the throat and was yelling 'I'm going to kill you, you bastard! I'm going to kill you!'

"Gates Brown grabbed Northrup from behind and said, 'You're not going to touch him until after we win the pennant. Then he's all yours.'"

❧

In the wake of the 1968 World Series, while Denny McLain was wowing Las Vegas audiences with his organ recitals and his outrageous, off-the-cuff comments, Jim Northrup was back home in Michigan, concocting a scheme of his own. He was going to make himself and his Tiger teammates some extra money, too.

Northrup's plan: He and his playmates would pose in the nude. The world champions would become calendar pinups.

Remember, this was 1968. The Tigers were incredibly popular, but the country was still relatively prudish.

"Burt Reynolds had posed naked for MS Magazine or something and I said, 'Hell, I'll get 11 other

"He's the original flim-flam man. Any day I expect him to come riding on a Conestoga wagon selling elixir out the back end as he's leaving town. Probably being run out of town. But that's Denny," says former teammate Jim Northrup. One of McLain's endeavors was an organ-playing lounge act, which resulted in a record release. Photos by Mark Cunningham, Creative Impressions Inc.

ballplayers to do the same thing and we'll sell more calendars than they can make,'" Northrup recalled.

"But I could only come up with nine guys. We were three short. A lot of other guys wanted to do it, but they knew they would have real problems with their wives at home. We weren't going to show anything. You know, you pose with your hand or your arm in a certain place. But back in those days, that just wasn't done. Today, everybody would say, 'Ho-hum.' But can you imagine the commotion we would have caused back then?"

Not that the Tigers' Denny McLain ever needed any help causing a commotion. He thrived on attention and controversy. When none existed, he would create some. With McLain around, life was never dull.

Early in the '68 season, McLain accused Tiger fans of being "the biggest front-runners in the world."

When those same fans roared their approval after his 30th win, Denny declared they were "the best fans in the world."

That was Denny being Denny.

After the Minnesota Twins belted two of his trademark high fastballs for home runs, McLain blasted venerable Tiger Stadium, claiming the ballpark was so small "the owners could take it and throw it in the Atlantic Ocean."

"I hate this park," he announced. "I hate it, I hate it, I hate it."

And the quote-conscious press ate it all up. When the Tigers caught fire midway through the 1968 season, McLain credited the fact that Detroit's two daily newspapers were on strike.

He dyed his hair red and blamed the color change on "Mother Nature." He "revealed" he had been pitching with a torn shoulder muscle. At the time McLain's record was 25-4. After he had made headlines with those outrageous comments, Denny quickly retracted both statements without blinking.

"I consider myself the best pitcher in the league on nights when I go out to pitch," declared the cocky, controversial right-hander, who was married to Hall of Famer Lou Boudreau's daughter.

"You accept what he is, and work with that," Tiger manager Mayo Smith explained with a shrug.

Until McLain, plucked from the Chicago White Sox farm system for a paltry $8,000, burst onto the scene, no pitcher in either league had reached the magical 30-victory mark since Dizzy Dean won 30 and lost seven for the 1934 St. Louis Cardinals. No American League pitcher had reached that lofty plateau since Lefty Grove in 1931.

The fact that both Grove and Dean had each achieved four of their victories in relief, while McLain was strictly a starter, made Denny's 31-6 effort, which included six shutouts, 280 strikeouts, and 28 complete games, all the more amazing.

Even more remarkable is the fact that the Tigers had tried to trade McLain to the Baltimore Orioles for Hall of Fame shortstop Luis Aparicio after the gut-wrenching 1967 season. Fortunately, the Orioles declined the offer.

In 1968, McLain was sitting on top of the baseball world. He played the organ, appeared on the popular *Ed Sullivan Show*, socialized with singer Glen Campbell and the Smothers Brothers, flew airplanes around the country, cut a couple of records, formed his own paint company, and drank a case of Pepsi-Cola every day. Of course, he was given the organs and airplanes and the Pepsi for free.

"Money impresses me," McLain declared. "I'm a mercenary. I want to be a billionaire."

When the 1968 World Series celebration was over, McLain, still basking in the limelight of his Most Valuable Player/Cy Young Award season, flew to Las Vegas, where he played the organ and sang before packed audiences at the Riviera Hotel and Casino.

There, Denny continued to put his foot in his mouth.

On stage the first night in Las Vegas, McLain informed his audience, "I wouldn't trade a dozen Mickey Loliches for one Bob Gibson."

The crowd, which had come to see and hear McLain, the controversial baseball player—not Denny, the organ-playing crooner—loved it. They assumed McLain was being intentionally outrageous once again.

When McLain realized he had misspoken—Lolich, after all, had accounted for three of the Tigers' Series victories—he went back on stage the following night, determined to retract his earlier words, as he had so often done with the sporting press.

Instead, he made the same ridiculous statement again.

Finally, on the third night, McLain got it straight. "I wouldn't trade a dozen Bob Gibsons for one Mickey Lolich," he said. "That's what I meant to say."

And for the third evening in a row, the audience roared.

But Denny McLain was no singer. "A Frank Sinatra, I'm not," he admitted. Obviously he wasn't much of a stand-up comedian, either.

Two years later, he would be suspended three times—first for his highly publicized involvement with Michigan bookmakers, then for dumping buckets of water over the heads of two unsuspecting sportswriters, and finally for carrying a gun.

But McLain's mystique remained. When Denny's off-the-field transgressions finally caught up with him in 1970, prompting commissioner Bowie Kuhn to suspend him for half the season for his association with gamblers dating back to 1967, Tiger manager Mayo Smith proudly pointed to the World Series ring on his finger and declared: "Denny McLain helped put that there."

When McLain returned from his first suspension on July 1, 1970, a crowd of 53,863—Tiger Stadium's largest in eight years—turned out to welcome the prodigal pitcher back. It was an incredible scene—McLain's last hurrah in Detroit.

At the conclusion of the 1970 season, the Tigers traded Denny to the Washington Senators in the blockbuster deal that brought shortstop Eddie Brinkman, third baseman Aurelio Rodriguez and pitcher Joe Coleman to Detroit.

In 1971, McLain led the AL in losses. By 1973, his career was over. Soon, he was promoting rock concerts, hustling golf games, and hosting TV and radio talk shows.

Since then, the legend of Denny McLain has been seriously sullied by bankruptcy, pension fraud and two tours in prison. His Florida home burned down. His first conviction, for racketeering, loan-sharking and extortion, was overturned in August of 1987, on a technicality. McLain is currently behind bars, serving time for looting the employees' pension firm of a meat packing company he owned. But for one fabulous season, in the sultry summer of 1968, brash, bespectacled 24-year-old Denny McLain was one of the very best pitchers baseball had ever seen.

John Hiller, the former chubby, fun-loving pitcher signed off the sandlots of Toronto, was the only Tiger player to bridge the gap from Mayo Smith to Sparky Anderson, with Billy Martin and Ralph Houk in between.

Not bad for a ballplayer whose career was once pronounced dead.

Hiller was relaxing at his home in Duluth, Minnesota, on January 11, 1971, sipping a beer, smoking a cigarette and thinking about spring training when he suddenly felt a stabbing pain in his chest. Hiller was so unconcerned that he finished his brew and lit another cigarette.

Then he felt the pain again, and again. The third jolt was much worse than the first two. That finally got Hiller's attention.

After phoning his doctor, Hiller went out into the cold northern Minnesota winter, hoisted his snowmobile off the back of his pick-up truck, and drove himself to the hospital. There, doctors told him he had suffered not one, not two, but three heart attacks. John Hiller was 27 years old, making $20,000 a year.

"I had no money," he later recalled. "All I knew how to do was play baseball."

So Hiller kept his heart attack secret. He had heard new Tiger manager Billy Martin say he was counting on John to be one of his starting pitchers that season, and Hiller was scared to death (no pun intended) of losing his job.

Finally, after undergoing a new medical procedure known as "intestinal bypass surgery," Hiller conjured up enough nerve to call Tiger general manager Jim Campbell on February 13—the day before he was scheduled to report to training camp.

Billy Martin and the Tigers immediately wrote Hiller out of their future pitching plans.

Hiller took a job selling appliances at a discount department store in Duluth. After a year, he called Campbell and begged for a chance to resume his baseball career. Reluctantly, Tiger management obliged. Hiller reported to Lakeland in the spring of 1972 as a minor-league pitching coach and batting practice pitcher. His new salary was $7,500 a year.

In an effort to make ends meet and support his growing family back home in Detroit, Hiller slept on the floor in the Tigers' minor-league locker room. He dined on ham and cheese sandwiches and kept a light on all night to frighten the roaches away. Sometimes he would walk to a nearby bar, order a draft beer, and nurse it until closing. "I was living like a bum," he later admitted.

Depressed, he gave up, went back to Duluth and asked if he could have his old job selling refrigerators back.

Then on July 6, 1972, Jim Campbell called. This time it was Hiller's turn to be surprised. "Get down to Chicago," the Tiger GM ordered. "We want to see if you can still throw." The Tigers were desperately in need of relief pitchers.

Fiery Billy Martin played for the Tigers in 1958 before returning as a manager in 1971. Under Martin, the Tigers never finished lower than third. Burton Historical Society

Two days later, Hiller was back on the mound, in a big-league uniform. "Hiller's back from the dead," Billy Martin announced with typical bluntness.

A year later, Hiller saved 38 games—a major-league record at the time.

In 1958, an aging Billy Martin had played second base for the Tigers. In 1971, he returned to manage the team, which had grown complacent under Mayo Smith after winning the 1968 World Series. With Brash Billy calling the shots, the fading Tiger heroes of '68—bolstered by the addition of veterans Frank Howard, Tony Taylor, and Woodie Fryman—clawed their way to the AL East title in 1972. Because the season had been shortened by a brief players' strike in the spring, the Tigers won half the pennant by a scant half-game.

But the Tigers were ousted by the Oakland A's in the 1972 playoff, which was marred by a bench-clearing brawl after Detroit pitcher Lerrin LaGrow, acting on orders from Martin, intentionally hit Oakland speedster Bert Campaneris with a pitch. Campaneris responded by flinging his bat at LaGrow.

The Tigers had hired the fiery Martin against the advice of his previous employers, the Minnesota Twins, because they liked the way he handled the men. Late in the 1973 season, they fired him because Tiger owner John Fetzer and GM Jim Campbell didn't like the way Martin handled himself.

By then, Martin was drinking heavily. He actually quit the team for a day in a snit during spring training. He skipped team flights and sometimes showed up late to the ballpark on the road. He criticized the front office and fought with one of his players in a nightclub parking lot during spring training. Finally, Fetzer and Campbell got fed up. Billy had to go. However, he wasn't the only one.

Al Kaline and Norm Cash retired in 1974. Jim Northrup and Dick McAuliffe were traded away. A year later, Mickey Lolich and Gates Brown were gone. In 1977, Willie Horton was shipped to Texas.

Northrup later recalled how, as a member of the Baltimore Orioles near the end of the 1975 season after the Tigers had traded him, he arrived at Tiger Stadium several hours early one afternoon to say goodbye. "I sat in the dugout, I walked all the way around the field on the warning track, and when I walked out of the ballpark that night, that was it," said Northrup, one of the heroes of the 1968 Series. "From that point on, Tiger Stadium was history for me."

Sadly, the era was over.

"I think about 1968 all the time," Kaline admitted. "I think about the tremendous amount of fun I had. The more you talk about it, the more things you remember. What I remember is a great bunch of guys who put a tremendous amount of effort into winning. You know, I only played on two winning teams in all my years in Detroit."

AL KALINE

Right Field
Bats: Right ◆ Throws: Right
6'2" ◆ 180 lbs.
Played with Tigers: 1953-74
Born: 12/19/34

As a youngster Al Kaline was an unlikely baseball hero. He was diagnosed with a bone disease known as osteomyelitis, and when he was eight years old, doctors removed two inches of bone from Kaline's left foot, leaving a permanent deformity.

Kaline was plagued by pain in his foot throughout his career. "It's like a toothache in the foot," he once explained.

But few people ever knew. Al never used that as an excuse. He never complained.

Instead, he patrolled right field so flawlessly that some of the seats in foul territory down the right field line were removed to accommodate him and that section of Briggs and later Tiger Stadium became known as "Kaline's Corner."

At the plate, he collected 3,007 hits, belted a team-record 399 homers and earned 10 Gold Gloves. He was only the 10th player ever ushered into the Hall of Fame in his first year on the ballot.

Kaline's 22-year career, spent entirely with the Tigers, was a model of consistency and excellence.

But when he reported to the ballpark in Philadelphia straight out of high school for his first night in the big leagues in 1953, the Tigers didn't even have a uniform small enough to fit him. Shy, skinny 18-year-old Al Kaline, the frightened kid with the slightly deformed left foot, spent the first night of his Hall of Fame career wearing the batboy's uniform.

Days later, when the Tigers returned home, the guard on duty at Briggs Stadium wouldn't let Kaline through the gate.

"He said, 'Where do you think you're going, kid?'" Kaline recalled.

"I said, 'I'm a new player.'

"The guard said, 'Yeah, sure.' Something to that effect. I was real skinny, 150 pounds. I'm sure I looked just like a lot of kids off the street."

"I finally convinced him I was a new kid," Kaline said. "It was a beautiful late June afternoon and to see that ball field for the first time, with the green grass and the green seats, it was just outstanding."

Kaline was born in a working-class section of Baltimore. The Kaline family was poor, but proud. Al's father, Nicholas, worked in a broom factory and his mother, Naomi, scrubbed floors to make ends meet.

Down the street from the Kalines' brick row house was a vacant lot. There, workers from a nearby gas and electric company would gather at lunchtime to play softball. When their abbreviated game was over, young Al Kaline, not yet old enough to be enrolled in school, would race full speed around the dusty base paths, sliding with reckless abandon into make-believe bases.

By the time he was six, Kaline was shagging fly balls for the workers and warming up pitchers before their lunchtime interlude.

Al's dad and two uncles had played semipro baseball on Maryland's Eastern Shore, a baseball hotbed. Because the elder Kaline had himself been a catcher, he first taught young Al to be a pitcher when he was seven years old. But Al was always happiest when he had a bat in his hands—even if was only one of his father's broomsticks.

By the time Kaline was 10, the grown men from the gas and electric company let him join in their games.

At first, it was Al's arm that attracted the loudest raves. At age 11, Kaline set an elementary school record by flinging a softball 173 feet, six inches at a school picnic. No one could recall ever seeing a skinny little 11-year-old throw a ball that far. In a hardball league of 10- to 12-year-olds, Al won 10 and lost none and hit .800 as his neighborhood team went undefeated.

In high school, Kaline was at first dismissed as a five-foot-seven, 115-pound string bean—until people saw him play. When Kaline showed up at a Brooklyn Dodgers tryout camp as a high school freshman, the scouts took one look at the frail youngster and sent him home.

That winter, Kaline ate and exercised. By the time he began his sophomore season in high school, he stood 5'11" and weighed 135 pounds. No one ever told Al Kaline he was too little to play baseball again.

But by then his high school coach had decided Kaline was too small to succeed as a pitcher and too fragile to play second base, and moved him to the outfield. In his four years in high school, Al batted .333, .418, .469, and .488 and was named to the All-Maryland team each season. No other player had done that since the New York Yankees' Charlie Keller.

During the summer months, Kaline played on as many different teams in as many different leagues as he could. Sometimes that meant he played two or three games, on different fields in different parts of Baltimore, on the same day. His father and uncles would shuttle him from game to game, while young Al changed uniforms in the back seat.

"I suffered a lot as a kid playing in all those games," Kaline later admitted. "You know how Baltimore is real hot in the summer? When everybody was going on their vacations, going swimming with all the other kids, here I was on Sundays, playing doubleheaders.

"All because I knew I wanted to be a ballplayer. And my dad always told me, 'You're gonna have to work hard and you're gonna have to suffer if you're gonna be a ballplayer. You're gonna have to play and play all the time.'

"There were a couple times when I told my dad I wasn't gonna play on Sunday. I was going to go down to the beach with my girl or with a bunch of the guys to go swimming. And my dad said, 'Now look, like I told you in the beginning when you agreed to play for these people, they're gonna be counting on you. So if you're not gonna play, tell 'em to tear your contract up.' So I would go play. It was these things he did to me that showed me the right way and pushed me the right way."

By the time Kaline signed with the Tigers for $35,000 straight out of high school in 1953, he had actually played more baseball than many minor leaguers.

In American Legion ball, Kaline developed so quickly, flawlessly playing center field and sometimes

second base while hitting .418, that he was picked to play in an All-Star game in New York.

Away from home for the first time, Kaline belted a home run into the upper deck in left field at the Polo Grounds and collected a couple of singles. He was voted the game's Most Valuable Player.

The next day Kaline witnessed his first big-league game, featuring the New York Yankees against the St. Louis Browns. Kaline could not take his eyes off another young phenom, a Yankee outfielder named Mickey Mantle.

By now, the big-league scouts all knew Al Kaline. The Philadelphia Phillies and St. Louis Cardinals were particularly interested. The Dodgers had also realized their earlier mistake and climbed on the bandwagon. But Ed Katalinas, a scout for the Detroit Tigers, seemed to have the inside track.

As Kaline's high school graduation drew nearer and his remarkable development as a ballplayer continued, Al grew anxious to sign with the Tigers. His mother needed eye surgery and he wanted to pay off the mortgage on the family home.

However, the Tigers also had their eye on another big bonus-baby pitcher from Pennsylvania named Tom Qualters. And Tigers' farm director John McHale informed Katalinas the club couldn't afford both.

Fortunately for the Tigers, Qualters signed with the Philadelphia Phillies a few days before Kaline was scheduled to graduate. Forced by the bonus rule to spend the 1953 season in the major leagues, Qualters spent the entire year on the Phillies' bench, never once getting into a ballgame even in a mop-up role. In 34 appearances over three years, Qualters never won or lost a big-league game.

Meanwhile, knowing a number of other teams were also preparing to make offers to Kaline, Katalinas asked the elder Kaline if he could speak to Al at one minute past midnight on June 17, 1953.

"That won't be necessary, Ed," Nicholas Kaline replied. "Around 10 in the morning will be okay."

Young Al was waiting alone in the living room when a nervous Katalinas arrived the next morning. He made the Tigers' offer: $35,000, including a $15,000 bonus. Katalinas had McHale waiting near a phone back in Detroit, just in case the Tigers had to go a little higher.

"Let me talk to my parents," Al said.

Minutes later, he returned to the living room. "When do I have to report?" he asked.

At the age of 20, Al Kaline became the youngest-ever batting champion. Brace Photo

Kaline, who nearly two decades later would turn down the Tigers' offer of a $100,000 contract because he didn't believe he had earned it, handed his entire bonus check over to his mom and dad.

That paid off the mortgage on their modest home and paid for an operation to save his mother's failing eyesight. Kaline felt he owed his parents. They had always encouraged him to play as much baseball as possible, often as many as three games a day during the summer months. As a youngster, Kaline never had a part-time job or a paper route. He played baseball.

Because of baseball's bonus rules in those days, the Tigers couldn't send Kaline to the minor leagues, where he admittedly might have benefited from a year or two of seasoning. Under the rules, he had to report immediately to the big-league team. He never did spend a day in the minors.

In the top half of the eighth inning of Kaline's second night in the big leagues, Tiger manager Fred Hutchinson turned to the nervous young man sitting beside him on the bench and said:

"Play right field when Philadelphia bats."

Kaline, a pitcher, second baseman and center fielder in amateur ball, had never played right field before in his life. When Kaline stepped up to the plate for his first big-league at-bat, he flied out to center field on the first pitch.

When the Tigers returned home from their road top, young Al got his first glimpse of the storied gray ballpark at the intersection of Michigan and Trumbull that would be his home away from home, in one capacity or another, for the next half century.

"It was 3 or 4 o'clock in the morning and we were coming on the team bus down Michigan Avenue from the old train station," Kaline recalled. "I was sitting next to Johnny Pesky and he leaned over to me and said, 'Look out the left window. That's going to be your home for the next two or three years.' It was dark, but I peeked out. I thought [Briggs Stadium] looked like a great big battleship."

Some in the Tigers organization wondered if Kaline would ever hit with enough power and enough consistency to justify his presence in the outfield. But Katalinas remained convinced. "To me, he was the prospect a scout creates in his mind and then prays that someone like that comes along," Katalinas said.

Kaline never doubted his own ability, either.

"The only reason I signed with Detroit was because I wanted to play right away," he later explained.

"I didn't want to go someplace and sit on the bench and not play. That was my one fear. Quite honestly, [Philadelphia and Boston] offered me more money than Detroit.

"But I knew if I played a lot and played well, I'd make a pretty good salary. Besides I wasn't worried about money at that time. I just wanted to play baseball.

"Before I signed with Detroit I asked Ed Katalinas, 'Who is the Tigers' best minor-league outfielder?'" Kaline recalled. "He said, 'It's a guy named Bill Tuttle.'

"I asked, 'What did he hit last year?'

"Katalinas said, 'He hit about .280 at Buffalo.'

"I was stupid enough to say to myself, 'Well, I can hit .280.'"

In 1955, Kaline did better than that. In his second full season in the big leagues, and his first as a regular, the 20-year-old Kaline batted .340 to win the American League batting crown by 21 points over Philadelphia's Vic Power. Thus Kaline became the youngest man ever to win that coveted title, dethroning Ty Cobb, the greatest Tiger of them all, by a single day.

Cobb won his first of 12 batting crowns when he was also 20. But Cobb's birth date was December 18. Kaline didn't turn 21 until December 19, 1955.

However, unlike Cobb, Kaline never led the league in hitting again.

For that reason he never received all of the credit he rightfully deserved. After his success in 1955, Tiger fans expected him to do it again and again. Frequently, the quiet, introverted Kaline became depressed.

"The worst thing that happened to me in the big leagues was the start I had," Kaline said a few years later. "Everybody said, 'This guy's another Ty Cobb, another Joe DiMaggio.'

"What they didn't know is I'm not that good a hitter. They kept saying I do everything with ease. But it isn't that way. I have to work as hard if not harder than anybody in the league. I'm in spring training a week early every year. I've worked with a heavy bat in the winter, swinging it against a big bag. I've squeezed rubber balls all winter long to strengthen my hands. I've lifted weights. I've done push-ups. But my hitting is all a matter of timing,

"I don't have the kind of strength that Mantle or Mays have, where they can be fooled on a pitch and still get a good piece of the ball. I've got to have my timing down perfect or I'm finished. Now you take a hitter like me, with all the concentration and effort I have to put into it—I'm not crying about it, it's just a fact—and imagine how it feels to be compared to Cobb. He was the greatest ballplayer that ever lived. To say that I'm like him is the most foolish thing that anyone can make a comparison on."

Early in Al's career, the Boston Red Sox reportedly proposed trading an aging Ted Williams for Kaline. But the Tigers wisely turned the deal down. "There's a hitter," Williams himself once said of Kaline. "In my book, he's the greatest right-handed hitter in the league."

Kaline's heroics in the outfield soon became legendary. He once threw a runner out from the sitting position in right field.

At Yankee Stadium one day, the Tigers were leading by one run when the Yankees put two runners aboard after two were out in the bottom of the ninth. Suddenly Mickey Mantle blasted a drive to right field. In the broadcast booth, New York announcer Mel Allen exclaimed, "The Yankees win!"

In the still-vacant visitors' locker room, the attendant flipped off the radio and prepared for the disappointed Tigers to come moping in with their heads down. Instead, moments later, they burst through the door, laughing and yelling and slapping one another on the back.

Kaline had raced to the outfield wall, placed his bare hand on the auxiliary scoreboard to support himself, and leaped high into the air. Somehow he caught Mantle's would-be home run backhanded before it could disappear into the seats.

Kaline lost the equivalent of one full year to injuries: There was a twisted knee in 1954, a broken cheekbone in '59, a broken collarbone in '62, a busted finger in '67 and a broken arm in '68.

"I had major injuries," Kaline said. "I didn't have any little injuries. I didn't pull any muscles or things like that. Usually when I got hurt, it was a broken bone. When I got hurt it was worth four, five, six weeks at a time."

The fractured collarbone in 1962 was the worst. "That was a devastating year for me even though I ended up having a good year," he recalled. "It probably would have been my best year ever. I was leading the league in everything."

As a young player Kaline always felt uncomfortable talking about himself to the press. But the writers all wanted to interview the young batting king. When Kaline didn't respond, they labeled him arrogant and stuck-up.

Meanwhile, the Tiger front office also was urging the talented young outfielder to be more outgoing. Uncomfortable during the early years of his career almost anywhere but on a baseball field, uncommunicative and often monosyllabic in his conversations with management and the media, Kaline was urged by Tiger officials to become something he was not.

"They wanted me to be more of a flashy type player," Kaline recalled. "They'd call me in and say, 'You've got to be a drawing card.' That kind of startled me because I thought just putting up numbers for the team was enough.

"But they wanted me to do a lot of stuff like sliding on my face, diving after balls, and cutting up. But that just wasn't my nature. I wasn't a yelling-type guy. I'd get mad at myself, but I wouldn't get on my teammates. That just wasn't the way I was.

"They told me to be more colorful, that I could bring more people into the ballpark if I was more colorful. But how could I do that? I could jump up and down on the field and make an ass out of myself arguing with umpires, but I'm not made that way. I could make the easy catches look hard but I'm not that way either."

Instead, Kaline continued to do everything quietly, with style and dignity and class.

As he began his 50th season with the ball club in 2002 as a special assistant and advisor to new Tiger president Dave Dombrowski, Kaline looked back at his career and with typical modesty declared: "I should have been a better player than I was.

"I had a lot of tools," admitted the man who hit more home runs (399) and played in more games (2,834) than any Tiger who ever lived. "I could do a lot of things. I think losing with bad teams, year in and year out, knowing every year going into September that we had no chance to win, finishing down near the bottom every year, beat me down.

"If you look at my record, when I played in the All-Star Games I did really well. When I played in the World Series, I did really well. If I was challenged I usually did pretty well.

"Maybe it was my fault," Kaline said with typical humility. "Maybe if I had elevated my game, we would have been a little bit better."

Alan Trammell (left) and Lou Whitaker were teammates for 19 years, making them the longest-running keystone tandem in baseball history.

5

SPARKY, TRAM & SWEET LOU

The Sparky Anderson Era, 1976-1992

In the wake of the Tigers' dramatic, emotional World Series triumph in 1968, the team again lapsed into another lengthy funk, just as it did after the 1907-08-09 pennant surge and again after the world championship of 1945.

For some reason, the Tigers have never seemed to be able to sustain prolonged prosperity.

Only the refreshing antics of curly-mopped young Mark "The Bird" Fidrych, whose presence on the mound coincided with nearly 60 percent of the Tigers' home attendance in 1976, and the arrival of home-grown speedster and ex-convict Ron LeFlore interrupted the monotonous years of losing as the Tigers were once again forced to rebuild.

However, by 1984, when Michigan pizza baron Tom Monaghan purchased the Tigers from John Fetzer for $53 million, the pieces of another championship team—namely Alan Trammell, Lou Whitaker, Lance Parrish, Kirk Gibson and Jack Morris—were neatly in place.

Even before the dramatic 1984 season began, Sparky Anderson, the Tigers' white-haired, pipe-smoking future Hall of Fame manager, boldly predicted, "The '84 Tigers will be the best team Detroit has ever seen."

After the Tigers got off to an incredible 35-5 start, few dared to disagree. The Tigers led the American League East from wire to wire in 1984 and drew a franchise record 2,704,794 fans.

After one late-season game, several of the Tigers were watching the 11 o'clock news on the clubhouse television when the announcer reverently referred to the 1968 Tigers and their previous success.

"The hell with the '68 Tigers!" one of the half-dressed players shouted. "We're the '84 Tigers!"

Around the cramped clubhouse, his teammates, brimming with newfound confidence, whooped and hollered in agreement.

But the party was just beginning.

In the middle of one chaotic 1984 clubhouse celebration, Kirk Gibson and Lance Parrish accidentally sliced open Sparky Anderson's head when they tried to douse their little manager with bottles of champagne. Suddenly, the bubbly and the blood were streaming together down the manager's well-weathered face.

"I've been very lucky in my life, I've been involved with a lot of baseball celebrations," Anderson said after things had calmed down in the clubhouse. "But I can honestly say that none of them ever matched anything like this."

Gibson dumped a cooler filled with partially melted ice and water over the head of millionaire owner Tom Monaghan. Pitchers Jack Morris and Dave Rozema did an abbreviated strip tease. All that the Tigers had done up until that point was win the AL East title—there were two more big battles yet to come.

However, there simply was no stopping the '84 Tigers as they easily rolled over Kansas City in the AL playoffs and then over San Diego in the World Series.

"I want the world to see how good this team can be," Sparky Anderson said, on the eve of the Series opener in San Diego. In the fifth and final game of the '84 World Series, the world saw precisely that.

With the Tigers leading the Padres, 5-4, Kirk Gibson, today the Tigers' bench coach, stepped up to the plate in the bottom of the eighth inning to face San Diego's relief ace Goose Gossage. In the Tigers' dugout, Anderson, who had scuffled with the physically imposing Gibson years earlier when he felt the young slugger wasn't living up to his potential, now held up the four fingers. Anderson felt certain the Padres would intentionally walk the highly competitive Gibson to load the bases. It was the logical strategy, the safe move, and the smart thing to do.

From the on-deck circle, Gibson, his eyes wide, glared back at his manager.

"I opened and closed my hand twice," Gibson later recalled with a grin. "Five and five."

Gibson wanted to bet his manager 10 bucks that Gossage would pitch to him. It was a wager Sparky would gladly lose.

In the San Diego dugout, Padres manager Dick Williams also held up four fingers, a signal that he wanted Gossage to walk Gibson. Williams and Anderson were on the same wavelength. But out on the mound, Gossage had other ideas. Gibson had already belted one home run in the game. Now with Tiger runners on second and third and the Padres trailing in the Series, three games to one, Williams hurried out to the mound.   Gossage was full of himself. He had enjoyed considerable success against Gibson over the years and was convinced he could handle the Tigers' slugger once again.

Williams was well known as a manager who was sometimes willing to play a hunch. Gossage quickly talked his manager into letting him pitch to Gibson.

"He don't want to walk you!" Anderson shouted from the dugout when he realized what was happening. Sparky was challenging Gibson to rise to the occasion.

On the second pitch, Gossage threw Gibson a slider. "The ball was up, but it was yelling, 'Hit me!'" Gibson later explained.

The rest is well-documented baseball history. Not to be outdone by close friend and teammate and eventual World Series MVP Alan Trammell, who had belted a pair of homers to account for all of the victorious Tigers' runs in Game 4, Gibson blasted a three-run homer into the upper deck in right field that buried the Padres and guaranteed the Tigers their first world championship since 1968.

Pandemonium prevailed. As 51,901 fans roared their approval, Gibson circled the bases, pumping his fist in the air. At the plate, he slammed Lance Parrish's outstretched hand with an emphatic high five. As Gibson neared the Tiger dugout, he jumped into the air with his fists clenched and both arms raised above his head, and screamed triumphantly. It was a classic picture that quickly came to represent both Gibson and the '84 Tigers.

It was one of the grandest moments in Detroit baseball history.

"I go blind," said Willie Hernandez, the Tigers' relief ace who won both the American League's Most Valuable Player and Cy Young Awards in 1984, after he had secured the final out in the top of the ninth. "My heart pumps so fast, I think I'm having a heart attack. My dream comes true and I went blind."

"Don't forget this moment," Sparky told his jubilant players when they finally reached the champagne-soaked locker room. "You did it all.

"The World Series," Sparky observed, "is Christmas and prom night and wedding day and New Year's Eve, all wrapped into one."

Unfortunately, outside the triumphant Tigers' locker room, the rest of the victory celebration was not so glorious.

After the Tigers fled from the field, near-riots erupted both inside Tiger Stadium and on the streets surrounding the ballpark. Unlike the world championship celebrations that enveloped the city in 1935, '45, and '68, the crowd quickly turned ugly in 1984. Spectators flooded the field, ripping up the sod and tearing out signs and seats. Outside the stadium, fans who had gathered during the game to drink and follow the action on car radios and portable TVs threw bottles, set fires, overturned vehicles and burned a police car.

By the time peace was restored, one person was dead, 42 people had been arrested and 80 had been injured.

Just as Sparky had hoped, the eyes of the world were focused on Detroit that balmy October Sunday evening. But what they saw gave the Motor City a huge black eye.

☙

Eight years earlier, Detroit had also been the center of national attention, but for a far different, more wholesome reason.

For four fabulous months in the Bicentennial summer of 1976, flaky, free-spirited, frizzy-haired 21-year-old Mark Fidrych was the most famous baseball player in the land. His faded blue jeans, his tattered T-shirts, his frayed sneakers and his habit of talking to the baseball, telling it exactly where to go, soon became well known, coast to coast.

Mark Fidrych truly was a phenomenon—a once-in-a-lifetime happening. He was arguably baseball's most prominent shooting star ever.

"Babe Ruth didn't cause this much excitement in his brightest day," declared Paul Richards, the elderly manager of the Chicago White Sox, whose playing career began in 1932.

"Playing against him was one of the most exciting things in my life," said White Sox outfielder Ralph Garr. "And I was there when Hank Aaron hit his 715th home run."

But the most remarkable thing was that, through it all, Fidrych himself remained unspoiled and unfazed. "I'm just a human being that my mom and dad made," he said.

"If he tells himself he's human, he's lying to himself," insisted Gene Mauch, manager of the Minnesota Twins. "He's not human—he's The Bird."

Fidrych, who was the 232nd player chosen in the 1974 amateur draft, where he wasn't picked until the 10th round, had earned his nickname in the minor leagues where Jeff Hogan, one of the Tigers' instructors, thought Mark's awkward, arm-flapping gait reminded him of Big Bird on TV's "Sesame Street."

As his popularity grew, Fidrych, who wasn't even on the major-league roster when the Tigers went to spring training in 1976, was so innocent he often worried about the high cost of answering his growing avalanche of fan mail. "Ten letters a day times 13 cents a stamp is a lot of money," groaned the kid, who was packing Tiger Stadium every time he pitched, but only making the major-league minimum $16,500 salary at the time.

Legend has it that Fidrych was so overjoyed when he learned late in spring training that he had made the major-league team that he smuggled a young lady into deserted Marchant Stadium that evening and celebrated by making love on the pitcher's mound.

Pitching sensation Mark "The Bird" Fidrych drew unheard-of crowds during his brief career with the Tigers. Collection of Jim Hawkins Productions Inc.

On the road with his Tiger teammates, Fidrych would flit through airports in the wee hours of the morning, poking his finger into the coin return slots of the telephones that lined the concourse walls in the hope that some frazzled traveler had forgotten to reclaim his dime. It never occurred to Fidrych that some might consider such conduct unbecoming a big-league ballplayer. It seemed perfectly natural to him.

On the mound, Fidrych would drop down on one knee and smooth out the dirt on the hill with his left hand before the start of each inning. He sprinted to and from his position, and would dart over to shake the hand of an infielder who turned in a particularly fine play.

Whenever an enemy batter managed a hit off him, Fidrych would discard the guilty ball and ask the umpire for a new one. "It's in my mind that ball has a hit in it," Fidrych explained. "The umpire has gotta give me another one. If he doesn't, I won't pitch. I'll stop the game. I'll just stand there until he gives me a new ball.

Mark "The Bird" Fidrych played four short, but stunning years with the Tigers before arm injuries forced him to retire in 1980. Collection of Jim Hawkins Productions Inc.

"I want that ball to get back in the ball bag and goof around with the other balls. I want him to talk to the other balls. I want the other balls to beat the shit out of him. Maybe that'll smarten him up so when he comes out the next time, he'll pop up."

According to Fidrych, talking to the ball before every pitch was no big deal. "Haven't you ever talked to yourself walking down the street?" he would ask.

Off the field, Fidrych was hunted and haunted, home and away. Girls followed him onto the Tigers' team bus in quest of a kiss. Others lined up outside the locker room door in pursuit of who knows what.

Shortstop Tom Veryzer, Fidrych's roommate on road trips, revealed that The Bird received at least 20 phone calls a day, even though the pair kept their phone off the hook until after noon. Fans and reporters and camp followers often lined up outside Fidrych's hotel room while he slept, patiently waiting for baseball's newest phenomenon to wake up.

In Detroit, Fidrych didn't even bother to have a telephone installed in his sparsely furnished suburban apartment. Instead, he used a pay phone in a supermarket down the street.

"Whenever I want to talk to somebody, I put in a dime and call collect," he explained.

Each day at Tiger Stadium, the incoming mail contained dollar bills for The Bird, some cash coming from as far away as San Francisco and Portland, Maine. From coast to coast, baseball fans felt sorry for Fidrych, who was making Major League Baseball's minimum salary while winning the hearts of the nation.

In Hell, Michigan, fans passed the hat and collected $103 for the beloved Bird. A blank cashier's check arrived from Pennsylvania, made out to "Mark Fidrych" and signed by a bank official. All Fidrych had to do was fill in the amount—any amount—and cash it. That check, along with all of the others, was returned, uncashed, with a polite thank-you note.

"He gets more mail in three days than I got in my whole career," observed veteran Tiger pitcher John Hiller, who had the locker next to The Bird in 1976.

During one hectic week in late June and early July, at the height of the hysteria, when Fidrych filled Tiger Stadium twice and beat both the Yankees and the Orioles, five would-be agents knocked on his door offering to negotiate a new deal for him. Everyone worried about how much money Fidrych was making—everyone except The Bird. "If they tore up my contract and wrote a new one, it might go to my head," he explained in typical "Bird-ese."

Besides, pitching in the big leagues certainly beat pumping gas for two bucks an hour at Pierce's Sunoco back home in Northboro, Massachusetts, which was what Fidrych had done before he began playing professional baseball.

"I don't need a raise," Fidrych declared. "I'm playing baseball. That's what counts."

Although he was relegated to the bullpen for the first five weeks of the 1976 season and didn't make his first start until May 15, The Bird nevertheless won 19 games for the fifth-place Tigers—the most by any Tiger rookie in 68 years. He completed 24 of his 29 starts and his 2.34 earned run average was the lowest of any starting pitcher in the American League. Incredibly, more than 900,000 fans, home and away, paid to see him pitch.

For the games Fidrych started at Tiger Stadium, the average attendance was 33,649. For the rest of their home games, the Tigers averaged 13,893. The Tigers claimed sales at the concession stands actually dropped on the nights when Fidrych pitched because nobody wanted to leave their seats and risk missing one precious moment.

"The whole season was like one giant trip," Fidrych gushed. "I can't explain it any other way. It was all unbelievable. Like a big bubble blowing up and exploding all year long. It was weird. I even had reporters follow me into the bathroom to talk to me. They just sat down next to me."

A book was written about his brief career two months before he had completed his rookie season. A Hollywood producer talked about putting him in the movies. In the Michigan legislature a lawmaker suggested Fidrych should be named the state bird, officially replacing the robin. A young Detroit couple named their newborn son Mark Fidrych.

While the Tigers were playing in California late in the '76 season, Fidrych was invited to appear on Bill Cosby's television show.

"They gave me some lines to read, but I couldn't read 'em," Fidrych later admitted. "So they said, 'Go ahead, do it your way.'

"I'm no actor. I can't even read. I'm just a ballplayer. That's all I want to be."

Utterly unimpressed with himself, Fidrych turned down invitations to appear with Johnny Carson, Mary Tyler Moore and Dinah Shore. He also rejected ABC's *Good Morning, America.*

"They wanted me to get up at five o'clock in the morning to be on that show!" shrieked The Bird. "Can you believe that? Five o'clock in the morning!

"I met Elton John and the Beach Boys. That was a thrill for me. Out in L.A., I got to meet Cary Grant, Monty Hall, Don Rickles and Frank Sinatra. That's more for my folks. I mean, what am I supposed to say to Frank Sinatra, 'Hi there, old Blue Eyes?'"

Late in the season, the Tiger players' wives gave Fidrych his first haircut in two months and then auctioned off his curly locks for charity. The freshly shorn Bird was asked if he was familiar with the story of Samson and Delilah.

"Goliath, you mean?" responded Fidrych. "Samson and Goliath? No, I never heard about them."

Tiger slugger Willie Horton was one of the first to take the impressionable young Fidrych under his wing. During spring training, Horton regularly hosted barbecues for his big-league teammates in the Lake-

land, Florida, Holiday Inn parking lot. Fidrych, who had to live in the Tigers' minor-league dormitory because he wasn't yet on the big league roster, didn't have a car, so Willie would personally pick The Bird up and bring him to the cookouts.

"I could tell he was everyday people," Horton explained.

Their friendship carried over into the regular season. When the Tiger clubhouse attendant decided he could no longer afford to provide free soft drinks for the players, Horton and Fidrych went into business for themselves.

Horton bought a cooler and several cases of pop and the pair set up shop in one corner of the clubhouse. They called their enterprise "The B & B Pop Shop"—The Boomer and The Bird.

"The guys don't have to pay for the pop," Horton explained. "If they want to give a donation, they can."

When Horton went on the disabled list in June, he left Fidrych in charge. When Willie returned a couple of weeks later, he found his partner in a frenzy.

"They robbed us blind!" The Bird shrieked. "They wiped us out!"

While Fidrych was minding the store, the players had simply helped themselves to the soda.

Horton wrapped one of his muscular arms around the skinny farm kid from Massachusetts and both players doubled over in laughter.

Near the end of the 1976 season, the Tigers finally rewarded Fidrych for his remarkable rookie season with a three-year contract, calling for annual salaries of $55,000, $90,000 and $125,000 in 1977-79.

Fidrych's father, Paul, who was doubling as The Bird's agent, never hesitated. "Take the three-year deal," he told his son.

"I could have signed a one-year contract for a lot of money," The Bird admitted afterwards. "But what if I died out next year? All that money would die out, too.

"You've got to look ahead to when you're 45 or 60. I figured if I got a three-year contract, I'd know I had my pension."

Of course, Fidrych did "die out" the following season, tragically injuring his knee in spring training, and subsequently ruining his arm.

Fidrych was shagging fly balls in the outfield alongside Rusty Staub on the fateful evening late in the spring of '77 when the whole fairy tale came to a screeching halt.

"Rusty was lecturing me," Fidrych recalled. "He

Outfielder Ron LeFlore spent time in prison when he was not playing baseball. This is his mugshot from State Prison of Southern Michigan where he spent 38 months for armed robbery. Collection of Jim Hawkins Productions Inc.

was saying, 'Now, Mark, slow down. Take it easy. We've got a week of spring training left.'

"And I was going, 'Yeah, yeah, yeah, Rusty.' But I wasn't really listening. Everybody was talking about the sophomore jinx. The sophomore jinx? I used to laugh it off. After all, I went through my sophomore year in high school all right.

"Then somebody hit a fly ball out our way. I said, 'Rusty, you want it?'

"Rusty said, 'Naw, you can have it.'

"I can picture it in my mind right now. I can see myself running for the ball, jumping for the ball, and coming down hard on my leg. When I came back, I said to Rusty, 'I think I screwed my knee up.'"

Fidrych had torn the cartilage in his left knee. He needed surgery. When he returned to the mound on May 27, 1977, 44,207 fans showed up at Tiger Stadium for The Bird's belated season debut.

Although Fidrych won six of his first eight starts in 1977, on July 12 he again was forced to leave the field after just 15 pitches because of pain in his right

shoulder. The Bird had a torn rotator cuff. Some said he tried to come back and pitch too soon. Others suggested he had injured his arm in a barroom scuffle. The rumors swirled.

Whatever the reason, The Bird never soared again. He won just four more games in his all-too-brief big-league career.

In 1971, young convict Ron LeFlore watched baseball's All-Star Game on TV in the noisy mess hall of the foreboding maximum security Southern Michigan State Prison in Jackson, the largest walled prison in the world.

Along with some of the other inmates, LeFlore had asked the warden for special permission to remain out of his cell past the normal 9:30 p.m. curfew in order to watch the end of the All-Star Game, which was being played that year at Tiger Stadium—a 90-minute drive, but nevertheless a world away.

For the first time in his troubled life, LeFlore saw players such as Hank Aaron, Reggie Jackson and Roberto Clemente. Back in the neighborhood where LeFlore had grown up, most of the kids weren't baseball fans. Most, like LeFlore, had never even played the game. They were too busy getting into trouble and committing crimes.

Watching that 1971 All-Star Game on TV, LeFlore could not, in his wildest dreams, have imagined himself playing in baseball's gala midsummer exhibition just five years later.

LeFlore, who grew up on Detroit's crime-infested east side, had gotten involved in drugs and crime at an early age. He had been sent to a reform school. In 1970, when he was 21, LeFlore was sentenced to serve five to fifteen years in prison for a botched armed robbery. It was not LeFlore's first offense. It was just one of the few times he had gotten caught.

In prison LeFlore began playing baseball—not out of any great love for the game but rather because he noticed that the guys on the prison baseball team enjoyed certain perks that were not readily available to the other inmates. LeFlore envisioned baseball as one more way to beat the system.

Although LeFlore had never played organized baseball at any level, either in school or on the sandlots, he immediately batted .569 in his first season on the prison team. Behind bars, surrounded by hardened criminals who were starved for any sort of entertainment or diversion, LeFlore quickly became a celebrity.

On an off day during the 1973 season, Tigers' manager Billy Martin, along with a couple of players and coaches, made a goodwill visit to Jackson Prison at the behest of a friend. There, Martin was introduced to LeFlore.

As the two men chatted, surrounded by other inmates in the prison yard, Martin halfheartedly invited LeFlore to a tryout at Tiger Stadium when Ron was eventually released. The other inmates cheered, and Martin, assuming he would never hear from LeFlore again, immediately forgot all about the incident.

However, several weeks later, LeFlore, who would soon be eligible for parole, was given a weekend furlough. He immediately phoned Martin, requesting the tryout that he had been promised.

Much to the surprise of Martin and other members of the Tiger organization, LeFlore impressed everyone with his speed and his power during his informal Saturday morning workout.

For the first time in his troubled life, LeFlore had somebody respectable, somebody influential, on his side. The Tigers were almost as eager to see LeFlore released from prison as Ron was.

Manager Billy Martin (left), former Tiger Ron LeFlore (center) and actor LaVar Burton pause during the 1978 filming of the TV movie One in a Million *about LeFlore's life.* Collection of Jim Hawkins Productions Inc.

They assured prison officials that he had a job waiting, and signed LeFlore to a minor-league contract as soon as he was paroled.

For the first time in his life Ron LeFlore had a future—on the right side of the law.

Incredibly, after a brief stint in the minors, LeFlore reached the big leagues—one year and one week after he was released from prison.

By 1976, a season in which he hit safely in 30 consecutive games, LeFlore was voted the American League's starting left fielder in the All-Star Game. "This means I'm a part of something I've never been a part of before," LeFlore said softly, as he sat in front of his cubicle in the visitors' clubhouse at Philadelphia's Vet-

erans Stadium before the game. "It means I'm a part of society."

Before the game, the procession of dignitaries that was slowly making its way around the clubhouse eventually arrived at LeFlore's locker.

"We Michiganders have got to stick together," the smiling man in the middle of the entourage said, extending his right hand.

LeFlore shook the well-dressed man's hand, then quickly sat back down on his stool as Gerald R. Ford, surrounded by secret service agents, moved on to greet the next All-Star.

"How about that?" LeFlore sighed. "The President of the United States knows who I am."

Meanwhile, back in Jackson Prison, along with millions of other Americans, hundreds of hardcore prisoners—murderers and rapists and bank robbers—gathered around TV sets to watch their new hero, ex-convict and former fellow inmate Ron LeFlore.

Unfortunately, LeFlore's past continued to haunt him.

In the middle of his 1976 30-game hitting streak—the longest the American League had seen in 27 years—LeFlore's younger brother, Gerald, was shot and killed during an argument in Detroit. An autopsy revealed codeine, morphine and methadone in his system.

LeFlore, who had been running from the police earlier in his life, averaged over 50 steals a season for nine years in the big leagues—the first six with the Tigers. In 1978 he lead the American League with 78 thefts, the most by any Tiger since Ty Cobb.

"Stealing was my specialty," he admitted with an impish grin. "As far back as I can remember, I was stealing things and getting away with it."

A book was written about LeFlore's remarkable life and made into a TV movie. Nevertheless, after the 1979 season, in which LeFlore hit .300 and stole 78 bases, he was traded from the Tigers to the Montreal Expos after repeatedly running afoul of managers Ralph Houk and Sparky Anderson. At the time, there were unconfirmed rumors that LeFlore was again using drugs.

In spite of what the Tigers had done to help him straighten out his life, LeFlore felt he had been cheated in Detroit. After he departed, he called the Tigers cheap.

"[Alan] Trammell was there three years," LeFlore complained. "I was there five years. I had good stats every year. They paid him [$2.8 million for seven years]. But they didn't feel it was necessary to pay me any more money."

Later, after he had been shipped from Montreal to Chicago, LeFlore ran afoul of White Sox manager Tony LaRussa, who accused him of being out of shape, missing workouts, and sleeping in the clubhouse. For LeFlore, the last straw came late in the 1982 season when he was arrested at his Chicago apartment in possession of amphetamines and an unlicensed gun. LeFlore claimed the pills and pistol belonged to someone else and was acquitted. But the damage had been done. His remarkable behind-bars-to-the-big-leagues baseball career was over.

The following January, LeFlore's 49-day-old son John Christopher died, apparently of Sudden Infant Death Syndrome. LeFlore said the baby had died in his arms.

The Florida Department of Health and Rehabilitative Services investigated a complaint from the county sheriff that neglect or abuse may have contributed to the child's death, but no criminal charges were filed.

Five years later, in 1988, long-time American League umpire Marty Springstead was exiting the Sarasota, Florida airport one afternoon, when he was surprised to hear one of the baggage handlers calling him by name.

"This guy says, 'Hey, Marty, how ya' doing?'" Springstead recalled. "I looked at him and said, 'Do I know you?'

"He stuck out his hand and said, 'I'm Ron LeFlore.'"

With Springstead's help, LeFlore enrolled in umpire school in an effort to get back into baseball. But it was too late. He was too old to start over again.

Before he was incarcerated, LeFlore had been a con man, a hustler. That was part of the reason he got into trouble in the first place. That brazen attitude helped him convince the Tigers to give him a second chance in life. But it also haunted him throughout his career.

As a ballplayer, he was often boastful and bombastic. He had little regard for rules or authority. He was chronically late, a character flaw that did not endear him to managers Ralph Houk and Sparky Anderson. The tardy LeFlore would walk into the manager's office with a grin on his face and flip the money to pay his fine onto the desk.

Once, when Anderson gave LeFlore an order, the outfielder replied, "I'll think about it."

"Hurry up," Sparky replied, "because the game starts soon."

LeFlore was not above bending the truth.

In the spring of 1974, 10 months removed from prison and still on probation, LeFlore was sent to Lakeland, Florida, to continue his professional baseball career. He told his girlfriend to rent a two-bedroom apartment, costing $225 a month. Then LeFlore invited Billy Baldwin, another promising young Tiger outfielder, to move in with them.

"I told Billy he and I would split the rent, $112.50 each," LeFlore recalled. "That was fine with him. Then

I told my girlfriend she and I would split the rent, $112.50 apiece, and let Baldwin stay with us for free since we had an extra bedroom. Billy was paying $112.50, my girlfriend was paying $112.50, and I was living for free."

As far as LeFlore was concerned, that was the way life should be.

In 1999, LeFlore returned to Detroit for ceremonies commemorating the final game at Tiger Stadium. LeFlore, along with his new wife and his mother, were among the many guests at parties and festivities honoring many of the former players who had played such a prominent role in the Tigers' past.

Immediately following the game, LeFlore, who was still in uniform savoring the moment with dozens of other former Tiger players, was arrested in the clubhouse for nonpayment of child support and taken to jail, where he unceremoniously remained until the next afternoon.

In the wake of arbitrator Peter Seitz's historic December 23, 1975 decision to make pitchers Andy Messersmith and Dave McNally instant free agents, baseball changed dramatically.

Salaries soared as players, suddenly emancipated after being unconditionally tied to their teams for nearly a century by the reserve clause, sought to sell their services to the highest bidders.

For the most part, the conservative, old-fashioned Tigers declined to participate. "I could be a hero if I went out and spent millions on players, but who is going to pay the price when the chips are down?" frugal Tiger owner John Fetzer asked rhetorically.

As a result, the Tigers' performance on the field suffered while teams such as the spendthrift New York Yankees flourished thanks to free agency.

In 1976, they drafted the rights to negotiate with nine players and eventually signed 33-year-old second baseman Tito Fuentes. But other than that the Tigers generally stayed out of the annual free agent auctions.

The Tigers did pursue Bobby Grich before he moved from Baltimore to California in 1977, but they did not offer nearly enough to get the talented infielder's attention. "I went to war with a switch," groaned GM Jim Campbell, who believed, as many members of the game's old guard did, that free agency would eventually lead to baseball's demise.

When Oakland A's owner Charley Finley called Campbell offering to sell star pitcher Vida Blue to the Tigers for $1 million, Campbell immediately sought Fetzer's approval. With his boss's blessing, Campbell quickly agreed to the deal.

But while Campbell impatiently waited by the phone to hear back from Finley, assuming Blue would soon become a Tiger, the Yankees jumped in and offered Finley $1.5 million for Blue. Finley accepted the new offer on the spot. He never even bothered to call the Tigers back.

The matter became moot when baseball commissioner Bowie Kuhn nullified the sale, as well as that of Joe Rudi and Rollie Fingers to the Boston Red Sox, on the grounds that they would distort the competitive balance of the game.

Frustrated by his failure to acquire either Grich or Blue, Campbell became gun-shy where the free agent market was concerned. "We learned a lesson: There is no limit," the Tigers' GM said.

"I think the elimination of the reserve clause is going to ruin the competitive balance of baseball," Campbell predicted.

His boss, John Fetzer, agreed.

"I've got the ability to go out and spend as much money as any of the owners, and probably more than most of them, for ballplayers," the Tigers' owner said. "And I could enjoy the biggest ego ride you ever saw. I could be a hero every day if I went out and spent a million here and a million there.

"But what would that do to my peers? What would it do to their payrolls? Some of them couldn't afford it. They don't have the resources. They don't have the town. They don't have the support. What am I doing to them? Do I have an obligation to my brothers or not? It's as simple as that. And I think I do.

"I think it's more of a justice to the people of the city of Detroit to see that we have a solid franchise in Detroit that can stand the test of time."

In fact, the Tigers did not make a major free agent acquisition until they signed Darrell Evans in 1984.

Years earlier, Campbell had refused to even speak to pitcher Earl Wilson's agent, Bob Woolf. Campbell continued to treat agents as the enemy even as the players' representatives gained more and more power under baseball's free agency and arbitration systems.

In 1980, Alan Trammell, Lou Whitaker, and Steve Kemp all took their salary disputes to arbitration and won. In 1983, Whitaker, Jack Morris, Dan Petry, Chet Lemon and Larry Herndon all won their cases. Time and again the arbitrators thought the Tigers were offering too little.

In 1979, the Tigers ranked 24th in salaries. By 1982, they had climbed all the way to 23rd.

Meanwhile, Campbell continued to try to build a winner the old-fashioned way, trading for pitcher Aurelio Lopez, outfielders Herndon and Lemon, and developing players such as Trammell, Whitaker, Lance Parrish, Kirk Gibson, Morris, Tom Brookens, and Petry in the farm system.

Midway through the 1979 season, without warning, Campbell hired Sparky Anderson, who had been unexpectedly fired by Cincinnati the previous fall.

"I've been too loyal," Campbell admitted when he was asked why he, in turn, had suddenly fired manager Les Moss, who had worked his way up in the Tigers' farm system, after less than half a season.

"I kept the 1968 team too long. I screwed myself and I screwed the whole organization."

Campbell was not about to make that same mistake again.

In 1983, Dan Petry and others took their salary disputes to arbitration and won. Petry pitched for the Tigers for 11 years. Collection of Jim Hawkins Productions Inc.

The Tigers' chief executive was in Anaheim midway through the 1979 season, watching the Tigers play the California Angels, when quite by accident he bumped into Anderson at the ballpark. Sparky, who was still being paid by the Reds in addition to doing promotional work for Burger King and feature reports for an L.A. TV station, had decided he would return to baseball in 1980 as the manager of the Chicago Cubs. An agreement was in place. All Sparky needed to do was sign the contract.

At 11 a.m. the next morning, Campbell began calling Sparky at home. At first, their conversations were casual. Sparky had already made up his mind. He wasn't interested in coming to Detroit. But Campbell refused to take "no" for an answer. Seven phone calls later—all placed that same day—Anderson agreed to become the Tigers' new manager.

"One of the hardest things I ever had to do in my life was to dismiss Les Moss," Campbell said later. "But he lacked charisma. And you only get the chance to hire a manager like Sparky Anderson once in your lifetime."

❦

The once highly excitable, hot-tempered George Lee Anderson was in the third season of his mediocre 10-year minor-league career as a player in 1955 when the Class AA team's radio announcer, commenting on Anderson's animated argument with an umpire, noted: "The sparks are really flying tonight."

"Sparks" became "Sparky." And the nickname stuck.

"I was embarrassed," Sparky admitted. "It took me a while to get used to it."

Anderson was born on February 22, 1934, in Bridgewater, South Dakota, the son of a house painter. The family's modest home didn't even have indoor plumbing. During the rugged South Dakota winters, Sparky's father, LeRoy, would cover the windows with cardboard in an effort to keep the cold out.

When Sparky was nine years old, the Anderson family moved to Los Angeles. The neighborhood, which later became known as Watts, was already rough. But at least the bathroom was indoors.

There young Georgie Anderson, as Sparky was first known, soon became hooked on baseball, serving as batboy for the University of Southern California team, which practiced near his home.

When Anderson was in the fifth grade, some of his friends decided to rob a gas station. They invited Georgie to join them.

"I said, 'No, no, I ain't going,'" Sparky recalled years later. "I said, 'I gotta go to baseball practice.'

"The next day the cops came and took all those kids down to juvenile court."

As a playground player, young Anderson made the utmost of his limited ability. He constantly hustled, striving for perfection. One pro scout told Anderson's father that young Georgie reminded him of major-leaguer Eddie Stanky.

Ironically, Anderson's Rancho Playground team was known as the Tigers. And in 1951, Anderson's American Legion team won the national championship in Detroit's Briggs Stadium.

Less than an hour after Anderson graduated from high school, he signed a $3,000 contract to play baseball in the Brooklyn Dodgers' farm system.

When he reported to training camp in Vero Beach, Florida, the following spring, Anderson encountered 512 players who would be competing for places on 26 minor-league teams. Based strictly on ability, Anderson estimated that at least 510 of those players had more talent than he did. "Ray Charles could have looked at those guys and seen they were better than me," he admitted.

Yet during each of the seven seasons Anderson spent with Toronto in the International League, he was annually voted the "smartest player in the league."

"They weren't talking about books, either," Sparky said.

In 1964, after a playing career that could charitably be described as undistinguished, Anderson was named Toronto's manager. Immediately, he bragged to the media, "If I can't win with this club, I ought to be fired."

Toronto, under Anderson, finished fifth. True to his prediction, Sparky was fired.

The following season he managed at Class A Rock Hill, South Carolina. There, Sparky's fiery temper almost ended his managerial career when, in the middle of a heated argument on the field, Sparky grabbed an umpire by the throat.

Banished to the locker room, Sparky assumed he was history. He had broken one of baseball's most sacred rules. He began packing his bags to go home.

But the umpire entered the locker room and approached Sparky. "You know something," the umpire said. "I bumped you first. I apologize for that. Why don't we forget what happened and let's go from there."

Sparky thanked the umpire and assured him he had learned his lesson. From that day forward whenever he left the dugout to debate an umpire, Sparky always buried his hands in his back pockets.

It was the turning point in Anderson's managerial career. Rock Hill, at the time, was in the St. Louis Cardinals' farm system. And Bob Howsam, who would later become boss of the Cincinnati Reds, was the Cardinals' GM.

To make ends meet at home, Anderson had to work in the off season. One winter he stocked shelves at Sears & Roebuck. Another year he sold doughnuts. He worked as a pipe cutter, he ran a drill press, and he spent two winters selling automobiles.

However, Sparky was not very successful at selling cars. He was too honest.

"I'd look at their credit statement and tell them they couldn't afford a new car," he recalled. "I'd tell them to invest some money in their old car and drive it 'til it died."

In this whole world there are only a handful of celebrities who can be universally identified simply by mentioning their first names. There is only one "Michael," one "Magic," one "Elvis," one "Tiger," one "Babe."

And only one "Sparky."

Nothing more need be said.

Sparky Anderson, the winningest manager in Tiger history (1,331 wins), and the game's third winningest manager of all time, reigned as one of the national pastime's greatest showmen—and one of its greatest ambassadors. He was often compared to fellow Hall of Famers Casey Stengel and Tommy Lasorda.

The once painfully shy Anderson, whose formal education came to a screeching halt immediately after high school, won 2,194 games. Only Connie Mack and John McGraw ever won more. He is the only manager ever to win 100 or more games in each major league.

Along the way, he also met three presidents, countless celebrities, and the Pope, and warmed the hearts of millions of fans.

"I always felt, even as a young kid, that I was the greatest thing God ever made," Sparky once boasted.

However, that outward bravado was all part of his act.

As the years passed, the inexhaustible cauldron of confidence grew more humble and introspective. "I know I'm the real Sparky," he later philosophized. "But Sparky ain't the real me.

"There's Sparky Anderson, he's the one who manages a baseball team. He talks to the nation and appears all over the country. Baseball is show business. That's the way it should be. And that's where Sparky belongs.

"Then there's George Anderson. He's the guy from Bridgewater. He's the guy who knows he's no smarter or no better than the guy next door. George Anderson is me."

Sparky never saw a camera he didn't like or a reporter's notepad that he couldn't fill with pithy quotes. He would talk to anyone about anything at any time for as long as they pleased. He was constantly on stage.

But he never lost sight of who he was or where he came from.

In the fall of 1979, following his first season at the helm of the Tigers, Anderson was invited to Las Vegas to appear on a television show. When he walked into the lobby of the hotel, gamblers in the adjacent casino suddenly stopped pulling the handles on their slot machines and started shouting, "Hey, Sparky! Hey, Sparky! Hey, Sparky!"

The next summer while the Tigers were playing in New York, Anderson and four friends were invited to tour the New York Stock Exchange.

When the frenzied brokers spotted Anderson they suddenly stopped shouting, waving their arms, and swapping stocks, and rushed over to shake Sparky's hand.

"I must have signed autographs for half an hour," Sparky said. "Here they are, dealing in millions, and I'm signing autographs for their kids and friends."

The brokers paid virtually no attention to two of Anderson's companions—merely a couple of Hall of Famers named Al Kaline and George Kell.

In 1984, when the Tigers were by far the hottest team in baseball and well on their way to the world championship, Anderson was eating breakfast in an Anaheim, California, hotel one morning when he noticed the man in the next booth staring at him.

Sparky assumed the man either wanted an autograph or was offended by the pipe the Tiger manager was smoking.

Finally, the customer walked over and introduced himself. "I'm from Dayton, [Ohio] and I was a big fan of yours when you managed the Cincinnati Reds," he said.

Although his breakfast had been interrupted, Sparky thanked the man for the kind words and waited for more accolades.

"By the way," the fan added, "what are you doing now?"

❧

As soon as he arrived in Detroit on June 14, 1979, Sparky, who had been fired the previous fall by the Cincinnati Reds despite two world championships, promised Tiger fans a World Series within five years. "That five-year deal just sorta popped into my head," the exuberant new Tiger manager later confessed.

When the once-shy Anderson, who had batted a puny .218 in his brief big-league playing career, arrived at the corner of Michigan and Trumbull, he immediately introduced himself as "Chief Walking Eagle."

"I'm so full of feathers I can't fly," Sparky boasted on the evening of his debut on the Tiger bench.

Incredibly, in 1984, in Sparky's fifth full season on the Tiger bench, the outspoken, white-haired skipper made good on his promise as the Tigers ran away with the American League pennant following a 35-5 start, then flattened the San Diego Padres in five games in the World Series thanks to the clutch hitting of Kirk Gibson and Alan Trammell.

Not since the vaunted 1927 New York Yankees juggernaut had any American League team gone wire to wire, leading in the standings from the first day of the season until the last. The 1984 Tigers were that dominating, that good.

They not only shattered the all-time Tiger Stadium record for attendance, drawing more than 2.7 million people at home, they also led the major leagues in attendance on the road.

For one season anyway, the Tigers became America's Team. Even TV star Tom Selleck wore a Tigers cap.

"I have to admit that I wanted to prove the Reds wrong for firing me," Anderson said after he became the first manager in baseball history to win world championships with teams from both leagues. "I wanted to show them I could win without them.

"I'd burned inside ever since I was fired in Cincinnati. When the Tigers won in '84, I finally felt vindicated.

Beloved manager Sparky Anderson waves to the crowd in this Sept. 23, 1984 photo after the Tigers beat the New York Yankees. The victory gave the Tigers their 100th victory of the season enroute to a World Championship. AP/Wide World Photos

"But I ain't no dummy," Anderson admitted. "I knew the kind of baseball talent I was getting when I came to Detroit. Howdy Doody could have seen all those good young players in their organization."

Those young players included the keystone combination of Alan Trammell and Sweet Lou Whitaker, pitching ace Jack Morris, catcher Lance Parrish, and Kirk Gibson.

However, it wasn't always easy, or automatic.

With the young Tigers gathered at Metro Airport for their first road trip under Anderson in 1979, Sparky couldn't believe his eyes. The players were all wearing blue jeans, sneakers and T-shirts. Disgusted, Anderson asked one of his coaches if the team was going to a rodeo.

From that day forward, the Tigers wore coats and ties on most road trips. Alcohol was banned from team flights. "If you're a slob, you'll be sloppy on the job, too," Anderson explained.

On June 23, nine days after he took the Tiger job, Anderson had second thoughts.

"We dropped a doubleheader to the Orioles in Baltimore and we were 2-9 since I took over as manager," Sparky recalled. "I'll never forget how low I was feeling that night.

"I called my wife back in California and I told her, 'Honey, we've made the gravest mistake of our lives. We had our pick of half a dozen teams and we picked absolutely the wrong one. I've never seen a team so unprofessional. They're satisfied just to come to the park and finish fifth or sixth every year. They actually like the fact that there's no pressure on them.'"

A few days later Anderson exploded in the locker room and behind closed doors and in no uncertain terms he told his young team the same thing.

"You're a bunch of frauds!" Sparky shouted at his stunned players. "You walk through the clubhouse door and pretend you're major-leaguers. You go to your lockers and put on a major-league uniform, but you're really a bunch of frauds.

"They wouldn't tolerate this in the places I've been. They wouldn't tolerate losing. God didn't put me on this earth to be a loser."

Five years later, on August 7, 1984, Anderson would again close the door to the clubhouse and privately address his team. Only this time, his message was quite different.

Sparky stood up and told his players, again in no uncertain terms: "I have never witnessed such great character in a team."

Slowly but surely, Anderson had molded the talented young Tigers into world champions.

On the eve of the Tigers' 1983 season opener in Minnesota, Anderson summoned Kirk Gibson, whom Sparky himself had once billed as "the next Mickey Mantle," to his clubhouse office and informed the intense, highly competitive Gibson that he would no longer be starting every game.

"You've been acting like an idiot," Sparky said, staring at his high-strung outfielder.

Gibson immediately became livid. Physically, he was much bigger than Sparky, and at least twice as strong. He was also half his age.

Gibson charged the little Tiger manager, attempting to pin him into the corner of his own office. He threatened to break Sparky in half.

"I almost had him and I swear I was going to bust him," Gibson later confessed. "But Sparky eluded my grasp, ran to the doorway and turned."

"Gibson!" Sparky bravely shouted. "One of these days, you'll find out who the boss is around here, and it ain't you!"

Then Anderson went out the door.

Eventually, Gibson grew up and came to see the game the same way Sparky saw it. "Sparky," Gibson admitted years later, "taught me how to play."

In the 1984 World Series, and again in 1988 with the Los Angeles Dodgers, Gibson demonstrated that he was the consummate big game player.

"Half of Gibby's game plan was to intimidate the opposition," Anderson observed. "He was the ultimate team player. When he went three-for-four and we lost, he could bite off the head of a rattlesnake. When he went zero-for-four and we won, he ran around the clubhouse like he had hit two grand slams and stole the mustard off somebody's hot dog."

The Tigers' offensive leader during the 1984 regular season was Lance Parrish, the muscular catcher the other players respectfully referred to as "The Big Wheel." Although he batted just .237 in 1984, Parrish smacked 33 homers and knocked in 98 runs. Along with free agent acquisition Darrell Evans, Parrish was a leader in the clubhouse.

On the field, Parrish had plenty of help. Gibson belted 27 homers and had 91 RBIs, and Chet Lemon contributed 20 HRs and 76 RBIs.

But the heart of the 1984 Tigers' team was their double play combination of Alan Trammell and Lou Whitaker. Trammell batted a team-leading .314 in 1984 while Whitaker hit .289.

From the day Trammell and Whitaker first joined the Tigers on a road trip in Boston in September of 1977, it was obvious they were going to be something special. They also were inseparable.

On their first day in Tiger uniforms, the two kids, who had flown in from Montgomery, Alabama, where they had just led the Tigers' Double-A subsidiary to the Southern League title, were the special guests on Hall of Fame announcer George Kell's pregame TV show.

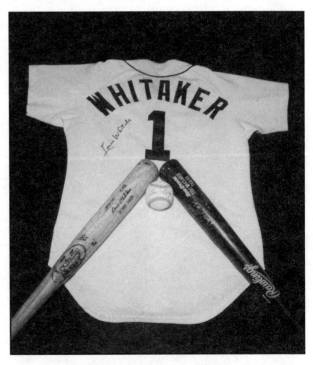

Lou Whitaker-autographed memorabilia. Mark Cunningham, Creative Impressions Inc.

Whitaker, who was 20 years old at the time, ignored Kell's opening question and instead waved at the camera.

"I want to say hello to my mother and my grandmother and all my friends in Virginia," the skinny second baseman announced.

It never occurred to Whitaker that the Tigers' telecast wouldn't be carried on television back at his rural Virginia home.

At the conclusion of the brief interview, the 19-year-old Trammell thrust his right fist into the air. "Go Rebels!" he exclaimed in tribute to the minor-league teammates he and Sweet Lou had left behind earlier that week.

By the time the pair retired, Whitaker in 1995 and Trammell in 1996, they had appeared in an American League-record 1,918 games together, turned more than 1,200 double plays, combined for nearly 5,000 base hits, and spent 19 years as teammates, making them the longest-running keystone tandem in baseball history.

Jack Morris, a fierce competitor who had arrived in the big leagues a few weeks before Trammell and Whitaker, became the winningest pitcher in the majors during the '80s. "Morris," Sparky Anderson once observed, "had the stubbornness of a mule and the grace of a thoroughbred.

"If I had three more Jack Morrises," Anderson added, "I'd be a certified genius."

Morris, who relied on his split-finger fastball, once boldly wondered aloud how some of the game's greatest hitters would have fared against him.

"Most people believe Babe Ruth was the greatest baseball player ever," Morris said with characteristic cockiness. "I wonder if he could have hit the split-finger? Ty Cobb? I've seen his swing. I know he couldn't hit it."

Jack Morris delivers a pitch against the Oakland A's May 14, 1980 in Tiger Stadium. AP/Wide World Photos

In 1984, armed with his split-finger pitch, Morris posted a 19-11 record to lead a starting staff that also featured fellow right-handers Dan Petry (18-8) and Milt Wilcox (17-8). At 34, Wilcox, who had pitched for Sparky Anderson years earlier in Cincinnati, was the senior citizen on the staff.

However, the secret of much of the Tigers' 1984 success could be found in the bullpen, where left-handed screwball specialist Willie Hernandez, acquired during spring training from Philadelphia, and hard-throwing right-hander Aurelio Lopez, who was known as "Senor Smoke," made the Tigers almost unbeatable in the late innings.

"I still can't believe we got Willie Hernandez and Dave Bergman for Glenn Wilson and John Wockenfuss," Anderson later admitted.

Hernandez, who had recorded only 35 saves during the preceding seven seasons, saved 32 games and won nine others himself in 1984 and was rewarded with both the Most Valuable Player and Cy Young Awards—a rare sweep. "The Cy Young and MVP awards ought to be renamed in honor of him," Sparky gushed.

Lopez, meanwhile, was 10-1 with 14 saves of his own. "Without Willie and Aurelio Lopez," Anderson observed, "we would have been so far back we would have solidified."

In addition, the Tigers benefited greatly from the signing of free agent slugger Darrell Evans, who provided the same leadership in the locker room that veteran Eddie Mathews had provided in the Tiger clubhouse in 1968.

During the 1984 season Anderson, the master manipulator, often astounded his own coaches with some of his starting lineups, as he cleverly deployed role players such as Dave Bergman, Rusty Kuntz and Marty Castillo in an effort to keep the entire team focused and fresh.

"You never knew when he was going to call on somebody at any point in the game," recalled Trammell. "He was so sharp that he knew a certain player in just the right situation could mean the difference in a game. It didn't matter if it was early in a game or late, everybody had better be ready. That kept everybody sharp. When the playoff and World Series rolled around, everybody was at their peak."

Before the postseason playoff against Kansas City began, outspoken utility man Marty Castillo informed Sparky Anderson that he thought he was crazy.

"I'll show you how crazy I am," Sparky replied. "I'm starting you at third base in the playoffs."

"Well, I'll show you how crazy I am," Castillo shot back. "I'm going to be the MVP."

After the Tigers swept the Kansas City Royals three straight in the playoff, Jack Morris opened the World Series with a 3-2 win in San Diego, thanks in a large part to the play on which the Padres' Kurt Bevacqua was gunned down on a perfect seventh-inning relay from Kirk Gibson to Lou Whitaker to third baseman Castillo.

The Padres rallied to win Game 2, but then the Series shifted to Tiger Stadium, where the Tigers easily reeled off three wins in a row, outscoring the stunned Padres, 17-8.

But the World Series Most Valuable Player was not Gibson, the home run hero of the dramatic fifth game. It was Alan Trammell, who grew up as a Padres fan in San Diego and batted .450 against his former favorite team in his only appearance in baseball's Fall Classic.

As a baseball-crazed youngster listening first to the Los Angeles Dodgers and later to the Padres' games on radio, Trammell's boyhood idols were Willie Mays and Roberto Clemente. In 1969 he proudly acquired Mays's autograph when the San Francisco Giants made their first trip to San Diego to play the expansion Padres.

That October Trammell's sixth grade teacher brought a television set to school and let Alan sit alone at the back of the room to watch the New York Mets battle the Baltimore Orioles in the World Series. Periodically Alan would update the rest of the class. "He knew I loved baseball," Trammell explained.

When Trammell was 12 he began sneaking into San Diego Stadium to watch the Padres play. "I was so skinny," he said, "I could slide underneath the gate." Trammell and his buddies witnessed 30 to 35 games a year that way.

Once Trammell asked Chicago Cubs third baseman Ron Santo for an autograph.

"It didn't just say, 'To Alan,'" Trammell recalled. "He signed it: 'To Alan, Best of Luck, Your Buddy, Ron Santo.'"

After the game, the 14-year-old Trammell waited outside the ballpark to shake his new best friend's hand. "Santo came out smoking a cigarette," Trammell said. "I had never seen a ballplayer smoke a cigarette before. And he was drinking a Coors beer.

"He put his arm around me and asked me to hold his Coors while he signed some autographs for some other kids."

Alan Trammell was thrilled.

Trammell retired as a player after the 1996 season, joining Ty Cobb and Al Kaline as the only Tigers ever to play 20 or more years in a Detroit uniform. After working for two years in the front office, Trammell returned to the field in 1999 as the Tigers' hitting coach under one-year manager Larry Parrish.

However, when Parrish was fired and Phil Garner was hired following the third-place '99 season, Trammell was fired, too, replaced by four-time National

League batting champ Bill Madlock, who had also briefly played for the Tigers.

Trammell returned to his native San Diego, where he was hired as a coach by the Padres.

Soon after the horrendous 2002 season, Trammell triumphantly returned to Detroit with a three-year contract to manage the Tigers.

In November of 1977, John Fetzer sold Tiger Stadium, worth an estimated $8 million, to the City of Detroit for one dollar. The city then leased the ballpark back to the Tigers for the next 30 years. Although a new electronic scoreboard was added, replacing the old, hand-operated model, and the traditional green wooden seats were replaced by blue and orange plastic ones, the stadium remained basically the same as it had been in Walter O. Briggs's heyday.

Prior to the 1984 season, the aging Fetzer, who was systematically dismantling his extensive financial empire in order to form a foundation because he had no heirs to whom he could will his fortune, sold the Tigers to Michigan pizza baron Tom Monaghan for $53 million—nearly 10 times the price Fetzer's syndicate had paid for the team in 1956.

Monaghan's archrival in the pizza business, Mike Ilitch, who had played in the Tigers' minor-league system in the 1950s, was also eager to buy the ball club. But Campbell, who had considerable input into Fetzer's deliberations and decision, had some personal concerns about Ilitch and quietly steered Fetzer toward Monaghan.

"Monaghan will serve the best interests of the city of Detroit and the fans of the Tigers," Fetzer explained.

Eight years later, when Ilitch purchased the Tigers from Monaghan for $85 million, he exacted his revenge, reportedly ordering Monaghan to fire both Campbell, who had remained in control of the team,

Detroit native and actor Tom Selleck shows his support for the Tigers in the dugout with Alan Trammell. Dan Ewald Jr.

and former University of Michigan football coach Bo Schembechler, who had been hired by Monaghan as club president, before the sale could be consummated.

Like their predecessors in 1968, the 1984 Tigers made one more grab for glory before they disbanded, winning the 1987 AL East title.

After trailing the Toronto Blue Jays by three and a half games with just eight to play, the Tigers rallied to win the Eastern half of the pennant in what Anderson called his most satisfying season. Ever the optimist,

Sparky himself had privately picked the 1987 Tigers to finish no better than fourth.

"No team ever made me feel prouder than that one," he said. "We were supposed to finish way down, somewhere in South America."

However, the Tigers succumbed to the Minnesota Twins' huge home-field advantage in the playoff.

By then Lance Parrish was gone. In spite of his 212 home runs and his unquestioned leadership in the locker room, Tiger management was worried about Lance's injured back. As a result they only offered him a one-year contract, worth $1.2 million, for 1987.

Parrish felt unappreciated and fled to Philadelphia for substantially less money. That, Lance later admitted, was one of the dumbest things he had ever done in his life.

"It was a bizarre thing, and it was very frustrating for me," recalled Parrish, who rejoined the Tigers as a coach in 1999, and after a stint in the TV booth became one of Alan Trammell's coaches in 2003. "I felt the organization wasn't dealing with me fairly. I felt they put me in a corner and forced me to make a decision. I had worked very hard to put myself in a position where I would be able to make the kind of money I felt I deserved. But that was right at the height of the collusion era, and the Tigers had both feet in the collusion bucket.

"I made a decision based on what I thought was best at the time," he continued. "Obviously, it didn't work out the way that I had hoped. The grass is not always greener on the other side. I found that out. But you make your bed and you've got to sleep in it. It's just a bad memory now."

Despite Parrish's love for the Tigers, he was fired as a coach by Phil Garner with one year remaining on his $120,000-a-year contract following the disappointing 2001 campaign.

However that injustice was quickly rectified when Parrish's good friend, Alan Trammell, became the Tigers' manager in 2003. In 1989, beset by injuries, and lacking both talent and team leadership, Sparky Anderson's Tigers lost 103 games. The pressure and pain of losing night after night, coupled with a family crisis at home, proved too much for Sparky to bear. On May 19, 1989 on doctor's orders, Anderson took a leave of absence and returned home to Thousand Oaks, California, to regroup and rest.

"It was time for me to set my priorities straight," he explained. Seventeen days later he returned to the bench.

"I never got over the point of bleeding a little inside after every loss," he said. "But I finally learned to let go. I gave up that obsession for always having control."

In 1992, Monaghan, whose public image had taken a pounding because of the decision to retire venerable Hall of Fame announcer Ernie Harwell and the team's public demands for a new stadium, sold the Tigers to fellow pizza-maker Mike Ilitch for a profitable $85 million.

From the outset, the relationship between Anderson and the Ilitch organization was tenuous, at best. Years later, Sparky admitted he should have resigned when Campbell and Schembechler were fired.

"I always felt guilty that I stuck around after what happened to them," Anderson confessed. "I should have listened to my heart. I have always maintained that when the people who were so close to you were ever mistreated, you go with them. Jim Campbell and Bo Schembechler deserved more from me."

But Sparky was making more than $1 million per year at the time. For once in his life, he let money rule his mind. "I really didn't have a job no more," he admitted. "It was totally different."

In spite of all his success, Anderson's stellar, record-setting career with the Tigers was concluded under a cloud of controversy. Sparky was on the last year of his contract when he walked away from the Tigers in spring training 1995 and went home to California rather than manage replacement players—a principled stance that sealed his fate in the eyes of Ilitch, who immediately placed him on unpaid leave.

No other manager took such a staunch stance. "There were 27 other managers and I didn't see no parade following me down the highway," Anderson recalled. "But I really didn't want no entourage."

Ilitch was outraged. He reportedly wanted to fire Sparky on the spot. Other owners privately turned against Anderson. Some other managers questioned the wisdom of what Sparky had done.

Baseball commissioner Bud Selig phoned Anderson to ask how he would have handled the ugly, prolonged players' strike.

"Put locks on all the spring training doors and hide all the keys 'til the thing is settled," Anderson replied.

The walkout cost Anderson $150,000 and any chance he may have had to return to manage the Tigers in 1996 or beyond. But he never looked back. "I'll swear under oath I never regretted my decision for a second," he said.

"My daddy never raised me to be a hero," Anderson later declared. "But he damn sure taught me always to do the right thing, no matter what it cost. I know I did the right thing in 1995.

"What if a teachers' union went on strike? Would the school board drive around the city to hire a bunch of people who weren't busy, just to keep the classes open?"

"Sparky wasn't for the players, he wasn't for the owners," former Tigers coach Billy Consolo, Anderson's lifelong friend, explained. "He was thinking of baseball."

After suffering a heart attack in 1999, Anderson underwent triple bypass surgery. When he awoke from the surgery, Anderson turned to his wife, Carol, and said in typical Sparky-speak: "I did good, didn't I?"

On July 23, 2000, Sparky Anderson, the winningest manager in the history of the Tigers, the winningest manager in the history of the Cincinnati Reds, the third winningest manager in the history of the game, was ushered into baseball's Hall of Fame.

At his induction, Anderson asked, "How can a young man from Bridgewater, South Dakota, with 600 people, who couldn't even play, ever become the third winningest manager in baseball?"

Manager Sparky Anderson acknowledges the crowd upon his return to the game in 1989.
Dan Ewald Jr.

Mark Cunningham, Creative Impressions Inc.

6

FROM THE CORNER
TO COMERICA
1993-present

In their first 93 seasons in the American League, the Tigers won nine pennants, four World Series, and three division crowns—and finished under the .500 mark in just thirty-one years, or thirty-three percent of the time. Never during all of those nine-plus decades did they fail to win more ballgames than they lost for more than four summers in a row.

But from 1994 through 2002, the Tigers won zero pennants, zero World Series, and zero division titles—and finished below .500 for nine agonizing years in succession—as they habitually lapsed into yet another lengthy funk in the years following their smashing 1984 success and their surprising 1987 division title.

Their latest drought has been their worst of all.

Hope soared in Detroit on August 26, 1992 when local businessman and former Tiger farmhand Mike Ilitch and his wife Marian purchased the floundering franchise from financially troubled fellow pizza magnate Tom Monaghan for $85 million.

Fans optimistically assumed that Ilitch—a native Detroiter who had signed with the Tigers in 1952 and batted .340 in his first three seasons as a minor-league infielder before a knee injury cut short his playing career—would be able to eventually turn the struggling baseball team around just as he had done with the city's previously moribund Detroit Red Wings of the National Hockey League.

That enthusiasm was buoyed early on when Ilitch reassured fans by signing slugging first baseman Cecil Fielder to a lucrative long-term contract and rehiring beloved radio announcer Ernie Harwell, who had been

fired a year earlier by radio station WJR and the Tigers.

The Tigers also embarked on an $8 million renovation and modernization of Tiger Stadium. And in 1993, Ilitch's first full season at the helm, attendance soared to 1,971,421—sixth highest in franchise history—as the team won eighty-five games under Sparky Anderson and finished in a tie for third in the American League East.

Unfortunately for Tiger fans, that success and that joy were short-lived.

On August 12, 1994, with the Tigers languishing in fifth place, 18 games off the pace, baseball was struck with its eighth and by far its most devastating work stoppage since 1972.

The lengthy, acrimonious strike by the players' union wiped out the 1994 World Series and cost the national pastime the allegiance of millions of fans. It also cost the Tigers the most successful manager in team history, as Anderson refused to have anything to do with baseball's ill-advised attempt to install replacement players in the spring of 1995. As a result, Anderson was unceremoniously excused by a still angry, unforgiving Mike Ilitch at the conclusion of the strike-shortened 1995 campaign.

The 1995 home opener, delayed until May 2 to give teams time to conduct an abbreviated spring training after the labor dispute finally ended, was indicative both of the damage done by the strike and of the deteriorated state of baseball in Detroit. The Tigers were clobbered 11-1 by the Cleveland Indians as a disgusted, less-than-capacity crowd of 39,398 interrupted the game by hurling cans, cups, bottles and assorted other debris onto the playing field.

Just prior to the dismal '95 season, Ilitch hired new team president John McHale Jr.—whose dad was a former Tiger player and front office executive. Shortly after the season, he hired general manager Randy Smith, whose own father was a longtime baseball exec.

McHale's mission was clearly defined: His goal was to get a new ballpark built in Detroit.

Smith's job, rebuilding the team on the field, would prove more difficult. One of Smith's first moves was to hire new manager Buddy Bell.

World Series hero Kirk Gibson, who returned to the team in 1993 after an earlier fallout with owner Tom Monaghan, had retired along with Lou Whitaker at the end of the '95 season. Cecil Fielder was traded to the New York Yankees in 1996. Alan Trammell called it quits at the end of that year. The Tigers were a team in transition.

The arrival of outfielder Bobby Higginson, first baseman Tony Clark, third baseman Travis Fryman, speedster Brian Hunter, relief ace Todd Jones and

pitcher Willie Blair appeared to give the team a solid nucleus around which to build as Bell piloted the Tigers to an encouraging 79-83 record and a third-place finish in 1997.

However, within five years, Bell, Clark, Fryman, Jones, Hunter and Blair would all be gone. And the Tigers would be no closer to contention than they were when their unprecedented skid began.

❧

The more things change, the more things remain the same.

Ty Cobb, the Greatest Tiger of Them All, was tainted by a 1926 betting scandal and forced to conclude his brilliant Hall of Fame career with the Philadelphia Athletics. Denny McLain, the Tigers' mercurial 31-game winner in 1968, was suspended three times during the 1970 season—once for consorting with bookmakers—and later served two stints in prison.

Influential early 20th century Tiger owner Frank Navin was an avid gambler and former bookie who,

Third baseman Travis Fryman takes a big swing for the Tigers in 1991. Dan Ewald Jr.

A fan says farewell to Tiger Stadium during the last game there on September 27, 1999. Tom Pearson

according to legend, may have purchased his stake in the team in 1907 with the proceeds from an all-night poker game. Marian Ilitch, the wife of Tiger owner Mike who was originally listed as co-owner and secretary/treasurer of the team herself, is the part owner of one of Detroit's 21st century casinos.

Lifelong Tiger fan and longtime team owner Walter O. Briggs abruptly fired manager Mickey Cochrane in 1938, less than three years after Black Mike piloted the Tigers to their first world championship ever. Former Tiger farmhand Mike Ilitch, who as a youngster shagged fly balls for Hank Greenberg, shoved Sparky Anderson out the door after the 1995 season—and a team-record 1,331 wins.

❧

On September 27, 1999, the Tigers concluded nearly a century of play at the corner of Michigan and Trumbull with an 8-2 victory over the Kansas City Royals before 43,356 sentimental, cheering fans—

many of whom watched the emotional finale with tears in their eyes. An era truly had ended.

Satchel Paige pitched at the corner of Michigan and Trumbull, five years before Jackie Robinson broke baseball's infamous color barrier. Nolan Ryan tossed one of his seven no-hitters there. Sparky Anderson played shortstop at Briggs Stadium in the 1951 American Legion World Series.

Joe Louis and Jake LaMotta fought there. So did Ty Cobb and Babe Ruth.

Fielding Yost's "Point-A-Minute" Michigan Wolverines played football at The Corner. So did Jim Thorpe, Pop Warner, the Detroit Lions and Notre Dame. Lions receiver Chuck Hughes died there.

Perry Como, Pat Boone, Patti Page, Nat King Cole, Rod Stewart, Kiss, the Eagles, and the Three Tenors sang there. Billy Graham, Eugene McCarthy, and Nelson Mandela preached there.

Now the House that Cobb helped to build under the watchful eye of owlish bean counter Frank Navin, the ballpark that industrialist Walter O. Briggs ex-

The fans are on their feet in the filled-to-capacity stadium during the final inning ever at the historic ballpark on the corner of Michigan and Trumbull. Tom Pearson

panded thanks to guys named Greenberg, Gehringer, Cochrane and Goslin, the stadium that Fidrych filled and Gibson rocked, was no more.

"I'm not bitter, I've had a great time here," said businessman and former Ford Motor Co. worker Neil Heffernan, who owned and operated Sportsland USA, a Michigan Avenue souvenir shop in the shadow of Tiger Stadium, for 25 years. "People who used to come in here as kids are coming back as men to say goodbye. People are coming from all over the country. Places you never heard of. All coming just to see Tiger Stadium."

But all that heartfelt emotion at that final game at Tiger Stadium—and the fact that 2,026,441 loyal fans showed up during that final season to bid their fond farewell—failed to mask the fact that the Tigers finished a distant 27 1/2 games out of first place in the American League Central Division in 1999 with a 69-92 record.

Many people blamed Tiger management, beginning at the top with Mike Ilitch, who seven seasons earlier had been hailed as a savior.

"I just don't have any use for the Ilitch people," shopkeeper Neil Heffernan said. "I don't like the way they operate. I'll never forget the day Ilitch took over in August of 1992. I watched 20 or 30 longtime Tiger employees walking out of the ballpark in the middle of the afternoon, carrying all of their belongings. They had just been told they didn't have jobs anymore. I said to myself, 'These Ilitches are not good people.'

"These Ilitch people think they're running a flea market instead of a baseball team. They're just a bunch of shoe clerks."

The Tigers went to spring training in 2000 with an effervescent new manager in Phil Garner, an attractive new marquee slugger in Juan Gonzalez, and a glitzy new state-of-the-art stadium in Comerica Park. They even had one employee whose only duty was to improve the players' hand-eye coordination. And they had their own clubhouse shrink.

When Garner boldly opened spring training by serving notice on the rest of the American League that they shouldn't take the Tigers' annual mediocrity for granted anymore, heads turned. "Cleveland is vulnerable," the Tiger manager declared, immediately setting his sights on the reigning division champions.

Despite a horrendous start, the Tigers eventually climbed to three games above .500, within sight of the wild card race. For the first time in six years, as Garner had predicted, the Central Division rival Indians failed to make the playoffs. At last there was hope again in Detroit. But there was more disappointment, too.

Comerica Park, built at a cost of $300 million—1,000 times the cost of new Navin Field, forerunner to Tiger Stadium, in 1912—attracted just 2.5 million curious fans to the Tigers' new home on Woodward Avenue. That was a near-record number of fans for the Tigers, but not nearly the throng of three million that most people, including Tiger management, expected.

With little to play for except pride, the Tigers had plenty of time to fool around. With Garner's blessing, on Oct. 1, the final day of the 2000 season, utility man Shane Halter became just the fourth player in big-league history to play all nine positions in a single game. All in all, he enjoyed quite a day.

Halter began the day at first base, moved over to third in the second inning, and went to right field in the third. He played center field in the fourth inning, left field in the fifth, and returned to the infield, at shortstop, in the sixth. Halter was behind the plate in the seventh inning, and on the mound in the eighth. After walking Minnesota's Matt LeCroy, the only batter he faced, Halter switched to second base.

In addition to playing all nine positions, Halter also collected four hits and scored the winning run in the ninth inning of the Tigers' 12-11 victory.

Juan Gonzalez, admittedly a gamble, turned out to be a dud. The petulant, enigmatic slugger immediately spurned the Tigers' stunning initial offer of $148 million for eight years—the richest contract in baseball history at the time—and quickly soured on spacious Comerica Park, where many of his line drives that would have been home runs elsewhere became merely long outs.

Although Juan couldn't wait to get out of town, the ever-optimistic Garner was encouraged by the adjustments the rest of his players had made to their new stadium and to Garner's get-on-base style of play. Furthermore, the manager had privately been led to be-

Several giant white tiger sculptures adorn the exterior of Comerica Park. Mike Litaker

lieve that the Tigers' middle-of-the-pack $60 million payroll would be increased by as much as $20 million in 2001.

However, unexpected cost overruns during construction, debt service on the new ballpark, and the shortfall in attendance at Comerica Park compelled Mike Ilitch to renege on his earlier promise to do everything in his power to produce a winner as soon as the Tigers moved into their new stadium.

Instead, the mercurial, often-reclusive Tiger owner, who reportedly was twice thwarted in attempts to consolidate and refinance $205 million of Comerica Park debt, ordered spending on salaries slashed to $49 million in 2001.

The hasty departure of Gonzalez and the inability to dabble in the free agent market as planned forced GM Randy Smith to trade veteran catcher Brad Ausmus and clubhouse leader Doug Brocail to Houston—where

Brian Moehler was the starting pitcher for the Tigers' first game in their new stadium, Comerica Park on April 11, 2000. Mike Litaker

actually show up. Contrast that with the Tigers' American League opener a century earlier, when 10,023 eager citizens overflowed the wooden stands at primitive Bennett Park.

By the end of the season, Hall of Famer Al Kaline was so disgusted that he refused to join the twice-delayed team picture. Mike Ilitch sprinted off the field after the photo shoot rather than risk having to answer any embarrassing questions from his puzzled employees or the prying press.

Roger Cedeno was benched for the duration of the season after openly defying Phil Garner during a workout following the September 11 terrorist attacks that rocked the nation and temporarily suspended play. Robert Fick had to be physically restrained after he engaged the manager in an obscenity-laced dugout confrontation over pitch selection. And ace pitcher Jeff Weaver complained publicly after his teammates failed to come to his aid during a Kansas City brawl.

"I was here in 1996 when we lost 109 games," said pitcher Jose Lima, reacquired from Houston in a midseason swap for Dave Mlicki, "but I've never seen a ball club like this. This is the worst."

No one disagreed.

The 2001 season ended amidst a flurry of rumors that the financially strapped Ilitch might soon sell all or part of the ball club. "If that wasn't the bottom of the barrel," Garner acknowledged, "that's some barrel."

After years of inexplicably snubbing their former heroes, the Tiger organization finally began to embrace them again in 2002.

At the encouragement of Al Kaline, who was beginning his 50th year with the team, former stars Willie Horton, Jack Morris and Bill Freehan were all invited to spring training to work with the team.

"I want to reestablish the pride and the tradition and the great history of the Tigers and the English D," said Kaline, who relinquished his broadcast duties to become a special assistant to new team president Dave Dombrowski. "I have to try."

"I wore this for 13 years," Morris said, proudly patting the Olde English D on his jersey.

"This is where my life is," Horton declared.

Smith's father, Tal, was the Astros' team president—for speedy outfielder Roger Cedeno, catcher Mitch Meluskey, and pitcher Chris Holt.

All three of the new players failed to produce in 2001. That, plus injuries to power-hitting third baseman Dean Palmer and starting pitcher Brian Moehler spelled disaster as the Tigers, their clubhouse racked by turmoil, faded to 30 games under .500 and 25 games off the pace.

When the Tigers threw a party of sorts at state-of-the-art Comerica Park on April 25, 2001 to celebrate the 100th anniversary of their American League debut, only about 9,000 die-hard fans cared enough to

Former Tigers' greats (from left) Al Kaline, George Kell and Willie Horton participate in pre-game ceremonies for the first game at Comerica Park on April 11, 2000. Mike Litaker

The awkward departures of coaches Alan Trammell and Lance Parrish—later rehired as a TV commentator—left some wondering if Phil Garner was uncomfortable in the presence of former Tiger stars.

"I'm not worried, I'm not scared in that regard," insisted Garner, who had passed up the opportunity to manage the Chicago Cubs to take charge of the Tigers in 2000. "I'm comfortable with it. We want to have our history play a part in our future. If I'm going to get fired here, I can do that on my own accord."

Six games, and six losses, into the 2002 season, he did.

A yellow taxi pulled up in the parking lot outside the entrance to the Tigers' Marchant Stadium clubhouse a few days before the official start of spring training in 1999. None of the half-dozen autograph hounds positioned along the fenced walkway, their arms loaded with baseball cards, balls and photos, paid any attention as a young man wearing a T-shirt and blue jeans climbed out of the cab.

He retrieved his oversized duffel from the trunk of the taxi and headed toward the beige cinder-block building that serves as the Tigers' clubhouse each spring. Not one fan asked for his signature.

The lanky young man walked past the entrance and continued around the building, past the entrance to the batting cages, past the door to the weight room, past the entrance to the executive offices, back to the front of the building again.

"Is this where we're supposed to go in?" 22-year-old Jeff Weaver asked.

Soon he would become the ace of the Tigers' pitching staff and one of the top young hurlers in the American League.

Nevertheless, in early July of 2002, the Tigers traded Weaver to the New York Yankees in a three-way swap that brought Oakland A's first baseman Carlos

Pena, minor-league reliever Franklyn German and a minor-leaguer pitcher Jeremy Bonderman to the Detroit organization. Another of the Tigers' brightest hopes for the future is Matt Anderson, the right-hander with the 103 mph fastball and the pierced tongue.

The blazing fastball was a gift. "Coming out of high school I was pretty mediocre," Anderson admitted. "The only scholarship offer I got was to Rice. Then my fastball started developing, my speed kept creeping up every year."

The pierced tongue proved a bit more painful. "Oh, yeah, it hurt all right—it hurt for about a week," Anderson admitted. "Your tongue swells up real fat. It's not something you want to do twice. It's not much fun."

No one was more enthusiastic about the Tigers' future than first baseman Dmitri Young, acquired in a trade with Cincinnati prior to the 2002 campaign.

Right handed pitcher Matt Anderson has been a contributor for the Tigers since 1998. Duane Burleson, AP/Wide World Photos

"I just got traded to heaven!" declared Young, who promptly demonstrated his sincerity by eschewing pending free agency to sign a six-year contract potentially worth as much as $44 million with options. "And I'm not going to wake up for six years. I love this place!"

But, he too, was soon forced to face reality as the most prolonged slump in Detroit franchise history continued.

When the Tigers opened the 2002 season with six consecutive losses, Dombrowski dismissed both manager Phil Garner and GM Randy Smith, along with several Tiger coaches.

The Tigers proceeded to lose their first five games under new manager Luis Pujols, too, extending their losing streak to 11 before they finally managed their first win.

Dombrowski assumed the role of general manager himself, in addition to his duties as Tiger president and CEO, and immediately began revamping the roster, building for the future as the Tigers continued down the path toward their ninth losing season in a row.

An unlikely new Tiger hero emerged in 2002 in the person of Robert Fick.

During spring training in 2001, Phil Garner summoned Fick to his Marchant Stadium office and informed Robert in no uncertain terms that he had caught his last game as a Tiger. Fick became so enraged that he was stopped twice and received two speeding tickets on the short drive home. Without a position, Fick's days as a Tiger certainly seemed numbered.

In April of that year, Fick was involved in a late-night incident in a bar across the street from Comerica Park, accused of hurling a racial slur at a black bouncer. Outfielder Wendell Magee, who is black and who was with Fick at the time, insisted his excitable teammate had done no such thing.

In July, after Garner had been forced to eat his earlier words and make Fick a catcher again because of injuries to Mitch Meluskey and Brandon Inge, Robert got into an obscenity-laced dugout confrontation with the Tiger manager and had to be restrained.

In September, after Fick complained publicly about his lack of playing time, he was summoned to Garner's office for another closed-door chat. Then, just as Fick was preparing to fly to Lakeland, Florida, for 2002 spring training, his close friend, San Diego Padre Mike Darr, was killed in a car crash.

Pressed into service in right field, Fick surprised skeptics during the opening days of the 2002 season. Then his sister Carolyn died suddenly at age 52 when her colon ruptured.

At the urging of family members, Fick remained in Detroit with the Tigers rather than fly home to California for the funeral. "My family told me there was no reason to be there," explained Fick, whose father died of congestive heart failure in 1998, shortly after Robert was first called up to the major leagues. "They told me to go out there and hit a home run for her."

On April 26, the day of his sister's funeral, with the Tigers and Minnesota Twins tied at 2-2, Fick led off the bottom half of the 10th inning with a game-winning homer over the right center field scoreboard.

"I swear I didn't hit," a somber Fick said. "She and my dad did."

Nevertheless, the 2002 season quickly degenerated into another Tiger disaster: They batted out of order due to an error on the lineup card; alcohol was banned from the team's charter flights after players became drunk and obnoxious; one player showed up at the ballpark after an off day with a black eye, reportedly obtained in a bar brawl; players openly yelled at one another after miscues on the field; players could sometimes be seen flirting with women in the stands during the games; and CEO Dave Dombrowski openly mocked a number of players by name because of the high salaries and low productivity, then went on radio several days later to apologize.

Dean Palmer, disabled all season, called it, "one of the worst years I've had.

"I've actually been embarrassed to where you don't want people to know you're a major-league baseball player," the straightforward Palmer admitted. "We had a lot of off-field distractions and stuff that really shouldn't happen. It's one thing to have a bad team. But then when you draw attention to other embarrassing stuff, it makes it more embarrassing."

The Tigers lost a total of 106 games in 2002, including 10 of their last 11 and 21 of their final 16. It marked the second time in seven years that the Tigers lost 100 or more games, and the fifth time since 1952. During their first 51 years of existence, the Tigers never once lost as many as 100 games.

After the 2002 season ended, Robert Fick, the Tigers' only All-Star was released and Tiger of the Year Randall Simon was traded.

Manager Phil Garner speaks with the umpires before the first game at Comerica on April 11, 2000. Mike Litaker

During the 2001-2002 seasons, the Tigers lost a total of 202 games—the worst two-year performance in franchise history.

The day after the season ended, Dombrowski dismissed Luis Pujols and all of his coaches—although hitting coach Merv Rettenmund, who had been hired by Phil Garner and praised by several players, including catcher Brandon Inge, had submitted his resignation two days earlier.

The 2002 season also marked the end of Hall of Fame announcer Ernie Harwell's 55-year broadcasting career. In his honor, the press box at Comerica Park was renamed the Ernie Harwell Media Center.

It was one of the few things the Tigers did right all year.

In October, Alan Trammell was hired as the team's manager and former Tigers heroes Kirk Gibson and Lance parrish returned to the dugout as coaches.

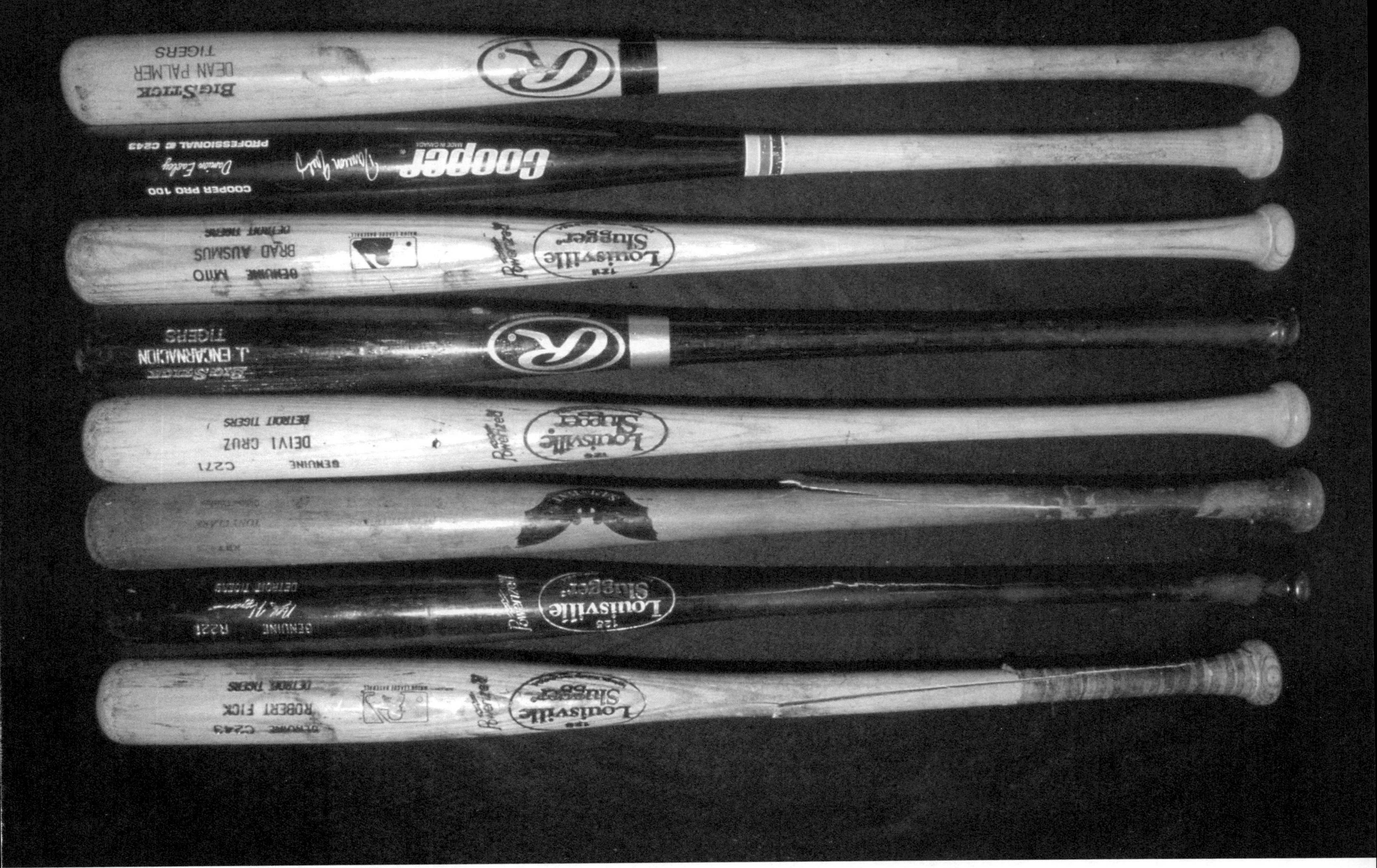

Mark Cunningham, Creative Impressions Inc.

7

ALL-TIME TIGER TALES

Players who have had the privilege of wearing the distinctive Olde English "D" for at least one game during their careers comprise one of the most exclusive clubs in all of professional sports. Since the Tigers became a charter member of the American League in 1901, almost 1,500 players share that distinction.

A handful went on to be inducted into baseball's Hall of Fame. Each player, however, left an imprint on the hearts of all Tiger fans. Sometimes it didn't take an All-Star career to carve memories that have survived more than a century. Here are some of the finest players and most memorable characters who have been part of the proud tradition.

A

Hank Aguirre
LHP Bats: R Throws: L
6'4" 205 lbs.
Played with Tigers: 1958-67
Born: 1/31/31 Died: 9/5/94

If baseball had a Will Rogers award for good guys, High Henry would have won it every year. Besides a lively fastball and a snappy curve, Aguirre's secret to success was knowing how to bear down on the field without taking himself too seriously away from the park. Everybody loved High Henry.

Acquired days before the start of spring training in 1958, Aguirre enjoyed the 10 finest seasons of his 16-year major-league career in Detroit. And he allowed Tiger fans to share in every joyous moment.

While Aguirre developed into a reliable pitcher who would be welcomed on any staff today, his legend grew as much through his anemic batting skills as it did through the prowess of his tireless left arm.

Playing before the designated hitter rule, Aguirre finished with a lifetime batting average of .085 (33/388). He had no home runs, but insisted he hit a ball to the warning track once during batting practice. Regardless of the score, fans sat on the edge of their seats waiting to see if Aguirre might somehow put a ball into play.

"I think I might be the only player in history to get a standing ovation for fouling off a pitch before striking out," Aguirre once cracked.

He also established a bittersweet distinction in 1962. While leading the American League with a 2.21 earned run average, he also set the mark for the lowest personal batting average by an ERA champ. He batted .027 on two hits in 75 at-bats.

"With any luck, though, I could have had three or four," he joked.

Aguirre joined the Tigers as a reliever. When moved to the starting rotation during the 1962 season, he posted a 16-8 record to go with his 2.21 ERA. He made a total of 42 appearances and completed 11 of his 22 starts.

Aguirre pitched one year for the Dodgers (1968)

and two for the Cubs (1969-70), ending his career with a 75-72 record and 3.25 ERA.

Born in Azusa, California, Aguirre called Detroit his home. Proud of his Mexican heritage, he eventually established a multimillion-dollar auto parts supply company that employed thousands from Detroit's growing Hispanic community.

Dale Alexander
1B Bats: R Throws: R
6'3"210 lbs.
Played with Tigers: 1929-32
Born: 4/26/03   Died: 3/2/79

Dale Alexander was the classic example of what could have been.

The big first baseman exploded with promise in his rookie season of 1929. Four years later, he was out of baseball after his career had crashed as drastically as the stock market.

His dramatic demise may have been partially caused by a burn on his leg—inflicted while he was being treated for a sprained knee—which became gangrenous. Whatever the cause, after 1930, Alexander was never the same.

In his rookie season, Alexander batted .343 and led the league with 215 hits. He also poked 25 homers and drove home 137 runs. He followed that with a .326 mark, 20 homers and 135 RBIs in 1930.

And then his career began to spiral downward. He was traded to the Red Sox in 1932 and retired after the 1933 season, perhaps wondering what might have been.

Doyle Alexander
RHP Bats: R Throws R
6'3" 190 lbs.
Played with Tigers: 1987-89
Born: 9/14/50

Doyle Alexander is remembered by Tiger fans as the present who arrived in exchange for the future.

Tiger fans also remember that when given the opportunity, the right-hander responded with more than could have been expected from a gritty veteran who survived 19 major-league seasons.

With the Tigers pushing themselves for an unlikely run at the East Division title in 1987, Alexander was acquired on August 12 in a trade with the Atlanta

Braves for 20-year-old minor-leaguer John Smoltz. Smoltz, of course, went on to become a fixture of the celebrated Braves' staff.

Had it not been for Alexander, though, the Tigers would not have won the East Division title for their second postseason appearance in a four-year span.

Alexander turned 37 just three weeks after his arrival in Detroit. Pitching with savvy and the pop of a pitcher half his age, he posted a 9-0 record and a 1.53 ERA for the Tigers when each game was a matter of survival. Down the stretch, in fact, he beat the second-place Blue Jays twice in what turned out to be one of the closest races in history.

The following year, Alexander made the All-Star team and finished with a 14-11 record. Finally, at age 39 in 1989, he ran out of gas and retired after the season.

The short, happy Tiger career of Alexander, however, is one that fans will long remember—especially that incredible stretch run to the 1987 East Division crown.

Elden Auker
RHP Bats: R Throws: R
6'2" 195 lbs.
Played with Tigers: 1933-38
Born: 9/21/10

Elden Auker was what modern players call nasty. It had nothing to do with his personality. It came from the right-hander's delivery, which was downright vicious.

A three-sport standout at Kansas State University, Auker suffered a shoulder injury in football that forced him to alter his pitching style. He developed a submarine, almost under-handed delivery that kept hitters on guard and very careful about digging in at the plate.

Auker spent the first six of his 10 big-league seasons with the Tigers. During his second year, in 1934, the Tigers captured their first pennant since 1909. Auker established himself quickly and finished the year with a 15-7 record and 3.42 ERA. He notched a complete-game 10-4 victory over the St. Louis Cardinals in Game 4 of the World Series. He suffered the loss to the legendary Dizzy Dean in Game 7.

In 1935, Auker did not get a decision against the Chicago Cubs when the Tigers won their first World

Series. However, the wicked underhander did his part to lead Detroit to the pennant by posting an 18-7 record for a league-leading .720 winning percentage.

As the players would say, he was nasty.

B

Dave Bergman
1B Bats: L Throws: L
6'2" 185 lbs.
Played with Tigers: 1984-92
Born: 6/6/53

It was merely one at-bat.

But for delirious Tiger fans in the magical year of 1984, it became one for the ages.

Before a packed house and a national television audience on June 4, Dave Bergman turned that one at-bat into a symbol of Detroit's undeterred ride to a world championship.

It was about a 10-minute duel between Toronto pitcher Roy Lee Jackson and Bergman that packed the drama of a two-hour Alfred Hitchcock classic. With two men on base and the score tied at three-all in the last of the 10th inning, Bergman went to war with Jackson. Foul ball after foul ball after foul ball kept a city on edge and TV viewers glued to their screens.

Finally, on the fateful 13th pitch, Bergman delivered a shot into the right field upper deck for a 6-3 victory.

During his nine-year Tiger career, however, Bergman proved over and over again that he was not a one at-bat wonder.

"Dave's the essence of the ultimate professional," commented longtime Tiger great Alan Trammell. "He's always prepared and does all the little things to help a team win."

Although rarely a regular, Bergman was a team leader with his hustle and preparedness for every situation. Manager Sparky Anderson often referred to him as being an extra coach on the bench.

Bergman was more than a deadly clutch hitter. He also was an unparalleled first baseman who often was inserted for defense late in a game.

After finishing his baseball career with the Tigers, Bergman chose to make Detroit his home. Through the same dedication he practiced on the field, he has developed into an equally successful financial planner. He remains committed to a variety of charities in the Detroit area.

Ray Boone
3B Bats: R Throws: R
6'0" 170 lbs.
Played with Tigers: 1953-58
Born: 7/27/23

He's the granddaddy of baseball's celebrated Boone Clan. And he was a dandy.

Ray Boone spent 13 years as a big-league infielder and enjoyed his most productive seasons wearing the Olde English "D."

Ray's son, Bob, spent 19 years as a major-league catcher. When he retired, Bob held the major-league record for most games caught. He then went on to a major-league managing career. Bob's sons, Bret and Aaron, are also major-leaguers. Bret is the All-Star second baseman for Seattle. He led the league in RBIs in 2001.

But it all began with Ray and his knack for big hits when they counted most.

"Ray was the kind of guy who every player looked up to," said former teammate and Hall of Famer Al Kaline. "He was steady."

In 1955, Boone and Kaline were a potent one-two punch. Kaline became the youngest player to win an American League batting title with a .340 average. Boone chipped in with a .295 mark and tied Boston's Jackie Jensen for the league lead with 116 RBIs.

Known as "Ike" to his friends, Boone hit at least 20 home runs in four consecutive seasons. In 1958, he belted four grand slams—two for Detroit and two for Cleveland.

Boone came to Detroit as part of an eight-player trade in 1953. The Tigers acquired him as a replacement for George Kell, who later was elected to Baseball's Hall of Fame.

On September 20, 1953, Boone received perhaps the highest compliment of his career in a *Detroit News* story that carried the headline: "He Made the Fans Forget George Kell."

Well, maybe not quite. But Ray Boone certainly gave Tiger fans enough clutch hits and gritty play for which to remember him.

Tommy Bridges
RHP   Bats: R Throws: R
5'10"   155 lbs.
Played with Tigers: 1930-46
Born: 12/28/06   Died: 4/19/68

Tommy Bridges spent his entire 16-season career with the Tigers proving to American League hitters that what they saw wasn't always what they got.

A quiet, unassuming, slender figure, Bridges more resembled his physician father than the terror he came to be for enemy hitters. After he graduated from the University of Tennessee, it was expected that Bridges would follow his father's footsteps into medicine.

Shortly after choosing baseball instead, Bridges made those enemy hitters wish he had chosen a scalpel instead of his deceptive fastball and frustrating curve.

Bridges was a "big game" pitcher. He appeared in four World Series and posted a 4-1 record, including the seventh-game victory over the Cubs in 1935. In that Series-clinching complete-game performance,

Fearsome pitcher Tommy Bridges played in four World Series, was named to six All-Star games and played all 16 years of his career with Detroit. Burton Historical Society

Bridges displayed the tenacity that marked his career. With the score tied at three-all, Chicago's Stan Hack opened the ninth with a triple. Bridges then bore down to retire the next three batters, leaving Hack stranded at third. The Tigers rallied in the last of the ninth for their first world championship.

Bridges was named to six All-Star teams and picked up the victory in 1939 at Yankee Stadium.

He didn't need the physique or flair of many of his contemporaries. He relied on tenacity, savvy and hard-breaking pitches to establish himself as one of the most reliable pitchers of his era.

Bridges won 22 games in 1934, 21 in 1935, and led the league with 23 in 1936. He led the league in strikeouts in 1935 and 1936. On August 5, 1932, he came within on out of pitching a perfect game at Navin Field. After yielding a single, he retired the next batter for one of his three one-hitters.

Bridges finished his career with 192 victories. He most certainly would have reached 200 if not for having missed the 1944 season when he was called into military service at the age of 37. He was inducted into the Michigan Sports Hall of Fame in 1963.

Ed Brinkman
SS   Bats: R Throws: R
6'0"   170 lbs.
Played with Tigers: 1971-74
Born: 12/8/41

He was called "Steady Eddie" for his reliable play at shortstop. Willie Horton affectionately nicknamed him "Wimpy" for his slightly less than athletic looking physique.

But Ed Brinkman couldn't care less about what anyone might call him. All that really mattered was that he be called into the starting lineup for every game.

Brinkman came to Detroit in 1971 after spending the first 10 years of his major-league career with the old Washington Senators. He, along with pitcher Joe Coleman and third baseman Aurelio Rodriguez, were part of the celebrated trade that sent Denny McLain to the Senators.

Although he spent just four seasons in Detroit, Brinkman made the most of them. In 1972 when the Tigers won the East Division championship, he won a Gold Glove and set four single-season records for shortstops: fielding percentage (.990); consecutive errorless

Shortstop Eddie Brinkman, 1972 Tiger of the Year, receives his award on the field at Tiger Stadium from Jim Hawkins, chairman of the Detroit Chapter of the Baseball Writers Association of America. Collection of Jim Hawkins Productions Inc.

games (72); fewest errors (7); and consecutive errorless chances (331).

After the Tigers clinched the title, Brinkman unwittingly caused an awkward moment for local TV crews. In the excitement of the celebrating clubhouse, part of Brinkman's spontaneous answer to a reporter's question on live TV was: "This is the best bunch of *%&@ing guys I ever played with."

Brinkman was a bonus baby from Cincinnati and wound up playing shortstop for the Senators right out of high school. One of his amateur teammates was Pete Rose, who signed for considerably less money with the hometown Reds.

Tom Brookens
3B Bats: R Throws: R
5'10" 165 lbs
Played with Tigers: 1979-88
Born: 8/10/53

Tom Brookens had a wry sense of humor that kept all of his teammates loose in the tightest situation.

"I hate when they play that song," he once told a teammate on the steps of the dugout after the conclusion of the National Anthem. "Every time they play it, I have a bad day."

Brookens brought more than a sense of humor to the park. He brought a tough, scrappy blue-collar work ethic that allowed him to realize more success than his natural talents allowed.

"From the first time Tommy came up, I kept looking around for someone to play third base," manager Sparky Anderson recalled. "Tommy never complained. He stuck around, worked hard and eventually played his way into the position."

Determination marked the essence of Brookens. Not only was he popular with his teammates, his blue-collar grit made him a favorite with the fans. No one ever left the park thinking Brookens hadn't given everything he had.

Brookens's single-game highlight came on August 20, 1980 at Milwaukee. In that game, Brookens went five-for-five with a triple and a home run. He stole a base and had the distinction of starting a triple play.

A product of the Tiger farm system, Brookens played 10 of his 11 major-league seasons for Detroit.

William "Gates" Brown
OF Bats: L Throws: R
5'11" 220 lbs.
Played with Tigers: 1963-75
Born: 5/2/39

He was "The Gator" and he still is. Throughout the entire metropolitan Detroit area, the name is still filled with magic.

His story is familiar and was made into an Emmy-winning documentary hosted by Joe Garagiola in 1973. The signing of William "Gates" Brown in November 1959 was a gamble by the Tigers that the Gator turned into a windfall for the franchise. Signed out of prison in Crestline, Ohio, the Gator not only turned his life completely around, but also gave the Tigers one of the most colorful characters in franchise history.

Though rarely used as a regular, the Gator combined his stone-cold patience and uncanny ability to dissect a pitcher to make himself one of the game's all-time premier pinch hitters.

The Gator thrived on pressure, which made his role as a pinch hitter a perfect fit. He wasted no time giving Tiger fans a taste of things to come when he delivered a pinch home run in his first major-league-at bat on June 19, 1963. In the world championship sea-

son of 1968, he was deadly coming off the bench and batted .370. On August 11 of that year, he single-handedly beat the Boston Red Sox in both games of a doubleheader. His 11th-inning pinch home run won the opener. He followed that with a game-winning RBI single in the ninth inning of the second game. He retired with 16 career pinch-hit homers.

"He was the one player during a game that scared me more than anyone in the league," Hall of Fame Baltimore manager Earl Weaver said. "I used to stare in their dugout watching every move he made. I tried everything I could to keep him out of a game."

There was one time, however, when manager Mayo Smith caught the Gator by surprise by sending him to the plate early in a game.

"I knew Mayo never called on me till at least the seventh inning," the Gator explained. "So in about the third or fourth inning, I was hiding at the end of the dugout munching on a hot dog. When he told me to grab a bat and go up to hit, I stuffed the dog inside my jersey so he couldn't see."

The Gator ripped a line drive down the right field line and legged it into a double with a headfirst slide into second. When he stood up to brush off the dirt, his jersey was splashed with mustard, to the amusement of the umpire and the players on both sides.

The Gator was extremely popular with his teammates, and his natural charisma made him an instant fan favorite. After his playing career, he served as a Tiger batting coach and was part of the 1984 championship team.

He still makes Detroit his home and remains actively involved with a variety of community and charitable activities. He was elected to the Michigan Sports Hall of Fame in 2002.

The Gator. No other words are necessary to bring a smile to any Tiger fan's face.

Jim Bunning
RHP Bats: R Throws: R
6'3" 190 lbs.
Played with Tigers: 1955-63
Born: 10/23/31

Jim Bunning is the only United States senator privileged to sit on the stage at the annual Baseball Hall of Fame induction ceremonies in Cooperstown. That's

Bunning finished his career with a 224-184 record and 3.27 ERA. At the time of his retirement after the 1971 season, Bunning was second to the legendary Walter Johnson with 2,855 strikeouts. He turned his economics degree from Xavier University into a post-baseball career in politics. He served in the U.S. House of Representatives before successfully running for a senatorial seat.

He also put his education to work while he was in the game. He was a founding member of the players' union and was instrumental in starting the players' pension fund.

Bunning was elected to baseball's Hall of Fame by the Veterans Committee in 1996. He was inducted into the Michigan Sports Hall of Fame in 1981.

Donie Bush
SS   Bats: B Throws: R
5'6"   140 lbs.
Played with Tigers: 1908-21
Born: 10/8/87   Died: 3/28/72

Former pitcher Jim Bunning is the only senator in the Baseball Hall of Fame. Burton Historical Society

because the Republican senator from Kentucky is an officially elected member of baseball's most exclusive club.

The former Tiger and Phillies pitcher earned his way into the prestigious Hall by winning more than 100 games and striking out more than 1,000 batters with each team. He became the first pitcher since Cy Young—and the lone modern-day pitcher—to reach those numbers in both leagues.

Bunning fired a no-hitter for Detroit on July 20, 1958 at Boston when he shut out the Red Sox, 3-0. Pitching for the Phillies on June 21, 1964, he notched a 6-0 perfect game over the Mets at New York.

Jim was a fierce competitor with an intimidating sidearm delivery that often had right-handed batters scrambling for cover. He led the American League with a 20-8 record in 1957. It was the first of seven straight seasons with double-digit victories for the Tigers. He led the league in strikeouts in 1959 and 1960, notching 201 in each season.

In his own way, Donie Bush was a better table setter than a head waiter at a five-star restaurant.

The diminutive switch-hitting shortstop was one of the best leadoff hitters of his era. He got on base for the big boys in the batting order and then proceeded to drive pitchers crazy with his antics on the base paths.

In the pennant-winning year of 1909, Bush had 53 stolen bases and led the league with 88 walks. It marked the first of four straight seasons in which he led the league in bases on balls. After "slipping" to 80 walks in 1913, he bounced back to lead the league with 112 the following season.

While teammate Ty Cobb was the acknowledged base-stealing champion of the world, Bush served as a perfect complement. From 1909 through 1915, Bush never stole fewer than 35 in a season.

Although he finished his career with a lifetime batting average of just .250, he stole 403 bases and walked 1,158 times. Along with Cobb, Bush was a spark plug. He was an outstanding defensive shortstop and a friend to all pitchers.

After 14 seasons with the Tigers, Bush finished his career with Washington and wound up as the Senators' manager.

C

Les Cain
LHP   Bats: L Throws: L
6'1"   200 lbs.
Played with Tigers: 1968-1972
Born: 1/13/48

Les Cain left a greater impact on baseball off the field than he did on. The lefty filed a workman's compensation claim against the club, which was upheld by the Michigan Bureau of Workman's Compensation. Cain contended that Tiger manager Billy Martin forced him to pitch with a sore arm that resulted in the end of his career. Cain was awarded $111 per week for the rest of his life. Later, he and the Tigers agreed to a lump sum settlement. It's the only judgment in baseball history whereby a club was required to pay a lifetime stipend.

Although his career was short, he was part of the 1968 world championship team and the 1972 East Division champions. He won 12 games in 1970 and 10 in 1971.

Cain also holds the distinction of being the last Tiger pitcher to hit a home run before the designated hitter rule was put into place in 1973. He belted a homer off Chicago's Tom Bradley on August 28, 1971.

Norm Cash
1B   Bats: L Throws: L
6'0"   185 lbs.
Played with Tigers: 1960-74
Born: 11/10/34   Died: 10/12/86

Norm Cash may not have been the best player to have ever worn the Tiger uniform. Countless teammates and Tiger fans, however, would argue that he was the most popular.

"Stormin' Norman" earned the nickname for more than his ferocious play on the field. He attacked life with the same voracious appetite he had for the game. There was nothing halfway about Norm Cash. And everybody loved him for it.

"There was no one else like him," said former teammate Gates Brown. "He might have been hurt... he might have stayed out all night... or it might have been a combination of both and he *still* would go into that lineup and play harder than anyone else on the field. He made life fun for everyone around him. He was a real man."

Cash mastered the trick of playing the game as hard as he could without taking himself too seriously. His enthusiasm was contagious.

In 1973 at Tiger Stadium when California's Nolan Ryan was firing a no-hitter at the Tigers, Cash tried to break the tension. Striding to the plate for his final attempt at Ryan, Cash carried a table leg instead of a bat. The umpire asked him what he was doing.

"I can't hit him with a bat," Cash cracked. "I might as well try this."

Norm Cash (left) receives a bat full of holes to symbolize his 1,081 career strikeouts from Jim Hawkins, chairman of the Detroit Chapter of the Baseball Writers Association of America on Norm Cash Day at Tiger Stadium August 12, 1973. Collection of Jim Hawkins Productions Inc.

Cash was a classic left-handed power hitter. He finished his career with 377 home runs, all but four with the Tigers. Except for Al Kaline (399), no player has hit more for the Tigers. He hit 25 or more in a season seven times. His most memorable year was 1961 when the Tigers made a run at the Yankees with 101 victories. Cash led the league with a booming .361 average. He also set career highs with 41 homers and 132 RBIs.

Even when he struck out, Cash did so with bravado. And when he connected, there was usually little doubt. He was the first Tiger to hit a ball completely out of Tiger Stadium. He cleared the right field roof on June 11, 1961. Ted Williams was the first to hit one over the roof and Mickey Mantle did it three times before Cash connected. Cash, however, did it three times later and is the only player to have done it four times.

Along with his penchant for clutch hits, Cash was a dazzling first baseman. He picked errant throws out of the dirt like a professional pickpocket. He could chase a foul pop fly down the right field line in his sleep. No one who played in Tiger Stadium ever did it better.

Cash made the most of his one World Series opportunity. In 1968 he collected 10 hits, including a homer, for a .385 average. He scored five runs and batted in five.

The numbers are impressive. But numbers were never the measure of Norm Cash. He was one of a kind. And Tiger fans will never forget him. He was inducted into the Michigan Sports Hall of Fame in 1984.

Ty Cobb (see page 26)

Mickey Cochrane (see page 52)

Rocky Colavito
OF Bats: R Throws: R
6'3" 190 lbs.
Played with Tigers: 1960-63
Born: 8/10/33

He was the hamburger who was traded for steak.

At least, that's the way Cleveland general manager Frank Lane described the deal that sent home run champion Rocky Colavito from the Indians to Detroit in exchange for batting champ Harvey Kuenn just before the start of the 1960 season.

The Detroit Free Press summarized the deal in a headline: 42 Home Runs for 140 Singles.

It was one of the most controversial trades in the game's history. Fans in both cities were irate after it was announced. Colavito's raw power and matinee idol good looks, however, quickly won Tiger fans to his side.

Colavito delivered the power the Tigers were looking for. In his four Detroit seasons he hit 35, 45, 37 and 22 home runs. He knocked in 140 runs in 1961 and followed that with 112.

Rocky became a fan favorite, especially with the young girls. His routine before getting into the batter's box was worth the price of admission. Twisting and stretching like a yoga instructor, he'd finish with the bat high over his head and then make the sign of the cross. Once in the box, he'd point the bat straight at the pitcher.

Colavito also was known for his well-publicized contract battles with GM Jim Campbell. In the end, however, he took any frustration out on enemy pitchers.

Joe Coleman, Jr.
RHP Bats: R Throws: R
6'3" 180 lbs.
Played with Tigers: 1971-76
Born: 2/3/47

Joe Coleman, Jr. got his first taste of big-league life when he was a boy and his father pitched for Philadelphia and Baltimore during a 10-year career. By the time he was grown, Coleman had more talent than his journeyman father ever had.

Coming to the Tigers as part of the famous Denny McLain trade to Washington, Coleman enjoyed his finest seasons in Detroit. He posted a 20-9 record with a 3.15 ERA in his first season. When the Tigers won the East Division title in 1972, Coleman was a workhorse with a 19-14 record and a sizzling 2.80 ERA. In 1973, Coleman notched a personal high of 23 victories.

He wound up with a career mark of 142-135 with a 3.69 ERA for 15 major-league seasons. He certainly did make his daddy proud.

Harry Coveleski
LHP Bats: B Throws: L
6'0" 180 lbs.
Played with Tigers: 1914-18
Born: 4/23/86 Died: 8/4/50

Harry Coveleski earned the nickname "The Giant Killer" for beating the New York Giants three times in five days in the middle of a pennant race during his rookie season with the Phillies in 1908.

He never recaptured that glory until he joined the Tigers in 1914. He strung together three straight seasons of at least 21 victories and pitched more than 303 innings in each. Although his career ended after one game in 1918, he finished with an 81-55 record and a 2.39 ERA.

Sam Crawford (see page 38)

Alvin "General" Crowder
RHP Bats: L Throws: R
5'10" 170 lbs.
Played with Tigers: 1934-36
Born: 1/11/99 Died: 4/3/72

His Detroit stay was brief, but extremely effective. General Crowder was one of those pitchers who made the most of a situation.

Traded to Detroit from Washington toward the end of the 1934 season, Crowder went 5-1 in nine games as the Tigers won the pennant. Starting in the rotation the following year when the Tigers won their first world championship, Crowder posted a 16-10 record and also won Game 4 against the Cubs in the World Series.

Crowder's finest seasons came while he was with Washington. He led the league in victories in 1932 and 1933 with 26 and 24. He participated in the first All-Star Game in 1933. He finished with a major-league mark of 167-115.

In addition to his contributions on the mound, Crowder was also known for the tattoo he had received while serving in the navy. A picture of a naked lady ran from his shoulder to his elbow on his right arm.

D

Hooks Dauss
RHP Bats: R Throws: R
5'10" 170 lbs.
Played with Tigers: 1912-26
Born: 9/22/89 Died: 7/27/63

His given name was George, but everyone called him "Hooks" in tribute to his wicked curveball. And the right-hander from Indianapolis certainly made the most of it.

Dauss turned his talent of cracking a curve into a 15-year big-league career—all with the Tigers. After going 1-1 in two appearances in 1912, Dauss never again won fewer than 12 games in any season the rest of his career. He was a 20-game winner three times and set a personal high of 24 in 1915.

Dauss was amazingly consistent and almost always stuck around in a game long enough to get a decision. He posted 10 winning seasons and had 15 or more victories in seven of them. He is the all-time Tiger leader with 221 victories and also has the most losses (182). He is second all-time in Tiger appearances (538) and third (388) in games started.

Dauss retired in 1927 because of a heart ailment.

Bill "Wild Bill" Donovan
RHP Bats: R Throws: R
5'11" 190 lbs.
Played with Tigers: 1903-1912, 1918
Born: 10/13/76 Died: 12/9/23

Bill Donovan was tagged with the name "Wild Bill" for the large number of walks he yielded, particularly at the beginning of his career. But he had a lot of lively stuff to go with it and turned himself into one of the most important characters during Detroit's pennant-winning years of 1907-09.

Perhaps another reason for the name was his fiery spirit that landed him in countless brawls. One particularly celebrated incident occurred with acknowledged Detroit mobster Bill Constantine. Donovan took it upon himself to give the underworld figure a taste of his own medicine after catching him flirting with his wife.

It was on the mound, though, that Donovan made most of his noise. He was phenomenal in 1907 when the Tigers captured their first pennant, going 25-4 with a 2.19 ERA. He also led the league with 25 wins while pitching for Brooklyn in the National League in 1901.

Donovan left the Tigers in 1915 to become player-manager for the New York Yankees. He returned to Detroit in 1918 for a couple of games and retired after the season.

Donovan finished with a lifetime mark of 186-139 and a 2.69 ERA. He won 141 games for the Tigers with a 2.49 ERA.

E

Darrell Evans
1B Bats: L Throws: R
6'2" 205 lbs.
Played with Tigers: 1984-88
Born: 5/26/47

Darrell Evans's short career with the Tigers was a sweet one, not only for the power-hitting lefty, but also for the fans.

After becoming Detroit's first major free agent player, prior to the championship 1984 season, Evans drilled a three-run homer in the season opener at Minnesota. It was merely a sign of the good things to come.

Evans contributed 16 homers during his first Tiger season. He followed that with 40 the next to become the oldest player (38) to lead the league in homers.

Along with being a dangerous clutch hitter, Evans was credited with being a steadying influence on a young, developing, winning team.

Evans played in the major leagues for 21 years. He finished with 414 home runs and 1,354 RBIs. At the time he retired, he was eighth on the all-time list with 1,605 walks.

Walter "Hoot" Evers
OF Bats: R Throws: R
6'2" 185 lbs.
Played with Tigers: 1941, 1946-52, 1954
Born: 2/8/21 Died: 1/25/91

In 1985, Darrell Evans was the oldest player, at age 38, to lead the league in home runs with 40. He still had a powerful swing in 1988 when this photo was taken. Dan Ewald Jr.

Hoot Evers enjoyed a solid career, though not quite the spectacular one that the Tigers had expected after signing him out of the University of Illinois in 1941.

His biggest contributions to the organization came after his playing career, when he moved from Cleveland's front office to Detroit's to become the farm director. Evers was a strict disciplinarian and a stickler for detail. It was during his tenure that the farm system developed the nucleus of players who would win the world championship in 1984.

Evers was a fierce competitor who wasn't afraid to let his emotions show. Perhaps the spectacular promise he had flashed would have been realized had it not been for World War II. After playing one game for the Tigers at the end of the 1941 season, he was returned to the minor leagues. His career was put on hold in 1943 when he was called into service in the Army Air

Corps. He didn't return to the Tigers till 1946 and missed half that year with a broken ankle.

Still, there were high points. From 1948 through 1950, he never batted lower than .303. He enjoyed his finest season in 1950, batting .323 with 21 homers and 103 RBIs. He was traded during the 1952 season and played for several teams before retiring after the 1956 season.

On September 7, 1950 against the Indians, Evers hit for the cycle. In that same year, the steady center fielder set an American League record for outfielders with a .997 fielding percentage. He went 115 games without making an error.

Evers picked up the nickname "Hoot" from his childhood days, when he idolized cowboy movie star Hoot Gibson. The name stuck. So did his passion for the game, which paid dividends for the Tigers.

F

Mark "The Bird" Fidrych
RHP Bats: R Throws: R
6'3" 175 lbs.
Played with Tigers: 1976-80
Born: 8/14/54

He talked to the ball. He manicured the mound by hand before the start of each inning. And in the process, he stole the hearts of baseball fans all over the country.

It was 1976—the summer of "The Bird." It was magical, mystical—almost make-believe. And true to any fairy tale, it was all too brief.

It happened so suddenly and disappeared just as quickly. But the memories Mark Fidrych left baseball were good enough for several lifetimes.

"I don't believe any one player ever dominated the game for one season the way that Mark did," said the late Tiger president and general manager Jim Campbell. "You almost had to see it to believe it."

The Bird's popularity actually transcended the game. Fidrych earned his nickname because his long curly blond hair and awkward gait resembled the Big Bird character on the TV show *Sesame Street*. He wore T-shirts and blue jeans. A pair of clean gym shoes were his one concession to convention.

And this gangly, unpretentious 21-year-old captured the imaginations of fans of every age.

"He was a rock star in a baseball uniform," former Tiger Bill Freehan remarked. "What else can you say? He was great for the game. Everybody loved him."

Fidrych filled Tiger Stadium every time he pitched. He did the same thing on the road, which prompted several general managers to beg the Tigers for a Fidrych start and a hefty payday. Once, when he wasn't pitching, Fidrych set up a table behind home plate during batting practice and signed autographs for kids. Of course, all for free.

After a couple of relief appearances at the start of the 1976 season, Fidrych worked his way into the starting rotation. Once he did, a legend was born.

With the precision of a laser, Fidrych nipped each corner of the plate. He tangled up even the most celebrated hitters with a fastball, slider, and a mystique that no one, to this day, can fully understand.

Fidrych finished the season with a 19-9 record. He led the league with a 2.34 ERA and completed an unheard-of 24 of 31 starts. He was the runaway winner of the Rookie of the Year Award.

As suddenly as his star began to sparkle, however, it just as suddenly crashed to earth. Knee and arm injuries limited Fidrych to just 11 starts the following year. He made a total of 16 starts in parts of each of the following three years.

"I'm not bitter," Fidrych said of his personal misfortune, which was as much a loss for the fans as it was for him. "Look at all the good things that happened to me. How many guys can say they got a chance to pitch in the big leagues? If the Tigers hadn't given me a chance, I probably would have pumped gas for a living."

He retired after the 1980 season and purchased a farm near his home in Worcester, Massachusetts. He drives a truck and lives quietly with his wife and daughter.

What he did for the game that one magical summer, baseball will never be able to fully re-pay.

Cecil Fielder
1B   Bats: R   Throws: R
6'3"   250 lbs.
Played with Tigers: 1990-96
Born: 9/21/63

He looked like a lineman who must have made the wrong turn and reported to Tiger Stadium instead of to the Lions when he arrived in Detroit.

Cecil Fielder was big. He was strong. He resembled a defensive nose tackle stuffed inside the Tigers' double-knit uniform. He had an intimidating physical presence that was overshadowed by his charismatic personality.

Together, those two traits quickly vaulted the slugger into the hearts of all Tiger fans.

And it didn't take long for all fans around the American League to discover what those in Japan already knew. The gentle giant was a run-producing machine.

After spending a year in Japan, Fielder signed as a free agent with the Tigers just prior to the 1990 season. By the time of the All-Star Game that summer, enemy pitchers were ready to pay his way back across the ocean.

Fielder didn't just arrive in Detroit. He exploded. Reviving his major-league career like a magician, he became the first American Leaguer to crack the 50-home run plateau since Roger Maris 29 years earlier. Fielder finished with 51. The one on August 25 off Oakland's Dave Stewart cleared Tiger Stadium's left field roof. With the blast, Fielder became only the third player, and the first Tiger, to accomplish the feat.

"I just wanted my chance and the Tigers gave it to me," Fielder humbly summarized his monstrous season.

And there was more to come.

After leading the major leagues with 51 homers and 132 RBIs in his first Tiger season, he followed that with 44 and 133 in 1991, and 25 and 124 in 1992. In that three-year span, Fielder joined the legendary Babe Ruth as the only players to lead the majors in RBIs for three straight seasons.

Fielder's power numbers were as prodigious as his physical presence. During his almost seven seasons with the Tigers, Fielder hit 245 home runs and knocked in 758 runs.

Before being traded to the Yankees on July 31, 1996, however, Fielder left his mark in Detroit with more than awesome displays of power. Because of his

Travis Fryman congratulates heavy-hitting Cecil Fielder at home plate after Fielder belted one of many out in 1992. Cecil "Big Daddy" Fielder was the first Tiger to blast a home run over Tiger Stadium's left field roof. Dan Ewald Jr.

size and his always-calm demeanor that made him a clubhouse leader, he was known as "Big Daddy" to his teammates. He became involved with a variety of charities that made him a leader in the community as well as with the team.

Bob "Fats" Fothergill
OF   Bats: R   Throws: R
5'10"   230 lbs.
Played with Tigers: 1922-30
Born: 8/16/97   Died: 3/20/38

Bob Fothergill was never mistaken for a model in a physical fitness magazine. Of course, none of those chiseled models could come close to swinging a bat the way Fothergill did.

Nicknamed "Fats" for his burly physique, Fothergill was a born designated hitter. Although often a liability in the outfield, he made up for his defensive deficiencies with the bat. For the decade of "The Roaring Twenties," he was definitely one of Detroit's most colorful characters.

Throughout his nine-year Tiger career, he batted under .300 only once. For three straight seasons (1925-27) he batted over .350. And in 1927 he knocked in 114 runs.

Pete Fox
OF Bats: R Throws: R
5'11"165 lbs.
Played with Tigers: 1933-40
Born: 3/8/09 Died: 7/5/66

Pete Fox played in the shadows of Hall of Fame teammates Charlie Gehringer, Hank Greenberg and Mickey Cochrane.

But during the pre-World War II decade when the Tigers won three pennants and a World Series, Fox was an anchor of the outfield and one of Detroit's steadiest hitters.

Fox had just enough speed and daring to turn many of his hits into extra bases. He never hit below .285 for the Tigers and for three straight years (1935-37) batted over .300. In the championship year of 1935, Fox hit .321 with 15 homers and 73 RBIs. He also scored 116 runs. At one point during the season he had a 35-game hitting streak.

Bill Freehan
C Bats: R Throws: R
6'3" 205 lbs.
Played with Tigers: 1961-76
Born: 11/29/41

Bill Freehan understood the concept of catching perhaps better than anyone who ever wore the mask and chest protector for the Tigers.

"I wanted to hit well, of course," he explained his philosophy. "I just never put that ahead of my primary responsibility. The catcher has to be the captain of the field. I felt if I did my job behind the plate, I was contributing to the team in the best way I could."

And there's no question. He did contribute.

Freehan became a fixture behind the plate two years after signing a $100,000 bonus contract in 1961 while he was a baseball and football star at the University of Michigan. Once he broke into Detroit's starting lineup, it was impossible to get him out.

He was, without question, the most dominant American League catcher of his era. Beginning in 1964, he was selected to 10 straight All-Star Games. After missing the one in 1974, he again was selected the next year. The only Tiger with more appearances in the Midsummer Classic is Al Kaline, with 18. In addition, starting in 1965, Freehan won five straight Gold Glove Awards.

Freehan's style of quiet leadership was best demonstrated during the world championship season of 1968. He was almost flawless, directing a pitching staff that dominated the American League. At the plate that year, he also belted a career-high 25 home runs and knocked in 84 runs. He finished second to 31-game winner Denny McLain in the MVP voting.

Freehan was instrumental in one of the most memorable plays in Tiger history. In Game 5 of the Series, he blocked home plate to prevent the speedy Lou Brock from scoring and kept the Tigers alive for their thrilling comeback.

Freehan was a better-than-average hitting catcher and still ranks in the top ten of a variety of club categories. He finished with a .262 batting average, 200 home runs and 758 RBIs.

Freehan retired after the 1976 season and spent some time as a Tiger broadcaster and also embarked on a successful business career. In 1989 he was named head baseball coach of the University of Michigan. He currently serves as a minor-league catching coach for the Tigers.

Freehan was inducted into the Michigan Sports Hall of Fame in 1982.

Travis Fryman
3B Bats: R Throws: R
6'1" 195 lbs.
Played with Tigers: 1990-97
Born: 3/25/69

Although he concluded his career with the Cleveland Indians, Travis Fryman made his mark with the Tigers.

And no Tiger fan will ever forget him.

Third baseman Travis Fryman excelled at the plate, in the field and on the basepaths. Dan Ewald Jr.

"He's one of those few players who comes to the park every day and wants to be in the lineup regardless of the standings, the weather or how he feels," said former manager Sparky Anderson. "He's one of the most intense players I ever managed. Travis could have played in any era of the game."

In the field, at the plate or on the base paths, Fryman's passion for perfection was relentless. His quiet determination often served as a spark plug for other players.

G

Charlie Gehringer (see page 58)

Kirk Gibson
OF   Bats: L   Throws: L
6'3"   215 lbs.
Played with Tigers: 1979-87; 93-95
Born: 5/28/57

Kirk Gibson was James Bond in baseball knickers. In big games, he was always around to save his teammates at the end. When all the cards had been dealt and everything was on the line, no player in the game delivered more dramatically.

"I was blessed with a lot of great players in my career," said former manager Sparky Anderson. "But I don't believe I ever saw one who consistently came up with more big hits in tight situations than Gibby."

Gibson delivered two of the most dramatic home runs in World Series history. His second home run of Game 5 in the 1984 Series sealed the Tigers' victory over San Diego. His arms-in-the-air celebration at home plate symbolized the accomplishments of the season.

His game-ending pinch-hit home run off Oakland's Dennis Eckersley in Game 1 of the 1988 World Series powered the Dodgers to a Series victory and also is one of the most often-run clips of baseball TV footage the game has ever produced.

There were others—too many to count.

"I dreamed about coming up in big situations," Gibson explained. "As a player, that's what I lived for."

Gibson was a major-league enigma. He brought the fiery intensity of a football standout to the baseball park where he had spent so many days and nights in the bleachers as a kid.

Gibson was an All-American wide receiver for Michigan State University and was a projected first-round draft choice before the Tigers beat the NFL to the punch and made him their top pick in 1978.

Neither Gibson nor the Tigers ever regretted the decision.

Gibson combined devastating power with dazzling speed that provided Tiger fans with memories for a lifetime. But it was Gibson's drive and his ability to perform against all odds that etched his name in baseball history.

In the championship season of 1984, Gibson hit .282 with 27 homers and 91 RBIs. He also became the first Tiger to hit 20 homers and steal 20 bases in a season. In the playoff against Kansas City, Gibson hit .417 and was named the LCS Most Valuable Player.

Kirk Gibson made the right choice when he joined the Tigers instead of the NFL in 1978. Collection of Jim Hawkins Productions Inc.

In 1987 when the Tigers made a miracle come-back to win the East Division, Gibson prevented a four-game sweep by the Blue Jays in Toronto by hitting a home run and a game-winning single. In the last three games of the season the following weekend in Detroit, the Tigers swept the Blue Jays for the title.

Statistics meant little to Gibson, however. The only numbers that counted were those in the victory column.

Gibson left the Tigers through free agency after the 1987 season. He returned for three more seasons starting in 1993. And as usual, they were memorable.

Gibson later became a Tiger TV analyst and a successful radio commentator. In 2002, he donned a Tiger uniform again as Alan Trammell's bench coach. He was inducted into the Michigan Sports Hall of Fame in 1999.

Leon "Goose" Goslin
OF   Bats: L Throws: R
5'11"   185 lbs.
Played with Tigers: 1934-37
Born: 10/16/00   Died: 5/15/71

He was one of the fabled "G-Men" along with Charlie Gehringer and Hank Greenberg.

And even though his Detroit career was brief, Leon "Goose" Goslin made it a memorable one by helping the Tigers win their first world championship in 1935. It was Goslin's ninth-inning single that scored Mickey Cochrane to snap a three-all tie and send the city into a raucous celebration.

"I hadn't had a hit all day in that game," Goslin later explained. "When I came up to bat there in the ninth with the score tied, two out and Mickey Cochrane on second, I said to the umpire, 'If they pitch that ball over this plate, you can go take that monkey suit off.' Sure enough, the first ball Larry French threw in there—zoom."

Goslin was brought to Detroit from Washington at the end of his career precisely for his knack of deliv-ering clutch hits. Playing for Washington in the 1924 Series, he set a record with six straight hits. He held the record alone until New York's Thurman Munson tied it in 1976.

Goslin made the most of every World Series op-portunity he had. He appeared in five and posted a .287 average with seven home runs and 18 RBIs.

Goslin joined the Tigers in 1934 and batted .305 with 100 RBIs as the Tigers won the first of two straight pennants. In the championship year of 1935, he bat-ted .292 with 109 RBIs. The following season he bat-ted .315 with 125 RBIs.

During his 18-year career, Goslin knocked in at least 100 runs in 11 seasons. Of course, the most memo-rable ones for Tiger fans came when he played in De-troit. And there were plenty.

Goslin was inducted into the Michigan Sports Hall of Fame in 1965 and baseball's Hall of Fame in 1968.

Hank Greenberg (see page 64)

Personable Hall of Famer Goose Goslin swings for the fences. **Brace Photo**

H

Richie Hebner
3B Bats: L Throws: R
6'1" 195 lbs.
Played with Tigers: 1980-82
Born: 11/26/47

Richie Hebner still digs graves during the off season near his hometown of Boston. Some habits are hard to break. With his bat during his brief two-and-a-half-year stay with the Tigers, Hebner certainly buried a lot of American League pitchers.

Until an August injury to his right instep limited him to pinch hitting duties during his first Tiger season, Hebner was unstoppable with men in scoring position. He collected 82 RBIs that year in just 341 at-bats.

Hebner was a brash, blue-collar player with an impeccable work ethic that mirrored the city. He has served as a minor-league hitting coach for several organizations.

Harry Heilmann (see page 46)

Mike Henneman
RHP Bats: R Throws: R
6'4" 210 lbs.
Played with Tigers: 1987-95
Born: 12/11/61

Mike Henneman never received the fanfare usually associated with today's successful closers. In his quiet steady manner, however, the right-hander finished his Tiger career with 154 saves than any pitcher in club history.

"Publicity never meant a lot to me," he said. "My manager and teammates knew if I was doing my job."

Rarely were they disappointed. Henneman took over as the team's top closer almost from the time he joined the Tigers during the 1987 season. When Willie Hernandez struggled as the closer during the pennant race of that season, Henneman stepped in and performed like a time-tested veteran. He finished the season with an 11-3 record and seven saves. Two victories and a save came during the final four games against the Toronto Blue Jays.

For his 2.98 ERA, Henneman was named *The Sporting News* American League Rookie Pitcher of the Year. And there was more to follow.

Before being traded to Houston during the 1995 season, Henneman notched 154 saves for the Tigers to bypass John Hiller who held the club record with 125.

Not too bad for a career of anonymity.

Ray Herbert
RHP Bats: R Throws: R
5'11" 185 lbs.
Played with Tigers: 1950-51, 1953-54
Born: 12/15/29

Ray Herbert was the local boy who never reached his potential until he went away from home. Signed out of Detroit's Catholic Central High School, Herbert spent his first four years with the Tigers before moving to three other teams during a 14-year big-league career. He was 12-14 while with Detroit.

Herbert went 20-9 and led the league with a .690 winning percentage for the White Sox in 1962. He finished with a career mark of 104-107. After retiring, Herbert returned to the Detroit area and often served as a Tiger batting practice pitcher. He now resides in the northern part of Michigan's Lower Peninsula.

Willie Hernandez
LHP Bats: L Throws: L
6'3" 185 lbs.
Played with Tigers: 1984-89
Born: 11/14/54

For the magical season of 1984, Willie Hernandez was more untouchable than Eliot Ness. No closer had ever enjoyed such a season.

"For that season, he was the greatest thing since TV remote control," said manager Sparky Anderson. "Just press a button, call him in, and get ready to say good night."

Hernandez led the league that year and set a Tiger club record with 80 appearances. He had 33 save opportunities and cashed in on all but one. He coupled that with a 9-3 record and 1.92 ERA. For that unprecedented effort, Hernandez won both the American League's MVP and Cy Young Awards.

Relief pitcher Willie Hernandez celebrates with catcher Lance Parrish after he recorded the final out in Game 5 to win the 1984 World Series. Ron Heflin, AP/Wide World Photos

"He made me look pretty smart," Sparky cracked.

No one—not even the Tigers—realized at the time of the trade of John Wockenfuss and Glenn Wilson for Hernandez and Dave Bergman on March 24 that the deal would turn into highway robbery.

Hernandez masterfully mixed his fastball and his back-door screwball to completely baffle enemy hitters, who averaged a meager .194 against him. He finished all three playoff games and notched a save. He finished three games in the World Series and picked up two saves.

Hernandez recorded 31 saves the next season and 24 the year after that. He began to run out of steam and finished his 13-year career with a 70-63 record and 147 saves after the 1989 season.

For the make-believe season of 1984, however, he was the unstoppable stopper.

Larry Herndon
OF   Bats: R   Throws: R
6'3"   195 lbs.
Played with Tigers: 1982-88
Born: 11/3/53

The image of Larry Herndon racing in to snag the last out of the final game of the 1984 World Series is permanently etched in the memories of all Tiger fans.

Herndon was an unassuming player whose penchant for big plays belied his pleasant personality and his desire to be considered merely a member of the team.

Herndon triggered Detroit's first-game 3-2 victory in the World Series with a two-run homer in the fifth inning. Instead of talking about it after the game in the media interview room, however, Herndon chose to dash out of the stadium—still in uniform—and return to the hotel.

"I was just happy for the team," he later explained. "I happened to hit a homer. Any one of us could have done it. I didn't want to talk about it."

In the season-ending game that decided the East Division championship of 1987, Frank Tanana rode Herndon's second-inning home run into a 1-0 complete-game victory.

And no Tiger fan is likely to forget his home run on Opening Day of that season. Facing New York's Dennis Rasmussen, Herndon unloaded a Herculean blast that smashed off the center field upper deck above the 440-foot sign.

After his retirement in 1988, Herndon served as a Tiger hitting coach. He was a man of few words who was able to carry his message to so many fans.

John Hiller
LHP   Bats: R   Throws: L
6'0"   195 lbs.
Played with Tigers: 1965-70; 1972-80
Born: 4/8/43

He was called "Ratso" for his resemblance to the character portrayed by Dustin Hoffman in the movie

Pitcher John Hiller (right), 1973 Comeback Player of the Year and Fireman of the Year, is presented with a new watch by **The Sporting News** *correspondent Jim Hawkins. Collection of Jim Hawkins Productions Inc.*

Midnight Cowboy. Ironically, it was John Hiller's life that had the ingredients of a movie.

The Canadian born left-hander was a mediocre pitcher who bounced between starting and relief after breaking in with the Tigers in 1965. On January 11, 1971, his whole life changed.

Hiller suffered a heart attack as he prepared for spring training. After bypass surgery and relentless recuperation, he returned to the team in mid-1972. The following season had all the trimmings of a genuine Hollywood screenplay.

Hiller won the Comeback of the Year Award by saving a then club-record 38 games. He posted a 10-5 record with a 1.44 ERA. He led the league with 65 appearances.

He learned it the hard way, but Hiller developed the perfect demeanor for the roller-coaster role of a stopper.

"After my heart attack, I learned what was im-

portant in life," he explained. "I always wanted to pitch well. But I also learned baseball is a game. As a stopper, sometimes you're going to get them and sometimes they're going to get you. If they get you, you have to get over it fast. The next night might belong to you."

Hiller spent his entire 15-year major-league career with the Tigers. He leads the franchise with 545 appearances. He was inducted into the Michigan Sports Hall of Fame in 1989 and also is a member of Canada's Baseball Hall of Fame. He resides in Michigan's Upper Peninsula.

Billy Hoeft
LHP Bats: L Throws: L
6'3" 180 lbs.
Played with Tigers: 1952-59
Born: 5/17/32

Billy Hoeft was one of those colorful left-handed pitchers who fell a few steps short of stardom, but was always fun to be around.

Hoeft and shortstop Harvey Kuenn were a pair of prospects from Wisconsin who provided plenty of entertainment for teammates and fans during the carefree decade of the '50s. He debuted with the Tigers in 1952. He didn't break the .500 barrier until 1955, when he made his lone All-Star appearance and finished the season at 16-7 with a 2.99 ERA. He set a personal high the following year with a 20-14 mark.

On July 14, 1957, Hoeft made his mark with the bat instead of on the pitcher's mound when he belted two home runs. He was traded during the 1959 season and played for five different teams until he retired in 1966. He still makes his home in the Detroit area.

Willie Horton
OF Bats: R Throws: R
5'11" 220 lbs.
Played with Tigers: 1963-77
Born: 10/18/42

Willie Horton was born to wear a Tiger uniform, and a statue honoring him in Comerica Park is a tribute that will keep alive the memories he created for generations to come.

"If you cut out my heart and put it on a table, you'd see it has the Olde English 'D' all over it," Horton said.

Horton grew up within walking distance of Tiger Stadium. He worked as a junior usher, dusting off seats before games, just to get into the park for free. Before graduating from Northwestern High School, he had established himself as a sandlot legend.

Playing in the Public School League championship game, the powerful right-handed hitter drilled a ball far up into the upper deck of right center field. In the spring of his senior year, scouts from several teams were knocking on his door. There was no doubt in Horton's mind, however. He was determined to sign with the Tigers.

A classic power hitter, no park was large enough to contain one of his shots when he got his muscles into it. Left field, center or right, it made no difference to Horton.

Horton broke in with the Tigers in 1963. In his first full season in 1965, he established himself as one of the league's deadliest power hitters, belting 29 homers and driving in 104 runs.

Horton was plagued by a variety of injuries throughout his career. He nevertheless persisted, finishing in the top ten of a variety of club records before he was traded to Texas at the start of the 1977 season.

Playing for Seattle in 1979, he won the Comeback Player of the Year Award by slamming 29 homers with 106 RBIs. He finished his career with 325 homers and 1,163 RBIs.

Horton provided the power during the championship season of 1968 when he poked 36 homers and drove home 85 runs. But it was his defensive gem that turned the Series around for Detroit. In Game 5, with Detroit trailing three games to one, Horton pounced on a hit to left field and fired a strike to catcher Bill Freehan, who tagged out the speedy Lou Brock to spark a dramatic Detroit comeback.

One of the strongest men ever to play for the Tigers, Horton once won the local 18-year-old Golden Gloves competition when he was just 13.

But his physical strength belies his gentle nature.

Horton remains in the Detroit area and is tireless in his efforts for charity and youth-oriented organizations. He serves as a special assistant to Tiger president Dave Dombrowski. The club retired his number (23)

in 2000 and he was inducted into the Michigan Sports Hall of Fame in 1987.

Frank House
C Bats: L Throws: R
6'1" 190 lbs.
Played with Tigers: 1950-51, 1954-57, 1961
Born: 2/18/30

Frank House was called "Pig," although his ruggedly handsome looks made the ladies of the era when he played for the Tigers disagree. The nickname allegedly was given by his teammates for the catcher's choice of fine clothes and manicured nails.

For the decade of the '50s, House was an unusually big catcher. And though his Tiger career was brief and far from remarkable, he developed into an outstanding receiver behind the plate.

House was a bonus baby from Alabama. He received $45,000 and two cars to sign. He played in a few games in 1950-51 and then became the primary catcher in 1954. His best year at the plate was 1955, when he hit 15 homers and drove home 53 runs. After the 1957 season he was part of the multiplayer deal with Kansas City that brought Billy Martin to Detroit.

After his career, House returned to Alabama, where he became involved with politics.

Art Houtteman
RHP Bats: R Throws: R
6'2" 190 lbs.
Played with Tigers: 1945-53
Born: 8/7/27

Art Houtteman was one of those pitchers who had a right to ask what might have been. A series of personal off-field setbacks perhaps prevented the right-hander from Detroit's Catholic Central High School from reaching the potential that had promised much more.

During spring training in 1949, he suffered a fractured skull in an auto accident. He still posted a 15-10 record and followed that with a 19-12 mark the next year. After the 1950 season, he was inducted into the army, but was released the following September because of severe headaches attributed to the accident. Shortly thereafter, Houtteman's seven-month-old daughter died tragically.

He was traded to Cleveland in 1953 and contributed a 15-7 record to the pennant-winning Indians of 1954. Still, the haunting off-field circumstances left many wondering what could have been.

Frank Howard
1B   Bats: R   Throws: R
6'7"   255 lbs.
Played with Tigers: 1972-73
Born: 8/8/36

Frank Howard was a giant wrapped in baseball knickers. And though his Tiger career was a mere blink of an eye, he left his mark on the team and fans alike.

Howard was a classic slugger who was acquired from the Texas Rangers for the pennant run of 1972. Although most of his power had been spent by then, he was a steadying clubhouse influence and was one-half of the largest pair of roommates in Tiger history when he teamed with Willie Horton.

While playing for the Washington Senators, Howard became just the second player to hit a ball over Tiger Stadium's left field roof. Playing for the Senators, he was nicknamed "The Capital Punisher." From 1968-70, he belted 44, 48 and 44 home runs. He finished his career with 382.

Fred Hutchinson
RHP   Bats: L   Throws: R
6'2"   200 lbs.
Played with Tigers: 1939-41, 1946-53
Born: 8/12/19   Died: 11/12/64

Fred Hutchinson was a fiery competitor who invented his own ways to vent frustration.

Once after losing a game as a Tiger pitcher, he broke every light in the tunnel that led from the dugout to the clubhouse. After a particularly tough loss when he managed the Tigers, he walked along Michigan Avenue all the way to his Dearborn home some 10 miles away.

Hutchinson spent his entire 10-year pitching career with the Tigers. He was consistent and could have been better except for a five-year military stint during World War II. When he returned, he posted six straight

seasons of double-digit victories. He was a pitcher-manager in 1952 and 1953 before settling into full-time managing in 1954.

In spite of his fiery temper, Hutchinson had a soft heart. After his managerial career ended, he returned to his Seattle home and helped to establish the Fred Hutchinson Cancer Research Center.

J

Davy Jones
OF   Bats: L   Throws: R
5'10"   165 lbs.
Played with Tigers: 1906-12
Born: 6/30/80   Died: 3/31/72

Davy Jones was like a drummer in a rock band. Everyone knows he's there, but hardly anyone knows his name.

Jones was the unsung third man of an outfield that featured Hall of Famers Ty Cobb and Sam Crawford. But he certainly knew how to set the table for the big boys.

Jones generally batted leadoff during his seven Tiger seasons. Although he never hit a home run, he stole 140 bases and never was caught. During his major-league career, record books show that he was never thrown out in 207 attempts. They also show that he never struck out as a Tiger.

For the World Series of 1907-08-09, Jones had a combined average of .265.

Jones was as valuable to the team off the field as he was on. He was one of the few friends the tempestuous Cobb had on the team.

Todd Jones
RHP   Bats: R   Throws: R
6'3"   230 lbs.
Played with Tigers: 1997-01
Born: 4/24/68

In the volatile world of the stopper, Todd Jones established himself as one of the most popular Tigers of recent years. Although his Tiger career was brief, the likeable right-hander from Alabama was steeped in team tradition. For the last game at Tiger Stadium, Jones asked Tiger legend Al Kaline if he could use the glove Al once proudly wore.

"Al Kaline is the Detroit Tigers," Jones explained. "I just felt a little piece of him should be on the field that day."

Jones packed a career full of statistics into his four-year stay with the Tigers. He finished with 142 saves, second only to Mike Henneman's club record of 154. In 2000, he posted a club record 42 saves, surpassing John Hiller's mark of 38 set in 1973.

K

Al Kaline (see page 103)

George Kell (see page 78)

Steve Kemp
OF Bats: L Throws: L
6'0" 195 lbs.
Played with Tigers: 1977-81
Born: 8/7/54

Steve Kemp was introduced to Detroit with a heavy burden on his shoulders. He was picked to replace the popular Willie Horton as the regular left fielder. The No. 1 pick in the January, 1976 free agent draft answered the call and was a consistent run producer during his five-year Tiger career.

Kemp took over the job in 1977. In 1979 and 1980 he knocked in 105 and 101 runs. After the 1981 season, he was traded to the White Sox for Chet Lemon who went on to establish himself as another Tiger fan favorite.

Ed Killian
LHP Bats: L Throws: L
5'11" 170 lbs.
Played with Tigers: 1904-10
Born: 11/12/76 Died: 7/18/28

Back in the days when fans traveled to the park via horse and buggy, Ed Killian established the importance of a left-handed pitcher. He joined the Tigers in 1904 after one year with Cleveland. He pitched for the Tigers through 1910, when he retired with a career mark of 102-78.

Killian won 23 games in 1905 and led the Tigers to their first pennant in 1907 with 25 wins and a 1.78 ERA. During the pennant drive of 1909, Killian tightened his belt and beat the Red Sox in both games of a doubleheader.

Bruce Kimm
C Bats: R Throws: R
5'11" 175 lbs.
Played with Tigers: 1976-77
Born: 6/29/51

Bruce Kimm didn't see much action when he played for the Tigers. But when Mark "The Bird" Fidrych was spinning his magical season in 1976, Kimm had the best seat in the house. That's because the backup catcher was in the starting lineup every time Fidrych pitched.

"We hit it off good," Fidrych explained simply. "He knew what he was doing behind the plate. Bruce made it easy."

Kimm hit the lone home run of his major-league career in 1976. He batted .263 in 63 games. After playing in just 14 games in 1977, he was traded to the Cubs' organization. He played nine games for the Cubs in 1979 and 100 for the White Sox in 1980 and then retired to get into coaching. He has served as manager of the AAA Iowa Cubs and had an interim stint at the helm of the big-league Cubs in 2002.

His major-league playing career was brief, but he'll always have 1976.

Harvey Kuenn
SS Bats: R Throws: R
6'2" 190 lbs.
Played with Tigers: 1952-59
Born: 12/4/30 Died: 2/28/88

Clubhouse legend still insists that Harvey Kuenn could roll out of bed and shoot at least three line drives to different parts of the field.

Clubhouse legend also holds that that often was the case.

With an uncanny ability to put the bat on the ball regardless where it was pitched, the fun-loving

Kuenn was one of the most consistent hitters of any era. In almost 7,000 times at bat, he only struck out 404 times.

He stood at the plate with a golf-ball–sized wad of tobacco stuffed inside his cheek, daring pitchers to try to throw one by him. In the end, it was Kuenn who usually won.

And regardless of the situation, Kuenn was always there, ready to play.

In 1953 and 1954, he led the league in at-bats. He also led the league in hits and doubles three times. He won the Rookie of the Year Award in 1953 when he batted .308 and set a major-league record for rookies with 679 at-bats.

Signed off the campus of the University of Wisconsin, Kuenn broke in with the Tigers in 1952 and batted .325 in 19 games. It was merely a sign of things to come. A line drive hitter who used a bat like a cue stick, he batted over .300 in seven of his eight Tiger seasons.

Kuenn was switched from shortstop to center field in 1958. The change of scenery obviously didn't bother him, as he won the 1959 batting title with a .353 average.

Just before the start of the next season, he was sent to Cleveland in exchange for home run champ Rocky Colavito in one of baseball's most controversial trades. Kuenn spent one year in Cleveland and then bounced to four different National League teams before retiring in 1966. He finished with a .303 average with 2,092 hits.

One of Kuenn's happiest years came in 1982, when he managed the Milwaukee Brewers into the World Series in his home state of Wisconsin.

L

Gene Lamont
C Bats: L Throws R
6'1" 195 lbs.
Played with Tigers: 1970-72, 1974-75
Born: 12/25/46

Gene Lamont made his biggest baseball marks managing the Chicago White Sox and Pittsburgh Pirates.

But the former catcher will forever remain a pivotal part of Tiger trivia.

For instance:
- On September 2, 1970, he homered in his first major-league at-bat in Boston;
- In 1965, he was Detroit's top pick in the first major-league free agent draft;
- He was selected ahead of Johnny Bench, who wasn't picked by Cincinnati till the second round.

Though his playing career was brief and unspectacular, his rise to managerial status was anything but trivial.

Frank Lary
RHP Bats: R Throws: R
5'11" 180 lbs.
Played with Tigers: 1954-64
Born: 4/10/30

He was nicknamed "Taters," but Tiger fans will always remember Frank Lary as "The Yankee Killer."

When facing the best that baseball had to offer, the slender right-hander from Alabama always had something better. During his 10-year Tiger career, Lary posted a remarkable 28-13 record against the bombers from the Bronx.

He started the roll in 1956 when he went 5-1 against the Yankees en route to a 21-13 overall record. In 1958, Lary's record slipped to 16-15. He notched seven of those victories against New York without suffering one loss. It marked the first time since 1916 that any pitcher had beaten the Yankees seven times in one year.

In 1959, Lary followed that performance by defeating the Yankees five straight times. Between August 26, 1957 and August 4, 1959, Lary posted a 13-1 record against the bullies from New York.

Lary's best single season came in 1961, when the Tigers made a run at the Yankees for the pennant. He finished at 23-9 with a 3.24 ERA.

After suffering an injury on Opening Day 1962, Lary never recovered and won only six games in three remaining seasons with the Tigers.

Ron LeFlore
OF Bats: R Throws: R
6'0" 200 lbs.
Played with Tigers: 1974-79
Born: 6/16/48

Ron LeFlore was a natural who wound up in the big leagues in a most unnatural way. Signed out of Jackson State Prison in July 1973, the speedy outfielder became the Tigers' regular center fielder by the middle of the next season.

His storybook life was portrayed in a book that was turned into a TV movie starring LeVar Burton.

LeFlore had the physique of a body builder and the speed of a sprinter. In his prime, he may have been baseball's fastest runner.

"He makes mistakes in the outfield," said former Tiger manager Ralph Houk. "But he's quick enough to outrun them."

After his partial season in 1974, LeFlore never stole fewer than 28 bases for the Tigers. He led the league with 68 in 1978 and followed that with 78. He was traded to Montreal in 1980 and led the National League with 97 stolen bases.

LeFlore batted .325 and scored 100 runs in 1977. The following year he led the league with 126 runs scored.

As the title of his book and the movie on his life aptly state, he was *One in a Million*.

Chet Lemon
OF Bats: R Throws: R
6'0" 185 lbs.
Played with Tigers: 1982-89
Born: 2/12/55

Chet Lemon was a boundless bundle of energy who had a tendency to run until he scored or was tagged out—whichever came first. He was the dependable, and sometimes spectacular, defensive player needed to cover the spacious territory of Tiger Stadium's center field.

Lemon was acquired from the White Sox in exchange for Steve Kemp. And though the Tigers traded one of their most productive hitters, they acquired a piece of the puzzle that had to be filled in order to win.

In the championship season of 1984, Lemon also contributed 20 home runs, 76 RBIs

and a .287 average. He hit at least 20 homers in three seasons for the Tigers.

Mickey Lolich
LHP Bats: R Throws: L
6'1" 210 lbs.
Played with Tigers: 1963-75
Born: 9/12/40

The argument is impossible to settle. But there are many who believe that Mickey Lolich is the best pitcher not yet to make it into baseball's Hall of Fame. Lolich was loved by the fans, because he was one of them. He had a potbelly and a ready smile. He showed up to work every day and never missed a turn when it was his time to pitch.

When he fired those three complete-game victories in the 1968 World Series to win the MVP, it was

When Chet Lemon was traded from the Chicago White Sox to Detroit for Steve Kemp, his home run production went up and he became a valuable contributor on the basepaths. Collection of Jim Hawkins Productions Inc.

like doing it for all his friends. What Lolich meant to the pitching staff can't be measured by numbers alone.

"What made him so valuable was that it was like having an extra arm on the staff," said his catcher Bill Freehan. "When it was Mickey's turn to pitch, the rest of the staff could take the day off."

He was a manager's dream. He regularly notched more complete games in one season than most modern pitchers accumulate in a career.

For his career, he completed 195 of 496 starts. In 1971, when he led the league with 25 victories, he also was the leader in starts (45), complete games (29), strikeouts (308) and a phenomenal 376 innings pitched. From 1971-74, he never threw fewer than 308 innings in a season.

"There's no way to explain Mickey's arm," Freehan remarked, "other than it's a gift."

Lolich was the perfect blue-collar pitcher for a blue-collar town. From 1964 to 1974, he won at least 14 games each season. He won 12 in 1975 and was traded to the Mets for Rusty Staub.

Lolich holds the club record for most starts (459), strikeouts (2,679) and shutouts (39). He is third on the list with 207 victories and in the top ten in various other categories. He finished with a lifetime mark of 217-191 and 3.44 ERA.

Lolich was inducted into the Michigan Sports Hall of Fame in 1982. He still resides in the Detroit area.

Aurelio Lopez
RHP Bats: R Throws: R
6'0" 220 lbs.
Played with Tigers: 1979-85
Born: 9/12/48 Died: 9/22/92

Aurelio Lopez had a fastball that earned him the nickname "Señor Smoke." He also had a sheepish smile, a twinkle in his eye and an engaging personality that made him an instant hit with the fans. And best of all, he was brilliant in relief.

Lopez began his Tiger career in 1979 after being traded by the Cardinals. It didn't take long for the deal to be considered an overwhelming success. He posted a 10-5 record and 2.41 ERA with 21 saves. He spent the next four seasons as the Tiger closer before giving way to Willie Hernandez in 1984.

Lopez quickly adjusted to his setup role and posted a 10-1 record and 2.94 ERA as the Tigers coasted

to the world championship. In the Game 5 clincher, Lopez got the victory with 2.1 scoreless innings.

Don Lund
OF Bats: R Throws: R
6'0" 200 lbs.
Played with Tigers: 1949, 1952-54
Born: 5/18/23

Don Lund's Tiger career was neither long nor particularly impressive. But it was the fulfillment of a childhood dream.

Lund was raised on the city's east side and was one of Detroit's finest all-around athletes. Before turning professional, he went to the University of Michigan, where he became one of the school's rare nine-letter winners—three each in football, basketball and baseball.

Upon graduation, he signed a contract with the Brooklyn Dodgers. He was traded to the St. Louis Browns before joining his hometown Tigers in 1949. After playing two games for the Tigers that season, he was shipped to the minor leagues. He returned to Detroit in 1952 and ended his career in 1954.

He served as farm director for the Tigers before returning to the University of Michigan, where he retired as associate athletic director. He was inducted into the Michigan Sports Hall of Fame in 1987.

M

Heinie Manush
OF Bats: L Throws: L
6'1" 200 lbs.
Played with Tigers: 1923-27
Born: 7/20/01 Died: 5/12/71

From his little hometown of Tuscumbia, Alabama, Heinie Manush took his ability to hit a baseball all the way to Cooperstown and enshrinement into baseball's Hall of Fame. Of course, the left-handed-hitting outfielder had a pretty good teacher.

Manush broke in with the Tigers in 1923 under the leadership of player-manager Ty Cobb. And Manush made the most of the opportunity. The usually cantankerous Cobb took a liking to Manush and

Heinie Manush was a solid hitter for the Tigers until a disastrous trade sent him to the St. Louis Browns. Burton Historical Society

adjusted his approach to hitting. Cobb convinced Manush to choke up on the bat and hit the ball to the opposite field.

Obviously, the advice paid dividends. Manush batted .334 in his rookie season. Three years later he won the American League batting championship with a .378 mark. On the last day of that season, Manush went six-for-nine in a doubleheader to beat out another pretty fair hitter—Babe Ruth—for the title.

In a nightmare trade by the Tigers, Manush and Lu Blue were sent to the St. Louis Browns for Harry Rice, Elam Vangilder and Chick Galloway. Manush again hit .378 in his first season with St. Louis and finished with a career mark of .330 and a spot in the Hall of Fame. Manush was inducted into the Michigan Sports Hall of Fame in 1964.

Billy Martin
SS/3B Bats: R Throws: R
5'11" 165 lbs.
Played with Tigers: 1958
Born: 5/16/28 Died: 12/25/89

Billy Martin left his mark on the Detroit Tigers when he managed the club from 1971-73. But he first wore the Olde English "D" as a player in 1958. He was acquired from Kansas City and traded to the Indians after the season. After playing second base for the Yankees, Martin played 131 games at shortstop and third base for the Tigers and batted .255.

Little did anyone know at the time that 13 years later, he would be managing the club.

Eddie Mathews
3B Bats: L Throws: R
6'1" 190 lbs.
Played with Tigers: 1967-68
Born: 10/13/31 Died: 2/18/01

Eddie Mathews spent the last season of his 17-year major-league career with the Tigers for one reason—he knew how to win. And the Hall of Fame third baseman, who finished with 512 home runs, certainly did the job for Detroit.

Mathews was acquired toward the end of the 1967 season when the Tigers were in a heated pennant race from which they were not eliminated until the final day. The next season, of course, the Tigers battled their way to a world championship.

Although Mathews appeared in only 67 games for Detroit, his presence in the clubhouse and on the field was a steadying force.

Charlie Maxwell
OF Bats: L Throws: L
5'11" 185 lbs.
Played with Tigers: 1955-62
Born: 4/8/27

Charlie Maxwell was nicknamed "Paw Paw" after his hometown near Kalamazoo, Michigan. He also was known as the "Sunday Punch" for his propensity to hit Sunday homers. Of his 148 career home runs, 40 came on Sunday.

His most prodigious power display occurred on May 3, 1959 in Detroit in a doubleheader against New York. Maxwell homered in his final at-bat of the opener. He then proceeded to homer his first three times up in the second game to tie a major-league record of four consecutive home runs.

Of course, it was on Sunday.

Maxwell finished the 1959 season with career highs of 31 home runs and 95 RBIs. 12 of those homers and 33 RBIs were delivered on Sunday.

Maxwell was inducted into the Michigan Sports Hall of Fame in 1997.

Dick McAuliffe
2B/SS   Bats: L   Throws: R
5'11"   175 lbs.
Played with Tigers: 1960-73
Born: 11/29/39

Dick McAuliffe was a scrappy little infielder with flashes of power and enough spit and vinegar to spark a whole team. McAuliffe wasn't the greatest infielder ever to play for Detroit, but he played like someone had forgotten to tell him that.

The scouting report on McAuliffe before he broke in with the Tigers in 1960 read: "He can't hit, he can't field and he's not the fastest runner. But there's something about him that will take him to the big leagues."

That something was a belly full of determination, which made him one of the most popular players on the team. McAuliffe broke in as a shortstop and made the All-Star team at the position in 1965 and 1966. He was moved to second base and again made the All-Star team in 1967.

McAuliffe's high-kick batting style was one of the most distinctive stances of the era. It produced plenty of power for a middle infielder and he finished his career with 197 home runs. He was inducted into the Michigan Sports Hall of Fame in 1986.

Barney McCosky
OF   Bats: L   Throws: R
6'1"   185 lbs.
Played with Tigers: 1939-42, 1946
Born: 4/11/17   Died: 9/6/96

Barney McCosky was a hometown boy who will always be remembered as the player who brought George Kell to Detroit. McCosky was traded to the Philadelphia Athletics in exchange for Kell during the 1946 season. Kell, of course, was eventually elected to baseball's Hall of Fame and became a fixture as a Tiger broadcaster.

Although McCosky's career was less prodigious, he was an outstanding hitter and outfielder whose career was cut short by a back injury.

After graduating from Detroit's Southwestern High School, McCosky hit .311 for the Tigers in 1939. He stole 20 bases and scored 120 runs. The following year he hit .340 with 123 runs and led the league with 200 hits. He batted .324 and .293 the next two years before going into military service for three years.

McCosky finished an 11-year career in 1953 with a career mark of .312. He was inducted into the Michigan Sports Hall of Fame in 1995.

John McHale
1B   Bats: L   Throws: R
6'0"   200 lbs.
Played with Tigers: 1943-45, 1947-48
Born: 9/21/21

John McHale was a part-time first baseman for the Tigers whose baseball career blossomed after he stepped down as a player. McHale worked his way up to general manager of the Tigers. He later served in the same capacity for the Milwaukee Braves, Atlanta Braves and Montreal Expos. His son, John Jr., later served as president of the Tigers.

Denny McLain
RHP   Bats: R   Throws: R
6'0"   185 lbs.
Played with Tigers: 1963-70
Born: 3/29/44

There was no happy ending to the fairy-tale baseball life of Denny McLain. Instead, he left a legacy of incomparable pitching brilliance defamed by the ignominy of two prison terms.

There was no other ball player quite like McLain. Ironically, it was the same irrepressible bravado that had spurred him to baseball greatness that insidiously consumed his personal life and eventually landed him behind bars.

"For a five-year period, there was no pitcher like

Sandy Koufax," said former Tiger Dick Tracewski, who roomed with the Hall of Famer when both played for the Dodgers. "But for just one year—that one special year of 1968—I never saw anyone as dominating as Denny McLain."

McLain transcended baseball that season to become a national phenomenon. He became the first pitcher since Dizzy Dean in 1934 to win 30 games. McLain finished with a 31-6 record and a 1.96 ERA to win both the MVP and Cy Young Awards. He made the games fast. He made the games fun. And he did it with a cocksure attitude that dared any hitter to cross him on his nonstop trip toward immortality.

McLain followed that season with a 24-9 mark in 1969. Then in a turn of events that caught everyone by surprise, the career and life of baseball's brightest star unraveled as swiftly as his fortune had been built.

In 1970 he was slapped with three suspensions, including one for associating with alleged gamblers, another for dumping water on a pair of sports writers and a third for carrying a gun on a team trip.

Frustrated by his star pitcher's insistence on living over the edge, Tiger general manager Jim Campbell traded McLain to Washington after the 1970 season in a deal that "stole" pitcher Joe Coleman, shortstop Ed Brinkman and third baseman Aurelio Rodriguez.

McLain, who was inducted into the Michigan Sports Hall of Fame in 1991, is currently serving time in prison.

Denny McLain (right) is presented with a bucket of writer repellant in 1983 to remind him of his 1970 clubhouse dousing of Jim Hawkins (left) and another sportswriter. The dousing resulted in one of three suspensions that McLain served that year. Collection of Jim Hawkins Productions Inc.

Gene Michael
SS Bat: B Throws: R
6'2" 185 lbs.
Played with Tigers: 1975
Born: 6/2/38

Before he became a permanent fixture in George Steinbrenner's unpredictable scheme of things with the Yankees, Gene Michael played shortstop for the Tigers in 1975.

Michael gained more baseball notoriety once he finished his playing career. Several times, in no particular order, Michael served as scout, manager and even general manager for the Yankees. He still is highly regarded as a Yankee super scout. But he did wear the Olde English "D" for one summer. He also was a crack card player, as some of his less fortunate teammates discovered the hard way.

Jack Morris
RHP Bats: R Throws: R
6'3" 210 lbs.
Played with Tigers: 1977-90
Born: 5/16/55

Jack Morris could be ornery. There were times when he was rude. Just before he went out to pitch, he put a cap on his head and a scowl on his face—and not necessarily in that order.

Temperamental pitcher Jack Morris takes a break from baseball to do some fly fishing. Dan Ewald Jr.

And with the game on the line, there was no one better to have on your side.

"So what if he was ornery?" former manager Sparky Anderson said. "That's the way all the great ones are. That's how much he wanted to win. When all the chips were on the line, Jack was at his best. He loved pitching the big games. That's what he lived for. And he rarely let us down. I've seen a lot of great ones. For that one big game, I'll take Jack."

That's high praise from a Hall of Fame manager who probably understood pitchers better than any manager of modern times. But the plaudits for Morris were well deserved.

"We had our differences," Sparky said. "He said his piece and I said mine. When it was done, it was over. Jack's pretty smart. He learned from his mistakes. All he cared about was winning. That's all that mattered to Jack."

Morris fired two complete-game victories for the Tigers in the 1984 World Series. He also won the first game of the playoffs and posted a 19-11 mark during the regular season. On April 7 at Chicago, he fired Detroit's first no-hitter since 1958.

Morris left the Tigers through free agency after the 1990 season and signed with his hometown Minnesota Twins. At the Metrodome in 1991, he turned in one of the most memorable performances of World Series history. In the Game 7 clincher, Morris was a giant as he fired a 10-inning complete-game 1-0 victory over Atlanta.

For his Herculean effort, he was named Series MVP.

Morris's list of records is longer than the faces on the frustrated hitters who were fooled by his split-finger or devastating fastball. Not only does he rank in the top ten of most Tiger pitching categories, he also holds the American League record for most consecutive starting assignments (515). He currently ranks 24th in all-time major-league strikeouts, 29th in starts, tied for 36th in wins and 44th in innings pitched. He holds the major-league record for most putouts by a pitcher (387).

Morris started 11 straight Opening Days for the Tigers. He made five All-Star teams and started three games.

Morris was inducted into the Michigan Sports Hall of Fame in 2001. He served as an assistant pitching coach for the Tigers in spring training of 2002.

Don Mossi
LHP Bats: L Throws: L
6'1" 195 lbs.
Played with Tigers: 1959-63
Born: 1/11/29

For any real Tiger fan, the first things that come to mind when thinking about Don Mossi are the ears. For a man his size, his ears were unusually large.

Of course, he was a pretty good pitcher after coming over from Cleveland.

After establishing himself as a reliable reliever for the Indians, the lefty was moved into Detroit's starting rotation. He responded with a 17-9 mark in his first Tiger season of 1959. He also posted 15 complete games. In 1961 when the Tigers made a run at the pennant, Mossi went 15-7 and led the staff with a 2.96 ERA.

But it is the ears that everyone remembers.

George Mullin
RHP Bats: R Throws: R
5'11" 190 lbs.
Played with Tigers: 1902-13
Born: 7/4/80 Died: 1/7/44

George Mullin flipped a coin and wound up winning more games for the Tigers (209) than any pitcher in club history with the exception of Hooks Dauss.

After a successful sandlot career in Wabash, Indiana, Mullin signed major-league contracts with the Tigers and Brooklyn Dodgers. After much deliberation, he decided it was wiser to stick closer to home. And Tiger fans are glad he did.

Mullin was powerfully built and had an intimidating fastball. He also kept hitters off-balance by talking to them when they came to the plate.

The tactics obviously worked. Mullin won at least 12 games in each of the 11 full seasons he pitched for Detroit. In six of those seasons he pitched over 300 innings. He was a 20-game winner five times. In the pennant-winning year of 1909, he led the league with 29 victories.

On July 4, 1912, Mullin celebrated his 32nd birthday by firing a no-hitter against the St. Louis Browns at Bennett Park. In a September 22, 1906 doubleheader, Mullin started and won both games.

George Mullin is the only Tiger hurler to pitch a no-hitter on his birthday. Mullin beat the Cardinals 7-0 on July 4, 1912 on his 32nd birthday. Brace Photo

He was inducted into the Michigan Sports Hall of Fame in 1962.

N

John Neun
1B Bats: B Throws: L
5'10" 175 lbs.
Played with Tigers: 1925-28
Born: 10/28/00 Died: 3/28/90

For Johnny Neun, the highlight of his career was over with the speed of a line drive. It happened on May 31, 1927 and remains as much a piece of trivia today as it did three-quarters of a century ago.

In the top of the ninth inning, with Detroit leading 1-0, Cleveland put runners on first and second base. With Neun playing first base, Homer Summa drilled a line drive, which Neun speared. He quickly tagged Charlie Jamieson, who'd been caught off first, and then made a mad dash to touch second to catch Glenn Myatt for an unassisted triple play. Only the day before, Pittsburgh's Johnny Cooney had performed the same trick against Chicago.

Too bad ESPN wasn't around to feature the highlights.

Hal Newhouser (see page 70)

Louis "Bobo" Newsom
RHP Bats: R Throws: R
6'3" 200 lbs.
Played with Tigers: 1939-41
Born: 8/11/07 Died: 12/7/62

Louis "Bobo" Newsom was big. He was colorful. He wasn't afraid to do some friendly boasting. And he had the talent to back it up.

While pitching for St. Louis, Bobo was promised a new suit by owner Don Barnes if he won the season opener. Bobo did and Barnes went to the clubhouse after the game to give his pitcher the money.

"Keep the money," Bobo told the owner. "I already bought it. The bill is on your desk."

Bobo also had a heart as big as his powerful right arm. Pitching an opener for the Senators in Washington, he was struck by a ball and suffered a fractured jaw. He refused to come out of the game.

"Are you crazy?" he rationalized. "Come out of a game against the Yankees with the President of the United States sitting in the stands? Not old Bobo."

Bobo won the game, 1-0.

Bobo demonstrated even more courage pitching for the Tigers in the 1940 World Series against the Cincinnati Reds. The night after watching his son fire a complete-game victory in Game 1, Bobo's father died of a heart attack. Newsom fought through his personal grief and tossed a three-hit shutout in Game 5. He was just as strong in Game 7 when he went the distance again. However, the Reds nipped the Tigers, 2-1, for the world championship.

Bobo was with the Tigers for only three seasons. But he made the most of them. He won 17 games in 1939, 21 in 1940 and 12 in 1941.

Bobo was one of the most well-traveled players in history during his career. He was traded 17 times. He never took the time to learn the names of his ever-changing teammates. To him, everyone was Bobo.

Bobo was a workhorse and finished his career with a dubious distinction. With a lifetime mark of 211-222, he is one of only two pitchers to win over 200 games and still have a losing record.

Jim Northrup
OF Bats: L Throws: R
6'3" 190 lbs.
Played with Tigers: 1964-74
Born: 11/24/39

Jim Northrup was one of the State of Michigan's finest all-around athletes. He was a standout in baseball, football, basketball, track and golf at Alma College. He almost signed a professional football contract with the old New York Titans before deciding to play baseball for his hometown Tigers. And the Tigers were glad he did.

Tiger fans vividly remember Northrup's seventh-inning drive over the head of center fielder Curt Flood that turned into a two-run triple in Game 7 of the 1968 World Series. It was the game-winning hit that dumped St. Louis and sent Detroit into pandemonium.

Northrup had a knack for delivering big hits. In one week of the 1968 season, he set a major-league record by clubbing three grand slams. On June 24 he belted two against the Indians. Five days later against Chicago, he hit another. He led the club with 90 RBIs that season.

On August 29, 1969, Northrup enjoyed another robust day. Against the Athletics, he went six-for-six, including a home run over Tiger Stadium's right field roof.

Northrup also enjoyed a reputation for being unafraid to voice his opinions. And there were plenty. There were several celebrated conflicts between the smooth left-handed hitter and the volatile Billy Martin when Martin managed the Tigers.

Because of his premature gray hair, Northrup was dubbed "The Gray Fox." After retiring, he spent time on the Tiger TV team. He was inducted into the Michigan Sports Hall of Fame in 2000. He makes his home in the Detroit area.

O

Marv Owen
3B Bats: R Throws: R
6'0" 175 lbs.
Played with Tigers: 1931, 1933-37
Born: 5/22/06 Died: 6/22/91

Marv Owen was the steady third baseman on one of baseball's most potent all-time infields. In 1934 when the Tigers won the pennant, first baseman Hank Greenberg, second baseman Charlie Gehringer, shortstop Billy Rogell and Owen combined for 462 RBIs. Owen's contribution was 96.

But the usually reliable Owen will always be remembered for his part in one of the most celebrated incidents in World Series history.

In the sixth inning of the seventh game of the 1934 Series, the Cardinals' Joe "Ducky" Medwick hit a triple and slid in hard on Owen at third base.

"I stepped on his foot accidentally," Owen told the press after the game.

Obviously Medwick didn't see it that way. He bounced to his feet and the scuffle was on.

When the dust settled and Medwick went to left field in the last half of the inning, the real commotion began. Fans in the stands peppered the Cardinal outfielder with hot dogs, paper cups and a potpourri of refuse.

Commissioner Landis, who was sitting in the stands, called a momentary halt to the game. In order to allow the game to continue, he ejected Medwick. Behind Dizzy Dean, the Cardinals won, 11-0.

Owen was Detroit's regular third baseman for six seasons. He knocked in 105 runs in 1936 when he batted .295. But he'll always be remembered for the World Series scuffle, which actually had no effect on the outcome.

Ray Oyler
SS Bats: R Throws: R
5'11" 165 lbs.
Played with Tigers: 1965-68
Born: 8/14/38 Died: 1/26/81

His teammates teased that he couldn't hit his way out of a paper bag. With the numbers Ray Oyler posted, that was hardly an endorsement for the strength of the bag.

But with the way Oyler played shortstop, the Tigers could afford his anemic bat. He had the hands of a pickpocket and the range of a radar screen.

He hit just .135 for the 1968 championship team. But he was the secretary of defense and was appreciated by his teammates.

P

Lance Parrish
C Bats: R Throws: R
6'3"   220 lbs.
Played with Tigers: 1977-86
Born: 6/15/56

In his own peculiar way, Lance Parrish was a baseball revolutionary. Not so much for his bat or glove, but for his physical training techniques that are now practiced by every major-league club.

Parrish had the physique of a body builder even before he reported to the Tigers. He easily could have graced the cover of any muscle magazine. He looked like he could have played in the NFL and, in fact, turned down a football scholarship to his hometown UCLA to sign as Detroit's top pick in the 1974 free agent draft.

"I've always enjoyed working out," Parrish explained. "I think it helped to make me a better player. I never went strictly for bulk. I was careful to keep my flexibility."

At the time of his arrival in the big leagues, his philosophy clashed with traditional baseball thinking, which frowned upon players lifting weights. Over the years, of course, traditional thinking mellowed into contemporary compromise. Now clubs furnish workout facilities equipped as well as any commercial enterprise. And special conditioning coaches have been added to each staff.

Parrish brought more than muscle to the Tigers. Through the same diligence with which he went about his own workouts, Parrish developed into an outstanding defensive catcher. In his second big-league season in 1978, he led the league with 21 passed balls. Five years later, he started a string of three straight Gold Glove seasons.

Parrish pushed himself as intently at the plate. After hitting .219 in his first full season, he evolved into an uncharacteristically potent power hitter not often associated with the position of catcher.

In 1982, Parrish slugged 32 homers to break Yogi Berra's American League record for catchers. In 1984, he hit 33 and knocked in 98 runs.

Parrish was named to six All-Star teams with the Tigers and another two after he left the team via free agency.

In addition to all of the offensive and defensive weapons he added to the team, Parrish brought another quality not measured by statistics. Although soft-spoken by nature, his presence was voluminous. He was a true team leader who needed few words to get his message across.

He was known as the "Big Wheel" by his teammates. As he rolled, so did the team.

For a couple of seasons, Parrish served as a major-league coach for the Tigers. In 2002, he spent his first season as a Tiger TV analyst and also was inducted into the Michigan Sports Hall of Fame.

In 2003, Parrish was back in uniform as a Tiger coach again.

Dan Petry
RHP Bats: R Throws: R
6'4"   210 lbs.
Played with Tigers: 1979-87, 1990-91
Born: 11/13/58

Dan Petry followed a reverse route from many of the modern young players. Born and raised near Anaheim Stadium in California, Petry chose to make his permanent home in the Detroit area after two tours of duty with the Tigers.

"I know a lot of the California guys like to go home after their careers are finished," Petry explained. "But there's something about Detroit that makes me feel at home. It's a working-class city and the people here have always been good to me. Besides, the Tigers are my team."

The right-hander was also pretty good to the fans. He had a lively fastball and as wicked a slider as there was in the league. With Jack Morris, the Tigers featured a potent one-two punch that most hitters hoped to escape when playing Detroit.

Petry reached a personal high of 19 wins and led the league with 38 starts in 1983 when the young Tigers were maturing for a run at the championship. The following year when they completed that run, Petry posted an 18-8 record.

Petry remains in the Detroit area and devotes a lot of time to charitable endeavors.

R

Aurelio Rodriguez
3B   Bats: R   Throws: R
5'10"   180 lbs.
Played with Tigers: 1971-79
Born: 12/28/47   Died: 9/23/00

Aurelio Rodriguez was known as "The Happy Mexican" during his stay in Detroit. He quickly established himself as one of the most popular Tigers, with a contagious smile that could break the tension of any situation.

Rodriguez came equipped with more than an infectious smile. Although he rarely hit for average or power, he was a vacuum cleaner at third base and possessed what many lifetime coaches, executives and scouts believed to be the strongest arm any had ever seen at that position.

From his knees and sometimes even while lying flat on his back, Rodriguez could fire a strike to the first baseman as accurately as most third basemen do from their feet.

Rodriguez, along with pitcher Joe Coleman and shortstop Eddie Brinkman, came to Detroit as part of the infamous trade that sent Denny McLain to Washington following the 1970 season. The deal paid off handsomely, as the Tigers won the East Division title in 1972. Before ending his career, Rodriguez appeared in playoffs for Detroit, New York and Chicago. He played in the 1981 World Series for the Yankees and batted .417.

Long after his career was over, Rodriguez remained popular with Detroit's Hispanic community. He often returned to Detroit, where he died tragically after being struck by a car while walking from a restaurant.

Dan Petry sends a pitch to the plate in 1991. Dan Ewald Jr.

Billy Rogell
SS   Bats: B   Throws: R
5'10"   165 lbs.
Played with Tigers: 1930-39
Born: 11/24/10

Billy Rogell is remembered in Detroit as much for what he did off the field as for what he did on it.

Part of one of the most potent infields of all time, Rogell became part of another prominent team after his playing days were over. The former shortstop ran for a spot on Detroit's city council and didn't retire from that team until almost 40 years had passed.

"There was something about Detroit that I always loved," Rogell said.

He had the chance to pick from about a half-dozen clubs who sought his services when he had been returned to the minor leagues in St. Paul, Minnesota in 1929. One of them was the Yankees.

"The manager asked which one I liked most," Rogell recalled. "I told him I wanted to go to Detroit."

The move paid off for Rogell and the Tigers, who wound up in the World Series in 1934 and 1935.

Rogell teamed with second baseman Charlie Gehringer to form one of the most dominant keystone combinations of any era. They led the league in double plays twice while playing together. From 1935-37, Rogell led all American League shortstops in fielding percentage.

Rogell was a forerunner of the modern game. He was a shortstop who could hit. The 1934 infield of Hank Greenberg at first base, Gehringer at second, Marv Owen at third and Rogell at short produced 462 RBIs. Rogell's contribution was 100. He also scored 114 runs.

After his playing career, Rogell became an outspoken and conscientious member of Detroit's city council. He was honored by having a Detroit municipal golf course named after him, as well as a main road that leads into Metropolitan Airport.

He was inducted into the Michigan Sports Hall of Fame in 1970.

Lynwood "Schoolboy" Rowe
RHP Bats: R Throws: R
6'4" 210 lbs.
Played with Tigers: 1933-42
Born: 1/11/10 Died: 1/8/61

Lynwood Rowe picked up the nickname "Schoolboy" when he was just 15. Pitching for a semipro team in his hometown of El Dorado, Arkansas, Rowe defeated a collection of former major-leaguers.

Legend holds that some of the locals taunted the former professionals: "Beaten by a schoolboy."

Apocryphal or not, the name stuck—all the way, in fact, throughout Rowe's personal professional career.

The son of a circus performer, Rowe was quite a character himself. Because of his size, strength and gritty determination, he became a fan favorite throughout the decade of the '30s.

Rowe was a dogged competitor who absolutely detested being removed from a game. He proved that

in the 1934 World Series when he went all 12 innings of Game 2 to beat the Cardinals, 3-2. He also went the distance in Game 6, but came up on the short end of a 4-3 decision.

It was a fabulous season for Rowe, on the way to the American League pennant. In just his second season, he juggled his fastball, curve and change-up effectively for a 24-8 record. In the process, he tied the American League record shared by Walter Johnson, Lefty Grove and "Smokey" Joe Wood of 16 straight victories.

"I eat a lot of vittles, climb that mound, wrap my fingers around the old baseball and say to it, 'Edna honey, let's go,'" Rowe said by way of explaining his winning streak. Edna was the name of his fiancee.

Rowe was filled with superstitions and carried several good luck charms in his pockets every time he pitched.

Schoolboy Rowe was a notorious prankster and pitched ten seasons for the Tigers. Brace Photo

Rowe was the victim of arm problems throughout his career. He rebounded with a 16-3 mark to help the Tigers to the pennant in 1940, but suffered two losses to the Cincinnati Reds in the World Series.

At 34, Rowe was called into World War II and missed the 1944-45 seasons. He came back to win 38 games over the next four seasons for the Phillies.

Along with his guts on the mound, Rowe also was a contributor at the plate. He finished with a .263 average with 18 home runs and153 RBIs. In a game in 1935, he went five-for-five with a double, triple and three RBIs. He was a dangerous pinch hitter who led the National League with 15 hits in 1943.

Rowe was inducted into the Michigan Sports Hall of Fame in 1961.

S

Herman "Germany" Schaefer
IF Bats: R Throws: R
5'9"   175 lbs.
Played with Tigers: 1905-09
Born: 2/14/77 Died: 5/16/19

Germany Schaefer was a marketing genius almost a century ahead of his time. He played less than five years with the Tigers. But he always gave the fans their money's worth even though he had limited ability.

Schaefer and teammate Charlie O'Leary teamed together on a vaudeville act. It was their song and dance routine that inspired the famous song "Take Me Out to the Ball Game."

He also brought his theatrical flair to the field. In a game in 1906 he wore a raincoat in the outfield for an inning. But that was nothing compared to the performance he offered when he announced his appearance to the fans as he walked to the plate.

"Ladies and gentlemen," he bellowed. "You are now looking at Herman Schaefer, better known as Herman the Great, acknowledged by one and all to be the greatest hitter in the world. I am now going to hit the ball into the left field bleachers. Thank you."

As the hometown fans were howling, Schaefer proceeded to hit a home run. As he trotted around the infield, he slid into each base, announcing his progress as he went along.

Who needed Bill Veeck with Germany Schaefer around?

Charles "Boss" Schmidt
C Bats: B Throws: R
5'11"   200 lbs.
Played with Tigers: 1906-11
Born: 9/12/80 Died: 11/14/32

Boss Schmidt had more punch in his fists than he did in his bat. But the muscular catcher was a defensive stalwart and played on three straight pennant-winning teams from 1907-09.

Schmidt was a powerful man who once fought heavyweight champion Jack Johnson in an exhibition boxing match. He also tangled with the tempestuous Ty Cobb several times in scuffles that were anything but exhibitions. And he usually finished on top.

Mickey Stanley
OF Bats: R Throws: R
6'1"   195 lbs.
Played with Tigers: 1954-78
Born: 7/20/42

Mickey Stanley was one of the finest center fielders in the history of the Tigers. But he'll always be remembered for his seven games at shortstop in the 1968 World Series.

The daring switch was pulled to spike more offense into the Tiger lineup. Jim Northrup moved from right field to Stanley's spot in center. Al Kaline, who had been injured much of the season, returned to his regular position in right. Willie Horton remained in left.

Switching a center fielder to shortstop is risky at any time of the season. For a World Series, it can be suicidal. Stanley performed as if he had played the position his entire career.

Of course, Stanley was no ordinary athlete. He had enough natural ability to excel at any position and probably any sport. Before he retired he played every position except pitcher and catcher. Ironically, the year he switched to shortstop for the Series marked the first of four Gold Glove seasons for Stanley.

He wasn't the fastest center fielder to patrol Tiger Stadium's spacious middle. But he was quick and had a natural instinct for getting a jump on the ball.

"Sometimes you thought he could never get to some drive up the gap," recalled Horton. "Somehow he always made the play. He took a lot of pressure off the other outfielders."

A native of Grand Rapids, Michigan, Stanley worked his way through the Tiger farm system and spent his entire 15-year career with the Tigers. He was one of the most popular players ever to wear the Tiger uniform. He was inducted into the Michigan Sports Hall of Fame in 1994 and still resides in Michigan.

Rusty Staub
OF Bats: L Throws: R
6'2" 200 lbs.
Played with Tigers: 1976-79
Born: 4/1/44

Rusty Staub was a born designated hitter long before the rule was conceived. He was a mule on the bases and a mediocre fielder at best. His arm never scared any runner from going for an extra base. But the redhead from New Orleans could hit. And he was at his best with men on base in tight situations.

Staub played only three seasons for the Tigers. That's all he needed to show American League pitchers what their National League counterparts already had found out the hard way.

In his three full seasons for Detroit he knocked in 96, 101 and 121 runs. He played for five teams during his 23-year major-league career and finished with 1,466 RBIs. At the time of his retirement in 1985, he ranked seventh in baseball history for years played.

Ed Summers
RHP Bats: B Throws: R
6'2" 180 lbs.
Played with Tigers: 1908-12
Born: 12/5/84 Died: 5/12/53

Rheumatism ended the pitching career of Ed Summers after just five years, all with the Tigers. But the knuckle-balling right-hander certainly made the most of them.

He set a record for rookies by winning 24 games in 1908 as the Tigers won the second of three straight pennants. On September 25, he demonstrated his durability by pitching two complete game victories over Philadelphia.

The following year he won 19 games and again showed his determination. On July 16 he went all 18 innings against Washington in a game that was declared a tie.

Normally a light hitter, Summers exploded at the plate on Sept. 17, 1910 when he hit the only two home runs of his career at Bennett Park. Both balls bounced over the outfield fence and in the era of the dead ball were considered homers.

T

Frank Tanana
LHP Bats: L Throws: L
6'3" 180 lbs.
Played with Tigers: 1985-92
Born: 7/3/53

It took a while for Frank Tanana to realize his childhood dream of pitching for his hometown Tigers. When he got the chance, though, he made the most of it.

Tanana was traded to the Tigers by Texas midway through the 1985 season. By the time he left after 1992, he had compiled a 96-82 record.

Tanana was a fireballing lefty when he was made the Angels' top pick after graduating from Detroit's Catholic Central High. He teamed with Nolan Ryan to give the Angels one of the most devastating one-two punches in the league.

Arm problems struck Tanana early in his career, however. The injury that could have ended the career of many pitchers was used by Tanana to completely reinvent himself. He turned his once-vicious fastball into an equally wicked curve, which helped him stick in the majors for 21 seasons He finished with a 240-236 record and 3.66 ERA.

Tanana's best season with the Tigers came in 1987, when he went 15-10. On the final game of the season, he nursed a second-inning Larry Herndon home run into a complete game 1-0 victory to clinch the East Division title. Tanana still resides in the Detroit area.

Left-handed hurler Frank Tanana won his 200ᵗʰ career game on April 28, 1990 as Detroit topped Milwaukee, 13–5. Brace Photo

George "Birdie" Tebbetts
C Bats: R Throws: R
5'11"   170 lbs.
Played with Tigers: 1936-42; 46-47
Born: 11/10/12   Died: 3/24/99

When he was just 15 years old, Birdie Tebbetts impressed Frank Navin so much that the Tiger owner financed the catcher's education at Providence College. It was there that Tebbetts got stuck with the nickname "Birdie," allegedly for talking so much.

After college, Tebbetts spent seven seasons with the Tigers with a three-year absence for military service in World War II.

Tebbetts was a reliable defensive catcher who made the All-Star team in 1941 and 1942. He played for Boston and Cleveland after leaving the Tigers. After retiring, Tebbetts established himself as one of the game's most productive scouts.

Dick Tracewski
IF Bats: R Throws: R
5'11"   160 lbs.
Played with Tigers: 1966-69
Born: 2/3/35

For a light-hitting utility infielder, Dick Tracewski finished his career with a World Series record that most celebrated stars can't come close to matching. The former Tiger infielder and long-time coach appeared in four World Series—three as a player and one as a coach—and walked away with four championship rings. He was part of the Los Angeles Dodgers when they won the Series in 1963 and 1965. He was a reserve on the 1968 Tigers and a coach on the 1984 championship team.

After spending four years with the Tigers, he became a coach in 1970. He held the position through his retirement in 1995. The popular Tiger was occasionally called upon to fill in as manager during emergencies.

Alan Trammell
SS Bats: R Throws: R
6'0"   175 lbs.
Played with Tigers: 1977-96
Born: 2/21/58

Former manager Sparky Anderson called him Huck Finn for his boyish grin and the twinkle in his eye that never faded. Twenty years after he first reported to the Tigers in 1977, Alan Trammell still was one of the most popular players ever to play in Detroit. In fact, Tiger fans thought he would be at shortstop forever.

"You know you've got a good one when you don't even think about him out at shortstop," Anderson explained. "It's such a key position. I've seen players with more talent. But nobody got more out of what he had than Alan Trammell."

It's a high compliment and one well deserved. For the entire decade of the '80s in the American League, there was no one better. Trammell and his second base partner, Lou Whitaker, were as closely linked as Laurel and Hardy throughout their careers. It seemed almost sinful to think about one without the other. Both played their entire careers for the Tigers and left with a major-

Milwaukee's Paul Molitor and Detroit's Alan Trammell talk baseball before the game in April 1990. Dan Ewald Jr.

league record that may never be challenged—1,915 games together as the keystone combination.

Throughout his career, Trammell was the epitome of consistency. In the field and at the plate he was as reliable as the seventh-inning stretch. He hit over .300 seven times and won four Gold Glove Awards. He was named to the All-Star team six times. He ranks in the club's all-time top ten in a variety of categories.

Trammell's performance in the 1984 World Series was the highlight of his career. He hit .450 with two homers and six RBIs and was named the MVP. In 1987 when the Tigers miraculously rallied to capture the East Division title, he enjoyed his finest single season. He batted .343 with 205 hits and set a club record for shortstops with 28 homers and 105 RBIs.

After his retirement, he served as a Tiger coach and remained extremely active in Detroit area charities. He served as a coach for the San Diego Padres before he accepted the Tigers' manager position in 2003. He was inducted into the Michigan Sports Hall of Fame in 2000.

Paul "Dizzy" Trout
RHP Bats: R Throws: R
6'2" 195 lbs.
Played with Tigers: 1939-52
Born: 6/29/15 Died: 2/28/72

Paul "Dizzy" Trout was a workhorse on the mound and later took his humor to the broadcast booth, where he shared his wit, wisdom and "down home" stories with the fans.

Trout pitched for the Tigers for his first 13 years in the big leagues and was part of the 1940 pennant winner and the 1945 world championship team.

During the championship season, Trout tightened his belt during a particularly grueling part of the pennant push and pitched six games in a nine-game period. He won four of them. He fired a five-hitter to win Game 4 of the World Series over the Chicago Cubs.

Trout led the American League with 20 wins in 1940. It was nothing compared to what he did the following season. Coupled with Hal Newhouser, who led the league with 29 wins, Trout added 27 and led the league with a 2.12 ERA, 40 starts, 33 complete games and a whopping 352.1 innings pitched. He finished his career with a 170-161 mark. He also flashed some power of his own with 20 home runs.

Trout was known for his country humor, his glasses and for always having a red handkerchief sticking out of his back pocket when he pitched. After retiring, Trout spent a few seasons in the radio booth as a color analyst.

Virgil Trucks
RHP Bats: R Throws: R
5'11" 200 lbs.
Played with Tigers: 1941-43, 1945-52, 1956
Born: 4/26/19

During the worst season of his 17-year major-league career, Virgil Trucks became a piece of baseball trivia. He went 5-19 in 1952, but was untouchable in two of his victories. On May 15, the right-hander threw a no-hitter against the Washington Senators. He put the exclamation point on that performance on August 25 when he no-hit the Yankees. Nolan Ryan, Allie Reynolds, Johnny Vander Meer and Trucks are the only pitchers ever to fire a pair of no-hitters in one season.

Before his no-hitter against the Senators, Trucks was having trouble putting on his spikes because his feet were hurting. Art Houtteman told him to borrow his because they were bigger. They were the same spikes Houtteman wore when he lost a no-hitter with two out in the ninth.

Trucks didn't get his no-hit victory until the bottom of the ninth when Vic Wertz snapped a scoreless tie with a home run.

Trucks was an unspectacular, but reliable starter for the Tigers. He returned from World War II in time to pitch one regular-season game in 1945. However, he pitched a complete-game victory over the Cubs in the World Series. He was inducted into the Michigan Sports Hall of Fame in 1985.

V

Bobby Veach
OF Bats: L Throws: R
5'11" 160 lbs.
Played with Tigers: 1912-23
Born: 6/29/88 Died: 8/7/45

Bobby Veach had to hit his way out from a lot of shadows when he joined the Tigers in 1912. The shadows of Ty Cobb, Sam Crawford and later Harry Heilmann can be quite overwhelming. But the left-handed hitter from Island, Kentucky certainly wasn't intimidated and finished his career as one of the best outfielders ever to play for Detroit.

Veach broke into professional baseball as a pitcher. But his ability to hit made him more valuable in the regular lineup. He had a remarkable knack for putting the bat on the ball. He consistently finished among league leaders in hits, doubles and triples. In 1919, for instance, he led the league in hits (191), doubles (45) and triples (17). He finished the year with a career-high .355 mark, second to Cobb's .384. He also led the league in RBIs three times.

Dominican infielder Ozzie Virgil became the Tigers' first black player when he started at third base on June 6, 1958. Brace Photo

On September 20, 1920, Veach became the first Tiger to hit for the cycle when he went six-for-six in a 12-inning game against the Boston Red Sox. He left the Tigers after the 1923 season and finished his career with a .310 average to cast quite a shadow of his own.

Ozzie Virgil
IF Bats: R Throws: R
6'0"   175 lbs.
Played with Tigers: 1958, 1960-61
Born: 5/17/33

On June 6, 1958, Ozzie Virgil became a permanent part of Tiger trivia, even though many still question the technicality of his holding the distinction.

It was on that night that the utility infielder started the game at third base at Briggs Stadium. Virgil thus became the first African American ever to play for the Tigers—even though he was a native of the Dominican Republic. Hence, some African-American and Caucasian fans and historians question the accuracy of the claim.

Regardless of the political debate, all Virgil wanted to do was to play. And he certainly gave the 29,000 in the stands something to cheer about. With each pair of eyes boring down on his every move, Virgil went five-for-five against the Senators to become an instant hit with the fans.

W

Dick Wakefield
OF Bats: L Throws: R
6'4"   210 lbs.
Played with Tigers: 1941, 1943-44,
1946-49
Born: 5/6/21 Died: 8/26/85

Dick Wakefield was baseball's first "bonus baby" whose "can't miss" career never quite came to fruition due to various twists of fate.

Wakefield was big, handsome, and the son of Howard Wakefield, who had pitched three years (1905-07) in the major leagues. Unlike his father, Wakefield was a born hitter with a smooth left-handed swing. He was signed off the campus of the University of Michigan for a then unheard-of $52,000. He appeared in seven games in 1941 before returning to the Tigers in 1943 to explode in his first full season. He played in every game and led the league in at-bats (633), hits (200) and doubles (38). He finished with a .316 average.

He spent half of the following year in the navy, but still managed to bat .355 in 78 games. He missed the world championship 1945 season because of military service and never regained his hitting touch after the war.

He finished his career in 1952 with the New York Giants and ended with a lifetime .293 average.

Don Wert
3B   Bats: R   Throws: R
5'10"   165 lbs.
Played with Tigers: 1963-70
Born: 7/29/38

Don Wert was more highly regarded for his glove at third base than for his bat. But his single to drive home the game-winning run that clinched the pennant on September 17, 1968 will be remembered for a long time.

Wert was steady and sometimes spectacular at the corner and teamed with shortstop Ray Oyler to give the championship Tigers the most solid left side of the infield in the league.

Wert played eight years for the Tigers and then was part of the Denny McLain deal with Washington. He retired in 1971.

Vic Wertz
OF/1B   Bats: L   Throws: R
6'0"   185 lbs.
Played with Tigers: 1947-52, 1961-63
Born: 2/9/25   Died: 7/7/83

Willie Mays's spectacular back-to-the-infield catch in the eighth inning of the first game of the 1954 World Series is one of baseball's most rerun pieces of TV footage. Vic Wertz was part of the colorful play, although many people still remain unaware of his involvement.

Playing for Cleveland at the time, it was Wertz who unloaded the monstrous 460-foot shot to center field to become a part of baseball trivia. The big first baseman/outfielder had plenty of other defining moments in which he came out on top.

Wertz broke in with the Tigers in 1947 and had two tours with the team. He enjoyed his finest seasons with Detroit, where he developed into a prodigious power hitter. He hit 74 home runs in the last three years of his first stint with the Tigers.

He became a symbol of determination when he returned to action in 1956, after being diagnosed with non-paralytic polio in August 1955. He finished his 17-year career with 266 home runs. In the 1954 Series, he collected eight hits in 16 at-bats with a home run.

Wertz was a personable character who enjoyed sharing his good fortune with those who needed it most. After retiring, he made his home in the Detroit area and was instrumental in raising money for charity. He was inducted into the Michigan Sports Hall of Fame in 1983.

Lou Whitaker
2B   Bats: L   Throws: R
5'11"   165 lbs.
Played with Tigers: 1977-95
Born: 5/12/57

It's one of those questions that is impossible to answer. But for pure baseball talent, Lou Whitaker may have been the most gifted player to perform for the Tigers in the last half-century.

"I've never seen a second baseman with a better arm," remarked former manager Sparky Anderson. "He had all the tools. It seemed like he could turn them on at will."

And he certainly left Tiger fans with many memories to savor.

Whitaker teamed with shortstop Alan Trammell for a major-league-record 1,915 games together at the keystone positions. It's a record that may never be broken.

Whitaker became an instant hit with the fans almost from the day he debuted in 1977. A chorus of "Lou, Lou, Lou" would buzz through the park every time he strode to the plate or made another amazing play in the field.

Going up the middle or far to his left in the hole, Whitaker was a magician with his range and ability to

"Sweet Lou" Whitaker played his entire 19-year career with the Tigers and was one of the most gifted ballplayers to don a Tigers uniform. Brace Photo

season four times, including a personal high of 28 in 1989. In 1985 he hit one over Tiger Stadium's right field roof. He ranks among the all-time Tiger leaders in several important categories.

Whitaker's list of individual awards is as long as his two-decade stay with the Tigers. He made five All-Star teams and won three Gold Gloves. He was voted the 1978 Rookie of the Year. Whitaker and Joe Morgan are the only second basemen in history to have over 2,000 hits, 2,000 games and 200 home runs.

He will always be remembered by Tiger fans simply as "Sweet Lou."

Whitaker was inducted into the Michigan Sports Hall of Fame in 2000.

Earl Whitehill
LHP Bats: L Throws: L
5'9"   175 lbs.
Played with Tigers: 1923-32
Born: 2/7/99 Died: 10/22/54

Earl Whitehill earned the nickname "The Earl" for his flashy wardrobe and sometimes flamboyant lifestyle. He was married to Violet Oliver, the model on the Sun-Maid Raisin box.

fire strikes to first base regardless of where he was on the field. It's impossible to calculate how many potential rallies were aborted by his gifted glove and arm.

Defense was only half of the artillery Whitaker could flash on the field, almost at will. During his first few years, he was primarily an opposite field hitter. Through experience and strength, he learned to use the entire field and actually possessed a dangerous amount of power. He hit more than 20 home runs in a

Whitehill was a dashing figure with a volatile temper that even Ty Cobb feared on occasion. It was Cobb, as the player/manager, who promoted Whitehill to the Tigers at the end of the 1923 season.

Whitehill won 17 games in his first full season. He won in double digits throughout his Tiger career, which ended in 1932.

After developing arm trouble in the spring of 1925, Whitehill was told by Cobb to throw more curves and off-speed pitches. When Whitehill, following orders, managed to win only 11 games, Cobb blamed the lefty for Detroit's failure to win the pennant as he had predicted. The two rarely communicated after that.

Whitehill was traded to Washington in 1933 and responded with a personal-high 22 victories. He is the only pitcher with more than 200 victories (218) and an ERA above 4.00 (4.36).

Milt Wilcox
RHP Bats: R Throws: R
6'2" 185 lbs.
Played with Tigers: 1977-85
Born: 4/20/50

Milt Wilcox may have been the best six-inning pitcher of the 1984 world championship season. Mixing Wilcox's spunk and savvy with one of the game's most reliable bullpens, manager Sparky Anderson nursed the veteran to a personal high of 17 victories.

Wilcox made 33 starts without completing one game that year to wind up as the best No. 3 starter anywhere in the game. In the playoff-clinching game against Kansas City, Wilcox extended his stay on the mound and went eight innings for a 1-0 victory before Willie Hernandez closed out the ninth. Wilcox went back to six innings and won Game 3 of the World Series against San Diego.

"Milt knew his role and performed it as well as anyone could have asked," Anderson explained. "He had a lot of guts and gave you everything he had every time he took the ball."

Wilcox wasn't flashy. He was merely always ready to battle.

After going 6-2 in his first Tiger season in 1977, he strung together seven straight double-digit-victory seasons.

On April 15, 1983, Wilcox joined Tommy Bridges as the only Tiger pitchers to come within one out of pitching a perfect game. With even the Chicago crowd cheering Wilcox in his bid for baseball history, pinch hitter Jerry Hairston singled through the hole. Wilcox then retired the next batter for a 6-0 victory.

Wilcox still resides in the Detroit area.

Earl Wilson
RHP Bats: R Throws: R
6'3" 215 lbs.
Played with Tigers: 1966-70
Born: 10/2/34

Earl Wilson was brought to Detroit in 1966 to help the Tigers win a world championship. And the powerful right-hander didn't disappoint them.

As the Tigers were growing into legitimate contenders, they traded Don Demeter and Julio Navarro to the Red Sox for Wilson on June 14, 1966. Wilson responded with a 13-6 mark in 23 games.

When the Tigers made a spirited pennant run that ended on the last day of the 1967 season, Wilson led the charge by leading the league with 22 victories. He was 13-12 when the Tigers went all the way in 1968 and also posted a career-best 2.85 ERA.

Wilson was an intimidating force on the mound who challenged batters with a sizzling fastball. He also was a force with the bat in his hands. When he retired in 1970, he was tied with Warren Spahn for fourth on the lifetime home run list for pitchers, with 35. Often he was used as a pinch hitter.

After retirement, Wilson made Detroit his home and became a successful businessman.

Y

Rudy York
C/1B Bats: R Throws: R
6'1" 210 lbs.
Played with Tigers: 1934, 1937-45
Born: 8/17/13 Died: 2/5/70

Red Smith, the celebrated New York sports writer, summed up Rudy York the best when he wrote: "No matter where he was stationed in the field, York always played the same position. He played bat. He was slow, unskilled, awkward, sincere, tireless, and stronger than dirt."

Rudy York was a slugger for whom the Tigers had to find a position.

Versatile Rudy York warms up at catcher before a game. York was often moved to various positions to keep his powerful bat in the lineup.
Brace Photo

He moved from catcher to third base and then to the outfield before settling in at first base. The Tigers even had to pay Hank Greenberg a bonus to move to left field so that York could replace him at first.

York could simply overpower the ball and likely would have broken all kinds of records had he played in contemporary times. He's best known for the August of his rookie year in 1937. That's when he dismantled American League pitching and broke Babe Ruth's record by slugging 18 home runs. He also set a major-league record with 49 RBIs for the month. The home run record stood until Sammy Sosa eclipsed it with the rocket ball of the current era.

Playing in just 104 games that rookie season, York was unstoppable. He hit .307 and belted 35 home runs and drove in 103. He followed that year with 33 homers and 127 RBIs in 1938. In 1943, York led the league with 34 homers and 118 RBIs.

York's idea of finesse was trotting around the bases after hitting one over the fence. He did everything hard without holding anything back.

Because of his tireless work ethic and awesome displays of brute force, he became a favorite with the fans. He stayed with the Tigers through 1945 and played all seven games in each of the World Series in 1940 and 1945.

York made the All-Star team in five of his 13 years in the major leagues and finished with 277 homers and 1,152 RBIs. He was inducted into the Michigan Sports Hall of Fame in 1972.

8

THE MEN WHO MANAGED

rior to the start of the 1984 playoff in Kansas City, Tiger manager Sparky Anderson referred to Alan Trammell as "my Huckleberry Finn."

"He's got that special kind of enthusiasm you don't see in too many players," Anderson said of his bouncy yet always reliable shortstop to a collection of national baseball writers.

"He's curious. He's always trying to learn how to play this game a little better. He can't get enough."

It was Trammell's first real slice of national media exposure. And, of course, he made the most of his first postseason opportunity by winning the Most Valuable Player Award of the World Series. Throughout a 20-year major-league playing career—all with the Tigers—Trammell never lost that twinkle of magic that only a baseball Huck Finn enjoys.

And it came to shine brighter than ever when he was named manager of the Tigers on Oct. 9, 2002. The youngster who broke in with the Tigers as a 19-year-old in 1977 now has come full circle and returns as the field general a quarter-century later. Trammell is signed to manage the Tigers for at least three seasons.

And the best part about it—Trammell hasn't changed. He still has the same bounce in his step. His eyes sparkle and his ears perk up at the first mention of baseball.

More importantly is the fact that the passion he felt for the Tigers during his distinguished playing career appears to have risen to a new level as he undertakes a challenge he has been preparing for since the end of his playing days.

"This is a day I'm very proud of," Trammell said on the day of his hiring. "This Olde English 'D' will always be part of my life. I'll be a Tiger wherever I happen to be.

"To put into words what the opportunity to manage the team I love so much means is almost impossible. It's a privilege beyond anything I could imagine. I know only one way to succeed in baseball. That's to give it everything I've got. That's the way I played and that's the way I'll manage. That's a promise I can easily make to every Tiger fan."

Trammell brings a sense of honesty and integrity to the position. In the last quarter-century, no other player brought more to the franchise than Trammell.

Trammell succeeded Luis Pujols, who was fired after posting a 55-100 record in the disastrous and strife-filled 2002 season. It was a season marred by clubhouse dissension and little team purpose other than getting through the schedule.

"Let's not kid ourselves," Trammell said after being hired. "We've got a lot of work to do. It's not going to be easy. We've got to get back to a point of putting pride into the Olde English 'D.'

"I care about this place. I think you all know that. That's how I played. Nothing else would make my life satisfied than to say that we were able to help turn this thing around."

Trammell credits much of his baseball success and knowledge to the tutelage he received under Sparky Anderson. Trammell played for Sparky throughout the Hall of Fame manager's 17-year Detroit tenure.

"Sparky taught all of us so much," Trammell said.

President and GM Dave Dombrowski presents a team shirt to newly hired manager Alan Trammell during a news conference in Detroit October 9, 2002. Paul Sancya, AP/Wide World Photos.

"He taught us how to play the game and how to respect it. More than anything else, he taught us how to be men. That's the challenge of a manager. I hope I can do some of the same."

Over the course of more than a century, Trammell is only the 35th manager in Tiger history. Considering that he is the sixth since 1996, that's quite a select group.

The two most successful Tiger managers appeared at opposite ends of the 20th century.

From 1907 through 1920, Hughie Jennings helped to establish the foundation of a tough and almost always competitive franchise. The son of a rugged Pennsylvania coal miner, Jennings was the perfect fit for Detroit's evolving industrial personality.

Jennings led the Tigers to three straight pennants in 1907-09. He managed the Tigers for 14 seasons and posted 1,131 victories in 2,103 games. He left after the 1920 season with club records that appeared likely to stand forever.

Then along came Sparky Anderson in 1979.

If Jennings laid a foundation for toughness, Sparky brought a luster to Detroit that shone over his Tigers and over the game itself. Before he unceremoniously departed following the 1995 season, Sparky rewrote the Detroit record books with 1,331 victories in 2,579 games.

Anderson and Jennings are the legitimate bookends for a franchise filled with managerial brilliance. In between the two, the Tigers were blessed with some of the most colorful characters ever to manage in the major leagues.

Anderson, of course, managed Detroit's most recent world championship team in 1984. The three other World Series-winning Tiger managers were Mickey Cochrane in 1935, Steve O'Neill in 1945, and Mayo Smith in 1968. Pennant-winning managers were Jennings (1907-08-09), Cochrane (1934-35), Del Baker (1940), O'Neill (1945), Smith (1968) and

Anderson (1984). Division-winning managers were Billy Martin (1972) and Anderson (1984 and '87).

From George Stallings in 1901 to current manager Alan Trammell, the history of Detroit managers is as colorful as the Tiger tradition itself. Consider the following:

- Six former Tiger managers are members of baseball's Hall of Fame – Ed Barrow, Hughie Jennings, Ty Cobb, Bucky Harris, Mickey Cochrane and Sparky Anderson.
- Six spent at least six years at the helm—Sparky Anderson (17), Hughie Jennings (14), Bucky Harris (7), Ty Cobb (6), Del Baker (6) and Steve O'Neill (6).
- Ten, including two interims, spent only one season.
- Three managed at least 1,000 games for Detroit—Sparky Anderson (2,579), Hughie Jennings (2,103) and Bucky Harris (1,073).
- Two (although they served only as interims) finished undefeated—Dick Tracewski (2-0 in 1979) and Billy Hitchcock (1-0 in 1960).
- One odd couple was Les Moss, who had the vocabulary of a sphinx and Sparky Anderson, who would talk to anyone or anything, including a sphinx.
- One won a battlefield promotion from private to major and a Silver Star during World War II—Ralph Houk.
- One quit the team in spring training only to return the next day and then be fired in September—Billy Martin.
- Two were considered the most ornery men on the planet—Ty Cobb and Mickey Cochrane.
- One was renowned for cooking chili for his players—Charlie Dressen.
- One served a season as a Tiger radio broadcaster after three years as the manager—Bob Scheffing.
- One served a whole day as an interim and after a rainout without managing a game, was promoted to the full-time position the following day—Luis Pujols.

Over the years, a few managers seemed to wear out their welcomes even before they had a chance to show what they could do. For others their stays were far too brief.

Regardless of who is officially charged with making out the starting lineup, in the chest of every Tiger fan beats the heart of a would-be manager.

Here, in order of number of Tiger victories, are profiles of those privileged to have led the Tigers—if only for one game.

Sparky Anderson
1979-95
Won: 1,331 Lost: 1,248

Sparky Anderson not only won more games than any other Tiger manager, he also was one of the most successful managers in baseball history.

With 2,194 victories during his 26-year career, his records en route to induction into the Hall of Fame in 2000 are overwhelming:

- 2,194 victories, third all-time behind Connie Mack and John McGraw.
- Only manager to lead two franchises in victories—Detroit (1,331) and Cincinnati (863).
- Only manager to win a World Series in both leagues.
- Only manager to record a 100-win season in both leagues.
- Only manager to be named Manager of the Year twice in both leagues.

Numbers, however, paint an incomplete picture of Sparky. No amount of numbers can show how much excitement and pride he provided to Detroit during his 17 years after doing the same for Cincinnati for nine seasons. Sparky's managerial savvy swallowed the opposition. His boundless optimism, friendliness and magnetic personality transcended the game.

"When Sparky came to Detroit, I was in awe of him," said longtime Tiger shortstop and current manager Alan Trammell. "I knew what he had done at Cincinnati. He was exactly what we needed. We needed to be corralled. We needed direction. We hadn't yet learned how to act as major-leaguers. He was the guy who got us going.

"When Sparky Anderson walks into a room, he immediately grabs your attention. You know he's in charge."

Sparky's gift for managing involved much more than such mundane matters as batting, throwing and running. His real strength lies with his insight into people.

Manager George "Sparky" Anderson looks on during a playoff game against the Kansas City Royals in Oct. 1984. AP/Wide World Photos

kick a guy that needed patting. And he didn't pat those that needed a kick. And he didn't do either one to guys who just needed to be left alone."

Kirk Gibson was one of those guys to whom Sparky wisely chose to give a boot in the butt to help him realize his big-league potential.

"I went through a period of my life where my priorities were misaligned," Gibson admitted. "I wasn't focused on what I was there for. Sparky didn't like what he saw and he challenged me.

"When it was all said and done, Sparky wanted me and all of us to be proud of what we did in the game and be proud of ourselves as persons. That's the definition of Sparky Anderson."

With his snow-white hair, natural ability to draw a crowd, and penchant for speaking nonstop fractured English for as long as anyone would listen, Sparky became a national personality.

Sparky joined the Tigers on June 14, 1979 and immediately promised that the Tigers would win the World Series within the next five years. He delivered when the Tigers jumped out to an unprecedented 35-5 start in 1984 before sweeping Kansas City in the playoff and then defeating San Diego in five games in the World Series for Detroit's first world championship in 16 years. Despite not having a 100-RBI hitter or a 20-game winner, the Tigers set club records with 104 victories and an attendance of 2,704,794 under Sparky in 1984.

In 1987, the Tigers rallied from an 11-19 start to win the East Division title.

"Of all the teams I was privileged to manage, that one in 1987 was real special," Sparky said. "We had no business winning the division. But that team simply refused to quit."

For all of Sparky's accomplishments on the field, it was his decision not to take the field and manage replacement players in 1995 during a players' strike that perhaps best symbolized Sparky's commitment to the game.

"Everyone was in a kind of panic stage," Trammell said. "Sparky's a little different. He thought, 'Wait a

"Sparky would have been a helluva psychologist," said Pete Rose, who starred for Anderson at Cincinnati. "That's what managing is. It doesn't matter what field it is. It's amazing how people try to run their businesses and don't know their personnel.

"Sparky knew his personnel. He always knew who he could put into a situation where they might fail and it wouldn't bother them. They were kind of kick-ass guys and were up for the challenge. Other people can't be put into a situation where they're going to fail because they'll fail every time. Sparky knew the difference.

"You can kick a guy in the ass—you can pat him on the back—or you can leave him alone. Sparky didn't

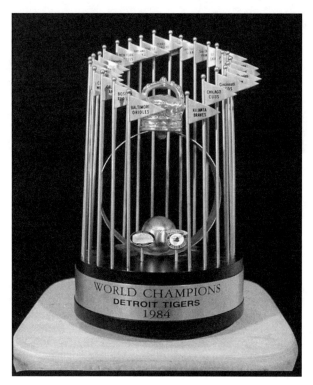

The Tigers won the 1984 World Series against the Padres.
Mark Cunningham, Creative Impressions Inc.

minute. I've got my principles. This is a joke.' When it gets down to a matter of ethics, Sparky Anderson is not going to be part of any joke. No amount of money would ever make Sparky Anderson compromise what he believes in."

Sparky's decision not only shocked the Tigers, it rocked the whole baseball world.

"Sparky is not a hypocrite," Gibson said. "He constantly preached principles to his players his whole career. For him to manage those replacement players would have been wrong for the game. It went against everything he had ever told anyone who had ever played for him."

Compromising principles is simply not part of Sparky's make-up. And compromising the game's integrity was something he could never do.

"I wasn't taking sides with the big-league players," Sparky explained. "I wasn't taking sides with the owners. And I certainly didn't feel anything against the replacements.

"What I did was strictly for baseball. Using replacement players was wrong. It didn't help the game. It embarrassed it."

Sparky didn't return until baseball invited the major-league players to camp. The walkout cost Sparky about $150,000 in salary and reportedly infuriated Tiger owner Mike Ilitch. Speculation immediately arose that Anderson would not be retained after the season.

None of that concerned Sparky. Doing what was right was the only thing that mattered.

Sparky finished his career as one of the game's most colorful characters. There'll never be another like him.

Hughie Jennings
1907-20
Won: 1,131 Lost: 972

Hughie Jennings was a manager a half-century ahead of his time. With his blue eyes, freckled face, ruggedly handsome looks and a natural gift for words that allowed him to communicate with people at every level, Jennings was a prime-time performer long before TV became the creator of instant sports legends.

Had he managed in the modern era instead of the early years of the 20th century, he most certainly would have become a household name.

However, memories of his managerial brilliance have been diluted by the media hype of the modern game.

That's unfortunate, because Jennings truly established himself as a pioneer.

Jennings's background was as colorful as his managerial style. The son of a tough Pennsylvania coal miner, Jennings got his first job as a young boy working the mines for 90 cents a day. He supplemented his income by playing semipro ball in the last quarter of the 19th century for the unheard-of sum of five dollars for Saturday afternoon games.

Although hardly a good student when he began his formal education, Jennings drove himself relentlessly and wound up graduating from Cornell with a law degree. After being admitted to the bar, he joined his brother's law firm, where his ability to articulate eloquently made him an accomplished trial lawyer.

Despite his success in the courtroom, baseball remained his passion. After playing infield for several seasons in the National League, Jennings was hired by Frank Navin to manage the 1907 Tigers.

Jennings wasted no time rewarding the faith that the Tiger owner had placed in him. Although he never

Showman manager Hughie Jennings showed his enthusiasm with a high leg kick and an "Ee-yah!" Burton Historical Society

managed a World Series winner, Jennings led the Tigers to their first three American League pennants in 1907-09.

Perhaps because of his rugged personal background, Jennings never lost touch with his feelings for the common man. He believed that baseball was America's most reachable outlet for the ordinary working man. And he believed strongly that any person paying a price to watch a professional game was entitled to the best show in town.

Although the success of a manager has always been dependent upon the talent of players on the field, Jennings did his part to give the fans a show. He worked the third base coaching box and became known throughout the league for kicking his leg high into the air and shouting "Ee-yah! Ee-yah!" to help his team start a rally.

The crowds appreciated his enthusiasm and returned his cries with similar chants of their own.

In spite of his crowd-pleasing antics, Jennings was a contemplative man who used his wits as well as his enthusiasm to extract the most from a team.

"You never waste your time or energy scolding a man in anger," he once explained. "It does no good. When you are angry, your reasoning isn't sound. If you must scold a player, let him know that by taking time with him, you are paying him the highest compliment possible."

One of Jennings's greatest personal accomplishments was learning how to coexist with the tempestuous Ty Cobb. Although Cobb had few friends on the team, in time he came to appreciate his manager's sincerity. The distinctly diverse duo eventually befriended each other. They spent countless hours away from the park discussing baseball theories and devising plans to make the ball club better.

From the day Jennings arrived in Detroit, he recognized the emerging brilliance of his young star. He also recognized Cobb's stubborn nature and decided to deal with it in a manner he felt would be most beneficial for the team.

"There isn't anything I can teach you about baseball," Jennings told Cobb. "Do as you please. You have my support. You can teach yourself how to play this game better than anyone else can teach you."

After winning three straight pennants, the Tigers never again returned to the World Series under Jennings. In 1915, the Tigers set a club record with 100 wins, but finished second, two and a half games behind Boston. During Jennings's 14-year career, the Tigers finished under .500 only four times.

After finishing seventh with only 61 victories in 1920, Jennings tendered his resignation. He had tired of the grind and the pressures that accompanied a losing team. He had begun to drink heavily and thought it wise to step down.

It was Jennings among others, who urged Navin to promote Cobb to the position of player/manager.

Despite having made a small fortune from investments in real estate and securities, Jennings never forgot from where he had come. He often returned to the Pennsylvania mining towns of his youth and bought groceries for families in need.

His Detroit managerial records lasted until the arrival of Sparky, more than a half-century later. Despite the fact that Jennings belonged to what now is considered an ancient era, he was Detroit's first great manager.

Jennings was an outstanding hitter and shortstop for Baltimore in the early years of the National League. He helped the Orioles to three straight pennants in 1894-96. His best season en route to a .314 career batting average was 1896, when he hit .398, stole 73 bases and set a record in his specialty—being hit by the pitch—49 times.

Jennings was inducted into baseball's Hall of Fame in 1945.

Bucky Harris
1929-33, 1955-56
Won: 516 Lost: 557

Bucky Harris enjoyed the most disjointed Detroit managerial tenure.

He joined the Tigers as a player/manager in 1929. Twenty-two years after managing his final Tiger game in 1933, Harris returned in 1955 for a two-year stint.

Harris was a baseball lifer who spent more than four decades as a player, manager and executive. With 2,157 victories, Harris ranks fourth on the all-time list behind Sparky Anderson.

Harris won two pennants and the 1924 World Series as a player/manager for Washington. In 1947, he managed the New York Yankees to a world championship.

During his first round as Tiger manager, Harris fell into disfavor with the fans after feuding with and trading away the popular Harry Heilmann and Fats Fothergill. Nevertheless, he enjoyed a lengthy major-league career, which eventually led to his 1975 induction into the Hall of Fame.

Steve O'Neill
1943-48
Won: 509 Lost: 414

Steve O'Neill was highly regarded for his patience and talent for developing young players.

As with all managers, his patience was tested during World War II when so many bright stars were called into military service. After the Tigers finished second by just one game in 1944, O'Neill led the Tigers to a

pennant and only their second world championship in 1945.

Describing O'Neill, legendary New York sports writer Red Smith commented:

"To this tough-looking muffin-faced catcher out of the anthracite mines of Minooka, Pennsylvania, Einstein and e.e. cummings and the Bolshoi Ballet were strictly for the birds, but he could sniff out baseball talent in the heaviest cover and he had a rare knack for keeping players relaxed."

Throughout O'Neill's Detroit tenure, the Tigers were always competitive. He never had a losing season during his 14 years as a big-league manager.

Ty Cobb
1921-26
Won: 479 Lost: 444

Ty Cobb never wanted to be the Tiger manager. But the all-time great tackled the job with the same stubborn intensity he demonstrated from the first day he laced up his spikes.

Owner Frank Navin was preparing to offer the job to Chicago's Pants Rowland. Cobb had no respect for Rowland and accepted the player/manager position at the urging of the outgoing Hughie Jennings.

In spite of his reluctance, Cobb attacked his new role with a passion.

Cobb's relentless fury perhaps undermined his ability to excel as a manager. He found it difficult to accept when players of lesser talent did not perform with the intensity he displayed. His finest season as a manager was 1923, when the Tigers finished second with an 83-71 mark.

Cobb's greatest managerial contribution was the development of Harry Heilmann and Charlie Gehringer. Cobb corrected a flaw in Heilmann's batting style, and Heilmann then proceeded to win four batting titles. Cobb also is credited with convincing owner Frank Navin to sign Gehringer. Heilmann and Gehringer both went on to Hall of Fame careers.

Never willing to admit defeat, Cobb defended his managerial record.

"In no way do I consider myself a failure as a manager," he said. "I took over a seventh-

Ty Cobb reluctantly served as player/manager for the Tigers from 1921-26. AP/Wide World Photos

Yankee pitcher Bump Hadley congratulates catcher/manager Mickey Cochrane upon his return to active management when the two teams opened a series on July 27, 1937. Cochrane was forced out of action when Hadley beaned him early in the season. AP/Wide World Photos

place club in 1921 and, with one exception, all of my clubs won more games than they lost. We finished in the first division four times. We played interesting and exciting ball."

Mickey Cochrane
1934-38
Won: 413 Lost: 297

Mickey Cochrane didn't earn the nickname "Black Mike" for playing like an Eagle Scout. He was tougher than dirt and straight as spit when it came to playing old-fashioned hardball.

"He had a certain look in his eyes," recalled Charlie Gehringer. "No one on the opposing team, and certainly no one on our club, wanted to cross him. All he wanted to do was win. He was a good man."

The pugnacious catcher/manager was brought to Detroit by owner Frank Navin for one reason—to win a World Series.

Cochrane actually had been Navin's second choice to become manager in 1934. Navin tried to lure Babe Ruth to Detroit. When The Babe balked, Navin purchased Cochrane from Connie Mack's Philadelphia Athletics for $100,000.

Cochrane wasted no time making the investment look like a steal. He won the Most Valuable Player Award and led the Tigers to the 1934 pennant. In 1935, he took them all the way to their first world championship.

Life quickly turned sour for Cochrane after the championship. As much as his fire had sparked the Tigers to victory, his intensity during less successful times led to a nervous breakdown in the middle of the 1936 season. Cochrane was sent to a Wyoming ranch to recuperate and didn't return to the team until early August. By that time, the Tigers had settled their own fate. They finished the season 19 1/2 games out of first place.

In 1937, Cochrane nearly died after being struck in the head by a pitch thrown by the Yankees' Bump

Hadley. Cochrane spent several days in the hospital with a triple skull fracture. Doctors considered his condition critical. He returned to the team on July 25, but his playing days were over. He served strictly as the manager for the rest of the year. Midway through the 1938 season, he was fired.

Cochrane is still regarded as one of the club's all-time favorite figures. After he was inducted into the Hall of Fame, one of the streets bordering Tiger Stadium was named in his honor.

Mayo Smith
1967-70
Won: 363 Lost: 285

Mayo Smith was not the first choice to manage the Tigers in 1967. But the nondescript former outfielder turned out to be the right man in the right place when he led the Tigers to a world championship in 1968.

After failing to talk Al Lopez into taking the job, the Tigers startled the baseball world by signing Smith in October 1966. Mayo inherited a club on the brink of maturing into a powerhouse. The Tigers took the 1967 race to the last day of the season. The following year, they waltzed to the pennant.

Although often criticized for his laid-back approach, Smith capitalized on two major gambles during the 1968 World Series to define his otherwise blasé career.

Looking to get the injured Al Kaline back into the lineup for the Series, Smith switched Gold Glove center fielder Mickey Stanley to shortstop. The bold move proved to be a stroke of genius. Kaline led the team with a .379 average and eight RBIs and Stanley played superbly at short.

Smith made an equally bold decision in Game 5. Behind by a run in the game and trailing the Series three games to one, Smith decided not to pinch hit for starter Mickey Lolich. Lolich delivered a bloop single and went on to finish the second of his three complete-game victories.

The Tigers slipped to second in 1969 and fourth in 1970, resulting in Smith's dismissal.

Ralph Houk
1974-78
Won: 363 Lost: 443

Ralph Houk knew he was in for a beating when he took the Tiger job. But his respect for GM Jim Campbell and the Tiger tradition prompted him to stay for five years.

"He knew it was going to be rough," Campbell said. "At the time, we needed a leader like Ralph. He took a lot of heat and helped us get through a rough period. I can't thank him enough."

The Tigers had embarked on a major rebuilding program. The talent cupboard was bare and it was up to Houk to keep the Tigers respectable until it was replenished.

The Tigers finished last in 1974 and 1975 before Mark "The Bird" Fidrych captured the nation's attention in 1976 under Houk.

During World War II, Houk won a Silver Star and a battlefield promotion from private to major. He spent 20 years as a manager with the New York Yankees, Detroit and Boston.

Del Baker
1933 (Interim), 1938-42
Won: 358 Lost: 317

Del Baker was the traditional baseball "organization man" who fell one game short of making his managerial opportunity complete. Baker's Tigers were edged in seven games by Cincinnati in the 1940 World Series after surprisingly jumping up to win the American League pennant.

The Tigers clinched the pennant on the season's final weekend, when Baker started the seldom-used Floyd Geibell against Cleveland great Bob Feller. Geibell held the second-place Indians scoreless and Rudy York drilled a two-run home run for a 2-0 victory.

After serving as an interim manager, Baker finally took over permanently for Mickey Cochrane in 1938. Baker spent 19 of his 22 seasons as a catcher in the minor leagues. He played with the Tigers in 1914-16. He served as a minor-league manager and then a major-league coach.

Red Rolfe
1949-52
Won: 278 Lost: 256

Red Rolfe came to the Tigers wearing a "Yankee luster." Unfortunately, that luster produced little more than a mediocre four-year record in Detroit.

In 1950, backed by George Kell's .340 batting average, Rolfe led the Tigers to a second-place finish, three games behind the perennially powerful Yankees. For that surprising performance, Rolfe was named Manager of the Year by *The Sporting News.*

Rolfe played third base for the Yankees from 1931-42. He posted a .289 lifetime average with 69 homers and 497 RBIs.

Billy Martin
1971-73
Won: 253 Lost: 208

Billy Martin was known as a spark plug. Love him or hate him, he had a gift for turning rust to gold. And though he did indeed ignite the underachieving Tigers—for which he had been brought to Detroit—he imploded himself in the process.

Manager Red Rolfe (right) poses with coaches (from left) Ted Lyons, Rick Ferrell (top) and Dick Bartell. **Burton Historical Society**

"Between the foul lines he was as good a manager as there was in the game,"acknowledged general manager Jim Campbell.

But the foul lines don't leave the park once the game is over. Martin's off-field escapades sealed his dismissal before the end of his third year.

Throughout his Tiger tenure, Martin managed with the bravado of a swashbuckling pirate. He was fearless in his moves and kept opposing managers off balance. His peppery personality and defiance of authority lifted him to folk hero status with Detroit's blue-collar work force.

Unfortunately, Martin's defiant behavior finally offset his on-field accomplishments, but not until after the Tigers won the East Division title in 1972.

Martin kept his Tigers in the race through most of 1973 until his personal life began to unravel. Still his popularity with the fans was as strong as on the first day he had worn a Tiger uniform.

Martin had extracted the most from an aging veteran team. By the time he was fired in September 1973, it had become apparent that the Tigers were facing a major rebuilding program.

Throughout his nearly three-year stay, however, Martin gave the fans plenty to talk about. He always left them wondering what would happen next.

Charlie Dressen
1963-66
Won: 221 Lost: 189

Charlie Dressen was known for his dignity and his class.

"We had a lot of good young prospects coming up at the time," explained general manager Jim Campbell. "We felt it important for them to learn about the major leagues the right way. Everybody respected and loved Charlie."

Dressen managed 16 years in the major leagues. He took the 1952 and 1953 Brooklyn Dodgers to the World Series.

Dressen never got the chance to enjoy the fruits of Detroit's rich farm system. He returned from one heart attack, which he suffered in spring training of 1965. After suffering a second one on May 16, 1966, however, he never returned. The popular manager went home and died of coronary arrest on August 10.

Bob Swift had replaced him on an interim basis. Shortly before the All-Star Game a tumor was detected on Swift's lung. Swift was sent home and replaced by Frank Skaff. Swift died on October 17, marking the first time two managers from one team had died in the same year.

Bob Scheffing
1961-63
Won: 210 Lost: 173

The Tigers wanted to hire Casey Stengel for the 1961 season. Instead, they had to settle for Bob Scheffing and an unexpected run for the pennant against the history-making Yankees.

Owner John E. Fetzer tried to lure Stengel to the Tigers after they had slipped to only 71 wins in 1960. Stengel was tempted, but wound up with the first-year New York Mets instead.

Scheffing, a former National League catcher, made the most of his opportunity by leading the Tigers to 101 wins. Scheffing possessed a calming motivational personality that enabled him to communicate well with young players.

The Tigers and Yankees were even until Labor Day in 1961. With Roger Maris bidding to break Babe Ruth's home run record, New York got hot and fin-

ished with 109 victories.

After the unexpected pennant run, Detroit's youth and inexperience showed. In 1962 they fell to fourth place. They tumbled all the way to ninth the following year, and Scheffing was dismissed.

Buddy Bell
1996-98
Won: 184 Lost: 277

Buddy Bell faced an uphill battle from the day he took the job. First, he had to follow a legend in Sparky Anderson. Secondly, he was charged with leading a club in the middle of a perpetual rebuilding program, along with a new front office staff that had yet to learn Detroit.

In the long run, nothing worked according to plans.

After the 1996 team set a club record with 109 losses, Bell led the 1997 team to a third-place finish with 79 wins. The nondescript team again regressed in 1998, leaving Bell seemingly relieved when he was fired near the end of the season.

Despite the frustrations he endured in Detroit, Bell is considered to be one of the game's classiest individuals. The former All-Star third baseman is the son of former Cincinnati slugger Gus Bell. Two of Buddy's sons also made it to the major leagues.

Fred Hutchinson
1952-54
Won: 155 Lost: 235

Above all else, Fred Hutchinson is remembered for two things: his class and his temper.

Hutchinson was revered by his players—almost to the point of veneration. In the face of tough losses, there were never any excuses. In the wake of bad breaks, there was never any whining.

Hutchinson vented his frustrations in his own peculiar ways. Furniture was thrown. Lights were sometimes smashed. Yet he never offered an alibi and never singled out one of his players for a careless misplay.

Occasionally, after particularly tough losses, Hutchinson would walk from the ballpark to his home in Dearborn—about 10 miles away.

As a pitcher, Hutchinson was a tough competitor who compiled a lifetime 95-71 record despite losing four years to the war. He was named Detroit's player/manager in July 1952 with the team heading toward its first last place finish.

After leaving Detroit, he managed St. Louis from 1956-58. He managed Cincinnati from 1959-64 and took the Reds to the World Series in 1961. At age 45, Hutchinson suffered from cancer, which forced him to resign in August 1964. He died that November.

Bill Armour
1905-06
Won: 150 Lost: 152

Bill Armour was one of the early game's truly colorful characters. Seeking to establish his authority over the players, Armour dressed in street clothes and wore a straw hat for the games.

Armour came loaded with a litany of superstitions. If he spotted a butterfly, he requested the game to be halted until one of his players could kill the bad-luck omen.

Armour's luck ran out after two seasons and 150 wins.

George Moriarty
1927-28
Won: 150 Lost: 157

While George Moriarty lasted only two seasons as the Tiger manager, his feisty spirit made him a favorite with Navin Field fans. From opposing players to umpires to heckling fans, Moriarty was never shy about making his feelings known.

Serving as an umpire in 1932 after his managerial career had ended, Moriarty challenged the entire Chicago White Sox team to a fight, one player at a time. The White Sox apparently misunderstood the challenge and attacked Moriarty en masse.

Moriarty was hospitalized with a broken hand and head injuries, but quickly returned to his job on the base paths.

Manager Buddy Bell peers out of the dugout during another loss enroute to a record 109 losses in the dismal 1996 season. Duane Burleson, AP/Wide World Photos

Phil Garner
2000-02
Won: 145 Lost: 185

Phil Garner brought a string of seven straight losing seasons as the Milwaukee manager when he came to Detroit. When he left, he had tied the legendary Connie Mack for the second most with 10. Mack, who owned the Philadelphia Athletics, also holds the record of 13 straight losing seasons as a manager.

Garner also set the dubious record for getting the earliest managerial ax when he was fired after six straight losses to start the 2002 season.

Garner was hired by owner Mike Ilitch to give the Tigers an established veteran as they moved into a new park for 2000. Ilitch and the front office were impressed with Garner's experience as a manager and his fiery intensity as a player.

Unfortunately for the Tigers, neither had an impact in Detroit.

In 2000, the Tigers won 79 games and showed late-season signs of improvement. They slipped to 66 wins in 2001 and there was widespread speculation that Garner had lost the confidence and control of the team.

Six games into the next season, Ilitch and new Tiger president Dave Dombrowski decided they had seen enough.

Garner was an intense player who earned the nickname "Scrap Iron." He played second base for at least parts of 16 seasons in the major leagues. He was a member of the 1974 Oakland world champions and the 1979 Pittsburgh world champions. He was a three-time All-Star.

Phil Garner was fired as the Tigers' manager after losing six straight in 2002. Mike Litaker

Jimmy Dykes
1959-60
Won: 118 Lost: 115

Jimmy Dykes was a valuable, versatile player who earned the highest praise from the legendary Connie Mack.

"Having one Dykes is like having five or six players and only having one to feed, clothe and pay," Mack commented.

But Dykes is best remembered by baseball trivia buffs for being one-half of the only managerial trade in history.

With Detroit and Cleveland headed nowhere fast in the 1960 season, the Tigers shipped Dykes to Cleveland for Indians Manager Joe Gordon.

Although his name will always remain a part of baseball trivia, Dykes's major-league career was far from trivial.

In 13 full seasons playing for Mack's Athletics, Dykes averaged 125 games a year. He hit over .300 five times and played in three straight World Series (1929-31).

Dykes managed for two undistinguished seasons in Detroit, but finished his career with 21 years of major-league managing.

Jack Tighe
1957-58
Won: 99 Lost: 104

Likeable Jack Tighe spent a half-century in the Tiger organization and had a knack for bringing a smile to everyone's face. The Tiger "lifer" had a dry sense of humor and the honesty of a judge.

When one of the partners from the John Fetzer ownership syndicate commented on the troubles of his struggling team, Tighe quickly cracked, "You'd have trouble too if you had to manage this cast of characters every day."

Because of his candor, wit and keen eye for talent, Tighe was a favorite with baseball writers across the country. Even after his dismissal as manager the Tigers kept him in the organization as a valued scout for decades.

Jimmy Dykes is best known for being one of the managers involved in the only managerial trade ever. Dykes was traded to Cleveland for manager Joe Gordon.
Burton Historical Society

Tighe joined the organization as a minor-league catcher in 1935. He played in the minors for five years and then managed in the minors beginning in 1940.

While managing Buffalo, Tighe roomed with Jim Campbell, who was serving as an executive in the minor-league system. When Campbell became general manager, he remembered his friend and promoted him to special scout.

Ed Barrow
1903-04
Won: 97 Lost: 117

Ed Barrow left a major imprint on baseball. But it was with the New York Yankees rather than the Tigers during his brief stint.

Barrow managed for five seasons in the majors, including two for Detroit. In 1918 he managed the Boston Red Sox to a pennant.

But it was after Barrow became chairman of the board of the Yankees that he really made his mark. During his 24-year tenure, New York won 14 pennants and 10 World Series. He is credited with having converted Babe Ruth from pitcher to outfielder.

Barrow was 35 when he managed the Tigers and had a reputation for being a tough competitor. He often challenged his own players to "come into the office, and only one of us will walk out."

Larry Parrish
1998 (Interim), 1999
Won: 82 Lost: 104

Despite a losing record, Larry Parrish will be remembered as a piece of Tiger trivia. He's the last man to manage Detroit in Tiger Stadium.

Parrish was a stopgap between Buddy Bell and Phil Garner as the Tigers ran through a string of managers after the departure of Sparky Anderson following the 1995 season.

George Stallings
1901
Won: 74 Lost: 61

George Stallings was the only Tiger manager to own a piece of the club. He was given a small portion of the team in addition to his position as manager when the Tigers became charter members of the American League in 1901.

The ownership relationship between Stallings and primary owner Jim Burns was stormy. Each accused the other of financial chicanery.

American League founder Ban Johnson offered his new league as an alternative to the brawling National League. Johnson did not condone Stallings's reckless style of play, which led to several fines. Johnson also tired of Detroit's financial bickering and forced a sale of the franchise.

Always a fiery competitor, Stallings led the Tigers to a third-place finish in their first year of American League existence.

After leaving Detroit, Stallings managed the Boston Braves to one of the most dramatic comebacks in history. In 1914, the Braves won 52 of their last 66 games to capture the National League pennant. They swept the World Series from the Philadelphia Athletics.

Bill Norman
1958-59
Won: 58 Lost: 64

After succeeding Jack Tighe in mid-1958, Bill Norman was fired following a 2-15 start the following year.

Norman's only managerial experience before getting the Tiger job came in the minor leagues. He was a utility outfielder for the White Sox in 1931-32.

Bob Swift
1965 (Interim), 1966 (Interim)
Won: 56 Lost: 43

Bob Swift was a two-time interim manager who fell one game short of 100 games managed in the big leagues.

The former Tiger catcher, who was part of the 1945 world champions, filled in twice for Charlie Dressen, who had suffered heart attacks. In 1966, Swift had to be replaced after the All-Star Game when a tumor was discovered on his lung. He died on October 17, 1966.

On August 19, 1951, Swift had the distinction of being the catcher against the St. Louis Browns when maverick owner Bill Veeck sent three-foot, seven-inch Eddie Gaedel to the plate.

Swift had a wry sense of humor. "We go first class," he once cracked during his managerial stint. "When we check out of hotels, we don't take towels. We take TV sets."

Luis Pujols
2002
Won: 55 Lost: 100

Luis Pujols knew he was stepping into a hornet's nest when he took over the reins only six games into the 2002 season. And he wound up getting stung— 100 times.

Pujols was promoted when Phil Garner was fired after the Tigers dropped the first six games of the season. After the team won just 55 of 155 games under Pujols, another managerial switch was made one day after the season ended.

Some suggest Pujols never had a chance with the team he inherited, coupled with massive front office uncertainty. Nevertheless, he got his one shot at the big time after managing successfully in the Tiger minor-league system.

Years from now, some fans may wonder "Who was that guy who took over the manager's job before the 2002 season was even a week old?"

Frank Dwyer
1902
Won: 52 Lost: 83

In spite of finishing in seventh place, Frank Dwyer's one season as Tiger manager met a better fate than his announced successor.

Win Mercer was supposed to take over the team as a pitcher/manager in 1903, but never made it. On January 12, 1903, Mercer committed suicide in a San Francisco hotel.

Frank Skaff
1966 (Interim)
Won: 40 Lost: 39

Frank Skaff had the dubious distinction of serving as an interim for the interim manager.

In the bizarre year of 1966 when Charlie Dressen and Bob Swift both died, it was Skaff who finished the season. Skaff was a longtime organizational man who concluded his career as a scout.

Bobby Lowe
1904 (Interim)
Won: 30 Lost: 44

Bobby Lowe's managerial career was brief, but he does hold the distinction of replacing Ed Barrow, who turned the Yankees into a dynasty after his Tiger career. Lowe finished the 1904 season after Barrow was fired.

Les Moss
1979
Won: 27 Lost: 26

Les Moss's claim to fame is that he was replaced by the most celebrated manager in Tiger history.

Moss posted a 27-26 record before Sparky Anderson was named as the new manager on June 12, 1979. Moss, a former catcher with the St. Louis Browns and Chicago White Sox, had served as Detroit's Class AAA manager before being promoted to Detroit.

Joe Gordon
1960
Won: 26 Lost: 31

Obviously, Joe Gordon didn't like the trade.

Gordon resigned as Tiger manager in 1960 after being traded to Detroit from Cleveland for Jimmy Dykes in midseason. It stands as the only managerial trade in history.

Gordon resigned before general manager Bill DeWitt could fire him.

Joe Schultz
1973 (Interim)
Won: 9 Lost: 10

Joe Schultz finished the 1973 season as interim manager after Billy Martin was fired. The longtime coach was not retained for the next season.

Dick Tracewski
1979 (Interim)
Won: 2 Lost: 0

Dick "Trixie" Tracewski was one of the classiest Tigers ever to wear the Olde English "D."

After spending four seasons as a Tiger utility infielder (1966-69), he served as a Tiger coach until he retired after the 1995 season.

Tracewski was called upon to serve as the interim manager for two games until Sparky Anderson could make it to Detroit after being named the manager on June 12, 1979.

Trixie made the most of his opportunity.

On June 12 in Detroit, the Tigers hammered Oakland, 9-2. The following evening at Tiger Stadium, the Tigers dumped Seattle, 7-3.

Before being traded to Detroit, Tracewski spent four years (1962-65) playing for the Los Angeles Dodgers. During his career, he was a player or coach on four teams that made it to the World Series—two with the Dodgers and two with the Tigers. All four teams won world championships.

Billy Hitchcock
1960 (Interim)
Won: 1 Lost: 0

Billy Hitchcock made the most of his one-game opportunity to manage the Tigers.

Hitchcock was the third base coach when the Tigers and Indians traded managers on August 3, 1960. While Joe Gordon was packing his belongings to come to Detroit, Hitchcock was called upon to serve as the interim for one day.

The Tigers were playing at Yankee Stadium and hammered the Bronx Bombers, 12-2.

9

THE EXECS UPSTAIRS

No other factor more clearly defines the personality of any baseball era than the evolution of the game's owners. As the business philosophies of the owners are defined, so too is the game.

There was a time when owners fiercely guarded against mixing their baseball and regular business operations. The separation was as sacred as that between religion and state. The owners were called sportsmen and their vigilance protected the purity of the game.

There was no seventh-inning stretch presented by some cash-paying sponsor, no pitching change with the intrusion of a commercial plug, and certainly no cross-promotional campaign between the ball club and the owner's other business interests.

None of that was necessary.

But times change, as do owners.

The evolution of the game into today's prevailing "corporate ball" is neither good nor bad. It simply is. Indeed, the tidal wave of marketing makes it difficult to believe things were ever any other way.

Tiger history, which spans more than a century, is marked by five distinct ownership eras—Frank Navin, Walter O. Briggs, John E. Fetzer, Tom Monaghan and Mike Ilitich.

Frank Navin
1904-1935

Frank Navin was the owner who built the foundation from which the franchise evolved. Arguably, his contributions to the club and to the city of Detroit make him the most significant single figure in Tiger history.

Under Navin, the Tigers solidified themselves as charter members of the American League, established a ballpark that endured for nearly a century, and won Detroit's first world championship in 1935.

Despite his historic influence, Navin remains one of the franchise's most misunderstood figures. Perhaps part of the problem was Navin's physical appearance and peculiar personality. He was tall and corpulent with a bald head. His penchant for conservative three-piece suits and passive neckties portrayed the image of a bookkeeper, which he had trained to be. He didn't drink, smoke or chew tobacco like many of his era's players and some of his colleagues.

"[Navin] did not make friends easily," said longtime *Detroit News* sports editor H. G. Salsinger. "But once you got to know him, you could see his rare sense of humor. And he was one of the most charitable men around, always helping those who needed help, especially former players who were down on their luck."

Navin wore a perpetual poker face, perhaps the result of his service as a croupier in one of Detroit's turn-of-the-century gambling houses. Win or lose, in good times or bad, whatever he felt inside was never betrayed by outward appearances.

He once confessed that he wished he could more openly express his emotions.

"But it's just not me," he concluded.

Beneath his calculating appearance, Navin harbored a passion to provide the city with the best team and finest park in baseball.

Navin was the right man at the right time in history to couple baseball's beautiful simplicity with the city's emergence as the automobile capital of the world.

In 1896, Detroit's population totaled approximately 250,000. With Henry Ford's development of the Model T in 1908 and the construction of the Ford plant in 1910, the demand for employees was huge and immediate. Dodge, General Motors and Packard soon joined the automobile boom.

Men seeking employment in the new industry came from everywhere, including Eastern Europe, to work in the factories. Despite the language barriers, the immigrants seemed to enjoy baseball. The Tigers quickly became a common denominator among cultures. The game provided a respite from the daily drudgery of factory work.

By 1929, the "Motor City" had been established. With a population of 1.6 million, Detroit was the nation's fourth largest city.

As Detroit's population exploded, Navin invested wisely to make his park and players an integral part of the community that would sustain the team to the present day.

Navin carefully coupled his calculating business instincts with his gut feeling for the game to establish the Tigers as one of the most solid franchises in either major league.

"Navin was one of the few owners who knew the playing end of the game as well as he knew the business end," Salsinger wrote. "Few of his players ever matched him in his understanding of the technical aspects of the game. He made a study of baseball and knew more about pitching than anyone around. He never criticized his players, except if he felt they were lazy and weren't putting out their best effort. For this reason, they liked playing for him. None of them got rich but they always thought he was fair in dealing with them."

Navin, a 31-year-old clerk in the insurance office of Samuel F. Angus, was promoted to bookkeeper in 1902 after Angus headed a syndicate that purchased the Tigers from Jim Burns and George Stallings. Burns had purchased the club for $12,000 from George Vanderbeck on March 6, 1900, one year before the creation of the American League. Stallings, who hit the first home run at the celebrated corner, owned a small interest in the club as part of his compensation as manager.

When Angus's business interests began to fail, he sold the club to William H. Yawkey, who had inherited a $10 million lumber fortune from his father. Navin received a 10 percent interest in the club for brokering the $50,000 deal.

Navin immediately moved into the front office and soon became enamored with his all-encompassing role with the Tigers. With the 28-year-old Yawkey too busy pursuing his whims as a multi-millionaire playboy to worry about the Tigers, Navin quickly immersed himself in every facet of the day-to-day operations of the Tigers.

Serving as secretary, treasurer, business manager, farm director, chief ticket seller, advertising manager and any other position that demanded immediate attention, Navin wore almost as many hats as the members of the team.

And he cherished every hectic moment.

In 1905, shortly after assuming part ownership, Navin arranged the deal that brought Ty Cobb to Detroit. During spring training, he spotted the fleet-footed outfielder who was playing for Augusta of the Sally League. While some Tiger players mocked Cobb's insatiable intensity, Navin was stunned by the youngster's potential. At the end of the season, Navin plucked Cobb for $750.

Prior to the 1907 season, Navin hired Hughie Jennings to manage the club. Jennings responded by becoming the Tigers' first great manager and led the team to three pennants in his first three years. He remained through the end of the 1920 season and held every club managerial record until Sparky Anderson surpassed all of them more than a half-century later.

Prior to the 1934 season, Navin swung a deal that brought the rambunctious Mickey Cochrane to the Tigers as a player/manager. Not only did the Tigers win the pennant in Cochrane's first season, but they brought the city its first world championship in 1935, only six weeks before Navin died.

While Navin's eye for talent and organization was impeccable, his true genius was the vision he exercised to firmly establish the Tigers at the celebrated corner of Michigan and Trumbull until the turn of the next century.

Thanks to Navin's tireless efforts and Detroit's first pennant-winning season in 1907 with a scrappy club that featured the tempestuous Cobb, the Tigers set an attendance record of 297,079. Nevertheless, Detroit

Owner Frank Navin is credited with bringing volatile star Ty Cobb to Detroit in 1905. Brace Photo

had yet to establish itself as one of baseball's hotbeds. The city was still a few years away from blossoming into the world-class industrial giant with the emergence of the auto industry. Many critics, in fact, questioned whether Detroit would ever become one of the game's major players.

In short, Detroit had not yet developed into the "baseball town" it was destined to become.

Apathy toward Tiger fortunes prompted Bill Yawkey to sell a half-interest in the club to Navin just prior to the 1907 World Series. Yawkey remained a silent partner until he died in 1919. After Yawkey's death, Walter O. Briggs and John Kelsey each bought a quarter-share of the Tigers for $250,000 apiece.

For all intents and purposes, however, the club belonged to Navin.

Perhaps spurred by his gambling instincts and an unshakeable confidence in his own tireless efforts, Navin decided to expand Bennett Park.

After the club won its first pennant in 1907, Navin embarked on a project that doubled the park's capacity for the next season. With the additional seating and second straight pennant, the 1908 Tigers set an attendance record of 436,199. With a third straight pennant in 1909, attendance rose to 490,490.

Navin's vision for Detroit and his Tigers took an even greater leap of faith after the 1911 season when he and partner Yawkey invested $300,000 to build a new park, doubling its capacity to 23,000 with a covered pavilion that connected each end of the grandstand from foul pole to foul pole.

On April 20, 1912, the Tigers played their first game in Navin Field, a ballpark that would be part of the city's essence throughout the remainder of the 20th century. In 1924, Navin added a second deck of seats from third base to first base, increasing the capacity to 30,000.

Despite the energy and heroics of luminaries such as Ty Cobb, Harry Heilmann, Sam Crawford and Bobby Veach, the team never recaptured the magic of its three straight early pennants. Soon the nation became mired in the worst depression of its history.

After the 1933 season, Navin—like all owners—was looking for a way to generate interest in his team. Attendance had sagged to a mere 320,972. With eventual Hall of Famers such as Charlie Gehringer and Hank Greenberg wreaking havoc on American League pitching, Navin was convinced he was one ingredient short of finally returning the team to the World Series.

Navin initially tried to lure Babe Ruth to Detroit to manage the club. When Ruth put him off, Navin purchased Mickey Cochrane for $100,000 from Connie Mack's Philadelphia Athletics. The deal turned into a bonanza that even The Babe couldn't have matched.

With the peppery Cochrane serving as both catcher and manager, the Tigers won a record 101 games in front of 919,161 spectators on their way to the 1934 pennant. For the fourth straight time under Navin, however, they lost the World Series when the Cardinals defeated them in seven games.

After the Tigers lost the sixth game, a friend tried to bolster Navin's spirits, "You got beat today, Frank, but this means a seventh game and some $50,000 extra for you." Uncharacteristically, Navin blistered, "To hell with $50,000. I'd give the $50,000 and five times that much to have won today."

Navin wondered if he would ever taste baseball's ultimate prize. With a team that many historians argue is still the greatest in franchise history, however, the Tigers bounced back in 1935 to whip the Chicago Cubs in six games to give the city its first world championship.

After it had been reported that the World Series victory had earned Navin about $150,000, the 64-year-old workaholic publicly announced the profit would be used to expand and enhance the ballpark.

Navin never got the chance to realize his final dream. Less than six weeks after celebrating the World Series victory, he suffered a heart attack while riding one of his horses and died on November 13.

Navin had a love for horses and racetrack gambling on which he risked thousands of dollars. Because of Navin's considerable stature within the game, commissioner Kenesaw Mountain Landis conveniently looked the other way when assessing his friend's personal indulgences.

Navin's first passion, however, was always his Tigers and his ballpark.

Navin was respected by the fans, his players and also by fellow owners in both leagues.

"He would sit silent for hours at meetings while arguments raged all around him," Salsinger wrote. "They would finally ask for his opinion and he always came up with the solution to their problems."

Albeit silently, Navin's contributions to the Tigers and the city are still apparent today.

He may have been the most significant individual in Tiger history.

Walter O. Briggs
1936-1952

Walter O. Briggs wasn't merely a passive beneficiary of Detroit's booming automobile economy. He was an active part of it. Briggs coupled his tireless drive and daring to become a self-made multimillionaire in the burgeoning industry. And then he capitalized on the opportunity to realize his baseball dreams—first as a silent partner with Frank Navin and then as sole owner of the Tigers for almost two decades.

Briggs first began working in Detroit car shops as a fifteen-year-old body trimmer. In 1909 he pur-chased the trim and paint shop of a boyhood friend and turned it into the Briggs Manufacturing Company. He worked tirelessly to develop the new enterprise into the country's largest independent manufacturer of auto bodies. There was a time when Briggs owned 16 plants, including nine in Detroit and one in England. With a workforce of 40,000, Briggs serviced all the major auto companies.

Briggs's passion for the Tigers preceded Navin's ownership of the team. Briggs was a regular customer at Bennett Park and also spent many afternoons at West End Park, where the Tigers played Sunday games when they weren't allowed at "The Corner" because of Detroit's "blue laws." The Sunday contests were rowdy affairs, and it's reported that Briggs found himself in the middle of several incidents involving players, umpires and fans.

Briggs's patience as a fan was put to its stiffest test before the start of the 1907 World Series. Legend has it that Briggs vowed to someday buy the club after he had trouble purchasing tickets to the Series opener. The budding 30-year-old industrialist finagled his way into a meeting with Navin before the start of the Series. Not only was he successful in purchasing his tickets, the encounter set the stage for a much more significant meeting 13 years later.

After Navin's partner, Bill Yawkey, died in 1919, Briggs and industrialist John Kelsey each paid $250,000 for quarter-shares of the club.

Briggs purchased Kelsey's quarter-share in 1927 to become half owner. Almost immediately after Navin died in November 1935, Briggs purchased the remainder of the stock for $1 million to become the team's first sole owner.

From the day he took control of the team until the day of his death on January 17, 1952, Briggs treated the Tigers more as part of his family than a business venture.

"My goal is to give Detroit the best team in the finest park in the country," Briggs proclaimed in 1936.

And despite a rash of erratic proclivities emanating from his enigmatic personality, that's precisely what Briggs did.

The club was not always successful on the field. But Briggs's sincerity was never questioned. And the park he provided for his players and the fans was regarded as the finest in either league.

As a silent partner to Navin, Briggs was relentless in his pursuit of excellence. For instance, it was Briggs who persuaded Navin to snatch Mickey Cochrane as a manager in 1934. And it also was Briggs who underwrote the $100,000 price tag out of his own pocket.

"I'll pay for him," Briggs told his partner. "I'll lend the club whatever's needed to get him. You just get him and win the pennant."

That bold move was a sign of things to come when Briggs became sole owner of the ball club.

In 1936, Briggs made good on Navin's promise to invest the profits from the previous season's world championship in expanding the park. The right field pavilion and bleachers were double-decked to increase seating to 36,000. In 1938, Briggs put a second deck onto the left and center field stands to bring seating to 53,000.

Briggs renamed his new baseball cathedral "Briggs Stadium," and the structure remained basically the same until the final game was played there to end the 1999 season.

Legendary New York sports writer Red Smith succinctly depicted Briggs's legacy to the game when he wrote a tribute after the owner's passing:

"Walter O. Briggs was, in the narrowest and best and most exacting sense of the term, a big-leaguer. Among owners of baseball clubs, real big-leaguers form a small and dwindling company, a company that has shrunk further with the death of the owner of the Detroit Tigers. Baseball cannot afford to lose his kind.

"Mr. Briggs was a sportsman, one of the very few in a game that has become, over the years, more and more a business and less a sport. He was not in baseball to make money, which he didn't need. He wasn't in it for personal publicity, which he didn't want.

"He did not look upon Briggs Stadium as a monument to himself. He considered it a place to play baseball, a place where fans like him could watch baseball, and because he was a fan and a big-leaguer, he wanted it to be the best possible setting for the best possible baseball."

Without a doubt, that's precisely what Briggs did.

Briggs ensured that fans remained as close as possible to the action on the field, regardless of their seat location. He installed a modern center field scoreboard that allowed fans to keep up with the Tiger games as well as all other major-league contests in both leagues. He created an inviting hitting environment second to none. With dark green outfield walls and a clutter-free hitting background, home and visiting players alike were able to utilize all of their hitting skills. Players

readily proclaimed that the infield and outfield provided a surface like a putting green.

"The outfield was just like a carpet," said Doc Cramer, who played in the park as both a Tiger and a visitor. "You could dive for a ball out there and you'd scoot across that grass. You wouldn't stick in the ground. A lot of these ballparks, the ground gets a little wet and you wind up sticking your shoulder into it."

It was Briggs who pioneered the use of a nylon tarpaulin to cover the infield during rainstorms. From his private box near the Tiger dugout, he would time the grounds crew while they stretched it over the infield. He also installed the major leagues' first underground sprinkling system to keep his immaculate field greener than any shamrock in Ireland.

Not only did Briggs maintain a critical eye for the surroundings of the players, but he did so for the fans as well. He had the seats and walls of the park painted every year. He stationed attendants in the ladies' restrooms. And his generosity with free tickets to youth groups was unparalleled in the game.

Like his predecessor, Briggs was opposed to night baseball. Navin once predicted that "night baseball will be the ruination of baseball. It changes the players from athletes to actors."

Nevertheless, Briggs eventually succumbed to the nudging evolution of the game. He had placed an order for light towers prior to the December 7, 1941 bombing of Pearl Harbor. When America went to war, Briggs donated the steel to the war effort, and night games in Detroit were put on hold. In addition to that generous donation, Briggs ordered the Tigers to offer 25 cents in war bond stamps for every foul ball returned to the field from the stands. Through that program and a string of exhibition games, the Tigers raised $70,000 for the war effort.

By 1948, only the Tigers and Chicago Cubs still played in parks without lights. When Briggs finally had them installed, of course, he made the Tigers' system the best in the game. At a cost of $400,000, Briggs had eight towers constructed that featured a total of 1,458 lights.

While Briggs encountered highly publicized salary disagreements with such players as Mickey Cochrane, Hank Greenberg and Rudy York, the owner's reputation for lavishly pampering his players was widely known throughout both leagues.

Despite Briggs's benevolence toward his players and the fans, the owner's reluctance to sign black play-

Multi-decked Briggs Stadium, as seen in 1951, had a seating capacity of over 53,000. It did not have lights for night games, however, until 1948. AP/Wide World Photos

ers was a stigma that haunted his legacy even after his death. When Briggs died, the Tigers and Boston Red Sox were the only big-league teams that had not signed a black player to a major-league contract.

Briggs was struck by another embarrassing predicament in January, 1940, just before the team was preparing for its unexpected American League pennant. Briggs had been diagnosed with polio, and the incident occurred after his health had begun to deteriorate and general manager John A. Zeller had been entrusted with more authority.

The Tigers were slapped with a stiff penalty by Commissioner Landis for allegedly entering into a scheme to hide minor-league players through a system of illegal contracts and other paper-shuffling diversions. The commissioner ordered 91 players, including five

on the major-league roster, to be released. In addition, the Tigers had to pay $47,250 to 15 other players.

Zeller denied the charges. Embarrassed by the incident, Briggs accepted responsibility.

"We have surely been penalized for any mistakes or wrongdoings within the organization," Briggs said. "The cost of this is mine and will be properly taken care of."

Zeller, who accepted public responsibility for the affair and denied Briggs's awareness of the situation, was not fired.

The 1940 Tigers shocked the American League and won the pennant, only to lose the World Series to Cincinnati in seven games. Five years later, with baseball just beginning to recover from the effects of World War II, Briggs finally realized his dream when the Tigers won the 1945 World Series in seven games over the Chicago Cubs.

The Tigers triumphed with a collection of veteran players who had either returned from the war or had been too old to serve. Briggs was asked by Zeller about his determination to sign established players instead of waiting for them to develop in the minor leagues.

"Because I don't think I will be here long enough to see them develop," Briggs replied. "My life is not certain. I want to be the head of a winning ball club before I am called out at the plate. And if I am taken and go to the Great Beyond, I want to be in a position to say, when I meet my old pal, Frank Navin, 'I've carried on your tradition of giving Detroit, the best ball town in the world, a championship team. I got one, too, Frank.'"

Briggs died on January 17, 1952 at the age of 74. His legacy was complicated. He gave Detroit the finest ballpark in the game and tirelessly tried to provide the best teams. He was generous with his contributions to youth groups and the American war effort. But his record on integration haunted his memory.

Never, though, was there any question about the fact that he was the Tigers' most rabid fan.

As Red Smith aptly summarized: "Walter O. Briggs was a sportsman, he was a big-leaguer, and most of all, he was a fan."

John Fetzer
1956-1983

No one summarized John E. Fetzer's baseball legacy more succinctly than the former owner himself.

"I don't regard myself as owner of the Tigers," he explained. "I serve only as their guardian. The franchise really belongs to the fans."

Fetzer's philosophy was simple. He believed in the purity of the game and keeping baseball within the reach of the common working man.

"Mr. Fetzer no more needed to buy the Tigers than the man in the moon," said Hall of Fame third baseman and longtime Tiger broadcaster George Kell. "He already had distinguished himself as a radio and television pioneer. He had made hundreds of millions. But he loved baseball and had a soft spot in his heart for the Tigers. He was one of the finest owners the game has ever known."

Fetzer served as sole owner of the club from 1961 through 1983 after being part of a syndicate that purchased the team from the Briggs's estate in 1956. Not only did Fetzer develop the Tigers into one of the most prized franchises in professional sports, his patience, wisdom and integrity lifted him into the position of serving as baseball's unofficial conscience.

"He doesn't say much and, by design, he stands in the background," observed longtime Chicago sports writer Jerome Holtzman during Fetzer's tenure. "But there's no question that John Fetzer is the most powerful force in baseball."

Fetzer was literally the power behind baseball's throne. When he spoke, all his fellow owners, the commissioner and presidents of both leagues listened.

"Mr. Fetzer was a man of vision," explained longtime Tiger general manager Jim Campbell. "He sincerely cared about the long-term well being of the game. He realized that for the game to thrive, all clubs had to do well. He always made decisions based upon what they meant to the game as a whole even when—for the moment—they may not have been in Detroit's best interests. He knew that in the long run, what was good for the game was good for all teams."

Fetzer's ubiquitous influence was felt by everyone in the game.

"There are two kinds of owners," former commissioner Bowie Kuhn observed. "One always wants to know 'How does it affect my club?' Then there are those who think first of how it affects the game. Emphatically, John belonged at the top of the latter group. He was always looking out for the best interests of baseball. He was a man of considerable wealth, a religious man with a fine ethical sense who always sought the good course. John didn't struggle with himself."

Fetzer was concerned with keeping baseball a game for the working man. At owners' meetings he spoke vigorously about the inherent spirit of baseball as part of the American work ethic.

"He loved the game dearly and was concerned about its future," former longtime baseball executive and American League president Lee MacPhail explained. "Even when he tried to remove himself from certain committees, we always convinced him that he had to stay. The owners recognized he was always looking out for the good of the game and not just the selfish interests of the Tigers."

Kell was awed by Fetzer's insight.

"He was such an intelligent man," Kell recalled.

"At times when I was talking with him, I almost felt afraid. Not because of the way he acted, but because he was so intelligent he almost seemed to know what you were thinking.

"There is no question that for the greater part of Mr. Fetzer's ownership he was the power behind the throne. It didn't matter if he was on a particular committee or not. If there was a major decision to be made and baseball was concerned about it, all the owners would call him to find out firsthand what he thought about the matter. Whichever way he viewed an issue usually sealed the deal."

Years ago, even Bill Veeck, the colorful maverick owner who lost out to Fetzer in his bid to buy the Tigers in 1956, acknowledged Fetzer's power.

"[Yankees owner] George Steinbrenner would like to be the new [Walter] O'Malley," Veeck said. "But I don't think he can do it. The strong man in the American League is John Fetzer. He's very intelligent, very balanced, very thoughtful. And he's as wealthy as any. He's a man of substance. He could influence me more than all the rest because he makes sense."

Fetzer's entry into baseball was not motivated by money. And he certainly didn't need the game to validate his already successful career.

"If I had gone into baseball to make a profit off the team, it would have been one of the most ill-advised business decisions of my career," Fetzer said.

Fetzer simply had a lifelong love affair with the game of baseball. And his particular passion was the Tigers, a team he had followed since his boyhood in Decatur, Indiana.

Fetzer was persuaded to get involved with the Tigers by fellow broadcast owner Fred Knorr, who was putting together a syndicate to purchase the team from the Briggs Family Trust. After Walter O. Briggs died in 1952, the Tigers were put into a trust from which Walter Jr. (Spike Briggs) was expected to buy them. Lawyers for the trust, however, did not deem the club to be a sound financial investment and ordered the team to be sold.

Eight groups of investors, including such sports luminaries as Bill Veeck, Charles O. Finley, George Halas and Jack Kent Cooke, bid for the storied franchise. In a move devised by Fetzer, his group bumped its bid by a half-million dollars to snatch the club from Veeck at the last minute. At the time, the bid of $5.5 million constituted the most ever paid for a baseball franchise. The 11-man syndicate took possession of the team on October 1, 1956.

With 11 owners tripping over each other trying to run the team, operation of the Tigers was disastrous. The team's chaos in the front office was reflected by its mediocre play on the field.

"There were so many owners it looked like most just wanted to be around a major-league team," Campbell reflected. "They wanted to make decisions about things they really knew nothing about. One man—Mr. Fetzer—seemed to stand above the rest, even though he did more observing than speaking."

Fetzer was busy analyzing the situation. He came to the conclusion that the only chance for success would be a one-man rule. He carefully proceeded to buy out each of his partners and on November 14, 1961, he became sole owner. He remained so until October 10, 1983 when he sold the club to Tom Monaghan.

"We had become the laughing stock of the city, the league, and the game," Fetzer recalled. "Baseball had become so complicated that it was extremely difficult to administer the affairs by group ownership. I had learned that a team should be run by one individual who had the authority to make decisions and carry them out. It cost me a lot of money and a lot of blood to finally figure that out."

After he did, Fetzer made some significant changes. First he renamed the park "Tiger Stadium" to reflect the fans' "ownership" of the team. Even more importantly, he promoted Campbell to general manager. Campbell served the Tigers his entire professional career. He didn't leave until August, 1992 when Mike and Marian Ilitch purchased the club from Monaghan and had Campbell dismissed.

Fetzer and Campbell shared the same honesty, integrity and passion for the Tigers and the community. Fetzer trusted Campbell to run the day-to-day operations as if the team were his own.

It can be argued that without Campbell, Fetzer would not have enjoyed the success he did in the game. And Campbell, without Fetzer, never would have had the opportunity to grow into the historical baseball figure he did.

Campbell briefed Fetzer daily about every aspect of the team. Based upon Campbell's advice, Fetzer made all major decisions.

"Throughout my whole career, I have never seen a better match than Mr. Fetzer and Jim Campbell,"

Tigers owner John Fetzer (right) and general manager Jim Campbell sit in the Tigers' dugout. **Collection of Jim Hawkins Productions Inc.**

tom of the locality," through 1962, African-American players were given the choice of lodging in the Tigertown barracks or being placed in the home of a local black family. White major-league players were housed at a local hotel.

Fetzer was dismayed at this injustice and ordered Campbell to rectify the situation. Regardless of race, Fetzer insisted that all players be treated equally.

Realizing that Fetzer would entertain the idea of moving his team's spring training to Arizona, the civic leaders of Lakeland agreed to allow the Tigers to enter into an agreement with the local Holiday Inn. Beginning with spring training, 1963, all major-league players lived in non-segregated housing at the hotel.

Fetzer also demonstrated his loyalty to the City of Detroit when he refused to move the franchise out of Detroit when suburban Pontiac courted the Tigers before plucking the Lions from the city.

"After we won the world championship in 1968, I made a promise to myself never to move the team from Detroit," Fetzer revealed. "After the civil riots during the previous season, I realized how much that franchise means to the city."

That championship was the culmination of a dream for Fetzer, the Tigers, and the entire community. Fetzer believed in building a championship team the old-fashioned way—from within. The 1968 champions were a classic example.

"How you win must become equally important to winning at any price," Fetzer reasoned. "Greed, ego-mandering, undercutting, and selfish self-centering for the sake of aggrandizement are far too prevalent. Too often these characteristics prevail over the public interest.

"We created teamwork in the front office, teamwork in the farm system and teamwork on the playing field of Tiger Stadium. Unless teamwork starts at the top, it never will show itself on the field. What we saw

MacPhail said. "Both were men of unimpeachable integrity. Both were concerned with the good of the Tigers and the long-term good of the game. They were part of history. Together, they wrote history. I'm not sure we'll witness that type of mutual loyalty in the game ever again."

In 1965, Fetzer provided baseball with the most significant fiscal package in the game's history. Almost single-handedly, he carved a network TV contract that virtually assured all franchises of financial stability.

"There's no question that John's original television contract was the forerunner of today's package," Bowie Kuhn affirmed.

And without the ubiquitous tube, where would baseball be today?

Although often overlooked, Fetzer made an equally historical decision for the Tigers that, at the time, called for considerable courage.

Except for three years during World War II (1943-45), the Tigers have conducted their spring training in Lakeland, Florida since 1934. In keeping with the "cusin 1968 was a result of seven years of toil and sweat."

Throughout Fetzer's guardianship of the team, the Tigers remained competitive. When it was time to sell, Fetzer was able to turn over a debt-free team to his handpicked successor.

Fetzer realized the time to sell was drawing near when he tired of the endless player labor-relations problems and the pervading commercialism that threatened to swallow the game's purity.

"He clearly saw the handwriting on the wall," Bowie Kuhn observed. "He saw the changes that were coming and he wanted no part of them.

"John Fetzer was a living symbol of everything baseball represented. There's no question he could never have tolerated the path which baseball ultimately chose."

On October 10, 1983, Fetzer sold the club to Monaghan for $53 million. Announcement of the sale stunned the sporting world. A condition set by Fetzer demanded that all negotiations were to be kept secret. Fetzer remained with the Tigers as chairman of the board for several seasons after the sale. The team Monaghan purchased was primed for the world championship that it delivered in his first year of ownership.

The era of John Fetzer is now history. He died on February 20, 1991. His passing ended an epoch that will never be repeated.

Fortunately for Tiger fans, that beautifully unfettered Fetzer era belonged to Detroit.

Mark Cunningham, Creative Impressions Inc.

Tom Monaghan
1983-1992

Tom Monaghan paid $53 for his ticket into major-league baseball.

Little did the now former pizza chain magnate realize, however, that after purchasing the Tigers on October 10, 1983, he was in for a first-year ride like no rookie owner could imagine.

The following spring the Tigers shocked the community, themselves and the entire world of baseball by setting a major-league record for the best 40-game start in history.

The Tigers jumped to a 35-5 start, which had Tiger fans everywhere thinking about the World Series even before Memorial Day. The unthinkable streak included a no-hitter by Jack Morris at Chicago.

Masterfully led by manager Sparky Anderson, the Tigers set a club record of 104 victories. They also established the home attendance mark of 2,704,794. The

Kirk Gibson's 545-foot home run over the right-field roof of Tiger Stadium on June 14, 1983 cemented his place in Tigers history as one of their most exciting players. Brace Photo

Tigers swept the Kansas City Royals to claim the American League pennant and needed just five games to dispose of the San Diego Padres in the World Series. With two home runs in Game 4, Alan Trammell was named the Series' Most Valuable Player. With two home runs in Game 5, Kirk Gibson claimed the unofficial award as most electrifying player.

Who could blame Monaghan for thinking life in baseball was a whole lot more fun than an oven full of pizzas oozing with cheese, pepperoni and mushrooms?

But like the perfect pizza, even the good times eventually get gobbled up.

Monaghan became a self-made multimillionaire by turning Domino's from a one-store operation in

Ypsilanti, Michigan into the nation's second largest pizza chain. Tiger owner John E. Fetzer was impressed by Monaghan's makeup and sense of morality. He hand-picked the entrepreneur with the Midas touch to succeed him as owner of the Tigers.

Monaghan purchased a young team that was on the brink of maturing into greatness. The shortstop/second base combination of Alan Trammell and Lou Whitaker set a major-league record for longevity. Lance Parrish developed into an offensive and defensive force as the most feared catcher in either league. Kirk Gibson emerged as one of the most electrifying players to hit the American League in many years. Jack Morris was the winningest starting pitcher of his time. The list of young stars to graduate from the Tiger minor-league system went on and on.

And when they needed that one player to push them to the top of the hill, Monaghan approved Detroit's first major free agent purchase with the signing of Darrell Evans.

Although they won just one World Series and the 1987 East Division title during the decade of the '80s, no other team had more success.

In 1990, inching closer to retirement, Jim Campbell relinquished his position as president to become the chairman of the board. He was replaced by legendary University of Michigan football coach Bo Schembechler.

Although some questioned Schembechler's knowledge of baseball, he wasted no time proving again how forceful and gifted a leader he was. Almost immediately, Schembechler made improvements throughout the farm system to bolster the organization. He added coaches and training facilities at each minor-league affiliate. He built a state-of-the-art training facility along with an oversized indoor batting range at the spring training complex. He added scouts and upgraded the medical and training program throughout the system. Schembechler had initiated immediate bold action to prove he was on track to become Detroit's next great president.

Shortly after those improvements, however, the good life began to sputter for Monaghan. The meltdown affected everyone within the organization. The Tigers were pinched by player losses to free agency. First it was Lance Parrish. Then it was Kirk Gibson. Finally Jack Morris walked away. The Tigers tried to patch the cracks, but eventually paid a price for so many front-line losses.

Worse for Monaghan was the avalanche of financial losses that struck Domino's. With the ball club teetering on perhaps the worst financial footing in its history, Monaghan was forced to put the franchise up for sale in 1992. Even the closest observers never guessed he would eventually sell his prized possession to Mike and Marian Ilitch, owners of one of his fiercest rivals in the highly competitive pizza industry.

The ride was not extraordinarily long. In good times and bad, though, it was a wild one for Monaghan. And the teams that played under him created plenty of good memories for Tiger fans everywhere.

Mike Ilitch
1992-Present

The era of "corporate ball" arrived in Detroit on August 26, 1992 when Mike and Marian Ilitch announced they had purchased the Tigers.

There had been an increase of marketing maneuverings in the latter years of Tom Monaghan's ownership. But under the Ilitches, the team became immersed in the methods of the modern game.

The industry had moved from encouraging fans to spend a night in the bleachers toward enticing large and small corporations to spend an evening in a luxury suite.

The Ilitch regime reflects baseball's changing philosophy regarding the traditional portrait of a franchise owner. For instance, baseball's unwritten rule restricting an owner from owning a team in another professional sport no longer applies. The Ilitches, of course, are the longtime owners of the highly successful Detroit Red Wings in the National Hockey League. Owners used to be strictly prohibited from holding any semblance of gambling interests. A few years after purchasing the Tigers, the Ilitch family invested in a Detroit casino.

Ilitch actually wanted to purchase the team before John Fetzer hand-picked Tom Monaghan to be his successor. Ilitch once had dreams of playing shortstop for the Tigers until a knee injury—and perhaps the emergence of a rising Harvey Kuenn—forced him out of Class B ball. When the opportunity to buy the club arose again, Ilitch was relentless in his pursuit.

Ilitch's chief competition to purchase the club came from Edsel Ford II, an heir to the Ford family fortune. When Ilitch bid $83 million, the competition was over.

Monaghan was the sole owner of Domino's Pizza, the nation's second largest pizza chain. Ilitch still owns Little Caesars, which at the time was ranked third. The sale of the Tigers from one pizza competitor to another stunned the entire community.

Ilitch inserted several executives from his pizza empire and other holdings into the Tiger front office. They brought an array of marketing gimmicks, but the team on the field struggled.

In August 1994, Ilitch and the rest of the owners were faced with an even stickier problem when the

A groundskeeper hoists home plate high above his head as they prepare it to be ceremoniously moved to the new stadium, Comerica Park. Tom Pearson

major-league players went on strike, leading to the cancellation of the playoffs and World Series.

Baseball initiated a replacement player plan for the following spring training. After Sparky Anderson left camp refusing to manage replacements, speculation immediately arose that he would not be rehired when his contract expired at the end of the season. The day after the season ended, Sparky announced he was leaving Detroit and thus prevented a potentially ugly situation. Since his departure, the Tigers have had five managers. Under Ilitch, the Tigers have also had four general managers.

One goal that Ilitch achieved, where two previous owners had been unsuccessful, was the building of a new ballpark. Prior to the 1995 season, Ilitch hired John McHale, Jr. as president. McHale was charged with brokering a deal that eventually led to the construction of Comerica Park. It was agreed in the deal that Ilitch would invest approximately $175 million

with approximately $145 million of public financing coming from such institutions as Wayne County, the State of Michigan and the Detroit Downtown Development Strategic Fund.

Ground breaking for the stadium, which sits across the street from Ilitch's Fox Theater, took place on October 29, 1997. On April 11, 2000 before a packed house, the Tigers played their first game at their new home and defeated the Seattle Mariners, 5-2.

The park reflects baseball's modern penchant for entertainment. In addition to numerous luxury suites, the park features a merry-go-round and Ferris wheel.

Prior to the 2002 season, Ilitch signed Dave Dombrowski to a five-year contract as president and chief executive officer. Six games into the season, Dombrowski fired Randy Smith and assumed his duties of general manager.

Ilitch has stated that Dombrowski will provide the stability to lead the Tigers back into playoff contention.

10

BEHIND THE MIKE

Detroit Tiger broadcasting history dates back to 1927 when Ty Cobb was still dashing madly around the bases in Detroit and Babe Ruth was leading the Yankees' "Murderer's Row" in New York.

And since Ty Tyson made that first Tiger broadcast three-quarters of a century ago, Detroit has been treated to some of the most knowledgeable and entertaining men behind the mike anywhere in baseball. Ernie Harwell. George Kell. Al Kaline. Harry Heilmann. Those are just a handful of colorful names that have turned Tiger broadcasts into lifelong memories for generation after generation.

With a full menu of nightly telecasts and radio coverage throughout the season, baseball has become as much a studio sport as one to be enjoyed at the ballpark. More than any other sport, baseball offers broadcasters the opportunity to become vital parts of the total package.

If the broadcasters are good, the game is that much better. Tiger fans have been spoiled by the best.

Ernie Harwell set the standard for radio excellence. And he did it for more than half a century, the last 42 for the Tigers. Grandchildren came to enjoy his familiar voice and coined phrases the same way their grandparents did when they were young.

George Kell and Al Kaline set a standard for television teams that may never be equaled. Both were Hall of Fame players and then settled into a side-by-side TV combination that provided as much entertainment to the viewers as the games themselves.

Kell and Kaline were not the first "jocks in the box" tandem. But they sure lifted the concept to another level, as evidenced by the consistently high ratings that they enjoyed throughout their broadcast careers. No other broadcast team brought more star power and baseball expertise to the booth than Kell and Kaline. No other pair enjoyed more loyalty from the fans.

No one knows for certain when the "jock in the box" trend first began in sports broadcasting. Since its inception, however, there has been no end to the former players working behind a microphone.

In their 75 years of broadcasting history, the Tigers have featured four former players who also are members of baseball's Hall of Fame. The first was Harry Heilmann, who made his broadcast debut in 1934. He was followed by Mel Ott and then, of course, George Kell and Al Kaline. Ernie Harwell was the recipient of the Hall of Fame's Ford Frick Award.

The Tigers refined the concept of the "jock in the box" with an impressive lineup of former players turned broadcasters. Besides Heilmann, Ott, Kell and Kaline, that lineup included Dizzy Trout, Lary Sorensen, Jim Price, Hank Aguirre, Norm Cash, Bill Freehan, Jim Northrup, and Kirk Gibson. For one season, former Tiger manager Bob Scheffing shared his expertise.

All brought their particular strengths and peculiarities to the booth. Each has shaped memories for millions of Tiger fans.

For the more than three-quarters of a century of Tiger broadcast history, 34 announcers have shared the radio and TV microphones. A few were around for only a couple of years. Only Ernie Harwell did it for 42.

Ernie Harwell smiles from the booth after the final broadcast of his career in Toronto on September 29, 2002.
Frank Gunn, AP/Wide World Photos.

Ernie Harwell

When Rocky Colavito came to Detroit from Cleveland in the stunning trade for Harvey Kuenn just prior to the start of the 1960 season, Ernie Harwell was a rookie in the Tiger broadcast booth.

It's strange to hear Harwell referred to as a rookie anything. And was that really 43 years ago?

Harwell came from Baltimore, where he had been doing Orioles' games, to serve as George Kell's partner. The two split time between radio and a limited number of televised games.

At that time, not even Harwell could have imagined that his Tiger career would last through the 2002 season, three years after the team had moved into a new ballpark.

"It's happening, because it's time," Harwell said, explaining his decision to retire. "No other reason, it's just time."

Harwell's retirement concluded 55 years of calling major-league games, including 42 for the Tigers. His career spanned seven decades, which gave him a distinct perspective for interpreting the game's evolution all the way back to World War II.

In a sport that places so much emphasis on statistics, it's impossible to imagine any significant number or award that Harwell hasn't achieved.

Arguably, the two most distinguished awards bestowed upon the Georgia native were the 1981 Ford C. Frick Award, presented by the National Baseball Hall of Fame for excellence in broadcasting, and his 1998 induction into the Radio Hall of Fame.

Perhaps the most amazing statistic established by the soft-spoken former U.S. Marine is the number of major-league games he called from behind the mic.

"I saw a list that said I've done about 8,400," Harwell mentioned at his retirement announcement

Hall of Fame broadcaster Ernie Harwell, right, gives a high-five to co-host Jim Price after the last out was called in the game with the New York Yankees in Detroit, Sunday, Sept. 22, 2002. Retiring after 55 years of broadcasting, 42 with the Tigers, this was Harwell's last game in Detroit. Carlos Osorio, AP/Wide World Photos

in spring training 2002. "But I think they missed a few. It's pretty hard to figure."

What isn't hard to figure is that Harwell enjoyed a stranglehold on listener loyalty as strong as any broadcaster in the history of the profession. When Harwell's contract was not renewed for the 1992 season, the Tigers experienced a fan and media backlash that carried the fury of a hurricane waiting to be given an official name.

Some fans vowed not to attend any more Tiger games or threatened to boycott Domino's Pizza, property of then Tiger owner Tom Monaghan.

Radio and television commentators and writers from newspapers and magazines around the state mercilessly ambushed the Tigers, even though their attack was misdirected.

Radio station WJR actually initiated the action to remove Harwell from its broadcasts and the booth. It is believed that the station was looking to increase broadcast ratings through a younger audience and sought a younger broadcast team. Marketing executives from the station and the Tigers devised a plan that would have fired Harwell immediately.

Tiger President Bo Schembechler, who was unjustly vilified in the media barrage, actually stepped up to the plate for Harwell and insisted the broadcaster remain for another year with a significant increase in pay. In addition, Harwell was offered a pregame show for future years.

For unknown reasons, the majority of the media refused to accept the facts of the incident and Schembechler was made the scapegoat of the volatile affair.

Soon after Mike and Marian Ilitch purchased the Tigers in August, 1992, they rehired Harwell.

Harwell is credited with coining such phrases as "Loooong gone" when describing a home run and "He stood there like a house at the side of the road" for a called third strike. Yet his style was simple, direct and laid back. It complemented the blue-collar and baseball-wise Tiger audience.

When asked what advice he would give to aspiring young broadcasters, Harwell answered simply: "Be yourself. Decide what kind of broadcaster you want to be. Don't try to create gimmicks. Just be yourself. You're on the air for three hours. The audience will learn if you're being an actor or yourself."

Throughout his career, Harwell certainly practiced what he preached.

When Harwell left after the 2002 season, the Tigers unveiled a stature of his likeness to stand in front of Comerica Park. In addition, they named the press box the Ernie Harwell Media Center.

Before joining the Tigers, Harwell did play-by-play for the Brooklyn Dodgers beginning in 1948. He was behind the mic for Bobby Thomson's historic playoff home run in 1951. He later worked for the New York Giants and Baltimore Orioles before coming to Detroit. He has done network games for CBS and

NBC, including playoff, World Series and All-Star Games.

For everyone in Michigan, though, Ernie will forever be a Tiger.

George Kell

"Hello everybody—I'm George Kell."

The opening words to a Tiger telecast by George Kell were magic to fans for decades.

The former third baseman first captivated Tiger fans with his hard-nosed play on his way to the Hall of Fame. Then during his nearly four decades as a Tiger broadcaster, he stole everybody's heart.

Kell was the grandfather every mother and father wanted for their kids. He was kind, patient, wise, and humble. And he may have been the finest broadcaster who was a former player that the game has ever seen.

"I treated that broadcast booth with the same respect I treated the field when I was a player," Kell ex-

Ernie Harwell (left) and George Kell shared the Tigers' broadcast booth from 1960-63. Ted Patterson

plained. "I had to work hard as a player to develop the gifts that God gave me. I took the same attitude to the booth. I promised myself to make every sacrifice and do whatever it took to become a respected baseball broadcaster.

"I wanted people to accept me as a professional announcer. I didn't want them to think I got the job just because I used to play third base for the Tigers or because I happen to be in the Hall of Fame. I wanted people to know I was proud to be the voice of the Detroit Tigers."

Born and raised in Swifton, Arkansas, where he still makes his home, Kell ingratiated himself with the fans with his gentle southern drawl and calm insight. There was no secret to Kell's success. He was simple. He was straightforward. Above all else, he was refreshingly honest.

"I'm not a flashy guy," Kell explained. "I never tried to get too fancy with words or descriptions. If a player made a good play, I called it a good play. If it was a bad play, I called it a bad play. If a broadcaster tries to cover up what every viewer has seen with his own eyes, then that announcer's credibility is zero. If a ball club wants their man to do something like that, then they don't want a broadcaster. They want a cheerleader.

"I had, and always will have, an undying love affair for the Tigers. But I was very careful not to give any appearance of being a cheerleader. When an announcer is a homer, he insults the intelligence of every viewer and listener of the game. Baseball fans, especially Tiger fans, know the game. You can't fool them. They can see right through that little trick."

Generation after generation came to appreciate Kell's soothing style and the honesty within it. Kell credits former Tiger owner John E. Fetzer with providing him the best advice he ever received before taking his first step into the booth.

"Just be yourself," Fetzer told him. "Don't try to be something you are not, because it will never work. The fans will see through that immediately. I hired you because you are George Kell and you have a gift for calling a game. Now just go out and be George Kell."

Although Kell has retired to his hometown of Swifton, he still considers Detroit "more than a second home."

In return, generations of Tiger fans can still feel the warmth he so generously gave.

Al Kaline

Al Kaline's pursuit of perfection during his 22-year playing career with the Tigers was reflected by the determination he brought to the broadcast booth. Never known for his speaking skills while he wore the uniform, Kaline was relentless in driving himself to become perhaps the most insightful color analyst the Tigers have ever employed.

It was Kaline's diligence in the booth that finally persuaded George Kell to alter an opinion about his broadcast partner.

"When I first knew Kaline as a player, there had been some talk about him possibly becoming a manager when his career was finished," Kell said. "To be honest, I never thought of him as a managerial type. Even after my first year in the booth with him, I wasn't convinced he would have made a good manager. My opinion changed, though. After spending more time with Al, I'm convinced he could have managed the Tigers and would have done a terrific job. Al Kaline knows baseball like no one else knows the game."

Admittedly, Kaline struggled the first couple of years after making his TV broadcasting debut in 1976. He knew the game. But he had to get a grasp on his new profession. So he practiced. He prepared meticulously for each broadcast. He learned from his mistakes. And then he worked some more.

"That's the only way Al tackles anything," Kell explained. "He's a worker. He wants to be the best."

Almost from the first day, even while Kaline was learning from the rookie mistakes of his new profession, Tiger fans sensed they were in for something special. A team like Kell and Kaline only comes around once in a lifetime.

The two learned to play off one another with the same grace Alan Trammell and Lou Whitaker displayed turning a double play.

Doing the play-by-play, Kell sensed precisely when it was time for Kaline to lend viewers his expertise on some subtle matter that might have significant importance in the game.

"Al would have made a good manager, but I'm glad he chose the broadcast booth, because it was an honor to work with him for all those years," Kell concluded.

Kaline admits that the switch from player to broadcaster was not easy.

"Sometimes people think that just because you were a big-league player it's easy to go up into the booth and broadcast a game," Kaline said. "Let me tell you, it doesn't work that way. It takes a lot of work and a lot of adjustment."

Kell was instrumental in helping Kaline make the adjustment.

"I can never thank George enough for all that he did for me when I broke in," Kaline said. "He's so generous and he was so natural behind the mic."

The chemistry between the two Hall of Famers was magical. The duo became as much a part of the Tiger entertainment package as the game itself.

Kell and Kaline worked together through the 1996 season, after which Kell retired. Kaline remained in the booth until midway through the 2001 season, when he stepped down to accept an executive position with the Tigers. He currently serves as special assistant to president Dave Dombrowski.

Since signing with the Tigers in June, 1953 when he was 18 years old, Kaline has served the club in some capacity for 51 consecutive years.

Harry Heilmann

Harry Heilmann crafted a magnificent major-league career that led him into the Hall of Fame in 1952. He was called one of the game's all-time great right-handed hitters by none other than Ted Williams, who may have been baseball's greatest hitter ever.

Heilmann also holds the distinction of becoming Detroit's first "jock in the box" when he joined Ty Tyson in the broadcast booth almost 70 years ago.

With a "down home" knack for spinning stories from his playing days, Heilmann was the perfect foil for Tyson's polished style. The two worked together harmoniously for nine years and Heilmann stayed on for another eight until arthritis forced him into retirement after the 1950 season.

Tyson's style was to choose his words carefully, often leaving gaps of dead air time between pitches. Heilmann spewed a litany of sentences, half-sentences and who knows what kind of phrases, as if he were getting paid for the number of words spoken.

But the fans loved his laid-back style and colorful anecdotes.

"His friendly, chatty style and infectious laugh earned him the admiration and respect of fans, sportscasters and players alike," remarked one critic.

Although his style was laid back, his approach to the job was serious, as witnessed by the elocution lessons he took to improve his grasp of an industry still in its infancy.

Tyson's admiration for his former partner was evidenced in 1951 when he returned for one season after Heilmann had to retire. Tyson bridged a gap until the Tigers could find a permanent replacement.

Heilmann died on July 9, 1951 in Southfield, Michigan. He was mourned, both by the fans he thrilled with his play on the field and those who came to love him as a "good ol' boy" talking about baseball.

Mel Ott

Mel Ott was the second member of the Hall of Fame to make it to the Tiger broadcasting booth. Unfortunately, his three-year Tiger stint was far too short. At the age of 49, Ott was killed in a head-on auto collision with a drunk driver on November 21, 1958.

Ott served as the color analyst for Van Patrick. With his Louisiana accent and a sincere, yet subtle approach to the game, Ott endeared himself to the fans with his warm-hearted insight.

He played his entire career with the New York Giants from 1926 to 1947. He became the first National Leaguer to slug 500 home runs and finished with 511.

Tiger fans never got a chance to see his power. But they certainly enjoyed the class and dignity he brought to the broadcast booth.

Ty Tyson

There were no standards by which to measure Ty Tyson when he assumed the radio broadcasting job for the Tigers in 1927.

Tyson was the standard bearer.

The "Roaring Twenties" were a magnificent time for all of professional sports. And radio began to share in that glory all across the country.

Imagine the overwhelming sense of freedom Tyson must have felt knowing that whatever he did with the Tiger broadcasts, it was being done for the first time.

Tyson certainly made the most of the unusual opportunity. By the time he retired about a quarter of a century later, he had become one of the state's most

Pioneer Ty Tyson broadcast the first baseball game in Detroit over the WWJ airwaves on April 19, 1927. This photo was taken in 1953 before his retirement. Ted Patterson

with his sense of drama to allow his listeners to appreciate the simple brilliance of baseball.

Tyson had a dry sense of humor and simply reported the action as it occurred. He was not considered to be a "homer," which would have run contrary to his deliberate professional style.

"He couldn't sound partial [to the Tigers]," Barber cracked. "He didn't use enough words between pitches and plays to give you an idea how he felt."

The fans loved Tyson. And Tyson loved the new position he had created.

In 1934, when the Tigers played in the World Series, commissioner Kenesaw M. Landis was going to prohibit Tyson from broadcasting the games so as to avoid any hint of partiality. Tiger fans were outraged and deluged the commissioner's office with 600,000 letters of protest. Landis relented and Tyson called the games on WWJ. To avoid confrontation in the 1935 World Series, which Detroit won, NBC added Tyson to its staff.

Tyson didn't travel with the team for road games during the regular season. He reconstructed them from telegraph messages that were received in the studio of WWJ. Coupling his natural acting talent and the experience he had gained from doing home games, he had the ability to make listeners believe he was sitting right behind home plate.

celebrated personalities for having served as the "voice of the Tigers."

Tyson earned his legendary status by developing a simple, no-frills style that allowed his listeners to become immersed in the game without having to dodge a string of wasted verbiage.

Tyson was a master with words and therefore felt they were precious. He chose them meticulously and used them with sparing care. Often there were several seconds of dead air between pitches. Those holes prompted New York broadcaster Red Barber to suggest that Tyson's "shortage of words at times bordered on being rude."

Tyson, however, became a master at recounting a game. He had been trained in acting while a student at Penn State University. He coupled his feel for the game

Tyson retired after the 1942 season, having missed only one game throughout his career. He returned to broadcast the Tigers' first televised game in 1947 and continued to do TV through 1952. He also returned to the radio booth for one season in 1951 after his longtime friend and partner, Harry Heilmann, had to retire for medical reasons.

Only one man gets the opportunity to be a true pioneer in any field. Tyson got that chance. And he certainly made the most of it.

Ty Tyson is shown in the Tigers' booth during his early broadcasting career. Ted Patterson

Patrick served as the radio "voice of the Tigers" from 1952 through 1959. His tenure would have lasted considerably longer had there not been a major sponsorship change. Stroh's Beer purchased the rights to Tiger broadcasts, ending a long run by Goebel Brewery. Because Patrick had been used in various promotional activities for Goebel, the new sponsor felt the association was too close and gave Patrick his release.

Patrick was a transplanted Texan, who was accused by many of having an ego the size of his home state. But he was a true professional and good enough to develop a strong national reputation, as well as the one he enjoyed locally.

Along with his demanding Tiger duties, Patrick also broadcast the Detroit Lions on radio and TV from 1950 through 1973. In addition, he served as sports director for the Mutual Broadcasting System and covered Notre Dame football, as well as a variety of major weekend events in golf, auto racing and basketball.

Patrick was a stickler for professionalism and often feuded with partner Dizzy Trout for his partisan remarks about the Tigers.

Patrick worked tirelessly and invested wisely. At the time of his death in 1974 he owned four radio stations.

Paul Carey

Paul Carey was described as having the "voice of God." The tone was rich and resonant. There was no mistaking Carey whenever he spoke.

Carey, who was nicknamed "four-five-and-six" for working the middle three innings of every Tiger radio broadcast from 1973-91, was the longest-running partner of legendary Ernie Harwell.

Carey was the consummate professional who won numerous broadcasting awards during his distinctive career that began in 1949. A graduate of Central Michigan University, Carey was experienced in a variety of sports before finishing his career in baseball. He handled Detroit Pistons broadcasts and also was known for his Friday night high school football roundup on station WJR.

Van Patrick

Van Patrick earned the nickname of the "Ol' Announcer" for the incredible number of events on his sports broadcasting menu.

Kirk Gibson

Kirk Gibson and Van Patrick may not have lasted together for one entire game.

While Gibson was as outspoken as an announcer as he was during his playing career, his allegiance to the team that remains so close to his heart was as clear as a cloudless sky in August.

Nevertheless, he attacked his job as color man on the Fox telecasts with the same intensity he attacked the game on the field.

Gibson was a fierce competitor throughout his 17-year big league career. He was the spark plug of the 1984 world champion Tigers and played the same role for Los Angeles when the Dodgers won the World Series in 1988. In his first National League season, Gibson won the Most Valuable Player Award.

Gibson completed five years on the Tiger telecasts and also served as a cohost on a daily radio sports talk show. As his playing career developed from his rookie season in 1979, so too did his broadcasting career, because of the intensity he brings to any task he tackles.

In 2003, Gibson left the broadcast booth to become the Tigers' bench coach.

Paul "Dizzy" Trout

Paul "Dizzy" Trout was a pitcher from Harvey, Illinois, who spun stories like the "good ol' boys" swigging a beer on the back porch. He did it during his 14-year Tiger career in which he won 161 games, and he continued when he moved to the broadcast booth in 1953.

Broadcaster Jim Price shares a laugh with partner Ernie Harwell just after Harwell announced his retirement.
Duane Burleson, AP/Wide World Photos

Some of the stories may have been true. Some may have been apocryphal. All were entertaining and were delivered with enough down-home malapropisms to make Dizzy Dean blush.

Frank Beckmann

Frank Beckmann is a classic case of the hometown boy doing well. And he did it the old-fashioned way—as a truly professional broadcaster.

Beckmann is a journalist whose direct, unbiased reporting carefully depicts each unfolding event with the precision of a camera. He is knowledgeable, prepared and brimming with enthusiasm for each game.

Frank served as the Tigers' radio play-by-play announcer from 1995 through 1998. Since 1999, he has served the same role for UPN-50 telecasts.

Beckmann is a 30-year veteran in Detroit broadcasting. He began his career in 1972, as the youngest news reporter ever hired by station WJR. As a news reporter he won a National Headliner Award for his coverage of the Jimmy Hoffa disappearance. He is a three-time winner of the Michigan Sportscaster of the Year Award.

Beckmann's versatility is limitless. He has served on broadcasts for the Lions, Pistons and Red Wings. He recently completed his 22nd season as the play-by-play broadcaster for University of Michigan football.

Jim Price

Jim Price was a backup catcher on the 1968 Tiger world championship team. But he has moved to the first team in his broadcasting career.

Price has served as the color commentator on Tiger radio broadcasts since 1998. Prior to his current assignment, he worked for several years on cable telecasts.

Ray Lane

Although he never made it to the big leagues as a player, Ray Lane brought plenty of baseball experience to the Tiger broadcasting booth.

The Detroit native played in the Chicago White Sox farm system after playing for Michigan State University.

Lane served as George Kell's TV partner from 1965-66. He then was Ernie Harwell's radio sidekick from 1967 through 1972. He later broadcast Cincinnati Reds games and still fills in occasionally on Tiger telecasts.

Larry Osterman

Before Al Kaline joined George Kell in the television booth, there was Larry Osterman. Osterman served as Kell's partner from 1967-77.

The partnership was a classic case of role reversal, with Kell, the former player, serving as the play-by-play man and Osterman, the trained professional broadcaster, serving as the color analyst. But the team clicked and was well received by TV viewers.

Osterman later broadcast Minnesota Twins games for five years before returning to Detroit as a radio sports commentator and also as the play-by-play man for Tiger cable telecasts.

The graduate of the University of Nebraska worked as the sports director for Tiger owner John E. Fetzer's Kalamazoo TV station for several years.

Dan Dickerson

Dan Dickerson worked his way through a variety of assignments at Detroit and Grand Rapids radio stations before joining Ernie Harwell and Jim Price on the Tiger broadcast team in 1998.

Dickerson has handled a variety of sports assignments, including those with the Detroit Lions and University of Michigan football. He is the winner of several Associated Press broadcasting awards.

In 2003, after Harwell's retirement, he became the Tigers' lead radio announcer.

Rick Rizzs

Rick Rizzs accepted the biggest challenge of his professional career when he replaced Ernie Harwell as the Tigers' radio play-by-play broadcaster in 1992.

Some members of the local media and many fans unfairly criticized his enthusiastic style. Quietly, he and partner Bob Rathbun withstood all the barbs to deliver a thoroughly professional package.

Prior to joining the Tigers, Rizzs spent nine seasons broadcasting Seattle Mariner games on radio and TV. After being released from the Tigers following the 1994 season, he returned to Seattle, where he is again handling Mariners' games.

Bob Rathbun

Along with his partner Rick Rizzs, Bob Rathbun encountered an uneasy welcome when he was brought in to replace Paul Carey for the 1992 season.

With 14 years of experience under his belt before he arrived in Detroit, however, Rathbun demonstrated poise under pressure to deliver a first-rate job.

Before coming to Detroit, Rathbun served as the play-by-play broadcaster for Atlanta's Triple-A team for several years. He now does some Braves games on cable TV and also does college football and basketball games broadcasts in the southeast.

Bob Scheffing

Bob Scheffing holds the distinction of being the only former Tiger manager to land a full-time position in the broadcast booth.

Scheffing managed the Tigers in 1961-62 and part of 1963 until he was fired and replaced by Charlie Dressen. Under Scheffing, the Tigers made an unexpected pennant run in 1961 and wound up second with 101 wins.

Tiger owner John E. Fetzer was impressed by Scheffing's dignity and class. He personally helped tutor the former manager before his lone season as Ernie Harwell's partner in 1964.

Scheffing obviously loved the game more than he did broadcasting and wound up being named general manager of the New York Mets.

TIGERS RADIO

Years	Broadcasters	Local Station(s)	Years	Broadcasters	Local Station(s)
1927-42	*Ty Tyson	WWJ-AM	1967-72	Ernie Harwell Ray Lane	WJR-AM
1934-42	*Harry Heilmann	WXYZ-AM	1973-91	Ernie Harwell Paul Carey	WJR-AM
1943-48	Harry Heilmann	WXYZ-AM	1992	Rick Rizzs Bob Rathbun	WJR-AM
1949	Harry Heilmann Van Patrick	WXYZ-AM	1993	Ernie Harwell Rick Rizzs	WJR-AM
1950	Harry Heilmann	WXYZ-AM/ WJBK-AM		Bob Rathbun	
1951	Ty Tyson WJBK-AM Paul Williams	WXYZ-AM/	1994	Rick Rizzs Bob Rathbun	WJR-AM
1952	Van Patrick	WKMH-AM/ WJBK-AM	1995-98	Frank Beckmann Lary Sorensen	WJR-AM
1953	#Van Patrick Dizzy Trout	WKMH-AM/ WJBK-AM	1998	Frank Beckmann Jim Price	WJR-AM
1954-55	#Van Patrick Dizzy Trout	WKMH-AM	1999	Ernie Harwell Jim Price	WJR-AM
1956-58	#Van Patrick Mel Ott	WKMH-AM	2000	Ernie Harwell Jim Price Dan Dickerson	WJR-AM
1959	#Van Patrick George Kell	WKMH-AM	2001-02	Ernie Harwell Jim Price Dan Dickerson	WXYT-AM
1960-63	%George Kell Ernie Harwell	WKMH-AM/ WJR-AM/ WWJ-AM	2003	Dan Dickerson Jim Price	WXYT-AM
1964	%Ernie Harwell Bob Scheffing	WJR-AM			
1965-66	Ernie Harwell Gene Osborne	WJR-AM			

TIGERS OVER-THE-AIR TELEVISION

Years	Broadcasters	Local Station(s)	Years	Broadcasters	Local Station(s)
1947-52	Ty Tyson Harry Heilmann Paul Williams	WWDT-TV (renamed WWJ)	1960-63	%George Kell Ernie Harwell	WJBK-TV
			1964	%Ernie Harwell Bob Scheffing	WJBK-TV
1953-55	#Van Patrick Dizzy Trout	WJBK-TV	1965-66	George Kell Ray Lane	WJBK-TV
1956-58	#Van Patrick Mel Ott	WJBK-TV	1967-74	George Kell Larry Osterman	WJBK-TV
1959	#Van Patrick George Kell	WJBK-TV	1975	George Kell Larry Osterman Don Kremer	WWJ-TV

Years	Broadcasters	Local Station(s)	Years	Broadcasters	Local Station(s)
1976	George Kell	WWJ-TV	1980-94	George Kell	WDIV-TV
	Larry Osterman			Al Kaline	
	Don Kremer		1995-96	George Kell	WKBD-TV
	Al Kaline			Al Kaline	
1977	George Kell	WWJ-TV		Jim Price	
	Larry Osterman		1997	Ernie Harwell	WKBD-TV
	Al Kaline			Al Kaline	
	Joe Pellegrino			Jim Price	
1978	George Kell	WWJ-TV	1998	Ernie Harwell	WKBD-TV
	Al Kaline			Al Kaline	
	Joe Pellegrino		1999-2001	Frank Beckmann	WKBD-TV
	Mike Barry			Al Kaline	
1979	George Kell	WDIV-TV	2002	Frank Beckmann	WKBD-TV
	Al Kaline			Lance Parrish	
	Mike Barry		2003	Frank Beckman	WKBD-TV
				Jack Morris	

TIGERS CABLE TELEVISION

Years	Broadcasters	Local Station(s)	Years	Broadcasters	Local Station(s)
1981-83	Larry Adderly	ON-TV	1994	Ernie Harwell	PASS
	Hank Aguirre			Jim Northrup	
	Norm Cash			Jim Price	
1984	Larry Osterman	PASS	1995-97	Ernic Harwell	PASS
	Bill Freehan			Fred McLeod	
1985	Larry Osterman	PASS		Jim Price	
	Bill Freehan		1998-2001	Josh Lewin	Fox Sports Net
	Jim Northrup			Kirk Gibson	
1986-92	Larry Osterman	PASS	2002	Mario Impemba	Fox Sports Net
	Jim Northrup			Kirk Gibson	
1993	Jim Northrup	PASS	2003	Mario Impremba	Fox Sports Net
	Jim Price			Rod Allen	

*Home games only, no Sunday games (1930-32), no weekend games (1933)
#Simulcast on radio and television
%Split time between radio and television

YOU CAN LOOK IT UP

Statistics

ALL-TIME ROSTER

𝒜

ABBOTT, GLENN (RHP)	1983-84
ABER, AL (LHP)	1953-57
ACEVEDO, JUAN (RHP)	2002
ADAMS, BOB (C)	1977
AGUIRRE, HANK (LHP)	1958-67
AHEARNE, PAT (RHP)	1995
AINSMITH, EDDIE (C)	1919-21
AKERS, BILL (IF)	1929-31
ALDRED, SCOTT (LHP)	1990-92, 1996
ALEXANDER, DALE (IF/OF)	1929-32
ALEXANDER, DOYLE (RHP)	1987-89
ALLANSON, ANDY (C)	1991
ALLEN, DUSTY (IF/OF)	2000
ALLEN, ROD (OF)	1984
ALTEN, ERNIE (LHP)	1920
ALUSIK, GEORGE (OF)	1958, 1961-62
ALVARADO, LUIS (IF)	1977
ALVAREZ, GABE (IF)	1998-00
ALVAREZ, OSSIE (IF)	1959
AMOROS, SANDY (OF)	1960
ANDERSON, BOB (RHP)	1963
ANDERSON, MATT (RHP)	1998-
ARCHER, JIMMY (C/IF)	1907
ARCHIE, GEORGE (IF)	1938
ARNDT, HARRY (IF/OF)	1902
ARROYO, FERNANDO (RHP)	1975, 1977-79
AUKER, ELDEN (RHP)	1933-38
AUSMUS, BRAD (C)	1996, 1999-00
AVERILL, EARL (OF)	1939-40
AYERS, DOC (RHP)	1919-21

𝔅

BAILEY, BILL (LHP)	1918
BAILEY, HOWARD (LHP)	1981-83
BAIR, DOUG (RHP)	1983-85
BAKER, DEL (C)	1914-16

BAKER, DOUG (IF)	1984-87
BAKER, STEVE (RHP)	1978-79
BAKO, PAUL (C)	1998
BALDWIN, BILLY (OF)	1975
BANDO, CHRIS (C)	1988
BARE, RAY (RHP)	1975-77
BARFOOT, CLYDE (RHP)	1926
BARNES, FRANK (LHP)	1929
BARNES, SAM (IF)	1921
BARNES, SKEETER (IF/OF)	1991-94
BARRETT, JIMMY (OF)	1901-05
BARTEE, KIMERA (OF)	1996-99
BARTELL, DICK (IF)	1940-41
BASHANG, AL (OF)	1912
BASSLER, JOHNNY (C)	1921-27
BATES, JASON (IF)	1998-2000
BATTS, MATT (C)	1952-54
BAUMANN, PADDY (IF/OF)	1911-14
BAUMGARTNER, HARRY (RHP)	1920
BAUMGARTNER, JOHN (IF)	1953
BAUTISTA, DANNY (OF)	1993-96
BAUTISTA, JOSE (RHP)	1997
BEAMON, TREY (OF/DH)	1998
BEAN, BILLY (OF)	1987-89
BEANE, BILLY (OF)	1988
BEARD, DAVE (RHP)	1989
BEARDEN, GENE (LHP)	1951
BECK, ERVE (IF/OF)	1902
BECK, WALTER (RHP)	1944
BECKENDORF, HEINIE (C)	1909-10
BECKER, RICH (OF)	2000-01
BELARDI, WAYNE (IF/OF)	1954-56
BELCHER, TIM (RHP)	1994
BELL, BEAU (OF)	1939
BENTON, AL (RHP)	1938-42, 1945-48
BERBERET, LOU (C)	1959-60
BERENGUER, JUAN (RHP)	1982-85
BERGMAN, DAVE (IF)	1984-92
BERGMAN, SEAN (RHP)	1993-95
BERNAZARD, TONY (IF)	1991

BERNERO, ADAM (RHP)	2000-	BUCHA, JOHNNY (C)	1953
BERO, JOHNNY (IF)	1948	BUDDIN, DON (IF)	1962
BERROA, GERONIMO (DH/OF)	1998	BUELOW, FRITZ (C/IF)	1901-04
BERRY, NEIL (IF)	1948-52	BULLARD, GEORGE (IF)	1954
BERTOIA, RENO (IF/OF)	1953-58, 1961-62	BUNNING, JIM (RHP)	1955-63
BEVERLIN, JASON (RHP)	2002	BURKE, LES (IF/C)	1923-26
BEVILLE, MONTE (C/IF)	1904	BURNS, BILL (LHP)	1912
BILKO, STEVE (IF)	1960	BURNS, GEORGE (IF)	1914-17
BILLINGHAM, JACK (RHP)	1978-80	BURNS, JACK (IF)	1936
BILLINGS, JOSH (RHP)	1927-29	BURNS, JOE (OF)	1913
BIRRER, BABE (RHP)	1955	BURNS, JOHN (IF)	1903-04
BLACK, BUD (LHP)	1952-56	BURNSIDE, PETE (LHP)	1959-60
BLAIR, WILLIE (RHP)	1999-00, 2001	BURNIDE, SHELDON (LHP)	1978-79
BLESSITT, IKE (OF)	1972	BUSH, DONIE (IF)	1908-21
BLOMDAHL, BEN (RHP)	1995	BUTERA, SAL (C)	1983
BLOODWORTH, JIMMY (IF)	1942-43, 1946	BYRD, HARRY (RHP)	1957
BLUE, LU (IF/OF)	1921-27		
BOCACHICA, HIRAM (OF)	2002-		

ℭ

BOCHTLER, DOUG (RHP)	1998	CABELL, ENOS (IF/OF)	1982-83
BOCKUS, RANDY (RHP)	1989	CADARET, GREG (LHP)	1994
BOEHLER, GEORGE (RHP)	1912-16	CAIN, BOB (LHP)	1951
BOEVER, JOE (RHP)	1993-95	CAIN, LES (LHP)	1968, 1970-72
BOGART, JOHN (RHP)	1920	CALVERT, PAUL (RHP)	1950-51
BOHANON, BRIAN (LHP)	1995	CAMPBELL, BILL (RHP)	1986
BOLAND, BERNIE (RHP)	1915-20	CAMPBELL, BRUCE (OF)	1940-41
BOLLING, FRANK (IF)	1954, 1956-60	CAMPBELL, DAVE (IF)	1967-68
BOLLING, MILT (IF)	1958	CAMPBELL, PAUL (IF)	1948-50
BOLTON, CLIFF (C)	1937	CANCEL, ROBINSON (C)	2002
BOLTON, TOM (LHP)	1993	CANTRELL, GUY (RHP)	1930
BOONE, DANNY (RHP)	1921	CAPPUZZZELLO, GEORGE (LHP)	1981
BOONE, RAY (IF)	1953-58	CARDONA, JAVIER (C)	2000-02
BORKOWSKI, DAVE (RHP)	1999-2001	CARISCH, FRED (C)	1923
BOROM, RED (IF)	1944-45	CARR, CHARLIE (IF)	1903-04
BOROS, STEVE (IF)	1957-58, 1961-62	CARREON, MARK (OF)	1992
BOROWY, HANK (RHP)	1950-51	CARROLL, OWNIE (RHP)	1925, 1927-30
BOSWELL, DAVE (RHP)	1971	CARSWELL, FRANK (OF)	1953
BRADY, JIM (LHP)	1956	CARY, CHUCK (LHP)	1985-86
BRANCA, RALPH (RHP)	1953-54	CASALE, JERRY (RHP)	1961-62
BRIDEWESER, JIM (IF)	1956	CASANOVA, RAUL (C)	1996-98
BRIDGES, ROCKY (IF)	1959-60	CASEY, DOC (IF)	1901-02
BRIDGES, TOMMY (RHP)	1930-43, 1945-46	CASEY. JOE (C/OF)	1909-11
BRINKMAN, ED (IF)	1971-74	CASH, NORM (IF/OF)	1960-74
BRITO, TILSON (IF)	1999-2000	CASH, RON (IF/OF)	1973-74
BROCAIL, DOUG (RHP)	1996-2000	CASTER, GEORGE (RHP)	1945-46
BROGNA, RICO (IF)	1992	CASTILLO, FRANK (RHP)	1998
BROOKENS, IKE (RHP)	1975	CASTILLO, MARTY (IF/C/OF)	1981-85
BROOKENS, TOM (IF/OF/C)	1979-88	CATALANOTTO, FRANK (IF)	1997-99
BROWER, LOU (IF)	1931	CAVET, PUG (LHP)	1911, 1914-15
BROWN, CHRIS (IF)	1989	CEDENO, ANDUJAR (IF)	1996
BROWN, DARRELL (OF)	1981	CEDENO, ROGER (OF)	2001
BROWN, DICK (C)	1961-62	CERUTTI, JOHN (LHP)	1991
BROWN, GATES (OF/IF)	1963-75	CHANCE, DEAN (RHP)	1971
BROWN, IKE (IF/OF)	1969-74	CHAVEZ, ANTHONY (RHP)	2000
BROWNING, FRANK (RHP)	1910	CHAVEZ, ENDY (OF)	2001-02
BRUCE, BOB (RHP)	1959-61	CHITI, HARRY (C)	1960-61
BRUCKMILLER, ANDY (RHP)	1905	CHRIS, MIKE (LHP)	1979
BRUMLEY, MIKE (IF/OF)	1989	CHRISLEY, NEIL (OF/IF)	1959-60
BRUNSBERG, ARLO (C)	1966	CHRISTIAN, BOB (IF/OF)	1968
BRUNSON, WILL (LHP)	1998-99	CHRISTMAN, MARK (IF)	1938-39
BRUTON, BILLY (OF)	1961-64	CHRISTOPHER, MIKE (RHP)	1995-96

CICOTTE, AL (RHP)	1958
CICOTTE, EDDIE (RHP)	1905
CLAIRE, DANNY (IF)	1920
CLARK, DANNY (IF/OF)	1922
CLARK, JERMAINE (IF)	2001
CLARK, MEL (OF)	1957
CLARK, PHIL (OF)	1992
CLARK, TONY (IF)	1995-2001
CLARKE, NIG (C)	1905
CLARKE, RUFE (RHP)	1923-24
CLAUSS, AL (LHP)	1913
CLIFTON, FLEA (IF)	1934-37
COBB, JOE (PH)	1918
COBB, TY (OF/IF/RHP)	1905-26
COCHRANE, MICKEY (C)	1934-37
COFFEY, JACK (IF)	1918
COFFMAN, SLICK (RHP)	1937-39
COLAVITO, ROCKY (OF)	1960-63
COLBERT, NATE (IF)	1975
COLE, BERT (LHP)	1921-25
COLEMAN, JOE, SR. (RHP)	1955
COLEMAN, JOE, JR. (RHP)	1971-76
COLEMAN, VINCE (OF)	1997
COLES, DARNELL (IF/OF)	1986-87, 1990
COLLIER, ORLIN (RHP)	1931
COLLINS, DAVE (OF)	1986
COLLINS, KEVIN (IF/OF)	1970-71
COLLINS, RIP (RHP)	1923-27
COMER, WAYNE (OF/C)	1967-68, 1972
COMSTOCK, RALPH (RHP)	1913
CONGER, DICK (RHP)	1940
CONKWRIGHT, ALLEN (RHP)	1920
CONNELLY, BILL (RHP)	1950
COOK, EARL (RHP)	1941
COOLEY, DICK (OF)	1905
COOMBS, JACK (RHP)	1920
COOPER, WILBUR (LHP)	1926
CORCORAN, TIM (OF)	1977-80
CORDERO, FRANCISCO (RHP)	1999
CORNEJO, NATE (RHP)	2001-
CORRIDEN, RED (IF)	1912
COTTIER, CHUCK (IF)	1961
COUCH, JOHNNY (RHP)	1917
COUGHLIN, BILL (IF)	1904-08
COURTNEY, ERNIE (IF)	1903
COVELESKI, HARRY (LHP)	1914-18
COVINGTON, BILL (RHP)	1911-12
COWENS, AL (OF)	1980-81
COX, RED (RHP)	1920
CRADLE, RICKEY (OF)	1998-99
CRAMER, DOC (OF)	1942-48
CRAWFORD, JIM (LHP)	1976-78
CRAWFORD, SAM (OF/IF)	1903-17
CRIMIAN, JACK (RHP)	1957
CRISTANTE, LEO (RHP)	1955
CROCKETT, DAVEY (IF)	1901
CRONIN, JACK (RHP)	1901-02
CROUCHER, FRANK (IF)	1939-41
CRWO, DEAN (RHP)	1998
CROWDER, GENERAL (RHP)	1934-36

CRUMPLER, RAY (LHP)	1920
CRUZ, DEIVI (IF)	1997-2001
CRUZ, FAUSTO (IF)	1996
CRUZ, JACOB (OF)	2001-02
CRUZ, NELSON (RHP)	1999-2000
CULLENBINE, ROY (OF/IF)	1938-39, 1945-47
CUMMINGS, JOHN (LHP)	1996-97
CUNNINGHAM, GEORGE (RHP/OF)	1916-19, 1921
CURRY, JIM (IF)	1918
CURTIS, CHAD (OF)	1995-96
CUTSHAW, GEORGE (IF)	1922-23
CUYLER, MILT (OF)	1990-95

D

DALTON, JACK (OF)	1916
DALTON, MIKE (LHP)	1991
DANIEL, CHUCK (RHP)	1957
DATZ, JEFF (C/DH)	1989
DAUGHERTY, DOC (PH)	1951
DAUSS, HOOKS (RHP)	1912-26
DAVIE, JERRY (RHP)	1959
DAVIS, ERIC (OF)	1993-94
DAVIS, HARRY (IF)	1932-33
DAVIS, STORM (RHP)	1993-94
DAVIS, WOODY (RHP)	1938
DEAL, CHARLIE (IF)	1912-13
DEER, ROB (OF)	1991-93
DEERING, JOHN (RHP)	1903
DEFATE, TONY (IF)	1917
DEJESUS, IVAN (IF)	1988
DEJOHN, MATK (IF)	1982
DELAHANTY, JIM (IF)	1909-12
DE LOS SANTOS, LUIS (OF)	1991
DELSING, JIM (OF)	1952-56
DEMETER, DON (OF/IF)	1964-66
DEMETER, STEVE (IF)	1959
DEMMITT, RAY (OF)	1914
DENEHY, BILL (RHP)	1971
DESAUTELS, GENE (C)	1930-33
DESILVA, JOHN (RHP)	1993
DEVIVEIROS, BERNIE (IF)	1927
DIDIER, BOB (C)	1973
DILLARD, STEVE (IF)	1978
DILLON, POP (IF)	1901-02
DISCH, GEORGE (P)	1905
DISHMAN, GLENN (LHP)	1997
DITTMER, JACK (IF)	1957
DOBSON, PAT (RHP)	1967-69
DOBY, LARRY (OF)	1959
DOHERTY, JOHN (RHP)	1992-95
DOLJACK, FRANK (OF/IF)	1930-34
DONAHUE, RED (RHP)	1906
DONOHUE, JIM (RHP)	1961
DONOVAN, DICK (RHP)	1954
DONOVAN, WILD BILL (RHP/IF/OF)	1903-12, 1918
DORAN, TIM (C)	1905
DOWD, SNOOKS (IF)	1919
DOWNS, RED (IF/OF)	1907-08

DOYLE, JESS (RHP)	1925-27
DRAKE, DELOS (OF/IF)	1911
DRESSEN, LEE (IF)	1918
DRILL, LEW (C/OF/IF)	1904-05
DROPO, WALT (IF)	1952-54
DUBOIS, BRIAN (LHP)	1989-90
DUBUC, JEAN (RHP)	1912-16
DUGAN, JOE (IF)	1931
DURAN, ROBERTO (LHP)	1997-98
DUSTAL, BOB (RHP)	1963
DYER, BEN (IF/OF/RHP)	1916-19
DYER, DUFFY (C)	1980-81

E

EARL, SCOTT (IF)	1984
EASLEY, DAMION (IF)	1996-
EASON, MAL (RHP)	1903
EASTERLING, PAUL (OF)	1928, 1930
EATON, ZEB (RHP)	1944-45
ECKENSTAHLER, ERIC (LHP)	2002-
EGAN, DICK (LHP)	1963-64
EGAN, WISH (RHP)	1902
EHMKE, HOWARD (RHP)	1916-17, 1919-22
EISCHEN, JOEY (LHP)	1996
EISENSTAT, HARRY (LHP)	1938-39
ELBERFELD, KID (IF)	1901-03
ELDER, HEINIE (LHP)	1913
ELLISON, BERT (IF/OF)	1916-20
ENCARNACION, JUAN (OF)	1997-2001
ENGLE, DAVE (IF/OF/C)	1986
ENGLISH, GIL (IF)	1936-37
ERICKSON, ERIC (RHP)	1916, 1918-19
ERICKSON, HAL (RHP)	1953
ERWIN, TEX (C)	1907
EUBANK, JOHN (RHP)	1905-07
EVANS, DARRELL (IF)	1984-88
EVERS, HOOT (OF)	1941, 1946-52, 1954

F

FACE, ROY (RHP)	1968
FAHEY, BILL (C)	1981-83
FAIN, FERRIS (IF)	1955
FARLEY, BOB (IF/OF)	1962
FARMER, ED (RHP)	1973
FARNSWORTH, JEFF (RHP)	2001-02
FARRELL, JOHN (RHP)	1996
FAUL, BILL (RHP)	1962-64
FEDEROFF, AL (IF)	1951-52
FELIX, JUNIOR (OF)	1994
FELLER, JACK (C)	1958
FERNANDEZ, CHICO (IF)	1960-63
FERRY, CY (RHP)	1904
FICK, ROBERT (C/OF)	1998-2002
FIDRYCH, MARK (RHP)	1976-80
FIELDER, CECIL (IF)	1990-96
FIELDS, BRUCE (OF)	1986
FINIGAN, JIM (IF)	1957

FINNERAN, HAPPY (RHP)	1918
FISCHER, BILL (RHP)	1958, 1960-61
FISCHER, CARL (LHP)	1933-35
FISHER, ED (RHP)	1902
FISHER, FRITZ (LHP)	1964
FLAGSTEAD, IRA (OF/IF)	1917, 1919-23
FLAHERTY, JOHN (C)	1994-96
FLEMING, LES (OF)	1939
FLETCHER, SCOTT (IF)	1995
FLETCHER, TOM (LHP)	1962
FLETCHER, VAN (RHP)	1955
FLORIE, BRYCE (RHP)	1998-99
FLOWERS, BEN (RHP)	1955
FLOYD, BUBBA (IF)	1944
FLYNN, DOUG (IF)	1985
FOILES, HANK (C)	1960
FOOR, JIM (LHP)	1971-72
FORD, GENE (RHP)	1905
FOSTER, LARRY (RHP)	1963
FOTHERGILL, BOB (OF)	1922-30
FOUCAULT, STEVE (RHP)	1977-78
FOX, PETE (OF)	1933-40
FOX, TERRY (RHP)	1961-66
FOYTACK, PAUL (RHP)	1953, 1955-63
FRANCIS, RAY (LHP)	1923
FRANCONA, TITO (OF)	1958
FRANKLIN, MURRAY (IF)	1941-42
FRASIER, VIC (RHP)	1933-34
FREEHAN, BILL (C)	1961, 1963-76
FREESE, GEORGE (PH)	1953
FRIED, CY (LHP)	1920
FRIEND, OWEN (IF)	1953
FRISK, EMIL (RHP/OF)	1901
FROATS, BILL (LHP)	1955
FRYMAN, TRAVIS (IF)	1990-97
FRYMAN, WOODIE (LHP)	1972-74
FUCHS, CHARLIE (RHP)	1942
FUENTES, TITO (IF)	1977
FULLER, FRANK (IF)	1915-16
FUNK, LIZ (OF)	1930

G

GAGNON, CHICK (IF)	1922
GAILLARD, EDDIE (RHP)	1997
GAINER, DEL (IF)	1909, 1911-14
GAKELER, DAN (RHP)	1991
GALLAGHER, DOUG (LHP)	1962
GALLOWAY, CHICK (IF/OF)	1928
GAMBLE, JOHN (IF)	1972-73
GARBEY, BARBARO (IF/OF)	1984-85
GARBOWSKI, ALEX (PR)	1952
GARCIA, KARIM (OF)	1999-2000
GARCIA, LUIS (IF)	1999
GARCIA, PEDRO (IF)	1976
GARDINER, MIKE (RHP)	1993-95
GARVER, NED (RHP)	1952-56
GEHRINGER, CHARLIE (IF)	1924-42
GELBERT, CHARLEY (IF)	1937
GENTRY, RUFE (RHP)	1943-44, 1946-48

GERMAN, FRANKLYN (RHP)	2002-
GERNERT, DICK (IF/OF)	1960-61
GESSLER, DOC (OF)	1903
GIBSON, FRANK (C/OF)	1913
GIBSON, KIRK (OF/DH)	1979-87, 1993-95
GIBSON, PAUL (LHP)	1988-91
GIBSON, SAM (RHP)	1926-28
GIEBELL, FLOYD (RHP)	1939-41
GILBRETH, BILL (LHP)	1971-72
GILL, GEORGE (RHP)	1937-39
GILLESPIE, BOB (RHP)	1944
GINSBERG, JOE (C)	1948, 1950-53
GLADDEN, DAN (OF)	1992-93
GLADDING, FRED (RHP)	1961-67
GLAISER, JOHN (RHP)	1920
GLEASON, KID (IF)	1901-02
GLEATON, JERRY DON (LHP)	1990-91
GLYNN, ED (LHP)	1975-78
GOHR, GREG (RHP)	1993-96
GOLDSTEIN, IZZY (RHP)	1932
GOLDY, PURNAL (OF)	1962-63
GOMEZ, CHRIS (IF)	1993-96
GONZALES, DAN (OF)	1979-80
GONZALEZ, JUAN (OF)	2000
GONZALEZ, JULIO (IF)	1983
GONZALEZ, LUIS (OF/DH)	1998
GORSICA, JOHNNY (RHP)	1940-44, 1946-47
GOSLIN, GOOSE (OF)	1934-37
GRABOWSKI, JOHNNY (C)	1931
GRAHAM, BILL (RHP)	1966
GRAHAM, KYLE (RHP)	1929
GRATER, MARK (RHP)	1993
GRATEROL, BEIKER (RHP)	1999
GRAY, TED (LHP)	1946, 1948-54
GREEN, LENNY (OF)	1967-68
GREENBERG, HANK (IF/OF)	1930, 1933-41, 1945-46
GREENE, ALTAR (OF)	1979
GREENE, WILLIE (IF)	1903
GREISINGER, SETH (RHP)	1998, 2002
GREMMINGER, ED (IF)	1904
GRIGGS, ART (IF)	1918
GRILLI, STEVE (RHP)	1975-77
GRISSOM, MARV (RHP)	1949
GROMEK, STEVE (RHP)	1953-57
GROOM, BUDDY (LHP)	1992-95
GROTH, JOHNNY (OF)	1946-52, 1957-60
GROVER, BERT (RHP)	1913
GRUBB, JOHN (OF)	1983-87
GRZENDA, JOE (LHP)	1961
GULLICKSON, BILL (RHP)	1991-94
GUMPERT, DAVE (RHP)	1982-83
GUTIERREZ, CESAR (IF)	1969-71

H

HAAS, DAVID (RHP)	1991-93
HALE, SAMMY (IF/OF)	1920-21
HALL, CHARLEY (RHP)	1918
HALL, HERB (RHP)	1918

HALL, JOE (OF)	1995, 1997
HALL, MARC (RHP)	1913-14
HALLER, TOM (C)	1972
HALTER, SHANE (IF)	2000-
HAMELIN, BOB (IF/DH)	1997
HAMILTON, EARL (LHP)	1916
HAMILTON, JACK (RHP)	1964-65
HAMLIN, LUKE (RHP)	1933-34
HANEY, FRED (IF)	1922-25
HANKINS, DON (RHP)	1927
HANNAN, JIM (RHP)	1971
HARDING, CHARLIE (RHP)	1913
HARE, SHAWN (OF)	1991-92
HARGRAVE, PINKY (C)	1928-30
HARLEY, DICK (OF)	1902
HARPER, BRIAN (OF/IF/C)	1986
HARPER, GEORGE (OF)	1916-18
HARPER, TERRY (OF)	1987
HARRIGER, DENNY (RHP)	1998
HARRINGTON, ANDY (PH)	1925
HARRIS, BOB (RHP)	1938-39
HARRIS, BUCKY (IF)	1929, 1931
HARRIS, GAIL (IF)	1958-60
HARRIS, GENE (RHP)	1994
HARRIS, NED (OF)	1941-43, 1946
HARRIST, EARL (RHP)	1953
HASELMAN, BILL (C)	1999
HATFIELD, FRED (IF)	1952-56
HATTER, CLYDE (LHP)	1935, 1937
HAVENS, BRAD (LHP)	1989
HAYWORTH, RAY (C)	1926, 1929-38
HAZLE, BOB (OF)	1958
HEATH, BILL (C)	1967
HEATH, MIKE (C)	1986-90
HEBNER, RICHIE (IF)	1980-82
HEFFNER, DON (IF)	1944
HEGAN, JIM (C)	1958
HEILMANN, HARRY (OF/IF)	1914, 1916-29
HEINKEL, DON (RHP)	1988
HENNEMAN, MIKE (RHP)	1987-95
HENNESSEY, LES (IF)	1913
HENRIQUEZ, OSCAR (RHP)	2002-
HENRY, DWAYNE (RHP)	1995
HENSHAW, ROY (LHP)	1942-44
HERBERT, RAY (RHP)	1950-54
HERMAN, BABE (OF)	1937
HERNANDEZ, FERNANDO (RHP)	1997
HERNANDEZ, WILLIE (LHP)	1984-89
HERNDON, LARRY (OF)	1982-88
HERRING, ART (RHP)	1929-33
HERZOG, WHITEY (OF)	1963
HETLING, GUS (IF)	1906
HIATT, PHIL (IF/OF)	1996
HICKMAN, CHARLIE (IF/ OF)	1904-05
HICKS, BUDDY (IF)	1956
HIGGINS, PINKY (IF)	1939-44, 1946
HIGGINSON, BOBBY (OF)	1995-
HIGH, ED (LHP)	1901
HIGH, HUGH (OF)	1913-14
HILJUS, ERIK (RHP)	1999-2000

HILLER, JOHN (LHP)	1965-70, 1972-80
HITCHCOCK, BILLY (IF)	1942, 1946, 1953
HOEFT, BILLY (LHP)	1952-59
HOGSETT, CHIEF (LHP)	1929-36, 1944
HOLDSWORTH, FRED (RHP)	1972-74
HOLLING, CARL (RHP)	1921-22
HOLLOWAY, KEN (RHP)	1922-28
HOLMAN, SHAWN (RHP)	1989
HOLMES, DUCKY (OF)	1901-02
HOLT, CHRIS (RHP)	2001
HOLTGRAVE, VERN (RHP)	1965
HOOVER, JOE (IF)	1943-45
HOPP, JOHNNY (IF/OF)	1952
WILLIE HORTON (OF)	1963-77
HOSLEY, TIM (C/IF)	1970-71
HOST, GENE (LHP)	1956
HOSTETLER, CHUCK (OF)	1944-45
HOUSE, FRANK (C)	1950-51, 1954-57, 1961
HOUSE, FRED (RHP)	1913
HOUTTEMAN, ART (RHP)	1945-50, 1952-53
HOWARD, FRANK (IF/OF)	1972-73
HOYT, WAITE (RHP)	1930-30
HUBER, CLARENCE (IF)	1920-21
HUDSON, CHARLES (RHP)	1989
HUELSMAN, FRANK (OF)	1904
HUGHES, TOM (OF)	1930
HUISMANN, MARK (RHP)	1988
HUMPHREY, TERRY (C)	1975
HUMPHREYS, BOB (RHP)	1962
HUNTER, BRIAN (OF)	1997-99
HURST, JIMMY (OF)	1997
HUTCHINSON, FRED (RHP)	1939-41, 1946-53
HYERS, TIM (IF/OF)	1996

ℑ

IGNASIAK, GARY (LHP)	1973
INCAVIGLIA, PETE (OF)	1991, 1998
INFANTE, OMAR (IF)	2002-
INGE, BRANDON (C)	2001-
INGRAM, RICCARDO (OF)	1994
IRVIN, ED (IF)	1912
IVIE, MIKE (DH)	1982-83

ℑ

JACKSON, CHARLIE (RHP)	1905
JACKSON, DAMIAN (IF)	2002-
JACKSON, RON (IF)	1981
JACKSON, RYAN (OF/IF)	2001-
JACOBSON, BABY DOLL (OF/IF)	1915
JAEGER, CHARLIE (RHP)	1904
JAMES, ART (OF)	1975
JAMES, BILL (RHP)	1915-19
JAMES, BOB (RHP)	1982-83
JARVIS, KEVIN (RHP)	1997
JATA, PAUL (IF/OF)	1972
JEFFERIES, GREGG (IF/OF)	1999-2000
JENNINGS, HUGHIE (IF)	1907, 1909, 1912, 1918

JENSEN, WILLIE (RHP)	1912
JENSEN, MARCUS (C)	1997
JIMENEZ, JASON (LHP)	2002
JOHNS, AUGIE (LHP)	1926-27
JOHNSON, ALEX (OF)	1976
JOHNSON, BRIAN (C)	1997
JOHNSON, DAVE (RHP)	1993
JOHNSON, EARL (LHP)	1951
JOHNSON, HOWARD (IF/OF)	1982-84
JOHNSON, KEN (LHP)	1952
JOHNSON, MARK (RHP)	2000
JOHNSON, ROY (OF)	1929-32
JOHNSON, SYL (RHP)	1922-25
JONES, ALEX (LHP)	1903
JONES, BOB (IF)	1917-25
JONES, DALTON (IF/OF)	1970-72
JONES, DAVY (OF)	1906-12
JONES, DEACON (RHP)	1916-18
JONES, ELIJAH (RHP)	1907, 1909
JONES, KEN (RHP)	1924
JONES, LYNN (OF)	1979-83
JONES, RUPPERT (OF)	1984
JONES, SAM (RHP)	1962
JONES, TODD (RHP)	1997-2001
JONES, TOM (IF)	1909-10
JONES, TRACY (OF)	1989-90
JORDAN, MILT (RHP)	1953
JUSTIS, WALT (RHP)	1905

𝔎

KAISER, JEFF (LHP)	1991
KALINE, AL (OF/IF/DH)	1953-74
KALLIO, RUDY (RHP)	1918-19
KANE, HARRY (LHP)	1903
KAPLER, GABE (OF)	1998-99
KAVANAGH, MARTY (IF/OF)	1914-16
KEAGLE, GREG (RHP)	1996-89
KELL, GEORGE (IF)	1946-52
KELLEHER, MICK (IF)	1981
KELLER, KRIS (RHP)	2002
KELLER, CHARLIE (OF)	1950-51
KELLY, BRYAN (RHP)	1986-87
KEMP, STEVE (OF)	1977-81
KENNEDY, BOB (IF/OF)	1956
KENNEDY, VERN (RHP)	1938-39
KERNS, RUSS (PH)	1945
KERR, JOHN (IF/OF)	1923-24
KIDA, MASAO (RHP)	1999-2000
KIELY, JOHN (RHP)	1991-93
KILKENNY, MIKE (LHP)	1969-72
KILLEFER, RED (IF/OF)	1907-09
KILLIAN, ED (LHP)	1904-10
KIMM, BRUCE (C)	1976-77
KIMSEY, CHAD (RHP)	1936
KING, CHICK (OF)	1954-56
KING, ERIC (RHP)	1986-88, 1992
KINGSALE, GENE (OF)	2002-
KINNEY, DENNIS (LHP)	1981

KINZER, MATT (RHP)	1990
KIRKE, JAY (IF/OF)	1910
KISINGER, RUBE (RHP)	1902-03
KITSON, FRANK (RHP)	1903-05
KLASSEN, DANNY (IF)	2003-
KLAWITTER, AL (RHP)	1913
KLINE, RON (RHP)	1961-62
KLIPPSTEIN, JOHNNY (RHP)	1967
KNEISCH, RUDY (LHP)	1926
KNIGHT, RAY (IF)	1988
KNOTTS, GARY (RHP)	2003-
KNOX, JOHN (IF)	1972-75
KNUDSEN, KURT (RHP)	1992-94
KOCH, ALAN (RHP)	1963-64
KOCHER, BRAD (C)	1912
KOENIG, MARK (IF/RHP)	1930-31
KOLLOWAY, DON (IF)	1949-52
KOPLITZ, HOWIE (RHP)	1961-62
KORINCE, GEORGE (RHP)	1966-67
KOSTRO, FRANK (IF/OF)	1962-63
KRENCHICKI, WAYNE (IF)	1983
KRESS, CHUCK (IF/OF)	1954
KRESS, RED (IF)	1939-40
KRETLOW, LOU (RHP)	1946, 1948-49
KREUTER, CHAD (C)	1992-94
KRUEGER, BILL (LHP)	1993-94
KRYHOSKI, DICK (IF)	1950-51
KUENN, HARVEY (IF/OF)	1952-59
KUNTZ, RUSTY (OF/IF/DH)	1984-85

𝕷

LABINE, CLEM (RHP)	1960
LAFITTE, ED (RHP)	1909, 1911-12
LAGA, MIKE (IF)	1982-86
LAGROW, LERRIN (RHP)	1970, 1972-75
LAKE, EDDIE (IF)	1946-50
LAKE, JOE (RHP)	1912-13
LAKEMAN, AL (C)	1954
LAMONT, GENE (C)	1970-75
LANCASTER, LES (RHP)	1992
LANDIS, JIM (OF)	1967
LANE, MARVIN (OF)	1971-74, 1976
LAPOINT, DAVE (LHP)	1986
LARKIN, STEVE (RHP)	1934
LARY, FRANK (RHP)	1954-64
LASHER, FRED (RHP)	1967-70
LATHERS, CHICK (IF)	1910-11
LAU, CHARLIE (C)	1956, 1958-59
LAWRENCE, BILL (OF)	1932
LAWSON, ROXIE (RHP)	1933, 1935-39
LAXTON, BILL (LHP)	1976
LAZORKO, JACK (RHP)	1986
LEACH, RICK (IF/OF)	1981-83
LEDBETTER, RAZOR (RHP)	1915
LEE, DON (RHP)	1957-58
LEFLORE, RON (OF)	1974-79
LEINHAUSER, BILL (OF)	1912
LEITER, MARK (RHP)	1991-93

LELIVELT, BILL (RHP)	1909-10
LEMANCZYK, DAVE (RHP)	1973-76
LEMON, CHET (OF)	1982-90
LENHARDT, DON (OF)	1952
LENTINE, JIM (OF)	1980
LEONARD, DUTCH (LHP)	1919-25
LEPCIO, TED (IF)	1959
LEPINE, PETE (OF/IF)	1902
LERCHEN, GEORGE (OF)	1952
LESHNOCK, DON (LHP)	1972
LEWIS, RICHIE (RHP)	1996
LEWIS, MARK (IF)	1995-96
LIMA, JOSE (RHP)	1994-96, 2001-
LINDBECK, EM (PH)	1960
LINDEMAN, JIM (DH/OF/IF)	1990
LINDSAY, CHRIS (IF)	1905-06
LINDSEY, ROD (OF)	2000
LINHART, CARL (PH)	1952
LIPON, JOHNNY (IF)	1942, 1946, 1948-52
LIRA, FELIPE (RHP)	1995-97, 1999
LITTLEFIELD, DICK (LHP)	1952
LIVELY, JACK (RHP)	1911
LIVINGSTONE, SCOTT (IF)	1991-94
LOCHHEAD, HARRY (IF)	1901
LOGAN, BOB (LHP)	1937
LOLICH, MICKEY (LHP)	1963-75
LOMBARD, GEORGE (OF)	2002-
LONG, HERMAN (IF)	1903
LOPEZ, AURELIO (RHP)	1979-85
LORENZEN, LEFTY (LHP)	1913
LOUDELL, ART (RHP)	1910
LOUDEN, BALDY (IF/OF)	1912-13
LOUX, SHANE (RHP)	2002-
LOVE, SLIM (LHP)	1919-20
LOVULLO, TOREY (IF)	1988-89
LOWDERMILK, GROVER (RHP)	1915-16
LOWE, BOBBY (IF/OF)	1904-07
LOWRY, DWIGHT (C)	1984, 1986-87
LUDOLPH, WILLIE (RHP)	1924
LUGO, URBANO (RHP)	1990
LUMPE, JERRY (IF)	1964-67
LUND, DON (OF)	1949, 1952-54
LUSADER, SCOTT (OF)	1987-90
LUSH, BILLY (OF/IF)	1903
LYNN, FRED (OF)	1988-89
LYNN, RED (RHP)	1939

𝕸

MAAS, DUKE (RHP)	1955-57
MACCORMACK, FRANK (RHP)	1976
MACDONALD, BOB (LHP)	1993
MACHEMER, DAVE (IF)	1979
MACIAS, JOSE (IF)	1999-2002
MADDEN, MORRIS (LHP)	1987
MADDOX, ELLIOTT (IF/OF)	1970
MADISON, DAVE (RHP)	1952-53
MADISON, SCOTTI (IF/DH)	1985-86
MADLOCK, BILL (IF/DH)	1987

MAGEE JR., WENDELL (OF)	2000-	MCMANUS, MARTY (IF)	1927-31
MAHARG, BILLY (IF)	1912	MCMILLON, BILLY (OF)	2000-01
MAHLER, MICKEY (LHP)	1985	MCMULLIN, FRED (IF)	1914
MAIER, BOB (IF/OF)	1945	MCNABB, CARL (PH)	1945
MAIN, ALEX (RHP)	1914	MCNAIR, ERIC (IF)	1941-42
MAISEL, GEORGE (OF)	1916	MCRAE, NORM (RHP)	1969-70
MAKOWSKI, TOM (LHP)	1975	MCTIGUE, BILL (LHP)	1916
MALLOY, HERM (RHP)	1907-08	MEACHAM, RUSTY (RHP)	1991
MALMBERG, HARRY (IF)	1955	MEANEY, PAT (IF)	1912
MANDERS, HAL (RHP)	1941-42, 1946	MEELER, PHIL (RHP)	1972
MANION, CLYDE (C/IF)	1920-24, 1926-27	MELUSKEY, MITCH (C)	2001-02
MANKOWSKI, PHIL (IF)	1976-79	MELVIN, BOB (C)	1985
MANTO, JEFF (IF/DH)	1998	MERCADO, ORLANDO (C)	1987
MANUEL, JERRY (IF)	1975-76	MERCER, WIN (RHP)	1902
MANUSH, HEINIE (OF/IF)	1923-27	MERRITT, HERM (IF)	1921
MAPES, CLIFF (OF)	1952	METHA, SCAT (IF)	1940
MARBERRY, FIRPO (RHP)	1933-35	METRO, CHARLIE (OF)	1943-44
MARENTETTE, LEO (RHP)	1965	MEYER, DAN (OF/IF)	1974-76
MARLOWE, DICK (RHP)	1951-56	MEYER, DUTCH (IF)	1940-42
MAROTH, MIKE (LHP)	2002-	MICELI, DAN (RHP)	1997
MARROW, BUCK (RHP)	1932	MICHAEL, GENE (IF)	1975
MARSHALL, MIKE (RHP)	1967	MIDDLETON, JIM (RHP)	1921
MARTIN, BILLY (IF)	1958	MIERKOWICZ, ED (OF)	1945, 1947-48
MARTIN, JOHN (LHP)	1983	MILLER, BOB G. (LHP)	1953-56
MASON, ROGER (RHP)	1984	MILLER, BOB L. (RHP)	1973
MASTERSON, WALT (RHP)	1956	MILLER, EDDIE (OF)	1982
MATCHICK, TOM (IF)	1967-69	MILLER, HACK (C)	1944-45
MATHEWS, EDDIE (IF)	1967-68	MILLER, MATT (LHP)	2001-02
MAVIS, BOB (PR)	1949	MILLER, ORLANDO (IF)	1997
MAXCY, BRIAN (RHP)	1995-96	MILLER, ROSCOE (RHP)	1901-02
MAXWELL, CHARLIE (OF/IF)	1955-62	MILLER, TREVER (LHP)	1996
MAY, MILT (C)	1976-79	MITCHELL, CLARENCE (LHP)	1911
MAYO, EDDIE (IF)	1944-48	MITCHELL, WILLIE (LHP)	1916-19
MCALLISTER. SPORT (OF/IF/C)	1901-03	MLICKI, DAVE (RHP)	1999-2001
MCAULIFFE, DICK (IF)	1960-73	MOEHLER, BRIAN (RHP)	1996-2002
MCCARTHY, ARCH (RHP)	1902	MOFORD, HERB (RHP)	1958
MCCOSKY, BARNEY (OF)	1939-42, 1946	MOHARDT, JOHN (OF)	1922
MCCOY, BENNY (IF)	1938-39	MOLINARO, BOB (OF)	1975, 1977, 1983
MCCREERY, ED (RHP)	1914	MONBOUQUETTE, BILL (RHP)	1966-67
MCCULLERS, LANCE (RHP)	1990	MONGE, SID (LHP)	1984
MCCURRY, JEFF (RHP)	1996	MONROE, CRAIG (OF)	2002-
MCDERMOTT, MICKEY (LHP)	1958	MONTEJO, MANNY (RHP)	1961
MCDERMOTT, RED (OF)	1912	MOORE, ANSE (OF)	1946
MCDILL, ALLEN (LHP)	2000	MOORE, BILL (RHP)	1925
MCFARLANE, ORLANDO (C)	1966	MOORE, JACKIE (C)	1965
MCGARR, JIM (IF)	1912	MOORE, MIKE (RHP)	1993-95
MCGARVEY, DAN (OF)	1912	MOORE, ROY (LHP)	1922-23
MCGEHEE, PAT (RHP)	1912	MOOTY, JAKE (RHP)	1944
MCGUIRE, DEACON (C/IF)	1902-03, 1912	MORALES, JERRY (OF)	1979
MCHALE SR., JOHN (IF)	1943-45, 1947-48	MORAN, HARRY (LHP)	1912
MCINTYRE, MATTY (OF)	1904-10	MORELAND, KEITH (IF/DH/C)	1989
MCKAIN, ARCHIE (LHP)	1939-41	MORGAN, CHET (OF)	1935, 1938
MCKEE, RED (C)	1913-16	MORGAN, TOM (RHP)	1958-60
MCLAIN, DENNY (RHP)	1963-70	MORIARTY, GEORGE (IF/OF)	1909-15
MCLAUGHLIN, PAT (RHP)	1937, 1945	MORRIS, JACK (RHP)	1977-90
MCLELAND, WAYNE (RHP)	1951-52	HAL MORRIS (IF)	2000
MCMACKIN, SAM (LHP)	1902	MORRISETTE, BILL (RHP)	1920
MCMAHON, DON (RHP)	1968-69	MORRISON, JIM (IF)	1987-88
MCMANUS, FRANK (C)	1904	MORTON, BUBBA (OF/IF)	1961-63

MOSEBY, LLOYD (OF)	1990-91
MOSES, JERRY (C)	1974
MOSES, JOHN (OF)	1991
MOSSI, DON (LHP)	1959-63
MUELLER, LES (RHP)	1941, 1945
MULLEN, BILLY (IF)	1926
MULLIN, GEORGE (RHP/OF)	1902-13
MULLIN, PAT (OF)	1940-41, 1946-53
MUNOZ, MIKE (LHP)	1991-93
MUNSON, ERIC (IF/C)	2000-
MURPHY, DWAYNE (OF)	1988
MURPHY, JOHN (IF)	1903
MURRAY, HEATH (LHP)	2001
MYATT, GLENN (C)	1936
MYERS, MIKE (LHP)	1995-97

N

NAGELSON, RUSS (OF/IF)	1970
NAHORODNY, BILL (PH)	1983
NANCE, DOC (OF)	1901
NARLESKI, RAY (RHP)	1959
NAVARRO, JULIO (RHP)	1964-66
NEKOLA, BOTS (LHP)	1933
NELSON, LYNN (RHP)	1940
NESS, JACK (IF)	1911
NETTLES, JIM (OF)	1974
NEUN, JOHNNY (IF)	1925-28
NEVIN, PHIL (OF/IF/C)	1995-97
NEWHOUSER, HAL (LHP)	1939-53
NEWSOM, BOBO (RHP)	1939-41
NICHOLLS, SIMON (IF)	1903
NICHOLSON, FRED (OF)	1917
NIEKRO, JOE (RHP)	1970-72
NIEMAN, BOB (OF)	1953-54
NIEVES, MELVIN (OF/DH)	1996-97
NISCHWITZ, RON (LHP)	1961-62
NITKOWSKI, C.J. (LHP)	1995-96, 1999-2001
NOKES, MATT (C)	1986-90
NOLES, DICKIE (RHP)	1987
NOMO, HIDEO (RHP)	2000
NORTH, LOU (RHP)	1913
NORTHRUP, JIM (OF/IF)	1964-73
NOSEK, RANDY (RHP)	1989-90
NUNEZ, EDWIN (RHP)	1989-90

O

OANA, PRINCE (RHP)	1943, 1945
O'CONNELL, JOHN (IF)	1902
OGLIVIE, BEN (IF/OF)	1974-77
OKRIE, FRANK (LHP)	1920
OLDHAM, RED (LHP)	1914-15, 1920-22
O'LEARY, CHARLEY (IF/OF)	1904-12
OLIVARES, OMAR (RHP)	1996-97
OLIVER, JOE (C)	1998
OLSEN, OLE (RHP)	1922-23
OLSON, GREGG (RHP)	1996
OLSON, KARL (OF)	1957

O'MARA, OLLIE (IF)	1912
O'NEAL, RANDY (RHP)	1984-86
ONSLOW, EDDIE (IF)	1912-13
ONSLOW, JACK (C)	1912
ORENGO, JOE (IF)	1944
O'ROURKE, FRANK (IF)	1924-26
ORRELL, JOE (RHP)	1943-45
OSBORNE, BOBO (IF)	1957-62
OUTLAW, JIMMY (OF)	1943-49
OVERMIRE, STUBBY (LHP)	1943-49
OWEN, FRANK (RHP)	1901
OWEN, MARV (IF)	1931, 1933-37
OYLER, RAY (IF)	1965-68

P

PACELLA, JOHN (RHP)	1986
PAGE, PHIL (LHP)	1928-30
PALMER, DAVID (RHP)	1989
PALMER, DEAN (IF)	1999-
PANIAGUA, JOSE (RHP)	2002-
PAPI, STAN (IF)	1980-81
PAQUETTE, CRAIG (IF)	2002-
PAREDES, JOHNNY (IF)	1990-91
PARENT, MARK (C)	1996
PARKER, CLAY (RHP)	1990
PARKER, SALTY (IF)	1936
PARKS, SLICKER (RHP)	1921
PARRISH, LANCE (C)	1977-86
PARSONS, DIXIE (C)	1939, 1942-43
PARTENHEIMER, STEVE (IF)	1913
PASEK, JOHNNY (C)	1933
PASHNICK, LARRY (RHP)	1982-83
PATRICK, BOB (OF)	1941-42
PATTERSON, DANNY (RHP)	2000-
PATTERSON, DARYL (RHP)	1968-71
PATTERSON, JARROD (IF)	2001
PAYNE, FRED (C)	1906-08
PEARSON, TERRY (RHP)	2002
PEASLEY, MARV (LHP)	1910
PEDRIQUE, AL (IF)	1989
PEMBERTON, RUDY (OF)	1995
PENA, CARLOS (IF)	2002
PENA, ORLANDO (RHP)	1965-67
PENA, RAMON (RHP)	1989
PENN, SHANNON (IF)	1995-96
PENTZ, GENE (RHP)	1975
PEPLOSKI, PEPPER (IF)	1913
PEPPER, DON (IF)	1966
PERISHO, MATT (LHP)	2001-02
PERKINS, CY (C)	1934
PERNOLL, HUB (LHP)	1910, 1912
PERRANOSKI, RON (LHP)	1971-72
PERRITT, POL (RHP)	1921
PERRY, BOYD (IF)	1941
PERRY, CLAY (IF)	1908
PERRY, HANK (OF)	1912
PERRY, JIM (RHP)	1973
PESKY, JOHNNY (IF)	1952-54

PETERS, JOHN (C)	1915	REGAN, PHIL (RHP)	1960-65
PETERS, RICK (IF/OF)	1979-81	REIBER, FRANK (C/OF)	1933-36
PETRY, DAN (RHP)	1979-87, 1990-91	REMNEAS, ALEX (RHP)	1912
PETTIS, GARY (OF)	1988-89, 1992	RENFER, ERWIN (RHP)	1913
PETTYJOHN, ADAM (LHP)	2001	RENSA, TONY (C)	1930
PHILLEY, DAVE (IF/OF)	1957	REYNOLDS, BOB (RHP)	1975
PHILLIPS, BUBBA (IF)	1955, 1963-64	REYNOLDS, ROSS (RHP)	1914-15
PHILLIPS, EDDIE (C)	1929	RHIEL, BILLY (IF/OF)	1932-33
PHILLIPS, JACK (IF/OF)	1955-57	RIBANT, DENNIS (RHP)	1968
PHILLIPS, RED (RHP)	1934, 1936	RICE, HARRY (OF/IF)	1928-30
PHILLIPS, TONY (IF)	1990-94	RICHARDS, PAUL (C)	1943-46
PIERCE, BILLY (LHP)	1945-48	RICHARDSON, NOLEN (IF)	1929, 1931-32
PIERCE, JACK (IF)	1975	RICHIE, ROB (OF)	1989
PIET, TONY (IF)	1938	RIEBE, HANK (C)	1942-49
PILLETTE, HERMAN (RHP)	1922-24	RIGNEY, TOPPER (IF)	1922-25
PINEDA, LUIS (RHP)	2001	RIPKEN, BILLY (IF)	1998
PINELLI, BABE (IF)	1920	RITZ, KEVIN (RHP)	1989-92
PIPP, WALLY (IF)	1913	RIVERA, MICHAEL (C)	2001-02
PIPPEN, COTTON (RHP)	1939-40	ROARKE, MIKE (C)	1961-64
PITTARO, CHRIS (IF)	1985-86	ROBBINS, BRUCE (LHP)	1979-80
PLATTE, AL (OF)	1913	ROBERTS, BIP (OF/IF/DH)	1998
PODRES, JOHNNY (LHP)	1966-67	ROBERTS, DAVE (LHP)	1976-77
POFFENBERGER, BOOTS (RHP)	1937-38	ROBERTS, LEON (OF)	1974-75
POLONIA, LUIS (DH/OF)	1998-2000	ROBERTS, WILLIS (RHP)	1999
POOLE, JIM (LHP)	2000	ROBERTSON, JERRY (RHP)	1970
PORTER, J.W. (C/OF/IF)	1955-57	ROBINSON, AARON (C)	1949-51
POST, LEW (OF)	1902	ROBINSON, EDDIE (IF)	1957
POWELL, BRIAN (RHP)	1998, 2002	ROBINSON, JEFF (RHP)	1987-90
POWELL, RAY (OF)	1913	ROBINSON, RABBIT (IF/OF)	1904
POWER, TED (RHP)	1988	RODNEY, FERNANDO (RHP)	2002-
PRATT, DEL (IF)	1923-24	RODRIGUEZ, AURELIO (IF)	1971-79
PRESKO, JOE (RHP)	1957-58	RODRIGUEZ, STEVE (IF)	1995
PRICE, JIM (C)	1967-71	ROGALSKI, JOE (RHP)	1938
PRIDDY, JERRY (IF)	1950-53	ROGELL, BILLY (IF/OF)	1930-39
PRIDE, CURTIS (OF)	1996-97	ROGOVIN, SAUL (RHP)	1949-51
PROCTOR, JIM (RHP)	1959	ROJAS, MEL (RHP)	1999
PRUDHOMME, AUGIE (RHP)	1929	ROMAN, BILL (IF)	1964-65
PUGH, TIM (RHP)	1997	ROMERO, ED (IF)	1990
PURTELL, BILLY (IF)	1914	RONDEAU, HENRI (C/IF)	1913
PUTMAN, ED (C)	1979	ROOKER, JIM (LHP)	1968
		ROSS, DON (IF/OF)	1938, 1942-45
		ROSSMAN, CLAUDE (IF)	1907-09
		ROTHSCHILD, LARRY (RHP)	1981-82
Q		ROWAN, JACK (RHP)	1906
		ROWE, SCHOOLBOY (RHP)	1933-42
QUELLICH, GEORGE (OF)	1931	ROWLAND, RICH (C)	1990-93
		ROZEMA, DAVE (RHP)	1977-84
		RUBLE, ART (OF)	1927
R		RUCKER, DAVE (LHP)	1981-83
		RUEL, MUDDY (C)	1931-32
RADATZ, DICK (RHP)	1969	RUHLE, VERN (RHP)	1974-77
RADCLIFF, RIP (OF/IF)	1941-43	RUNYAN, SEAN (LHP)	1998-2000
RAKOW, ED (RHP)	1964-65	RUSSELL, JACK (RHP)	1937
RANDA, JOE (IF)	1998		
RAPP, EARL (OF)	1949		
RAY, JIM (RHP)	1974	**S**	
RAYMOND, BUGS (RHP)	1904		
REDMAN, MARK (LHP)	2001, 2002	SABEL, ERIK (RHP)	2002
REDMOND, WAYNE (OF)	1965, 1969	SAGER, A.J. (RHP)	1996-98
REED, BOB (RHP)	1969-70	SALAS, MARK (C)	1990-91
REED, JODY (IF)	1997	SALAZAR, LUIS (IF)	1988
REESE, RICH (IF/OF)	1973		

SALAZAR, OSCAR (OF/IF/DH)	2002	SIMS, DUKE (C/OF)	1972-73
SAMFORD, RON (IF)	1955, 1957	SINATRO, MATT (C)	1989
SAMUEL, JUAN (IF)	1994-95	SINGLETON, DUANE (OF)	1996
SAMUELS, JOE (RHP)	1930	SISLER, DAVE (RHP)	1959-60
SANCHEZ, ALEJANDRO (OF)	1985	SKEELS, DAVE (RHP)	1910
SANDERS, REGGIE (IF)	1974	SKIZAS, LOU (OF/IF)	1958
SANDERS, SCOTT (RHP)	1997	SKOPEC, JOHN (LHP)	1903
SANTANA, MARINO (RHP)	1998	SLATON, JIM (RHP)	1978, 1986
SANTANA, JULIO (RHP)	2002-	SLAYBACK, BILL (RHP)	1972-74
SANTANA, PEDRO (IF)	2001	SLEATER, LOU (LHP)	1957-58
SANTIAGO, RAMON (IF)	2002-	SMALL, JIM (OF)	1955-57
SANTOS, VICTOR (RHP)	2001	SMITH, BOB (LHP)	1959
SARGENT, JOE (IF)	1921	SMITH, CLAY (RHP)	1940
SAUCIER, KEVIN (LHP)	1981-82	SMITH, GEORGE C. (IF)	1963-65
SAUNDERS, DENNIS (RHP)	1970	SMITH, GEORGE S. (RHP)	1926-29
SCANLAN, BOB (RHP)	1996	SMITH, HEINIE (IF)	1903
SCARBOROUGH, RAY (RHP)	1953	SMITH, JACK (IF)	1912
SCHAEFER, GERMANY (IF/OF)	1905-09	SMITH, RUFUS (LHP)	1927
SCHALLER, BIFF (OF/IF)	1911	SMITH, WILLIE (LHP)	1963
SCHANG, WALLY (C)	1931	SNELL, NATE (RHP)	1987
SCHATZEDER, DAN (LHP)	1980-81	SODOWSKY, CLINT (RHP)	1995-96
SCHEIBECK, FRANK (IF)	1906	SORRELL, VIC (RHP)	1928-37
SCHERMAN, FRED (LHP)	1969-73	SOSA, ELIAS (RHP)	1982
SCHERRER, BILL (LHP)	1984-86	SOUCHOCK, STEVE (OF/IF)	1951-55
SCHIAPPACASSE, LOU (OF)	1902	SPARKS, STEVE (RHP)	2000-
SCHMIDT, BOSS (C/OF)	1906-11	SPARMA, JOE (RHP)	1964-69
SCHU, RICK (IF)	1989	SPEER, KID (LHP)	1909
SCHUBLE, HEINIE (IF)	1929, 1932-35	SPENCER, GEORGE (RHP)	1958, 1960
SCHULTZ, BARNEY (RHP)	1959	SPENCER, TUBBY (C/IF)	1916-18
SCHULTZ, BOB (LHP)	1955	SPIKES, CHARLIE (OF)	1978
SCHWABE, MIKE (RHP)	1989-90	SPILMAN, HARRY (IF)	1986
SCRIVENER, CHUCK (IF)	1975-77	STAINBACK, TUCK (OF)	1940-41
SEALE, JOHNNIE (LHP)	1964-65	STALEY, GERRY (RHP)	1961
SEARCY, STEVE (LHP)	1988-91	STANAGE, OSCAR (C/IF)	1909-20, 1925
SEATS, TOM (LHP)	1940	STANLEY, MICKEY (OF/IF)	1964-78
SECORY, FRANK (OF)	1940	STATON, JOE (IF)	1972-73
SEELBACH, CHUCK (RHP)	1971-74	STAUB, RUSTY (OF)	1976-79
SEMPROCH, RAY (RHP)	1960	STEEN, BILL (RHP)	1915
SEWELL, RIP (RHP)	1932	STEGMAN, DAVE (OF)	1978-80
SHARON, DICK (OF)	1973-74	STEINER, BEN (PR)	1947
SHAW, AL (C/IF)	1901	STEVERSON, TODD (OF)	1995
SHAW, BOB (RHP)	1957-58	STEWART, LEFTY (LHP)	1921
SHEA, MERV (C)	1927-29, 1939	STIDHAM, PHIL (RHP)	1994
SHEETS, LARRY (OF)	1990	STODDARD, BOB (RHP)	1985
SHELBY, JOHN (OF)	1990-91	STONE, JOHN (OF)	1928-33
SHELLEY, HUGH (OF)	1935	STONER, LIL (RHP)	1922, 1924-29
SHERIDAN, PAT (OF)	1986-89	STOVALL, JESSE (RHP)	1904
SHERRY, LARRY (RHP)	1964-67	STRAHLER, MIKE (RHP)	1973
SHEVLIN, JIMMY (IF)	1930	STRAMPE, BOB (RHP)	1972
SHIVER, IVEY (OF)	1931	STRANGE, DOUG (IF)	1989
SHOOP, RON (C)	1959	STREULI, WALT (C)	1954-56
SHORTEN, CHICK (OF/C)	1919-21	STROUD, SAILOR (RHP)	1910
SIDDALL, JOE (C)	1998	STUART, MARLIN (RHP)	1949-52
SIERRA, RUBEN (OF/DH)	1996	STUBBS, FRANKLIN (IF/OF)	1995
SIEVER, ED (LHP)	1901-02, 1906-08	STUMP, JIM (RHP)	1957, 1959
SIGAFOOS, FRANK (IF)	1929	STURDIVANT, TOM (RHP)	1963
SIMMONS, AL (OF/IF)	1936	SUGDEN, JOE (IF)	1912
SIMMONS, HACK (IF/OF)	1910	SUGGS, GEORGE (RHP)	1908-09
SIMMONS, NELSON (OF)	1984-85	SULLIVAN SR., BILLY (C)	1916
SIMON, RANDALL (IF)	2001-02	SULLIVAN JR., BILLY (C/IF)	1940-41

SULLIVAN, CHARLIE (RHP)	1928, 1930-31
SULLIVAN, JACKIE (IF)	1944
SULLIVAN, JOE (LHP)	1935-36
SULLIVAN, JOHN E. (C)	1905
SULLIVAN, JOHN P. (C)	1963-65
SULLIVAN, RUSS (OF)	1951-53
SUMMERS, CHAMP (OF)	1979-81
SUMMERS, ED (RHP)	1908-12
SUSCE, GEORGE C. (C)	1932
SUSCE, GEORGE D. (RHP)	1958-59
SUTHERLAND, GARY (IF)	1974-76
SUTHERLAND, SUDS (RHP)	1921
SWEENEY, BILL (IF/OF)	1928
SWIFT, BOB (C)	1944-53
SYKES, BOB (LHP)	1977-78
SZOTKIEWICZ, KEN (IF)	1970

𝕿

TANANA, FRANK (LHP)	1985-92
TAVENER, JACKIE (IF)	1921, 1925-28
TAYLOR, BEN (IF)	1952
TAYLOR, BILL (OF)	1957-58
TAYLOR, BRUCE (RHP)	1977-79
TAYLOR, GARY (RHP)	1969
TAYLOR, TONY (IF/OF)	1971-73
TAYLOR, WILEY (RHP)	1911
TEBBETTS, BIRDIE (C)	1936-42, 1946-47
TERRELL, WALT (RHP)	1985-88, 1990-92
TERRY, JOHN (P)	1902
TETTLETON, MICKEY (C/DH)	1991-94
THOMAS, BUD (RHP)	1939-41
THOMAS, FROSTY (RHP)	1905
THOMAS, GEORGE (IF/OF)	1957-58, 1961, 1964-65
THOMAS, IRA (C)	1908
THOMPSON, JASON (IF)	1976-80
THOMPSON, JUSTIN (LHP)	1996-99
THOMPSON, SAM (OF)	1906
THOMPSON, TIM (C)	1958
THURMAN, GARY (OF)	1993
THURMOND, MARK (LHP)	1986-87
TIMMERMANN, TOM (RHP)	1969-73
TINGLEY, RON (C)	1995
TOBIK, DAVE (RHP)	1978-82
TOBIN, JIM (RHP)	1945
TOLAR, KEVIN (LHP)	2000-01
TOLMAN, TIM (OF)	1986-87
TOMBERLIN, ANDY (OF/DH)	1998
TORGESON, EARL (IF)	1955-57
TORRES, ANDRES (OF)	2002-
TRACEWSKI, DICK (IF)	1966-69
TRAMMELL, ALAN (IF)	1977-96
TRAMMELL, BUBBA (OF/DH)	1997
TRAVERS, ALLAN (RHP)	1912
TRESH, TOM (OF/IF)	1969
TRIANDOS, GUS (C)	1963
TROUT, DIZZY (RHP)	1939-52
TROY, BUN (RHP)	1912
TRUBY, CHRIS (IF)	2002
TRUCKS, VIRGIL (RHP)	1941-43, 1945-52, 1956

TRUJILLO, MIKE (RHP)	1988-89
TSITOURIS, JOHN (RHP)	1957
TURNER, JERRY (OF)	1982
TUTTLE, BILL (OF)	1952, 1954-57
TUTWILER, GUY (IF/OF)	1911, 1913

𝖀

UHL, BOB (RHP)	1940
UHLE, GEORGE (RHP)	1929-33
UJDUR, JERRY (RHP)	1980-83
UNDERWOOD, PAT (LHP)	1979-83
UNSER, AL (C/IF)	1942-44
URBANI, TOM (LHP)	1996

𝖁

VALENTINETTI, VITO (RHP)	1958
VANGILDER, ELAM (RHP)	1928-29
VAN HEKKEN, ANDY (LHP)	2002-
VAN POPPEL, TODD (RHP)	1996
VEACH, BOBBY (OF)	1912-23
VEAL, COOT (IF)	1958-60, 1963
VEDDER, LOU (RHP)	1920
VERES, RANDY (RHP)	1996
VERYZER, TOM (IF)	1973-77
VICO, GEORGE (IF)	1948-49
VILLAFUERTE, BRANDON (RHP)	2000
VIRGIL, OZZIE (IF/C)	1958, 1960-61
VITT, OSSIE (IF/OF)	1912-18

𝖂

WADE, JAKE (LHP)	1936-38
WAGNER, HAL (C)	1947-48
WAGNER, MARK (IF)	1976-80
WAKEFIELD, DICK (OF)	1941, 1943-44, 1946-49
WAKELAND, CHRIS (OF)	2001
WALBECK, MATT (C)	1997, 2002-
WALEWANDER, JIM (IF)	1987-88
WALKER, DIXIE (OF)	1938-39
WALKER, FRANK (OF)	1917-18
WALKER, GEE (OF)	1931-37
WALKER, HUB (OF)	1931, 1935, 1945
WALKER, JAMIE (LHP)	2002-
WALKER, LUKE (LHP)	1974
WALKER, MIKE (RHP)	1996
WALKER, TOM (RHP)	1975
WALKUP, JIM E. (RHP)	1939
WALKUP, JIM H. (LHP)	1927
WALSH, JIM (LHP)	1921
WAPNICK, STEVE (RHP)	1990
WARD, GARY (IF/OF)	1989-90
WARD, HAP (OF)	1912
WARDEN, JON (LHP)	1968
WARNER, JACK (IF)	1925-28
WARNER, JOHN (C)	1905-06
WATSON, JOHNNY (IF)	1930

WEAVER, JEFF (RHP)	1999-2002
WEAVER, JIM (OF)	1985
WEAVER, ROGER (RHP)	1980
WEBB, EARL (OF/IF)	1932-33
WEBB, SKEETER (IF)	1945-47
WEHMEIER, HERM (RHP)	1958
WEIK, DICK (RHP)	1953-54
WELCH, MILT (C)	1945
WELLS, DAVID (LHP)	1993-95
WELLS, ED (LHP)	1923-27
WERT, DON (IF)	1963-70
WERTZ, VIC (OF/IF)	1947-52, 1961-63
WHEATLEY, CHARLIE (RHP)	1912
WHILLOCK, JACK (RHP)	1971
WHITAKER, LOU (IF)	1977-95
WHITE, DERRICK (OF/IF)	1995
WHITE, HAL (RHP)	1941-43, 1946-52
WHITE, JO-JO (OF)	1932-38
WHITEHILL, EARL (LHP)	1923-32
WHITESIDE, SEAN (LHP)	1995
WICKANDER, KEVIN (LHP)	1995
WICKERSHAM, DAVE (RHP)	1964-67
WIGGS, JIMMY (RHP)	1905-06
WIGHT, BILL (LHP)	1952-53
WILCOX, MILT (RHP)	1977-85
WILLETT, ED (RHP)	1906-13
WILLIAMS, BRIAN (RHP)	1996
WILLIAMS, EDDIE (OF/IF/DH)	1996
WILLIAMS, FRANK (RHP)	1989
WILLIAMS, JOHNNIE (RHP)	1914
WILLIAMS, KEN (OF)	1989-90
WILLIAMS, LEFTY (LHP)	1913-14
WILLIS, CARL (RHP)	1984
WILSON, EARL (RHP)	1966-70
WILSON, GLENN (OF)	1982-83
WILSON, ICEHOUSE (PH)	1934
WILSON, JACK (RHP)	1942
WILSON, MUTT (RHP)	1920
WILSON, RED (C)	1954-60
WILSON, SQUANTO (C)	1911
WILSON, WALTER (RHP)	1945
WINGO, AL (OF/IF)	1924-28
WINTER, GEORGE (RHP)	1908
WISE, CASEY (IF)	1960
WISE, HUGHIE (C)	1930
WOCKENFUSS, JOHN (C/OF/IF)	1974-83
WOJEY, PETE (RHP)	1956-57
WOOD, BOB (C)	1904-05
WOOD, JAKE (IF/OF)	1961–67
WOOD, JASON (IF/DH)	1998-99
WOOD, JOE (IF)	1943
WOODALL, LARRY (C)	1920-29
WOODESHICK, HAL (LHP)	1956, 1961
WOODS, RON (OF)	1969
WORKS, RALPH (RHP)	1909-12
WORRELL, TIM (RHP)	1998
WUESTLING, YATS (IF)	1929-30
WYATT, JOHN (RHP)	1968
WYATT, WHIT (RHP)	1929-33

Y

YDE, EMIL (LHP)	1929
YEAGER, JOE (IF/RHP/OF)	1901-03
YELLE, ARCHIE (C)	1917-19
YEWCIC, TOM (C)	1957
YORK, RUDY (IF/C/OF)	1934, 1937-45
YOST, EDDIE (IF)	1959-60
YOUNG, DMITRI (OF)	2002-
YOUNG, JOHN (IF)	1971
YOUNG, KIP (RHP)	1978-79
YOUNG, RALPH (IF)	1915-21

Z

ZACHARY, CHRIS (RHP)	1972
ZAMLOCH, CARL (RHP)	1913
ZEPP, BILL (RHP)	1971
ZERNIAL, GUS (OF/IF)	1958-59
ZUVERINK, GEORGE (RHP)	1954-55

TEAM YEARLY DATA

Detroit Tigers

American League

Year	Pos	W-L	Pct	GA/GB	Manager	Attendance
1901	3	74-61	.548	8.5	George Stallings	259,430
1902	7	52-83	.385	30.5	Frank Dwyer	189,469
1903	5	65-71	.478	25	Ed Barrow	224,523
1904	7	62-90	.408	32	Ed Barrow Bobby Lowe*	177,796
1905	3	79-74	.516	15.5	Bill Armour	193,384
1906	6	71-78	.477	21	Bill Armour	174,043
1907^	1	92-58	.613	1.5	Hughie Jennings	297,079
1908^	1	90-63	.588	0.5	Hughie Jennings	436,199
1909^	1	98-54	.645	3.5	Hughie Jennings	490,490
1910	3	86-68	.558	18	Hughie Jennings	391,288
1911	2	89-65	.578	13.5	Hughie Jennings	484,988
1912	6	69-84	.451	36.5	Hughie Jennings	402,870
1913	6	66-87	.431	30	Hughie Jennings	398,502
1914	4	80-73	.523	19.5	Hughie Jennings	416,225
1915	2	100-54	.649	2.5	Hughie Jennings	476,105
1916	3	87-67	.565	4	Hughie Jennings	616,772
1917	4	78-75	.510	21.5	Hughie Jennings	457,289
1918	7	55-71	.437	20	Hughie Jennings	203,719
1919	4	80-60	.571	8	Hughie Jennings	643,805
1920	7	61-93	.396	37	Hughie Jennings	579,650
1921	6	71-82	.464	27	Ty Cobb	661,527
1922	3	79-75	.513	15	Ty Cobb	861,206
1923	2	83-71	.539	16	Ty Cobb	911,377
1924	3	86-68	.558	6	Ty Cobb	1,015,136
1925	4	81-73	.526	16.5	Ty Cobb	820,766
1926	6	79-75	.513	12	Ty Cobb	711,914
1927	4	82-71	.536	27.5	George Moriarty	773,716
1928	6	68-86	.442	33	George Moriarty	474,323
1929	6	70-84	.455	36	Bucky Harris	869,318
1930	5	75-79	.487	27	Bucky Harris	649,450
1931	7	61-93	.396	47	Bucky Harris	453,056
1932	5	76-75	.503	29.5	Bucky Harris	397,157
1933	5	75-79	.487	25	Bucky Harris Del Baker*	320,972
1934^	1	101-53	.656	7	Mickey Cochrane	919,161
1935‡	1	93-58	.616	3	Mickey Cochrane	1,034,929
1936	2	83-71	.539	19.5	Mickey Cochrane	875,948
1937	2	89-65	.578	13	Mickey Cochrane	1,072,276
1938	4	84-70	.545	16	Mickey Cochrane Del Baker	799,557

Year	Pos	W-L	Pct	GA/GB	Manager	Attendance
1939	5	81-73	.526	26.5	Del Baker	836,279
1940^	1	90-64	.584	1	Del Baker	1,112,693
1941	T4	75-79	.487	26	Del Baker	684,915
1942	5	73-81	.474	30	Del Baker	580,087
1943	5	78-76	.506	20	Steve O'Neill	606,287
1944	2	88-66	.571	1	Steve O'Neill	923,176
1945‡	1	88-65	.575	1.5	Steve O'Neill	1,280,341
1946	2	92-62	.597	12	Steve O'Neill	1,722,590
1947	2	85-69	.552	12	Steve O'Neill	1,398,093
1948	5	78-76	.506	18.5	Steve O'Neill	1,743,035
1949	4	87-67	.565	10	Red Rolfe	1,821,204
1950	2	95-59	.617	3	Red Rolfe	1,951,474
1951	5	73-81	.474	25	Red Rolfe	1,132,641
1952	8	50-104	.325	45	Red Rolfe / Fred Hutchinson	1,026,846
1953	6	60-94	.390	40.5	Fred Hutchinson	884,658
1954	5	68-86	.442	43	Fred Hutchinson	1,079,847
1955	5	79-75	.513	17	Bucky Harris	1,181,838
1956	5	82-72	.532	15	Bucky Harris	1,051,182
1957	4	78-76	.506	20	Jack Tighe	1,272,346
1958	5	77-77	.500	15	Jack Tighe / Bill Norman	1,098,942
1959	4	76-78	.494	18	Bill Norman / Jimmy Dykes	1,221,221
1960	6	71-83	.461	26	Jimmy Dykes / Joe Gordon	1,167,669
1961	2	101-61	.623	8	Bob Scheffing	1,600,710
1962	4	85-76	.528	10.5	Bob Scheffing	1,207,881
1963	T5	79-83	.488	25.5	Bob Scheffing / Chuck Dressen	821,952
1964	4	85-77	.525	14	Chuck Dressen	816,139
1965	4	89-73	.549	12	Chuck Dressen / Bob Swift*	1,029,645
1966	3	88-74	.543	10	Dressen-Swift / Frank Skaff*	1,124,293
1967	T2	91-71	.562	1	Mayo Smith	1,447,143
1968‡	1	103-59	.636	12	Mayo Smith	2,031,847

American League East

Year	Pos	W-L	Pct	GA/GB	Manager	Attendance
1969	2	90-72	.556	19	Mayo Smith	1,577,481
1970	4	79-83	.488	29	Mayo Smith	1,501,293
1971	2	91-71	.562	12	Billy Martin	1,591,073
1972†	1	86-70	.551	0.5	Billy Martin	1,892,386
1973	3	85-77	.525	12	Billy Martin / Joe Schultz*	1,724,146

Year	Pos	W-L	Pct	GA/GB	Manager	Attendance
1974	6	72-90	.444	19	Ralph Houk	1,243,080
1975	6	57-102	.358	37.5	Ralph Houk	1,058,836
1976	5	74-87	.460	24	Ralph Houk	1,467,020
1977	4	74-88	.457	26	Ralph Houk	1,359,856
1978	5	86-76	.531	13.5	Ralph Houk	1,714,893
1979	5	85-76	.528	18	Les Moss Sparky Anderson	1,630,929
1980	5	84-78	.519	19	Sparky Anderson	1,785,293
1981	4	60-49	.550	2	Sparky Anderson	1,149,144
	T2	29-23	.558	1.5	(2nd Half)	
	4	31-26	.544	3.5	(1st Half)	
1982	4	83-79	.512	12	Sparky Anderson	1,636,058
1983	2	92-70	.568	6	Sparky Anderson	1,829,636
1984‡	1	104-58	.642	15	Sparky Anderson	2,704,794
1985	3	84-77	.522	15	Sparky Anderson	2,286,609
1986	3	87-75	.537	8.5	Sparky Anderson	1,899,437
1987†	1	98-64	.605	2	Sparky Anderson	2,061,830
1988	2	88-74	.543	1	Sparky Anderson	2,081,162
1989	7	59-103	.364	30	Sparky Anderson	1,543,656
1990	3	79-83	.488	9	Sparky Anderson	1,495,785
1991	T2	84-78	.519	7	Sparky Anderson	1,641,661
1992	6	75-87	.463	21	Sparky Anderson	1,423,963
1993	T3	85-77	.525	10	Sparky Anderson	1,971,421
1994	5	53-62	.461	18	Sparky Anderson	1,184,783
1995	4	60-84	.417	26	Sparky Anderson	1,180,979
1996	5	53-109	.327	39	Buddy Bell	1,168,610
1997	3	79-83	.488	19	Buddy Bell	1,365,157

American League Central

Year	Pos	W-L	Pct	GA/GB	Manager	Attendance
1998	5	65-97	.401	24	Buddy Bell Larry Parish*	1,409,391
1999	3	69-92	.429	27.5	Larry Parish	2,026,441
2000	3	79-83	.488	16	Phil Garner	2,533,752
2001	4	66-96	.407	25	Phil Garner	1,921,305
2002	5	55-106	.342	38.5	Phil Garner Luis Pujols	1,503,353

Totals	Seasons	W-L	Pct	Attendance
	102 Seasons	8,035-7,750	.505	113,538,584

*Interim manager
^AL Championships
‡World Championship
†Division title

ALL-TIME COACHES

Adair, Rick	1996-99	Kress, Red	1940
Alou, Felipe	2002	Landestoy, Rafael	2002
Appling, Luke	1960	Leifield, Lefty	1927-28
Baker, Del	1933-38	Lund, Don	1957-58
Bartell, Dick	1949-52	Lyons, Ted	1949-53
Blackburn, Wayne	1963-64	Matlack, Jon	1996
Bresnahan, Roger	1930-31	Madlock, Bill	2000-01
Bridges, Tommy	1946	Mansolino, Doug	2000-02
Brinkman, Ed	1979	McBride, George	1925-26, 1929
Brown, Gates	1978-84	McCatty, Steve	2002
Burke, Jimmy	1914-17	McGuire, Deacon	1911-16
Carisch, Fred	1923-24	Meyer, Benny	1928-30
Cavaretta, Phil	1961-63	Melvin, Bob	2000
Cluck, Bob	2003	Miller, Bing	1938-41
Coleman, Bob	1932	Mills, Art	1944-48
Consolo, Billy	1979-92	Moses, Wally	1967-70
Coombs, Jack	1920	Muffett, Billy	1985-94
Craig, Roger	1980-84	Mullin, Pat	1963-66
Cramer, Doc	1948	Myatt, George	1962-63
Cuccinello, Tony	1967-68	O'Neill, Steve	1941
Deal, Cot	1973-74	Ott, Ed	2001-02
Donovan, Bill	1918	Overmire, Stubby	1963-66
Dubuc, Jean	1930-31	Parrish, Lance	1999-01, 2003
Ens, Jewel	1932	Parrish, Larry	1997-98
Ezell, Glenn	1996	Perkins, Cy	1934-39
Ferrell, Rick	1950-53	Pinson, Vada	1985-91
Ferrick, Tom	1960-63	Pujols, Luis	2002
Fields, Bruce	2003	Resinger, Grover	1969-70
Fowler, Art	1971-73	Rettenmund, Merv	2002
Francona, Terry	1996	Roarke, Mike	1965-66, 1970
Gehringer, Charlie	1942	Roof, Gene	1992-95
Gibson, Kirk	2003	Rowe, Schoolboy	1954-55
Gladding, Fred	1976-78	Sain, Johnny	1967-69
Gordon, Joe	1956	Samuel, Juan	1999-
Grammas, Alex	1980-91	Schultz, Joe	1971-76
Grodzicki, Johnny	1979	Shaughnessy, Shag	1928
Hamilton, Steve	1975	Shea, Merv	1939-42
Harrah, Toby	1998	Shellenback, Jim	1946-47
Hatfield, Fred	1977-78	Silvera, Charlie	1971-73
Heffner, Don	1961	Skaff, Frank	1965-66, 1971
Hegan, Jim	1974-78	Sweeney, Bill	1947-48
Henrich, Tommy	1958-59	Swift, Bob	1953-54, 1963-66
Herndon, Larry	1992-98	Tighe, Jack	1942
Hill, Perry	1997-99	Tracewski, Dick	1972-95
Hitchcock, Billy	1955-60	Trammell, Alan	1999
Hopp, Johnny	1954	Treuel, Ralph	1995
Howley, Dan	1919, 1921-22	Vincent, Al	1943-44
Hudlin, Willis	1957-59	Warthen, Dan	1999-02
Jones, Jeff	1995, 1998-00, 02	White, Jo Jo	1960
Kendall, Fred	1996-98	Whitmer, Dan	1992-94
Kelleher, Mick	2003	Williams, Otto	1925

GAMES PLAYED, BY POSITION

Catcher	Games
Bill Freehan	1581
Oscar Stanage	1073
Lance Parrish	1039
Johnny Bassler	730
Ray Hayworth	643
Bob Swift	629
Birdie Tebbetts	620
Larry Woodall	484
Red Wilson	473
Boss Schmidt	447

First Base	Games
Norm Cash	1912
Hank Greenberg	1019
Rudy York	945
Lu Blue	894
Cecil Fielder	748
Tony Clark	681
Jason Thompson	602
Dave Bergman	582
George Burns	469
Dale Alexander	437

Second Base	Games
Lou Whitaker	2308
Charlie Gehringer	2206
Dick McAuliffe	918
Ralph Young	873
Damion Easley	794
Frank Bolling	779
Eddie Mayo	544
Germany Schaefer	483
Jerry Lumpe	446
Jerry Priddy	431

Shortstop	Games
Alan Trammell	2139
Donie Bush	1846
Billy Rogell	1148
Harvey Kuenn	747
Deivi Cruz	702
Dick McAuliffe	663
Charley O'Leary	634
Ed Brinkman	628
Johnny Lipon	590
Jackie Travener	537

Third Base	Games
Aurelio Rodriguez	1236
Don Wert	1036
Tom Brookens	979
Pinky Higgins	842
George Kell	826
Bob Jones	774
Travis Fryman	767
Marv Owen	717
George Moriarty	634
Bill Coughlin	591

Outfield	Games
Ty Cobb	2723
Al Kaline	2488
Sam Crawford	1906
Bobby Veach	1565
Harry Heilmann	1488
Mickey Stanley	1290
Jim Northrup	1190
Willie Horton	1179
Chet Lemon	1170
Bobby Higginson	1081
Pete Fox	934
Kirk Gibson	833
Matty McIntyre	786
Ron LeFlore	745
Hoot Evers	732
Gee Walker	714
Larry Herndon	696

Designated Hitter	Games
Rusty Staub	420
Kirk Gibson	296
Willie Horton	266
Darrell Evans	253
Cecil Fielder	237
Al Kaline	147
Dave Bergman	133
Gates Brown	132
Larry Herndon	120
Champ Summers	110

Pitcher	Games
John Hiller	545
Hooks Dauss	538
Mickey Lolich	508
Dizzy Trout	493
Mike Henneman	491
Hal Newhouser	460
George Mullin	435
Jack Morris	430
Tommy Bridges	424
Willie Hernandez	358

SINGLE SEASON BATTING LEADERS

Games Played

	G	Season
Rocky Colavito	163	1961
Jimmy Barrett	162	1904
Jake Wood	162	1961
Dick McAuiliffe	162	1964
Don Wert	162	1965
Ed Brinkman	162	1973
Rusty Staub	162	1978
Cecil Fielder	162	1991
Brian Hunter	162	1997

At-Bats

	AB	Season
Harvey Kuenn	679	1953
Ron LeFlore	666	1978
Jake Wood	663	1961
Travis Fryman	659	1992
Brian Hunter	658	1997
Harvey Kuenn	656	1954
Ron LeFlore	652	1977
Lou Whitaker	643	1983
Rusty Staub	642	1978
Charlie Gehringer	641	1936
George Kell	641	1950

Runs

	R	Season
Ty Cobb	147	1911
Ty Cobb	144	1915
Charlie Gehringer	144	1930
Charlie Gehringer	144	1936
Hank Greenberg	144	1938
Hank Greenberg	137	1937
Charlie Gehringer	134	1934
Charlie Gehringer	133	1937
Charlie Gehringer	133	1938
Lu Blue	131	1922
Charlie Gehringer	131	1929

Hits

	H	Season
Ty Cobb	248	1911
Harry Heilmann	237	1921
Ty Cobb	227	1912
Charlie Gehringer	227	1936
Ty Cobb	225	1917
Harry Heilmann	225	1925
George Kell	218	1950

Sam Crawford	217	1911
Ty Cobb	216	1909
Dale Alexander	215	1929
Charlie Gehringer	215	1929

Doubles

	2B	Season
Hank Greenberg	63	1934
Chalie Gehringer	60	1936
George Kell	56	1950
Gee Walker	55	1936
Harry Hielmann	50	1927
Charlie Gehringer	50	1934
Hank Greenberg	50	1940
Hank Greenberg	49	1937
Ty Cobb	47	1911
Charlie Gehringer	47	1930
Dale Alexander	47	1931

Triples

	3B	Season
Sam Crawford	26	1914
Sam Crawford	25	1903
Ty Cobb	24	1911
Ty Cobb	23	1912
Sam Crawford	23	1913
Ty Cobb	23	1917
Sam Crawford	21	1912
Ty Cobb	20	1908

Home Runs

	HR	Season
Hank Greenberg	58	1938
Cecil Fielder	51	1990
Rocky Colavito	45	1961
Hank Greenberg	44	1946
Cecil Fielder	44	1991
Hank Greenberg	41	1940
Norm Cash	41	1961
Hank Greenberg	40	1937
Darrell Evans	40	1985
Norm Cash	39	1962

Runs Batted In

	RBI	Season
Hank Greenberg	183	1937
Hank Greenberg	170	1935
Hank Greenberg	150	1940
Hank Greenberg	146	1938

Ty Cobb	144	1911
Rocky Colavito	140	1961
Harry Heilmann	139	1921
Hank Greenberg	139	1934
Dale Alexander	137	1929
Dale Alexander	135	1930

Eddie Yost	125	1960
Norm Cash	124	1961
Mickey Tettleton	122	1992
Eddie Lake	120	1947
Hank Greenberg	119	1938
Donie Bush	118	1915
Ty Cobb	118	1915

Extra-Base Hits

	XBH	Season
Hank Greenberg	103	1937
Hank Greenberg	99	1940
Hank Greenberg	98	1935
Hank Greenberg	96	1934
Charlie Gehringer	87	1936
Hank Greenberg	85	1938
Rudy York	85	1940
Dale Alexander	83	1929
Hank Greenberg	82	1939
Ty Cobb	79	1911

Total Bases

	TB	Season
Hank Greenberg	397	1937
Hank Greenberg	389	1935
Hank Greenberg	384	1940
Hank Greenberg	380	1938
Ty Cobb	367	1911
Harry Heilmann	365	1921
Dale Alexander	363	1929
Hank Greenberg	356	1934
Charlie Gehringer	356	1936
Norm Cash	354	1961

Batting Average

	AVG	Season
Ty Cobb	.420	1911
Ty Cobb	.410	1912
Harry Heilmann	.403	1923
Ty Cobb	.401	1922
Harry Heilmann	.398	1927
Harry Heilmann	.394	1921
Harry Heilmann	.393	1925
Ty Cobb	.390	1913
Ty Cobb	.389	1921
Ty Cobb	.385	1910

Walks

	BB	Season
Roy Cullenbine	137	1947
Eddie Yost	135	1959
Tony Phillips	132	1993

Strikeouts

	SO	Season
Cecil Fielder	182	1990
Rob Deer	175	1991
Melvin Nieves	158	1996
Melvin Nieves	157	1997
Dean Palmer	153	1999
Cecil Fielder	151	1991
Cecil Fielder	151	1992
Travis Fryman	149	1991
Dean Palmer	146	2000
Travis Fryman	144	1992
Tony Clark	144	1997

Slugging Percentage

	SLG	Season
Hank Greenberg	.683	1938
Hank Greenberg	.670	1940
Hank Greenberg	.668	1937
Norm Cash	.662	1961
Rudy York	.651	1937
Harry Heilmann	.632	1923
Hank Greenberg	.628	1935
Hank Greenberg	.622	1939
Ty Cobb	.621	1911
Harry Heilmann	.616	1927

Stolen Bases

	SB	Season
Ty Cobb	96	1915
Ty Cobb	83	1911
Ron LeFlore	78	1979
Ty Cobb	76	1909
Brian Hunter	74	1997
Ty Cobb	68	1916
Ron LeFlore	68	1978
Ty Cobb	65	1910
Ty Cobb	61	1912
Ron LeFlore	58	1976

Consecutive-Game Hitting Streaks

	Games	Season
Ty Cobb	40	1911
Ty Cobb	35	1917
John Stone	34	1930
Goose Goslin	30	1934
Ron LeFlore	30	1976
Dale Alexander	29	1930
Pete Fox	29	1935
Ron LeFlore	27	1978
Gee Walker	27	1937
Ty Cobb	25	1906
John Stone	25	1931

SINGLE SEASON PITCHING LEADERS

Games

	G	Season
Mike Myers	88	1997
Sean Runyan	88	1998
Mike Myers	83	1996
Willie Hernandez	80	1984
Willie Hernandez	74	1985
Richie Lewis	72	1996
Aurelio Lopez	71	1984
Danny Miceli	71	1997
Doug Brocail	70	1999
Fred Scherman	69	1971
Mike Henneman	69	1990
Matt Anderson	69	2000

Games Started

	GS	Season
Mickey Lolich	45	1971
George Mullin	44	1904
George Mullin	42	1907
Mickey Lolich	42	1973
George Mullin	41	1905
Denny McLain	41	1968
Denny McLain	41	1969
Mickey Lolich	41	1972
Joe Coleman	41	1974
Mickey Lolich	41	1974

Complete Games

	CG	Season
George Mullin	42	1904
Roscoe Miller	35	1901
George Mullin	35	1905
George Mullin	35	1906
George Mullin	35	1907
Wild Bill Donovan	34	1903
Ed Killian	33	1905
Dizzy Trout	33	1944
Ed Killian	32	1904
George Mullin	31	1903

Shutouts

Name	SHO	Season
Denny McLain	9	1969
Ed Killian	8	1905
Hal Newhouser	8	1945
George Mullin	7	1904
Dizzy Trout	7	1944
Billy Hoeft	7	1955

Innings Pitched

	IP	Season
George Mullin	382.1	1904
Mickey Lolich	376.0	1971
George Mullin	357.1	1907
Dizzy Trout	352.1	1944
George Mullin	347.2	1905
Denny McLain	336.0	1968
Roscoe Miller	332.0	1901
Ed Killian	331.2	1904
George Mullin	330.0	1972
Mickey Lolich	327.1	1972

Walks

	BB	Season
Joe Coleman	158	1974
Paul Foytack	142	1956
George Mullin	138	1905
Hal Newhouser	137	1941
George Mullin	131	1904
Howard Emhke	124	1920
Virgil Trucks	124	1949
Mickey Lolich	122	1969
Tommy Bridges	119	1932
Earl Whitehill	118	1931
Bobo Newsom	118	1941

Strikeouts

	SO	Season
Mickey Lolich	308	1971
Denny McLain	280	1968

Hal Newhouser	275	1946
Mickey Lolich	271	1969
Mickey Lolich	250	1972
Joe Coleman	236	1971
Jack Morris	232	1983
Mickey Lolich	230	1970
Mickey Lolich	226	1965
Jack Morris	223	1986

Wins

	W	Season
Denny McLain	31	1968
George Mullin	29	1909
Hal Newhouser	29	1944
Dizzy Trout	27	1944
Hal Newhouser	26	1946
Ed Killian	25	1907
Wild Bill Donovan	25	1907
Hal Newhouser	25	1945
Mickey Lolich	25	1971

Losses

	L	Season
George Mullin	23	1904
George Mullin	21	1905
Hooks Dauss	21	1920
Mickey Lolich	21	1974
Ed Killian	20	1904
George Mullin	20	1907
Bobo Newsom	20	1941
Art Houtteman	20	1952

Saves

	SV	Season
Todd Jones	42	2000
John Hiller	38	1973
Willie Hernandez	32	1984
Willie Hernandez	31	1985
Todd Jones	31	1997
Todd Jones	30	1999
Todd Jones	28	1998
Juan Acevedo	28	2002
Tom Timmerman	27	1970
Willie Hernandez	24	1986

Earned Run Average

	ERA*	Season
Ed Summers	1.64	1908
Ed Killian	1.71	1909
Ed Killian	1.78	1907
Hal Newhouser	1.81	1945
Ed Siever	1.91	1902
Hal Newhouser	1.94	1946
Denny McLain	1.96	1968
Harry Covelski	1.97	1916
Al Benton	2.02	1945
Wild Bill Donovan	2.08	1908

Earned Runs Allowed

	ER	Season
Mickey Lolich	142	1974
Joe Coleman	137	1974
Howard Ehmke	131	1922
Mickey Lolich	131	1973
Vic Sorrell	130	1929
Bobo Newsom	128	1941
Hooks Dauss	127	1923
Roxie Lawson	127	1937
Earl Whitehill	126	1929
Jack Morris	125	1990

Hits Allowed

	H	Season
George Mullin	346	1907
George Mullin	345	1904
Roscoe Miller	339	1901
Mickey Lolich	336	1971
Ed Siever	334	1901
Hooks Dauss	331	1923
George Mullin	315	1906
Mickey Lolich	315	1973
Dizzy Trout	314	1944
Mickey Lolich	310	1974

Home Runs Allowed

	HR	Season
Denny McLain	42	1966
Jack Morris	40	1986
Jack Morris	39	1987
Jim Bunning	38	1963
Mickey Lolich	38	1974
Jim Bunning	37	1959
Jack Morris	37	1982
Dan Petry	37	1983
Mickey Lolich	36	1971
Denny McLain	35	1967
Mickey Lolich	35	1973
Bill Gullickson	35	1992

*Minimum 1.0 innings pitched per game

CAREER BATTING LEADERS

Games Played

	G	Career
Al Kaline	2834	1953-74
Ty Cobb	2805	1905-26
Lou Whitaker	2390	1977-95
Chalie Gehringer	2323	1924-42
Alan Trammell	2293	1977-96
Sam Crawford	2114	1903-17
Norm Cash	2018	1960-74
Harry Heilmann	1991	1914, 1916-29
Donie Bush	1872	1908-21
Bill Freehan	1774	1961, 1963-76

At-Bats

	AB	Career
Ty Cobb	10591	1905-26
Al Kaline	10116	1953-74
Charlie Gehringer	8860	1924-42
Lou Whitaker	8570	1977-95
Alan Trammell	8288	1977-96
Sam Crawford	7984	1903-17
Harry Heilmann	7297	1914, 1916-29
Donie Bush	6970	1908-21
Norm Cash	6593	1960-74
Bill Freehan	6073	1961, 1963-76

Runs

	R	Career
Ty Cobb	2088	1905-26
Charlie Gehringer	1774	1924-42
Al Kaline	1622	1953-74
Lou Whitaker	1386	1977-95
Donie Bush	1242	1908-21
Alan Trammell	1231	1977-96
Harry Heilmann	1209	1914, 1916-29
Sam Crawford	1115	1903-17
Norm Cash	1028	1960-74
Hank Greenberg	980	1930, 1933-41, 1945-46

Hits

	H	Career
Ty Cobb	3900	1905-26
Al Kaline	3007	1953-74
Charlie Gehringer	2839	1924-42
Harry Heilmann	2499	1914, 1916-29
Sam Crawford	2466	1903-17
Lou Whitaker	2369	1977-95
Alan Trammell	2365	1977-96
Bobby Veach	1859	1912-23
Norm Cash	1793	1960-74
Donie Bush	1745	1908-21

Doubles

	2B	Career
Ty Cobb	665	1905-26
Charlie Gehringer	574	1924-42
Al Kaline	498	1953-74
Harry Heilmann	497	1914, 1916-29
Lou Whitaker	420	1977-95
Alan Trammell	412	1977-96
Sam Crawford	402	1903-17
Hank Greenberg	366	1930, 1933-41, 1945-46
Bobby Veach	345	1912-23
Harvey Kuenn	244	1952-59

Triples

	3B	Career
Ty Cobb	286	1905-26
Sam Crawford	249	1903-17
Charlie Gehringer	146	1924-42
Harry Heilmann	145	1914, 1916-29
Bobby Veach	136	1912-23
Al Kaline	75	1953-74
Donie Bush	73	1908-21
Dick McAuliffe	70	1960-73
Hank Greenberg	69	1930, 1933-41, 1945-46
Lu Blue	66	1921-27

Home Runs

	HR	Career
Al Kaline	399	1953-74
Norm Cash	373	1960-74
Hank Greenberg	306	1930, 1933-41, 1945-46
Willie Horton	262	1963-77
Cecil Fielder	245	1990-96
Lou Whitaker	244	1977-95
Rudy York	239	1934, 1937-45
Lance Parrish	212	1977-86
Bill Freehan	200	1961, 1963-76
Kirk Gibson	195	1979-87, 1993-95

Runs Batted In

	RBI	Career
Ty Cobb	1804	1905-26
Al Kaline	1583	1953-74
Harry Heilmann	1442	1914, 1916-29
Charlie Gehringer	1427	1924-42
Sam Crawford	1264	1903-17

Hank Greenberg	1202	1930, 1933-41, 1945-46
Norm Cash	1087	1960-74
Lou Whitaker	1084	1977-95
Bobby Veach	1042	1912-23
Alan Trammell	1003	1977-96

Extra-Base Hits

	XBH	Career
Ty Cobb	1063	1905-26
Al Kaline	972	1953-74
Charlie Gehringer	904	1924-42
Harry Heilmann	806	1914, 1916-29
Hank Greenberg	741	1930, 1933-41, 1945-46
Lou Whitaker	729	1977-95
Sam Crawford	723	1903-17
Norm Cash	654	1960-74
Alan Trammell	652	1977-96
Bobby Veach	540	1912-23

Total Bases

	TB	Career
Ty Cobb	5466	1905-26
Al Kaline	4852	1953-74
Charlie Gehringer	4257	1924-42
Harry Heilmann	3778	1914, 1916-29
Lou Whitaker	3651	1977-95
Sam Crawford	3576	1903-17
Alan Trammell	3442	1977-96
Norm Cash	3233	1960-74
Hank Greenberg	2950	1930, 1933-41, 1945-46
Bobby Veach	2653	1912-23

Batting Average

	AVG*	Career
Ty Cobb	.368	1905-26
Harry Heilmann	.343	1914, 1916-29
Bob Fothergill	.337	1922-30
George Kell	.326	1946-52
Heinie Manush	.321	1923-27
Charlie Gehringer	.320	1924-42
Hank Greenberg	.319	1930, 1933-41, 1945-46
Gee Walker	.317	1931-37
Harvey Kuenn	.314	1952-59
Barney McCosky	.312	1939-42, 1946

Walks

	BB	Career
Al Kaline	1277	1953-74
Lou Whitaker	1197	1977-95
Charlie Gehringer	1185	1924-42
Ty Cobb	1148	1905-26
Donie Bush	1125	1908-21
Norm Cash	1025	1960-74
Alan Trammell	850	1977-96
Dick McAuliffe	842	1960-73
Harry Heilmann	792	1914, 1916-29
Hank Greenberg	748	1930, 1933-41, 1945-46

Strikeouts

	SO	Career
Lou Whitaker	1099	1977-95
Norm Cash	1081	1960-74
Al Kaline	1020	1953-74
Willie Horton	945	1963-77
Dick McAuliffe	932	1960-73
Travis Fryman	931	1990-97
Kirk Gibson	930	1979-87, 1993-95
Cecil Fielder	926	1990-96
Alan Trammell	874	1977-96
Lance Parrish	847	1977-86

Slugging Percentage

	SLG*	Career
Hank Greenberg	.616	1930, 1933-41, 1945-46
Harry Heilmann	.518	1914, 1916-29
Ty Cobb	.517	1905-26
Rudy York	.503	1934, 1937-45
Tony Clark	.502	1995-2001
Rocky Colavito	.501	1960-63
Cecil Fielder	.498	1990-96
Norm Cash	.490	1960-74
Ray Boone	.482	1953-58
Bob Fothergill	.482	1922-30

Stolen Bases

	SB	Career
Ty Cobb	865	1905-26
Donie Bush	400	1908-21
Sam Crawford	317	1903-17
Ron LeFlore	294	1974-79
Alan Trammell	236	1977-96
Kirk Gibson	194	1979-87, 1993-95
George Moriarty	190	1909-15
Bobby Veach	189	1912-23
Charlie Gehringer	181	1924-42
Lou Whitaker	143	1977-95

*Minimum 2,000 At-Bats

CAREER PITCHING LEADERS

Games

	G	Career
John Hiller	545	1965-70, 1972-80
Hooks Dauss	538	1912-26
Mickey Lolich	508	1963-75
Dizzy Trout	493	1939-52
Mike Henneman	491	1987-95
Hal Newhouser	460	1939-53
George Mullin	435	1902-13
Jack Morris	430	1977-90
Tommy Bridges	424	1930-43, 1945-46
Willie Hernandez	358	1984-89

Games Started

	GS	Career
Mickey Lolich	459	1963-75
Jack Morris	408	1977-90
George Mullin	395	1902-13
Hooks Dauss	388	1912-26
Hal Newhouser	373	1939-53
Tommy Bridges	362	1930-43, 1945-46
Dizzy Trout	305	1939-52
Earl Whitehill	287	1923-32
Frank Lary	274	1954-64
Dan Petry	274	1979-87, 1990-91

Complete Games

	CG	Career
George Mullin	336	1902-13
Hooks Dauss	245	1912-26
Wild Bill Donovan	213	1903-12, 1918
Hal Newhouser	212	1939-53
Tommy Bridges	207	1930-43, 1945-46
Mickey Lolich	190	1963-75
Dizzy Trout	156	1939-52
Jack Morris	154	1977-90
Earl Whitehill	148	1923-32
Ed Killian	142	1904-10

Shutouts

	SHO	Career
Mickey Lolich	39	1963-75
George Mullin	34	1902-13
Tommy Bridges	33	1930-43, 1945-46
Hal Newhouser	33	1939-53
Wild Bill Donovan	29	1903-12, 1918
Dizzy Trout	28	1939-52
Denny McLain	26	1963-70

Jack Morris	24	1977-90
Hooks Dauss	22	1912-26
Virgil Trucks	20	1941-43, 1945-52, 1956
Frank Lary	20	1954-64

Innings Pitched

	IP	Career
George Mullin	3394	1902-13
Hooks Dauss	3391	1912-26
Mickey Lolich	3362	1963-75
Jack Morris	344	1977-90
Hal Newhouser	2944	1939-53
Tommy Bridges	2826	1930-43, 1945-46
Dizzy Trout	2592	1939-52
Earl Whitehill	2172	1923-32
Wild Bill Donovan	2139	1903-12, 1918
Frank Lary	2009	1954-64

Walks

	BB	Career
Hal Newhouser	1227	1939-53
Tommy Bridges	1192	1930-43, 1945-46
George Mullin	1106	1902-13
Jack Morris	1086	1977-90
Hooks Dauss	1067	1912-26
Mickey Lolich	1014	1963-75
Dizzy Trout	978	1939-52
Earl Whitehill	831	1923-32
Dan Petry	744	1979-87, 1990-91
Virgil Trucks	732	1941-43, 1945-52, 1956

Strikeouts

	SO	Career
Mickey Lolich	2679	1963-75
Jack Morris	1980	1977-90
Hal Newhouser	1770	1939-53
Tommy Bridges	1674	1930-43, 1945-46
Jim Bunning	1406	1955-63
George Mullin	1380	1902-13
Hooks Dauss	1201	1912-26
Dizzy Trout	1199	1939-52
Denny McLain	1150	1963-70
Wild Bill Donovan	1079	1903-12, 1918

Wins

	W	Career
Hooks Dauss	222	1912-26
George Mullin	209	1902-13

Mickey Lolich	207	1963-75
Hal Newhouser	200	1939-53
Jack Morris	198	1977-90
Tommy Bridges	194	1930-43, 1945-46
Dizzy Trout	161	1939-52
Wild Bill Donovan	141	1903-12, 1918
Earl Whitehill	133	1923-32
Frank Lary	123	1954-64

Losses

	L	Career
Hooks Dauss	182	1912-26
George Mullin	179	1902-13
Mickey Lolich	175	1963-75
Dizzy Trout	153	1939-52
Jack Morris	150	1977-90
Hal Newhouser	148	1939-53
Tommy Bridges	138	1930-43, 1945-46
Earl Whitehill	119	1923-32
Frank Lary	110	1954-64

Saves

	SV	Career
Mike Henneman	154	1987-95
Todd Jones	142	1997-2001
John Hiller	125	1965-70, 1972-80
Willie Hernandez	120	1984-89
Aurelio Lopez	85	1979-85
Terry Fox	55	1961-66
Al Benton	45	1938-42, 1945-48
Hooks Dauss	41	1912-26
Larry Sherry	37	1964-67
Fred Scherman	34	1969-73
Dizzy Trout	34	1939-52

Earned Run Average

	ERA*	Career
Harry Covelski	2.34	1914-18
Ed Killian	2.38	1904-10
Wild Bill Donovan	2.49	1903-12, 1918
Ed Siever	2.61	1901-02, 1906-08
George Mullin	2.76	1902-13
John Hiller	2.83	1965-70, 1972-80
Ed Willett	2.89	1906-13
Jean Dubuc	3.06	1912-16
Hal Newhouser	3.07	1939-53
Bernie Boland	3.09	1915-20

Earned Runs Allowed

	ER	Career
Mickey Lolich	1289	1963-75
Jack Morris	1262	1977-90
Hooks Dauss	1245	1912-26
Tommy Bridges	1122	1930-43, 1945-46
George Mullin	1042	1902-13
Earl Whitehill	1004	1923-32
Hal Newhouser	1003	1939-53
Dizzy Trout	922	1939-52
Vic Sorrell	828	1928-37
Dan Petry	787	1979-87, 1990-91

Hits Allowed

	H	Career
Hooks Dauss	3407	1912-26
George Mullin	3206	1902-13
Mickey Lolich	3093	1963-75
Jack Morris	2767	1977-90
Tommy Bridges	2675	1930-43, 1945-46
Hal Newhouser	2639	1939-53
Dizzy Trout	2504	1939-52
Earl Whitehill	2329	1923-32
Frank Lary	1975	1954-64
Wild Bill Donovan	1862	1903-12, 1918

Home Runs Allowed

	HR	Career
Mickey Lolich	329	1963-75
Jack Morris	321	1977-90
Jim Bunning	223	1955-63
Denny McLain	195	1963-70
Dan Petry	187	1979-87, 1990-91
Frank Tanana	182	1985-92
Tommy Bridges	181	1930-43, 1945-46
Frank Lary	180	1954-64
Paul Foytack	165	1953, 1955-63
Milt Wilcox	143	1977-85

*Minimun 1,000 innings pitched

YEAR-BY-YEAR BATTING LEADERS

1901

Category	Player	Mark
AVG	Kid Elberfeld	.310
Runs	Jimmy Barrett	110
Hits	Jimmy Barrett	159
2B	Ducky Holmes	28
3B	Kid Gleason	12
HR	Jimmy Barrett	4
	Ducky Holmes	
RBI	Kid Elberfeld	76
SB	Ducky Holmes	35

1902

Category	Player	Mark
AVG	Jimmy Barrett	.303
Runs	Jimmy Barrett	93
Hits	Jimmy Barrett	154
2B	Jimmy Barrett	19
3B	Dick Harley	8
HR	Doc Casey	3
RBI	Kid Elberfeld	64
SB	Jimmy Barrett	24

1903

Category	Player	Mark
AVG	Sam Crawford	.335
Runs	Jimmy Barrett	95
Hits	Sam Crawford	184
2B	Charlie Carr	23
	Sam Crawford	
3B	Sam Crawford	25*
HR	Sam Crawford	4
RBI	Sam Crawford	69
SB	Jimmy Barrett	27

1904

Category	Player	Mark
AVG	Jimmy Barrett	.268
Runs	Jimmy Barrett	83
Hits	Jimmy Barrett	167
2B	Sam Crawford	22
3B	Sam Crawford	16
HR	Three players	2
RBI	Sam Crawford	73
SB	Sam Crawford	20

1905

Category	Player	Mark
AVG	Sam Crawford	.297
Runs	Sam Crawford	73
Hits	Sam Crawford	171
2B	Sam Crawford	38
3B	Sam Crawford	10
HR	Sam Crawford	6
RBI	Sam Crawford	75
SB	Sam Crawford	22

1906

Category	Player	Mark
AVG	Sam Crawford	.295
Runs	Sam Crawford	65
Hits	Sam Crawford	166
2B	Sam Crawford	25
3B	Sam Crawford	16
HR	Four players	2
RBI	Sam Crawford	72
SB	Bill Coughlin	31
	Germany Schaefer	

1907

Category	Player	Mark
AVG	Ty Cobb	.350*
Runs	Sam Crawford	102*
Hits	Ty Cobb	212*
2B	Sam Crawford	34
3B	Sam Crawford	17
HR	Ty Cobb	5
RBI	Ty Cobb	116*
SB	Ty Cobb	49*

1908

Category	Player	Mark
AVG	Ty Cobb	.324*
Runs	Matty McIntyre	105*
Hits	Ty Cobb	188*
2B	Ty Cobb	36*
3B	Ty Cobb	20*
HR	Sam Crawford	7*
RBI	Ty Cobb	101*
SB	Germany Schaefer	40

1909

Category	Player	Mark
AVG	Ty Cobb	.377*
Runs	Ty Cobb	116*
Hits	Ty Cobb	216*
2B	Sam Crawford	35*
3B	Sam Crawford	14
HR	Ty Cobb	9*
RBI	Ty Cobb	115*
SB	Ty Cobb	76*

1910

Category	Player	Mark
AVG	Ty Cobb	.385*
Runs	Ty Cobb	106*
Hits	Ty Cobb	196
2B	Ty Cobb	35
3B	Sam Crawford	19*
HR	Ty Cobb	8
RBI	Sam Crawford	120*
SB	Ty Cobb	65

1911

Category	Player	Mark
AVG	Ty Cobb	.420*
Runs	Ty Cobb	147*
Hits	Ty Cobb	248*
2B	Ty Cobb	47*
3B	Ty Cobb	24*
HR	Ty Cobb	8
RBI	Ty Cobb	144*
SB	Ty Cobb	83*

1912

Category	Player	Mark
AVG	Ty Cobb	.410*
Runs	Ty Cobb	119
Hits	Ty Cobb	227*
2B	Ty Cobb	30
	Sam Crawford	
3B	Sam Crawford	23
HR	Ty Cobb	7
RBI	Sam Crawford	109
SB	Ty Cobb	61

1913

Category	Player	Mark
AVG	Ty Cobb	.390*
Runs	Donie Bush	98
Hits	Sam Crawford	193

2B	Sam Crawford	32
3B	Sam Crawford	23*
HR	Sam Crawford	9
RBI	Sam Crawford	83
SB	Ty Cobb	52

1914

Category	Player	Mark
AVG	Ty Cobb	.368*
Runs	Donie Bush	97
Hits	Sam Crawford	183
2B	Three players	22
3B	Sam Crawford	26*
HR	Sam Crawford	8
RBI	Sam Crawford	104*
SB	Donie Bush	35
	Ty Cobb	

1915

Category	Player	Mark
AVG	Ty Cobb	.369*
Runs	Ty Cobb	144*
Hits	Ty Cobb	208*
2B	Bobby Veach	40*
3B	Sam Crawford	19*
HR	G. Burns	5
RBI	Sam Crawford	112
	Bobby Veach	
SB	Ty Cobb	96*

1916

Category	Player	Mark
AVG	Ty Cobb	.371
Runs	Ty Cobb	113*
Hits	Ty Cobb	201
2B	Bobby Veach	33
3B	Bobby Veach	15
HR	Ty Cobb	5
RBI	Bobby Veach	91
SB	Ty Cobb	68*

1917

Category	Player	Mark
AVG	Ty Cobb	.383*
Runs	Donie Bush	112*
Hits	Ty Cobb	225*
2B	Ty Cobb	44*
3B	Ty Cobb	24*
HR	Bobby Veach	8
RBI	Bobby Veach	103*
SB	Ty Cobb	55*

1918

Category	Player	Mark
AVG	Ty Cobb	.382*
Runs	Ty Cobb	83
Hits	Ty Cobb	161
2B	Bobby Veach	21
3B	Ty Cobb	14*
HR	Harry Heilmann	5
RBI	Bobby Veach	78*
SB	Ty Cobb	34

1919

Category	Player	Mark
AVG	Ty Cobb	.384*
Runs	Ty Cobb	92
Hits	Ty Cobb	191^
	Bobby Veach	
2B	Bobby Veach	45*
3B	Bobby Veach	17*
HR	Harry Heilmann	8
RBI	Bobby Veach	101
SB	Ty Cobb	28

1920

Category	Player	Mark
AVG	Ty Cobb	.334
Runs	Bobby Veach	92
Hits	Bobby Veach	188
2B	Bobby Veach	39
3B	Bobby Veach	15
HR	Bobby Veach	11
RBI	Bobby Veach	113
SB	Donie Bush	15

1921

Category	Player	Mark
AVG	Harry Heilmann	.394*
Runs	Ty Cobb	124
Hits	Harry Heilmann	237*
2B	Harry Heilmann	43
	Bobby Veach	
3B	Ty Cobb	16
HR	Harry Heilmann	19
RBI	Harry Heilmann	139
SB	Ty Cobb	22

1922

Category	Player	Mark
AVG	Ty Cobb	.401
Runs	Lu Blue	131
Hits	Ty Cobb	211
2B	Ty Cobb	42
3B	Ty Cobb	16
HR	Harry Heilmann	21
RBI	Bobby Veach	126
SB	Topper Rigney	17

1923

Category	Player	Mark
AVG	Harry Heilmann	.403*
Runs	Harry Heilmann	121
Hits	Harry Heilmann	211
2B	Harry Heilmann	44
3B	Harry Heilmann	11
	Topper Rigney	
HR	Harry Heilmann	18
RBI	Harry Heilmann	115
SB	Fred Haney	12

1924

Category	Player	Mark
AVG	Harry Heilmann	.346
Runs	Ty Cobb	115
Hits	Ty Cobb	211
2B	Harry Heilmann	45^
3B	Harry Heilmann	16
HR	Harry Heilmann	10
RBI	Harry Heilmann	113
SB	Ty Cobb	23

1925

Category	Player	Mark
AVG	Harry Heilmann	.393*
Runs	Red Wingo	104
Hits	Harry Heilmann	225
2B	Harry Heilmann	40
	Frank O'Rourke	
3B	Ty Cobb	12
HR	Harry Heilmann	13
RBI	Harry Heilmann	133
SB	Lu Blue	19

1926

Category	Player	Mark
AVG	Heinie Manush	.378*
Runs	Heinie Manush	95
Hits	Heinie Manush	188
2B	Harry Heilmann	41
3B	Charlie Gehringer	17
HR	Heinie Manush	14
RBI	Harry Heilmann	103
SB	Lu Blue	13

1927

Category	Player	Mark
AVG	Harry Heilmann	.398*
Runs	Charlie Gehringer	110
Hits	Harry Heilmann	201
2B	Harry Heilmann	50
3B	Heinie Manush	18
HR	Harry Heilmann	14
RBI	Harry Heilmann	120
SB	Johnny Neun	22

1928

Category	Player	Mark
AVG	Harry Heilmann	.328
Runs	Charlie Gehringer	108
Hits	Charlie Gehringer	193
2B	Harry Heilmann	38
3B	Charlie Gehringer	16
HR	Harry Heilmann	14
RBI	Harry Heilmann	107
SB	Harry Rice	20

1929

Category	Player	Mark
AVG	Harry Heilmann	.344
Runs	Charlie Gehringer	131*
Hits	Dale Alexander	215
	Charlie Gehringer	
2B	Charlie Gehringer	45^
	Roy Johnson	
3B	Charlie Gehringer	19*
HR	Dale Alexander	25
RBI	Dale Alexander	137
SB	Charlie Gehringer	27*

1930

Category	Player	Mark
AVG	Charlie Gehringer	.330
Runs	Charlie Gehringer	144
Hits	Charlie Gehringer	201
2B	Charlie Gehringer	47
3B	Charlie Gehringer	15
HR	Dale Alexander	20
RBI	Dale Alexander	135
SB	Matty McManus	23*

1931

Category	Player	Mark
AVG	John Stone	.327
Runs	Roy Johnson	107
Hits	John Stone	191
2B	Dale Alexander	47
3B	Roy Johnson	19*
HR	John Stone	10
RBI	Dale Alexander	87
SB	Roy Johnson	33

1932

Category	Player	Mark
AVG	Gee Walker	.323
Runs	John Stone	106
Hits	Charlie Gehringer	184
2B	Charlie Gehringer	44
3B	Harry Davis	13
HR	Charlie Gehringer	19
RBI	John Stone	108
SB	Gee Walker	30

1933

Category	Player	Mark
AVG	Charlie Gehringer	.325
Runs	Charlie Gehringer	103
Hits	Charlie Gehringer	204
2B	Charlie Gehringer	42
	Billy Rogell	
3B	Pete Fox	13
HR	Charlie Gehringer	12
	Hank Greenberg	
RBI	Charlie Gehringer	105
SB	Gee Walker	26

1934

Category	Player	Mark
AVG	Charlie Gehringer	.356
Runs	Charlie Gehringer	134*
Hits	Charlie Gehringer	214*
2B	Hank Greenberg	63*
3B	Marv Owen	9
HR	Hank Greenberg	26
RBI	Hank Greenberg	139
SB	Jo Jo White	28

1935

Category	Player	Mark
AVG	Charlie Gehringer	.330
Runs	Charlie Gehringer	123
Hits	Hank Greenberg	203
2B	Hank Greenberg	46
3B	Hank Greenberg	16
HR	Hank Greenberg	36
RBI	Hank Greenberg	170*
SB	Jo Jo White	19

1936

Category	Player	Mark
AVG	Charlie Gehringer	.354
Runs	Charlie Gehringer	144
Hits	Charlie Gehringer	227
2B	Charlie Gehringer	60*
3B	Charlie Gehringer	12
HR	Goose Goslin	24
RBI	Goose Goslin	125
SB	Gee Walker	17

1937

Category	Player	Mark
AVG	Charlie Gehringer	.371*
Runs	Hank Greenberg	137
Hits	Gee Walker	213
2B	Hank Greenberg	49
3B	Hank Greenberg	14
HR	Hank Greenberg	40
RBI	Hank Greenberg	183*
SB	Gee Walker	23

1938

Category	Player	Mark
AVG	Hank Greenberg	.315
Runs	Hank Greenberg	144*
Hits	Pete Fox	186
2B	Pete Fox	35
3B	Pete Fox	10
HR	Hank Greenberg	58*
RBI	Hank Greenberg	146
SB	Pete Fox	16

1939

Category	Player	Mark
AVG	Charlie Gehringer	.325
Runs	Barney McCoskey	120
Hits	Barney McCoskey	190
2B	Hank Greenberg	42
3B	Barney McCoskey	14
HR	Hank Greenberg	33
RBI	Hank Greenberg	112
SB	Pete Fox	23

1940

Category	Player	Mark
AVG	Hank Greenberg	.340
Runs	Hank Greenberg	129
Hits	Pinky Higgins	161
2B	Hank Greenberg	50*
3B	Barney McCoskey	19*
HR	Hank Greenberg	41*
RBI	Hank Greenberg	150*
SB	Barney McCoskey	13

1941

Category	Player	Mark
AVG	Barney McCoskey	.324
Runs	Rudy York	91
Hits	Pinky Higgins	161
2B	Rudy York	29
3B	Bruce Campbell	10
HR	Rudy York	27
RBI	Rudy York	111
SB	Barney McCoskey	8

1942

Category	Player	Mark
AVG	Barney McCoskey	.293
Runs	Rudy York	81
Hits	Barney McCoskey	176
2B	Pinky Higgins	34
3B	Barney McCoskey	11
HR	Rudy York	21
RBI	Rudy York	90
SB	Barney McCoskey	11

1943

Category	Player	Mark
AVG	Dick Wakefield	.316
Runs	Dick Wakefield	91
Hits	Dick Wakefield	200*
2B	Dick Wakefield	38*
3B	Rudy York	11
HR	Rudy York	34*
RBI	Rudy York	118*
SB	Ned Harris / Joe Hoover	6

1944

Category	Player	Mark
AVG	Pinky Higgins	.297
Runs	Pinky Higgins	79
Hits	Doc Cramer	169
2B	Pinky Higgins	32
3B	Doc Cramer	9
HR	Rudy York	18
RBI	Rudy York	98
SB	Eddie Mayo	9

1945

Category	Player	Mark
AVG	Eddie Mayo	.285
Runs	Roy Cullenbine	80
Hits	Rudy York	157
2B	Roy Cullenbine	27
3B	Doc Cramer	8
HR	Roy Cullenbine	18
	Rudy York	
RBI	Roy Cullenbine	93
SB	Earl Webb	8

1946

Category	Player	Mark
AVG	George Kell	.327
Runs	Eddie Lake	105
Hits	Eddie Lake	149
2B	Hank Greenberg	29
3B	George Kell	9
HR	Hank Greenberg	44*
RBI	Hank Greenberg	127*
SB	Eddie Lake	15

1947

Category	Player	Mark
AVG	George Kell	.320
Runs	Eddie Lake	96
Hits	George Kell	188
2B	George Kell	29
3B	Eddie Lake	6
	Pat Mullin	
HR	Roy Cullenbine	24
RBI	George Kell	93
SB	Eddie Lake	11

1948

Category	Player	Mark
AVG	Hoot Evers	.314
Runs	Pat Mullin	91
Hits	Hoot Evers	169
2B	Hoot Evers	33
3B	Pat Mullin	11
HR	Pat Mullin	23
RBI	Hoot Evers	103
SB	Johnny Lipon	4

1949

Category	Player	Mark
AVG	George Kell	.343*
Runs	George Kell	97
Hits	Vic Wertz	185

2B	George Kell	38
3B	George Kell	9
HR	Vic Wertz	20
RBI	Vic Wertz	133
SB	George Kell	7
	Don Kolloway	

1950

Category	Player	Mark
AVG	George Kell	.340
Runs	George Kell	114
Hits	George Kell	218*
2B	George Kell	56*
3B	Hoot Evers	11^
HR	Vic Wertz	27
RBI	Vic Wertz	123
SB	Johnny Lipon	9

1951

Category	Player	Mark
AVG	George Kell	.319
Runs	George Kell	92
Hits	George Kell	191*
2B	George Kell	36^
3B	Pat Mullin	6
	Jerry Priddy	
HR	Vic Wertz	27
RBI	Vic Wertz	94
SB	George Kell	10

1952

Category	Player	Mark
AVG	Johnny Groth	.284
Runs	Walt Dropo	56
	Johnny Groth	
Hits	Johnny Groth	149
2B	Jerry Priddy	23
3B	Pat Mullin	5
HR	Walt Dropo	23
RBI	Walt Dropo	70
SB	Pat Mullin	4

1953

Category	Player	Mark
AVG	Harvey Kuenn	.308
Runs	Harvey Kuenn	94
Hits	Harvey Kuenn	209*
2B	Harvey Kuenn	33
3B	Harvey Kuenn	7
HR	Ray Boone	22
RBI	Walt Dropo	96
SB	Harvey Kuenn	6

1954

Category	Player	Mark
AVG	Harvey Kuenn	.306
Runs	Harvey Kuenn	81
Hits	Harvey Kuenn	201
2B	Harvey Kuenn	28
3B	Bill Tuttle	11
HR	Ray Boone	20
RBI	Ray Boone	85
SB	Al Kaline	9
	Harvey Kuenn	

1955

Category	Player	Mark
AVG	Al Kaline	.340*
Runs	Al Kaline	121
Hits	Al Kaline	200*
2B	Harvey Kuenn	38*
3B	Al Kaline	8
HR	Al Kaline	27
RBI	Ray Boone	116
SB	Earl Torgeson	9

1956

Category	Player	Mark
AVG	Harvey Kuenn	.332
Runs	Three players	96
Hits	Harvey Kuenn	196*
2B	Al Kaline	32
	Harvey Kuenn	
3B	Al Kaline	10
HR	Charlie Maxwell	28
RBI	Al Kaline	128
SB	Harvey Kuenn	9

1957

Category	Player	Mark
AVG	Al Kaline	.295
Runs	Al Kaline	83
Hits	Harvey Kuenn	173
2B	Harvey Kuenn	30
3B	Frank Bolling	6
HR	Charlie Maxwell	24
RBI	Al Kaline	90
SB	Al Kaline	11

1958

Category	Player	Mark
AVG	Harvey Kuenn	.319
Runs	Frank Bolling	91
Hits	Harvey Kuenn	179
2B	Harvey Kuenn	39*
3B	Gail Harris	8
HR	Gail Harris	20
RBI	Al Kaline	85
SB	Red Wilson	10

1959

Category	Player	Mark
AVG	Harvey Kuenn	.353*
Runs	Eddie Yost	115*
Hits	Harvey Kuenn	198*
2B	Harvey Kuenn	42*
3B	Harvey Kuenn	7
HR	Charlie Maxwell	31
RBI	Charlie Maxwell	95
SB	Al Kaline	10

1960

Category	Player	Mark
AVG	Al Kaline	.278
Runs	Eddie Yost	78
Hits	Al Kaline	153
2B	Al Kaline	29
3B	Charlie Maxwell	5
HR	Rocky Colavito	35
RBI	Rocky Colavito	87
SB	Al Kaline	19

1961

Category	Player	Mark
AVG	Norm Cash	.361*
Runs	Rocky Colavito	129
Hits	Norm Cash	193*
2B	Al Kaline	41*
3B	Jake Wood	14*
HR	Rocky Colavito	45
RBI	Rocky Colavito	140
SB	Jake Wood	30

1962

Category	Player	Mark
AVG	Billy Bruton	.278
Runs	Norm Cash	94
Hits	Rocky Colavito	164
2B	Rocky Colavito	30
3B	Al Kaline	6
HR	Norm Cash	39
RBI	Rocky Colavito	112
SB	Jake Wood	24

1963

Category	Player	Mark
AVG	Al Kaline	.312
Runs	Rocky Colavito	91
Hits	Al Kaline	172
2B	Rocky Colavito	29
3B	Billy Bruton	8
HR	Al Kaline	27
RBI	Al Kaline	101
SB	Jake Wood	18

1964

Category	Player	Mark
AVG	Bill Freehan	.300
Runs	Dick McAuliffe	85
Hits	Jerry Lumpe	160
2B	Al Kaline	31
3B	Bill Freehan	8
HR	Dick McAuliffe	24
RBI	Norm Cash	83
SB	Jake Wood	14

1965

Category	Player	Mark
AVG	Willie Horton	.273
Runs	Don Wert	81
Hits	Don Wert	159
2B	Norm Cash	23
3B	Dick McAuliffe	6
HR	Norm Cash	30
RBI	Willie Horton	104
SB	Jerry Lumpe	7

1966

Category	Player	Mark
AVG	Al Kaline	.288
Runs	Norm Cash	98
Hits	Norm Cash	168
2B	Al Kaline	29
3B	Dick McAuliffe	8
HR	Norm Cash	32
RBI	Willie Horton	100
SB	Don Wert	6

1967

Category	Player	Mark
AVG	Al Kaline	.308
Runs	Al Kaline	94
Hits	Bill Freehan	146
2B	Al Kaline	28
3B	Dick McAuliffe	7
HR	Al Kaline	25
RBI	Al Kaline	78
SB	Mickey Stanley	9

1968

Category	Player	Mark
AVG	Willie Horton	.285
Runs	Dick McAuliffe	95*
Hits	Jim Northrup	153
2B	Jim Northrup	29
3B	Dick McAuliffe	10
HR	Willie Horton	36
RBI	Jim Northrup	90
SB	Dick McAuliffe	8

1969

Category	Player	Mark
AVG	Jim Northrup	.295
Runs	Norm Cash	81
Hits	Jim Northrup	160
2B	Jim Northrup	31
3B	Dick McAuliffe	5
	Jim Northrup	
HR	Willie Horton	28
RBI	Willie Horton	91
SB	Mickey Stanley	8

1970

Category	Player	Mark
AVG	Al Kaline	.278
Runs	Mickey Stanley	83
Hits	Mickey Stanley	143
2B	Al Kaline	24
3B	Mickey Stanley	11
HR	Jim Northrup	24
RBI	Jim Northrup	80
SB	Mickey Stanely	10

1971

Category	Player	Mark
AVG	Al Kaline	.294
Runs	Norm Cash	72
	Jim Northrup	
Hits	Aurelio Rodriguez	153
2B	Aurelio Rodriguez	30
3B	Aurelio Rodriguez	7
HR	Norm Cash	32
RBI	Norm Cash	91
SB	Jim Northrup	7

1972

Category	Player	Mark
AVG	Jim Northrup	.261
Runs	Aurelio Rodriguez	65
Hits	Aurelio Rodriguez	142
2B	Aurelio Rodriguez	23
3B	Mickey Stanley	6
HR	Norm Cash	22
RBI	Norm Cash	61
SB	Tony Taylor	5

1973

Category	Player	Mark
AVG	Willie Horton	.316
Runs	Mickey Stanley	81
Hits	Mickey Stanley	147
2B	Aurelio Rodriguez	27
3B	Jim Northrup	7
HR	Norm Cash	19
RBI	Aurelio Rodriguez	58
AB	Tony Taylor	9

1974

Category	Player	Mark
AVG	Bill Freehan	.297
Runs	Gary Sutherland	60
Hits	Gary Sutherland	157
2B	Al Kaline	28
3B	Bill Freehan	5
	Aurelio Rodriguez	
HR	Bill Freehan	18
RBI	Al Kaline	64
SB	Ron LeFlore	23

1975

Category	Player	Mark
AVG	Willie Horton	.275
Runs	Ron LeFlore	66
Hits	Willie Horton	169
2B	Aurelio Rodriguez	20
3B	Ron LeFlore	6
	Aurelio Rodriguez	
HR	Willie Horton	25
RBI	Willie Horton	92
SB	Ron LeFlore	28

1976

Category	Player	Mark
AVG	Ron LeFlore	.316
Runs	Ron LeFlore	93
Hits	Rusty Staub	176
2B	Rusty Staub	28
3B	Ron LeFlore	8
HR	Jason Thompson	17
RBI	Rusty Staub	96
SB	Ron LeFlore	58

1977

Category	Player	Mark
AVG	Ron LeFlore	.325
Runs	Ron LeFlore	100
Hits	Ron LeFlore	212
2B	Rusty Staub	34
3B	Ron LeFlore	10
	Tito Fuentes	
HR	Jason Thompson	31
RBI	Jason Thompson	105
SB	Ron LeFlore	39

1978

Category	Player	Mark
AVG	Ron LeFlore	.297
Runs	Ron LeFlore	126*
Hits	Ron LeFlore	198
2B	Ron LeFlore	30
	Rusty Staub	
3B	Lou Whitaker	7
HR	Jason Thompson	26
RBI	Rusty Staub	121
SB	Ron LeFlore	68*

1979

Category	Player	Mark
AVG	Steve Kemp	.318
Runs	Ron LeFlore	110
Hits	Ron LeFlore	180
2B	Steve Kemp	26
	Lance Parrish	
3B	Ron LeFlore	10
HR	Steve Kemp	26
RBI	Steve Kemp	105
SB	Ron Leflore	78

1980

Category	Player	Mark
AVG	Alan Trammell	.300
Runs	Alan Trammell	107
Hits	Alan Trammell	168
2B	Lance Parrish	34
3B	Tommy Brookens	9
HR	Lance Parrish	24
RBI	Steve Kemp	101
SB	Rick Peters	13
	Alan Trammell	

1981

Category	Player	Mark
AVG	Kirk Gibson	.328
Runs	Steve Kemp	52
	Alan Trammell	
Hits	Steve Kemp	103
2B	Steve Kemp	18
	Lance Parrish	
3B	Three players	4
HR	Lance Parrish	10
RBI	Steve Kemp	49
SB	Kirk Gibson	17

1982

Category	Player	Mark
AVG	Larry Herndon	.292
Runs	Larry Herndon	92
Hits	Larry Herndon	179
2B	Alan Trammell	34
3B	Larry Herndon	13
HR	Lance Parrish	32
RBI	Larry Herndon	88
SB	Alan Trammell	19

1983

Category	Player	Mark
AVG	Lou Whitaker	.320
Runs	Lou Whitaker	94
Hits	Lou Whitaker	206
2B	Lance Parrish	42
3B	Kirk Gibson	9
	Larry Herndon	
HR	Lance Parrish	27
RBI	Lance Parrish	114
SB	Alan Trammell	30

1984

Category	Player	Mark
AVG	Alan Trammell	.314
Runs	Kirk Gibson	92
Hits	Alan Trammell	174
2B	Chet Lemon	34
	Alan Trammell	
3B	Kirk Gibson	10
HR	Lance Parrish	33
RBI	Lance Parrish	98
SB	Kirk Gibson	29

1985

Category	Player	Mark
AVG	Kirk Gibson	.287
Runs	Lou Whitaker	102
Hits	Lou Whitaker	170
2B	Kirk Gibson	37
3B	Lou Whitaker	8
HR	Darrell Evans	40*
RBI	Lance Parrish	98
SB	Kirk Gibson	30

1986

Category	Player	Mark
AVG	Alan Trammell	.277
Runs	Alan Trammell	107
Hits	Alan Trammell	159
2B	Alan Trammell	33
3B	Alan Trammell	7
HR	Darrell Evans	29
RBI	Darnell Coles	86
	Kirk Gibson	
SB	Kirk Gibson	34

1987

Category	Player	Mark
AVG	Alan Trammell	.343
Runs	Lou Whitaker	110
Hits	Alan Trammell	205
2B	Lou Whitaker	38
3B	Lou Whitaker	6
HR	Darrell Evans	34
RBI	Alan Trammell	105
SB	Kirk Gibson	26

1988

Category	Player	Mark
AVG	Alan Trammell	.311
Runs	Alan Trammell	73
Hits	Alan Trammell	145
2B	Chet Lemon	29
3B	Tommy Brookens	5
	Pat Sheridan	
HR	Darrell Evans	22
RBI	Alan Trammell	69
SB	Gary Pettis	44

1989

Category	Player	Mark
AVG	Gary Pettis	.257
Runs	Gary Pettis	77
	Lou Whitaker	
Hits	Lou Whitaker	128
2B	Lou Whitaker	21
3B	Gary Pettis	6

HR	Lou Whitaker	28
RBI	Lou Whitaker	85
SB	Gary Pettis	43

1990

Category	Player	Mark
AVG	Alan Trammell	.304
Runs	Cecil Fielder	104
Hits	Alan Trammell	170
2B	Alan Trammell	37
3B	Lloyd Moseby	5
	Tony Phillips	
HR	Cecil Fielder	51*
RBI	Cecil Fielder	132*
SB	Tony Phillips	19

1991

Category	Player	Mark
AVG	Tony Phillips	.284
Runs	Cecil Fielder	102
Hits	Cecil Fielder	163
2B	Travis Fryman	36
3B	Milt Cuyler	7
HR	Cecil Fielder	44
RBI	Cecil Fielder	133*
SB	Milt Cuyler	41

1992

Category	Player	Mark
AVG	Lou Whitaker	.278
Run	Tony Phillips	114*
Hits	Travis Fryman	175
2B	Tony Phillips	32
3B	Travis Fryman	4
HR	Cecil Fielder	35
RBI	Cecil Fileder	124*
SB	Gary Pettis	13

1993

Category	Player	Mark
AVG	Tony Phillips	.313
Runs	Tony Phillips	113
Hits	Travis Fryman	182
2B	Travis Fryman	37
3B	Milt Cuyler	7
HR	Mickey Tettleton	32
RBI	Cecil Fielder	117
SB	Tony Phillips	16

1994

Category	Player	Mark
AVG	Lou Whitaker	.301
Runs	Tony Phillips	91
Hits	Tony Phillips	123
2B	Travis Fryman	34
3B	Travis Fryman	5
	Juan Samuel	
HR	Cecil Fielder	28
RBI	Cecil Fielder	90
SB	Tony Phillips	13

1995

Category	Player	Mark
AVG	Travis Fryman	.275
Runs	Chad Curtis	96
Hits	Chad Curtis	157
2B	Chad Curtis	29
3B	Travis Fryman	5
	Bobby Higginson	
HR	Cecil Fielder	31
RBI	Cecil Fielder	82
SB	Chad Curtis	27

1996

Category	Player	Mark
AVG	Bobby Higginson	.320
Runs	Travis Fryman	90
Hits	Travis Fryman	165
2B	Bobby Higginson	35
3B	Curtis Pride	5
HR	Tony Clark	27
RBI	Travis Fryman	100
SB	Kimera Bartee	20

1997

Category	Player	Mark
AVG	Bobby Higginson	.299
Runs	Brian Hunter	112
Hits	Brian Hunter	177
2B	Damion Easley	37
3B	Brian Hunter	7
HR	Tony Clark	32
RBI	Tony Clark	117
SB	Brian Hunter	74

1998

Category	Player	Mark
AVG	Tony Clark	.291
Runs	Bobby Higginson	92

Hits	Tony Clark	175
2B	Damion Easley	38
3B	Luis Gonzalez	5
HR	Tony Clark	34
RBI	Tony Clark	103
SB	Brian Hunter	42

1999

Category	Player	Mark
AVG	Deivi Cruz	.284
Runs	Dean Palmer	92
Hits	Tony Clark	150
2B	Deivi Cruz	35
3B	Luis Polonia	8
HR	Dean Palmer	38
RBI	Dean Palmer	100
SB	Juan Encarnacion	33

2000

Category	Player	Mark
AVG	Deivi Cruz	.302
Runs	Bobby Higginson	104
Hits	Bobby Higginson	179
2B	Deivi Cruz	46
3b	Juan Encrnacion	6
HR	Bobby Higginson	30
RBI	Bobby Higginson	102
	Dean Palmer	
SB	Juan Encarnacion	16

2001

Category	Player	Mark
AVG	Roger Cedeno	.293
Runs	Bobby Higginson	84
Hits	Roger Cedeno	153
2B	Shane Halter	32
3B	Roger Cedeno	11
HR	Robert Fick	19
RBI	Tony Clark	75
SB	Roger Cedeno	55

2002

Category	Player	Mark
AVG	Omar Infante	.333
Runs	Robert Fick	66
Hits	Robert Fick	150
2B	Robert Fick	36
3B	Shane Halter	6
HR	Carlos Pena	19
RBI	Randall Simon	82
SB	George Lombard	13

*League leader
^Tied for league lead

Abbreviations:
AVG—Batting Average
2B—Doubles
3B—Triples
HR—Home Runs
RBI—Runs Batted In
SB—Stolen Bases

YEAR-BY-YEAR PITCHING LEADERS

1901

Category	Player	Mark
G	Roscoe Miller	38
	Ed Siever	
IP	Roscoe Miller	332.0
SHO	Roscoe Miller	3
SO	Ed Siever	85
W	Roscoe Miller	23
L	Ed Siever	15
	Jack Cronin	
ERA	Joe Yeager	2.61
SV	Roscoe Miller	1
	Joe Yeager	

1902

Category	Player	Mark
G	George Mullin	35
	Win Mercer	
IP	Win Mercer	281.2
SHO	Win Mercer	4
SO	George Mullin	78
W	Win Mercer	15
L	Win Mercer	18
ERA	Ed Siever	1.91*
SV	3 players	1

1903

Category	Player	Mark
G	George Mullin	41
IP	George Mullin	320.2
SHO	George Mullin	6
SO	Wild Bill Donovan	187
W	George Mullin	19
L	Wild Bill Donovan	16
	Frank Kitson	
ERA	George Mullin	2.25
SV	George Mullin	2

1904

Category	Player	Mark
G	George Mullin	45
IP	George Mullin	382.1
SHO	George Mullin	7
SO	George Mullin	161
W	Wild Bill Donovan	17
	George Mullin	
L	George Mullin	23

ERA	George Mullin	2.40
SV	Frank Kitson	1
	George Mullin	

1905

Category	Player	Mark
G	George Mullin	44
IP	George Mullin	347.2*
SHO	Ed Killian	8
SO	George Mullin	168
W	Ed Killian	23
L	George Mullin	21
ERA	Ed Killian	2.27
SV	Ed Killian	1
	Frank Kitson	

1906

Category	Player	Mark
G	George Mullin	40
IP	George Mullin	330.0
SHO	Red Donohue	3
SO	George Mullin	123
W	George Mullin	21
L	George Mullin	18
ERA	Ed Siever	2.71
SV	Ed Killian	2
	John Eubank	

1907

Category	Player	Mark
G	George Mullin	46
IP	George Mullin	357.1
SHO	George Mullin	5
SO	George Mullin	146
W	Wild Bill Donovan	25
	Ed Killian	
L	George Mullin	20
ERA	Ed Killian	1.78
SV	George Mullin	3

1908

Category	Player	Mark
G	Ed Summers	40
IP	Ed Summers	301.0
SHO	Wild Bill Donovan	6
SO	Wild Bill Donovan	141
W	Ed Summers	24
L	George Mullin	13

Category	Player	Mark
ERA	Ed Summers	1.64
SV	Four players	1

1909

Category	Player	Mark
G	Ed Willett	41
IP	George Mullin	303.2
SHO	Wild Bill Donovan	4
SO	George Mullin	124
W	George Mullin	29*
L	Ed Willett	10
ERA	Ed Killian	1.71
SV	Wild Bill Donovan	2
	Ralph Works	

1910

Category	Player	Mark
G	George Mullin	38
IP	George Mullin	289.0
SHO	George Mullin	5
SO	Wild Bill Donovan	107
W	George Mullin	21
L	George Mullin	12
	Ed Summers	
ERA	Wild Bill Donovan	2.42
SV	Frank Browning	3

1911

Category	Player	Mark
G	Ed Willett	38
IP	George Mullin	234.1
SHO	Ralph Works	3
SO	George Mullin	87
W	George Mullin	18
L	Ed Willett	14
ERA	George Mullin	3.07
SV	Five players	1

1912

Category	Player	Mark
G	Ed Willett	37
	Jean Dubuc	
IP	Ed Willett	284.1
SHO	Jean Dubuc	2
	George Mullin	
SO	Jean Dubuc	97
W	Ed Willett	17
	Jean Dubuc	
L	George Mullin	17
ERA	Jean Dubuc	2.77
SV	Jean Dubuc	3

1913

Category	Player	Mark
G	Jean Dubuc	36
IP	Jean Dubuc	242.2
SHO	Hooks Dauss	2
SO	Hooks Dauss	107
W	Jean Dubuc	15
L	Jean Dubuc	14
	Ed Willett	
ERA	Hooks Dauss	2.68
SV	Jean Dubuc	2

1914

Category	Player	Mark
G	Hooks Dauss	45
IP	Harry Covelski	303.1
SHO	Harry Covelski	5
SO	Hooks Dauss	150
W	Harry Covelski	21
L	Hooks Dauss	15
ERA	Harry Covelski	2.49
SV	Hooks Dauss	4

1915

Category	Player	Mark
G	Harry Covelski	50
IP	Harry Covelski	312.2
SHO	Jean Dubuc	5
SO	Hooks Dauss	112
W	Hooks Dauss	24
L	Harry Covelski	13
	Hooks Dauss	
ERA	Harry Covelski	2.45
SV	Three players	4

1916

Category	Player	Mark
G	Harry Covelski	44
IP	Harry Covelski	324.1
SHO	Harry Covelski	3
SO	Harry Covelski	108
W	Harry Covelski	21
L	Hooks Dauss	12
	Bill James	
ERA	Harry Covelski	1.97
SV	Hooks Dauss	4

1917

Category	Player	Mark
G	George Cunningham	44
IP	Hooks Dauss	270.2

SHO	Hooks Dauss	6
SO	Hooks Dauss	102
W	Hooks Dauss	17
L	Howard Ehmke	15
ERA	Bill James	2.09
SV	Bernie Boland	6

1918

Category	Player	Mark
G	Hooks Dauss	33
IP	Hooks Dauss	249.2
SHO	Bernie Boland	4
SO	Hooks Dauss	73
W	Bernie Boland	14
L	Hooks Dauss	16
ERA	Bernie Boland	2.65
SV	Hooks Dauss	3

1919

Category	Player	Mark
G	Bernie Boland	35
IP	Hooks Dauss	256.1
SHO	Dutch Leonard	4
SO	Dutch Leonard	102
W	Hooks Dauss	21
L	Bernie Boland	16
ERA	Dutch Leonard	2.77
SV	Four players	1

1920

Category	Player	Mark
G	Doc Ayers	46
IP	Hooks Dauss	270.1
SHO	Doc Ayers	3
	Dutch Leonard	
SO	Doc Ayers	103
W	Howard Ehmke	15
L	Hooks Dauss	21
ERA	Howard Ehmke	3.29
SV	Howard Ehmke	3

1921

Category	Player	Mark
G	Red Oldham	40
IP	Dutch Leonard	245.0
SHO	Four players	1
SO	Dutch Leonard	120
W	Howard Ehmke	13
L	Hooks Dauss	15
ERA	Dutch Leonard	3.75
SV	Jim Middleton	7

1922

Category	Player	Mark
G	Howard Ehmke	45
IP	Howard Ehmke	279.2
SHO	Herman Pillette	4
SO	Howard Ehmke	108
W	Herman Pillette	19
L	Howard Ehmke	17
ERA	Herman Pillette	2.85
SV	Hooks Dauss	4

1923

Category	Player	Mark
G	Hooks Dauss	50
IP	Hooks Dauss	316.0
SHO	Hooks Dauss	4
SO	Hooks Dauss	105
W	Hooks Dauss	21
L	Herman Pillette	19
ERA	Hooks Dauss	3.62
SV	Bert Cole	5

1924

Category	Player	Mark
G	Ken Holloway	49
IP	Earl Whitehill	233.0
SHO	Earl Whitehill	2
SO	Rip Collins	75
W	Earl Whitehill	17
L	Hooks Dauss	11
	Lil Stoner	
ERA	Rip Collins	3.21
SV	Hooks Dauss	6

1925

Category	Player	Mark
G	Ken Holloway	38
IP	Earl Whitehill	239.1
SHO	Hooks Dauss	1
	Earl Whitehill	
SO	Earl Whitehill	83
W	Hooks Dauss	16
L	Three players	11
ERA	Hooks Dauss	3.16
SV	Jesse Doyle	8

1926

Category	Player	Mark
G	Three players	36
IP	Earl Whitehill	252.1

SHO	Ed Wells	4
SO	Earl Whitehill	109
W	Earl Whitehill	16
L	Earl Whitehill	13
ERA	Sam Gibson	3.48
SV	Hooks Dauss	9

1927

Category	Player	Mark
G	Earl Whitehill	41
IP	Earl Whitehill	236.0
SHO	Earl Whitehill	3
SO	Earl Whitehill	95
W	Earl Whitehill	16
L	Earl Whitehill	14
ERA	Earl Whitehill	3.36
SV	Ken Holloway	6

1928

Category	Player	Mark
G	George Smith	39
IP	Ownie Carroll	231.0
SHO	Ownie Carroll	2
SO	Earl Whitehill	93
W	Ownie Carroll	16
L	Earl Whitehill	16
ERA	Ownie Carroll	3.27
SV	Elam Vangilder	5

1929

Category	Player	Mark
G	Earl Whitehill	38
IP	George Uhle	249.0
SHO	Five players	1
SO	Earl Whitehill	103
W	George Uhle	15
L	Ownie Carroll	17
ERA	George Uhle	4.08
SV	Lil Stoner	4

1930

Category	Player	Mark
G	Charlie Sullivan	40
IP	George Uhle	239.0
SHO	Vic Sorrell	2
SO	George Uhle	117
W	Earl Whitehill	17
L	Earl Whitehill	13
ERA	George Uhle	3.65
SV	Charlie Sullivan	5

1931

Category	Player	Mark
G	Three players	35
IP	Earl Whitehill	271.1
SHO	Tommy Bridges	2
	George Uhle	
SO	Tommy Bridges	105
W	Vic Sorrell	13
	Earl Whitehill	
L	Tommy Bridges	16
	Earl Whitehill	
ERA	George Uhle	3.50
SV	Chief Hogsett	2
	George Uhle	

1932

Category	Player	Mark
G	Chief Hogsctt	47
IP	Earl Whitehill	244.0
SHO	Tommy Bridges	4
SO	Tommy Bridges	108
W	Earl Whitehill	16
L	Vic Sorrell	14
ERA	Tommy Bridges	3.36
SV	Chief Hogsett	7

1933

Category	Player	Mark
G	Chief Hogsett	45
IP	Firpo Marberry	238.1
SHO	Tommy Bridges	2
SO	Tommy Bridges	120
W	Firpo Marberry	16
L	Vic Sorrell	15
	Carl Fischer	
ERA	Tommy Bridges	3.09
SV	Chief Hogsett	9

1934

Category	Player	Mark
G	Schoolboy Rowe	45
IP	Tommy Bridges	275.0
SHO	Tommy Bridges	3
	Schooldboy Rowe	
SO	Tommy Bridges	151
W	Schoolboy Rowe	24
L	Tommy Bridges	11
ERA	Eldon Auker	3.42
SV	Chief Hogsett	3
	Firpo Marberry	

1935

Category	Player	Mark
G	Schoolboy Rowe	42
IP	Schoolboy Rowe	275.2
SHO	Schoolboy Rowe	6
SO	Tommy Bridges	163
W	Tommy Bridges	21
L	Schoolboy Rowe	13
ERA	Tommy Bridges	3.51
SV	Chief Hogsett	5

1936

Category	Player	Mark
G	Schoolboy Rowe	41
	Roxie Lawson	
IP	Tommy Bridges	294.2
SHO	Tommy Bridges	5
SO	Tommy Bridges	175
W	Tommy Bridges	23*
L	Elden Auker	16
ERA	Tommy Bridges	3.60
SV	Four players	3

1937

Category	Player	Mark
G	Elden Auker	39
IP	Elden Auker	252.2
SHO	Tommy Bridges	3
SO	Tommy Bridges	138
W	Roxie Lawson	18
L	Tommy Bridges	12
ERA	Elden Auker	3.88
SV	Jack Russell	4

1938

Category	Player	Mark
G	Slick Coffman	39
IP	Vern Kennedy	190.1
SHO	Elden Auker	1
	George Gill	
SO	Tommy Bridges	101
W	Tommy Bridges	13
L	Elden Auker	10
ERA	George Gill	4.12
SV	Harry Eisenstat	4

1939

Category	Player	Mark
G	Al Benton	37
IP	Bobo Newsom	246.0
SHO	Tommy Bridges	2
	Bobo Newsom	
SO	Bobo Newsom	164
W	Tommy Bridges	17
	Bobo Newsom	
L	Schoolboy Rowe	12
ERA	Bobo Newsom	3.37
SV	Al Benton	5

1940

Category	Player	Mark
G	Al Benton	42
IP	Bobo Newsom	264.0
SHO	Bobo Newsom	3
SO	Bobo Newsom	164
W	Bobo Newsom	21
L	Al Benton	10
ERA	Bobo Newsom	2.83
SV	Al Benton	17

1941

Category	Player	Mark
G	Bobo Newsom	43
IP	Bobo Newsom	250.1
SHO	Bobo Newsom	2
SO	Bobo Newsom	175
W	Al Benton	15
L	Bobo Newsom	20*
ERA	Al Benton	2.97
SV	Al Benton	7

1942

Category	Player	Mark
G	Hal Newhouser	38
IP	Al Benton	226.2
SHO	Hal White	4
SO	Al Benton	110
W	Virgil Trucks	14
L	Dizzy Trout	18
ERA	Hal Newhouser	2.45
SV	Hal Newhouser	5

1943

Category	Player	Mark
G	Dizzy Trout	44
IP	Dizzy Trout	246.2
SHO	Dizzy Trout	5
SO	Hal Newhouser	144
W	Dizzy Trout	20
L	Hal Newhouser	17

ERA	Tommy Bridges	2.39
SV	Dizzy Trout	6

1944

Category	Player	Mark
G	Dizzy Trout	49
IP	Dizzy Trout	352.1*
SHO	Dizzy Trout	7
SO	Hal Newhouser	187
W	Hal Newhouser	29
L	Three players	14
ERA	Dizzy Trout	2.12*
SV	Johnny Gorsica	4

1945

Category	Player	Mark
G	Dizzy Trout	41
IP	Hal Newhouser	313.1*
SHO	Hal Newhouser	8
SO	Hal Newhouser	212
W	Hal Newhouser	25*
L	Dizzy Trout	15
ERA	Hal Newhouser	1.81*
SV	Stubby Overmire	4

1946

Category	Player	Mark
G	Dizzy Trout	38
IP	Hal Newhouser	292.2
SHO	Hal Newhouser	6
SO	Hal Newhouser	275
W	Hal Newhouser	26
L	Dizzy Trout	13
ERA	Hal Newhouser	1.94*
SV	George Caster	4

1947

Category	Player	Mark
G	Hal Newhouser	40
IP	Hal Newhouser	285.0
SHO	Three players	3
SO	Hal Newhouser	176
W	Fred Hutchinson	18
L	Hal Newhouser	17*
ERA	Hal Newhouser	2.87
SV	Al Benton	7

1948

Category	Player	Mark
G	Art Houtteman	43
	Virgil Trucks	
IP	Hal Newhouser	272.1
SHO	Hal Newhouser	2
	Dizzy Trout	
SO	Hal Newhouser	143
W	Hal Newhouser	21*
L	Art Houtteman	16
ERA	Hal Newhouser	3.01
SV	Art Houtteman	10

1949

Category	Player	Mark
G	Virgil Trucks	41
IP	Hal Newhouser	292.2
SHO	Virgil Trucks	6
SO	Virgil Trucks	153
W	Virgil Trucks	19
L	Hal Newhouser	11
	Virgil Trucks	
ERA	Virgil Trucks	2.81
SV	Virgil Trucks	4

1950

Category	Player	Mark
G	Hal White	42
IP	Art Houtteman	274.2
SHO	Art Houtteman	4
SO	Ted Gray	102
W	Art Houtteman	19
L	Hal Newhouser	13
ERA	Art Houtteman	3.54
SV	Three players	4

1951

Category	Player	Mark
G	Dizzy Trout	42
IP	Ted Gray	197.1
SHO	Fred Hutchinson	2
SO	Ted Gray	131
W	Virgil Trucks	13
L	Ted Gray	14
	Dizzy Trout	
ERA	Fred Hutchinson	3.68
SV	Dizzy Trout	5

1952

Category	Player	Mark
G	Hal White	41
IP	Ted Gray	224.0
SHO	Virgil Trucks	3

	Bill Wight	
SO	Ted Gray	138
W	Ted Gray	12
L	Art Houtteman	20*
ERA	Hal Newhouser	3.74
SV	Hal White	5

1953

Category	Player	Mark
G	Ray Herbert	43
IP	Ned Garver	198.1
SHO	Steve Gromek	1
SO	Ted Gray	115
W	Ned Garver	11
L	Ted Gray	15
ERA	Ned Garver	4.45
SV	Ray Herbert	6

1954

Category	Player	Mark
G	Ray Herbert	42
IP	Steve Gromek	252.2
SHO	Steve Gromek	4
	Billy Hoeft	
SO	Billy Hoeft	114
W	Steve Gromek	18
L	Steve Gromek	16
ERA	Steve Gromek	2.74
SV	George Zuverink	4

1955

Category	Player	Mark
G	Al Aber	39
IP	Frank Lary	235.0
SHO	Billy Hoeft	7
SO	Billy Hoeft	133
W	Billy Hoeft	16
L	Ned Garver	16
ERA	Billy Hoeft	2.99
SV	Three players	3

1956

Category	Player	Mark
G	Paul Foytack	43
IP	Frank Lary	294.0*
SHO	Billy Hoeft	4
SO	Paul Foytack	184
W	Frank Lary	21*
L	Billy Hoeft	14
ERA	Frank Lary	3.15
SV	Al Aber	7

1957

Category	Player	Mark
G	Jim Bunning	45
	Duke Maas	
IP	Jim Bunning	267.1*
SHO	Frank Lary	2
	Duke Maas	
SO	Jim Bunning	182
W	Jim Bunning	20
L	Frank Lary	16
ERA	Jim Bunning	2.69
SV	Duke Maas	6

1958

Category	Player	Mark
G	Hank Aguirre	44
IP	Frank Lary	260.1*
SHO	Jim Bunning	3
	Frank Lary	
SO	Jim Bunning	177
W	Frank Lary	16
L	Frank Lary	15
ERA	Frank Lary	2.90
SV	Hank Aguirre	5

1959

Category	Player	Mark
G	Tom Morgan	46
IP	Jim Bunning	249.2
SHO	Frank Lary	3
	Don Mossi	
SO	Jim Bunning	201
W	Three players	17
L	Paul Foytack	14
ERA	Don Mossi	3.36
SV	Tom Morgan	9

1960

Category	Player	Mark
G	Dave Sisler	41
IP	Frank Lary	274.1*
SHO	Jim Bunning	3
SO	Jim Bunning	201
W	Frank Lary	15
L	Frank Lary	15
ERA	Jim Bunning	2.79
SV	Hank Aguirre	10

1961

Category	Player	Mark
G	Hank Aguirre	45
IP	Frank Lary	275.1
SHO	Jim Bunning	4
	Frank Lary	
SO	Jim Bunning	194
W	Frank Lary	23
L	Jim Bunning	11
ERA	Don Mossi	2.96
SV	Terry Fox	12

1962

Category	Player	Mark
G	Ron Nischwitz	48
IP	Jim Bunning	258.0
SHO	Hank Aguirre	2
	Jim Bunning	
SO	Jim Bunning	184
W	Jim Bunning	19
L	Don Mossi	13
ERA	Hank Aguirre	2.21*
SV	Terry Fox	16

1963

Category	Player	Mark
G	Terry Fox	46
IP	Jim Bunning	248.1
SHO	Hank Aguirre	3
SO	Jim Bunning	196
W	Phil Regan	15
L	Hank Aguirre	15
ERA	Hank Aguirre	3.67
SV	Terry Fox	11

1964

Category	Player	Mark
G	Mickey Lolich	44
IP	Dave Wickersham	254.0
SHO	Mickey Lolich	6
SO	Mickey Lolich	192
W	Dave Wickersham	19
L	Dave Wickersham	12
ERA	Mickey Lolich	3.26
SV	Larry Sherry	11

1965

Category	Player	Mark
G	Fred Gladding	46
IP	Mickey Lolich	243.2
SHO	Denny Mclain	4
SO	Mickey Lolich	226
W	Denny McLain	16
L	Dave Wickersham	14
ERA	Denny McLain	2.61
SV	Terry Fox	10

1966

Category	Player	Mark
G	Larry Sherry	55
IP	Denny McLain	264.1
SHO	Denny McLain	4
SO	Denny McLain	192
W	Denny McLain	20
L	Mickey Lolich	14
ERA	Earl Wilson	2.59
SV	Larry Sherry	20

1967

Category	Player	Mark
G	Fred Gladding	42
IP	Earl Wilson	264.0
SHO	Mickey Lolich	6
SO	Earl Wilson	184
W	Earl Wilson	22
L	Denny McLain	16
ERA	Mickey Lolich	3.04
SV	Fred Gladding	12

1968

Category	Player	Mark
G	Pat Dobson	47
IP	Denny McLain	336.0*
SHO	Denny McLain	6
SO	Denny McLain	280
W	Denny McLain	31*
L	Earl Wilson	12
ERA	Denny McLain	1.96
SV	Pat Dobson	7
	Daryl Patterson	

1969

Category	Player	Mark
G	Pat Dobson	49
IP	Denny McLain	325.0*
SHO	Denny McLain	9
SO	Mickey Lolich	271
W	Denny McLain	24*
L	Mickey Lolich	11
ERA	Denny McLain	2.80
SV	Don McMahon	11

1970

Category	Player	Mark
G	Tom Timmerman	61
IP	Mickey Lolich	272.2
SHO	Mickey Lolich	3
SO	Mickey Lolich	230
W	Mickey Lolich	14
L	Mickey Lolich	19*
ERA	Mickey Lolich	3.79
SV	Tom Timmerman	27

1971

Category	Player	Mark
G	Fred Scherman	69
IP	Mickey Lolich	376.0*
SHO	Mickey Lolich	4
SO	Mickey Lolich	308
W	Mickey Lolich	25*
L	Mickey Lolich	14
ERA	Mickey Lolich	2.92
SV	Fred Scherman	20

1972

Category	Player	Mark
G	Chuck Seelbach	61
IP	Mickey Lolich	327.1
SHO	Mickey Lolich	4
SO	Mickey Lolich	250
W	Mickey Lolich	22
L	Mickey Lolich	14
	Joe Coleman	
ERA	Mickey Lolich	2.50
SV	Chuck Seelbach	14

1973

Category	Player	Mark
G	John Hiller	65
IP	Mickey Lolich	308.2
SHO	Mickey Lolich	3
SO	Mickey Lolich	214
W	Joe Coleman	23
L	Joe Coleman	15
ERA	Joe Coleman	3.53
SV	John Hiller	38

1974

Category	Player	Mark
G	John Hiller	59
IP	Mickey Lolich	308.0
SHO	Mickey Lolich	3
SO	Mickey Lolich	202
W	John Hiller	17
L	Mickey Lolich	21*
ERA	Mickey Lolich	4.15
SV	John Hiller	13

1975

Category	Player	Mark
G	John Hiller	36
	Tom Walker	
IP	Mickey Lolich	240.2
SHO	Vern Ruhle	3
SO	Mickey Lolich	139
W	Mickey Lolich	12
L	Joe Coleman	18
	Mickey Lolich	
ERA	Mickey Lolich	3.78
SV	John Hiller	14

1976

Category	Player	Mark
G	John Hiller	56
IP	Dave Roberts	252.0
SHO	Mark Fidrych	4
	Dave Roberts	
SO	John Hiller	117
W	Mark Fidrych	19
L	Dave Roberts	17
ERA	Mark Fidrych	2.34*
SV	John Hiller	13

1977

Category	Player	Mark
G	John Hiller	45
IP	Dave Rozema	218.1
SHO	Three players	1
SO	John Hiller	115
W	Dave Rozema	15
L	Fernando Arroyo	18
ERA	Dave Rozema	3.09
SV	Steve Foucault	13

1978

Category	Player	Mark
G	John Hiller	51
IP	Jim Slaton	233.2
SHO	Jack Billingham	4
SO	Milt Wilcox	132
W	Jim Slaton	17
L	Dave Rozema	12

	Milt Wilcox	
ERA	Dave Rozema	3.14
SV	John Hiller	15

1979

Category	Player	Mark
G	Aurelio Lopez	61
IP	Jack Morris	197.2
SHO	Jack Morris	1
	Dave Rozema	
SO	Jack Morris	113
W	Jack Morris	17
L	Milt Wilcox	10
ERA	Jack Morris	3.28
SV	Aurelio Lopez	21

1980

Category	Player	Mark
G	Aurelio Lopez	67
IP	Jack Morris	250.0
SHO	Dan Petry	3
SO	Jack Morris	112
W	Jack Morris	16
L	Jack Morris	15
ERA	Dan Petry	3.94
SV	Aurelio Lopez	21

1981

Category	Player	Mark
G	Kevin Saucier	38
IP	Jack Morris	198.0
SHO	Dan Petry	2
	Dave Rozema	
SO	Jack Morris	97
W	Jack Morris	14
L	Dan Petry	9
	Milt Wilcox	
ERA	Dan Petry	3.00
SV	Kevin Saucier	13

1982

Category	Player	Mark
G	Dave Tobik	51
IP	Jack Morris	266.1
SHO	Jack Morris	3
SO	Jack Morris	135
W	Jack Morris	17
L	Jack Morris	16
ERA	Dan Petry	3.22
SV	Dave Tobik	9

1983

Category	Player	Mark
G	Aurelio Lopez	57
IP	Jack Morris	293.2*
SHO	Dan Petry	2
	Milt Wilcox	
SO	Jack Morris	232
W	Jack Morris	20
L	Jack Morris	13
ERA	Jack Morris	3.34
SV	Aurelio Lopez	18

1984

Category	Player	Mark
G	Willie Hernandez	80
IP	Jack Morris	240.1
SHO	Dan Petry	2
SO	Jack Morris	148
W	Jack Morris	19
L	Jack Morris	11
ERA	Dan Petry	3.24
SV	Willie Hernandez	32

1985

Category	Player	Mark
G	Willie Hernandez	74
IP	Jack Morris	257.0
SHO	Jack Morris	4
SO	Jack Morris	191
W	Jack Morris	16
L	Dan Petry	13
ERA	Jack Morris	3.33
SV	Willie Hernandez	31

1986

Category	Player	Mark
G	Willie Hernandez	64
IP	Jack Morris	267.0
SHO	Jack Morris	6
SO	Jack Morris	223
W	Jack Morris	21
L	Walt Terrell	12
ERA	Jack Morris	3.27
SV	Willie Hernandez	24

1987

Category	Player	Mark
G	Mike Henneman	55
	Eric King	
IP	Jack Morris	266.0

SHO	Doyle Alexander	3
	Frank Tanana	
SO	Jack Morris	208
W	Jack Morris	18
L	Jack Morris	11
ERA	Jack Morris	3.38
SV	Eric King	9

1988

Category	Player	Mark
G	Mike Henneman	65
IP	Jack Morris	235.0
SHO	Jack Morris	2
	Jeff Robinson	
SO	Jack Morris	168
W	Jack Morris	15
L	Walt Terrell	16
ERA	Jeff Robinson	2.98
SV	Mike Henneman	22

1989

Category	Player	Mark
G	Mike Henneman	60
IP	Frank Tanana	223.2
SHO	Three players	1
SO	Frank Tanana	147
W	Mike Henneman	11
L	Doyle Alexander	18*
ERA	Frank Tanana	3.58
SV	Willie Hernandez	15

1990

Category	Player	Mark
G	Mike Henneman	69
IP	Jack Morris	249.2
SHO	Jack Morris	3
SO	Jack Morris	162
W	Jack Morris	15
L	Jack Morris	18
ERA	Jack Morris	4.51
SV	Mike Henneman	22

1991

Category	Player	Mark
G	Paul Gibson	68
IP	Bill Gullickson	226.1
SHO	Frank Tanana	2
	Walt Terrell	
SO	Frank Tanana	107
W	Bill Gullickson	20
L	Walt Terrell	14
ERA	Frank Tanana	3.77
SV	Mike Henneman	21

1992

Category	Player	Mark
G	Mike Munoz	65
IP	Bill Gullickson	221.2
SHO	Bill Gullickson	1
	David Haas	
SO	Frank Tanana	91
W	Bill Gullickson	14
L	Bill Gullickson	13
ERA	Bill Gullickson	4.34
SV	Mike Henneman	24

1993

Category	Player	Mark
G	Bob MacDonald	68
IP	Mike Moore	213.2
SHO	Mike Moore	3
SO	David Wells	139
W	John Doherty	14
L	John Doherty	11
ERA	David Wells	4.19
SV	Mike Henneman	24

1994

Category	Player	Mark
G	Joe Boever	46
IP	Tim Belcher	162.0
SHO	David Wells	1
SO	Tim Belcher	76
W	Mike Moore	11
L	Tim Belcher	15
ERA	David Wells	3.96
SV	Mike Henneman	8

1995

Category	Player	Mark
G	Jim Boever	60
IP	Felipe Lira	146.1
SHO	Sean Bergman	1
SO	Felipe Lira	89
W	David Wells	10
L	Mike Moore	15
ERA	David Wells	3.04
SV	Mike Henneman	18

1996

Category	Player	Mark
G	Mike Myers	83
IP	Felipe Lira	194.2
SHO	Felipe Lira	2
SO	Felipe Lira	113
W	Omar Olivares	7
L	Felipe Lira	14
ERA	Felipe Lira	5.22
SV	Gregg Olson	8

1997

Category	Player	Mark
G	Mike Myers	88
IP	Justin Thompson	223.1
SHO	Omar Olivares	2
SO	Justin Thompson	151
W	Willie Blair	16
L	Brian Moehler	12
ERA	Justin Thompson	3.02
SV	Todd Jones	31

1998

Category	Player	Mark
G	Sean Runyan	88
IP	Justin Thompson	222.0
SHO	Brian Moehler	3
SO	Justin Thompson	149
W	Brian Moehler	14
L	Justin Thompson	15
ERA	Brian Moehler	3.90
SV	Todd Jones	28

1999

Category	Player	Mark
G	Doug Brocail	70
IP	Brian Moehler	196.1
SHO	Brian Moehler	2
SO	Dave Mlicki	119
W	Dave Mlicki	14
L	Brian Moehler	16*
ERA	Dave Mlicki	4.60
SV	Todd Jones	30

2000

Category	Player	Mark
G	Matt Anderson	69
IP	Jeff Weaver	200.0
SHO	Steve Sparks	1
SO	Hideo Nomo	181
W	Brian Moehler	12
L	Hideo Nomo	12
ERA	Jeff Weaver	4.32
SV	Todd Jones	42

2001

Category	Player	Mark
G	Matt Anderson	62
IP	Steve Sparks	232.0
SHO	Steve Sparks	1
SO	Jeff Weaver	152
W	Steve Sparks	14
L	Jeff Weaver	16
ERA	Steve Sparks	3.65
SV	Matt Anderson	22

2002

Category	Player	Mark
G	Juan Acevedo	65
IP	Mark Redman	203.0
SHO	Andy Van Hekken	1
SO	Mark Redman	109
W	Mark Redman	8
	Steve Sparks	
L	Steve Sparks	16
ERA	Brian Moehler	2.29
SV	Juan Acevedo	28

*League leader

Abbreviations:
G—Games Played
IP—Innings Pitched
SHO—Shutouts
SO—Strikeouts
W—Wins
L—Losses
ERA—Earned Run Average
SV—Saves

NO-HITTERS

By Detroit

Date	Pitcher	Opponent	Location	Score
7/14/1912	George Mullin	St. Louis	Navin Field, Detroit	7-0
5/15/1952	Virgil Trucks	Washington	Briggs Stadium, Detroit	1-0
8/25/1952	Virgil Trucks	New York	Yankee Stadium, New York	1-0
7/20/1958	Jim Bunning	Boston	Fenway Park, Boston	3-0
4/7/1984	Jack Morris	Chicago	Comiskey Park, Chicago	4-0

By Opponents

Date	Pitcher	Team	Location	Score
9/20/1902	Jim Callahan	Chicago	Comiskey Park, Chicago	3-0
9/6/1905	Frank Smith	Chicago	Bennett Park, Detroit	15-0
8/30/1912	Earl Hamilton	St. Louis	Navin Field, Detroit	5-1
6/3/1919	Dutch Leonard	Boston	Navin Field, Detroit	5-0
4/30/1922	Charlie Robertson	Chicago	Navin Field, Detroit	2-0*
6/20/1948	Bob Lemon	Cleveland	Briggs Stadium, Detroit	2-0
7/1/1951	Bob Feller	Cleveland	Cleveland Stadium, Cleveland	2-1
4/30/1967	Steve Barber	Baltimore	Memorial Stadium, Baltimore	1-2^
	Stu Miller			
9/10/1967	Joel Horlen	Chicago	Comiskey Park, Chicago	6-0
4/27/1973	Steve Busby	Kansas City	Tiger Stadium, Detroit	3-0
7/15/1973	Nolan Ryan	California	Tiger Stadium, Detroit	6-0
6/20/1990	Randy Johnson	Seattle	Kingdome, Seattle	2-0

*Perfect game
^Tigers victory

Tigers' No-Hitter Box Scores

Detroit (AL) 7, vs. St. Louis 0
July 4, 1912
Pitcher: George Mullin

St. Louis	AB	R	H	O	A	Detroit	AB	R	H	O	A
Shotton, cf	1	0	0	4	1	Vitt, 3b	5	1	0	0	0
Jantzen, rf	3	0	0	1	0	Bush, ss	3	1	1	4	1
Kutina, 1b	4	0	0	7	1	Cobb, cf	4	1	3	6	0
Pratt, ss	4	0	0	3	4	Crawford, rf	3	1	1	2	0
LaPorte, 2b	3	0	0	2	1	Delahanty, lf	3	1	1	0	0
Austin, 3b	1	0	0	3	1	Moriarty, 1b	4	0	1	6	1
Hogan, lf	2	0	0	1	0	Louden, 2b	3	2	3	1	3
Compton, lf	1	0	0	0	0	Stanage, c	4	0	1	7	1
Stephens, c	3	0	0	3	4	Mullin, p	4	0	3	1	3
Adams, p	1	0	0	0	1	Totals	33	7	14	27	9
Hamilton, p	1	0	0	0	0						
a-Stovall	1	0	0	0	0						
Mitchell, p	0	0	0	0	0						
Totals	25	0	0	24	13						

a-Batted for Hamilton in 8th

Errors: Pratt, Louden, Stephens. Doubles: Mullin, Delahanty. Stolen bases: Vitt, Austin, Louden, Shotton. Sacrifices: Jantzen, Delahanty. Double plays: Mullin, Moriarty and Bush; Shotton, Pratt and Stephens; Stephens, Kutina and Stephens; Pratt and LaPorte. Left on base: St. Louis 4, Detroit 6. Bases on balls: Mullin 5, Adams 1, Hamilton 1. Strikeouts: Mullin 5, Adams 1. Hits: Off Adams, 5 in 4 innings; Off Hamilton 3 in 3 innings; Off Mitchell, 6 in 1 inning. Hit by pitch: by Adams (Crawford). Losing pitcher: Adams. Umpires: Dinneen and Sheridan. Time-2:05.

St. Louis	000	000	000	—0
Detroit	111	000	04x	—7

Detroit (AL) 1, vs. Washington 0
May 15, 1952
Pitcher: Virgil Trucks

Washington	AB	R	H	O	A
Yost, 3b	3	0	0	2	1
Busby, cf	3	0	0	3	0
Jensen, rf	4	0	0	2	0
Vernon, 1b	4	0	0	9	0
Runnels, ss	3	0	0	3	3
Coan, lf	3	0	0	2	0
Marsh, 2b	3	0	0	1	2
Kluttz, c	2	0	0	4	2
Porterfield, p	3	0	0	0	0
Totals	28	0	0	26*	8

Detroit	AB	R	H	O	A
Lipon, ss	4	0	0	1	4
Kell, 3b	3	0	1	1	2
Mullin, lf	4	0	0	3	0
Wertz, rf	3	1	2	1	0
Souchock, 1b	3	0	0	9	0
Ginsberg, c	3	0	0	7	0
Groth, cf	3	0	0	5	0
Priddy, 2b	3	0	0	0	1
Trucks, p	3	0	1	0	0
Totals	29	1	4	27	7

*Two out when winning run scored. Errors: Priddy 3. RBI: Wertz. Doubles: Wertz. Home run: Wertz. Left on base: Washington 4, Detroit 4. Bases on balls: Trucks 1, Porterfield 2. Stikeouts: Trucks 7, Potterfield 5. Runs and earned runs: Porterfield 1-1. Hit by pitch: By Trucks (Yost, Busby). Winner: Trucks (1-2). Loser: Porterfield (3-4). Umpires: Duffy, Summers and McKinley. Time-1:32.

Washington	000	000	000	—0
Detroit	000	000	001	—1

Detroit (AL) 1, at New York 0
August 25, 1952
Pitcher: Virgil Trucks

Detroit	AB	R	H	O	A
Groth, cf	4	0	0	2	0
Pesky, ss	4	0	0	2	1
Hatfield, 3b	3	0	1	2	0
Dropo, 1b	4	1	2	4	3
Souchock, rf	4	0	1	3	0
Delsing, lf	4	0	0	2	0
Batts, c	2	0	1	6	1
Federoff, 2b	3	0	0	1	1
Trucks, p	2	0	0	4	2
Totals	30	1	5	27	8

New York	AB	R	H	O	A
Mantle, cf	3	0	0	3	0
Collins, 1b	4	0	0	10	1
Bauer, rf	4	0	0	0	1
Berra, c	3	0	0	7	0
Woodling, lf	3	0	0	3	0
Babe, 3b	3	0	0	3	2
Martin, 2b	3	0	0	1	4
Rizzuto, ss	2	0	0	0	5
a-Mize	1	0	0	0	0
Brideweser, ss	0	0	0	0	0
Miller, p	1	0	0	0	1
b-Noren	1	0	0	0	0
Scarborough, p	0	0	0	0	0
Totals	28	0	0	27	14

a-Fouled out for Rizzuto in 8th
b-Flied out for Miller in 8th

Errors: Batts, Pesky. RBI: Souchock. 2B: Dropo. Sacrifice: Miller. Double play: Babe, Martin and Collins. Left on base: Detroit 5, New York 3. Bases on balls: Miller 2, Trucks 1. Strikeouts: Miller 7, Trucks 8. Hits: Off Miller, 4 in 8 innings; Scarborough, 1 in 1 inning. Runs and earned runs: Miller (Batts). Winner: Trucks (5-15). Loser: Miller (3-5). Umpires: Robb, Grieve, Honochick and Passarella. Time-2:03.

Detroit	000	000	100	—1
New York	000	000	000	—0

Detroit (AL) 3, at Boston 0
July 20, 1958
Pitcher: Jim Bunning

Detroit	AB	R	H	RBI	E
Kuenn, cf	4	0	2	1	0
Martin, ss	4	0	1	0	0
Kaline, rf	4	0	0	0	0
Harris, 1b	4	1	1	0	0
Zernial, lf	4	1	2	1	0
Broth, pr, lf	0	0	0	0	0
F. Bolling, 2b	4	0	0	0	0
Virgil, 3b	4	0	1	0	0
Wilson, c	4	1	1	1	0
Bunning, p	3	0	1	0	0
Totals	35	3	9	3	0

Boston	AB	R	H	RBI	E
Stephens, cf	2	0	0	0	1
Runnels, 2b	1	0	0	0	0
Lepcio, 2b	3	0	0	0	0
Williams, lf	4	0	0	0	0
Malzone, 3b	3	0	0	0	0
Jensen, rf	2	0	0	0	0
Gernert, 1b	3	0	0	0	0
Berberer, c	3	0	0	0	0
Consolo, ss	3	0	0	0	0
Sullivan, p	1	0	0	0	0
Keough, ph	1	0	0	0	0
Byerly, p	0	0	0	0	0
Klaus, ph	1	0	0	0	0
Bowsfield, p	0	0	0	0	0
Totals	27	0	0	0	1

Detroit	000	030	000	—3
Boston	000	000	000	—0

2B-Zernial, Kuenn. 3B-Harris. DP-Boston 1. LOB-Detroit 5, Boston 3.

	IP	H	R	ER	BB	SO
Bunning (W 8-6)	9	0	0	0	2	12
Sullivan (L 8-3)	6	6	3	3	0	4
Byerly	2	2	0	0	0	1
Bowsfield	1	1	0	0	0	0

HBP-By Bunning (Jensen). U-Umont, Summers, Honochick, Soar. Time-2:02. Attendance-29,529.

Detroit (AL) 4, at CHI White Sox 0
April 7, 1984
Pitcher: Jack Morris

Detroit	AB	R	H	RBI	E
Whitaker, 2b	4	0	1	1	0
Trammell, ss	4	0	1	0	0
Garbey, 1b	3	0	0	0	0
Bergman, 1b	1	0	0	0	0
Parrish, c	3	1	0	0	0
Herndon, lf	4	0	0	0	0
Allen, dh	3	0	0	0	0
Grubb, ph	1	0	0	0	0
Lemon, cf	4	2	2	2	0
Gibson, rf	1	1	1	1	0
Brookens, 3b	2	0	0	0	0
Totals	30	4	5	4	0

Chicago	AB	R	H	RBI	E
R. Law, cf	3	0	0	0	0
Dybzinski, ss	0	0	0	0	0
Fisk, c	3	0	0	0	0
Baines, rf	3	0	0	0	0
Luzinski, dh	2	0	0	0	0
Stegman, pr	0	0	0	0	0
Kittle, lf	4	0	0	0	0
Paciorek, 1b	3	0	0	0	0
V. Law, 3b	1	0	0	0	0
Walker, ph	1	0	0	0	0
Hulett, 3b	0	0	0	0	0
Fletcher, ss	2	0	0	0	0
Hairston, ph, cf	1	0	0	0	0
Cruz, 2b	3	0	0	0	0
Totals	26	0	0	0	0

Detroit	020	020	000	—4
Chicago	000	000	000	—0

2B-Lemon, Gibson. HR-Lemon. SB-R. Law, Trammell. SAC-Brookens. DP-Detroit 1, Chicago 1. LOB-Detroit 3, Chicago 5.

	IP	H	R	ER	BB	SO
Morris (W 2-0)	9	0	0	0	6	8
Bannister (L 0-1)	6	4	4	4	2	3
Brennan	2	1	0	0	1	3
Barojas	1	0	0	0	0	1

Time-2:44. Attendance-24,616.

MILESTONES

ML Pitching Triple Crown

Year	Pitcher	W	SO	ERA
1945	Hal Newhouser	25	212	1.81

20-Game Winners

Year	Pitcher	Record
1901	Roscoe Miller	23-13
1905	Ed Killian	23-14
	George Mullin	21-21
1906	George Mullin	21-18
1907	Wild Bill Donovan	25-4
	Ed Killian	25-13
	George Mullin	20-20
1908	Ed Summers	24-12
1909	George Mullin	29-9
	Edgar Willett	21-10
1910	George Mullin	21-12
1914	Harry Coveleski	22-12
1915	Hooks Dauss	24-13
	Harry Coveleski	22-13
1916	Harry Coveleski	21-11
1919	Hooks Dauss	21-9
1923	Hooks Dauss	21-13
1934	Schoolboy Rowe	24-8
	Tommy Bridges	22-11
1935	Tommy Bridges	21-10
1936	Tommy Bridges	23-11
1939	Bobo Newsom	20-11
1940	Bobo Newsom	21-5
1943	Dizzy Trout	20-12
1944	Hal Newhouser	29-9
	Dizzy Trout	27-14
1945	Hal Newhouser	25-9
1946	Hal Newhouser	26-9
1948	Hal Newhouser	21-12
1956	Frank Lary	21-13
	Billy Hoeft	20-14
1957	Jim Bunning	20-8
1961	Frank Lary	23-9
1966	Denny McLain	20-14
1967	Earl Wilson	22-11
1968	Denny McLain	31-6
1969	Denny McLain	24-9
1971	Mickey Lolich	25-14
	Joe Coleman	20-9
1972	Mickey Lolich	22-14
1973	Joe Coleman	23-15
1983	Jack Morris	20-13
1986	Jack Morris	21-8
1991	Bill Gullickson	20-9

20-Save Pitchers

Year	Pitcher	Saves
1966	Larry Sherry	20
1970	Tom Timmerman	27
1971	Fred Scherman	20
1973	John Hiller	38
1979	Aurelio Lopez	21
1980	Aurelio Lopez	21
1984	Willie Hernandez	34
1985	Willie Hernandez	31
1986	Willie Hernandez	24
1988	Mike Henneman	22
1990	Mike Henneman	22
1991	Mike Henneman	21
1992	Mike Henneman	24
1993	Mike Henneman	24
1997	Todd Jones	31
1998	Todd Jones	28
1999	Todd Jones	30
2000	Todd Jones	42
2001	Matt Anderson	22
2002	Juan Acevedo	28

30 Stolen Bases

Year	Player	SB
1901	Ducky Holmes	35
	Doc Casey	34
	Kid Gleason	32
1906	Bill Coughlin	31
	Germany Schaefer	31
1907	Ty Cobb	49
	Davy Jones	30
1908	Germany Schaefer	40
	Ty Cobb	39
1909	Ty Cobb	76
	Donie Bush	53
	George Moriarty	34
	Sam Crawford	30
1910	Ty Cobb	65
	Donie Bush	49
	George Moriarty	33
1911	Ty Cobb	83
	Donie Bush	40
	Sam Crawford	37

Year	Player	
1912	Ty Cobb	61
	Sam Crawford	41
	Donie Bush	35
1913	Ty Cobb	52
	Donie Bush	44
	George Moriarty	33
1914	Ty Cobb	35
	Donie Bush	35
	George Moriarty	34
1915	Ty Cobb	96
	Donie Bush	35
1916	Ty Cobb	68
1917	Ty Cobb	55
	Donie Bush	35
1918	Ty Cobb	34
1932	Gee Walker	30
1961	Jake Wood	30
1976	Ron LeFlore	58
1977	Ron LeFlore	39
1978	Ron LeFlore	68
1979	Ron LeFlore	78
1983	Alan Trammell	30
1985	Kirk Gibson	30
1986	Kirk Gibson	34
1988	Gary Pettis	44
1989	Gary Pettis	43
1991	Milt Cuyler	41
1997	Brian Hunter	74
1998	Brian Hunter	42
1999	Juan Encarnacion	33
2001	Roger Cedeno	55

30 Home Runs

Year	Player	HR
1935	Hank Greenberg	36
1937	Hank Greenberg	40
	Rudy York	35
1938	Hank Greenberg	58
	Rudy York	33
1939	Hank Greenberg	33
1940	Hank Greenberg	41
	Rudy York	33
1943	Rudy York	34
1946	Hank Greenberg	44
1959	Charlie Maxwell	31
1960	Rocky Colavito	35
1961	Rocky Colavito	45
	Norm Cash	41
1962	Norm Cash	39
	Rocky Colavito	37
1965	Norm Cash	30
1966	Norm Cash	32
1968	Willie Horton	36
1971	Norm Cash	32
1977	Jason Thompson	31
1982	Lance Parrish	32
1984	Lance Parrish	33
1985	Darrell Evans	40
1987	Darrell Evans	34
	Matt Nokes	32
1990	Cecil Fielder	51
1991	Cecil Fielder	44
	Mickey Tettleton	31
1992	Cecil Fielder	35
	Mickey Tettleton	32
	Rob Deer	32
1993	Mickey Tettleton	32
	Cecil Fielder	30
1995	Cecil Fielder	31
1997	Tony Clark	32
1998	Tony Clark	34
	Dean Palmer	38
	Tony Clark	31
2000	Bobby Higginson	30

100 Runs Batted In

Year	Player	RBI
1907	Ty Cobb	116
1908	Ty Cobb	101
1909	Ty Cobb	107
1910	Sam Crawford	120
1911	Ty Cobb	144
	Sam Crawford	115
1912	Sam Crawford	109
1914	Sam Crawford	104
1915	Sam Crawford	112
	Bobby Veach	112
1917	Bobby Veach	103
	Ty Cobb	102
1919	Bobby Veach	101
1920	Bobby Veach	113
1921	Harry Heilmann	139
	Bobby Veach	128
	Ty Cobb	101
1922	Bobby Veach	126
1923	Harry Heilmann	115
1924	Harry Heilmann	113
1925	Harry Heilmann	133
	Ty Cobb	102
1926	Harry Heilmann	103
1927	Harry Heilmann	120
	Bob Fothergill	114

1928	Harry Heilmann	107
1929	Dale Alexander	137
	Harry Heilmann	120
	Charlie Gehringer	106
1930	Dale Alexander	135
1932	John Stone	108
	Charlie Gehringer	107
1933	Charlie Gehringer	105
1934	Hank Greenberg	139
	Charlie Gehringer	127
	Billy Rogell	100
	Goose Goslin	100
1935	Hank Greenberg	170
	Goose Goslin	109
	Charlie Gehringer	108
1936	Goose Goslin	125
	Charlie Gehringer	116
	Al Simmons	112
	Marv Owen	105
1937	Hank Greenberg	183
	Gee Walker	113
	Rudy York	103
1938	Hank Greenberg	146
	Rudy York	127
	Charlie Gehringer	107
1939	Hank Greenberg	112
1940	Hank Greenberg	150
	Rudy York	134
1941	Rudy York	111
1943	Rudy York	118
1946	Hank Greenberg	127
1948	Hoot Evers	103
1949	Vic Wertz	133
1950	Vic Wertz	123
	Hoot Evers	103
	George Kell	101
1955	Ray Boone	116
	Al Kaline	102
1956	Al Kaline	128
1961	Rocky Colavito	140
	Norm Cash	132
1962	Rocky Colavito	112
1963	Al Kaline	101
1965	Willie Horton	104
1966	Willie Horton	100
1977	Jason Thompson	105
	Rusty Staub	101
1978	Rusty Staub	121
1979	Steve Kemp	105
1980	Steve Kemp	101
1983	Lance Parrish	114
1987	Alan Trammell	105
1990	Cecil Fielder	132

1991	Cecil Fielder	133
1992	Cecil Fielder	124
1993	Cecil Fielder	117
	Mickey Tettleton	110
1996	Travis Fryman	100
1997	Tony Clark	117
	Travis Fryman	102
	Bobby Higginson	101
1998	Tony Clark	103
	Damion Easley	100
1999	Dean Palmer	100
2000	Bobby Higginson	102
	Dean Palmer	102

AL Home Run Championship

Year	Player	HR
1908	Sam Crawford	7
1909	Ty Cobb	9
1935	Hank Greenberg	36^
1938	Hank Greenberg	58
1940	Hank Greenberg	41
1943	Rudy York	34
1946	Hank Greenberg	44
1985	Darrell Evans	40
1990	Cecil Fielder	51
1991	Cecil Fielder	44^

^Tied

AL Batting Championship

Year	Player	AVG
1907	Ty Cobb	.350
1908	Ty Cobb	.324
1909	Ty Cobb	.377
1910	Ty Cobb	.385
1911	Ty Cobb	.420
1912	Ty Cobb	.410
1913	Ty Cobb	.390
1914	Ty Cobb	.368
1915	Ty Cobb	.369
1917	Ty Cobb	.383
1918	Ty Cobb	.382
1919	Ty Cobb	.384
1921	Harry Heilmann	.394
1923	Harry Heilmann	.403
1925	Harry Heilmann	.393
1926	Heinie Manush	.378
1927	Harry Heilmann	.398
1937	Charlie Gehringer	.371

1949	George Kell	.343
1955	Al Kaline	.340
1959	Harvey Kuenn	.353
1961	Norm Cash	.361

| 1979 | Steve Kemp | .318 | 105 | 26 |
| 1998 | Tony Clark | .291 | 103 | 34 |

*AL Triple Crown

20-20 Club

Year	Player	HR	SB
1984	Kirk Gibson	27	29
1985	Kirk Gibson	29	30
1986	Kirk Gibson	28	34
1987	Kirk Gibson	24	26
	Alan Trammell	28	21
1995	Chad Curtis	21	27
1997	Damion Easley	22	28

Ironmen—Consecutive Games

Games	Player	Dates
511	Charlie Gehringer	9/3/27 to 5/7/31
504	Charlie Gehringer	6/25/32 to 8/11/35
458	Rocky Colavito	6/21/60 to 5/21/63
434	Ed Brinkman	9/26/71 to 8/9/74

Cycle Hitters

Player	Date	Innings
Bobby Veach	9/17/20	12
Bob Fothergill	9/26/26	9
Gee Walker	4/20/37	9
Charlie Gehringer	5/27/39	9
Vic Wertz	9/14/47	9
George Kell	6/2/50	9
Hoot Evers	9/7/50	10
Travis Fryman	7/28/93	9
Damion Easley	6/8/01	9

Club Hitting Triple Crown

Year	Player	BA	RBI	HR
1903	Sam Crawford	.335	89	4
1905	Sam Crawford	.297	75	6
1907	Ty Cobb	.350	116	5
1909*	Ty Cobb	.377	107	9
1911	Ty Cobb	.420	144	8
1921	Harry Heilmann	.394	139	19
1923	Harry Heilmann	.403	115	18
1924	Harry Heilmann	.346	113	10
1925	Harry Heilmann	.393	133	13
1927	Harry Heilmann	.398	120	14
1928	Harry Heilmann	.328	107	14
1933	Charlie Gehringer	.325	105	12
1938	Hank Greenberg	.315	146	58
1940	Hank Greenberg	.340	150	41
1963	Al Kaline	.312	101	27
1967	Al Kaline	.308	78	25
1975	Willie Horton	.275	92	25

INSIDE-THE-PARK HOME RUNS

Date	Player	Opponent	Location
5/10/12	Sam Crawford	Boston	Fenway Park, Boston
9/21/12	Sam Crawford	Boston	Navin Field, Detroit
6/24/17	Ty Cobb	St. Louis	Navin Field, Detroit
7/29/22	Bob Jones	Philadelphia	Navin Field, Detroit
6/8/27	Charlie Gehringer	Boston	Fenway Park, Boston
6/22/30 (Gm 2)	Charlie Gehringer	Boston	Fenway Park, Boston
6/4/36	Mickey Cochrane	Philadelphia	Shibe Park, Philadelphia
7/28/36	Goose Goslin	NY Yankees	Navin Field, Detroit
9/27/38 (Gm 1)	Mark Christman	St. Louis	Briggs Stadium, Detroit
9/27/38 (Gm 2)	Hank Greenberg	St. Louis	Briggs Stadium, Detroit
5/16/41	Pat Mullin	Philadelphia	Shibe Park, Philadelphia
4/19/49	Johnny Groth	CHI White Sox	Briggs Stadium, Detroit
6/23/50	Hoot Evers	NY Yankees	Briggs Stadium, Detroit
7/20/50	Pat Mullin	Boston	Fenway Park, Boston
6/18/55	Bill Tuttle	Baltimore	Memorial Stadium, Baltimore
4/17/56*	Frank Lary	KC Athletics	Briggs Stadium, Detroit
6/13/61	Norm Cash	Boston	Tiger Stadium, Detroit
4/29/62	Jake Wood	LA Angels	Tiger Stadium, Detroit
6/14/63	Jake Wood	NY Yankees	Yankee Stadium, New York
9/1/64	Jerry Lumpe	CHI White Sox	Comiskey Park, Chicago
9/30/64	Al Kaline	NY Yankees	Yankee Stadium, New York
5/5/65	Dick McAuliffe	CHI White Sox	Tiger Stadium, Detroit
7/9/65	Norm Cash	KC Athletics	Municipal Stadium, Kansas City
7/29/66	Willie Horton	KC Athletics	Municipal Stadium, Kansas City
5/20/67	Dick McAuliffe	NY Yankees	Tiger Stadium, Detroit
7/31/71	Willie Horton	California	Tiger Stadium, Detroit
9/12/71	Tony Taylor	Boston	Tiger Stadium, Detroit
5/27/75	Ron LeFlore	Minnesota	Tiger Stadium, Detroit
7/20/75	Ben Oglivie	KC Royals	Tiger Stadium, Detroit
6/2/76	Ben Oglivie	Milwaukee	Tiger Stadium, Detroit
7/25/77	Ron LeFlore	Toronto	Tiger Stadium, Detroit
9/4/77	Steve Kemp	Oakland	Tiger Stadium, Detroit
8/13/78	Lou Whitaker	CHI White Sox	Comiskey Park, Chicago
5/25/83	Kirk Gibson	Toronto	Exhibition Stadium, Toronto
8/24/83	Lou Whitaker	Texas	Arlington Stadium, Arlington
7/13/84	Lou Whitaker	Minnesota	Metrodome, Minneapolis
10/2/85	Kirk Gibson	Toronto	Tiger Stadium, Detroit
9/10/86	Mike Heath	Milwaukee	Tiger Stadium, Detroit
7/15/91	Lou Whitaker	Texas	Tiger Stadium, Detroit
7/6/97	Bobby Higginson	Baltimore	Tiger Stadium, Detroit
9/2/2000	Juan Gonzalez	Texas	Comerica Park, Detroit
5/11/2001	Damion Easley	Anaheim	Comerica Park, Detroit
8/10/2001	Shane Halter	KC Royals	Kauffman Stadium, Kansas City
6/14/2002	Wendell Magee	Arizona	Bank One Ballpark, Phoenix

*Opening Day

HONOR ROLL

BBWAA Awards

Chalmers Award (AL MVP from 1911-14)

Year	Player	Position
1911	Ty Cobb	OF

American League Most Valuable Player

Year	Player	Position
1934	Mickey Cochrane	C
1935	Hank Greenberg	1B
1937	Charlie Gehringer	2B
1940	Hank Greenberg	OF
1944	Hal Newhouser	LHP
1945	Hal Newhouser	LHP
1968	Denny McLain	RHP
1984	Willie Hernandez	LHP

Cy Young Award

Year	Player	Position
1968	Denny McLain*	RHP
1969	Denny McLain^	RHP
1984	Willie Hernandez	LHP

*Unanimous selection
^Tied

AL Rookie of the Year

Year	Player	Position
1953	Harvey Kuenn	SS
1976	Mark Fidrych	RHP
1978	Lou Whitaker	2B

AL Manager of the Year

Year	Manager
1984	Sparky Anderson
1987	Sparky Anderson

The Sporting News Awards

ML Player of the Year

Year	Player	Position
1945	Hal Newhouser	LHP
1968	Denny McLain	RHP

AL Most Valuable Player

Year	Player	Position
1935	Hank Greenberg	1B
1937	Charlie Gehringer	2B
1940	Hank Greenberg	OF
1945	Eddie Mayo	2B

AL Player of the Year

Year	Player	Position
1955	Al Kaline	OF
1963	Al Kaline	OF
1990	Cecil Fielder	1B

AL Pitcher of the Year

Year	Player	Position
1968	Denny McLain	RHP
1969	Denny McLain	RHP
1981	Jack Morris	RHP
1984	Willie Hernandez	LHP

AL Fireman of the Year

Year	Player	Position
1973	John Hiller	LHP

AL Rookie Pitcher of the Year

Year	Player	Position
1976	Mark Fidrych	RHP
1977	Dave Rozema	RHP
1987	Mike Henneman	RHP

ML Manager of the Year

Year	Manager
1950	Red Rolfe
1968	Mayo Smith

Executive of the Year

Year	Executive
1940	Walter O. Briggs, Sr.
1968	James A. Campbell

AL Silver Slugger Award

Year	Player	Position
1980	Lance Parrish	C
1982	Lance Parrish	C
	Lou Whitaker	2B
1983	Lance Parrish	C
	Lou Whitaker	2B
1984	Lance Parrish	C
	Lou Whitaker	2B
1985	Lou Whitaker	2B
1986	Lance Parrish	C
1987	Matt Nokes	C
	Alan Trammell	SS
	Lou Whitaker	2B
1988	Alan Trammell	SS

1990	Cecil Fielder	1B
	Alan Trammell	SS
1991	Mickey Tettleton	C
	Cecil Fielder	1B
1992	Mickey Tettleton	C
	Travis Fryman	SS
1998	Damion Easley	2B
1999	Dean Palmer	3B

Other Awards

Rawlings Gold Glove Award

Year	Player	Position
1957	Al Kaline	OF
1958	Frank Boling	2B
	Al Kaline	OF
1959	Al Kaline	OF
1961	Al Kaline	OF
	Frank Lary	P
1962	Al Kaline	OF
1963	Al Kaline	OF
1964	Al Kaline	OF
1965	Al Kaline	OF
	Bill Freehan	C
1966	Al Kaline	OF
	Bill Freehan	C
1967	Al Kaline	OF
	Bill Freehan	C
1968	Bill Freehan	C
	Mickey Stanley	OF
1969	Bill Freehan	C
	Mickey Stanley	OF
1970	Mickey Stanley	OF
1972	Ed Brinkman	SS
1973	Mickey Stanley	OF
1976	Aurelio Rodriguez	3B
1980	Alan Trammell	SS
1981	Alan Trammell	SS
1982	Lou Whitaker	2B
1983	Lance Parrish	C
	Alan Trammell	SS
1984	Lance Parrish	C
	Alan Trammell	SS
	Lou Whitaker	2B
1985	Lance Parrish	C
	Lou Whitaker	2B
1988	Gary Pettis	OF
1989	Gary Pettis	OF

Babe Ruth Award (World Series MVP)

Year	Player	Position
1968	Mickey Lolich	LHP
1984	Jack Morris	RHP

AL Championship Series MVP

Year	Player	Position
1984	Kirk Gibson	OF

Sport Magazine World Series MVP

Year	Player	Position
1968	Mickey Lolich	LHP
1984	Alan Trammell	SS

AL Rolaids Relief Man

Year	Player	Position
2000	Todd Jones#	RHP

#Tied

AL Comeback Player of the Year

Year	Player	Position
1965	Norm Cash	1B
1971	Norm Cash	1B
1973	John Hiller	LHP
1983	Alan Trammell	SS

Roberto Clemente Award

Year	Player	Position
1973	Al Kaline	OF

Joseph E. Cronin Trophy

Year	Player	Position
1974	Al Kaline	DH

Lou Gehrig Trophy

Year	Player	Position
1970	Al Kaline	OF

Hutch Award

Year	Player	Position
1970	Al Kaline	OF
1973	John Hiller	LHP

National Baseball Hall of Fame

Name	Position	With Detroit	Induction
Sparky Anderson	Mgr	1979-95	2000
Earl Averill	OF	1939-40	1975
Ed Barrow	Mgr	1903-04	1953
Jim Bunning	RHP	1955–63	1996
Ty Cobb	OF/Mgr	1905-26	1936
Mickey Cochrane	C/Mgr	1934-38	1947
Sam Crawford	OF	1903-17	1957
Larry Doby	OF	1959	1998
Charlie Gehringer	2B	1924-42	1949
Goose Goslin	OF	1934-37	1968
Hank Greenberg	1B/OF	1930, 1933-41, 1945-46	1956
Bucky Harris	2B/Mgr	1929-33,1955-56	1975

Harry Heilmann	OF	1914, 1916-30	1952
Waite Hoyt	RHP	1930-31	1969
Hughie Jennings	1B/Mgr	1907, 1909, 1912-20	1945
Al Kaline	OF	1953-74	1980
George Kell	3B	1946-52	1983
Heinie Manush	OF	1923-27	1964
Eddie Mathews	3B/1B	1967-68	1978
Hal Newhouser	LHP	1939-53	1992
Al Simmons	OF	1936	1953
Sam Thompson	OF	1906	1974
Ernie Harwell	Broadcaster	1960-2002	1981

(Ford C. Frick Award)

†With NL Detroit Wolverines

Retired Numbers‡

Player	No.	Date Retired
Al Kaline	6	8/17/1980
Charlie Gehringer	2	7/12/1983
Hank Greenberg	5	7/12/1983
Hal Newhouser	16	7/27/1997
Willie Horton	23	7/15/2000

‡Numbers were not put on uniforms in the major leagues until 1929.

Detroit Tigers Awards

Tiger of the Year
(Selected by the Detroit Chapter of the BBWAA)

Year	Player	Position
1965	Don Wert	3B
1966	Denny McLain	RHP
1967	Bill Freehan	C
1968	Denny McLain	RHP
1969	Denny McLain	RHP
1970	Tom Timmerman	RHP
1971	Mickey Lolich	LHP
1972	Ed Brinkman	SS
1973	John Hiller	LHP
1974	Al Kaline	DH
1975	Willie Horton	DH
1976	Mark Fidrych	RHP
1977	Ron LeFlore	OF
1978	Ron LeFlore	OF
1979	Steve Kemp	OF
1980	Alan Trammell	SS
1981	Kirk Gibson	OF
1982	Lance Parrish	C
1983	Lou Whitaker	2B
1984	Willie Hernandez	RHP
1985	Darrell Evans	1B
1986	Jack Morris	RHP
1987	Alan Trammell	SS
1988	Alan Trammell	SS
1989	Lou Whitaker	2B
1990	Cecil Fielder	1B
1991	Cecil Fielder	1B
1992	Cecil Fielder	1B
1993	Tony Phillips	OF
1994	Kirk Gibson	DH/OF
1995	Travis Fryman	3B
1996	Travis Fryman	3B/SS
1997	Tony Clark	1B
	Bobby Higginson	OF
1998	Damion Easley	2B
1999	Dean Palmer	3B
2000	Bobby Higginson	OF
2001	Steve Sparks	RHP
2002	Randall Simon	1B

Tiger Rookie of the Year
(Selected by the Detroit Sports Broadcasters Association)

Year	Player	Position
1969	Mike Kilkenny	LHP
1970	Elliott Maddox	3B/OF
1971	No Award	
1972	Chuck Seelbach	RHP
1973	Dick Sharon	OF
1974	Ron LeFlore	OF
1975	Vern Ruhle	RHP
1976	Mark Fidrych	RHP
1977	Dave Rozema	RHP
1978	Lou Whitaker	2B
1979	Lynn Jones	OF
1980	Rick Peters	OF
1981	No Award	
1982	Glenn Wilson	OF
1983	Dave Gumpert	RHP
1984	Barbaro Garbey	1B
1985	Nelson Simmons	OF
1986	Eric King	RHP
1987	Matt Nokes	C
1988	Paul Gibson	LHP
1989	Kevin Ritz	RHP
1990	Travis Fryman	SS
1991	Milt Cuyler	OF
1992	Scott Livingstone	3B
1993	Chris Gomez	SS
1994	Chris Gomez	SS
1995	Bobby Higginson	OF
1996	Tony Clark	1B
1997	Deivi Cruz	SS
1998	Matt Anderson	RHP
1999	Gabe Kapler	OF
2000	Jose Macias	2B/3B
2001	Victor Santos	RHP
2002	Carlos Pena	1B

TIGERS ALL-STAR GAME SELECTIONS

2002
Robert Fick

2001
Tony Clark

2000
Todd Jones

1999
Brad Ausmus

1998
Damion Easley

1997
Justin Thompson

1996
Travis Fryman

1995
David Wells

1994
Travis Fryman
Mickey Tettleton

1993
Cecil Fielder
Travis Fryman

1992
Travis Fryman

1991
Cecil Fielder*

1990
Cecil Fielder
Alan Trammell

1989
Mike Henneman‡

1988
Doyle Alexander‡
Alan Trammell†

1987
Jack Morris

Matt Nokes
Alan Trammell
Lou Whitaker†

1986
Willie Hernandez
Lance Parrish*
Lou Whitaker*

1985
Willie Hernandez‡
Jack Morris*
Lance Parrish*†
Dan Petry
Alan Trammell
Lou Whitaker*
Manager: Sparky Anderson

1984
Willie Hernandez
Chet Lemon*
Jack Morris
Lance Parrish*
Alan Trammell†
Lou Whitaker*

1983
Aurelio Lopez‡
Lance Parrish
Lou Whitaker

1982
Lance Parrish

1981
Jack Morris*

1980
Lance Parrish
Alan Trammell

1979
Steve Kemp

1978
Jason Thompson

1977
Mark Fidrych†
Jason Thompson‡

1976
Mark Fidrych*
Ron LeFlore*
Rusty Staub*

1975
Bill Freehan‡

1974
John Hiller‡
Al Kaline

1973
Ed Brinkman
Bill Freehan‡
Willie Horton

1972
Norm Cash
Bill Freehan*
Mickey Lolich

1971
Norm Cash*
Bill Freehan*
Al Kaline
Mickey Lolich

1970
Bill Freehan*
Willie Horton

1969
Bill Freehan*
Mickey Lolich‡
Denny McLain
Manager: Mayo Smith

1968
Bill Freehan*
Willie Horton*
Denny McLain
Don Wert

1967
Bill Freehan*
Al Kaline*†
Dick McAuliffe

1966
Norm Cash

Bill Freehan*
Al Kaline
Dick McAuliffe*
Denny McLain*

1965
Bill Freehan*
Willie Horton*
Al Kaline
Dick McAuliffe*

1964
Bill Freehan‡
Al Kaline†
Jerry Lumpe‡

1963
Jim Bunning
Al Kaline*

1962 (Game 2)
Hank Aguirre
Jim Bunning‡
Rocky Colavito
Al Kaline

1962 (Game 1)
Hank Aguirre‡
Jim Bunning
Rocky Colavito

1961 (Game 2)
Jim Bunning
Norm Cash*
Al Kaline

1961 (Game 1)
Jim Bunning
Norm Cash*
Al Kaline
Frank Lary

1960 (Game 2)
Al Kaline
Frank Lary

1960 (Game 1)
Al Kaline
Frank Lary

1959 (Game 2)
Al Kaline
Harvey Kuenn†

1959 (Game 1)
Jim Bunning
Al Kaline
Harvey Kuenn

1958
Al Kaline
Harvey Kuenn

1957
Jim Bunning*
Al Kaline*
Harvey Kuenn*
Charlie Maxwell

1956
Ray Boone
Al Kaline*
Harvey Kuenn*
Charlie Maxwell‡

1955
Billy Hoeft‡
Al Kaline*
Harvey Kuenn*

1954
Ray Boone*
Harvey Kuenn‡

1953
Harvey Kuenn

1952
Vic Wertz‡

1951
Fred Hutchinson
George Kell*
Vic Wertz

1950
Hoot Evers*
Ted Gray
Art Houtteman
George Kell*

1949
George Kell*
Virgil Trucks
Vic Wertz

1948
Hoot Evers*
George Kell‡
Pat Mullin*
Hal Newhouser

1947
George Kell*
Pat Mullin‡
Hal Newhouser*
Dizzy Trout‡

1946
Hal Newhouser
Manager: Steve O'Neill

1945
Hank Greenberg‡^

1944
Pinky Higgins
Hal Newhouser
Dizzy Trout‡
Rudy York‡

1943
Hal Newhouser
Dick Wakefield*
Rudy York

1942
Al Benton
Hal Newhouser‡
Birdie Tebbetts*
Rudy York*

1941
Al Benton‡
Birdie Tebbetts‡
Rudy York*
Manager: Del Baker

1940
Tommy Bridges‡
Hank Greenberg*
Bobo Newsom

1939
Tommy Bridges
Hank Greenberg*
Bobo Newsom‡

1938
Charlie Gehringer*
Hank Greenberg†
Vern Kennedy‡
Rudy York

1937
Tommy Bridges
Charlie Gehringer*
Hank Greenberg‡
Gee Walker†

1936
Tommy Bridges†
Charlie Gehringer*
Goose Goslin
Schoolboy Rowe

1935
Tommy Bridges‡
Mickey Cochrane‡
Charlie Gehringer*
Schoolboy Rowe‡
Manager: Mickey Cochrane

1934
Tommy Bridges‡
Mickey Cochrane
Charlie Gehringer*

1933
Charlie Gehringer*

*Voted to start or started
†Selected, but replaced due to injury
‡Selected, but did not appear in game
^No game was played, but teams were selected

Most All-Star Game Selections

18	Al Kaline
11	Bill Freehan
8	Harvey Kuenn
7	Jim Bunning
6	Tommy Bridges
	Charlie Gehringer
	Hal Newhouser
	Lance Parrish
	Alan Trammell
5	Norm Cash
	George Kell
	Rudy York
	Hank Greenberg
	Lou Whitaker
4	Travis Fryman
	Willie Horton
	Jack Morris
3	Willie Hernandez
	Frank Lary
	Denny McLain
	Vic Wertz
	Cecil Fielder

Tiger Pitchers With a Decision in an All-Star Game

Year	Pitcher	Decision	Final
1939	Tommy Bridges	W	AL 3, NL 1
1949	Virgil Trucks	W	AL 11, NL 7
1950	Ted Gray	L	NL 4, AL 3
1957	Jim Bunning	W	AL 6, NL 5
1963	Jim Bunning	L	NL 5, AL 3
1976	Mark Fidrych	L	NL 7, AL 1
1985	Jack Morris	L	NL 6, AL 1

All-Star Games at Detroit

Year	Winning Mgr/Losing Mgr	Attendance	Final
1941	Del Baker, Det./Bill McKechnie, Cin.	54,674	AL 7, NL 5
1951	Eddie Sawyer, Phi./Casey Stengel, NYY	52,075	NL 8, AL 3
1971	Earl Weaver, Bal./Sparky Anderson, Cin.	53,559	AL 6, NL 4

FIRST-YEAR PLAYER FIRST-ROUND DRAFT PICKS

Date	Player, Position	Selection	Date	Player, Position	Selection
6/65	Gene Lamont, C	13th	6/80	Glenn Wilson, IF	18th
1/66	Tim Marting, P	13th	1/81	Jeff Rutledge, IF	18th
6/66	Rick Konik, IF	14th	6/81	Ricky Barlow, P	17th
1/67	James Carter, IF	16th	1/82	Thor Edgell, P	19th
6/67	Jim Foor, P	15th	6/82	Richard Monteleone, P	20th
1/68	James Carter, IF	17th	1/83	Jon Leake, IF	16th
6/68	Bob Robinson, OF	18th	6/83	Wayne Dotson, P	15th
1/69	Ralph Edwards, IF	20th	1/84	Chuck McHugh, P	26th
6/69	Jim Baxley, IF	19th	6/84	Rob Souza, P	52nd
1/70	Jim Steele, IF	19th	1/85	Ken Williams, P	26th
6/70	Terry Mappin, C	20th	6/85	Randy Nosek, P	26th
1/71	Jim Cates, IF	12th	1/86	Jeff Cesari, P	17th
6/71	Tom Veryzer, IF	11th	6/86	Phil Clark, C	18th
1/72	Al Callis, P	19th	1/87	Bill Henderson, C	21st
6/72	Jerry Manuel, IF	20th	6/87	Steve Pegues, OF	21st
1/73	Steve Trella, P	20th	6/88	Rico Brogna, IF	26th
6/73	Charley Bates, IF	19th	6/89	Greg Gohr, P	21st
1/74	Randall Nall, OF	15th	6/90	Tony Clark, IF	2nd
6/74	Lance Parrish, C	16th	6/91	Justin Thompson, P	32nd
1/75	Tom Brookens, IF	4th	6/92	Rick Greene, P	16th
6/75	Les Filkins, OF	3rd	6/93	Matt Brunson, IF	9th
1/76	Steve Kemp, OF	1st	6/94	Cade Gaspar, P	18th
6/76	Pat Underwood, P	2nd	6/95	Mike Drumright, P	11th
1/77	Kevin Richards, P	5th	6/96	Seth Greisinger, P	6th
6/77	Ray Hampton, OF	6th	6/97	Matt Anderson, P	1st
1/78	Chris Codiroli, P	11th	6/98	Jeff Weaver, P	14th
6/78	Kirk Gibson, OF	12th	6/99	Eric Munson, C	3rd
1/79	Mike Camp, P	14th	6/00	Matt Wheatland, P	8th
6/79	Rick Leach, OF	13th	6/01	Kenny Baugh, P	11th
6/79	Chris Baker, OF	23rd	6/02	Scott Moore, SS	8th
1/80	Mike Laga, IF	17th			

POSTSEASON APPEARANCES

The Standings—1907 American League

	Team	W	L	PCT	GB
1.	Detroit	92	58	.613	-
2.	Philadelphia	88	57	.607	1.5
3.	Chicago	87	64	.576	5.5
4.	Cleveland	85	67	.559	8.0
5.	New York	70	78	.473	21.0
6.	St. Louis	69	83	.454	24.0
7.	Boston	59	90	.396	32.5
8.	Washington	49	102	.325	43.5

1907 World Series: Chicago Cubs (NL) vs. Detroit Tigers (AL)

Game	Winning/Losing Pitchers	Date	Score	Attendance
1	Tie	Oct. 8	Detroit 3, Chicago 3 (Tie)	24,377
2	Pfeister/Mullin	Oct. 9	Detroit 1, Chicago 3	21,901
3	Reulbach/Siever	Oct. 10	Detroit 1, Chicago 5	13,114
4	Overall/Donovan	Oct. 11	Chicago 6, Detroit 1	11,306
5	Brown/Mullin	Oct. 12	Chicago 2, Detroit 0	7,370

Final: Chicago 4, Detroit 0

The Standings—1908 American League

	Team	W	L	PCT	GB
1.	Detroit	90	63	.588	-
2.	Cleveland	90	64	.584	0.5
3.	Chicago	88	64	.579	1.5
4.	St. Louis	83	69	.546	6.5
5.	Boston	75	79	.487	15.5
6.	Philadelphia	68	85	.444	22.0
7.	Washington	67	85	.441	22.5
8.	New York	51	103	.331	39.5

1908 World Series: Chicago Cubs (NL) vs. Detroit Tigers (AL)

Game	Winning/Losing Pitchers	Date	Score	Attendance
1	Brown/Summers	Oct. 10	Chicago 10, Detroit 6	10,812
2	Overall/Donovan	Oct. 11	Detroit 1, Chicago 6	17,760
3	Mullin/Pfeister	Oct. 12	Detroit 8, Chicago 3	14,543
4	Brown/Summers	Oct. 13	Chicago 3, Detroit 0	12,915
5	Overall/Donovan	Oct. 14	Chicago 2, Detroit 0	6,210

Final: Chicago 4, Detroit 1

The Standings—1909 American League

	Team	W	L	PCT	GB
1.	Detroit	98	54	.645	_
2.	Philadelphia	95	58	.621	3.5
3.	Boston	88	63	.583	9.5
4.	Chicago	78	74	.513	20.0
5.	New York	74	77	.490	23.6
6.	Cleveland	71	82	.464	27.5
7.	St. Louis	61	89	.407	36.0
8.	Washington	42	110	.276	56.0

1909 World Series: Pittsburgh Pirates (NL) vs. Detroit Tigers (AL)

Game	Winning/Losing Pitchers	Date	Score	Attendance
1	Adams/Mullin	Oct. 8	Detroit 1, Pittsburgh 4	29,264
2	Donovan/Camnitz	Oct. 9	Detroit 7, Pittsburgh 2	30,915
3	Maddox/Summers	Oct. 11	Pittsburgh 8, Detroit 6	18,277
4	Mullin/Leifeld	Oct. 12	Pittsburgh 0, Detroit 5	17,036
5	Adams/Summers	Oct. 13	Detroit 4, Pittsburgh 8	21,706
6	Willis/Mullin	Oct. 14	Pittsburgh 4, Detroit 5	10,535
7	Adams/Donovan	Oct. 16	Pittsburgh 8, Detroit 0	17,562

Final: Pittsburgh 4, Detroit 3

The Standings—1934 American League

	Team	W	L	PCT	GB
1.	Detroit	101	53	.656	-
2.	New York	94	60	.610	7.0
3.	Cleveland	85	69	.552	16.0
4.	Boston	76	76	.500	24.0
5.	Philadelphia	68	82	.453	31.0
6.	St. Louis	67	85	.441	33.0
7.	Washington	66	86	.434	34.0
8.	Chicago	53	99	.349	47.0

1934 World Series: St. Louis Cardinals (NL) vs. Detroit Tigers (AL)

Game	Winning/Losing Pitchers	Date	Score	Attendance
1	D. Dean/Crowder	Oct. 3	St. Louis 8, Detroit 3	42,505
2	Rowe/W. Walker	Oct. 4	St. Louis 2, Detroit 3	43,451
3	D. Dean/Bridges	Oct. 5	Detroit 1, St. Louis 4	34,073
4	Auker/W. Walker	Oct. 6	Detroit 10, St. Louis 4	37,492
5	Bridges/D. Dean	Oct. 7	Detroit 3, St. Louis 1	38,536
6	P. Dean/Rowe	Oct. 8	St. Louis 4, Detroit 3	44,551
7	D. Dean/Auker	Oct. 9	St. Louis 11, Detroit 0	40,902

Final: St. Louis 4, Detroit 3

The Standings—1935 American League

	Team	W	L	PCT	GB
1.	Detroit	93	58	.616	-
2.	New York	89	60	.597	3.0
3.	Cleveland	82	71	.536	12.0
4.	Boston	78	75	.510	16.0
5.	Chicago	74	78	.487	19.5
6.	Washington	67	86	.438	27.0
7.	St. Louis	65	87	.428	28.5
8.	Philadelphia	58	91	.389	34.0

1935 World Series: Detroit Tigers (AL) vs. Chicago Cubs (NL)

Game	Winning/Losing Pitchers	Date	Score	Attendance
1	Warneke/Rowe	Oct. 2	Chicago 3, Detroit 0	47,391
2	Bridges/Root	Oct. 3	Chicago 3, Detroit 8	46,742
3	Rowe/French	Oct. 4	Detroit 6, Chicago 5 (11 inn)	45,532
4	Crowder/Carleton	Oct. 5	Detroit 2, Chicago 1	49,350
5	Warneke/Rowe	Oct. 6	Detroit 1, Chicago 3	49,237
6	Bridges/French	Oct. 7	Chicago 3, Detroit 4	48,420

Final: Detroit 4, Chicago 2

The Standings—1940 American League

	Team	W	L	PCT	GB
1.	Detroit	90	64	.584	-
2.	Cleveland	89	65	.578	1.0
3.	New York	88	66	.571	2.0
4T.	Boston	82	72	.532	8.0
4T.	Chicago	82	72	.532	8.0
6.	St. Louis	67	87	.435	23.0
7.	Washington	64	90	.416	26.0
8.	Philadelphia	54	100	.351	36.0

1940 World Series: Cincinnati Reds (NL) vs. Detroit Tigers (AL)

Game	Winning/Losing Pitchers	Date	Score	Attendance
1	Newsom/Derringer	Oct. 2	Detroit 7, Cincinnati 2	31,793
2	Walters/Rowe	Oct. 3	Detroit 3, Cincinnati 5	30,640
3	Bridges/Turner	Oct. 4	Cincinnati 10, Detroit 13	52,877
4	Derringer/Trout	Oct. 5	Cincinnati 5, Detroit 2	54,093
5	Newsom/Thompson	Oct. 6	Cincinnati 0, Detroit 8	55,189
6	Walters/Rowe	Oct. 7	Detroit 0, Cincinnati 4	30,481
7	Derringer/Newsom	Oct. 8	Detroit 1, Cincinnati 2	26,854

Final: Cincinnati 4, Detroit 3

The Standings—1945 American League

	Team	W	L	PCT	GB
1.	Detroit	88	65	.575	-
2.	Washington	87	67	.565	1.5
3.	St. Louis	81	70	.536	6.0
4.	New York	81	71	.533	6.5
5.	Cleveland	73	72	.503	11.0
6.	Chicago	71	78	.477	15.0
7.	Boston	71	83	.461	17.5
8.	Philadelphia	52	98	.347	34.5

1945 World Series: Detroit Tigers (AL) vs. Chicago Cubs (NL)

Game	Winning/Losing Pitchers	Date	Score	Attendance
1	Borowy/Newhouser	Oct. 3	Chicago 9, Detroit 0	54,637
2	Trucks/Wyse	Oct. 4	Chicago 1, Detroit 4	53,636
3	Passeau/Overmire	Oct. 5	Chicago 3, Detroit 0	55,500
4	Trout/Prim	Oct. 6	Detroit 4, Chicago 1	42,923
5	Newhouser/Borowy	Oct. 7	Detroit 8, Chicago 4	55,189
6	Borowy/Trout	Oct. 8	Detroit 7, Chicago 8	41,708
7	Newhouser/Borowy	Oct. 10	Detroit 9, Chicago 3	41,590

Final: Detroit 4, Chicago 3

The Standings—1968 American League

	Team	W	L	PCT	GB
1.	Detroit	103	59	.636	-
2.	Baltimore	91	71	.562	12.0
3.	Cleveland	86	75	.534	16.5
4.	Boston	86	76	.531	17.0
5.	New York	83	79	.512	20.0
6.	Oakland	82	80	.506	21.0
7.	Minnesota	79	83	.488	24.0
8T.	California	67	95	.414	36.0
8T.	Chicago	67	95	.414	36.0
10.	Washington	65	96	.404	37.5

1968 World Series: Detroit Tigers (AL) vs. St. Louis Cardinals (NL)

Game	Winning/Losing Pitchers	Date	Score	Attendance
1	Gibson/McLain	Oct. 2	Detroit 0, St. Louis 4	54,692
2	Lolich/Briles	Oct. 3	Detroit 8, St. Louis 1	54,692
3	Washburn/Wilson	Oct. 5	St. Louis 7, Detroit 3	53,634
4	Gibson/McLain	Oct. 6	St. Louis 10, Detroit 1	53,634
5	Lolich/Hoerner	Oct. 7	St. Louis 3, Detroit 5	53,634
6	McLain/Washburn	Oct. 9	Detroit 13, St. Louis 1	54,692
7	Lolich/Gibson	Oct. 10	Detroit 4, St. Louis 1	54,692

Final: Detroit 4, St. Louis 3

The Standings—1972 American League

	Team-East	W	L	PCT	GB
1.	Detroit	86	70	.551	-
2.	Boston	85	70	.548	0.5
3.	Baltimore	80	74	.519	5.0
4.	New York	79	76	.510	6.5
5.	Cleveland	72	84	.462	14.0
6.	Milwaukee	65	91	.417	21.0

	Team-West	W	L	PCT	GB
1.	Oakland	93	62	.600	-
2.	Chicago	87	67	.565	5.5
3.	Minnesota	77	77	.500	15.5
4.	Kansas City	76	78	.494	16.5
5.	California	75	80	.484	18.0
6.	Texas	54	100	.351	38.5

1972 American League Championship Series: Oakland A's (W) vs. Detroit Tigers (E)

Game	Winning/Losing Pitchers	Date	Score	Attendance
1	Fingers/Lolich	Oct. 7	Detroit 2, Oakland 3	29,536
2	Odom/Fryman	Oct. 8	Detroit 0, Oakland 5	31,088
3	Coleman/Holtzman	Oct. 10	Oakland 0, Detroit 3	41,156
4	Hiller/Horlen	Oct. 11	Oakland 3, Detroit 4	37,615
5	Odom/Fryman	Oct. 14	Oakland 2, Detroit 1	50,276

Final: Oakland 3, Detroit 2

The Standings—1984 American League

	Team-East	W	L	PCT	GB
1.	Detroit	104	58	.642	-
2.	Toronto	89	73	.549	15.0
3.	New York	87	75	.537	17.0
4.	Boston	86	76	.531	18.0
5.	Baltimore	85	77	.525	19.0
6.	Cleveland	75	87	.463	29.0
7.	Milwaukee	67	94	.416	36.5

	Team-West	W	L	PCT	GB
1.	Kansas City	84	78	.519	_
2.	California	81	81	.500	3.0
3.	Minnesota	81	81	.500	3.0
4.	Oakland	77	85	.475	7.0
5T.	Chicago	74	88	.457	10.0
5T.	Seattle	74	88	.457	10.0
7.	Texas	69	92	.429	14.5

1984 American League Championship Series: Detroit Tigers (E) vs. Kansas City Royals (W)

Game	Winning/Losing Pitchers	Date	Score	Attendance
1	Morris/Black	Oct. 2	Detroit 8, Kansas City 1	41,973
2	Lopez/Quisenberry	Oct. 3	Detroit 5, Kansas City 3	42,019
3	Wilcox/Leibrandt	Oct. 5	Kansas City 0, Detroit 1	52,168

Final: Detroit 3, Kansas City 0

1984 World Series: Detroit Tigers (AL) vs. San Diego (NL)

Game	Winning/Losing Pitchers	Date	Score	Attendance
1	Morris/Thurmond	Oct. 9	Detroit 3, San Diego 2	57,908
2	Hawkins/Petry	Oct. 10	Detroit 3, San Diego 5	57,911
3	Wilcox/Lollar	Oct. 12	San Diego 2, Detroit 5	51,970
4	Morris/Show	Oct. 13	San Diego 2, Detroit 4	52,130
5	Lopez/Hawkins	Oct. 14	San Diego 4, Detroit 8	51,901

Final: Detroit 4, San Diego 1

The Standings—1987 American League

	Team-East	W	L	PCT	GB
1.	Detroit	98	64	.605	-
2.	Toronto	96	66	.593	2.0
3.	Milwaukee	91	71	.562	7.0
4.	New York	89	73	.549	9.0
5.	Boston	78	84	.481	20.0
6.	Baltimore	67	95	.414	31.0
7.	Cleveland	61	101	.377	37.0

	Team-West	W	L	PCT	GB
1.	Minnesota	85	77	.525	-
2.	Kansas City	83	79	.512	2.0
3.	Oakland	81	81	.500	4.0
4.	Seattle	89	84	.481	7.0
5.	Chicago	77	85	.475	8.0
6T.	California	75	87	.463	10.0
6T.	Texas	75	87	.463	10.0

1987 American League Championship Series: Minnesota Twins (W) vs. Detroit Tigers (E)

Game	Winning/Losing Pitchers	Date	Score	Attendance
1	Reardon/Alexander	Oct. 7	Detroit 5, Minnesota 8	55,269
2	Blyleven/Morris	Oct. 8	Detroit 3 Minnesota 6	55,245
3	Henneman/Reardon	Oct. 10	Minnesota 6, Detroit 7	49,730
4	Viola/Tanana	Oct. 11	Minnesota 5, Detroit 3	51,939
5	Blyleven/Alexander	Oct. 12	Minnesota 9, Detroit 5	50,276

Final: Minnesota 4, Detroit 1

ALL-TIME TIGER TRADES

1903
6/10   Acquired INFs Ernie Courtney and Herman Long from the Yankees for INF Kid Elberfield

1904
1/??   Acquired LHP Ed Killian and RHP Jesse Stovall from the Indians for OF Billy Lush
7/25   Acquired C Monte Beville from the Yankees for C Frank McManus
8/7   Acquired INF Piano Legs Hickman from the Indians for C Fritz Buelow and INF Charlie Carr

1909
8/13   Acquired INF Jim Delahanty from the Senators for INF Germany Schaefer and INF Red Killefer
8/20   Acquired INF Tom Jones from the Browns for INF Claude Rossman

1915
8/18   Acquired RHPs Bill James and RHP Grover Lowdermilk from the Browns for OF Baby Doll Jacobson

1919
1/17   Acquired C Eddie Ainsmith, LHP Slim Love and OF Chick Shorten from the Red Sox for INF Ossie Vitt
7/5   Acquired RHP Doc Ayers from the Senators for RHP Eric Erickson

1922
10/30   Acquired INF Del Pratt and RHP Rip Collins from the Red Sox for RHPs Carl Holling and Howard Ehmke, INF Danny Clark, OF Babe Herman and cash
11/24   Acquired LHP Ray Francis from the Senators for INF Chick Gagnon

1925
12/9   Acquired INF Homer Ezzell and OF Tex Vache from the Red Sox for INF Fred Haney

1927
1/15   Acquired C Pinky Hargrave and INFs Marty McManus and Bobby LaMotte from the Browns for LHP Lefty Stewart, INFs Frank O'Rourke and Billy Mullen and C Otto Miller
12/2   Acquired INF Chick Galloway, RHP Elam Vangilder and OF Harry Rice from the Browns for OF Heinie Manush and INF Lu Blue

1928
12/11   Acquired RHP George Uhle from the Indians for RHP Ken Holloway and INF Jackie Tavener
12/19   Acquired INF Bucky Harris from the Senators for INF Jack Warner

1930
5/30   Acquired RHP Waite Hoyt and INF Mark Koenig from the Yankees for RHP Ownie Carroll, INF Yats Wuestling and OF Harry Rice

1931
8/31   Acquired C Muddy Ruel from the Red Sox for INF Marty McManus

1932
6/12   Acquired OF Earl Webb from the Red Sox for INF Dale Alexander and OF Roy Johnson
12/14   Acquired LHP Carl Fischer and RHP Firpo Marberry from the Senators for LHP Earl Whitehill

1933
6/2   Acquired RHP Vic Frasier from the White Sox for RHP Whit Wyatt
12/12   Acquired C Mickey Cochrane from the Athletics for C Johnny Pasek and cash
12/20   Acquired OF Goose Goslin from the Senators for OF John Stone

1936
4/30   Acquired INF Jack Burns from the Browns for LHP Chief Hogsett

1937
12/2   Acquired RHP Vern Kennedy, INF Tony Piet and OF Dixie Walker from the White Sox for INF Marv
          Owen, C Mike Tresh and OF Gee Walker

1938
12/15   Acquired INF Pinky Higgins and LHP Archie McKain from the Red Sox for RHP Eldon Auker, LHP
          Jake Wade and OF Chet Morgan

1939
5/13   Acquired OF Beau Bell, RHPs Bobo Newsom and Jim Walkup and INF Red Kress from the Browns
          for RHPs Vern Kennedy, Bob Harris, George Gill and Roxie Lawson, OF Chet Laabs and INF Mark
          Christman
6/14   Acquired OF Earl Averill from the Indians for LHP Harry Eisenstat and cash
12/6   Acquired INF Dick Bartell from the Cubs for INF Billy Rogell

1940
1/20   Acquired OF Bruce Campbell from the Indians for OF Beau Bell

1941
12/12   Acquired OF Doc Cramer and INF Jimmy Bloodworth from the Senators for INF Frank Croucher and
          OF Bruce Campbell

1942
7/17   Acquired RHP Jack Wilson from the Senators for INF Eric McNair (McNair refused to report)

1943
10/11   Acquired C Bob Swift and INF Don Heffner from the Athletics for OF Rip Radcliff

1944
12/12   Acquired INF Skeeter Webb from the White Sox for INF Joe Orengo

1945
4/27   Acquired OF Roy Cullenbine from the Indians for INFs Don Ross and Dutch Meyer

1946
1/3   Acquired INF Eddie Lake from the Red Sox for INF Rudy York
5/18   Acquired INF George Kell from the Athletics for OF Barney McCosky

1947
5/20   Acquired C Hal Wagner from the Red Sox for C Birdie Tebbetts

1948
11/10   Acquired C Aaron Robinson from the White Sox for LHP Billy Pierce and cash

1949
5/7   Acquired INF Don Kolloway from the White Sox for OF Vern Rapp
12/14   Acquired INF Gerry Priddy from the Browns for RHP Lou Kretlow and cash
12/17   Acquired INF Dick Kryhoski from the Yankees for OF Dick Wakefield

1951
5/15   Acquired LHP Bob Cain from the White Sox for RHP Saul Rogovin

1952
2/14   Acquired C Matt Batts, OF Cliff Mapes, INF Ben Taylor and LHP Dick Littlefield from the Browns for LHPs Gene Bearden and Bob Cain
6/3   Acquired INFs Johnny Pesky, Walt Dropo and Fred Hatfield, OF Don Lenhardt and LHP Bill Wight from the Red Sox for INFs George Kell and Johnny Lipon, OF Hoot Evers and RHP Dizzy Trout
8/14   Acquired RHPs Ned Garver, Dave Madison and Bud Black and OF Jim Delsing from the Browns for OFs Vic Wertz and Don Lenhardt, RHP Marlin Stuart and LHP Dick Littlefield
10/27   Acquired OF Jake Crawford from the Browns for OF Cliff Mapes and INF Neil Berry
12/4   Acquired OF Bob Nieman, INF Owen Friend and OF/INF J.W. Porter from the Browns for RHPs Virgil Trucks and Hal White and OF Johnny Groth

1953
1/29   Acquired INF Billy Hitchcock from the Athletics for INF Don Kolloway
6/15   Acquired INF Ray Boone, RHPs Steve Gromek and Dick Weik and LHP Al Aber from the Indians for RHPs Art Houtteman and Bill Wight, C Joe Ginsberg and INF Owen Friend

1954
5/29   Acquired C Robert Wilson from the White Sox for C Matt Batts
6/9   Acquired INF Wayne Belardi from the Dodgers for INF Charley Kress, C John Bucha, RHP Ernie Nevel and cash
12/6   Acquired INFs Ferris Fain and Jack Phillips and RHP Leo Cristante from the White Sox for INF Walt Dropo, OF Bob Nieman and LHP Ted Gray

1955
11/30   Acquired RHP Virgil Trucks from the White Sox for OF Bubba Phillips

1956
5/15   Acquired INF Jim Brideweser and OF/INF Bob Kennedy from the White Sox for INF Fred Hatfield and OF Jim Delsing
12/3   Acquired RHPs Jack Crimian and Bill Harrington and INFs Eddie Robinson and Jim Finigan from the Athletics for RHPs Virgil Trucks and Ned Garver, LHP Gene Host and INF Wayne Belardi

1957
2/12   Acquired INF Jack Dittmer from the Braves for OF Charles King and cash
4/30   Acquired OF Karl Olson from the Red Sox for INF Jack Phillips
6/13   Acquired OF Dave Philley and cash from the White Sox for INF Earl Torgeson
11/20   Acquired INF Billy Martin, OFs Gus Zernial and Lou Skizas, RHP Tom Morgan, LHP Maury McDermott and C Charlie Thompson from the Athletics for OFs Bill Tuttle and Jim Small, RHPs Duke Maas and John Tsitouris, C Frank House, INF Kent Hadley and a player to be named (INF Jim McManus)

1958

1/28	Acquired INFs Ozzie Virgil and Gail Harris from the Giants for INF Jim Finigan and cash
2/18	Acquired LHP Hank Aguirre and C Jim Hegan from the Indians for C. J.W. Porter and LHP Hal Woodeshick
3/31	Acquired INF Milt Bolling and RHP Vito Valentinetti from the Indians for RHP Pete Wojey and cash
6/15	Acquired OF Tito Francona and RHP Bill Fischer from the White Sox for INF Ray Boone and RHP Bob Shaw
6/23	Acquired RHP Al Cicotte from the Senators for RHP Vito Valentinetti
7/27	Acquired C John Turk and cash from the Phillies for C Jim Hegan
11/20	Acquired RHP Ray Narleski, LHP Don Mossi and INF Ossie Alvarez from the Indians for INF Billy Martin and RHP Al Cicotte
12/5	Acquired C Lou Berberet from the Red Sox for RHP Herb Moford
12/6	Acquired INFs Eddie Yost and Rocky Bridges and OF Neil Chrisley from the Senators for INFs Reno Bertoia and Ron Samford and OF Jim Delsing

1959

1/29	Acquired OF Lary Doby from the Indians for OF Tito Francona
5/2	Acquired RHP Dave Sisler and INF Ted Lepcio from the Red Sox for LHP Billy Hoeft
10/15	Acquired INF Casey Wise, RHP Don Kaiser and C Mike Roarke from the Braves for C Charlie Lau and RHP Don Lee

1960

4/12	Acquired INF Norm Cash from the Indians for INF Steve Demeter
4/17	Acquired OF Rocky Colavito from the Indians for OF Harvey Kuenn
5/6	Acquired OF Sandy Amoros from the Dodgers for INF Gail Harris
6/15	Acquired RHP Clem Labine from the Dodgers for RHP Ray Semproch
7/22	Acquired RHP Bill Fischer from the Senators for RHP Tom Morgan
7/25	Acquired C Hank Foiles from the Indians for C Bob Wilson and INF Rocky Bridges
12/7	Acquired OF Bill Burton, INF Chuck Cottier, C Dick Brown and RHP Terry Fox from the Braves for INF Frank Bolling and OF Neil Chrisley

1961

5/10	Acquired INF Jim Baumer from the Reds for INF Dick Gernert
6/5	Acquired LHP Hal Woodeschick from the Senators for INF Chuck Cottier
6/7	Acquired RHP Jerry Casale from the Angels for RHP Jim Donohue
7/31	Acquired INF Reno Bertoia and RHP Gerry Staley from the Athletics for INF Ozzie Virgil and RHP Bill Fischer
9/8	Acquired INF Vic Wertz from the Red Sox for cash
12/1	Acquired RHP Sam Jones from the Colt 45's for RHPs Bob Bruce and Manny Montejo

1962

6/25	Acquired OF/INF Bob Farley from the White Sox for OF Charlie Maxwell
11/25	Acquired INF Bubba Phillips from the Indians for LHP Ron Nischwitz and RHP Gordon Seyfried
11/26	Acquired C Gus Triandos and OF Whitey Herzog from the Orioles for C Dick Brown
11/27	Acquired INF Steve Boros from the Cubs for RHP Bob Anderson

1963

3/23	Acquired OF Wayne Comer and cash from the Senators for INF Larry Osborne
5/8	Acquired OF Lou Johnson and cash from the Braves for INF Chico Fernandez
6/15	Acquired OF George Thomas and cash from the Angels for RHP Paul Foytack and INF Frank Kostro
11/18	Acquired INF Jerry Lumpe and RHPs Ed Rakow and Dave Wickersham from the Athletics for OF Rocky Colavito, RHP Bob Anderson and cash

| 12/4 | Acquired OF Don Demeter and RHP Jack Hamilton from the Phillies for RHP Jim Bunning and C Gus Triandos |

1964

| 4/9 | Acquired RHP Larry Sherry from the Dodgers for OF Lou Johnson and cash |
| 4/28 | Acquired RHP Julio Navarro from the Angels for OF Willie Smith |

1965

| 10/4 | Acquired RHP Bill Monbouquette from the Red Sox for OF George Thomas and INF George Smith |
| 12/15 | Acquired INF Dick Tracewski from the Dodgers for RHP Phil Regan |

1966

5/10	Acquired LHP Johnny Podres from the Dodgers for cash considerations
5/10	Acquired cash considerations from the Phillies for RHP Terry Fox
6/14	Acquired RHP Earl Wilson and OF Joe Christopher from the Red Sox for OF Dom Demeter and P Julio Navarro

1967

5/5	Acquired cash considerations from the Indians for RHP Orlando Pena
6/23	Acquired cash considerations from the Reds for OF Jake Wood
6/29	Acquired OF Jim Landis from the Astros for RHP Larry Sherry
8/17	Acquired INF Eddie Mathews from the Astros for RHP Fred Gladding and cash
11/28	Acquired RHP Dennis Ribant from the Pirates for RHP Dave Wickersham

1968

| 4/3 | Acquired INF Fred Moulder from the Dodgers for LHP Hank Aguirre |
| 7/26 | Acquired RHP Don McMahon from the White Sox for RHP Dennis Ribant |

1969

6/14	Acquired INF/OF Tom Tresh from the Yankees for OF Ron Woods
12/3	Acquired RHP Jerry Robertson from the Expos for RHP Joe Sparma
12/4	Acquired RHP Joe Niekro from the Padres for RHP Pat Dobson and INF Dave Campbell
12/13	Acquired INF Dalton Jones from the Red Sox for INF Tom Matchick

1970

| 5/22 | Acquired OF Russ Nagelson and LHP Bill Rohr from the Indians for RHP Fred Lasher |
| 10/9 | Acquired INFs Eddie Brinkman and Aurelio Rodriguez and RHPs Joe Coleman and Jim Hannan from the Senators for RHPs Denny McLain and Norm McRae, INF Don Wert and OF Elliott Maddox |

1971

3/29	Acquired RHP Bill Zepp from the Twins for INF Bob Adams and P Art Clifford
6/12	Acquired INF Tony Taylor from the Phillies for Ps Mike Fremuth and Carl Cavanaugh
12/2	Acquired C Tom Haller from the Dodgers for a player to be named (LHP Bernie Beckman) and cash

1972

5/9	Acquired INF/OF Reggie Sanders from the Athletics for LHP Mike Kilkenny
5/30	Acquired RHP Norm McRae from the Rangers for INF Dalton Jones
11/30	Acquired OF Dick Sharon from the Pirates for LHP Jim Foor and RHP Norm McRae

1973

| 3/27 | Acquired RHP Jim Perry from the Twins for RHP Danny Fife and cash |

4/2	Acquired C Charlie Sands from the Pirates for RHP Chris Zachary
5/14	Acquired C Bob Didier from the Braves for C Gene Lamont
6/15	Acquired RHP Ed Farmer from the Indians for RHP Tom Timmerman and INF Kevin Collins
10/23	Acquired OF Ben Oglivie from the Red Sox for INF Dick McAuliffe
12/3	Acquired RHP Jim Ray and INF Gary Sutherland from the Astros for LHP Fred Scherman and cash
12/6	Acquired LHP Ray Newman from the Brewers for RHP Mike Strahler

1974

3/19	Acquired C Gerry Moses from the Yankees and traded RHP Jim Perry to the Indians and RHP Ed Farmer to the Yankees in a three-way deal (The Indians traded RHP Rick Sawyer and OF Walt Williams to the Yankees)
11/18	Acquired INF Nate Colbert from the Padres for INF Eddie Brinkman, OF Dick Sharon and RHP Bob Strampe
12/4	Acquired RHP Tom Walker and C Terry Humphrey from the Expos for LHP Woodie Fryman
12/5	Acquired cash from the Pirates for RHP Jim Ray

1975

3/29	Acquired INF Jack Pierce from the Braves for INF Reggie Sanders
5/29	Acquired RHP Bob Reynolds from the Orioles for RHP Fred Holdsworth
12/6	Acquired C Milt May and LHPs Dave Roberts and Jim Crawford from the Astros for OF Leon Roberts, C Terry Humphrey and RHPs Gene Pentz and Mark Lemongello
12/12	Acquired OF Rusty Staub and LHP Bill Laxton from the Mets for LHP Mickey Lolich and OF Robert Baldwin

1976

6/8	Acquired cash considerations from the Cubs for RHP Joe Coleman
6/10	Acquired INF Pedro Garcia from the Brewers for INF Gary Sutherland

1977	
4/12	Acquired RHP Steve Foucault from the Rangers for OF Willie Horton
7/30	Acquired cash considerations from the Cubs for LHP Dave Roberts
12/9	Acquired OF Charlie Spikes from the Indians for INF Tom Veryzer
12/9	Acquired RHP Jim Slaton and LHP Rich Folkers from the Brewers for OF Ben Oglivie

1978

1/30	Acquired INF Steve Dillard from the Red Sox for Ps Michael Burns and Frank Harris and cash
3/6	Acquired RHP Jack Billingham from the Reds for OF John Valle and LHP George Cappuzzello
12/4	Acquired OF Jerry Morales and RHP Aurelio Lopez from the Cardinals for LHPs Bob Sykes and Jack Murphy

1979

3/13	Acquired RHP Mardie Cornejo from the Mets for LHP Ed Glynn
3/20	Acquired INF Steve Dillard from the Cubs for C Ed Putman
5/25	Acquired OF Champ Summers from the Reds for LHP Sheldon Burnside
7/20	Acquired C Randy Schafer and cash from the Expos for OF Rusty Staub
10/31	Acquired INF Richie Hebner from the Mets for INF Phil Mankowski and OF Jerry Morales
12/5	Acquired LHP Jeff Holly from the Twins for RHP Fernando Arroyo
12/7	Acquired cash considerations from the Padres for INF Aurelio Rodriguez
12/7	Acquired LHP Dan Schatzeder from the Expos for OF Ron LeFlore

1980

3/14	Acquired C Duffy Dyer from the Expos for INF Jerry Manuel

5/12	Acquired cash considerations from the Red Sox for RHP Jack Billingham
5/27	Acquired OF Al Cowens from the Angels for INF Jason Thompson
6/2	Acquired OF Jim Lentine from the Cardinals for LHP John Martin and OF Al Greene
12/10	Acquired LHP Kevin Saucier from the Rangers for INF Mark Wagner
12/12	Acquired LHP Dennis Kinney from the Padres for OF Dave Stegman

1981

4/1	Acquired INF Mick Kelleher from the Cubs for cash
8/22	Acquired INF Ron Jackson from the Twins for OF Tim Corcoran
11/27	Acquired OF Chet Lemon from the White Sox for OF Steve Kemp
12/9	Acquired OF Larry Herndon from the Giants for LHPs Dan Schatzeder and Mike Chris

1982

3/4	Acquired INF Enos Cabell and cash from the Giants for OF Champ Summers
3/23	Acquired OF Ed Miller from the Braves for RHP Roger Weaver
3/30	Acquired RHP Elias Sosa from the Expos for cash
4/21	Acquired cash considerations from the Angels for INF Mick Kelleher
10/7	Acquired cash considerations from the Padres for RHP Elias Sosa

1983

3/24	Acquired OF John Grubb from the Rangers for RHP Dave Tobik
3/25	Acquired C Sal Butera from the Twins for C Stine Poole
6/22	Acquired RHP Doug Bair from the Cardinals for a player to be named (LHP Dave Rucker)
6/30	Acquired INF Wayne Krenchicki from the Reds for LHP Pat Underwood
11/21	Acquired cash considerations from the Reds for INF Wayne Krenchicki

1984

3/27	Acquired LHP Willie Hernandez and INF Dave Bergman from the Phillies for OF Glenn Wilson and C John Wockenfuss
8/28	Acquired LHP Bill Scherrer from the Reds for a player to be named (RHP Carl Willis) and cash
12/7	Acquired RHP Walt Terrell from the Mets for INF Howard Johnson

1985

4/5	Acquired OF Alex Sanchez from the Giants for RHP Roger Mason
6/20	Acquired LHP Frank Tanana from the Rangers for RHP Duane James
10/7	Acquired LHP Dave LaPoint, C Matt Nokes and RHP Eric King from the Giants for RHPs Juan Berenguer and Scott Medvin and C Bob Melvin
11/13	Acquired OF Dave Collins from the Athletics for INF/OF Barbaro Garbey
12/12	Acquired INF/OF Darnell Coles from the Mariners for RHP Rich Monteleone

1986

1/18	Acquired INF/OF Dave Engle from the Twins for OF Alex Sanchez and INF Chris Pittaro
7/9	Acquired LHP Mark Thurmond from the Padres for LHP Dave LaPoint
8/9	Acquired C Mike Heath from the Cardinals for RHP Ken Hill and a player to be named (INF Mike Laga)

1987

1/27	Acquired OFs Terry Harper and Freddie Tiburcio from the Braves for RHP Randy O'Neal and LHP Chuck Cary
3/24	Acquired C Orlando Mercado from the Rangers for a player to be named (OF Ruben Guzman)
5/5	Acquired RHP Balvino Galvez from the Dodgers for C Orlando Mercado
6/22	Acquired RHP Karl Best from the Mariners for RHP Bryan Kelly

6/26	Acquired RHP Shawn Holman and INF Pete Rice from the Pirates for OF Terry Harper
8/7	Acquired INF Jim Morrison from the Pirates for OF/INF Darnell Coles and a player to be named (LHP Morris Madden)
8/12	Acquired RHP Doyle Alexander from the Braves for RHP John Smoltz
9/22	Acquired RHP Dickie Noles from the Cubs for a player to be named (Noles returned to the Cubs on 10/23)
12/5	Acquired OF Gary Pettis from the Angels for RHP Dan Petry

1988

2/24	Acquired INF Julius McDougal from the Twins for INF Doug Baker
2/27	Acquired INF Ray Knight from the Orioles for LHP Mark Thurmond
3/24	Acquired OF Billy Beane from the Twins for RHP Balvino Galvez
3/28	Acquired RHP Don Schulze from the Twins for RHP Karl Best
8/31	Acquired OF Fred Lynn from the Orioles for C Chris Hoiles, RHP Cesar Mejia and LHP Robinson Garces
8/31	Acquired RHP Ted Power from the Royals for LHP Mark Lee and C Rey Palacios
10/28	Acquired INF/OF Keith Moreland and INF Chris Brown from the Padres for RHP Walt Terrell

1989

3/23	Acquired INF Mike Brumley from the Padres for INF Luis Salazar
3/23	Acquired RHP Charlie Hudson from the Yankees for INF Tom Brookens
3/23	Acquired OF Kenny Williams from the White Sox for RHP Eric King
6/16	Acquired OF Tracy Jones from the Giants for OF Pat Sheridan
7/17	Acquired OFs Domingo Michel and Steve Green from the Dodgers for OF Billy Bean
7/28	Acquired LHP Brian Dubois from the Orioles for INF Keith Moreland
12/6	Acquired OF Jim Lindeman and RHP Matt Kinzer from the Cardinals for INF Pat Austin, RHP Marcos Betances and C Bill Henderson

1990

1/10	Acquired OF Larry Sheets from the Orioles for INF Mike Brumley
4/2	Acquired RHP Jerry Don Gleaton from the Royals for RHP Greg Everson
6/4	Acquired RHPs Lance McCullers and Clay Parker from the Yankees for C Matt Nokes
6/18	Acquired OF Darnell Coles from the Mariners for OF Tracy Jones
10/1	Acquired LHP Mike Munoz from the Dodgers for RHP Mike Wilkins

1991

1/12	Acquired C Mickey Tettleton from the Orioles for RHP Jeff Robinson
1/22	Acquired INF Todd Haney from the Mariners for LHP Dave Richards
3/19	Acquired RHP Mark Leiter from the Yankees for INF Torey Lovullo
3/30	Acquired C Andy Allanson from the Royals for C Jim Baxter
6/25	Acquired INF Victor Rosario from the Braves for RHP Dan Petry

1992

1/22	Acquired OF Mark Carreon and LHP Tony Castillo from the Mets for LHP Paul Gibson

1993

8/31	Acquired OF Eric Davis from the Dodgers for a player to be named (RHP John DeSilva)

1994

3/31	Acquired C Alan Zinter from the Mets for INF Rico Brogna
5/11	Acquired RHP Gene Harris from the Padres for INFs Scott Livingstone and Jorge Velandia

1995

4/13	Acquired OF Chad Curtis from the Angels for INF Tony Phillips
7/31	Acquired LHP C.J. Nitkowski, RHP Dave Tuttle and a player to be named (INF Mark Lewis) from the Reds for LHP David Wells
8/7	Acquired a player to be named (LHP Mike Myers) from the Marlins for LHP Buddy Groom
8/10	Acquired a player to be named (INF Phil Nevin) from the Astros for RHP Mike Henneman
8/29	Acquired a player to be named (OF Derek Hacopian) from the Brewers for LHP Kevin Wickander
9/8	Acquired a player to be named (OF Phil Hiatt) from the Royals for INF Juan Samuel

1996

1/23	Acquired OF Duane Singleton from the Brewers for LHP Henry Santos
3/11	Acquired RHP Randy Veres from the Marlins for INF Matt Brunson
3/22	Acquired RHP Ramon Fermin and INF Fausto Cruz from the Athletics for OF Phil Plantier
3/22	Acquired C Raul Casanova, OF Melvin Nieves and RHP Richie Lewis from the Padres for RHP Sean Bergman, OF Todd Steverson and RHP Cade Gaspar
4/26	Acquired RHP Gregg Olson from the Reds for INF Yuri Sanchez
5/14	Acquired RHP John Farrell from the Indians for RHP Greg Granger
5/31	Acquired OF Anton French from the Braves for OF Danny Bautista
6/7	Acquired LHP Tom Urbani and INF Miguel Inzunza from the Cardinals for OF Micah Franklin and RHP Brian Maxcy
6/18	Acquired C Brad Ausmus, INF Andujar Cedeno and RHP Russell Spear from the Padres for C John Flaherty and INF Chris Gomez
7/31	Acquired RHP Matt Drews, OF Ruben Sierra and cash from the Yankees for INF Cecil Fielder
7/31	Acquired INF Damion Easley from the Angels for RHP Greg Gohr
7/31	Acquired RHP Joey Eischen and LHP John Cummings from the Dodgers for OF Chad Curtis
8/26	Acquired two players to be named (RHP Kevin Gallaher and INF Pedro Santana) from the Astros for RHP Gregg Olson
9/11	Acquired cash considerations from the Astros for INF Andujar Cedeno
9/20	Acquired RHP Fernando Hernandez from the Padres for a player to be named (OF Justin Mashore)
10/28	Acquired OF Decomba Conner and RHP Ben Bailey from the Reds for OF Ruben Sierra and cash
11/1	Acquired RHP Dan Miceli from the Pirates for RHP Clint Sodowsky
12/9	Acquired INF Deivi Cruz and OF Juan Hernaiz from the Dodgers for INF Jeff Berblinger
12/10	Acquired OF Brian Hunter, RHPs Todd Jones and Doug Brocail, INF Orlando Miller and cash from the Astros for C Brad Ausmus, RHP Jose Lima, INF Daryle Ward and LHPs Trever Miller and C.J. Nitkowski
12/10	Acquired LHP Roberto Duran from the Blue Jays for OF Anton French
12/11	Acquired C Matt Walbeck from the Twins for RHP Brent Stentz
12/16	Acquired INF Jesse Ibarra from the Giants for INF Mark Lewis
12/17	Acquired RHP Willie Blair and C Brian Johnson from the Padres for LHP Joey Eischen and RHP Cam Smith

1997

3/22	Acquired INF Jody Reed from the Padres for OF Mike Darr and RHP Matt Skrmetta
7/16	Acquired C Marcus Jensen from the Giants for C Brian Johnson
7/16	Acquired OF Earl Johnson from the Padres for INF Dave Hajek
7/18	Acquired RHPs Scott Sanders and Dean Crow and INF Carlos Villalobos from the Mariners for RHPs Omar Olivares and Felipe Lira
11/11	Acquired RHP Donne Wall and C Paul Bako from the Reds for OF Melvin Nieves
11/18	Acquired INFs Joe Randa and Gabe Alvarez and RHP Matt Drews from the Diamondbacks for INF Travis Fryman
11/18	Acquired RHP Tim Worrell and OF Trey Beamon from the Padres for RHPs Dan Miceli and Donne Wall and INF Ryan Balfe
11/20	Acquired RHP Bryce Florie and cash from the Brewers for LHP Mike Myers, RHP Rick Greene and INF Santiago Perez

| 11/20 | Acquired RHP Nick Skuse from the Angels for INF Phil Nevin and C Matt Walbeck |
| 11/24 | Acquired cash considerations from the Red Sox for OF Jimmy Hurst |

1998

3/25	Acquired RHP Doug Bochtler from the Athletics for cash
6/23	Acquired a player to be named (INF Jason Wood) from the Athletics for OF Bip Roberts
6/24	Acquired OF Geronimo Berroa from the Indians for RHP Tim Worrell and OF Dave Roberts
12/4	Acquired RHP Willie Blair from the Mets for INF Joe Randa
12/10	Acquired cash considerations from the Red Sox for RHP Marino Santana
12/14	Acquired LHP Alberto Blanco from the Marlins for cash
12/14	Acquired RHP Beiker Graterol from the Blue Jays for RHP Eric Ludwick
12/28	Acquired OF Karim Garcia from the Diamondbacks for OF Luis Gonzalez

1999

1/14	Acquired C Brad Ausmus and LHP C.J. Nitkowski from the Astros for RHPs Dean Crow, Brian Powell and Mark Persails, C Paul Bako and INF Carlos Villalobos
4/16	Acquired RHPs Dave Mlicki and Mel Rojas from the Dodgers for RHPs Robinson Checo and Apostol Garcia and LHP Rick Roberts
4/28	Acquired two players to be named (LHP Andrew Vanhekken and OF Jerry Amador) from the Mariners for OF Brian Hunter
7/31	Acquired LHP Mike Maroth from the Red Sox for RHP Bryce Florie
7/31	Acquired RHP Brandon Villafuerte from the Marlins for RHP Mike Drumright
11/2	Acquired OF Juan Gonzalez, RHP Danny Patterson and C Gregg Zaun from the Rangers for LHP Justin Thompson, OF Gabe Kapler, RHP Francisco Cordero, INF Frank Catalanotto, C Bill Haselman and LHP Alan Webb

2000

3/7	Acquired cash considerations from the Royals for C Gregg Zuan
3/10	Acquired OF Wendell Magee, Jr. from the Phillies for LHP Bobby Sismondo
6/12	Acquired cash considerations from the Orioles for OF Karim Garcia
7/17	Acquired OF Dusty Allen from the Padres for INF Gabe Alvarez
7/18	Acquired INF Hal Morris from the Reds for cash considerations
12/11	Acquired OF Roger Cedeno, RHP Chris Holt and C Mitch Meluskey from the Astros for C Brad Ausmus and RHPs Doug Brocail and Nelson Cruz
12/15	Acquired LHP Matt Perisho from the Rangers for RHPs Kevin Mobley and Brandon Villafuerte

2001

6/23	Acquired RHP Jose Lima and cash considerations from the Astros for RHP Dave Mlicki
7/28	Acquired LHP Mark Redman from the Twins for RHP Todd Jones
12/11	Acquired INF/OF Dmitri Young from the Reds for OF Juan Encarnacion and RHP Luis Pineda

2002

7/5	Acquired INF Carlos Pena and RHPs Franklyn German and Jeremy Bonderman from the Athletics for RHP Jeff Weaver
7/23	Acquired INF David Espinosa, OF Gary "Noochie" Varner and RHP Jorge Cordova from the Reds for RHP Brian Moehler and OF Matt Boone
7/25	Acquired OF Hiram Bocachica from the Dodgers for RHPs Tom Farmer and Jason Frasor
11/15	Acquired OF Gene Kingsale from the Padres for C Michael Rivera
11/25	Acquired LHP Adrian Burnside and two minor-league players to be named from the Pirates for INF Randall Simon

SPRING TRAINING FACILITIES

Year	Site
1901	Detroit, MI
1902	Ypsilanti, MI
1903-04	Shreveport, LA
1905-07	Augusta, GA
1908	Hot Springs, AR
1909-10	San Antonio, TX
1911-12	Monroe, LA
1913-15	Gulfport, MS
1916-18	Waxahachie, TX
1919-20	Macon, GA
1921	San Antonio, TX
1922-26	Augusta, GA
1927-28	San Antonio, TX
1929	Phoenix, AZ
1930	Tampa, FL
1931	Sacramento, CA
1932	Palo Alto, CA
1933	San Antonio, TX
1934-42	Lakeland, FL
1943-45	Evansville, IN
1946-present	Lakeland, FL

Bibliography

Anderson, Sparky and Dan Ewald. *They Call Me Sparky.* Chelsea: Sleeping Bear Press, 1998.

Bak, Richard. *A Place For Summer.* Detroit: Wayne State University Press, 1998.

Benagh, Jim and Jim Hawkins. *Go, Bird, Go!* New York: Dell Publishing, 1976.

Bingay, Malcolm W. *Detroit Is My Home Town.* Indianapolis: Bobbs-Merrill, 1946.

Broeg, Bob. *The Pilot Light of the Gas House Gang.* St. Louis: Chalice Press, 1980.

Butler, Hal. *Al Kaline.* Chicago: Henry Regnery Co., 1973.

Cantor, George. *The Tigers of '68.* New York: Taylor Publishing, 1997.

Cantor, George. *World Series Fact Book.* Detroit: Visible Ink Press, 1996.

Curran, Williams. *Big Sticks.* New York: William Morrow & Co., 1990.

Detroit Free Press archives.

Detroit News archives.

Detroit Tigers, Various Media Guides and Programs.

detroit.tigers.mlb.com: official website of the Detroit Tigers.

Dewey, Donald and Nicholas Acocella. *The Biographical History of Baseball.* Chicago: Triumph Books, 2002.

Dickey, Glenn. *The History of American League Baseball.* New York: Stein and Day, 1980.

Drummond, Steven. *Wayne State Magazine.* Detroit: Winter 2002.

Ernie Harwell Collection, Detroit Public Library

Ewald, Dan. *John Fetzer: On A Handshake.* Champaign: Sagamore Publishing, 1997.

Falls, Joe. *The Detroit Tigers.* New York: Walker & Company, 1989.

Freehan, Bill, Steve Gelman and Dick Schaap. *Behind The Mask.* New York: World Publishing Co., 1970.

Goldstein, Richard. *Spartan Seasons.* New York: MacMillan Publishing, 1980.

Gutman, Dan. *Baseball Babylon.* New York: Penguin Books, 1992.

Hirshberg, Al. *The Al Kaline Story.* New York: Julian Messner, Inc., 1964.

Honig, Donald. *Baseball Between The Lines.* New York: Coward, McCann, & Geoghegan, 1976.

Honig, Donald. *The Man in the Dugout.* Chicago: Follett Publishing, 1977.

Kell, George and Dan Ewald. *Hello Everybody, I'm George Kell.* Champaign: Sports Publishing, 1989.

LeFlore, Ron and Jim Hawkins. *Breakout.* New York: Harper & Row, 1978.

Leib, Fred. *Baseball As I Have Known It.* New York: Grosset & Dunlap, 1977.

McLain, Denny and Mike Nahrstedt. *Strikeout.* St. Louis: Sporting News Publishing, 1988.

Oakland Press archives.

Peary, Danny. *Cult Baseball Players.* New York: Simon & Schuster, 1990.

Ritter, Lawrence S. *The Glory Of Their Times.* New York: MacMillan Publishing, 1966.

Ritter, Lawrence and Donald Honig. *The Image of Their Greatness.* New York: Crown Publishers, 1979.

Seymour, Harold. *Baseball, The Early Years.* New York: Oxford University Press, 1960.

Smith, Robert. *Baseball.* New York: Simon and Schuster, 1970.

Stump, Al. *Cobb.* Chapel Hill: Algonquin Books of Chapel Hill, 1994.

Veeck, Bill. *Veeck As In Wreck.* New York: G.P. Putnam's Sons, 1962.

Veeck, Bill. *The Hustler's Handbook.* New York: G.P. Putnam's Sons, 1967.

www.baseball-reference.com: Statistics from 1871 to the present for major league players, teams, and leagues.

Celebrate the Heroes of Baseball and Detroit Sports
in These Other Acclaimed Titles from Sports Publishing!

Detroit Red Wings: Greatest Moments and Players
by Stan Fischler
8.5 x 11 hardcover, 255 pages
100+ photos throughout
$29.95

Stanley's Back! The Detroit Red Wings Recapture the Cup
by *The Detroit News*
8.5 x 11 hardcover and softcover, 150+ pages
100+ color photos throughout
$26.95 (hardcover)
$19.95 (softcover)

Dominik Hasek: The Dominator
by Randy Schultz
8.5 x 11 hardcover
128 pages color photos throughout
$24.95

They Earned Their Stripes: The Detroit Tigers' All-Time Team
by *The Detroit News*
8.5 x 11 hardcover and softcover, 192 pages
photos throughout
$29.95 (hardcover)
$17.95 (softcover)

They Earned Their Stripes: The Detroit Tigers' All-Time Team (leatherbound edition)
by *The Detroit News*
8.5 x 11 leatherbound
192 pages, photos throughout
$74.95 • *All copies signed by George Kell, Al Kaline, John Hiller, & Bill Freehan!*

Home, Sweet Home: Memories of Tiger Stadium
by *The Detroit News*
8.5 x 11 hardcover and softcover, 176 pages
photos throughout
$29.95 (hardcover)
$19.95 (softcover)

The Big M: The Frank Mahovlich Story
by Ted Mahovlich
6 x 9 hardcover
244 pages
eight-page color-photo section
$24.95

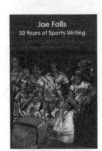

Joe Falls: 50 Years of Sports Writing
by Joe Falls
6 x 9 hardcover
225 pages
$22.95
2002 Baseball Hall of Fame inductee!

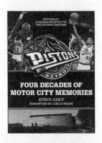

The Detroit Pistons: Four Decades of Motor City Memories
by Steve Addy
8.5 x 11 softcover, 263 pages
eight-page color-photo section
$19.95

Tales from Michigan Stadium
by Jim Brandstatter
5.5 x 8.25 hardcover
200 pages
photos & drawings throughout
$19.95

To order at any time, please call toll-free **877-424-BOOK (2665)**.
For fast service and quick delivery, order on-line at **www.SportsPublishingLLC.com**.